Developments in the International Harmonization of Accounting

The New Library of International Accounting

Series Editor: Christopher W. Nobes

PricewaterhouseCoopers Professor of Accounting, University of Reading, UK

1. Developments in International Accounting – General Issues and Classification
   Christopher W. Nobes

2. Developments in Country Studies in International Accounting – Europe
   Sally Aisbitt and Lisa Evans

3. Developments in Country Studies in International Accounting – Americas and the Far East
   Gary K. Meek

4. Developments in the International Harmonization of Accounting
   Christopher W. Nobes

Future titles will include:

Developments in Financial Reporting by Multinationals
Clare B. Roberts

Wherever possible, the articles in these volumes have been reproduced as originally published using facsimile reproduction, inclusive of footnotes and pagination to facilitate ease of reference.

For a list of all Edward Elgar published titles visit our site on the World Wide Web at www.e-elgar.com

Developments in the International Harmonization of Accounting

Edited by

Christopher W. Nobes

PricewaterhouseCoopers Professor of Accounting
University of Reading, UK

THE NEW LIBRARY OF INTERNATIONAL ACCOUNTING

An Elgar Reference Collection
Cheltenham, UK • Northampton, MA, USA

Published by
Edward Elgar Publishing Limited
Glensanda House
Montpellier Parade
Cheltenham
Glos GL50 1UA
UK

Edward Elgar Publishing, Inc.
136 West Street
Suite 202
Northampton
Massachusetts 01060
USA

A catalogue record for this book is available from the British Library.

Library of Congress Cataloguing in Publication Data

Developments in the international harmonization of accounting / edited by Christopher W. Nobes.
p. cm. — (New library of international accounting)
"An Elgar reference collection".
Includes bibliographical references and index.
1. Accounting—Standards. 2. Comparative accounting. I. Nobes, Christopher. II. Series.

HF5626.D48 2004
657'.02'18—dc22

2003068791

ISBN 1 84376 097 5

Printed and bound in Great Britain by MPG Books Ltd, Bodmin, Cornwall

Contents

Acknowledgements

The editor and publishers wish to thank the authors and the following publishers who have kindly given permission for the use of copyright material.

Accounting and Business Research for articles: Simon Archer, Pascale Delvaille and Stuart McLeay (1995), 'The Measurement of Harmonisation and the Comparability of Financial Statement Items: Within-Country and Between-Country Effects', *Accounting and Business Research*, **25** (98), Spring, 67–80; Don Herrmann and Wayne Thomas (1995), 'Harmonisation of Accounting Measurement Practices in the European Community', *Accounting and Business Research*, **25** (100), Autumn, 253–65; Asheq Rahman, Hector Perera and Siva Ganeshanandam (1996), 'Measurement of Formal Harmonisation in Accounting: An Exploratory Study', *Accounting and Business Research*, **26** (4), Autumn, 325–39; P. Weetman, E.A.E. Jones, C.A. Adams and S.J. Gray (1998), 'Profit Measurement and UK Accounting Standards: A Case of Increasing Disharmony in Relation to US GAAP and IASs', *Accounting and Business Research*, **28** (3), Summer, 189–208; Richard D. Morris and R.H. Parker (1998), 'International Harmony Measures of Accounting Policy: Comparative Statistical Properties', *Accounting and Business Research*, **29** (1), Winter, 73–86; Sally Aisbitt and Christopher Nobes (2001), 'The True and Fair View Requirement in Recent National Implementations', *Accounting and Business Research*, **31** (2), Spring, 83–90; Sally Aisbitt (2002), 'Harmonisation of Financial Reporting before the European Company Law Directives: The Case of the Nordic Companies Act', *Accounting and Business Research*, **32** (2), 105–17.

American Accounting Association for articles: Peter H. Collett, Jayne M. Godfrey and Sue L. Hrasky (2001), 'International Harmonization: Cautions from the Australian Experience', *Accounting Horizons*, **15** (2), June, 171–82; Ronald A. Dye and Shyam Sunder (2001), 'Why Not Allow FASB and IASB Standards to Compete in the U.S.?', *Accounting Horizons*, **15** (3), September, 257–71; Stephen A. Zeff (2002), '"Political" Lobbying on Proposed Standards: A Challenge to the IASB', *Accounting Horizons*, **16** (1), March, 43–54.

Blackwell Publishing Ltd for articles: Simon Archer, Pascale Delvaille and Stuart McLeay (1996), 'A Statistical Model of International Accounting Harmonization', *Abacus*, **32** (1), March, 1–29; Robert H. Parker and Richard D. Morris (2001), 'The Influence of U.S. GAAP on the Harmony of Accounting Measurement Policies of Large Companies in the U.K. and Australia', *Abacus*, **37** (3), October, 297–328.

Elsevier Science for articles: Emmanuel N. Emenyonu and Sidney J. Gray (1996), 'International Accounting Harmonization and the Major Developed Stock Market Countries: An Empirical Study', *International Journal of Accounting*, **31** (3), 269–79; Alan S. Dunk and Alan Kilgore (2000), 'The Reintroduction of the True and Fair Override and Harmonization with IASC

Standards in Australia: Lessons from the EU and Implications for Financial Reporting and International Trade', *International Journal of Accounting*, **35** (2), 213–26; Hervé Stolowy, Axel Haller and Volker Klockhaus (2001), 'Accounting for Brands in France and Germany Compared with IAS 38 (Intangible Assets): An Illustration of the Difficulty of International Harmonization', *International Journal of Accounting*, **36**, 147–67.

Taylor and Francis Ltd (http://www.tandf.co.uk/journals) for articles: Neil Garrod and Isabel Sieringhaus (1995), 'European Union Accounting Harmonization: The Case of Leased Assets in the United Kingdom and Germany', *European Accounting Review*, **4** (1), 155–64; R.H. Parker (1996), 'Harmonizing the Notes in the UK and France: A Case Study in *De Jure* Harmonization', *European Accounting Review*, **5** (2), 317–37; Lisa Evans and Christopher Nobes (1996), 'Some Mysteries Relating to the Prudence Principle in the Fourth Directive and in German and British Law', *European Accounting Review*, **5** (2), 361–73; Vera M. Krisement (1997), 'An Approach for Measuring the Degree of Comparability of Financial Accounting Information', *European Accounting Review*, **6** (3), 465–85; Karel Van Hulle (1997), 'The True and Fair View Override in the European Accounting Directives', *European Accounting Review*, **6** (4), 711–20; Lisa Evans and Christopher Nobes (1998), 'Harmonization of the Structure of Audit Firms: Incorporation in the UK and Germany', *European Accounting Review*, **7** (1), 125–48; Stephen A. Zeff, Willem Buijink and Kees Camfferman (1999), '"True and Fair" in the Netherlands: *Inzicht* or *Getrouw Beeld*?', *European Accounting Review*, **8** (3), 523–48; Leandro Cañibano and Araceli Mora (2000), 'Evaluating the Statistical Significance of *De Facto* Accounting Harmonization: A Study of European Global Players', *European Accounting Review*, **9** (3), 349–69; Sally Aisbitt (2001), 'Measurement of Harmony of Financial Reporting Within and Between Countries: The Case of the Nordic Countries', *European Accounting Review*, **10** (1), 51–72.

Every effort has been made to trace all the copyright holders but if any have been inadvertently overlooked the publishers will be pleased to make the necessary arrangement at the first opportunity.

In addition the publishers wish to thank the Marshall Library of Economics, Cambridge University and the Library of the University of Warwick for their assistance in obtaining these articles.

Introduction

Christopher W. Nobes

General

This volume takes up the literature on the harmonization of financial reporting where the first edition left off: in the middle of the 1990s. The coverage here is divided into two parts. Part I is concerned with the measurement of harmonization, and Part II contains analysis of, and comment on, harmonization. Most of the papers refer to harmonization as driven by the European Union (EU) or by the International Accounting Standards Committee (IASC). In many cases both the EU and the IASC are considered or contrasted, so it would not have been useful to try to separate the papers into a part on the EU and another part on the IASC, as in the first edition.

Measurement

The measurement of harmonization became a well-established area of academic research from the late 1980s, and the seminal papers were included in the first edition of the volume. The papers in this edition reveal a continuing interest in the topic by a large number of researchers. Many of the papers do not just use the handed-down statistical tools but seek to enhance them. As a result, the subject has advanced rapidly, with researchers building on the recently completed work of others.

Much of the work included here uses techniques that can be traced back to the ideas of van der Tas (1988) who developed three indices for measuring harmonization:

- the H index for harmonization within a country,
- the C index for harmonization within a country where there is multiple reporting, and
- the I index for harmonization between countries.

Herrmann and Thomas (Chapter 1, this volume) use the I index and the chi-square statistic to measure the harmony of nine accounting issues in eight European countries in 1992–3. Like many authors, they refer to harmonization (a process over time) when they mean harmony (a state of affairs at a particular date).

Archer, Delvaille and McLeay (Chapter 2, this volume) develop the C index by breaking it into within-country and between-country elements. They also tackle the problem of non-disclosure and propose solutions for non-disclosures of methods and of items. They apply their techniques to two important accounting issues (deferred tax and goodwill) in eight European countries for 1986–7 and 1990–1. They find little harmony or harmonization. In Chapter 3, the same authors use this data in a more complex analysis, in which they present a method of modelling statistically the process of harmonization.

Emenyonu and Gray (Chapter 4, this volume) examine the practices of companies from five major countries over the period 1971–2 to 1991–2. They use a chi-square test and the I index. For 26 measurement bases, they find mixed results: some increases in harmony and some decreases.

Krisement (Chapter 5, this volume) sets out to measure the comparability of financial reporting for particular transactions. She has some criticisms of the papers by van der Tas and Archer *et al.* Krisement uses a combination of the C index and a measure of entropy. This is applied to data on the practices of a large survey of European companies in 1989.

Morris and Parker (Chapter 6, this volume) examine the competing merits of the I index and the between-country C index. They use a simulation study of the use of three accounting valuations methods in ten countries. They find that the indices diverge as more countries are added, and that the C index is superior.

Cañibano and Mora (Chapter 7, this volume) use the C index but introduce a bootstrapping test in order to measure the significance of changes in the index over time. They look at four accounting issues for 85 'global players' from 13 European countries in order to measure harmonization from 1991–2 to 1996–7. They find evidence of harmonization that is spontaneous, i.e. not driven by changes in rules.

Aisbitt (Chapter 8, this volume) looks at harmonization in the Nordic region by studying harmony at four dates from 1981 to 1998. The paper finds some evidence of harmonization but is especially interesting for its investigation of problems relating to causal inference and to the properties of the indices.

In the last of the papers using the C index, Parker and Morris (Chapter 9, this volume) examine, for eleven accounting measurement issues, whether large UK and Australian companies are moving closer together because of the influence of US rules. For the measurement of national harmony, they use the H index; for international harmony, the C index and the chi-square test. Parker and Morris find international harmony for only three of the eleven issues.

The above papers study harmony or harmonization of *practices*. Rahman, Perera and Ganeshanandam (Chapter 10, this volume) propose a method for studying *de jure* harmony. They apply multiple discriminant analysis to the disclosure and measurement rules of Australia and New Zealand of 1993.

Weetman *et al.* (Chapter 11, this volume) study Forms 20-F for UK companies for 1988 and 1994. They find greater conservatism under US than under UK rules for both years, and increased disharmony. The biggest differences related to goodwill, deferred tax and pension accounting. Readers will be aware that all three issues have seen major changes to UK rules (and, in the case of goodwill, US rules also) since 1994.

Part II of this volume has a broadly chronological arrangement, not by publication but by topic. That is, we begin with harmonization before the European Directives, then move to the Fourth Directive, then the Eighth, then to the interaction of the European harmonization programme with the IASC, then to a recent harmonization issue connected to the United States.

In Chapter 12, Aisbitt examines harmonization in the four large Nordic countries through the twentieth century and particularly in the 1970s. There is an interesting mixture of influences from outside, particularly from Germany and from the UK.

The next six chapters cover issues related to the Fourth Directive. Parker (in Chapter 13, this volume) looks at the harmonization between the UK and France as caused by the Fourth Directive, on the subject of the rules relating to the notes to the financial statements. He considers that French accounting can be seen to have moved towards British accounting in this area, although the *annexe* in France is a separate document from the financial statements, whereas the notes in the UK are not. Evans and Nobes (Chapter 14, this volume) look at the treatment of prudence. Before the Directive, this principle was given special status in Germany and in the UK. However, its importance varies in different language versions of the Directive. Its importance has gradually waned in the rules of the UK but not those of Germany.

Chapters 15 to 17 look at various aspects of the true and fair view. Van Hulle (Chapter 15, this volume) examines the origins of the override in the Directive, reporting how various member states supported or opposed it. He also notes opposition from several countries to the override in IAS 1. Elsewhere, Walton (1997) looks at the detailed wording concerning 'true and fair' in the various drafts of the Directive. Like Van Hulle, he comments on the contributions of the various member states.

The next two papers look at implementations of the 'true and fair view' in specific member states. Zeff *et al.* (Chapter 16, this volume) investigates the phrases in Dutch law that could be seen as the equivalent of the original English words. The origins of those words pre-date the Directive. Elsewhere, Zeff (1990, see the first edition of Volume 2) examines which words should be best seen as the English equivalent. Aisbitt and Nobes (Chapter 17, this volume) analyse the implementations in Austria, Finland, Norway and Sweden. As with earlier implementations, there is interesting variety in the literal translations and in the strength of (or even presence of) the override.

In Chapter 18, Dunk and Kilgore examine the reluctant proposed reintroduction of the override in Australia caused by harmonization with International Accounting Standards. They draw parallels with developments in the EU. Collett *et al.* (Chapter 19, this volume) examine the political aspects of the adoption of international standards in Australia. The authors are fighting a rear-guard action for the survival of distinctive Australian standards.

Chapters 20 and 21 look at the harmonization of accounting for assets in some EU countries. In a brief paper, Garrod and Sieringhaus examine lease accounting in the UK and Germany. They show that the rules in both countries are vague and lead to different results. The arrival of the Fourth Directive did not bring about harmonization. Stolowy *et al.* (Chapter 21) examine the treatment of brands in France and Germany. They show that valuation and amortization approaches are substantially different even in these two countries that are often classified together.

Elsewhere, four papers contain a heated debate between three writers on the comparative merits and success of the harmonization programmes of the EU and the IASC. Flower (1997) looks at the implications of the EU's proposal of 1995 to allow European 'global players' to use IASs. He suggests that a problem for acceptance is that the IASC is 'dominated by the Anglo-American approach', and that the SEC is unlikely to accept IASs. In a comment of about twice the length of Flower's paper, Cairns (1997) suggests that the notion of Anglo-American accounting is out of date; indeed, that the whole activity of classification is misguided. As part of this, he rejects the idea of Anglo-American dominance of the IASC. Cairns provides a detailed description of the IASC and its relationships with other bodies. Nobes (1998) and Flower (1998) respond to Cairns' criticisms, although they do not share the same view on some major issues. Nobes suggests that classifications can be useful. The fact that a few German corporations were using US rules for consolidated statements does not change German accounting or mean that Anglo-American accounting cannot be presented as a contrast to it. To complete the picture, Flower replies briefly that he still believes in the main theses of his original paper.

In Chapter 22, Evans and Nobes turn attention to the Eighth Directive, and in particular the incorporation of audit firms. They examine the legal position in Germany and the UK before the Directive, the provisions of the Directive, and the implementations in the two countries' laws. There was legal change but little harmonization. Elsewhere, Evans and Nobes (1998) examine another aspect of Anglo-German audit harmonization: auditor independence.

The last two papers connect the US and the IASB. Dye and Sunder (Chapter 23, this volume) ask, in the form of a debate, whether international standards should be allowed to compete with domestic standards in the United States. Zeff reports (in Chapter 24) on the strength of political lobbying of the US standard setter. He notes the threat to the IASB on particular issues, such as accounting for stock options. These papers were written before the dramatic collapses of Enron and Andersen in 2001–2. The pressure in the USA to take notice of international aspects was greatly increased then, and will no doubt lead to many further papers in this area.

References

Cairns, D. (1997), 'The future shape of harmonization: a reply', *European Accounting Review*, **7** (2), 304–48.

Evans, L. and Nobes, C. (1998), 'Harmonization relating to auditor independence: the Eighth Directive, the UK and Germany', *European Accounting Review*, **7** (3), 493–516.

Flower, J. (1997), 'The future shape of harmonization: the EU versus the IASC versus the SEC', *European Accounting Review*, **6** (2), 281–303.

Flower, J. (1998), 'The future shape of harmonization: a reply', *European Accounting Review*, **7** (2), 331–3.

Nobes, C.W. (1998), 'The future shape of harmonization: some responses', *European Accounting Review*, **7** (2), 323–30.

Walton, P. (1997), 'The true and fair view and the drafting of the Fourth Directive', *European Accounting Review*, **6** (4), 721–30.

Zeff, S.A. (1990), 'The English language equivalent of "Geeft een Getrouw Beeld"', *De Accountant*, **2**, October, 83.

Part I
The Measurement of Harmonization

[1]

Accounting and Business Research, Vol. 25, No. 100, pp. 253-265, 1995

Harmonisation of Accounting Measurement Practices in the European Community

Don Herrmann and Wayne Thomas*

Abstract—This study attempts to determine the level of accounting harmonisation in the European Community by examining selected measurement practices from the 1992/93 annual reports of companies from Belgium, Denmark, France, Germany, Ireland, the Netherlands, Portugal and the UK. Harmonisation is tested using the chi-square statistic and measured using the *I* index. The chi-square statistic tests for the equality of the proportions of accounting measurement methods across countries. The *I* index measures the extent of concentration around a particular accounting measurement method. The results reveal that accounting for foreign currency translation of assets and liabilities, treatment of translation differences, and inventory valuation are harmonised, while accounting for fixed asset valuation, depreciation, goodwill, research and development costs, inventory costing, and foreign currency translation of revenues and expenses are not harmonised. The results also demonstrate that the extent of harmonisation is greater among fairness oriented countries than among legalistic countries.

Introduction

There are three primary questions of interest in the area of accounting harmonisation: Is there a need for harmonised accounting practices? What factors are the most favourable and the most obstructive to the harmonisation process? And to what extent are current practices harmonised? Answers to these questions are important to a wide variety of financial statement users, including stockholders, creditors, analysts, standard-setters, regulators and economic planners.

Regarding the first question, some have argued that harmonisation of accounting practices is not only unnecessary (Choi and Levich, 1991; Goeltz, 1992), but potentially harmful in certain contexts (Fantl, 1971; Samuels and Oliga, 1982). However, efforts by several international organisations indicate that these organisations consider harmonisation of accounting practices to be a worthwhile pursuit. Evident by the number of pronouncements issued, international political bodies (such as the United Nations, European Community and the Organisation for Economic Cooperation and Development) and international private standard-setting bodies (such as the International Accounting Standards Committee), have contributed significant resources towards improving the comparability of both the measurement and disclosure of accounting information. A variety of other institutions such as worldwide banks, labour unions, accounting firms and auditing firms can benefit from harmonised accounting practices through reduced information costs.

With respect to the factors favouring and obstructing harmonisation, Nobes and Parker (1991) and Radebaugh and Gray (1993) provide comprehensive discussions of the environmental factors that influence a nation's accounting system. Theoretically, environmental differences should cause accounting systems to differ while environmental likenesses should cause them to be similar. However, it is difficult to determine a priori which similarities represent the most favourable environment and which differences represent the largest obstacles for harmonisation.

The primary purpose of this paper addresses the third question: To what extent are current accounting practices harmonised? Specifically, we determine the extent of harmonisation of selected measurement practices (as opposed to disclosure practices or extant measurement and disclosure regulations) for companies within the EC. The EC was chosen because it provides a particularly interesting focus in the study of accounting harmonisation. Initiated by the Treaty of Rome (1957), the EC was established to provide for the free movement of persons, goods, services and capital among member countries.

Harmonisation of accounting practices is thought to be a major means to achieving a single common market. Whereas other regional and international bodies are only able to recommend or suggest international accounting standards, the EC requires member states to incorporate directives into national law. Many of the EC's member states are major industrialised countries with

*The authors are at the College of Business, Oregon State University and the School of Accounting, Oklahoma State University, respectively. They gratefully acknowledge the many helpful comments of Gary Meek, Grace Pownall, Tatsuo Inoue, participants of the accounting workshop at Oklahoma State University, participants at the American Accounting Association 1994 Midwest Regional Meeting, and two anonymous reviewers. Correspondence should be addressed to Professor Herrmann at the College of Business, Oregon State University, Corvallis, OR 97330-2603, USA.

well-established capital markets. Yet, the cultures of these countries are quite distinct. The outcome of the EC's harmonisation effort provides direction for the extent to which harmonisation is possible and the most effective strategy with which to proceed to harmonise accounting practices in other regions and around the world.

Defining harmonisation is not a simple task. The definitions used in prior research studies have varied. Therefore, for the purpose of this paper, harmonisation is concurrently defined in two ways. First, harmonisation is defined as the similarity in the frequency of accounting policy choices across countries. That is, harmonisation is achieved when the companies in each country select accounting policies with the same frequency. This type of de facto harmonisation will be measured using the chi-square test of independence. Second, harmonisation is defined as the extent of concentration around a particular accounting policy choice. The degree of harmonisation increases as the number of companies selecting the same accounting policy increases. This type of de facto harmonisation will be measured using a concentration index developed by Van der Tas (1988). While the second definition is the more strict of the two, an analysis of this study's results indicates little difference between the two definitions.

The remainder of this paper is organised as follows. The second section presents the contributions and improvements of this paper in relation to prior research. The third section discusses research methodology, including data selection, statistical analysis, measurement practices examined and a statement of the hypotheses, and section four provides an analysis of the results by measurement practice. Finally, the fifth section concludes with a summary of the findings, limitations and possibilities for future research.

Contributions and improvements

Many research studies examining the extent of harmonisation fall short in one or more of the following areas: distinction between measurement and disclosure issues; data selection; statistical tests of significance; and measurement of harmonisation.

The remainder of this section addresses each of these areas.

Distinction Between Measurement and Disclosure Issues

Research studies attempting to determine the extent of harmonisation frequently combine accounting measurement and disclosure issues without distinguishing between them (e.g., Nair and Frank, 1981; Choi and Bavishi, 1982; Evans and Taylor, 1982; McKinnon and Janell, 1984; and Purvis 1991). While the results are often shown according to accounting practice or standard, the extent of harmonisation is determined based on measurement and disclosure practices combined. The importance of distinguishing between the two is evident in a study by Hussein (1992). Comparing only two countries, the Netherlands and the US, Hussein found that measurement practices were harmonised but disclosure practices were not. The similarities of the markets and stock exchanges between the two countries were cited as the likely reason for measurement harmonisation, and differences in culture were given as the likely reason for lack of disclosure harmonisation. Thus, by clearly distinguishing measurement and disclosure issues, a greater understanding of the factors that have been the most conducive or obstructive to harmonisation of accounting practices can be obtained. This study will concentrate exclusively on measurement issues.

Data Selection

This study examines actual annual reports whereas many past studies in this area have employed survey data (e.g., Nair and Frank, 1981; McKinnon and Janell, 1984; Doupnik and Taylor, 1985; and Purvis 1991). One benefit of using survey data is that the tedious and time-consuming work of data collection is minimised. Also, several countries and practices can be examined since the data collection stage of the research project is practically eliminated. However, Nobes (1981) discusses some of the inherent limitations of using survey data when examining accounting practices. First, survey data may contain errors. Nobes illustrates numerous errors in the Price Waterhouse survey data, commonly used in classification and harmonisation studies.[1] Second, some answers, although strictly true, can be misleading, if taken out of the context of the survey. For instance, survey response in the Price Waterhouse survey data gives the impression that accounting in the UK and in Germany is equally conservative since both countries report similar scores for conservatism. However, the results fail to consider that the German definition of conservatism differs significantly from that in the UK. Finally, Nobes points out that in order to present data from surveys in an objective format, subjective choice must be made by the compilers of the survey data. Often, the compilers, staff accountants in the case of the Price Waterhouse survey data, have a different purpose in mind than do researchers who might use the data, resulting in potential measurement error from the standpoint of the researcher.

[1]Price Waterhouse collected data of accounting principles and reporting practices in various countries in 1973, 1975 and 1979. The 1973, 1975 and 1979 surveys included 38, 46 and 64 countries, respectively, and covered 233, 264 and 267 accounting practices, respectively.

Tay and Parker (1990) distinguish between de jure harmonisation (rules, standards, etc.) and de facto harmonisation (corporate financial reporting practices). It is possible to have one of these two forms of harmonisation without the other. This study tests de facto harmonisation in contrast to the majority of studies examining de jure harmonisation. We agree with Tay and Parker (1990, pp. 84–85):

> 'If harmonisation activities are the result of concern about the comparability of accounts produced by companies from different countries, then a measurement study should focus on actual reporting practices rather than regulations, that is, on de facto rather than de jure harmonisation. Actual reporting practices may be assessed most accurately from annual accounts, or detailed surveys of such accounts.'

A research project should clearly distinguish between whether it is measuring harmonisation of accounting standards or harmonisation of accounting practices. For example, the 1973 Price Waterhouse survey data is categorised as (1) required, (2) majority, (3) about half, (4) minority, (5) no application, and (6) not permitted.[2] Note that categories 1 and 6 refer to standards whereas categories 2, 3, 4 and 5 refer to practices. The fact that a particular practice is required by a professional standard does not necessarily indicate that it is practised by all companies. Meek and Saudagaran (1990, p. 147) point out that 'penalties for non-compliance with official accounting pronouncements are weak or ineffective in many countries. Examining only the required standards can result in a misleading picture of actual accounting practices in a country'.

Emenyonu and Gray (1992) examine the harmonisation of measurement practices in France, Germany and the UK, based on 1989 annual reports from 26 major companies located in each of the three countries. They find significant differences in the measurement practices of inventory valuation, depreciation, goodwill, fixed asset valuation and extraordinary items. Our study builds upon Emenyonu and Gray (1992) in the following ways: First, this study includes the reporting practices of companies from Belgium, Denmark, Ireland, the Netherlands and Portugal, in addition to France, Germany and the UK. Second, this study examines the measurement practices for foreign currency translation, inventory costing methods and accounting for research and development, in addition to the practices examined in Emenyonu and Gray.[3] Finally, this study examines the 1992/93 annual reports in contrast to the 1989 annual reports used in Emenyonu and Gray. This allows for a comparison of reporting practices in France, Germany and the UK over time. Differences in results between this study and Emenyonu and Gray are addressed in the relevant portions of the analysis section.

Statistical Tests of Significance

With the exception of Emenyonu and Gray (1992), past research studies have not employed a statistical test of significance when determining the degree of harmonisation across countries (e.g., Choi and Bavishi, 1982; Evans and Taylor, 1982; McKinnon and Janell, 1984; Doupnik and Taylor, 1985; and Freedman and Stagliano, 1992), relying simply on interpretations of means, percentages and ratios. The difference in the level of harmonisation across countries will be tested for statistical significance with the non-parametric chi-square test of independence.

Measurement of Harmonisation

The majority of the past research studies have not computed a single, objective measure of harmonisation (e.g., Choi and Bavishi, 1982; Evans and Taylor, 1982; McKinnon and Janell, 1984; and Freedman and Stagliano, 1992), instead they have relied primarily on descriptive statistics. Without a single measure on which to judge the level of harmonisation, the results tend to rely heavily on the researcher's interpretation as to the extent of harmonisation. Not until Van der Tas (1988) was a single, quantifiable measure proposed to assess international harmonisation, the *I* index. The *I* index will be used to determine the extent to which companies within EC countries concentrate around a particular accounting method.

Research methodology

Data

The data used in this study are from the most recent annual reports available at the time of collection (1992/93 year ends). Based on the information in *Europe's 15,000 Largest Companies* (1992), letters written in English requesting the most recent annual report were sent to the 65 largest companies, excluding financial institutions and insurance companies, from 10 of the 12 EC member nations. Greece and Luxembourg were excluded from the mailing as neither country had 65 companies large enough to be listed in our data source. Italy and Spain were subsequently excluded from the study as less than 10 serviceable annual reports were received from each of these two countries.

[2]The 1975 and 1979 Price Waterhouse surveys employed a similar format for classifying accounting practices.

[3]Emenyonu and Gray initially examined research and development but were unable to present results due to the lack of disclosure by companies, resulting in sample sizes too small for purposes of statistical tests.

This study examines the largest companies located in each country since accounting harmonisation is an especially important issue for large multinationals. Large firms are more likely to be listed on foreign stock exchanges and to attract the interest of international investors. The likelihood of response should also increase by sampling large multinationals. Sample selection was based on firm size (total sales), not industry code. However, a review of the final sample of firms does not reveal any particular industry bias by country.

Response to the original mailing request varied by country. Companies from the Netherlands and the UK provided the best response. Second requests were sent to non-responders in Belgium, Denmark, France, Germany, Ireland and Portugal eight weeks subsequent to the initial requests. The final sample includes 30 corporate annual reports from Denmark, France, Germany, Netherlands and the UK, 23 from Belgium, 24 from Ireland and 20 from Portugal, for a total sample size of 217 annual reports from eight of the 12 EC countries.

With the exception of Belgium and Portugal, all annual reports were English versions. Six of the 23 reports from Belgium were translated from French and 11 of the 20 reports from Portugal were translated from Portuguese with the aid of an interpreter. A comparison of the English reports and the domestic language reports for both Belgium and Portugal revealed no significant differences in reporting practices. Additionally, in cases where both an English and a domestic language report were received from a company, no differences were found for the six measurement practices examined.

Statistical Analysis

The general hypothesis of harmonisation is tested using the chi-square statistic. By comparing observed frequencies against expected frequencies, the chi-square statistic tests for the equality of the proportions of accounting measurement policy choices across countries. The computed test statistic is compared to the 0.01 critical value to determine whether the null hypothesis is rejected. Failure to reject the null hypothesis suggests harmonisation of accounting measurement practices and rejection of the null hypothesis suggests a lack of harmonisation of accounting measurement practices.

When employing the chi-square statistic, Cochran (1952) suggests that when 20% of the expected cell frequencies are less than five or when any one expected cell frequency is less than one, then the computed test statistic may be inflated, possibly resulting in inappropriate conclusions. To control for the inflation caused by small expected frequencies, this paper employs a commonly used method to adjust the computed test statistics. If either of the two conditions mentioned by Cochran exists, the chi-square statistic can be approximated by averaging the contributions of individual cells that have expected cell frequency of greater than five and then multiplying by the total number of cells. The resulting test statistic has an approximate chi-square distribution.

Van der Tas (1988) uses a Herfindahl concentration index (*H* index) to measure the harmonisation of an accounting method within a country. The *H* index is computed as:

$$H = \sum_{m=1}^{M} p_m^2$$

where:

H = Herfindahl index.
m = alternative accounting method m.
p_m = relative frequency of accounting method m.

Van der Tas (1988) devises two variants of the *H* index; the *C* index and the *I* index. The *C* index measures national harmonisation when a company provides information for several alternative methods of a particular accounting practice. The *I* index measures international harmonisation, i.e., harmonisation of accounting practices among two or more countries. The *I* index is computed as:

$$I = \left[\sum_{m=1}^{M}\left(\prod_{n=1}^{N} p_{m,n}\right)\right]^{\frac{1}{(N-1)}}$$

where:

I = *I* index.
m = alternative accounting method m.
n = country n.
p_{mn} = relative frequency of accounting method m in country n.

The *I* index is computed by multiplying across countries the proportion of companies practising a particular accounting alternative and then summing over all alternative practices. The correction factor in the exponent is used when more than two countries are examined. The *I* index is not meant to give an indication of the statistical significance of harmonisation, but rather a scale upon which to quantify harmonisation for comparative purposes.

Although the *I* index is a direct variant of the *H* index, it falls short in one particular area. The *H* index ranges from 1 (all companies using the same method) to 1/*M* (companies are proportioned evenly over *M* alternative methods). Therefore, the *H* index approaches 0 as the number of alternative methods all with the same frequency approaches infinity. The *I* index also ranges from 0 to 1 but, due to the multiplication involved, the *I* index is sensitive to zero proportions. The potential sensitivity increases as the number of countries surveyed increases. To control for this sensitivity, this paper employs a simple modification to the *I* index. In cases where all of the companies in a particular country chose one of the two alternative methods, the proportions are recorded as 0.99 for the

Figure 1
Comparison of the Unadjusted and Adjusted *I* Index for Each of the Three Scenarios

						Unadjusted *I* index	Adjusted *I* index
Scenario 1:							
	Country	*1*	*2*	*3*	*4*		
Method	A	20	20	0	0	0[1]	0.0581[2]
	B	0	0	20	20		
Scenario 2:							
	Country	*1*	*2*	*3*	*4*		
Method	A	20	20	10	0	0	0.1704
	B	0	0	10	20		
Scenario 3:							
	Country	*1*	*2*	*3*	*4*		
Method	A	20	20	20	0	0	0.2133
	B	0	0	0	20		

[1]For scenario 1, Unadjusted $I = [(1 \times 1 \times 0 \times 0) + (0 \times 0 \times 1 \times 1)]^{1/3} = 0$

[2]For scenario 1, Adjusted $I = [(0.99 \times 0.99 \times 0.01 \times 0.01) + (0.01 \times 0.01 \times 0.99 \times 0.99)]^{1/3} = 0.0581$

unanimous method and 0.01 for the non-practised method (instead of 1 and 0, respectively). The following illustration will demonstrate this point.

There are three scenarios with a sample of 20 companies from each of four countries. Each company may select accounting method A or B. In the first scenario, all of the companies in countries 1 and 2 select method A and all of the companies in countries 3 and 4 select method B. In the second scenario, half of the companies in country 3 switch from method B to method A. In the third scenario, all of the companies in country 3 select method A. From this, one would intuitively conclude that, going from scenario 1 to scenario 2 to scenario 3, harmonisation is increasing among the countries (i.e., a greater number of firms are choosing method A). However, use of the *I* index to measure harmonisation would not indicate this. The illustrations in Figure 1 compare the unadjusted and adjusted *I* index for each of the three scenarios.

Due to at least one zero existing in each row, the unadjusted *I* indices will be 0 for each of the three scenarios, indicating absolutely no harmonisation among the four countries. This does not seem reasonable from observation of the data since the number of firms choosing the same accounting method is increasing. Furthermore, the index is computed to be 0 even though as many as 75% of all companies choose method A (scenario 3). After adjusting the *I* index to account for the zeros, a more realistic measure of harmonisation among the four countries is given for each of the three scenarios. The adjusted *I* index increases, correctly indicating that the level of harmonisation increases as the number of companies clustering around method A increases.

As mentioned earlier, the chi-square statistic measures a different definition of harmonisation than does the *I* index. The chi-square statistic tests for equal proportions across countries and renders the power of statistics to determine significant differences. The *I* index measures the more intuitive definition of harmonisation but provides no test for statistical significance.[4]

Measurement Practices

Measurement practices must meet two criteria for inclusion in this study. First, the policy choices must significantly affect measures of net assets and/or profits. Second, the annual reports must contain sufficient disclosure to determine the policy choice selected. Potential measurement practices to be examined include fixed asset valuation, research and development, inventory valuation, inventory costing, investments, depreciation, deferred tax, extraordinary items, pensions, consolidations, goodwill and foreign currency translation. Van der Tas (1992) extensively measures the degree of harmonisation of deferred taxes in the EC. He finds that harmonisation of accounting for deferred taxes has improved over time. Investments, leases, pensions and consolidations are excluded from this study due to the more varied and complex wording of these disclosures as well as the difficulty of fitting these measurement practices into distinct categories.

[4]The possibility of confounding results may arise. That is, the *I* index could suggest a high level of harmonisation while the chi-square test statistic could concurrently reject this notion, and vice versa. However, this limitation does not seem to affect the results of this study. The Spearman rank correlation computed between the chi-square test statistics and the *I* indices across all accounting measurement issues resulted in a correlation coefficient of −0.7333 which is significantly different from 0 at the 0.05 significance level, but is not significantly different from −1. This indicates that high *I* indices are appropriately associated with low values of the chi-square test statistic.

Extraordinary items were originally examined, but later dropped due to the lack of a consistent definition of extraordinary items across countries and limited disclosure of the practice used in recording them. Inventory costing methods are combined with inventory valuation methods as the former represent a subset of the latter. Therefore, the six measurement practices selected for examination are fixed asset valuation, depreciation, goodwill, research and development, inventory, and foreign currency translation.

Hypothesis

Adopted by the EC Council of Ministers on 25 July 1978, the Fourth Directive outlines the formats of financial statements and rules of accounting. It aims to expedite the harmonisation of financial accounting practices. However, agreement on the Fourth Directive involved a long and difficult process. Radebaugh and Gray (1993, p. 148) conclude: 'The result of the Fourth Directive was a compromise between the continental European and the Anglo-Saxon systems with the emphasis more on disclosing the nature and effect of differences between countries.' It resulted in more of a disclosure document than a change in accounting measurement practices. While the Fourth Directive may have changed the status of measurement practices (e.g., in the UK they are now part of company law), financial statement users are ultimately concerned with companies' actual accounting measurement policy choices. The general hypothesis to be tested is stated below in the alternative form.

H_A: There are differences in the frequency of accounting measurement policy choices across the eight EC countries examined.

This hypothesis is tested by individually examining the accounting policy choices for fixed asset valuation, depreciation, goodwill, research and development costs, inventory, and foreign currency translation. Accounting for inventory consists of the valuation basis and the cost flow assumption for inventory. Accounting for foreign currency translation includes the translation of balance sheet items, translation of income statement items and the treatment of translation gains and losses.

Analysis of results

For each of the six measurement practices examined in this study, a discussion of the provisions under the EC Fourth Directive will be provided along with an analysis of the results, statistical tests and conclusions. Tables, summarising the results for each measurement practice, are located within each section. The categories of alternative accounting methods listed in the tables are based on the actual wording of the annual reports. A non-disclosure category is included for research and development, goodwill, inventory costing and foreign currency translation. Non-disclosure may simply signify that the particular accounting policy is not relevant (e.g. no research and development costs). In other cases, non-disclosure signifies that the company is not willing to reveal this information. Since most of the EC countries allow more than one alternative for each accounting policy choice, it is impossible to infer which accounting method the non-disclosing firm selects. As a result, the non-disclosure category is reported but excluded for the purposes of statistical tests and computation of I indices.

Fixed Asset Valuation

The standard valuation principle under the Fourth Directive is historical cost. Article 33 allows member states to use periodic revaluations, replacement values and valuation methods that consider the effects of inflation. The Fourth Directive requires the disclosure of valuations that are determined by tax rules rather than by commercial or company law provisions.

Table 1 summarises the results by country relating to fixed asset valuation. Germany is the only country where all sampled companies used strict historical cost. German law does not allow for the use of periodic revaluations. In France, fixed assets were revalued in 1978 at 1976 values. However, the majority of French companies disclose the use of historical cost to value fixed assets. Ireland and the

Table 1

Fixed Asset Valuation

	Belgium	*Denmark*	*France*	*Germany*	*Ireland*	*Netherlands*	*Portugal*	*UK*	*Total*
Historical cost	19	12	24	30	5	24	0	9	123
Modified historical	4	18	6	0	19	6	20	21	94
	23	30	30	30	24	30	20	30	217

$X^2 = 93.34$, p-value $= 0.0001$, I index $= 0.2852$

UK allow periodic revaluations on an ad hoc basis. In the Netherlands, often recognised for their use of replacement cost, only one company discloses replacement cost as the primary basis of fixed asset valuation. This company is included in the modified historical cost category. All Portuguese companies disclose the use of periodic revaluations. Based on the chi-square test statistic, we conclude that there is a significant difference in the fixed asset valuation methods chosen by large companies from the eight EC countries examined.

Depreciation Methods

The Fourth Directive has a flexible depreciation policy requirement as it does not specify the use of any particular depreciation method. Rather, straight-line, declining balance, or a combination of the two methods is allowed. Tax rules play an important role in the depreciation policy of some European countries. In countries such as Ireland, the Netherlands and the UK, depreciation for financial reporting purposes is separate from depreciation for tax purposes. In contrast, depreciation in Germany is very similar for financial reporting and tax purposes. It is common practice in Germany to use a declining balance method and then switch to the straight-line method in the later years of a fixed asset's useful life in order to obtain the maximum possible tax benefits.

Table 2 summarises the results regarding the depreciation methods used. With the exception of Germany, the vast majority of large EC companies use straight-line depreciation. Only two companies, both located in Denmark, strictly use declining balance methods. These two companies are included with the 39 companies disclosing the use of both straight-line and declining balance methods. The chi-square statistic is significant, due almost exclusively to the practice of Germany. We conclude that there is a significant difference in the depreciation methods used by large companies from the eight EC countries.

Examining only France, Germany and the UK, Emenyonu and Gray (1992) report an *I* index for depreciation methods of only 0.0076. Our results for these three countries represent an *I* index of 0.2417. However, the *I* index of 0.6245 for all eight countries is much higher, reflecting the fact that Germany appears to be a lone outlier in the consistent use of declining balance methods among EC countries. A subsequent analysis made without Germany reveals an insignificant chi-square test statistic and an *I* index of 0.9067 among the seven remaining countries.

Goodwill

Article 37 of the Fourth Directive permits goodwill, to the extent that it was acquired for valuable consideration, to be capitalised as an intangible asset on the balance sheet or to be immediately written off against reserves. If capitalised, goodwill should normally be written off over a maximum of five years. However, Article 37 allows companies to amortise purchased goodwill systematically over a period of time exceeding five years provided that this period does not exceed the useful economic life of the asset and is disclosed in the footnotes to the financial statements.

Table 3 provides a summary of the reporting practices for purchased goodwill by country. The split between those companies capitalising goodwill and those companies writing off goodwill immediately to reserves is approximately equal. Belgium, France, Germany and Portugal favour capitalisation of goodwill, whereas Denmark, Ireland, the Netherlands and the UK prefer immediate write-off of purchased goodwill against reserves. Based on the chi-square test statistic, we conclude that a significant difference exists for the recording of purchased goodwill by large companies from the eight EC countries examined. The *I* index reflects a low degree of harmonisation for this accounting policy.

The results are consistent with those reported in Emenyonu and Gray (1992) with the exception of Germany. Emenyonu and Gray in their examination of 1989 annual reports found a higher percentage of German firms writing off purchased

Table 2

Depreciation

	Belgium	*Denmark*	*France*	*Germany*	*Ireland*	*Netherlands*	*Portugal*	*UK*	*Total*
Straight-line	17	28	26	2	23	30	20	30	176
Straight-line and declining balance	6	2	4	28	1	0	0	0	41
	23	30	30	30	24	30	20	30	217

$X^2 = 134.82$, p-value = 0.0001, I index = 0.6245

Germany excluded:
$X^2 = 2.94$, p-value = 0.8158, I index = 0.9067

Table 3

Goodwill

	Belgium	*Denmark*	*France*	*Germany*	*Ireland*	*Netherlands*	*Portugal*	*UK*	*Total*
Write-off	0	18	0	9	17	25	0	29	98
Capitalise	20	5	30	20	3	2	8	1	89
Not disclosed	3	7	0	1	4	3	12	0	30
	23	30	30	30	24	30	20	30	217

$X^2 = 124.90$, p-value $= 0.0001$, I index $= 0.2457$

goodwill directly to reserves, whereas this analysis found a higher percentage of German firms capitalising purchased goodwill. German firms were not required to apply the Accounting Directives Law, which governs the treatment of goodwill in Germany, until fiscal years ending *after* 1989, which may explain the change in the German practice.

Research and Development

Similar to the case for goodwill, Article 37 of the Fourth Directive is flexible in the recording of research and development costs. Companies may capitalise the costs of research and development as an intangible asset and amortise this cost over future years, or they may record the cost immediately as an expense in the income statement. If capitalised, the costs should normally be written off over a maximum of five years. However, similar to purchased goodwill, a longer amortisation period is allowed under Article 37, provided that this longer amortisation period is disclosed in the footnotes to the financial statements.

The reporting practices for research and development costs by country are given in Table 4. Almost 50% of all companies examined failed to disclose their method of recording research and development costs. As pointed out by Tonkin (1989, p. 18), 'this lack of disclosure is especially discouraging considering the size and importance that research and development costs can have on a company's operations'. The majority of the disclosing companies record research and development costs as an expense in the income statement. In contrast, companies from Belgium and Portugal favour capitalising research and development costs. The chi-square test statistic is significant and we conclude that there is a significant difference in the recording of research and development costs by large companies from the eight EC countries examined. The I index indicates a higher degree of harmonisation for research and development than for fixed asset valuation or goodwill, but a lower degree of harmonisation than for depreciation. When Belgium and Portugal are excluded, the chi-square test statistic and the I index indicate a high degree of harmonisation among the remaining six countries.

Inventory

Article 39 of the EC Fourth Directive states that current assets should be valued at the lower of purchase price, productive cost, or market value. If current assets are adjusted for taxation purposes alone, the amount of the adjustments and the reasons for making them must be disclosed.

The categorisation of inventory valuation methods is based on the stated accounting policies of the reporting firms. In the EC, market generally means net realisable value. However, we did note two exceptions in France. These two companies, likely influenced by US accounting principles,

Table 4

Research and Development

	Belgium	*Denmark*	*France*	*Germany*	*Ireland*	*Netherlands*	*Portugal*	*UK*	*Total*
Expense	4	15	19	3	10	9	0	25	85
Capitalise	9	0	0	0	0	4	10	1	24
Not disclosed	10	15	11	27	14	17	10	4	108
	23	30	30	30	24	30	20	30	217

$X^2 = 38.76$, p-value $= 0.0001$, I index $= 0.4105$

Belgium and Portugal excluded:
$X^2 = 2.47$, p-value $= 0.7814$, I index $= 0.9381$

Table 5a
Inventory Valuation

	Belgium	*Denmark*	*France*	*Germany*	*Ireland*	*Netherlands*	*Portugal*	*UK*	*Total*
Lower cost/market	22	26	29	30	24	17	7	30	185
Cost	1	4	1	0	0	8	13	0	27
Market	0	0	0	0	0	5	0	0	5
	23	30	30	30	24	30	20	30	217

$X^2 = 17.89$, p-value $= 0.0127$, I index $= 0.7943$

defined market as replacement cost rather than net realisable value in recording inventories at the lower of cost or market.

Table 5a demonstrates that the majority (87.5%) of EC companies value inventories at the lower of cost or market. In contrast, approximately two thirds of the companies from Portugal report strict historical cost, while on third report the use of lower of cost or market. In the Netherlands, eight companies use strict historical cost, while five companies report the valuation of inventories at market values. These five companies are combined with those reporting lower of cost or market for the purpose of statistical tests. The chi-square test statistic is not significant and we conclude that there is no significant difference in the valuation methods selected by large companies in the eight countries examined. The *I* index indicates a greater degree of harmonisation for inventory valuation than for any of the measurement practices discussed previously. The results are consistent with Emenyonu and Gray with the exception of France.

Inventory costing methods are a subset of inventory valuation methods. Article 40 of the Fourth Directive is flexible as to the method of computing inventory cost. Cost can be calculated by the weighted average method, the 'first in, first out' (FIFO) method, the 'last in, first out' (LIFO) method, or some similar method. Many companies use a combination of these methods, applying different cost methods to different categories of inventory.

Referring to Table 5b, the diversity of practice for inventory costing methods is quite evident. Additionally, the low level of disclosure (less than 60%) is disappointing. Tonkin (1989, p. 18) summarises the situation well:

> 'The low level of policy disclosures, coupled with the inherent variability in measurement practices used when accounting for inventories represents yet another information inefficiency within the international capital markets.'

Companies disclosing a combination of costing methods are classified as FIFO, LIFO, or average cost based on the dominant method used. If a dominant method is not clearly evident, companies are classified in the combined category. The combined category is deleted for purposes of statistical tests. Based on the chi-square test statistic, we conclude that significant differences exist among the inventory costing methods used by large companies from the eight EC countries examined The *I* index also signifies a low level of harmonisation.

Foreign Currency Translation

EC directives provide little guidance in the area of foreign currency translation. The Seventh Directive on consolidated accounts refers to translation methods only in the requirement that the

Table 5b
Inventory Costing

	Belgium	*Denmark*	*France*	*Germany*	*Ireland*	*Netherlands*	*Portugal*	*UK*	*Total*
FIFO	2	9	5	0	8	9	2	7	42
LIFO	6	0	2	15	0	1	0	0	24
Average	8	2	11	3	0	0	9	2	35
Combination	3	1	6	1	0	1	8	3	23
Not disclosed	4	18	6	11	16	19	1	18	93
	23	30	30	30	24	30	20	30	217

$X^2 = 71.88$, p-value $= 0.0001$, I index $= 0.2295$

Table 6a

Foreign Currency Translation of Assets and Liabilities

	Belgium	*Denmark*	*France*	*Germany*	*Ireland*	*Netherlands*	*Portugal*	*UK*	*Total*
Current	17	21	30	19	21	27	9	29	173
Current/historical	3	0	0	11	0	1	0	0	15
Not disclosed	3	9	0	0	3	2	11	1	29
	23	30	30	30	24	30	20	30	217

$X^2 = 7.22$, p-value = 0.4062, I index = 0.9040

Table 6b

Foreign Currency Translation of Revenues and Expenses

	Belgium	*Denmark*	*France*	*Germany*	*Ireland*	*Netherlands*	*Portugal*	*UK*	*Total*
Average/actual	20	4	29	24	13	18	6	26	140
Current	0	17	1	6	5	9	2	4	44
Not disclosed	3	9	0	0	6	3	12	0	33
	23	30	30	30	24	30	20	30	217

$X^2 = 54.39$, p-value = 0.0001, I index = 0.6433

Denmark excluded:
$X^2 = 5.23$, p-value = 0.5143, I index = 0.7881

Table 6c

Treatment of Translation Differences

	Belgium	*Denmark*	*France*	*Germany*	*Ireland*	*Netherlands*	*Portugal*	*UK*	*Total*
Reserves	19	17	30	19	17	29	3	30	164
Income	0	1	0	10	2	0	2	0	15
Not disclosed	4	12	0	1	5	1	15	0	38
	23	30	30	30	24	30	20	30	217

$X^2 = 6.88$, p-value = 0.4416, I index = 0.8494

bases of foreign currency translation be disclosed in the notes to the accounts. Nobes and Parker (1991, p. 324) indicate that, in most of Europe, the choice of method is left to the company.

We began our examination of foreign currency translation by classifying policy choices into the current rate method, the temporal method, or other methods. However, it became evident that many companies, especially in Germany, did not consistently apply either the current rate method or the temporal method. For instance, some companies translate all assets and liabilities at current rates, consistent with the current rate method, but record the resulting translation gain or loss in the income statement, consistent with the temporal method. Therefore, a finer classification is employed, whereby the translation of balance sheet and income statement accounts, and the treatment of translation differences are examined separately. The results are presented in the three tables above: Table 6a provides the results for the translation of foreign subsidiary assets and liabilities, Table 6b provides the results for the translation of foreign subsidiary revenue and expenses, and Table 6c provides the results for the treatment of translation differences.

Table 6a demonstrates that use of the current rate in translating all assets and liabilities is the dominant practice among major corporations in the EC. The lone exception is Germany where 11 of the 30 companies examined use a combination of current and historical rates. The chi-square test statistic is not significant and the I index demonstrates a high level of harmonisation. We conclude that there are no significant differences in the translation of foreign subsidiary assets and liabilities.

The translation of foreign subsidiary income is not as uniform as the translation of assets and liabilities. The use of average or actual rates during the fiscal year is more common than the use of year-end rates. Denmark provides the lone exception where 80% of companies disclosing translation of foreign subsidiary income use the current (year-end) rates. The chi-square test statistic is significant and the *I*-index is much lower for the translation of income statement items than for the translation of balance sheet items. We conclude that there are significant differences in the translation of foreign subsidiary revenues and expenses. A subsequent analysis made with the exclusion of Denmark indicates that a considerable degree of harmonisation exists among the countries studied with the exception of Denmark. The recomputed chi-square test statistic is not significant and the *I* index is 0.7881.

The treatment of translation differences is surprisingly uniform. The majority of large companies in Europe report translation differences in the reserve section of the balance sheet, rather than taking translation differences to the income statement. Similar to translation of the assets and liabilities, Germany provides the lone exception by reporting translation differences in the income statement. Nevertheless, the *I* index depicts a high level of harmonisation. The chi-square test statistic is not significant and we conclude that there are no significant differences in the treatment of translation gains and losses.

Bicountry I indices

To further explore the extent of harmonisation in the EC, bicountry *I* indices are computed for all pairs of countries (28 pairs) for each measurement practice. The averages of the bicountry *I* indices over the nine measurement practices are shown in Table 7.

The UK and Ireland have the highest bicountry average *I* index of 0.8554. This would seem to indicate that, at least for the measurement practices and countries examined, the accounting practices in these two countries appear to be the most harmonised. Portugal and Germany produce the lowest bicountry average *I* index of 0.3824 indicating that the accounting systems between these two countries are the least harmonised.

It is interesting to observe the bicountry *I* indices when the eight countries are classified as either legalistic (Belgium, France, Germany and Portugal) or fairness oriented (Denmark, Ireland, the Netherlands and the UK). The bicountry *I* indices computed between the fairness oriented countries are higher than *all* of the bicountry *I* indices computed between a fairness oriented country and a legalistic country. Of the legalistic countries, France has the highest bicountry *I* indices when compared to each of the fairness oriented countries. Two reasons for this may be the adoption of Anglo-Saxon principles of consolidation by numerous French multinational companies (Nobes and Parker, 1991, p. 300) and the influence of the IASC's international accounting standards in France. While not as uniform as the fairness oriented countries, the bicountry *I* indices are generally higher between legalistic countries than between a legalistic and a fairness oriented country.

The overall averages of the bicountry *I* indices are shown in the last column of Table 7. They represent an average measure of a particular country's harmonisation with the other seven countries. Four of the five most harmonised countries are fairness oriented, with the UK being the most harmonised and Portugal being the least harmonised of the eight countries. The results of the bicountry *I* indices indicate that factors related to fairness oriented accounting systems are more conducive to harmonisation of accounting measurement practices than are factors related to legalistic accounting systems.

Table 7

Bicountry *I* Indices Averaged over the Nine Measurement Practices

	Denmark	*France*	*Germany*	*Ireland*	*Netherlands*	*Portugal*	*UK*	*Overall average*[a]
Belgium	0.5200	0.7559	0.5963	0.5595	0.5877	0.6429	0.5940	0.6081
Denmark		0.6457	0.4940	0.7835	0.7244	0.4795	0.7733	0.6315
France			0.6403	0.6842	0.6569	0.6091	0.7114	0.6719
Germany				0.5225	0.4950	0.3824	0.5321	0.5232
Ireland					0.7600	0.4950	0.8554	0.6657
Netherlands						0.4994	0.7750	0.6426
Portugal							0.5127	0.5173
UK								0.6791

[a]This column is computed by averaging the seven bicountry *I* indices of each country.

A final analysis is done by separating the fairness oriented countries and the legalistic countries into two groups. Computing the four-country *I* indices for both groups reveals a higher level of harmonisation among fairness oriented countries. The *I* indices of the fairness oriented countries are higher in seven of the nine measurement practices. The average four-country *I* index for the fairness oriented countries is 0.7945 while for the legalistic countries it is only 0.5501.

Conclusion

This study applies statistical tests to determine the degree of harmonisation of selected accounting measurement practices among eight EC countries. The non-parametric chi-square statistic is used in determining whether the level of harmonisation for a given accounting practice is the same or different across countries. An *I* index developed by Van der Tas (1988) is used to measure the extent of harmonisation with respect to a given accounting practice and then to compare across practices. Modifications to both the chi-square statistic and the *I* index are developed in this paper to allow for small cell sizes and the 'zero effect' naturally occurring in this type of research.

A summary of the *I* index values and chi-square test statistics by measurement practice is given in Table 8. The highest degree of harmonisation is found in the areas of foreign currency translation and inventory valuation. The relatively high level of harmonisation for foreign currency translation is surprising considering that the EC's directives provide little guidance in this area. The use of lower of cost or market for inventory valuation is the predominant method in the EC. Harmonisation of depreciation methods is also very high, with the exception of the German practice of combining declining balance and straight-line methods. However, the results of this analysis also demonstrate that significant differences exist in accounting for research and development cost, fixed assets, goodwill and inventory costing. Additionally, the lack of disclosure for certain measurement practices is disappointing. Approximately 50% of all companies examined fail to disclose their method of recording research and development costs; whereas another 40% of all companies examined fail to disclose their method of inventory costing.

Evident by the bicountry *I* indices, the UK and Ireland appear to have the most harmonised measurement practices while Germany and Portugal have the least. On a regional basis, the UK, Ireland and France appear to be more harmonised with the rest of the EC countries while Portugal and Germany seem to be the most different. The bicountry and four-country *I* indices reveal that fairness oriented countries are more harmonised than legalistic ones.

The results are subject to limitations. First, the largest companies from each country are examined. Therefore, the results may not be generalisable to the accounting practices of small and medium-sized companies from the respective eight countries. Second, as discussed in the research methodology section, we do not examine the practices of companies from Greece, Italy, Luxembourg and Spain. The results from these four countries would influence the overall impact of harmonisation in the EC. Finally, with the exception of six reports from Belgium and 11 from Portugal, all of the annual reports examined are in the English language. However, a comparison of results for companies reporting in English and companies reporting in their domestic language from both Belgium and Portugal reveal no significant differences in reporting practices between translations. In cases where both an English and a domestic language report are received from a company, no differences are found for the six measurement practices examined.

Research measuring the extent of accounting harmonisation is still in an early stage of development. Thus, numerous opportunities exist for future

Table 8

Summary of *I* Index Values and Chi-square Test Statistics

Measurement practices	*I indices*	*Chi-square test statistics*
1. Translation of the balance sheet	0.9040	7.22
2. Treatment of translation differences	0.8494	6.88
3. Inventory valuation	0.7943	17.89
4. Translation of the income statement	0.6433	54.39*
5. Depreciation method	0.6245	134.82*
6. Research and development	0.4105	38.76*
7. Fixed asset valuation	0.2852	93.34*
8. Goodwill	0.2457	124.90*
9. Inventory costing method	0.2292	71.88*

*significant at the 0.01 level

research. Examination of additional measurement practices such as pensions, leases, investments and/or consolidations is needed. Additionally, consideration of disclosure practices, such as segment reporting, has great potential. Practices of companies from countries attempting to enter the EC, such as Austria, Norway and Sweden, could be examined and compared to practices of companies in EC member states. For this study, harmonisation is examined by measurement practice across countries. Instead, harmonisation might be analysed by country across a large number of measurement practices. This would provide an indication of the level of national harmonisation in the EC. Harmonisation by industry is yet another area requiring further research. Finally, as the measurement of accounting harmonisation becomes further developed, the examination of changes over time and the factors causing the change in harmonisation needs to be studied.

References

Choi, F. D. S. and Bavishi, V. B. (1982), 'Financial Accounting Standards: A Multinational Synthesis and Policy Framework', *International Journal of Accounting*, Fall, pp. 159–183.

Choi, F. D. S. and Levich, R. M. (1991), 'International Accounting Diversity: Does it Affect Market Participants?', *Financial Analysts Journal*, July/August, pp. 73–82.

Cochran, W. G. (1952), 'The Chi-square Test of Goodness of Fit', *Annals of Mathematical Statistics*, 23, pp. 315–45.

Doupnik, S. and Taylor, M. E. (1985), 'An Empirical Investigation of the Observance of IASC Standards in Western Europe', *Management International Review*, Spring, pp. 27–33.

Emenyonu, E. N. and Gray, S. J. (1992), 'European Community Accounting Harmonisation: An Empirical Study of Measurement Practices in France, Germany and the United Kingdom', *Accounting and Business Research*, Winter, pp. 49–58.

Europe's 15,000 Largest Companies (1992) (ELC Publishing Ltd.).

Evans, T. G. and Taylor, M. E. (1982), 'Bottom-Line Compliance with the IASC: A Comparative Analysis', *International Journal of Accounting*, Fall, pp. 115–28.

Fantl, I. L. (1971), 'Case Against International Uniformity', *Management Accounting*, May, pp. 13–16.

Freedman, M. and Stagliano, A. J. (1992), 'European Unification, Accounting Harmonization and Social Disclosures', *International Journal of Accounting*, No. 2, pp. 112–22.

Goeltz, R. K. (1991), 'Commentary: International Accounting Harmonization: The Impossible (and Unnecessary?) Dream', *Accounting Horizons*, March, pp. 85–88.

Hussein, M. (1992), 'The Cultural Context of Financial Reporting: The Case of the US and the Netherlands', *1992 International Accounting Research Conference*.

McKinnon, S. M. and Janell, P. (1984), 'The International Accounting Standards Committee: A Performance Evaluation', *International Journal of Accounting*, Spring, pp. 19–34.

Meek, G. K. and Saudagaran, S. M. (1990), 'A Survey of Research on Financial Reporting in a Transnational Context', *Journal of Accounting Literature*, Vol. 9, pp. 145–82.

Nair, R. D. and Frank, W. C. (1981), 'The Harmonization of International Accounting Standards, 1973–1979', *International Journal of Accounting*, Fall, pp. 61–77.

Nobes, C. W. (1981), 'An Empirical Investigation of International Accounting Principles: A Comment', *Journal of Accounting Research*, Spring, pp. 268–270.

Nobes, C. W. and Parker, R. H. (1991), *Comparative International Accounting* (Prentice-Hall).

Purvis, S. E. (1991), 'The IASC and Its Comparability Project: Prerequisites for Success', *Accounting Horizons*, June, pp. 25–44.

Radebaugh, L. and Gray, S. J. (1993), *International Accounting and Multinational Enterprises* (John Wiley & Sons).

Samuels, J. M. and Oliga, J. C. (1982), 'Accounting Standards in Developing Countries', *International Journal of Accounting*, Fall, pp. 69–88.

Tay, J. S. W. and Parker, R. H. (1990), 'Measuring International Harmonization and Standardization', *Abacus*, Vol. 26, No. 1, pp. 71–87.

Tonkin, D. R. (1989), *World Survey of Published Accounts: An Analysis of 200 Annual Reports From the World's Leading Companies* (Lafferty Publications).

Van der Tas, L. G. (1988), 'Measuring Harmonisation of Financial Reporting Practice', *Accounting and Business Research*, Spring, pp. 157–69.

Van der Tas, L. G. (1992), 'Evidence of European Community Financial Reporting Practice Harmonization: The Case of Deferred Taxation', *European Accounting Review*, May, pp. 59–104.

[2]

Accounting and Business Research, Vol. 25, No. 98, pp. 67–80, 1995

The Measurement of Harmonisation and the Comparability of Financial Statement Items: Within-Country and Between-Country Effects

Simon Archer, Pascale Delvaille and Stuart McLeay*

Abstract—This paper reports on an analysis of accounting policy choices made by European companies with an international shareholding. The accounting policies analysed in depth in this paper comprise the treatment of goodwill and accounting for deferred taxation. In the paper, the van der Tas comparability index is developed by separating the index into two components relating to the within-country (intra-national) effects of domestic standardisation and the between-country (inter-national) effects of harmonisation. It is shown in this paper that the value of the index may be interpreted as the probability that two companies selected at random will report financial information that is comparable, and that the lowest level of comparability exists when the accounting methods are assumed to be distributed equiprobably over the companies, the outcome of a random selection of accounting policies. The paper also considers the problems of non-disclosure, and a comprehensive 'disclosure-adjusted' comparability index is proposed.

Introduction

This paper reports on an analysis of accounting policy choices made by European companies with an international shareholding. The companies in the sample are based in Belgium, France, Germany, Ireland, the Netherlands, Sweden, Switzerland and the UK. The accounting policies analysed in depth in this paper comprise the treatment of goodwill and accounting for deferred taxation.

The main purpose of our analysis is to study the impact of accounting harmonisation on the financial reporting practices or policy choices of the companies in our sample. These companies in particular are likely to be the focus of attention of financial analysts carrying out international comparisons. In this context, we have taken as our methodological starting point the comparability 'C' index introduced by van der Tas (1988), and later discussed in Tay and Parker (1990, 1992) and van der Tas (1992a, 1992b), a method that we develop by separating the index into two components relating to the within-country (intra-national) effects of domestic standardisation and the between-country (inter-national) effects of harmonisation. We also propose a comprehensive 'disclosure-adjusted' comparability index incorporating non-disclosures.

We also identify in this paper the minimum level of the comparability index. For any given numbers of companies and of different accounting methods for a particular financial statement item, the lowest level of comparability exists when the accounting methods are assumed to be distributed equiprobably over the companies, the outcome of a random selection. Other things being equal, comparability increases when the choices made by companies converge towards a generally accepted method or when the number of accounting methods in use is reduced.

The C index proposed by van der Tas as an indicator of harmonisation effects is a measure of the extent to which accounting information disclosed by companies is comparable. Indeed, the index can be interpreted as a model of interfirm comparison, as it measures the proportion of pairwise comparisons that are feasible given the alternative accounting methods adopted by different companies.

---

*The authors are, respectively, at the University of Surrey, Ecole Supérieure de Commerce de Paris, and the University of Wales, Bangor. They are grateful to Jean-Bruno Dufour and Wolfgang Dick for their research assistance, to the Institute of Chartered Accountants in England and Wales for financial support provided during the first phase of this project and to Groupe ESCP for financial support during the second phase. The authors also wish to thank Sid Gray for his useful comments as discussant, as well as other participants at the following conferences where an earlier version of the paper was presented: British Accounting Association, April 1994; European Accounting Association, April 1994; University of Wales Gregynog Colloquium, May 1994; and Association Française de Comptabilité, June 1994. Correspondence should be addressed to Professor S. McLeay at the School of Accounting, Banking and Economics, University of Wales, Bangor, Gwynedd LL57 2DG.

The C index is a measure of accounting *harmony* (a state) in a population of companies, while the change in the value of the C index over time is a measure of accounting *harmonisation* (a process). With respect to a given financial statement item subject to a particular area of accounting policy, the value of the index may be interpreted as the probability, p, that two companies selected at random will report financial information that is comparable. Essentially, p may be interpreted as the unconditional probability of interfirm comparability, as p is calculated as the proportion of pairs of companies that are comparable with respect to the financial statement item in question out of the maximum number of pairs that may be selected from the entire population of companies.[1] The C index thus measures the comparability of financial statements on an item-by-item basis. It is not a measure of their overall comparability.

The mathematics of the comparability index

The Basic C Index

The basic C index measures direct comparability of reported accounting numbers which are treated as comparable only in those cases where the same accounting method is used by any two companies. That is, the basic index is calculated without taking account of supplementary information of a kind which may assist the reader to make adjustments necessary to achieve comparability. It should be noted that van der Tas (1992a) also uses an extended index, which includes those cases where information reported in the notes to the accounts would allow the reader to re-estimate the reported numbers in accordance with one or more alternative methods. However, this paper is restricted to the issue of direct comparability where there exists a mutually exclusive choice between two or more alternative accounting methods.

As an example, consider a situation where a choice is to be made between two accounting methods by five companies, a, b, c, d and e. Companies a and b choose method 1 and companies c, d and e choose method 2. Therefore, the number of comparable sets of accounts is four; that is, comparison is possible in the case of (a, b), both of which adopt method 1, and (c, d), (d, e) and (c, e), all three of which adopt method 2.

To generalise using notation appropriate to combinatorial mathematics, the number of combinations of n companies taken r at a time is given by

$$\binom{n}{r} = \frac{n!}{(n-r)!r!}$$

which simplifies to $\frac{1}{2}n(n-1)$ for pairwise comparisons.[2] From the sample of size n, we are able to count the numbers of companies adopting each of the different accounting methods. We use the notation x_j to indicate the number of companies selecting the jth of 1 to J accounting methods, and the number of pairwise comparisons amongst the x_j companies using that particular method is given by

$$\binom{x_j}{2} = \tfrac{1}{2}x_j(x_j - 1)$$

where x_j is substituted for n and where $r = 2$. We obtain the total number of pairwise comparisons that are possible given the choices of method made by the companies in the sample (the numerator of the C index), $\frac{1}{2}\Sigma_j(x_j(x_j-1))$, by summing the combinations over the methods. Thus, in the case of the example above, the total number of pairwise comparisons is:

Number of pairwise comparisons

$$= \tfrac{1}{2}\Sigma_j(x_j(x_j - 1))$$
$$= \tfrac{1}{2}(2 \times 1) + \tfrac{1}{2}(3 \times 2) = 1 + 3 = 4.$$

The C index itself is a measure of the total number of feasible pairwise comparisons expressed as a proportion of the maximum possible number of comparisons that could be made in the event that all companies were to choose the same accounting method. This maximum, i.e. the denominator of the C index, is given by $\frac{1}{2}\Sigma_j x_j(\Sigma_j x_j - 1)$, where $\Sigma_j x_j$ is the total number of companies in the sample. Thus, for the five companies in the example above, the index is calculated as follows:

Van der Tas C index

$$= \tfrac{1}{2}\Sigma_j(x_j(x_j - 1))/\tfrac{1}{2}\Sigma_j x_j(\Sigma_j x_j - 1)$$
$$= (\tfrac{1}{2}(2 \times 1) + \tfrac{1}{2}(3 \times 2))/\tfrac{1}{2}(5 \times 4) = 4/10 = 0.40$$

The C index provides a measure of uniformity in accounting policy choice at a given point in time, and the change in the index provides a measure of the convergence of accounting policy choice for a particular financial statement item through time. This convergence may occur in response to new accounting standards or because companies voluntarily adopt what they perceive to be the method

---

[1]In statistical terms, p is the unconditional probability for the entire sample space, which in turn may contain subsets within which separate conditional probability statements may be made. One of the subsets in the case of harmonisation studies is the country in which a subsample of companies is registered, and a conditional probability of interfirm comparison will exist for each country. This issue is developed later in the paper.

[2]For n companies, the number of permutations is factorial n, that is $n! = n \times (n-1) \times (n-2) \ldots 3 \times 2 \times 1$, and the number of permutations of n companies taken r at a time is given by $n!/(n-r)!$ This simplifies to the second factorial $n(n-1)$ for pairwise permutations, and, to $\frac{1}{2}n(n-1)$ for pairwise combinations.

Table 1
The Basic Grid of Sample Counts x_{ij}

		jth accounting method 1	2	*Totals*
ith country	1	x_{11}	x_{12}	x_{1+}
	2	x_{21}	x_{22}	x_{2+}
Totals		x_{+1}	x_{+2}	x_{++}

generally accepted at the international level. For example, if, as a result of uniformity at the international level, national regulations were to converge on a single accounting method which companies adopt universally, comparability would increase in the case of the above illustration from 40% to 100%.

Measuring International Comparability

In previous research in this area, a distinction has been made between inter-national and intra-national comparability (van der Tas, 1988; Emenyonu and Gray, 1992). While the C index outlined above has been used as the appropriate measure of comparability at the national or global level, a separate index known as the I index has been used as a measure of inter-national, or between-country, comparability.[3]

It should be recognised, however, that the C index itself may be decomposed in a way that allows us to distinguish between comparability within countries and comparability between countries. In this way, the decomposition of a single index is able to provide a basis for distinguishing between, first, the impact of standardisation of accounting method on interfirm comparison within individual countries and, second, the effects of harmonisation on international interfirm comparison. This is illustrated below.

A two-dimensional array sets out the data for the examples that follow, showing the number of companies in the ith country adopting the jth accounting method, x_{ij}. The double subscripts refer to the position of the cells in the arrangement. For instance, x_{12} refers to the number of companies in country $i = 1$ adopting method $j = 2$. A 2×2 version of the grid is displayed in Table 1.

The marginal totals x_{i+} and x_{+j} are summed over the subscripts j and i, respectively, as indicated by replacing the relevant subscript with '+'. For example, the marginal total x_{1+} is the total number of companies in country $i = 1$ adopting both accounting methods $j = 1$ and $j = 2$. The marginal total x_{+1} is the total number of companies selecting method $j = 1$ in both countries $i = 1$ and $i = 2$. The total number of companies, n, is denoted as x_{++}.

The number of pairwise comparisons that may be made in the ith country amongst companies selecting the jth accounting method is $\frac{1}{2}x_{ij}(x_{ij} - 1)$. Therefore, the total number of comparisons that may be made between companies operating within the same countries is given by the sum of the combinations for the four cells, $\frac{1}{2}\Sigma_i\Sigma_j(x_{ij}(x_{ij} - 1))$, that is, for the 2×2 example,

$$\tfrac{1}{2}x_{11}(x_{11} - 1) + \tfrac{1}{2}x_{12}(x_{12} - 1) + \tfrac{1}{2}x_{21}(x_{21} - 1) + \tfrac{1}{2}x_{22}(x_{22} - 1).$$

This will be referred to as *within-country* comparability.

The number of pairwise comparisons that may be made between companies selecting the jth accounting method but operating in different countries is given by the sum of the products between cells within each category of accounting method, divided by two as these are combinations not permutations. This will be referred to as *between-country* comparability which, for the above grid, is equal to $x_{11}x_{21} + x_{12}x_{22}$ (the comparisons between countries $i = 1$ and $i = 2$ for, first, method $j = 1$ and, second, method $j = 2$). Given that the number of companies outside the ith country using the jth method is equal to $x_{+j} - x_{ij}$, it follows that between-country comparability may be expressed as $\frac{1}{2}\Sigma_i\Sigma_j(x_{ij}(x_{+j} - x_{ij}))$.

Within-country and between-country comparability indices may be constructed by dividing the numbers of feasible within-country and between-country pairwise combinations as stated above by their respective maxima, $\frac{1}{2}\Sigma_i(x_{i+}(x_{i+} - 1))$ and $\frac{1}{2}\Sigma_i(x_{i+}(x_{++} - x_{i+}))$. After multiplying all terms by 2, the resultant indices may be expressed as follows:

Within-country comparability index

$$\frac{\Sigma_i\Sigma_j(x_{ij}(x_{ij} - 1))}{\Sigma_i(x_{i+}(x_{i+} - 1))}$$

Between-country comparability index

$$\frac{\Sigma_i\Sigma_j(x_{ij}(x_{+j} - x_{ij}))}{\Sigma_i(x_{i+}(x_{++} - x_{i+}))}$$

The total number of feasible pairwise comparisons is the sum of the within-country and between-country totals, as follows:

$$\tfrac{1}{2}\Sigma_i\Sigma_j(x_{ij}(x_{ij} - 1)) + \tfrac{1}{2}\Sigma_i\Sigma_j(x_{ij}(x_{+j} - x_{ij})) = \tfrac{1}{2}\Sigma_j(x_{+j}(x_{+j} - 1))$$

It can be seen that, unlike its within-country and between-country components, the total number of

[3]The inter-national comparability index, I, is the sum, over the alternative methods $j = 1, \ldots, J$, of the squared geometric means of the frequencies of their use in the countries included in the sample. For $i = 1, \ldots, I$ countries, and where x_{ij}/x_{i+} is the frequency of use of method j in country i, the index may be stated as $\Sigma_j \Pi_i (x_{ij}/x_{i+})^{1/(I-1)}$.

Table 2
An Example of Minimum Comparability

A. Policy choices

		Accounting method			
		j = 1	*j = 2*	*j = 3*	*Totals*
Country	i = 1	5	5	5	15
	i = 2	10	10	10	30
	Totals	15	15	15	45

B. Pairwise comparisons

	Number of pairwise comparisons	*Maximum*	*Comparability indices*
Within-country comparability	165	540	30.6%
Between-country comparability	150	450	33.3%
Total	315	990	31.8%

feasible pairwise comparisons does not itself depend on the counts in individual cells, the x_{ij}s, but on the marginal counts, the x_{+j}s. Thus, the overall C index may be stated as follows:

Total comparability index

$$\frac{\Sigma_j(x_{+j}(x_{+j}-1))}{x_{++}(x_{++}-1)}$$

Minimum Comparability

The minimum level of comparability exists when companies choose equally between different accounting methods, the expected outcome in statistical terms of a random selection procedure. Accordingly, for J accounting methods, we may substitute x_{++}/J for x_{+j} and it may be seen that the minimum of the comparability index would be as follows:

$$\frac{J\left(\frac{x_{++}}{J}\left(\frac{x_{++}}{J}-1\right)\right)}{x_{++}(x_{++}-1)}$$

which tends to 1/J as the number of companies x_{++} increases. Departure from an equal distribution of choices would increase the number of feasible pairwise comparisons. For instance, the number of pairwise comparisons between companies selecting from any two methods in equal proportions is $\frac{1}{2}(x(x-1)+x(x-1))=x^2-x$, and a change of method by one company would result in a number of pairwise comparisons equal to $\frac{1}{2}([x+1]([x+1]-1)+[x-1]([x-1]-1))=x^2-x+1$, an increase of one.

Table 2 presents the comparability indices arising in the case of an example of equal choice amongst methods in each of two countries, where 15 companies in country 1 and 30 companies in country 2 select from three accounting methods. It can be seen in this example that the minimum level of comparability overall is 31.8% of the maximum, the latter being the number of comparisons that would occur if all firms were to select the same accounting method.

As indicated earlier, we may also distinguish pairwise combinations of companies in the same country selecting the same accounting method (within-country or intra-national comparison) from pairwise combinations of companies in different countries adopting the same method (between-country or inter-national comparison). For the distribution of choices shown here, the lack of national uniformity has reduced within-country comparability from a maximum of 540 to 165 pairwise comparisons, or 30.6%. The effect on international comparison has been to reduce between-country comparability from a maximum of 450 to 150 pairwise comparisons, or 33.3%.

It was shown above that computation of the overall C index requires information regarding only the marginal counts, the x_{+j}s. It follows that, although the minimum level of overall comparability is achieved when the numbers of companies choosing each accounting method are equal for the sample as a whole, this pattern does not have to hold in each country. Nevertheless, it is worth noting that the minimum number of within-country comparisons occurs when equal choices are made in each country (as in Table 2), while the minimum number of between-country comparisons will depend on sample design. A further example, this time illustrating the minimum level of between-country comparability, is given in Table 3.

Non-disclosure and the comparability index

Problems of Non-disclosure

The comparability index has been constructed in a restricted manner in previous studies, whereby

Table 3
An Example of Minimum Between-country Comparability

A. Policy choices

		Accounting method			
		j = 1	*j = 2*	*j = 3*	*Totals*
Country	i = 1	15	0	0	15
	i = 2	0	15	15	30
	Totals	15	15	15	45

B. Pairwise comparisons

	Number of pairwise comparisons	*Maximum*	*Comparability indices*
Within-country comparability	315	540	58.3%
Between-country comparability	0	450	0.0%
Total	315	990	31.8%

companies not reporting on a given item or not disclosing the accounting method used are excluded from the index. As a result, it is likely that increases in comparability reported in the past are attributable to an overwhelming extent to changes in the applicability of certain accounting methods as well as changes in the level of financial disclosure (McLeay, 1993). Below, we reconsider this issue and suggest some adjustments that might be made.

Non-disclosure of Method

In some instances, companies may provide insufficient information to allow the reader to determine the precise nature of the accounting method used. Without supplementary information, there are two interpretations of the behaviour of non-disclosers of method. First, a 'default assumption' can be made that the company in question has used the method applicable to its circumstances, such as the method required by law in its country of registration. In this case, the financial statements may be assumed to be comparable with others prepared using that method. Alternatively, it may not be possible to make such a default assumption, in which case the financial statements are not comparable with respect to the item in question.

In the first case, where a 'default' method can be assumed, it would be appropriate to include such a company in one of the comparable subsets, the x_{+j}s, from which the index numerator is calculated and, consequently, in the total x_{++} from which the denominator is calculated. In the latter case, however, it would seem appropriate to include the company only in the denominator of the comparability index, but not in the numerator. In the analysis reported later in this paper, there were no circumstances where we were able to make default assumptions.

Non-disclosure of Item

In some cases, a particular accounting item may not be reported in a company's financial statements. For example, this would be the case where a company reports no goodwill. Here, an assumption might be made that this reflects the fact that no acquisitions have taken place.[4] Where such an assumption can be made, implying that the company has not needed to make an accounting policy choice, the financial statements may be considered as comparable with other companies without acquisitions and with companies reporting goodwill, regardless of the method used. That is, the definition of comparability can include the universal comparability of such a company where the impact on the financial statements would remain the same whichever policy is considered, as the item is assumed to have been omitted because its value is zero. In this case, the numerator of the index would be increased by the number of pairwise comparisons between companies in subset j′ and all other companies, that is by $x_{+j'}(x_{++} - x_{+j'})$.

With respect to the two issues raised above, the solution proposed here is to compute a 'disclosure-adjusted' comparability index which includes the effect of non-disclosure of items and the use of default methods in the index numerator where appropriate and which includes all possible comparisons, including non-disclosures of method and of items in the index denominator. The proposed 'disclosure-adjusted' comparability index may be compared with the unadjusted C index as follows:

[4]An alternative assumption would be that the amount of goodwill arising is zero, such as in the case where the book value of acquired subsidiaries is equivalent to the purchase price. In countries where elimination of goodwill against reserves is allowed without the cumulative amount of such eliminations having to be disclosed in the Notes, there is also the possibility that all goodwill has been eliminated without trace.

Van der Tas C index
{Pairwise comparisons between companies using same method} ÷ {Maximum pairwise comparisons between companies disclosing method}

Disclosure-adjusted index
{Pairwise comparisons between companies using same method (including the default method) plus pairwise comparisons with and between companies which did not include the item in their financial statements} ÷ {Maximum pairwise comparisons between all companies (including all disclosers and non-disclosers)}

The analysis of accounting practices

In this section, we describe how we analysed the accounting practices studied in this paper for the purpose of measuring the degree to which harmony existed in 1986/87 and 1990/91 and hence the process of harmonisation (i.e. the change in harmony) between those years.

For the sample on which our analysis is based, we selected companies in eight European countries whose shares are traded internationally and which, therefore, are likely to be influenced by international factors and country-specific factors in the selection of accounting methods. The companies were first selected in 1986 (see Archer, McLeay and Dufour, 1989) and, for the purpose of this analysis, the financial statements of the same set of companies were reviewed again for the 1990 calendar year (or for accounting periods over 1990/91).

As we discussed in the second section of this paper, the measurement of accounting harmonisation raises some challenging issues of methodology. Comparability of a financial statement item obviously presupposes disclosure of that item in either the financial statements or the notes (disclosure harmony). Given disclosure harmony, comparability further depends on the similarity of the accounting recognition and valuation rules employed for the items disclosed (measurement harmony). In this context, it must be recognised that comparison involves a degree of subjective judgment as to what is comparable. In other words, how close does the similarity between the accounting methods used for a particular financial statement element need to be, in order for the figures for that component reported by different companies to be considered comparable? At what level of detail, therefore, should the degree of harmony be measured? For example, in the case of deferred taxation, we had to make a decision as to the materiality, for comparison purposes, of the difference between the 'deferred' and 'liability' methods, given what we saw as the major difference between the 'full provision' and 'partial provision' methods.

Likewise, there are problems of interpretation of the financial information that is disclosed. In the case of a group reporting no deferred tax, for example, does this mean that the relevant tax regimes are such that no significant temporary differences arise for group companies (i.e. that the answer is 'not applicable'), or that the group is ignoring them and the answer is that it is using the 'nil provision' or 'taxes payable' method? Generally, the notes on accounting policies allow such questions to be answered, but not in all cases.

In this paper, we consider two areas of accounting policy, deferred taxation and goodwill. Below, we describe our analysis of the selected accounting practices indicating how the methodological problems that have arisen have been dealt with.

Deferred Tax

Accounting policy issues. The rationale for accounting for deferred tax arises primarily from differences between reported profit before tax and taxable income which are not of a permanent nature, but result from charges or credits being recognised for tax purposes in different periods from those in which they are recognised for financial reporting purposes. As a result of these temporary differences,[5] tax on part of profits is paid either sooner or later than it would have been if the calculation of tax payable had been made on the basis of reported profits. However, the total amount of taxable profit over the life of the business is not affected, because the temporary differences 'reverse'. The reversal of a temporary difference causes a deferred tax liability or asset to 'crystallise', except to the extent that a new temporary difference arises to offset it.

The most common example is the use of different methods or economic lives for depreciation of fixed assets for reporting and for tax purposes. For example, the use of linear depreciation for reporting purposes and accelerated depreciation for tax purposes leads to a reduction of tax payable in the early years of the asset's life, which is liable to be compensated by an increase in tax payable as the differences reverse in the later years of its life. The principles of 'prudence' and 'matching' may be interpreted as requiring that provision be made for this anticipated increase in future tax payable (i.e., for the reversal of the temporary differences) by recognising a deferred tax liability which builds up through additional charges made against profit

[5]The term 'temporary differences' is used in SFASs 96 and 109 rather than '[reversible] timing differences' as used in APB 11 and SSAP 15. More generally, however, the term 'temporary differences' may be used to refer to differences between the value of a balance sheet item for tax purposes (its 'tax basis') and its value for financial reporting purposes.

during the years of reduced tax payable and reduces through credits made to profit during the years of increased tax payable as the temporary differences reverse. The effect of this (subject to applicable tax rates remaining constant) is to remove the effects of the temporary differences on reported profit after tax, which is calculated more or less as though the tax charge was based on reported profit before tax.

Such a procedure raises two kinds of issue:

1. Will deferred tax liabilities actually crystallise, or will the reversals be offset by new temporary differences arising on new asset acquisitions? In the latter case, is there any need to make provisions in respect of such temporary differences? This is the issue of *full* versus *partial* provision. The full provision method provides for all temporary differences; the partial provision method does not provide for temporary differences so long as they are not expected to reverse.

   This is essentially a recognition issue: should a liability be recognised that is not expected to crystallise because the related temporary differences are not expected to reverse?

   There are additional recognition issues arising from the 'prudence' principle in relation specifically to deferred tax assets when the temporary differences are such as to result in tax being paid sooner not later. For example, while SFAS 96 issued in the US required that net (or 'naked') deferred tax assets be recognised only to the extent that the enterprise can obtain a refund of taxes previously paid, its successor SFAS 109 treats the matter as a valuation issue to be dealt with by '[deducting] valuation allowances if it ... is more likely than not ... that some portion or other of the deferred tax assets will not be realised'. Neither of these US standards was in force during the period covered by our study, but they usefully illustrate different approaches to the issue in question.
2. Given that a liability (or asset) is to be recognised, how is its amount to be calculated? Should the tax rate applicable in the original year of recognition be used, or should the rate be used that is expected to be in force when the liability (or asset) is likely to crystallise, thus determining its expected amount? This is the issue of the *deferral* versus the *liability* method of provision. The deferral method uses the tax rate of the original year of recognition, the liability method normally the most recent tax rate. This is essentially a valuation or measurement issue.

From the analysis just given, it is apparent that there are in principle four main methods of accounting for deferred tax: (1) full provision, deferral method; (2) full provision, liability method; (3) partial provision, liability method; and (4) partial provision, deferral method. The logic of the fourth method might be questioned, on the grounds that the rationale of the partial provision basis of recognition is to avoid providing for non-existent liabilities, and that liabilities which are recognised should logically be valued in such a way as to provide the best estimate of the amount likely to be payable.

With regard to recommended practice, the initial framework for deferred tax accounting had been provided in the US by APB 11 and in the UK and in Ireland by SSAP 11. Both pronouncements recommended a full provision using the deferral method to calculate the provision. In the US, APB 11 was replaced by SFAS 96 in December 1987, and SSAP 11 was superseded in the UK and in Ireland by SSAP 15 in 1985. Both standards now favour the use of the liability method of calculating the amount payable at the current rate of tax, but, while SFAS 109 follows SFAS 96 in requiring full provision to be made for all future effects of temporary differences, SSAP 15 requires a partial provision. Surveys carried out in both Ireland and the UK, as reported by Brennan, O'Brien and Pierce (1992) and Gordon and Gray (1994), reveal that the interpretations placed on the partial provision are such that some companies provide for substantially all temporary differences and others for a negligible proportion, with no provision where the liability is not probable.

The Fourth and Seventh EC Directives contain no requirements in respect of deferred taxation. IAS 12, *Accounting for Taxation on Income*, is compatible with both SSAP 15 and SFAS 96.

National accounting standards and practices. In France, the 1986 Accounting Decree, which implemented the Seventh EC Directive, took the opposite position to that set down in law for individual company accounts and required that deferred tax should be accounted for in consolidated accounts. No method of calculating deferred tax was specified in the Decree, nor had this been mentioned previously in the consolidation instructions of the Plan Comptable of 1982 (Scheid and Walton, 1992). However, OECCA published a recommendation on deferred tax in 1987, specifying full provision on a liability basis.

In Germany, accounting for deferred taxation is governed by section 274 of the commercial code (*Handelsgesetzbuch*, or HGB), where it is required that the general provision for taxation should include any probable future tax charges arising from the difference between taxable profits and reported profits, although this is less likely to be the case in Germany due to the general consistency between the policies used for preparation of the annual financial statements and those used for tax computation. In addition, according to Ordelheide and Pfaff (1994), there is little difference in law between the treatment of deferred tax at present and the provision for taxation as understood prior to the 1985 modification of the HGB, and many companies have not modified their traditional practices. With regard to group accounts, where further tax effects may arise on consolidation, section 306 of the commercial code contains the more specific requirement that deferred taxation be separately reported. However, when reversal of temporary differences is not foreseen in the near future, the provision takes on a quasi-permanent nature and, as such, is again not reported separately.

In the Netherlands, the provision for deferred taxation must be stated separately, either on the face of the accounts or in the notes. According to Dijksma and Hoogendoorn (1993), a partial provision is not allowed under Dutch law, and this is the recommendation from the Council for Annual Reporting, the *Raad voor de Jaarverslaggeving*, as contained in its guideline RJ.2.53.509. Furthermore, the liability method is required under guideline RJ.2.53.515, although the deferral method was permitted until 1992. It is worth noting that some Dutch companies value deferred tax at discounted present value.

In Sweden, during the period of our study, neither the Accounting Act nor the Companies Act recognised deferred tax accounting, although the Swedish Institute of Authorised Public Accountants, the *Föreningen Auktoriserade Revisorer* (FAR), has recommended that, in consolidated accounts, deferred tax liabilities in acquired subsidiaries should be deducted from 'untaxed reserves' which are shown as part of equity (Heurlin and Peterssohn, 1992). Such 'untaxed reserves' are a feature of the Swedish and certain other business environments, being similar to the German *Sonderposten mit Rücklageanteil*, although the latter are shown below, and not included in, equity. Another aspect particular to Sweden during this period was the calculation of net profit after tax in two stages: in the first stage, pre-tax profit is adjusted by special debits or credits laid down by the tax code, in order to arrive at taxable profit; the applicable tax charge is then deducted. The corresponding balance sheet effects are taken to 'untaxed reserves', and not disclosed as a separate tax provision.

The situations in the UK and in Ireland have already been indicated above.

Classification of accounting policies for deferred tax. Within the framework established earlier, it can be seen that three potential combinations of deferred tax accounting methods were required or recommended in various European countries prior to and during the period of our study:

1. Full provision, deferral method (as required by APB 11 and SSAP 11, and, possibly but with less specific disclosure requirements, under the German Commercial code from 1987).
2. Full provision, liability method (as required by SFAS 96; in France, by the OECCA recommendation of 1987; and in the Netherlands from 1992).
3. Partial provision, liability method (as required by SSAP 15 applicable in both the UK and Ireland).

At the time when our 1986/87 data were being analysed (early 1989), SFAS 96 had not come into force; it did not do so until the fourth quarter of 1990, and then only on a voluntary basis. The main methods found in practice were similar either to APB 11 (which was still in force) or to SSAP 15. Thus, our data for 1986/87 do not distinguish between methods 1 and 2. In any event, from the comparability perspective, it seemed to us that the recognition difference between full and partial provision was likely to be much more significant than the measurement difference between deferral and liability. Only in the event of a very significant change in tax rates, or where deferred tax balances were large relative to net assets, would the latter difference be material.

Bearing in mind all of the above, in our analysis we decided on the following classification of policies in accounting for deferred tax:

Policy

A	Nil provision or 'taxes payable' approach;
B	Full provision;
C	Partial provision;
D1	Deferred tax recognised but method (full or partial provision) unspecified;
D2	Deferred tax recognised only for some group companies (normally foreign subsidiaries);
E	No recognition of deferred tax, and it is not known whether or not deferred tax accounting is applicable.

From the comparability perspective, this classification raises some further issues. As a general rule, groups are comparable with others in the same category, and only with those; but this is not the case for all categories. It seems reasonable to consider those companies following a 'nil provision' policy (method A) as comparable with others adopting A, those companies following a 'full provision' policy (method B) as comparable with others adopting B, and those following a 'partial provision' policy (method C) as comparable with others using C. On the other hand, companies not recognising any deferred tax (method E), without explaining whether they are

Table 4
Deferred Tax Cross-classifications

	1986/87						*1990/91*					
	Accounting method						*Accounting method*					
	A	*B*	*C*	*D*	*E*	*Total*	*A*	*B*	*C*	*D*	*E*	*Total*
Belgium	2	0	1	0	1	4	2	1	0	0	1	4
France	0	6	5	1	0	12	0	8	4	0	0	12
Germany	0	2	1	15	4	22	0	4	4	12	2	22
Ireland	0	0	3	0	1	4	1	0	3	0	0	4
Netherlands	0	6	2	4	0	12	0	6	1	4	1	12
Sweden	8	1	0	3	1	13	2	5	1	5	0	13
Switzerland	0	0	0	2	2	4	0	0	3	1	0	4
UK	0	0	18	0	0	18	0	0	18	0	0	18
Total	10	15	30	25	9	89	5	24	34	22	4	89

Key. A: Nil provision (taxes payable method); B: Full method; C: Partial method; D: Deferred tax recognised but method unspecified; E: No recognition of deferred tax and it is not known whether or not it is applicable.

following a 'nil provision' policy or have no temporary differences because of their particular tax situation, are not comparable even with others falling in category E.

The problematic categories are D1 and D2. It would seem that companies recognising deferred tax without specifying whether they are following the 'full' or the 'partial' provision policy (method D1) are not comparable even with others in that category. Typically, consolidated groups recognising deferred tax only for some group companies (normally foreign subsidiaries) also do not specify whether the full or partial provision policy is followed. Hence, we chose to consider companies falling in category D2 (of which there were very few) as not being comparable with others in that category. Consequently, we combined D1 and D2 in a single category for our analysis.

Analysis of deferred tax accounting policy choices. The cross-classification of methods of tax accounting adopted by 89 companies from eight countries in two separate periods 1986/87 and 1990/91 is set out in Table 4.

Overall, there was a decline in the number of companies using the taxes payable method and an increase in deferred tax accounting, both in the case of the partial provision method and the full provision method. Nevertheless, non-disclosure remained a serious barrier to comparability. A substantial number of companies recognising deferred tax did not disclose the deferred tax method used and a small number of companies not recognising deferred tax did not indicate whether or not it is applicable. However, in both cases, the number of companies not disclosing sufficient information decreased.

The conclusions reached above are reflected in the disclosure-adjusted comparability indices presented in Table 5. There is an increase in overall comparability, but from just 14.94% in 1986/87 to 21.63% in 1990/91. It should be recalled that, in calculating the comparability indices, the financial statements of companies falling in categories D (deferred tax method unspecified) and E (not known if deferred tax accounting is applicable) were treated as non-comparable. For instance, if there had been full disclosure of the deferred taxation accounting method by each company in the sample, then given a choice of three methods, the minimum level of comparability would have approximated 33%. However, in view of the levels of disclosure observed (55 disclosing companies choosing between three methods in 1986/87, increasing to 63 disclosing companies in 1990/91), the effective minimum level of comparability overall increased from 12.17% in 1986/87 to 16.09% in 1990/91. Thus, on the basis of these index values, the observed increase in the comparability index (+6.69) may be attributed in part to greater disclosure (+3.92) and to a lesser extent to the effects of harmonisation (+2.77).

It is also evident from the indices reported above that within-country comparability continues to be greatly influenced by the clustering of policy choices within countries. A majority of disclosing companies in France, the Netherlands and Sweden used the full provision method (method B) in 1990/91 while all British and Irish companies and

Table 5
Deferred Taxation Comparability Indices

	1986/87	*1990/91*
Within-country	37.09	37.91
Between-country	10.84	18.61
Total comparability	14.94	21.63

the majority of Swiss companies used the partial provision method (method C). Indeed, within-country comparability remained stable over the period (37.09% in 1986/87 and 37.91% in 1990/91). On the other hand, inter-national, or between-country, comparability increased substantially from 10.84% to 18.61%, due in particular to changes in accounting method by Swedish companies and also to greater disclosure by Swiss and German companies.

Goodwill Arising on Consolidation

Accounting policy issues. For some countries, such as Germany, the Seventh Directive required substantial changes in the method of calculation and the treatment of the difference arising on consolidation. This difference arises in respect of a given participating interest included in a consolidation because the amount ('carrying value') of the asset in the balance sheet of the company holding the participating interest (an asset that is eliminated on consolidation) differs from the amount of the holding company's pro-rata share of the capital and reserves of the company in which the participating interest is held, also eliminated on consolidation.

The Seventh Directive (Articles 19, 30 and 31) requires the 'purchase' or 'acquisition' method of capital consolidation to be used and, in appropriate circumstances, it also permits the 'pooling of interests' or 'merger' method as a member state option. According to the 'purchase' or 'acquisition' method, the consolidation difference is calculated at the date of the acquisition and, as far as possible, is attributed to assets or liabilities that have fair values above or below their book values in the acquired company's accounts, the residual difference being shown in the consolidated balance sheet with an appropriate heading. If positive, the item is to be treated as an asset and amortised through the consolidated profit and loss account according to the rules in the Fourth Directive for 'goodwill acquired for valuable consideration' (see below); alternatively, however, it may be deducted immediately from (or eliminated against) consolidated reserves. If negative, the amount may be transferred to the consolidated profit and loss account only (a) insofar as it reflects an expectation of future losses or costs, and these losses or costs materialise; or (b) insofar as it corresponds to a realised gain on disposal of relevant assets.

The Fourth Directive (Article 37.2) requires goodwill, to the extent that it was acquired for valuable consideration, to be treated as an asset and amortised through the profit and loss account over a period not exceeding five years; member states, however, may allow systematic amortisation over a longer period provided this does not exceed the economic life of the asset, and this member state option is very widely used.

The rules laid down by the directives had the effect of outlawing a method of capital consolidation previously used, particularly in Germany (and hence known as the 'former German method'). According to this method, there is no assignment of the consolidation difference to assets and liabilities whose fair values differ from their book values in the accounts of the company in which the participation has been acquired. Moreover, the difference is recalculated at each consolidation, and therefore changes as the reserves of the company in which the participation is held change as a result of retained profits or losses. This means that such retained profits and losses are excluded from the group result, which equals that of the parent company.

While the EC directives had the effect of eliminating this method (still used by two German companies in our sample in 1987), they still left room for different interpretations as to the method required. Not merely is considerable flexibility left regarding the disposition of positive goodwill (immediate elimination against reserves, or amortisation through profit and loss account either in the year of acquisition or over an arbitrary number of years supposedly corresponding to its estimated 'economic life'). In addition, the requirements leave open more than one method of calculating the difference arising on first consolidation, namely:

1. *The purchase method*

This method is known as the 'purchase' method in the US and as the 'acquisition' method in the UK, to distinguish it from the 'pooling of interests' or 'merger' method which is rarely used in Europe. Under the purchase method, all assets and liabilities of the company in which the participation has been acquired are restated to fair values for consolidation purposes. This has the effect that, where there is a minority interest, the minority interest is also restated to reflect the fair values of the attributable share of the net assets. Moreover, where the net assets at fair values exceed the cost of the participating interest, there arises an amount of 'negative goodwill'.[6]

[6]The US version of the purchase method differs in two respects from the UK version in the treatment of negative goodwill. First, in the US version, in the event that the assignable fair values of net assets acquired exceed the cost, the values of non-current assets acquired (excluding long-term investments in marketable securities) should be reduced proportionately. Excess of net assets over cost (negative goodwill) should not be recorded unless the values of all the non-current assets acquired (excluding long-term investments in marketable securities) have been reduced to zero. Second, in the US version, negative goodwill is treated as deferred income (a liability). In the UK version in force at the time of writing, negative goodwill is treated as a component of reserves.

2. *The German purchase method* (*Neubewertungsmethode in German*)

This is similar to the purchase method described above, except that the restatement of the assets and liabilities is restricted to the amount of the consideration given adjusted for any minority interest, so that no 'negative goodwill' can arise as a result of such restatement.

3. *The Book Value method* (*Buchwertsmethode in German*)

With this method, the restatement of the assets and liabilities of the company in which the participation has been acquired is restricted to the amount required to make the value of the pro-rata share of its net assets equal to the cost of the investment. There is no restatement of the share of net assets attributable to the minority interest. Moreover, as with the *Neubewertungsmethode*, the assets and liabilities are not restated to an amount in excess of the cost of the investment, so that no 'negative goodwill' can arise as a result of such restatement.

Use of the latter two variants of the 'purchase method' in calculating the difference on first consolidation by companies in our sample was confined (with one exception) to Germany. We had no reason to suppose that the use of these variants produced results materially different from those produced by using the purchase method as applied in the UK or US. Any such differences would hardly be more material than the differences resulting from the use of different 'economic lives'.

National accounting standards and practices. In France, the Decree of 17 February 1986 which implemented the Seventh Directive adopted the 'Anglo-US purchase method'. The elimination of goodwill against reserves is permitted only in exceptional circumstances, rather similar to those in which goodwill may be eliminated against a 'merger reserve' in the UK (see below). In the normal case, goodwill must be shown as an asset and amortised systematically according to a predetermined plan. In an opinion issued in 1990, the *Conseil National de la Comptabilité* stated that the amortisation period should normally be that over which the original justification for the investment had been calculated, with additional amortisation in exceptional circumstances. In a bulletin issued in January 1988, the *Commission des Opérations de Bourse* laid down a maximum amortisation period of 40 years (the same as in the US).

The situation in Germany following the passage of the 1985 *Bilanzrichtliniengesetz* (which modified the HGB) has already been mentioned above. The provisions concerning consolidated financial statements became applicable for financial years commencing after 31 December 1989, but could be (and in many cases were) adopted earlier. Either the *Buchwertsmethode* or the *Neubewertungsmethode* may be used. In addition, the 'pooling of interests' method is allowed when the (stringently defined) conditions for a merger have been met, but according to a survey carried out by the accounting firm Treuarbeit in 1990, it is virtually never used (Ordelheide and Pfaff, 1994). Goodwill may be amortised systematically either over four years or over the 'expected life' (no maximum is laid down). It may also be eliminated against consolidated reserves, though Ordelheide and Pfaff note that this is 'contrary to certain basic principles that in Germany have for years applied to the individual [company] accounts . . . and was accepted . . . only to avoid German enterprises being at a disadvantage in reporting profits' (op. cit. pp. 190–191).

In the Netherlands, according to the Commercial Code, goodwill may be shown as an asset and amortised systematically over its expected economic life, or charged directly to the income statement, or eliminated against reserves (Dijksma and Hoogendoorn, 1993). The 'pooling of interests' method is also allowed, but rarely used. In the case of systematic amortisation, no maximum period is laid down, but an explanation must be provided for the use of any period exceeding five years, and in the case of a permanent decline in value an additional write-off should be made.

In Sweden, the 'purchase' method is normally used; however, during the period of our study, the restatement of assets and liabilities of the acquired company was not required, resulting in a sort of hybrid between the 'purchase' method and the 'former German method'. According to a recommendation of the *Föreningen Auktoriserade Revisorer* (FAR, the Institute of Authorised Auditors), goodwill on consolidation should be systematically amortised to profit and loss over a maximum of 10 years, but this recommendation has not generally been followed. Accounting policies adopted have included amortisation over periods of up to 40 years, and elimination against reserves (Heurlin and Peterssohn, 1992). The 'pooling of interests method' is also permissible in Sweden, but only in cases where the business combination has the characteristics of a genuine merger (e.g., use of share exchange as the consideration, neither of the combining companies to be of dominant size compared to the other, continuity of the combined companies' activities). However, Heurlin and Peterssohn note that the 'pooling of interests method' has been used 'in more cases than would logically follow from the prerequisites indicated above' (op. cit. p. 777).

In the UK, the applicable accounting standards were SSAP 22, *Accounting for Goodwill*, and SSAP 23, *Accounting for Acquisitions and Mergers*. The Companies Act 1985 was also relevant. According to SSAP 22, the preferred treatment of goodwill is

Table 6
Goodwill Cross-classifications

	1986/87						*1990/91*					
	Accounting method						*Accounting method*					
	A	*B*	*C*	*D*	*E*	*Total*	*A*	*B*	*C*	*D*	*E*	*Total*
Belgium	0	0	0	4	0	4	0	0	0	4	0	4
France	0	1	0	11	0	12	0	1	0	11	0	12
Germany	3	10	2	6	1	22	0	11	0	8	3	22
Ireland	1	2	0	0	1	4	1	2	0	0	1	4
Netherlands	0	12	0	0	0	12	0	9	0	1	2	12
Sweden	1	2	0	10	0	13	0	4	0	9	0	13
Switzerland	0	0	0	2	2	4	0	2	0	2	0	4
UK	0	15	0	1	2	18	0	15	0	1	2	18
Total	5	42	2	34	6	89	1	44	0	36	8	89

Key. A: Written off against profit and loss acount in the year of acquisition; B: Eliminated against reserves in the year of acquisition; C: Shown as an asset and not amortised; D: Shown as an asset and amortised through the profit and loss account over more than one year; E: Other or unspecified.

elimination against reserves; systematic amortisation over the expected useful life is also allowed. SSAP 22 does not state a maximum amortisation period. However, the normal maximum of 20 years stated in the Accounting Standards Committee's Exposure Draft ED 47, *Accounting for Goodwill*, (published in February 1990) seems to be rarely exceeded in practice (Archer, Alexander, Collins and Pham, 1995).

At the time of the study, the 'pooling of interests' or 'merger' method was also allowed subject to the conditions laid down in SSAP 23 and the Companies Act 1985 as amended by the Companies Act 1989. In substance, these required that at least 90% of the equity of the 'mergee' company should have been acquired by means of a share exchange (Gordon and Gray, 1994, chapter 9). As an alternative to the 'merger' method, the Companies Act also allows the share premium arising on the shares issued as consideration in a share exchange to be converted into a 'merger reserve'. (With the permission of the courts, even an existing share premium account may be similarly converted.) Goodwill arising on the 'acquisition' may then be eliminated against the 'merger reserve'. The result is similar to what would have been produced by using the 'pooling of interests' method, except that the assets and liabilities of the 'mergee' company would be restated to their fair values.

Classification of accounting policies for goodwill. For the reasons given above, we have used in this paper the following classification of policies in accounting for the difference on first consolidation:

Policy

- A Written off against profit and loss in the year of acquisition;
- B Eliminated against reserves in the year of acquisition;
- C Shown as an asset and not amortised;
- D Shown as an asset and amortised through the profit and loss account over more than one year;
- E Other or unspecified.

For policy B, a variety of different reserves is used, especially by UK companies. However, in view of the different legal status of categories of reserves in the various countries, it did not seem reasonable to treat these differences as different accounting policies.

For policy D, as we have already noted, amortisation periods varied from five years or less, to over 20 years. A number of companies stated that they amortised goodwill 'over one to 20 years'. Again, it did not seem useful to treat the use of different amortisation periods as signifying different accounting policies. In any event, the very notion of 'economic life' for goodwill is problematic.

Analysis of goodwill accounting policy choices. The cross-classification of goodwill accounting methods used is given in Table 6.

There was little change overall. Two German companies, which in 1986/87 were still using the method formerly adopted in Germany (method C, shown as an asset and not amortised) abandoned that practice at a later date. Thus, given that there is no basis on which to consider method C as equiprobable, we may consider the choice to be between the three main alternative methods. Therefore, if there had been full disclosure, the minimum level of comparability would have been approximately 33% in 1990/91. However, in view of the level of disclosure observed (81 out of 89 companies choosing between the three main methods in both periods, and two companies

Table 7
Goodwill Comparability Indices

	1986/87	*1990/91*
Within-country	58.17	53.92
Between-country	34.66	37.71
Total comparability	38.33	40.25

capitalising goodwill without subsequent amortisation in the first period), the effective overall minimum level of comparability was 27% in both 1986/87 and 1990/91. Non-disclosure was not a particularly serious problem in the case of goodwill.

As shown in Table 7, there was a slight increase overall in the level of comparability between 1986/87 and 1990/91, from 38.33% to 40%. In both periods, this is greater than the minimum level that would have been observed if companies had selected their policies at random, and it may be inferred that an important degree of harmony was already in existence by 1986/87 with respect to goodwill. The results also demonstrate the effect that occurs when a relatively small number of companies switch from a minority practice to a more generally accepted practice (or vice versa), resulting in substantial increases (or decreases) in the number of pairwise comparisons. For instance, the decision by a small number of German companies to abandon the minority practices of either writing off against profit in the year of acquisition (method A) or showing as an unamortised asset (method C), and to adopt one of two more generally accepted practices (method B or method D), had a positive effect on comparability, particularly on inter-national, or between-country, comparability. The between-country index increased from 34.66% to 37.71%. On the other hand, the decision by a small number of Dutch companies which followed generally accepted Dutch practice (method B) in 1986/87 either to switch to another method that is generally accepted in several countries other than the Netherlands (method D) or to not specify the method used in their 1990/91 financial statements led to an overall decrease in within-country comparability. The within-country comparability index fell from 58.17% to 53.92%.

Summary and conclusions

The C (comparability) index developed by van der Tas may be used, with some restrictions, as a measure of the state of accounting harmony prevailing in a sample of companies with respect to a single financial statement item. It follows that the change in the value of the comparability index over a period of time is likewise a measure of the process of accounting harmonisation in the treatment of that item. However, we show that the C index is deficient in that it is insensitive to the interactions between intra-national and inter-national trends in accounting policy choice, and therefore is an imperfect measure of *international* harmonisation.

In this paper, we have as a first step developed the comparability index further by decomposing it formally into its within-country (intra-national) and its between-country (inter-national) components, whereas van der Tas (1988) calculated a separate I index for the latter.

With regard to the measures of the processes of harmonisation over the four-year period for deferred tax and goodwill, the following results of our analysis are worthy of mention.

Deferred Tax

The total comparability index for the eight-country sample (Belgium, France, Germany, Ireland, the Netherlands, Sweden, Switzerland and the UK) increased from 14.94 to 21.63, still a very low level of harmony. As within-country comparability remained fairly low and showed no significant increase over 1986/87, the increase in overall comparability was almost entirely attributable to an increase in between-country comparability. This was due in part to the choice by most Swedish companies to abandon the taxes payable method in favour (insofar as disclosure allowed us to determine) of the full provision method of deferred tax accounting. It was also due in part to fuller disclosure of the methods used in other countries.

The area of deferred tax is one where no standardisation was (or could readily have been) attempted in the Fourth Directive, national practices reflecting the divergences in the relationships between accounting for tax and for financial reporting. Where tax allowances, to be claimed, must be 'booked' for financial reporting purposes, there is no need for deferred tax accounting. Consequently, in countries where that is the case, there is typically no comprehensive national standard for deferred tax. Multinational groups with their holding company in such countries and subsidiaries in foreign countries are therefore left with various choices as to how the group deferred tax position is to be accounted for. This is reflected in turn in the diversity of accounting practices that we have observed, and, in spite of some discernible harmonisation effects during the period, in the relatively low level of comparability of financial statements with respect to deferred tax accounting.

Goodwill Arising on Consolidation

The total comparability index for the eight countries showed no significant increase (1986/87: 38.33; 1990/91: 40.25). As regards the levels of within-country and between-country comparability, the former actually decreased while the latter increased. Of the 89 sample companies, all but 11 in 1986/87 and nine in 1990/91 were divided into two groups of similar size: those which chose to eliminate goodwill against reserves, and those which treated goodwill as an asset to be amortised through the profit and loss account over its 'useful economic life'. This division did not change significantly over the four-year period, and reflects the options left by the Seventh Directive and also by IAS 22 prior to its revision.

The analysis of the sample data thus suggests that, for very large companies, the impact of the Seventh Directive had already taken place by 1986/87. For example, only two German companies were still using the 'former German method' at that time, although the 1985 *Bilanzrichtliniengesetz* permitted the continued use of the method during a transitional period ending in 1990. This suggests that almost all the large German groups in the sample decided to abandon a method that was not internationally recognised, in an area that had no German tax implications. Also, in 1986/87 the previously illegal practice of eliminating goodwill against reserves was already the most frequently used method in Germany, thanks to early adoption of the provisions of the 1985 Law; by 1990/91, only one further company was using the method.

Conclusions

Our analysis indicates that, in the two areas of deferred taxation and consolidated goodwill, little progress in harmonisation took place between 1986/87 and 1990/91, but that such progress as there was can be attributed to increases in between-country comparability, since the change in within-country comparability was either very small or negative.

The EC Directives have brought about a significant amount of *rapprochement* of national accounting standards in Europe, not just in the member states but also in potential member states and other countries having close links with the EU. However, both deferred taxation and consolidated goodwill are areas where the EC directives left considerable latitude to member states, and where national standards have continued in some cases to be somewhat flexible. Moreover, the German companies in our sample had mostly chosen to adopt the provisions of the 1985 Law well in advance of the deadline.

Van der Tas (1992a) distinguished between the international harmonisation of accounting standards ('formal' harmonisation) and of accounting practices ('substantive' harmonisation). Obviously, the distinction is important, not least because the harmonisation of national standards across countries is one of the major factors affecting the international harmonisation of practices.

The process of 'substantive' harmonisation in a population of multinational companies is, however, likely to be influenced by other factors, such as IASs and US GAAP, insofar as these are internationally recognised and the benefits of adopting internationally recognised accounting methods are seen to exceed the costs. Such factors may have an influence on a substantial part, but far from all, of the sub-population of companies in a country, leading to a *decrease* in the level of national (within-country) harmony in that country. This, in turn, may offset the effects (in terms of international comparability) of an increase in between-country harmony. Therefore, to have an understanding of the processes of harmonisation, we believe that it is crucial to be able to identify, as we have done here, the different impacts of changes in comparability at the within-country and the between-country levels.

References

Archer, G. S. H., Alexander, D., Collins, L. and Pham, D. (1995), *The Treatment of the Difference Arising on First Consolidation: Theory, Standards and Practices in the UK and France*, ICAEW Research Report.

Archer, G. S. H., McLeay, S. J. and Dufour, J.-B. (1989), *Audit Reports on the Financial Statements of European Multinational Companies: A Comparative Study*, ICAEW.

Brennan, N., O'Brien, F. J. and Pierce, A. (1992), *European Financial Reporting: Ireland*, Routledge.

Dijksma, J. and Hoogendoorn, M. (1993), *European Financial Reporting: The Netherlands*, Routledge.

Emenyonu, E. N. and Gray, S. J. (1992), 'European Community Accounting Harmonisation: An Empirical Study of Measurement Practices in France, Germany and the United Kingdom', *Accounting and Business Research*, Winter, pp. 49–58.

Gordon, P. D. and Gray, S. J. (1994), *European Financial Reporting: The United Kingdom*, Routledge.

Heurlin, S. and Peterssohn, E. (1992), 'Sweden' in Alexander, D. and Archer, G. S. H., *The European Accounting Guide*, Academic Press.

McLeay, S. J. (1993), 'The Measurement of Harmonisation', Working Paper (University of Wales, Bangor), November.

Ordelheide, D. and Pfaff, D. (1994), *European Financial Reporting: Germany*, Routledge.

Scheid, J.-C. and Walton, P. (1992), *European Financial Reporting: France*, Routledge.

Tas, L. G. van der, (1988), 'Measuring Harmonisation of Financial Reporting Practice', *Accounting and Business Research*, Spring, pp. 157–169.

Tas, L. G. van der, (1992a), *Harmonisation of Financial Reporting*, Datawyse Maastricht.

Tas, L. G. van der, (1992b), 'Measuring International Harmonization and Standardization: A Comment', *Abacus*, September, pp. 211–216.

Tay, J. S. W. and Parker, R. H. (1990), 'Measuring International Harmonisation and Standardization', *Abacus*, March, pp. 71–88.

Tay, J. S. W. and Parker, R. H. (1992), 'Measuring International Harmonization and Standardization: A Reply', *Abacus*, September, pp. 217–220.

[3]

ABACUS, Vol. 32, No. 1, 1996

SIMON ARCHER, PASCALE DELVAILLE AND STUART MCLEAY

A Statistical Model of International Accounting Harmonization

This article shows how the difference between the observed frequencies of accounting policy choice and the outcome of a random policy choice, where each available method has an equal chance of being selected, may be fully explained with a statistical model. The process of harmonization is described in a way that identifies departures from equiprobable accounting policy choice as either: (a) the systematic effects of harmonization, or (b) the effects of systematic divergence from international harmony where the frequency of adoption of differing accounting methods varies across countries, or (c) the effects of company-specific accounting policy choices.

The understanding of *harmony* that underlies previous attempts to measure harmonization is such that, with respect to a particular financial statement item, a situation of maximum harmony is reached when all companies in all countries use the same accounting method. From the standpoint of modelling the harmonization process, however, a different concept of harmony may be more useful. In this article, therefore, we posit a state of *distributional harmony* in which, other things being equal, the expected distribution of accounting policy choices is the same in each country. In this theoretical state, the odds of selecting a given accounting method from those available for a particular financial statement item are identical for each country. A major advantage of this benchmark is that it provides a basis for distinguishing between two possibly conflicting components of the international harmonization process: between-country harmonization and within-country standardization.

A hierarchy of nested statistical models is then used to describe accounting policy choices made by companies with an international shareholding and registered in Europe, where the European Union has been involved in a program of accounting harmonization. The accounting

---

SIMON ARCHER is a Professor in the Department of Management Studies, University of Surrey, PASCALE DELAVAILLE is a Lecturer in the Ecole Supérieure de Commerce de Paris, and STUART MCLEAY is a Professor in the School of Accounting, Banking and Economics, University of Wales, Bangor.

The authors are grateful to Jean-Bruno Dufour and Wolfgang Dick for their research assistance, to the Institute of Chartered Accountants in England and Wales for financial support provided during the first phase of this project and to Groupe ESCP for financial support during the second phase. The authors also wish to acknowledge the useful comments made by participants at the following conferences where an earlier version of the paper was presented: British Accounting Association, April 1994; European Accounting Association, April 1994; University of Wales Gregynog Colloquium, May 1994; Association Française de Comptabilité, June 1994.

policies analysed in depth in this article comprise the treatment of goodwill and accounting for deferred taxation. The results are compared with the comparability index method used previously in harmonization research studies.

Key words: Accounting policies; Deferred taxation; Goodwill; Harmonization; Standardization.

INTRODUCTION

The literature on the measurement of international accounting harmonization has focused almost exclusively on the use of index measures. In the first published paper on this subject, van der Tas (1988) considered a concentration index approach (the H index), derived from the Hirschman–Herfindal index of industrial concentration, before developing his own comparability index (the C index). We have discussed the mathematics of the comparability index elsewhere (Archer, Delvaille and McLeay 1995), and some further reference to the *C* index will also be made below. The aim of this article, however, is to present a method of modelling statistically the process of international accounting harmonization which, we believe, provides a richer insight into that process than the use of index measures.

The possibility of a statistical modelling approach is hinted at by Tay and Parker (1990, p. 85), in the context of a discussion in *Abacus* concerning the measurement of harmonization (see Tay and Parker, 1990, 1992; van der Tas, 1992a, 1992b, 1992c). They suggest that the level of harmony in the accounting practices adopted by companies in different countries may be assessed for a particular financial statement item by comparing 'the observed distribution of companies between different methods with either a random distribution or some expected distribution', and that a suitable representation of a random distribution could be 'a distribution in which equal numbers of companies would be expected to use each of the available alternatives'. Given this approach, Tay and Parker propose that 'evidence of harmony would then be the existence of a significant difference between the observed and expected distributions, as measured by some appropriate significance test, for example chi-square'.

In this article, we show how the difference between the observed frequencies of accounting policy choices and the outcome of a process of random choice can be fully explained by means of a statistical model. In so doing, we describe harmonization in a way that allows us to identify those departures from random, or equiprobable,[1] accounting policy choice which are associated with either national standardization or international harmonization, or which are company-specific.

The notion of harmony, as normally understood in the literature, is such that the process of harmonization will lead to a situation of maximum harmony with respect to a particular financial statement item when all companies in all countries use the same accounting method. This notion ignores the possibility that companies may be

[1] If an accounting policy choice is made by selecting an accounting method from those available by means of a random process, then each available method has an equal chance of selection, and the expected distribution of accounting policy choices will be an equiprobable, or uniform, distribution.

subject to different circumstances which arguably justify the use of correspondingly different accounting methods in respect of that item.[2] The approach envisaged in this article is based on the assumption that different commercial circumstances do indeed motivate the choice of different accounting methods. This implies an alternative notion of international harmony. According to this notion, a state of international harmony exists when, other things being equal, the odds of selecting a given accounting method are identical in each country. Hence, our statistical modelling approach incorporates a theoretical state of affairs which may be termed *distributional harmony*, and which allows measurement of the extent to which distributions of accounting policy choices are similar between countries.

We develop these ideas in the context of a hierarchy of nested statistical models based on logistic Poisson regression. These provide a description of (a) systematic effects of harmonization, (b) systematic divergence from a state of international harmony, and (c) non-systematic accounting policy choices made by individual companies.

The method is illustrated by an analysis of corporate accounting policy choices carried out during the period subsequent to the original empirical study (van der Tas, 1988) which prompted the debate in *Abacus*. The accounting policies analysed in depth here are the treatment of goodwill and accounting for deferred taxation. The companies in our sample are based in Belgium, France, Germany, Ireland, the Netherlands and the U.K., where the process of harmonization in the European Union is likely to have had an effect, and also Sweden and Switzerland where the accounting practices of multinational companies have been influenced by the EU directives. The particular companies in the sample are interlisted within Europe and are likely to be the focus of attention of financial analysts carrying out international comparisons.

In this article, we also reconcile our results with the indexation approach proposed by van der Tas (1988) and extended in Archer *et al.* (1995), and for this purpose we separate the comparability index, or C index, into two components relating to the within-country (intra-national) effects of domestic standardization and the between-country (inter-national) effects of harmonization. We show that the expected values from our model of harmonization, a model in which there are no country-specific or company-specific accounting policy choices, yield the same C index value overall as the observed data, and that it is the within-country and between-country components of the index which reflect the divergence from harmony caused by differing national standards and company-specific policy choices.

[2] One fairly obvious set of different circumstances is membership of different industries. Thus, for example, real estate companies might arguably be justified in treating buildings held as investments in a similar way to financial investments rather than as tangible fixed assets subject to systematic depreciation. Similarly, there may also be size effects. For example, smaller oil and gas extraction companies may choose the full cost method of accounting for hydrocarbon reserves, while the larger companies choose the successful efforts method.

A B A C U S

STATISTICAL MODELLING OF HARMONIZATION

Using a numerical example, this section develops the idea of a hierarchical sequence of statistical models to describe the harmonization process. A three-dimensional array in Table 1 shows for each year the number of companies in each country selecting each accounting method, cross-classified in this case for two years, two countries and three accounting methods.

TABLE 1

AN ILLUSTRATION OF POLICY CHOICES IN TWO PERIODS

	Year $k = 1$				Year $k = 2$				Combined			
Method	$j = 1$	$j = 2$	$j = 3$	Total	$j = 1$	$j = 2$	$j = 3$	Total	$j = 1$	$j = 2$	$j = 3$	Total
Country												
$i = 1$	51	61	38	150	19	169	12	200	70	230	50	350
$i = 2$	99	89	112	300	41	311	48	400	140	400	160	700
Total	150	150	150	450	60	480	60	600	210	630	210	1050

We increase the number of companies from 450 in year 1 to 600 in year 2 in order to demonstrate the functioning of the model with respect to such changes. It can be seen that, for the two countries combined, the distribution of accounting policy choices has changed from a uniform distribution in year 1 (33% : 33% : 33%) to a high degree of convergence in year 2 on method 2, the generally accepted practice adopted by 80 per cent of companies. It will be noted, however, that the aggregate frequencies in each of the two periods do not fit the individual *country* subsamples precisely.

The aim of the statistical model is to estimate from the observed patterns of policy choices the extent to which the changes may be attributed to a process of international harmonization rather than to behaviour that is specific to individual countries or companies. In order to develop a sequence of models which describe this kind of data adequately, we may generalize by letting x_{ijk} be the observed number of companies in the *i*th country selecting the *j*th accounting method in the *k*th year, where $i = 1, ..., I$ countries; $j = 1, ..., J$ methods; and $k = 1, ..., K$ years. The marginal totals are summed over the subscripts by replacing the relevant subscript with '+'. Thus, x_{+12} is the total number of companies selecting method $j = 1$ in year $k = 2$. The corresponding notation for the three-dimensional array of observed counts and the relevant marginal totals is set out in Table 2 giving, first, the general notation for an $I \times J \times K$ table and, second, the specific notation for a $2 \times 3 \times 2$ table.

The probability of a count falling in cell (*ijk*) is p_{ijk} and the corresponding expected value will be denoted as m_{ijk}. An estimate $\hat{m}_{ijk}$ of the expected value is obtained by multiplying the grand total x_{+++} by the estimated probability, $\hat{p}_{ijk}$, where the latter is estimated from the relationships between marginal totals that vary depending on the level of the model.

TABLE 2

$I \times J \times K$ ARRAY BY COUNTRY, ACCOUNTING METHOD AND YEAR

	Year $k = 1$				Year $k = 2$				Combined			
Method	$j = 1$	$j = 2$	$j = 3$	Total	$j = 1$	$j = 2$	$j = 3$	Total	$j = 1$	$j = 2$	$j = 3$	Total
Country												
$i = 1$	x_{ijk}	x_{ijk}	x_{ijk}	x_{i+k}	x_{ijk}	x_{ijk}	x_{ijk}	x_{i+k}	x_{ij+}	x_{ij+}	x_{ij+}	x_{i++}
$i = 2$	x_{ijk}	x_{ijk}	x_{ijk}	x_{i+k}	x_{ijk}	x_{ijk}	x_{ijk}	x_{i+k}	x_{ij+}	x_{ij+}	x_{ij+}	x_{i++}
Total	x_{+jk}	x_{+jk}	x_{+jk}	x_{++k}	x_{+jk}	x_{+jk}	x_{+jk}	x_{++k}	x_{+j+}	x_{+j+}	x_{+j+}	x_{+++}
	Year $k = 1$				Year $k = 2$				Combined			
Method	$j = 1$	$j = 2$	$j = 3$	Total	$j = 1$	$j = 2$	$j = 3$	Total	$j = 1$	$j = 2$	$j = 3$	Total
Country												
$i = 1$	x_{111}	x_{121}	x_{131}	x_{1+1}	x_{112}	x_{122}	x_{132}	x_{1+2}	x_{11+}	x_{12+}	x_{13+}	x_{1++}
$i = 2$	x_{211}	x_{221}	x_{231}	x_{2+1}	x_{212}	x_{222}	x_{232}	x_{2+2}	x_{21+}	x_{22+}	x_{23+}	x_{2++}
Total	x_{+11}	x_{+21}	x_{+31}	x_{++1}	x_{+12}	x_{+22}	x_{+32}	x_{++2}	x_{+1+}	x_{+2+}	x_{+3+}	x_{+++}

A suitable probability model for count data in the context of multicategory response such as multiple accounting choices is provided by the Poisson distribution. This distribution can take any non-negative integral value and may be used to describe the number of events (i.e., companies making accounting policy choices) which have occurred in a given period of time or in a given space, although no *a priori* knowledge of the total number of observations is assumed. However, a restriction may be imposed whereby the total sample size is fixed and, if the x_{ijk}s have been generated according to a Poisson sampling scheme, then the conditional distribution is multinomial, with the probability function as given in Bishop *et al.* (1975).[3] Further discussion of the relevant sampling scheme for cross-classified data is to be found in Fienberg (1977) and, with respect to measurements repeated through time, in Lindsey (1993).

When a Poisson-distributed error term is linked to a multinomial logistic regression, we may estimate simultaneously the probabilities, the p_{ijk}s, for the type of cross-classified categorical data dealt with in this article As closed-form solutions are not feasible for all levels of three-way interaction models with multiple responses, the estimation of the expected values, the m_{ijk}s, may be achieved by fitting parameters from a generalized linear model for the complete cross-classification by explanatory variable using iterative proportional fitting (Aitken *et al.*, 1989). In this article, the analysis was carried out using the generalized linear modelling system GLIM4 (Francis *et al.*, 1993).

[3] For a three-dimensional table with observed cell counts x_{ijk}, and $n = x_{+++}$, the probability function for the multinomial model is $\prod ((m_{ijk}/m_{+++})x_{ijk}) (x_{+++}!/\prod x_{ijk}!)$

Model 1: Complete Independence

For the model of complete independence, the expected value of accounting policy choices is equal in each cell, regardless of country or year.[4] However, when subsamples are unbalanced because there are different numbers of observations in each country and/or in each year, the model of complete independence has no descriptive validity, and the appropriate model of independence is one which reflects the sampling design, as below.

Model 2: Conditional Independence

For a population of company financial disclosures, the number of disclosing companies may vary as a result of population differences between countries and as a result of changes in the population of companies from one time period to another. This may be reflected in sampling design. Furthermore, if non-disclosure is not considered as one of the choices and, as a result, statistical modelling is restricted to accounting policy choices only, this may also cause variation in the country and year subsamples for the reduced set of data. The second model, the model of conditional independence, reflects these constraints imposed by sampling design.

As the model of conditional independence provides estimates of the effects associated with the numbers of observations by country and by year, the components of the model are a country factor (C), a year factor (Y) and the second-order interactions between countries and years ($C.Y$). The linear model of conditional independence is, therefore, denoted as

$$C + Y + C.Y \text{ (or, more succinctly, } C{*}Y)$$

where . represents the interaction between main effects, and $*$ indicates the inclusion of both main effects and interaction effects.[5]

For the example, the two-level country factor measures the relative odds of a company belonging to country 1 or country 2. Given the marginal totals indicated in Table 1 above, the relative odds of a company being in country 1 are $x_{1++}{:}x_{2++}$ = 350:700, or 1:2. Likewise, the two-level year factor is described by the odds ratio $x_{++1}{:}x_{++2}$ which, using the marginal totals in Table 1, gives the relative odds of an observation falling in year 1 as 450:600, or 3:4. From the logistic regression, we obtain each of these parameter estimates as a logit, that is, the logarithm of the relative odds ratio.

[4] In this case, the expected value is the grand mean (the only parameter in the model), where the total number of repeated observations, Σx_{ijk}, is divided by the number of cross-classifications from I policy choices in J countries over K years (for the example, the expected value in each cell would be given by x_{+++}/IJK or 105/(2 × 3 × 2), which is equal to 8.75).

[5] A corresponding algebraic representation of the linear structure is

$$\beta_o + \beta_i^{C} + \beta_k^{Y} + \beta_{ik}^{C.Y}$$

with levels i = 1, ..., I of the country variable and k = 1, ..., K of the year variable, where main effects allow the intercepts to vary and the interaction term allows the slopes to vary for all levels of C and Y. A useful introduction to the structure of generalized linear models is provided in Dobson (1990).

Under this model, $C*Y$, the estimated probability $\hat{p}_{ijk}$ of a count falling in cell (ijk) is equal to $(x_{i+k}/x_{+++})/J$, where J is the total number of methods.[6] For the model of conditional independence (and all higher-order models), the estimate $\hat{m}_{i+k}$ of the expected marginal count for each country in each year is equal to the observed marginal count x_{i+k}. However, for this model, the estimated marginal count for each method $\hat{m}_{+jk}$ is equal to x_{++k}/J, and not to the observed value. The expected values for the example are given in Table 3.

TABLE 3

EXPECTED VALUES UNDER CONDITIONAL INDEPENDENCE

	Year $k=1$				Year $k=2$				Combined			
Method	$j=1$	$j=2$	$j=3$	Total	$j=1$	$j=2$	$j=3$	Total	$j=1$	$j=2$	$j=3$	Total
Country												
$i=1$	50	50	50	*150*	67	67	67	*200*	117	117	117	*350*
$i=2$	100	100	100	*300*	133	133	133	*400*	233	233	233	*700*
Total	150	150	150	*450*	200	200	200	*600*	350	350	350	*1050*

Note: In this table, expected values are rounded to the nearest integer. Furthermore, in this table and those that follow, expected values which are equal to the observed data are given in italics.

The model of conditional independence reproduces the situation where the selection of an accounting method for a financial statement item from among the various possible methods is entirely random and where each of the possible methods thus has an equal chance of being used. We refer to this model as being one of *conditional* independence, since the expected number of companies selecting a particular method in a given country in a given year is conditional only on the total number of companies in that country sample for that year.[7]

We may consider model 2 to be the null model. By adding further terms, we are able to account for systematic effects relating to changes in policy choices. At subsequent levels of the model hierarchy, the increase in the goodness of fit that is achieved is divided through by the number of degrees of freedom lost by adding

[6] With regard to the $C.Y$ interaction effects, the logistic parameter values would differ from 0 (and, accordingly, the exponentiated odds ratios would differ from 1) if there were any differences between countries in the proportionate change in sample size from one period to another. In the case of the above example, for instance, the sample design is fully described by the C and Y main effects, and the $C.Y$ interaction effects are equal to zero.

[7] It may be noted that the benchmark of a 'uniform distribution' proposed by Tay and Parker (1990) relies implicitly upon a comparison of observed values with the expected values given by the basic model of conditional independence (model 2). An empirical study by Emenyonu and Gray (1992) bases its chi-square tests on a main effects model which is equivalent to our static model of harmony (model 3). As shown here, these approaches do not distinguish between the systematic effects of international harmony, the systematic effects of nationally generally accepted practices, and the non-systematic choices made by individual companies.

parameters to the model, thus providing the basis for tests of the usefulness of the additional parameters in the model. The inferential procedures are described in greater detail later in this section.

Model 3: The Static Model of Harmony

A situation of *distributional harmony* may be said to exist when accounting policy frequency distributions are identical across countries. When there is no harmonization between years, these frequency distributions also remain identical across years. That is, if we allow policy choices to depart from equiprobability and to vary overall, but not to depart from this pattern across countries, or from year to year, the resulting model describes the most likely pattern of policy choices in a state where there is an unchanging level of harmony for the period as a whole. This may be achieved by adding the three-level policy factor (P) to the model as a main effect, giving the following:

$$C + Y + P + C.Y \text{ (or } C{*}Y + P).$$

As a result of adding policy main effects, the estimates of expected values are distributed over the policy choices in the proportions observed for total policy choices for all years combined, that is x_{+j+}/x_{+++}, a distribution which remains constant for each country and for each year. The expected values from the static model of harmony for the example, which follow the pattern 1:3:1 throughout, are shown in Table 4.

TABLE 4

EXPECTED VALUES FROM THE STATIC MODEL OF HARMONY

	Year $k = 1$				Year $k = 2$				Combined			
Method	$j = 1$	$j = 2$	$j = 3$	Total	$j = 1$	$j = 2$	$j = 3$	Total	$j = 1$	$j = 2$	$j = 3$	Total
Country												
$i = 1$	30	90	30	*150*	40	120	40	*200*	70	210	70	*350*
$i = 2$	60	180	60	*300*	80	240	80	*400*	140	420	140	*700*
Total	90	270	90	*450*	120	360	120	*600*	*210*	*630*	*210*	*1050*

Under this model, the estimated probability $\hat{p}_{ijk}$ of a count falling in cell ijk is equal to $(x_{i+k}/x_{+++}) * x_{+j+}/x_{+++})$. For example, for the first accounting method in the first country in the first year, our probability estimate $\hat{p}_{111}$ is equal to

$$\frac{x_{1+1}}{x_{+++}} * \frac{x_{+1+}}{x_{+++}} = \frac{150}{1050} * \frac{210}{1050} = \frac{1}{35} = 0.0286$$

and the estimated expected value $\hat{m}_{111}$ is equal to $\hat{p}_{111} * x_{+++} = 30$.

Model 4: The Dynamic Model of Harmonization

If we allow policy choices to vary from year to year, but still not from country to country, the model describes the change in harmony from one period to the next. This is achieved by adding the interaction between years and policy choices (*Y.P*) to the model to give

$$C + Y + P + C.Y + Y.P \text{ (or } C_*Y + Y_*P).$$

The *Y.P* interaction terms represent, for each policy, the change from one year to the next in the relative odds of it being selected. These changes are identified in this study as the *harmonization effects*. Hence, this model describes the level of harmony year by year, given the aggregate distribution of policy choices for all countries as observed in each year, and consequently the harmonization effect between years. Thus, if the data are such that the distribution of aggregate policy choices converges on a smaller number of generally accepted methods over time, this increase in harmony will be reflected in the better fit of model 4 (the dynamic model) compared to model 3 (the static model). In this case, the sign of the estimated parameter values for the *Y.P* interactions between years and policies would be positive. In the case of a reduction in harmony, the sign of the estimated parameter values for those *Y.P* interaction effects would be negative.

The expected values for the example are shown in Table 5. It can be seen that the estimated expected marginal counts of policy choices by year, $\hat{m}_{+jk}$, are equal to the observed marginals x_{+jk}, which was not the case with the previous model where the distributions were constant over time. Within each country and for each year, the distribution of expected values reflects the proportions of total policy choices for each year, and the estimated probability $\hat{p}_{ijk}$ of a count falling in cell *ijk* is equal to $(x_{i+k}/x_{+++}) * (x_{+jk}/x_{+++})$. For example, the probability estimate $\hat{p}_{111}$ is now equal to

$$\frac{x_{1+1}}{x_{+++}} * \frac{x_{+11}}{x_{++k}} = \frac{150}{1050} * \frac{150}{450} = \frac{1}{21} = 0.0476$$

and the estimated expected value $\hat{m}_{111}$ is equal to $\hat{p}_{111} * x_{+++} = 50$.

TABLE 5

EXPECTED VALUES FROM THE DYNAMIC MODEL OF HARMONIZATION

	Year $k = 1$				Year $k = 2$				Combined			
Method	$j = 1$	$j = 2$	$j = 3$	Total	$j = 1$	$j = 2$	$j = 3$	Total	$j = 1$	$j = 2$	$j = 3$	Total
Country												
$i = 1$	50	50	50	*150*	20	160	20	*200*	70	210	70	*350*
$i = 2$	100	100	100	*300*	40	320	40	*400*	140	420	140	*700*
Total	*150*	*150*	*150*	*450*	*60*	*480*	*60*	*600*	*210*	*630*	*210*	*1050*

The paramaterization of model 4 may be compared instructively at this stage with that of the lower-order models 2 and 3 which, given that they contain a subset of its terms, are nested within model 4. The linear logits from each fit are given below and the corresponding exponentiated values are also listed:

	Model 2 (conditional independence)		Model 3 (static harmony)		Model 4 (dynamic harmonization)	
	logits	exponent	logits	exponent	logits	exponent
m_{111}	3.912	50.00	3.402	30.00	3.912	50.00
C2	+0.693	2.00	+0.693	2.00	+0.693	2.00
Y2	+0.288	1.33	+0.288	1.33	–0.916	0.40
C2.Y2	+0.000	1.00	+0.000	1.00	+0.000	1.00
P2			+1.099	3.00	+0.000	1.00
P3			+0.000	1.00	+0.000	1.00
Y2.P2					+2.079	8.00
Y2.P3					+0.000	1.00

As noted, the exponentiated parameter values are relative odds. An example of the computation of the linear predictor and the exponentiated expected value in the case of m_{222} is as follows:

	Model 2		Model 3		Model 4	
	logits	exponent	logits	exponent	logits	exponent
*m*111	3.912	50.00	3.402	30.00	3.912	50.00
C2	+0.693	*2.00	+0.693	*2.00	+0.693	*2.00
Y2	+0.288	*1.33	+0.288	*1.33	–0.916	*0.40
C2.Y2	+0.000	*1.00	+0.000	*1.00	+0.000	*1.00
P2			+1.099	*3.00	+0.000	*1.00
Y2.P2					+2.079	*8.00
m_{222}	4.893	133.33	5.482	240.00	5.768	320.00

For instance, for model 4, the odds of selecting method 2 rather than method 1 in the first year are evens (the exponent of P2 is equal to 1) while the relative odds of selecting the second method in the second year, as measured by the term Y2.P2, are 8:1

Model 5: The Full Model

The full second-order interaction model, model 5, allows policy choices to vary systematically from country to country from year to year. By adding the interactions between countries and policy choices (*C.P*), this model accounts for policy choices which depart from the overall pattern and are specific to individual countries. In other words, the increase of goodness of fit is attributable to the extent to which the distribution of national policy preferences differs from their distribution internationally. The components of the full model are

$$C + Y + P + C.Y + Y.P + C.P \text{ (or } C{*}Y + Y{*}P + C{*}P).$$

In this case, the probabilities are estimated using an iterative procedure. All expected marginal counts under model 5 are in agreement with observed marginals, now including $\hat{m}_{ij+} = x_{ij+}$, the sum over the years for each policy choice in each country. Thus, except for random variation attributable to non-systematic policy selection by individual companies, the full model is a perfect description of the data. The expected values for the full model applied to our example are given in Table 6.

TABLE 6

EXPECTED VALUES FROM THE FULL SECOND-ORDER INTERACTION MODEL

	Year $k = 1$				Year $k = 2$				Combined			
Method	$j = 1$	$j = 2$	$j = 3$	Total	$j = 1$	$j = 2$	$j = 3$	Total	$j = 1$	$j = 2$	$j = 3$	Total
Country												
$i = 1$	52	61	37	*150*	18	169	13	*200*	*70*	*230*	*50*	*350*
$i = 2$	98	89	113	*300*	42	311	47	*400*	*140*	*400*	*160*	*700*
Total	*150*	*150*	*150*	*450*	*60*	*480*	*60*	*600*	*210*	*630*	*210*	*1050*

Note: The expected values in this table are rounded to the nearest integer.

Model 5 is treated for all purposes in the following analysis as the full model, with all previous models being nested within it. The degrees of freedom for model 5 therefore provide the index for *F*-tests, as shown at the end of this description of the model hierarchy. The full model provides a description of systematic accounting policy choice, including effects of international harmonization (*Y.P*) and national standardization (*C.P*), the significance of each being reflected in the parameter estimates.

Model 6: The Saturated Model

Finally, by adding the three-way interaction effects (*C.Y.P*), which account for the residual random variation in the previous model, the data are fully saturated. This maximal model has the following structure

$$C + Y + P + C.Y = Y.P + C.P + C.Y.P \text{ (or } C*Y*P)$$

and fits expected values without error to the observed values, where $\hat{m}_{ijk} = x_{ijk}$. The sum of errors is therefore zero.[8] There are as many parameters as there are observations, and the degrees of freedom are consequently also zero. The difference

[8] In longer repeated measure studies, time (the variable *Y*) may be treated as continuous. This would add degrees of freedom to the analysis which may more than compensate for the loss in estimating accuracy and, if effective, could provide summary statistics for long-term harmonization effects described by the *Y.P* interaction — see model 4. It follows that model 6 would not necessarily fully saturate the data, leaving some residual error attributable to the smoothing of harmonization effects to a single slope parameter.

between models 5 and 6 is attributable to those policy choices by companies which are not systematic, that is, they are described neither by international harmonization nor by national patterns of accounting policy choice.

The hierarchical sequence of the models is summarised in Table 7.

TABLE 7

THE SEQUENCE OF NESTED HARMONIZATION MODELS

Model hierarchy, main effects and interaction effects	Description of models and effects
1 Grand mean	Model of complete independence
Add: Country*Year	Sample design effects
2 $(C*Y)$	Model of conditional independence
Add: Policy	Convergence effects
3 $(C*Y) + (P)$	Static model of harmony
Add: Year.Policy	Harmonization effects
4 $(C*Y)+(Y*P)$	Dynamic model of harmonization
Add: Country.Policy	Divergence effects
5 $(C*Y)+(Y*P)+(C*P)$	Full model
Add: three-way effects	Random company effects
6 $(C*Y*P)$	Saturated model

Measuring Goodness of Fit

The appropriate measure of goodness of fit for Poisson data is the log likelihood-ratio test statistic, referred to more generally as the deviance and calculated as the difference between the maximized log likelihoods for the fitted and saturated models, multiplied by –2. For the Normal model, the deviance is equal to the residual sum of squares, but in the case of the Poisson model it has an interpretation similar to that of the Pearson goodness of fit statistic (Francis *et al.*, 1993).

The relative goodness of fit of two nested models can be compared by examining the ratio of (a) the change in deviances from two models within the hierarchy divided by the change in degrees of freedom, to (b) the deviance for the full model (which we define as model 5 above, the model which reproduces all marginals exactly) divided by its degrees of freedom. That is, where the deviance of a higher-order model M_H is D_H on v_H degrees of freedom and the deviance of the lower-order model M_L containing a subset of the terms in model M_H is D_L on v_L degrees of freedom, and D_F is the deviance of the full model on v_F degrees of freedom, the ratio $[(D_L-D_H)/(v_L-v_H)]/(D_F/v_F)$ has an F-distribution on $(v_L-v_H), (v_F)$.[9]

[9] The deviance is proportional to a χ^2 variable. It follows under certain general conditions that the difference between deviances is asymptotically χ^2 with degrees of freedom equal to the number of independent parameters that are omitted in fitting the nested model. The ratio of two χ^2s has an F-distribution which is indexed (v_L-v_H), (v_F), as shown in the text.

A small *F*-statistic indicates that model M_H and model M_L may not be distinguished, as the residual deviance for the reduced model M_L is not much larger than for model m_H. The *F*-statistic provides a likelihood ratio test of the hypothesis that the variables added to the model have zero regression coefficients and do not contribute to the regression function, in the first case with respect to the accurate model or, in the case of the alternative test described above, with respect to successive higher-order models.

Non-Disclosure

In some cases, a particular item may not be reported in a company's financial statements. A possible explanation may be that there were no transactions of the relevant kind, thus obviating the need for an accounting policy in that area. A further possibility is that there were such transactions but the company chose not to recognize the item for reporting purposes. Another possibility is that the item was reported, while the company provided insufficient information to allow the reader to determine the accounting method used. One explanation of this may be that the company in question considered that it did not need to disclose the accounting method used because it took the view that readers of its financial statements would be able to make an informed default assumption on the basis, for instance, that only one method is permitted by law in the company's country of registration. An alternative explanation is that the company may have decided not to report the method used even though no default assumption was applicable.

In the context of a statistical model, we may wish to treat such a decision process either as stochastic, where there is an element of choice by the company, or as non-stochastic. In the analysis carried out in this article, we were unable to make any default assumptions. Accordingly, we first treat non-disclosure as stochastic by assuming that such non-disclosure is one of the choices available to a company alongside the J accounting methods (i.e., given $J = 3$ methods, there would exist four choices including non-disclosure). We then compare the results of model-fitting under the above assumption with those obtained under the alternative assumption that non-disclosure is not a matter of choice since there had been no relevant transactions for the companies in question. This is achieved by weighting non-disclosures out of the generalized regression, thus restricting the estimation of expected values to the subset of companies selecting one or other of the J accounting methods.

COMPARABILITY INDICES

In this article we also compare our results with the comparability index introduced by van der Tas (1988). The C index is best interpreted as a model of interfirm comparison, as it measures for a single financial statement item the proportion of pairwise comparisons that are feasible given the alternative accounting methods adopted by different companies. Thus, it represents the probability that, for the item in question, two companies selected at random will report financial information that is comparable. Other things being equal, comparability increases when the choices made by companies converge towards a generally accepted method or when the number of accounting methods in use is reduced.

The C index may be constructed for each model from the expected marginal counts in any year k. In this context, the C index would measure the total number of expected pairwise comparisons given a particular model (obtained by summing over the alternative accounting methods the expected numbers of pairwise comparisons in each subset using the same accounting method) expressed as a proportion of the maximum number of pairwise comparisons that would be made if all companies were to use the same accounting method. The expected value of the C index is as follows:

$$\frac{\Sigma_j \left(m_{+jk}(m_{+jk}-1)\right)}{m_{++k}(m_{++k}-1)}$$

where, for year k, m_{+jk} is the number of companies expected to select the jth method and m_{++k} is the total number of companies.[10]

For a given number of companies and a given number of different accounting methods for a particular financial statement item, the lowest level of comparability exists when the accounting methods are assumed to be selected with equal probability by companies.[11] Thus, the C index estimated from the model of conditional independence (model 2) is a measure of the minimum level of comparability for the sample, which converges each year on the reciprocal of the number of accounting methods, $1/J$, as sample size increases. The C index estimated from the static model of harmony (model 3) also remains constant through time as it measures the level of comparability that would exist in a state of unchanging distributional harmony. In contrast, the index value estimated from the expected values of the dynamic model of harmonization (model 4) varies over time as it measures the effects of harmonization on comparability.

The index values obtained for the example are given in Table 8. It can be seen that the minimum level of comparability with three methods is 33 per cent, the level estimated from the model of conditional independence. This would increase to a

[10] The comparability index assumes that comparison occurs in pairwise combinations. The number of combinations of n companies taken r at a time is given by

$$\binom{n}{r} = \frac{n!}{(n-r)!\,r!}$$

For n companies, the number of permutations is factorial n, and the number of permutations of n companies taken r at a time is given by $n!/(n-r)!$ This simplifies to the second factorial $n(n-1)$ for pairwise permutations, and, to $\frac{1}{2}n(n-1)$ for pairwise combinations.

[11] For J accounting methods, we may substitute m_{++k}/J for m_{+jk} in this minimum comparability model. It follows that the minimum of the comparability index would be

$$\frac{J\left(\frac{m_{++k}}{J}\left(\frac{m_{++k}}{J}\right)-1\right)}{m_{++k}(m_{++k}-1)} = \frac{1}{J}\left(\frac{m_{++k}-J}{m_{++k}-1}\right)$$

which tends to $1/J$ as the number of companies m_{++k} increases. Thus, under the model of conditional independence, inter-company comparability is at its minimum level. Even a marginal change in the overall distribution of accounting choices will increase the level of comparability, as there will be a marginal preference for one method over the others.

TABLE 8

COMPARABILITY INDICES

		Year 1	Year 2
Model 2	Conditional independence	33	33
Model 3	Static harmony	44	44
Model 4	Dynamic harmonization	33	66
Model 5	Full model	33	66
Model 6	Observed values	33	66

constant level of 44 per cent under the static model of harmony, where the distribution of policy choices remains unchanged from year to year. Allowing for harmonization, the C index increases from 33 per cent in year 1 to 66 per cent in year 2, as shown in Figure 1.

The C index values obtained from model 4 are equal to those obtained from models 5 and 6 (the full model and the saturated model), as all information required

FIGURE 1

COMPARABILITY INDICES

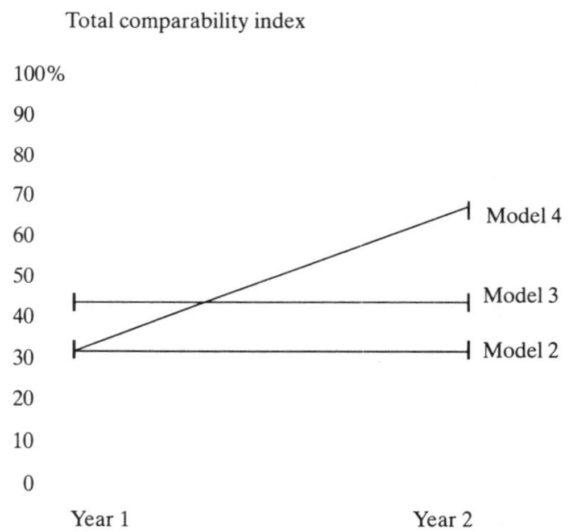

Key: Model 2 = Minimum comparability (conditional independence); Modal 3 = Harmony (static); Modal 4 = Harmonization (dynamic). Note that the total comparability index values are identical when estimated from the model of harmonization (model 4), the full model (model 5) and the actual data (observed values in the saturated model, model 6).

for the C index is accurately estimated by each of these models. It will be recalled that, in the earlier discussion of the sequence of nested models, the expected marginal counts were given as sufficient statistics whose accuracy increased for higher-order models. The equivalence between expected marginals and observed marginals may be summarized as follows:

Expected marginal	*Description of marginal*	*Models where expected marginal equals observed marginal*
m_{+++}	grand total	1,2,3,4,5,6
m_{i++}	counts in the *i*th country	2,3,4,5,6
m_{++k}	counts in the *k*th year	2,3,4,5,6
m_{i+k}	counts in the *i*th country in the *k*th year	2,3,4,5,6
m_{+j+}	counts of the *j*th policy choice	3,4,5,6
m_{+jk}	counts of the *j*th policy choice in the *k*th year	4,5,6
m_{ij+}	counts of the *j*th policy choice in the *i*th country	5,6

It can be seen that the expected number of companies selecting the *j*th accounting method in the *k*th year, m_{+jk}, is an accurate estimate in each of the higher-order models 4, 5 and 6.

It follows that the C index is not able to distinguish the within-country effects of national standardization that are allowed for in model 5 from the between-country effects of international harmonization in model 4, a feature of the C index which makes it deficient as a measure of international harmonization. Consequently, we also use in our analysis a within-country index of international comparability and between-country index of international comparability. The latter is a more appropriate index of international harmonization.

The number of pairwise comparisons that may be expected in the *i*th country amongst companies selecting the *j*th accounting method in the *k*th year is $\frac{1}{2}m_{ijk}(m_{ijk} - 1)$. Therefore, the expected total number of such within-country comparisons is given by summing over *I* countries and *J* methods. This is maximized for the *i*th country at $\frac{1}{2}m_{i+k}(m_{i+k} - 1)$ when all companies within that country use the same method. Thus, the within-country index for year *k* is given by

$$\frac{\Sigma_i \Sigma_j (m_{ijk}(m_{ijk} - 1))}{\Sigma_i (m_{i+k}(m_{i+k} - 1))}$$

Between-country comparability is based on the number of pairwise comparisons that may be expected between companies selecting the *j*th accounting method but operating in different countries. As the number of companies outside the *i*th country using the *j*th accounting method in the *k*th year is equal to $m_{+jk} - m_{ijk}$, it follows that between-country comparability index for year *k* may be expressed as

$$\frac{\Sigma_i \Sigma_j (m_{ijk}(m_{+jk} - m_{ijk}))}{\Sigma_i (m_{i+k}(m_{++k} - m_{i+k}))}$$

Finally, it should be noted that non-disclosure could influence the C index in a number of ways. If a company does not disclose a particular financial statement item because no such transactions took place, that company's accounts may be compared with those of all other companies, whichever method the other companies have adopted. If a company discloses a financial statement item but not the accounting method (which was referred to earlier as stochastic non-disclosure), comparison will not be possible with the accounts of other companies disclosing the item. In this article, we assume that all non-disclosures fall into the latter category and the comparability indices are calculated accordingly.

THE ANALYSIS OF ACCOUNTING PRACTICES

In this section, we describe how we analysed the accounting practices studied for the purpose of measuring the degree to which harmony existed in 1986/87 and 1990/91 and hence the process of harmonization (i.e., the change in harmony) between those years. For the sample on which our analysis is based, we selected from eight European countries those companies whose shares are traded internationally and which, therefore, are likely to be influenced by international factors, country-specific factors and company-specific factors in the selection of accounting methods. The companies were first selected in 1986 (see Archer, Dufour and McLeay 1989) and, for the purpose of this analysis, the financial statements of the same set of companies were reviewed again for the 1990 calendar year (or for accounting periods over 1990/91). The accounting policies considered are deferred taxation and goodwill, for which a more detailed description of the regulations and practices in each of the countries studied is given in Archer *et al.* (1995). Further discussion of financial reporting practices may be found in detailed studies of the countries involved: Belgium (Lefebvre and Flower, 1994), France (Scheid and Walton, 1992), Germany (Ordelheide and Pfaff, 1994), Ireland (Brennan *et al.*, 1992), the Netherlands (Dijksma and Hoogendoorn, 1993), Sweden (Heurlin and Peterssohn, 1995), Switzerland (Laffournier, 1995) and the United Kingdom (Gordon and Gray, 1994).

Deferred Taxation

The cross-classification of methods of tax accounting adopted by eighty-nine companies from eight countries in two separate periods 1986/87 and 1990/91 is set out in Table 9.

Overall, there was a decline in the number of companies using the taxes payable method and an increase in deferred tax accounting, in the cases of both the partial provision method and the full provision method. Nevertheless, non-disclosure remained a serious barrier to comparability. A substantial number of companies recognizing deferred tax did not disclose the deferred tax method used and a small number of companies not recognizing deferred tax did not indicate whether or not it was applicable. However, in both cases, the number of companies not disclosing sufficient information decreased.

The statistical analysis was carried out first for companies in all eight countries. Secondly, in order to exclude country–year and country–policy effects which could

TABLE 9

DEFERRED TAX CROSS-CLASSIFICATIONS

	1986/87						1990/91					
	Accounting method						Accounting method					
	A	B	C	D	E	Total	A	B	C	D	E	Total
Belgium	2	0	1	0	1	4	2	1	0	0	1	4
France	0	6	5	1	0	12	0	8	4	0	0	12
Germany	0	2	1	15	4	22	0	4	4	12	2	22
Ireland	0	0	3	0	1	4	1	0	3	0	0	4
Netherlands	0	6	2	4	0	12	0	6	1	4	1	12
Sweden	8	1	0	3	1	13	2	5	1	5	0	13
Switzerland	0	0	0	2	2	4	0	0	3	1	0	4
U.K.	0	0	18	0	0	18	0	0	18	0	0	18
Total	10	15	30	25	9	89	5	24	34	22	4	89

Key: A = Nil provision (taxes payable method); B = Full method; C = Partial method; D = Deferred tax recognized but method unspecified; E = No recognition of deferred tax and it is not known whether or not it is applicable.

not add significantly to explanation (due to the small number of observations), it was repeated for a subset that excluded the three smaller subsamples in Belgium, Ireland and Switzerland. The remaining five countries represent 87 per cent of the total sample.

With regard to policy choices, we treated the five categories A to E as stochastic in a first fit of the models and we repeated the procedures treating those companies which did not recognize deferred tax (category E) as non-stochastic. That is, in the latter cases, we assumed that selection was restricted to the four choices A to D.

A notable feature of the analysis reported in Table 10 is the small residual from the full model, attributable to random company effects. This has some influence on the F-tests of changes in goodness of fit with respect to the full model (reported as F_1 in Table 10), as explanations other than company-specific selection of accounting methods account for a high proportion of the deviance.

For the F_1 likelihood ratio test with respect to the full model, harmony (the addition of the policy choice main effect) and national divergence (the addition of the interaction between countries and policies) are both seen to be highly significant, with probabilities of a larger F-value being almost zero. Harmonization effects (the addition of the interaction between years and policies) are significant when the nuisance parameters associated with the small country samples are removed, as the p-value for the five-country analysis is reduced to 0.7 per cent. As recalled above, the F_1 test compares the harmonization effects with the impact of policy choices made by individual companies, of which relatively few are non-systematic. It can be seen that the reduction in deviance attributable to the systematic effects of harmonization is

INTERNATIONAL ACCOUNTING HARMONIZATION

TABLE 10

STATISTICAL ANALYSIS OF DEFERRED TAX HARMONIZATION

	Scope of stochastic model							
	All disclosures and non-disclosures				*Four main policy choices only*			
	Eight countries		Five countries		Eight countries		Five countries	
Models and effects	Deviance	*DF*	Deviance	*DF*	Deviance	*DF*	Deviance	*DF*
Null model	358.69	79	266.06	49	314.24	63	220.62	39
Country.Year	–60.91	–15	–9.86	–9	–64.71	–15	–7.13	–9
Conditional independence	297.78	64	256.20	40	249.53	48	213.49	30
Policy	–56.19	–4	–63.92	–4	–33.76	–3	–35.91	–3
F_1	*(19.07)*		*(33.38)*		*(16.75)*		*(41.28)*	
p	*(.000)*		*(.000)*		*(.000)*		*(.000)*	
F_2	*(3.49)*		*(2.99)*		*(2.35)*		*(1.82)*	
p	*(.012)*		*(.031)*		*(.085)*		*(.167)*	
Static harmony	241.59	60	192.28	36	215.77	45	177.58	27
Year.Policy	–6.21	–4	–6.23	–4	–4.09	–3	–5.69	–3
F_1	*(2.11)*		*(3.25)*		*(2.03)*		*(6.54)*	
p	*(.107)*		*(.039)*		*(.141)*		*(.007)*	
F_2	*(.369)*		*(.268)*		*(.271)*		*(.265)*	
p	*(.829)*		*(.896)*		*(.846)*		*(.850)*	
Dynamic harmonization	235.38	56	186.05	32	211.68	42	171.89	24
Country.Policy	–214.75	–28	–178.39	–16	–197.57	–21	–168.41	–12
$F_1 = F_2$	*(10.41)*		*(23.29)*		*(14.00)*		*(48.41)*	
p	*(.000)*		*(.000)*		*(.000)*		*(.000)*	
Full model	20.63	28	7.66	16	14.11	21	3.48	12
Random company effects	–20.63	–28	–7.66	–16	–14.11	–21	–3.48	–12

Notes:

1. Classification of policy variable
   Treated as stochastic in each analysis:
   A = Nil provision, or taxes payable approach
   B = Full provision
   C = Partial provision
   D = Deferred tax recognized but method unspecified

Treated as non-stochastic in the restricted analysis of four main policy choices:

E = No recognition of deferred tax, and it is not known whether or not deferred tax accounting is applicable

2. Countries included in each analysis: France, Germany, Netherlands, Sweden, U.K. Small samples included only in eight-country analysis: Belgium, Ireland, Switzerland.

3. The first *F*-test, F_1, compares the additional explanatory power of successive models with the random company effects, that is, it compares the reduction in deviance for successive models with the deviance after fitting the full model (model 5). The second *F*-test, F_2, compares the additional explanatory power of each model with the unexplained variation after fitting that model.

–5.69, compared to –3.48 for the non-systematic effects of company-specific accounting policy choice, suggesting that where companies departed from national preferences during the period investigated, they tended to select accounting policies which led to harmonization.

The F_2 test provides an alternative perspective on deferred tax accounting. Although some harmonization occurred during the period, as shown above, it did not have a significant effect on changing the level of harmony between the two years in question, as little explanatory power was offered by fitting the dynamic model instead of the static model.

Furthermore, a comparison of the model of conditional independence and the static model reveals that there was relatively little harmony when the model fit was restricted to the main policy choices only. The main characteristic of the data is the existence of national differences in deferred tax accounting. However, a stronger case that there is some harmony in tax accounting arises when non-disclosure, a decreasing practice, is treated as stochastic, with the low *p*-values of 1.2 per cent (eight countries) and 3.1 per cent (five countries) suggesting that the significant impact on harmonization has been greater disclosure.

As shown in Table 11, the parameter estimates obtained for all categories of policy choice when fitting model 4, the dynamic model of harmonization, indicate that there was during the test period a relatively high probability that companies would select

TABLE 11

PARAMETER ESTIMATES FOR DEFERRED TAX HARMONIZATION

	All countries		Five largest countries		EC countries	
	Policy effects	Year effects	Policy effects	Year effects	Policy effects	Year effects
A: Nil provision		–0.693		–1.386		+0.406
		(.881)		(.842)		(1.14)
B: Full method	+0.406	+1.163*	+0.629	+1.814*	+1.946*	–0.100
	(.408)	(.639)	(.437)	(.857)	(.755)	(.977)
C: Partial method	+1.099*	+0.818	+1.179*	+1.460	+2.708*	–0.406
	(.365)	(.602)	(.404)	(.836)	(.729)	(.948)
D: Method unspecified	+0.916*	+0.565	+1.056*	+1.295	+2.303*	–0.629
	(.374)	(.621)	(.410)	(.846)	(.741)	(.972)
E: Deferred tax not recognized	–0.105	–0.118	–0.470	+0.875	+1.099	–0.811
	(.459)	(.813)	(.570)	(1.08)	(.816)	(1.12)

Note: Parameter estimates are reported as log-relatives with respect to Policy A, and are not directly comparable between the full and reduced data sets. The boxed year-policy interaction effects are additive with respect to the main effects outside the box. The estimates are obtained by fitting model 4, the dynamic model of harmonization. The intercept estimate and the country effects are not included in the above table as they do not affect the interpretation of the policy, year and year–policy parameter values. Standard errors of log-adds are given in brackets and significant values are indicated with an asterisk.

the partial method or would choose not to disclose the method of deferred taxation used. The only change of any statistical significance concerns the increase in probability of selecting the full method. These inferences are unchanging under the full eight-country analysis and the restricted analysis of the five larger countries.

However, a further analysis restricted in this case to the EC countries in the sample (i.e., excluding Sweden and Switzerland), also reported in Table 11, reveals that the harmonizing effect with respect to the full method is no longer present to such a marked extent. This is because Swedish companies discontinued the use of the taxes payable method, with most of those disclosing the new policy indicating that the full method had been selected. Thus, we are able to conclude from results that have some statistical significance that an important harmonizing effect (although limited in its extent) had been the change in policy choice by European companies outside the EC at the time to one or other of the more generally accepted practices within the EC.

Nevertheless, this conclusion must be interpreted in the light of the main explanation arising from the F_2 test relating to the systematic behaviour of companies using methods that are widely adopted nationally but not internationally. All p-values reported in Table 10 for the comparison between dynamic harmonization and the full model (the difference being explained by country–policy effects) are virtually zero.

The conclusions reached above are reflected in the disclosure-adjusted comparability indices presented in Table 12 which have been constructed from the expected values given by each model for the eight-country analysis of all disclosures and non-disclosures. The financial statements of companies falling in categories D (deferred tax method unspecified) and E (not known whether deferred tax accounting is applicable) were treated as non-comparable with regard to deferred tax.

Constant comparability in a state of static harmony stands at 17.89 per cent overall, a low figure attributable in particular to the low levels of disclosure on average over the two periods about the method of deferred taxation used. The increase in disclosure from 1986/87 to 1990/91 and the greater use of deferred taxation brought about an increase in total comparability levels from 14.94 per cent

TABLE 12

DEFERRED TAXATION COMPARABILITY INDICES

	Within-country comparability		Between-country comparability		Total comparability	
	1986/87	1990/91	1986/87	1990/91	1986/87	1990/91
Conditional independence	8.51	8.51	12.00	12.00	11.46	11.46
Static harmony	14.96	14.96	18.44	18.44	17.89	17.89
Dynamic harmonization	12.10	18.65	15.47	22.18	14.94	21.63
Full model	35.07	38.09	11.21	18.58	14.94	21.63
Observed values	37.09	37.91	10.84	18.61	14.94	21.63

in 1986/87 to 21.63 per cent in 1990/91. As shown earlier in the article, these estimates of the total comparability index are equal under the dynamic model of harmonization, the full model and for the actual data.

Figure 2 shows the index values constructed from the fitted estimates under minimum comparability (model 2), dynamic harmonization (model 4) and the full model (model 5).

The measures of within-country and between-country comparability are greatly influenced by the national clustering of policy choices.[12] For instance, within-country comparability is substantially higher in both years when the expected index values from the full model, which allows for divergent country practices, are compared with those from the model of dynamic harmonization, which assumes distributional harmony. This is because a majority of disclosing companies in France, the Netherlands and Sweden use the full provision method (method B) while all British and Irish companies and the majority of Swiss companies use the partial provision method (method C). In contrast, the divergence from a harmonized state has an opposite effect on the expected between-country index values. For instance, the between-country index in 1990/91 stands at 22.18 per cent given the assumptions of distributional harmony compared to 18.58 per cent given the assumptions of systematic divergence from distributional harmony inherent in the full model.

FIGURE 2

DEFERRED TAXATION COMPARABILITY INDICES CONSTRUCTED FROM EXPECTED VALUES

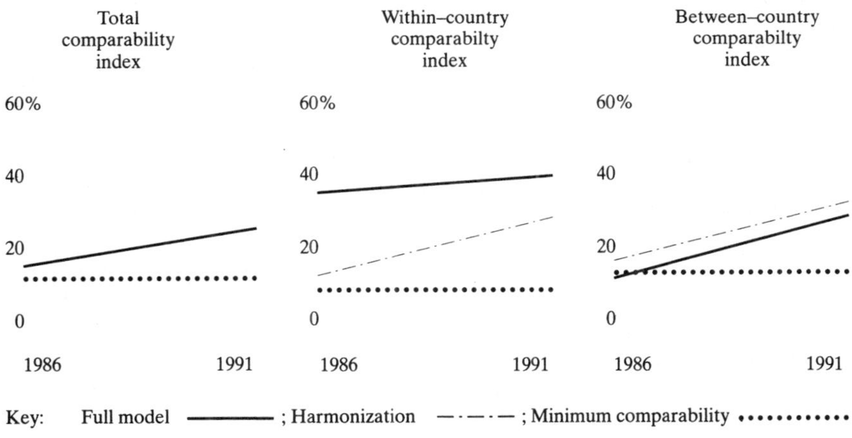

[12] The index values differ for within-country, between-country and total comparability due to sample design and index construction, as shown at the beginning of this article. There is also a differing proportional impact which can be seen in the relative index values from the dynamic harmonization and full models for within-country and between-country indices.

Finally, it may be noted that the non-systematic selection of deferred tax methods by individual companies has a negligible effect on comparability. The expected values of the between-country and within-country comparability indices obtained from the full second-order interaction model are similar to those obtained from the actual data.

Goodwill Arising on Consolidation

The cross-classification of goodwill accounting methods is given in Table 13. There was little change overall. Two German companies, which in 1986/87 were still using the method formerly adopted in Germany (method C, the capitalization of goodwill without subsequent amortization), abandoned that practice at a later date. We did not consider method C as equiprobable in either period of our study, and we treated the counts under method C as structural zeros for the purposes of stochastic analysis. In addition, we note that non-disclosure was not a serious problem in the case of goodwill.

TABLE 13

GOODWILL CROSS-CLASSIFICATIONS

	1986/87 Accounting method						1990/91 Accounting method					
	A	B	C	D	E	Total	A	B	C	D	E	Total
Belgium	0	0	0	4	0	4	0	0	0	4	0	4
France	0	1	0	11	0	12	0	1	0	11	0	12
Germany	3	10	2	6	1	22	0	11	0	8	3	22
Ireland	1	2	0	0	1	4	1	2	0	0	1	4
Netherlands	0	12	0	0	0	12	0	9	0	1	2	12
Sweden	1	2	0	10	0	13	0	4	0	9	0	13
Switzerland	0	0	0	2	2	4	0	2	0	2	0	4
U.K.	0	15	0	1	2	18	0	15	0	1	2	18
Total	5	42	2	34	6	89	1	44	0	36	8	89

Key: A = Written off against profit and loss account in the year of acquisition; B = Eliminated against reserves in the year of acquisition; C = Shown as an asset and not amortized; D = Shown as an asset and amortized through the profit and loss account over more than one year; E = Other or unspecified.

As previously, the statistical analysis was carried out for companies in all eight countries and also for a subset that might improve explanatory power by excluding the three smaller countries. With regard to policy choices, we first treated choices A, B, D and E as stochastic in the model fitting and then, in a second analysis, we treated as deterministic the behaviour of those companies which did not specify the method used,[13] thus restricting the estimation of fitted values to methods A, B and D. The results are summarized in Table 14.

[13] This group also includes two companies which each used a different non-standard method. Due to the non-comparability of their financial statements with respect to the treatment of goodwill, these have been classified under E (other or unspecified) together with non-disclosers.

A B A C U S

TABLE 14

STATISTICAL ANALYSIS OF GOODWILL HARMONIZATION

	Scope of stochastic model							
	Disclosures and non-disclosures				*Three main policy choices only*			
	Eight countries		Five countries		Eight countries		Five countries	
Models and effects	Deviance	*DF*	Deviance	*DF*	Deviance	*DF*	Deviance	*DF*
Null model	328.16	63	238.29	39	268.74	47	185.30	29
Country.Year	–60.92	–15	–9.87	–9	–58.73	–15	–6.05	–9
Conditional independence	267.24	48	228.42	30	210.01	32	179.25	20
Policy	–126.19	–3	–125.18	–3	–90.00	–2	–87.77	–2
F_1	*(63.14)*		*(111.0)*		*(91.57)*		*(146.3)*	
p	*(.000)*		*(.000)*		*(.000)*		*(.000)*	
F_2	*(13.42)*		*(10.91)*		*(11.25)*		*(8.64)*	
p	*(.000)*		*(.000)*		*(.000)*		*(.002)*	
Static harmony	141.05	45	103.24	27	120.01	30	91.48	18
Year.Policy	–3.24	–3	–7.19	–3	–3.02	–2	–5.59	–2
F_1	*(1.62)*		*(6.38)*		*(3.07)*		*(9.32)*	
p	*(.215)*		*(.008)*		*(.078)*		*(.008)*	
F_2	*(.329)*		*(.599)*		*(.361)*		*(.521)*	
p	*(.804)*		*(.622)*		*(.700)*		*(.604)*	
Dynamic harmonization	137.81	42	96.05	24	116.99	28	85.89	16
Country.Policy	–123.82	–21	–91.54	–12	–110.11	–14	–83.49	–8
$F_1 = F_2$	*(8.85)*		*(20.30)*		*(16.00)*		*(34.79)*	
p	*(.000)*		*(.000)*		*(.000)*		*(.000)*	
Full model	13.99	21	4.51	12	6.88	14	2.40	8
Random company effects	–13.99	–21	–4.51	–12	–6.88	–14	–2.40	–8

Notes:

1. Classification of policy variable

   Treated as stochastic in each analysis:
   A = Goodwill on consolidation is written off against profit and loss in the year of acquisition
   B = Goodwill on consolidation is eliminated against reserves in the year of acquisition
   D = Goodwill on consolidation is shown as an asset and amortized through the profit and loss account over more than one year

   Treated as structural zero:
   C = Goodwill on consolidation is shown as an asset and not amortized

   Treated as non-stochastic in the restricted analysis of three main policy choices:
   E = Other or unspecified

2. Countries included in each analysis: France, Germany, Netherlands, Sweden, U.K. Small samples included only in eight-country analysis: Belgium, Ireland, Switzerland.

3. The first *F*-test, F_1, compares the additional explanatory power of successive models with the random company effects, that is, it compares the reduction in deviance for successive models with the deviance after fitting the full model (model 5). The second *F*-test, F_2, compares the additional explanatory power of each model with the unexplained variation after fitting that model.

As in the case of deferred taxation, the analysis of goodwill accounting choices shows that policy main effects (i.e., static harmony) and country.policy interaction effects (i.e., divergence) account for most of the reduction in deviance in the full and restricted analyses. Accordingly, the F_1 and F_2 tests show that harmony was highly significant and that the nationally systematic behaviour of companies causing divergence from complete harmony was also highly significant.

Overall, there was little evidence that harmony increased during the period, with high *p*-values arising from the F_2 test which compares the deviances for the static and dynamic models. However, the F_1 test reveals (when calculated for the subset of five countries, thus removing the disturbance effects of the small subsamples) that harmonizing policy choices were significant by comparison with company-specific policy choices, suggesting that where companies departed from national preferences in goodwill accounting during the period investigated, they tended to select accounting policies which led to harmonization.

The parameter estimates obtained from fitting the dynamic model of harmonization confirm that there were no significant changes between 1986/87 and 1990/91 in the probability of selecting between the categories of policy choice. This applies to the analysis of the complete eight-country data set and to the reduced five-country set, and also to a further analysis of the countries in the EC at the time.

TABLE 15

PARAMETER ESTIMATES FOR GOODWILL HARMONIZATION

	All countries		Five largest countries		EC countries	
	Policy effects	Year effects	Policy effects	Year effects	Policy effects	Year effects
A: Written off against profit and loss		–1.386		–8.445		–1.609
		(1.31)		(20.7)		(1.29)
B: Eliminated against reserves	+2.303*	+1.335	+2.303*	+8.445	+2.128*	+1.656
	(.524)	(1.14)	(.524)	(20.7)	(.473)	(1.11)
C: Asset not amortized	+1.705*	+1.514	+1.946*	+8.514	+1.917*	+1.667
	(.544)	(1.16)	(.535)	(20.7)	(.479)	(1.12)
D: Asset amortized through profit and loss	–0.693	–5.094	–0.693	+0.693	–0.916	–5.548
	(.866)	(11.0)	(.866)	(29.3)	(.837)	(15.4)
E: Other or unspecified	+0.000	+2.079	–0.288	+9.292	+0.182	+1.897
	(.707)	(1.28)	(.764)	(20.7)	(.605)	(1.22)

Note: Parameter estimates are reported as log-relatives with respect to Policy A, and are not directly comparable between the full and reduced data sets. The boxed year-policy interaction effects are additive with respect to the main effects outside the box. The estimates are obtained by fitting model 4, the dynamic model of harmonization. The intercept estimate and the country effects are not included in the above table as they do not affect the interpretation of the policy, year and year–policy parameter values. Standard errors of log-adds are given in brackets and significant values are indicated with an asterisk.

Finally, disclosure-adjusted comparability indices were calculated using the expected values from each of the models. For this purpose, the non-comparability of companies in category E (other methods and methods not specified) was assumed.

TABLE 16

GOODWILL COMPARABILITY INDICES

	Within-country comparability		Between-country comparability		Total comparability	
	1986/87	1990/91	1986/87	1990/91	1986/87	1990/91
Conditional independence	14.66	14.66	18.75	18.75	18.11	18.11
Static harmony	36.01	36.01	39.82	39.82	39.22	39.22
Dynamic harmonization	35.00	37.17	38.95	40.82	38.33	40.25
Full model	54.87	56.35	35.27	37.26	38.33	40.25
Observed values	58.17	53.92	34.66	37.71	38.33	40.25

Constant comparability in a state of static harmony stands at 39.22 per cent overall, a much higher level than in the case of deferred taxation. The near absence of harmonization effects is reflected in the index values given under the dynamic model of harmonization which changed little from 38.33 per cent in 1986/87 to 40.25 per cent in 1990/91 (see Table 16).

Again, within-country comparability is increased by the clustering of policy choices within countries, and between-country comparability is reduced accordingly, as illustrated by the relative positions of the lines representing the full model and the dynamic harmonization model in Figure 3. It can be seen from the cross-classifica-

FIGURE 3

GOODWILL COMPARABILITY INDICES CONSTRUCTED FROM EXPECTED VALUES

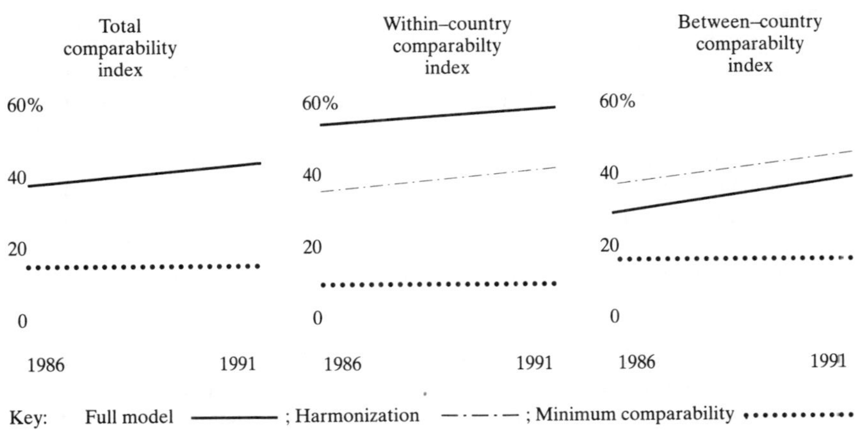

tions in Table 13 that most Dutch and British companies eliminated against reserves, most French and Swedish companies capitalized and then amortized through the profit and loss account, while the choices of German companies were mixed.

Finally, it may be noted that non-systematic choices by individual companies cause a noticeable change in the within-country comparability index based on observed values, which falls from 58.17 per cent in 1986/87 to 53.92 per cent in 1990/91.

CONCLUSIONS

In this article, we have shown how the measurement of harmonization over time can be analysed by means of a nested hierarchy of log-linear models. This hierarchy of models enables a distinction to be made between two sets of systematic effects: those which account for the level of international harmony (and the change in such levels through time which we have defined as international harmonization); and those systematic effects which account for international disharmony, which may be attributed to national differences in the distribution of accounting policy choices. In addition, the approach used permits the identification of any non-systematic policy choices by companies, that is, choices that are explained by neither international nor national patterns of choice and appear as residual values.

The models were fitted sequentially to the sample data, starting with a null model in which accounting policy choices are assumed to be random and, hence, equiprobable within each subsample for each country in each year. We then introduced the main policy effects, in which the frequencies of the policy choices for the total sample are assigned pro-rata to the country–year subsamples, so that neither the country nor the year affects the probabilities of the subsample policy choices.

The next step was to add the effect of changes in policy choices from year to year, but not from country to country. At this level, the model captures the process of harmonization at the international level, assuming that the distribution of policy choices is identical across countries in a given year but varying from year to year.

The final step was to add the interaction effect between countries and policy choices, to arrive at a full second-order interaction model, thus capturing the extent to which national standardization on different methods detracts from international harmonization. This full model provides a systematic statistical characterization of accounting policy choices, including the effects of both harmonization at the international level and differential standardization at the national level, the significance of each being reflected in its parameter estimates. The differences between the policy choices modelled in this full model and the actual data were the non-systematic or individualistic policy choices at the company level. For the samples considered in this article, such choices were unusual.

It was also shown how the goodness of fit of the model can be measured, and a test of significance for each step up the hierarchy can be applied by estimation of the relevant F-statistic.

We applied the hierarchy of models to two areas of accounting policy choice, deferred tax and consolidated goodwill. In each case, the full model was shown to capture the systematic policy choices reflected in the sample data very precisely and to reveal the small extent of harmonization, or change in harmony, during the period. In other words, neither individualistic policy choices, unsystematic in the sense of not being explained by either international harmony or differential national standardization, nor policy choices leading to an increase in the level of harmony, could be said to be common. This can be seen clearly in Figure 4, where the proportion of statistical variation attributable to each effect in the models is shown, based on the statistics reported earlier in Table 10 and Table 14.

However, there was some evidence, when the analysis was restricted to the five largest country subsamples (France, Germany, the Netherlands, Sweden and the U.K.) and the variability attributable to company-specific choices fell even further, that when companies did select policies which were not in line with national practice this tended to have a positive but small harmonizing effect.

Our analysis indicates that, in the two areas of deferred taxation and consolidated goodwill, little progress in harmonization took place between 1986/87 and 1990/91, but that such progress as there was can be attributed to increases in between-country comparability, since the change in within-country comparability was either very small or negative.

The EU Directives have brought about a significant amount of *rapprochement* of

FIGURE 4

PROPORTION OF STATISTICAL VARIATION
ATTRIBUTABLE TO EACH EFFECT

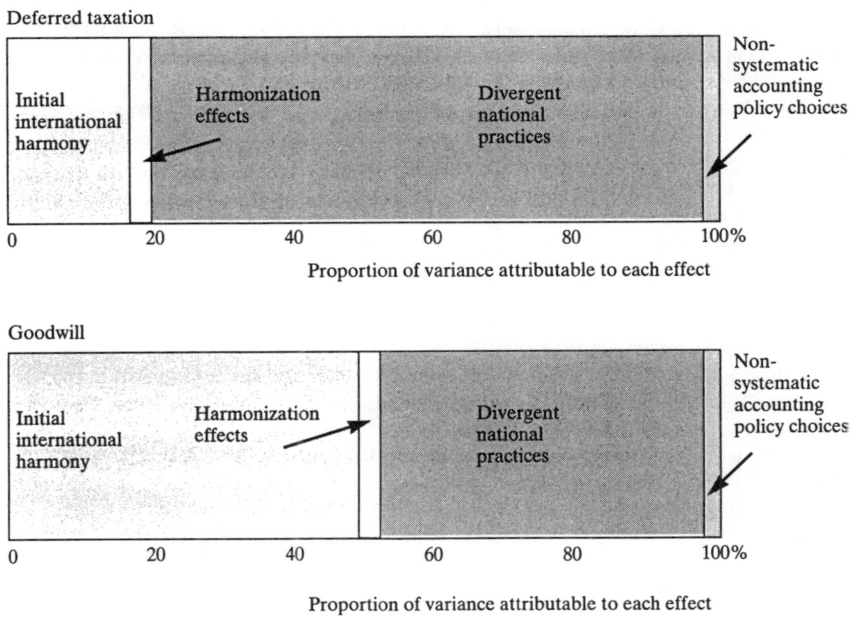

national accounting standards in Europe, not just in the member states but also in potential member states and other countries having close links with the EU. However, both deferred taxation and consolidated goodwill are areas where the EU Directives left considerable latitude to member states, and where national standards have continued in some cases to be somewhat flexible.

REFERENCES

Aitken, M. A., D. A. Anderson, B. J. Francis and J. P. Hinde, *Statistical Modelling in GLIM,* Oxford University Press, 1989.

Archer, G. S. H., P. Delvaille and S. J. McLeay, 'The Measurement of Harmonization and the Comparability of Financial Statement Items: Within-Country and Between-Country Effects', *Accounting and Business Research*, Spring 1995.

Archer, G. S. H., J.-B. Dufour and S. J. McLeay, *Audit Reports on the Financial Statements of European Multinational Companies: A Comparative Study*, ICAEW, 1989.

Bishop, Y. M., S. E. Fienberg and P. W. Holland, *Discrete Multivariate Analysis: Theory and Practice*, MIT Press, 1975.

Brennan, N., F. J. O'Brien and A. Pierce, *European Financial Reporting: Ireland*, Routledge, 1992.

Dijksma, J., and M. Hoogendoorn, *European Financial Reporting: The Netherlands*, Routledge, 1993.

Dobson, A. J., *An Introduction to Generalized Linear Models*, Chapman and Hall, 1990.

Emenyonu, E. N., and S. J. Gray, 'European Community Accounting Harmonization: An Empirical Study of Measurement Practices in France, Germany and the United Kingdom', *Accounting and Business Research*, Winter 1992.

Fienberg, S. E., *The Analysis of Cross-Classified Data*, MIT Press, 1977.

Francis, B. J., M. Green and C. D. Payne (eds), *GLIM4: The Statistical System for Generalized Linear Interactive Modelling*, Oxford University Press, 1993.

Gordon, P. D., and S. J. Gray, *European Financial Reporting: The United Kingdom*, Routledge, 1994.

Heurlin, S., and E. Peterssohn, 'Sweden', in D. J. Alexander and G. S. H. Archer (eds), *The European Accounting Guide* (2nd edn), Harcourt Brace, 1995.

Laffournier, B. 'Switzerland', in D. J. Alexander and G. S. H. Archer (eds), *The European Accounting Guide* (2nd edn), Harcourt Brace, 1995.

Lefebvre, C., and J. Flower, *European Financial Reporting: Belgium*, Routledge, 1994.

Lindsey, J. K., *Models for Repeated Measurements*, Oxford University Press, 1993.

Ordelheide, D., and D. Pfaff, *European Financial Reporting: Germany*, Routledge, 1994.

Scheid, J.-C., and P. Walton, *European Financial Reporting: France*, Routledge, 1992.

Tas, L. G. van der, 'Measuring Harmonization of Financial Reporting Practice', *Accounting and Business Research*, Spring 1988.

_____, 'Evidence of EC Financial Reporting Practice Harmonization: The Case of Deferred Taxation', *European Accounting Review*, May 1992a.

_____, *Harmonization of Financial Reporting*, Datawyse Maastricht, 1992b.

_____, 'Measuring International Harmonization and Standardization: A Comment', *Abacus*, September 1992.

Tay, J. S. W., and R. H. Parker, 'Measuring International Harmonization and Standardization', *Abacus*, March 1990.

_____, 'Measuring International Harmonization and Standardization: A Reply', *Abacus*, September 1992.

[4]

The International Journal of Accounting

International Accounting Harmonization and the Major Developed Stock Market Countries: An Empirical Study

Emmanuel N. Emenyonu and Sidney J. Gray
Sacred Heart University and the University of Warwick

Key Words: Harmonization; international; measurement

Abstract: *The purpose of this study is to assess the extent to which the accounting measurement and associated disclosure practices of large listed companies have become more harmonized internationally. An empirical study of companies based in the five major developed stock market countries, namely, France, Germany, Japan, the United Kingdom and the United States, examines the results of the efforts made so far to reduce or eliminate diversity in accounting practices internationally. An evaluation of changes over the 20 year period from 1971/72 to 1991/92 shows that while progress has been made in some respects, international accounting harmonization has remained an elusive goal.*

Technological innovations coupled with the deregulation of national capital markets have created a positive climate for the increasing integration of the world's capital markets. This phenomenon which has been variously described as "globalization" or "internationalization" has meant that companies are no longer limited in their fund raising and investment activities to their home countries. Similarly, investors incessantly search around the world for the best portfolios. This situation brings to the fore the issue of the accounting practices which underlie the numbers on which these cross-border financing and investing decisions are predicated. Furthermore, the increasing trend of multinationality of companies raises serious questions as to the adequacy and suitability of ethnocentric accounting guidelines, as conflicting standards of national reporting pose additional problems and costs both for multinational corporations and information users.

In recognition of the problems posed by international accounting diversity, leading professional accountancy bodies from Australia, Canada, France, Germany, Japan, Mexico, Netherlands, the United Kingdom and the United States of America established the International Accounting Standards Committee (IASC) in 1973 in a bid to promote the harmonization of international accounting practices.

Direct all correspondence to: Sidney J. Gray, University of Warwick, Warwick Business School, Coventry CV4 7AL, U.K.

The International Journal of Accounting, Vol. 31, No. 3, pp. 269-279 **ISSN: 0020-7063.**

Shortly after its establishment in 1973, the IASC predicted that "Provided that the initial enthusiasm and thrust with which the IASC was started is continued, its impact in the years to come will be important. It will take perhaps five to ten years before its full effects are recognized, but after that they will increase each year" (IASC, 1975). In retrospect, optimism about international harmonization or reductions in international accounting diversity may seem to have been misplaced, because in practice IASC standards have often been necessarily flexible in order to achieve consensus. They have also been difficult to enforce in countries such as Germany and Japan, where professional accounting organizations do not have a significant role in the standard setting process.

However, any progress in international accounting harmonization, or lack of it, is not just the responsibility of the IASC. Many other agencies have been involved such as the United Nations and OECD together with the European Union (EU) at the regional level. Nevertheless, the IASC is perhaps the only organization to claim prime responsibility for promoting international accounting harmonization or standardization on a world-wide basis.

It is against this background that the purpose of this study is to assess the extent to which the accounting measurement and associated disclosure practices of major companies based in five countries, namely, France, Germany, Japan, the U.K. and the U.S.A. have become more harmonized or less diverse in the context of efforts made since the 1970s to reduce or eliminate differences in accounting policies and practices internationally. Given that 1993 marked the 20th anniversary of the IASC's establishment, it would now seem an opportune time to assess how much progress has been made over this 20-year period in terms of a reduction in international accounting diversity. Furthermore, it would seem useful to identify areas of continuing concern which warrant the attention of international accounting harmonization agencies in the years ahead.

THE MEANING OF INTERNATIONAL ACCOUNTING HARMONIZATION

The terms "harmonization" and "standardization" tend to be used rather loosely and sometimes interchangeably. To clarify these concepts, it is probably helpful to think of a spectrum of practice ranging from total flexibility and diversity to total uniformity. In this context, harmonization is a process involving movement away from total diversity towards a state of harmony which may include total uniformity (Tay and Parker, 1990). Standardization is also a process involving movement away from total diversity towards total uniformity. Thus both harmonization and standardization involve a reduction in accounting diversity. The difference between them seems to lie in their relative flexibility or strictness in terms of their application to accounting regulation and practice. Harmonization seems to imply consensus and coordination in the context of a more flexible approach, (compared to standardization), with acceptance of a state of harmony which may be short of total uniformity. Standardization, on the other hand, implies a more strict approach resulting ultimately in a state of uniformity. These concepts are applicable at both the national and international level.

For the purposes of this study, the focus is on a reduction of international accounting diversity as an indicator of an increase in harmony. This is consistent with both the harmonization and standardization approaches but at the same time it does imply that uniformity is desirable, which may not necessarily be the case, i.e., some flexibility may be appropriate to reflect different circumstances.

It is also important to note the distinction between harmonization at the level of regulation as compared to the level of practice. Given that the ultimate concern is to enhance the comparability of financial statements to users, then any measure of success in the context of international harmonization or standardization would seem best focused on de facto accounting practices as is the case in this research.

PRIOR EMPIRICAL RESEARCH ON INTERNATIONAL HARMONIZATION

Earlier writers have written extensively on such issues as the benefits and costs of harmonization, obstacles and problems hindering harmonization, scope for harmonization, factors that are encouraging the harmonization drive and so on, (see, for example, Carey, 1970; Chevalier, 1977; Fantl, 1971; Gray, 1984; McComb, 1979; Moulin, 1988; Turley, 1983; Turner, 1983). Accordingly, this review of prior research will concentrate on those studies which are directly related to the measurement of international harmonization.

Nair and Frank (1981, p. 76) attempted to ascertain the impact of the harmonization endeavors of the IASC. Consequently, they surveyed the effect of IAS 1 to 10 on the accounting practices of some thirty seven countries, using the Price Waterhouse surveys of 1973, 1975, and 1979. Friedman's Analysis of Variance was used to analyze the data. They found that the period of the IASC's existence had coincided with an increase in the harmonization of accounting standards among the countries surveyed. It should be noted, however, that the Price Waterhouse Surveys are limited in terms of reliability not least by their focus on regulation rather than practice (Nobes, 1981).

Evans and Taylor (1982) with aims similar to those of Nair and Frank (1981), though more limited in terms of the scope of their research, studied the effect of IAS 2, 3, 4, 6 and 7 on financial reporting practices in France, Japan, U.K., U.S.A. and West Germany. This study relied on data in the financial reports of selected companies in each of the countries for the period from 1975 to 1988. The data were analyzed using percentages in respect of compliance. Based on their findings they concluded that the IASC had had very little effect on the accounting practices of the countries studied.

Doupnik and Taylor (1985) set out to assess the extent to which 16 Western European countries conformed to a "basic core of accounting practice," using IAS's 1-8. Data collected through a survey questionnaire and the Price Waterhouse 1979 survey were analyzed. The findings supported the hypothesis that many differences still existed in Western European accounting practices though some increased compliance with IASC standards was found. This latter finding was, however, disputed by Nobes (1987) who also concluded, from a recent study of accounting practices by U.S. multinationals, that compliance with IASC standards was negligible (Nobes, 1990).

The Federation des Experts Comptables Europeens (FEE) has also produced some noteworthy surveys. The 1989 Survey (FEE, 1989), covering 1987 accounts, sought to ascertain whether or not the implementation of the EC Fourth Directive on Annual Accounts has resulted in the increased harmonization of accounting practices within the member countries. Consequently, data were gathered from survey questionnaires and the annual reports of about 191 companies from nine countries. The survey concluded that for those areas covered comprehensively by the Fourth Directive a high level of harmonization can be observed. On the other hand, an apparent lack of harmonization was seen in those areas covered only partially by the Directive. An update and extension of this survey (FEE, 1991) based on 1989 accounts covered 441 companies from 15 European countries including three non-EC countries. A major finding of the survey was the suggestion that other factors besides the Fourth Directive are having a significant influence on accounting practice at national level. What both of these surveys do not do, however, is to attempt to quantify the existence of significant differences in practice and the current status of harmonization.

Van der Tas (1988), in an exploratory article, sought to quantify harmony, to determine when and to what extent harmonization has taken place and then to measure the impact of the organizations involved in international harmonization. In order to accomplish the set goals, three indices of concentration measurement were developed and adapted. The basic tool was the Herfindahl index, or H-index, one of many concentration measures. Variants of the H-index were developed: the C-index to handle national and the I-index to handle international harmonization measurement. Using these indices, Van der Tas measured levels of harmonization on the subject of accounting for Deferred Tax in the U.K., accounting for the Investment Tax Credit Equalization account in the Netherlands, and the Valuation of Land and buildings in the Netherlands. Finally, he attempted to compute a harmonization index for accounting for the Investment Tax Credit in the U.S. and the Netherlands. From these indices, which were computed over a period ranging from 1965-1985, it was possible at a glance to recognize periods of high and low harmonization. However, this was an exploratory article with substantial scope for development.

Tay and Parker (1990), after reviewing Van der Tas (1988) and other notable papers on the measurement of international harmonization, identified the following as major problems: data sources, operationalization of concepts, statistical methods employed, and distinguishing changes in accounting practice due to compliance with standards from changes due to other reasons. They also suggested an alternative approach to harmonization measurement—a study focused on the actual practices of companies as disclosed in their annual reports rather than as stated by regulatory requirements. Evidence of harmony could be derived by subjecting data extracted from companies' annual reports to tests of statistical significance using, for instance, the chi-square test and indices such as the I-index proposed by Van der Tas. Clearly, the question of how to measure harmonization requires further experimentation and development.

In summary, while there have been a number of empirical studies of comparative international accounting practices, these have been limited in scope. Further, much of the research is now somewhat dated. The main problem, however, is the lack of a comprehensive quantitative analysis of the nature and extent of harmonization in practice both at the present time and over time.

RESEARCH METHODOLOGY

Given that the purpose of this paper is to assess the nature and extent of international accounting harmonization (or reduction in international accounting diversity), how much progress has been made since 1973 when the IASC was established? What have been the major successes and what are the remaining problem areas? Some insights into these questions can be gained from an assessment of the measurement practices of companies based in countries which are hosts to the world's largest developed stock markets, i.e., France, Germany, Japan, the U.K. and the U.S. This assessment will be made by an examination of key accounting measurement issues as at 1991/92 and a comparison made with the position as at 1971/72. The aim here is to assess progress for a 20-year period starting from just before the IASC came into existence and when international harmonization issues were just beginning to be addressed by them and other agencies such as the OECD and UN. Progress in this context is defined in terms of a reduction in international accounting diversity.

From an initial sample objective of 45 multi-listed and 45 domestic listed industrial companies from each country, the final sample of companies used in the survey comprised a total of 293 companies who were found to be reporting in *both* 1971/72 and 1991/92. The size criterion used was that of sales turnover of at least US $250 million for the 1990/91 financial year. The country breakdown of the final sample was as follows: 25 from France, 42 from Germany, 54 from Japan, 82 from the U.K. and 90 from the U.S. Given the size of these companies and the importance of the countries involved, which are among the largest economies and stock markets in a global context, it would seem reasonable to expect that the impact of efforts to harmonize accounting internationally would be clearly discernible. Indeed, these parameters could be said to provide a favorable test environment given that all of the countries involved are founding members of IASC and strongly committed to the international harmonization objective. A much more severe test of harmonization would be to include all countries comprising membership of the IASC and to survey both large and small companies, listed and unlisted.

Annual Reports for the sample of 293 companies across the five countries were examined in respect of reports published during both of the periods 1971/72 and 1991/92. In general, English language reports were used but in the case of a number of French, German and Japanese reports it was necessary to translate the originals and also obtain advice on interpretation. Accounting measurement issues were assessed relating to choices of method and associated disclosures in each of the following major areas: group accounting and consolidations; goodwill; foreign currency translation; accounting for inventories; property, plant and equipment; depreciation; accounting for investments; accounting for borrowing costs; deferred taxation; extraordinary and exceptional items; research and development expenditures; pensions and retirement benefits; long-term contracts; and government grants. The issues chosen for analysis were based on the measurement issues covered by International Accounting Standards and especially those highlighted by the IASC in its recent comparability project designed to limit the accounting policy choices available (IASC, 1990).

First, an assessment was made of the extent to which changes in measurement and associated disclosure practices over the 20-year period to 1991/92 are significant using the Chi-square (χ^2) test (Siegel and Castellan, 1988) applied to the companies in aggregate.

Second, for each of the accounting measurement practices analyzed, a harmony index was constructed to assess the extent of international accounting harmonization as at both 1971/72 and 1991/92. This index provides a range of values from zero for extreme diversity to 1 for an absolute uniformity of accounting methods. The harmony index used, i.e., the I-index, was a variant of the Herfindahl index, a measure of concentration used by Van der Tas (1988) in his study of accounting harmonization. The general formula for the index, which includes a correction factor in the case of three or more countries, is stated as follows:

$$\text{I-Index} = [\sum_{i=1}^{n} (f^1 i \times f^2 i \times \ldots \times f^m i)]\ 1/(m-1)$$

where:

fi = relative frequency of method i in country m

m = number of countries

n = number of alternative accounting methods

The index is computed by multiplying the relative frequency or proportion of use of a particular accounting method across countries and subsequently adding the results for all alternative methods. As a result, the index rises when more companies across countries use the same method from the available accounting options. An example of a simple 2 country/2 method case is as follows:

Country	*1*	2
Accounting method 1	0.7	0.6
Accounting method 2	0.3	0.4
	1.0	1.0

Harmony index = (0.7 × 0.6 + 0.3 × 0.4)
= (0.42 + 0.12)
= 0.54

In most cases, the I-index would seem to give a fair impression of the extent and level of accounting harmonization between two or more countries. However, there are some instances when the I-index computation using the formula given above can lead to very misleading results. The following hypothetical case of a 4 country/2 method case vividly illustrates this point.

Country	*1*	2	*3*	*4*
Method 1	1.0	1.0	0.0	1.0
Method 2	0.0	0.0	1.0	0.0

$$I = (1.0 \times 1.0 \times 0.0 \times 1.0 + 0.0 \times 0.0 \times 1.0 \times 0.0)^{1/(4-1)} = 0.0^{1/3} = 0/0$$

The I-index score value of zero derived in the above illustration erroneously suggests that there is no degree of harmony whatsoever with respect to the four countries on this particular topic. This misleading result arises due to the fact that all the companies from country 3 adopted method 2 which was not used at all by any of the companies from the other three countries. From this it can be deduced that when the number of countries exceeds two, the practices of one or more of the countries can, in extreme cases, render the I-index score value totally meaningless. Therefore, for the purposes of this study, whenever a situation similar to the one described in the illustration above occurred, no attempt was made to compute the I-index score for that particular topic.

In reviewing the results of the statistical analyses it should be noted that the results derived from the chi-square tests should not be expected to accord with the rankings given by the I-index computations. For instance it is quite possible that on a particular item the chi-square test might indicate that there are no significant differences between the practices of the companies, whereas the I-index calculation might lead to a relatively low score. The reason for this likelihood is that both tools are intended to measure different concepts of harmonization.

The chi-square test measures the extent to which the preferences of some independent groups are matched. That is, whether or not companies use alternative accounting methods in similar proportions as between countries or between points in time. On the other hand, the I-index measures the extent to which the accounting practices of companies across countries are concentrated around one or more alternatives, i.e., more uniform.

In order to illustrate the above point, assume that on a given accounting topic there are three alternative methods. If an equal proportion of companies used the same alternative methods in each country, then the chi-square test will invariably indicate that there are no significant differences in the accounting practices of the countries concerned over time. On the other hand, the I-index will give a score of 0.33 percent which might relatively speaking be lower (less harmonized) than the score on another topic whose chi-square test result might have indicated that there are significant differences between countries.

RESULTS AND ANALYSIS

The results of the statistical tests and the harmonization analysis are reported in Tables 1 and 2.

In order to assess whether or not there are significant differences between the accounting measurement and associated disclosure practices adopted by the companies as between 1971/72 and 1991/92, 46 tests (17 disclosure-based and 29 policy-based) were conducted. As seen in Table 1, findings based on 36 issues (14 disclosure-based and 22 policy-based), indicate that there are significant differences in the accounting measurement and associated disclosure practices adopted by companies from the five countries in aggregate as between 1971/72 and 1991/92. On ten of the issues, however, no significant differences were observed. Therefore, it would appear from these tests that there is substantial support for the viewpoint that there have been significant changes over the period in respect of the accounting measurement and associated disclosure practices of the companies surveyed.

However, from Table 2 it can be seen that progress in reducing international accounting diversity over the last 20 years has been mixed and, taken overall, quite modest with an increase in the average I-index score from a moderate level of 0.6230 to only 0.6903. This is an average increase in international accounting harmonization of *only* 10.8% from 1971/72 to 1991/92.

The results for the 26 accounting measurement issues indicate that only in the case of 14 issues was there an *increase* in harmonization. In 12 cases there was in fact a *reduction* in harmonization or a higher level of accounting diversity. This would seem to be a situation of one step forward and one step back so far as harmonization is concerned.

Significant *increases* in international accounting harmonization since 1971/72 across the five countries are in respect of consolidation, with a very notable increase of 862.5% from 0.0963 to 0.9269, together with the treatment of exchange differences, the treatment of gains/losses on long-term investments, and the treatment of research and development

Table 1. Assessment of Changes in Measurement and Associated Disclosure Practices from 1971-72 to 1991-92

		Chi-Square Statistic	*Significance*
	Accounting Methods		
1.	Consolidation method	74.773	.0000*
2.	Business combinations (disclosure)	67.426	.0000*
3.	Business combinations (policy)	.712	.3985
4.	Accounting for Associates (policy)	28.026	.0000*
5.	Goodwill (disclosure of policy)	78.228	.0000*
6.	Goodwill (policy)	3.078	.0794
7.	Goodwill (amortisation period)	35.279	.0000*
8.	Foreign Income Statements (disclosure)	71.017	.0000*
9.	Foreign Income Statements: Translation Rate (policy)	57.770	.0000*
10.	Translation Differences (disclosure)	154.165	.0000*
11.	Translation Differences (policy)	1.109	.2922
12.	Foreign Currency Transactions (disclosure)	56.090	.0000*
13.	Foreign Currency Transactions (policy)	10.880	.0124*
14.	Exchange Differences (policy)	39.316	.0000*
15.	Disclosure of inventory valuation policy	27.331	.0000*
16.	Method used to assign cost to inventory	12.211	.0067*
17.	Measurement basis for recording inventory	13.134	.0766
18.	Definition of market value	8.412	.0149*
19.	Disclosure of policy for measuring property, plant and equipment	57.003	.0000*
20.	Cost basis of recording property, plant and equipment	3.816	.0508
21.	Gains or losses on disposal of property, plant and equipment	97.389	.0000*
22.	Disclosure of depreciation policy	79.766	.0000*
23.	Method of accounting for depreciation	19.362	.0007*
24.	Disclosure of policy on Long-term investments	0.114	.7347
25.	Method of valuing long-term investments	10.643	.0011*
26.	Disposal of long-term investments	69.315	.0000*
27.	Disclosure of policy on current investments	6.825	.0090*
28.	Measurement of current investments	19.674	.0002*
29.	Gain/loss on disposal of current investments	22.181	.0000*
30.	Disclosure of policy on borrowing costs	0.006	.9336
31.	Method of accounting for borrowing costs	72.447	.0000*
32.	Disclosure of deferred tax accounting policy	129.758	.0000*
33.	Basis of providing for deferred taxes	64.084	.0000*
34.	Method of treating deferred taxes	4.465	.0346*
35.	Disclosure of policy on extraordinary/exceptional items	1.641	.2001
36.	Treatment of extraordinary/exceptional items	5.899	.0151*
37.	Disclosure of policy on R & D expenditures	31.688	.0000*
38.	Treatment of research expenditures	67.365	.0000*
39.	Treatment of development expenditures	62.145	.0000*
40.	Disclosure of policy on pensions	102.139	.0000*
41.	Determination of cost of pensions	119.196	.0000*
42.	Past service costs/experience adjustments	7.109	.0077*
43.	Disclosure of policy on long-term contracts	22.118	.0000*
44.	Method of accounting for long-term contracts	2.204	.3321
45.	Disclosure of policy on government grants	21.016	.0000*
46.	Method of treating government grants	3.157	.0756

Note: *Significant at the 5% level.

Table 2. International Accounting Harmonization: I-Index and Changes from 1971/72 to 1991/92

		Index 1971/72	*Index 1991/92*	*Index Change*	*% Change*
	Accounting Methods				
1.	Consolidation method	0.0963	0.9269	+0.8306	+862.5
2.	Investments in Associates	0.7784	0.9376	+0.1592	+20.4
3.	Treatment of goodwill	0.6865	0.5441	–0.1424	–20.7
4.	Rate for translating Income Statement of Subsidiaries	0.5417	0.7039	+0.1622	+29.9
5.	Treatment of Translation Differences	0.5377	0.5063	–0.0314	–5.8
6.	Treatment of Exchange Differences	0.2323	0.8136	+0.5813	+250.2
7.	Method used to assign cost to inventories	0.3853	0.2825	–0.1028	–26.7
8.	Measurement basis for recording inventories	0.6781	0.7564	+0.0783	+11.5
9.	Definition of market value	0.6164	0.6990	+0.0826	+13.4
10.	Cost basis for recording property, plant and equipment	0.7629	0.7906	+0.0277	+3.6
11.	Gains/losses on disposal of property, plant and equipment	0.7093	0.9777	+0.2684	+37.8
12.	Method of accounting for depreciation	0.3294	0.2295	–0.0999	–30.3
13.	Method of valuing long-term investments	0.8471	0.6088	–0.2383	–28.1
14.	Gains/losses on disposal of long-term investments	0.5803	0.9889	+0.4986	+85.9
15.	Method of valuing current investments	0.5731	0.7662	+0.1931	+33.7
16.	Gains/losses on disposal of current investments	0.6999	0.9914	+0.2915	+41.6
17.	Method of accounting for borrowing costs	0.9426	0.3843	–0.5583	–59.2
18.	Basis for providing for deferred taxes	0.7732	0.2321	–0.5411	–70.0
19.	Method of treating deferred taxes	0.4005	0.3953	–0.0052	–1.3
20.	Accounting for extra-ordinary and exceptional items	0.9401	0.9950	+0.0549	+5.8
21.	Treatment of research expenditures	0.3592	0.9465	+0.5873	+163.5
22.	Treatment of development expenditures	0.4145	0.9098	+0.4953	+119.5
23.	Determination of the cost of pensions	0.9524	0.4882	–0.4642	–48.7
24.	Treatment of past service costs/experience adjustments	0.9439	0.8501	–0.0938	–9.9
25.	Method of accounting for long-term contracts	0.6670	0.5933	–0.0737	–11.0
26.	Method of treating government grants	0.7500	0.6300	–0.1200	–16.0
	Average I-Index Score	0.6230	0.6903	+0.0673	+10.8

expenditures. It is also noteworthy that there is a relatively high level of harmonization in respect of consolidation method, investments in associates, the treatment of gains/losses on the disposal of property, plant and equipment, the treatment of gains and losses on the disposal of current investments, and accounting for extraordinary and exceptional items.

At the same time, it is noteworthy that there are a number of issues where there have been significant *decreases* in international accounting harmonization since 1971/72 including the treatment of goodwill, the costing of inventories, the method of depreciation, the valuation of long-term investments, the treatment of borrowing costs, the basis for providing for deferred taxes and the method of determining the cost of pensions. Furthermore, it is also noteworthy that there is a relatively low level of harmonization especially in respect of the costing of inventories, accounting for depreciation, and the basis for providing for deferred taxes.

CONCLUSIONS

The results of this empirical study of the accounting measurement methods used by large listed companies in five major countries, i.e., France, Germany, Japan, the U.K. and the

U.S., show that the impact of efforts to reduce international accounting diversity over the 20-year period from 1971/72 to 1991/92 have been, in general terms, quite modest.

While there have been a number of significant changes since 1971/72, it seems that, taken overall, there has been an average increase in harmony of *only* 10.8%. Looking individually at 26 major accounting measurement issues the results are *mixed* with 14 cases showing *increases* in harmonization and 12 cases showing *decreases* in harmonization.

Given there is as yet no accepted benchmark for determining what constitutes a necessary level of harmony for the purposes of comparability, the significance of the I-index scores must remain a matter of judgement. A degree of flexibility, and the use of alternative methods, may well be acceptable. In respect of many measurement issues, however, it seems clear that the problems facing those promoting international accounting harmonization, most notably the IASC, continue to be substantial despite 20 years of effort. Although there has been a significant reduction in accounting diversity in respect of issues such as consolidation, the treatment of associates, and the method of accounting for exchange differences, there has also been an increasing diversity relating to issues such as the treatment of goodwill, accounting for depreciation, the treatment of borrowing costs, accounting for inventories, accounting for deferred taxes, and accounting for pensions.

While these empirical findings indicate areas of change in international accounting harmonization, it has been beyond the scope of this research to explain such changes. Rather the purpose here has been to assess whether change has taken place and, if so, whether or not international accounting diversity has been reduced or increased. This is likely to be of concern to international harmonization agencies and also of interest to the international investment community.

It may be that the IASC's recent Comparability Project (IASC, 1990) and subsequent changes to International Accounting Standards (effective for accounting periods ending on or after 31 December 1995) will reduce the level of international accounting diversity. Given the recent support of the International Organization of Securities Commissions (IOSCO), this may indeed be feasible in the longer term. In the meantime, international accounting harmonization remains a desirable but often elusive goal.

REFERENCES

Carey, J.L. 1970. "How can Barriers Against International Accounting be Eliminated?" *The International Journal of Accounting,* 6(1): 53-58.

Chevalier, G. 1977. "Should Accounting Practices be Universal?" *CA Magazine,* (July).

Doupnik S. and M.E. Taylor. 1985. "An Empirical Investigation of the Observance of IASC Standards in Western Europe," *Management International Review,* Vol. 2 (Spring).

Evans, T.G. and M.E. Taylor. 1982. "Bottom-line Compliance with the IASC: A Comparative Analysis," *The International Journal of Accounting,* 18(1): 115-128.

Fantl, I.L. 1971. "Case Against International Uniformity," *Management Accounting,* (May).

Federation des Experts Comptables Europeen. 1989. *European Survey of Published Financial Statements in the Context of the Fourth Directive.* Brussels: FEE.

Federation des Experts Comptables Europeen. 1991. *European Survey of Published Accounts.* Brussels: FEE/Routledge.

Gray S.J. 1984. (with L.B. McSweeney and J.C. Shaw). *Information Disclosure and the Multinational Corporation.* Chichester: Wiley.

International Accounting Standards Committee. 1975. *Work and Purpose of the International Accounting Standards Committee.* London: IASC.

International Accounting Standards Committee. 1990. *Statement of Intent on Comparability of Financial Statements.* London: IASC.

McComb, D. 1982. "International Accounting Standards and the EEC Harmonization Programme: A Conflict of Disparate Objectives," *International Journal of Accounting,* 17(2): 35-48.

Moulin, D.J. 1988. "Practical Means of Promoting Common Accounting and Auditing Standards," *Proceedings of the 13th Annual Conference of the International Organisation of Securities Commissions.* Montreal: IOSCO.

Nair, R.D. and W.G. Frank. 1981. "The Harmonization of International Accounting Standards, 1973-1979," *International Journal of Accounting,* 17(1): 61-78.

Nobes, C.W. 1981. "An Empirical Analysis of International Accounting Principles: A Comment," *Journal of Accounting Research,* 19(1): 268-270.

Nobes, C.W. 1987. "An Empirical Investigation of the Observance of IASC Standards in Western Europe: A Comment," *Management International Review,* Vol. 4 (Spring): 78-79.

Nobes, C.W. 1990. "Compliance by US Corporations with IASC Standards," *British Accounting Review,* Vol. 22 (Spring): 41-49.

Nobes, C.W. and R.H. Parker. 1991. *Comparative International Accounting.* London: Prentice-Hall.

Siegel, S. and N.J. Castellan. 1988. *Non-Parametric Statistics for the Behavioural Sciences.* Singapore: McGraw-Hill.

Tay, J.S.W. and R.H. Parker. 1990. "Measuring International Harmonization and Standardisation," *Abacus,* 26(1): 71-88.

Turley, W.S. 1983. "International Harmonization of Accounting: The Contribution of the EEC Fourth Directive on Company Law," *International Journal of Accounting,* 18(2): 13-28.

Turner, J.N. 1983. "International Harmonization: A Professional Goal," *Journal of Accountancy,* (January): 58-66.

Van der Tas, L.G. 1988. "Measuring Harmonization of Financial Reporting Practice," *Accounting and Business Research,* Vol. 18 (Spring): 151-171.

The European Accounting Review 1997, **6:3**, 465–485

An approach for measuring the degree of comparability of financial accounting information

Vera M. Krisement
Osterwicker Strasse 36, D-48653 Coesfeld, Germany

ABSTRACT

This contribution sets out to provide an index to measure comparability of financial accounting information concerning specific kinds of transactions or events. It suggests definitions for the terms of comparability of financial accounting information and of accounting method. Requirements are derived from these definitions which must be met by an index of comparability, and entropy is shown to be an appropriate measure fulfilling these requirements. The problem of multiple reporting is dealt with separately. Finally, the measurement concept developed is applied to an example from the FEE report for 1989.

INTRODUCTION

Financial accounting is the process of collecting and transforming information about transactions and events affecting the assets and liabilities, the financial position and the performance of an enterprise, and of presenting this information in the annual accounts, the notes thereto, and other supplementary accounts, e.g. a cash flow statement. In particular, the objective of financial accounting is to provide information that is relevant to the economical decisions of external users of the accounts with respect to the enterprise (IASC, 1992: 32).

To be relevant to the decisions of external users, information about an enterprise must be comparable through time and with information about other enterprises (IASC, 1992: 39). Since the preparation and presentation of financial accounts in different countries is determined by different rules and practices (Radebaugh and Gray, 1993: 79–140), the question arises as to the international comparability of financial accounting information. This question is tightly linked to the judgement of the various efforts to harmonize financial accounting.

Examples for harmonization efforts are (i) on the global level the standards of the International Accounting Standards Committee (IASC) (Fleming, 1991; Chandler, 1992) and (ii) on the European level the EC directives (van Hulle, 1992). The result of such efforts is discussed controversially in the

 0963–8180

literature (Nobes and Parker, 1991: 70–3, 77–9, 84; Choi and Mueller, 1992: 257–61). As a basis for judgement of these efforts, a precise definition of comparability of financial accounting information is needed.

Besides harmonization, multiple reporting is another approach to increase comparability of financial accounting information. Multiple reporting means that information is given on a specified transaction or event applying several alternative accounting methods simultaneously (van der Tas, 1988: 158). For example, the amount of a specific kind of assets may be disclosed both at historical cost and at replacement and market value. In particular, multiple reporting occurs in the case of a domestic enterprise quoted on a foreign stock exchange whereby the obligation arises to prepare supplementary accounts corresponding to the accounting rules required by that stock exchange (Parker, 1991: 124; Choi and Mueller, 1992: 306–17). To assess the results of the multiple reporting approach, a well-defined notion of comparability of financial accounting information has to be presupposed.

In this contribution, a formal definition of comparability of financial accounting information is put forward. Following from this definition, a suggestion is developed to quantify the degree of comparability. Concentration indices used in statistics are shown to be basically appropriate to this measuring problem with entropy, a particular concentration index, meeting all the qualifications required of a measure of comparability. Special problems of measuring comparability arising from multiple reporting are treated in a separate section. In conclusion, the feasibility of the measuring concept put forward is demonstrated, and the results of the present contribution are summarized.

COMPARABILITY OF FINANCIAL ACCOUNTING INFORMATION

Introductory remarks

To be comparable, all information is required to refer to facts of the same kind. For the problem under consideration, this means that the transactions and events affecting the assets and liabilities, the financial position and the performance of enterprises have to be classified into groups of similar events so that the treatment in financial accounting (or rather the resulting information presented) of transactions or events of the same class may be compared. Valuation of certain fixed or current assets, allocation of depreciable amounts to similar fixed assets or deferral of development cost to future periods are examples of classes of events and their treatment in financial accounting. Classes of transactions or events may be defined taking a broader or a narrower point of view depending on the concrete issue under consideration. In any case, comparability of financial accounting information is dealt with on the level of particular items of the annual accounts and not on the level of the accounts as a whole (van der Tas, 1988; 1992a: 72; 1992b: 418; 1992c: 235–7).

As a matter of principle, information on similar transactions or events are comparable to one another if they represent these transactions or events in the same way, i.e. if they have the same contents. In regard to the comparability of financial accounting information the question arises as to how information about similar transactions or events must be collected, transformed and presented to have the same contents. Obviously, the answer to this question depends on the accounting method(s) applied. Concerning the formal definition of comparability of financial accounting information, a thesis is put forward which shall be discussed in the following, namely: financial accounting informations on similar transactions or events are comparable to one another if they are collected and transformed applying the same accounting methods.

In consequence of this definition, multiple reporting will, as a rule, raise the degree of comparability of financial accounting information (van der Tas, 1988: 158; 1992a: 72; 1992c: 112–3; 199).[1] If for instance an enterprise accounting so far for specified fixed assets at historical cost only is going to disclose henceforth the replacement value of these assets in addition, the accounting information of this enterprise becomes comparable with the corresponding accounting information of other enterprises accounting for similar assets at replacement value only.

The conception of an accounting method

As a prerequisite for discussing the definition of comparability of financial accounting information, the notion of accounting method has to be agreed upon. Since comparability of information is dependent on its contents, the concept of accounting method comprises all methods of collecting and transforming information which influence the contents of the annual accounts.

To begin with, the recognition methods form part of the accounting methods. If events of some distinct kind are recognized in the annual accounts of an enterprise, while another enterprise does not recognize similar events in its accounts, comparability of information referring thereto is impaired. Moreover, methods of valuation and income determination are accounting methods as well (van der Tas, 1992a: 70–1; 1992b: 408; 1992c: 13, 36, 46).

Furthermore, the contents of financial accounting information are influenced by the choice between alternative disclosure policies. If information on a specific kind of events may be disclosed separately or combined with information on events of a different kind in a summary item, the latter alternative results in less detailed financial accounting information than the first one. However, if supplementary notes are added which allow breakdown of the summary item, the degree of detail of financial accounting information is not affected by the choice between the two alternatives which, in this case, is a matter of presentation and not of disclosure policy. Therefore, alternatives of disclosure are looked upon as accounting methods, whereas alternative methods of presentation are not.

Depending on which kind of accounting method is under consideration, comparability may be characterized as concerning the recognition, valuation, income determination or disclosure alternatives applied to collect and transform information on specific transactions or events.

Comparability of accounting information subject to environmental conditions

As is shown in the comparative accounting literature, there are numerous more-or-less important differences between national accounting systems (Radebaugh and Gray, 1993: 79–140). Apparently, these differences are caused by different economical, political, social and cultural environmental conditions that influence accounting in each country (Zeff, 1972; Choi and Mueller, 1992: 39–43). Law and taxation system, language, possible inflation etc. may be cited as examples for such environmental conditions (Nobes and Parker, 1991: 11–20; Choi and Mueller, 1992: 40–3). Environmental conditions are tightly linked to the fact that in different countries the various groups of users of external accounting information have differing means to enforce their partially diverging interests (Nobes and Parker, 1991: 12–5).

Considering these various national environmental factors, the question arises as to which accounting methods should be regarded as 'the same' under different environmental conditions according to the definition of comparability of financial accounting information. This question cannot be answered in general but only for special cases. For instance, such a special case is the occurrence of inflation. It makes no sense for an enterprise operating in a hyperinflationary economy to account for its assets at historical cost, since this information has no decision relevance for anyone and therefore does not create comparability with the corresponding financial accounting information of an enterprise in a non-inflationary country accounting for its assets also at historical cost. Comparability would more likely exist if the enterprise in the hyperinflationary country were accounting for its assets at replacement value, since historical cost in a non-inflationary environment may be considered as a replacement value in a special case.

It follows from the foregoing that the degree of comparability of financial accounting information is dependent on the number of alternative accounting methods for collecting and transforming information on a specific kind of transaction or event and on the number of enterprises applying each of these alternatives. Obviously, the highest possible degree of comparability is reached if all enterprises choose the same accounting alternative (or rather if only one accounting method exists, i.e. the choice between accounting alternatives is omitted).

In the following, an approach to quantify the degree of comparability of financial accounting information based on frequencies of application of each accounting alternative will be put forward. To begin with, several requirements following from the definition of comparability are set up which a measure must fulfil to qualify as an index of comparability. Subsequently, a method of measurement is described that complies with these requirements. Problems arising in connection with multiple reporting are deferred for later consideration.

MEASURING THE DEGREE OF COMPARABILITY BY MEANS OF THE ENTROPY

Requirements to be met by a measure of comparability

Resulting directly from the nature of the measuring problem under consideration, the first requirement to be fulfilled by a measure of comparability (briefly designated as index) reads as follows (by analogy to industrial concentrations: Jacquemin and de Jong, 1977: 42):

> The index sought shall increase or decrease steadily and monotonically with increasing comparability of financial accounting information.

The expression 'with increasing comparability' requires to be considered more closely. If any conceivable situation characterized by the frequencies of application of the alternative accounting methods could *ex ante* be arranged corresponding to its degree of comparability on an ordinal scale, the index sought should just transform the ordinal into an interval scale leaving the order unchanged. Requiring transformation on a ratio scale would not be appropriate (Münzner, 1963: 3–4). Actually, there are many situations which may not *ex ante* be ordered as to their respective degree of comparability. In these cases, the index sought shall allocate figures to the situations allowing them to order on an interval scale (by analogy to industrial concentrations: Paschen, 1969: 30–1; Paschen and Buyse, 1971: 5–6).

An inverse measure, i.e. an index increasing with decreasing degree of comparability, may well be suitable for the measuring problem under consideration and is therefore not excluded in the above-mentioned qualification. Furthermore, the index sought is required to be steady. Since proportionally small changes of the frequencies of application of the alternative accounting methods have only small implications on the degree of comparability, they should produce but small variations of the index. In other words, the measure of comparability may not feature points of unsteadiness (by analogy to industrial concentrations: Marfels, 1972: 462).

A second requirement of the index sought is concerned with the number of enterprises studied as to the comparability of their accounting information (by analogy to industrial concentrations: Hall and Tideman, 1967: 163):

> With constant relative frequencies of application of the accounting alternatives given, the index sought shall be independent of the number of enterprises studied as to their collecting and transforming of information about specific transactions or events.

The relative frequency of application of an accounting method is the number of the enterprises applying this accounting method in proportion to the number of all enterprises where the kind of transaction or event under consideration is found. Of course, all the enterprises where a certain kind of transaction or event is found may not be recorded in practice, in which case samples must be taken instead. In that case, the relative frequencies of application refer to the sample size, i.e. the number of enterprises studied where a specified kind of transaction or event is found. Obviously, the measure of comparability should not depend on the sample size, since this would be an arbitrary influence. This is why the second requirement postulates that the index sought be independent of the number of enterprises studied. In other words, the index should depend upon the relative but not upon the absolute frequencies of application of the accounting alternatives.

The third requirement is consideration of the elementary process which causes the degree of comparability to increase (by analogy to industrial concentrations: Curry and George, 1983: 204–7):

> If the relative frequency of application of an accounting method increases to the debit of the lower or equal relative frequency of application of an alternative accounting method, the index sought shall indicate that the degree of comparability of financial accounting information is increasing.

To illustrate this requirement, a specific transaction is considered which may be treated in the annual accounts applying two alternative accounting methods. Comparability of corresponding accounting information is at its maximum (under the assumption of equal environmental conditions) if all enterprises studied, where the transaction under consideration is found, give information about it applying the same accounting method. The degree of comparability decreases with more and more enterprises turning to apply the other accounting alternative. The minimum degree of comparability is reached if each of the two accounting alternatives is applied by exactly half of the enterprises studied. Thus, the third requirement is describing a step on the way from minimum to maximum degree of comparability.

The fourth and last requirement to be met by a measure to quantify comparability results from the necessity of practical applicability (by analogy to industrial concentrations: Marfels, 1971: 143):

> The index calculated for the enterprises operating in a larger geographical unit (for example Europe) shall be decomposable additively into the contributions of the

enterprises operating in segments (for example countries or groups of countries) forming part of that geographical unit.

If for example the result of harmonization efforts in Europe has to be judged, the degree of comparability would not only be of interest regarding all Europe but also regarding the two groups of countries formed by the member states and the non-members of the EC and regarding each individual European country. If the corresponding values of the index for the countries and the groups of countries can be additively isolated from the index for all Europe, the measuring concept of comparability is simple to handle, and the results produced may be interpreted meaningfully.

Entropy as a qualified comparability measure

Since the degree of comparability of financial accounting information is determined by the number and the relative frequencies of application of alternative accounting methods, concentration indices seem basically to be appropriate for its measurement. Namely, these indices quantify concentration as accumulation of a quantity at single elements of a set of objects (Rosenbluth, 1955: 57, 61; Marfels, 1971: 143; Paschen and Buyse, 1971: 2; Jacquemin and Kumps, 1971: 60). In the case under consideration, the objects are the alternative accounting methods, and the quantity is the relative frequency of application by the enterprises. Concentration indices, in any case, meet the first three of the four requirements for a measure of comparability (Curry and George, 1983: 207–12), but entropy is the only one of the current concentration indices to be also additively decomposable (Hildenbrand and Paschen, 1964; Paschen and Buyse, 1971).

Entropy is computed as follows (Curry and George, 1983: 208):

$$E = \sum_{i=1}^{N} y_i \cdot \ln \frac{1}{y_i}$$

with i = numeral characterizing the alternative accounting methods to collect and transform information on a specific kind of transaction or event, N = number of existing alternative accounting methods, y_i = relative frequency of application of accounting method i and ln = natural logarithm. In the literature, entropy is calculated using logarithms to different bases (Theil, 1967: 293; Horowitz and Horowitz, 1968: 197; Marfels, 1971: 150). Natural logarithm is choosen here for convenience.

Entropy is an inverse measure of the degree of comparability. Given the number N of alternative accounting methods, the maximum value of entropy, $E = \ln N$, is reached where the degree of comparability is at minimum, i.e. if the frequencies of application are equally distributed among the alternative accounting methods (by analogy to Theil, 1967: 291). If the degree of comparability is at its maximum, which is the case with application concentrated on a single accounting alternative, entropy takes the value $E = 1$ (by analogy to Theil, 1967: 291).

Additive decomposition of entropy

In the following, the additive decomposition of entropy will be described taking as an example the decomposition of the index calculated for the geographical unit of Europe into the contributions from groups of countries (in the following, briefly called regions; e.g. member-states of the EC versus non-members) and from individual European countries. To this end, some symbols have to be introduced:

l = numeral characterizing the individual European countries.

r = numeral characterizing the groups of individual European countries (i.e. the regions).

M_r = set of all countries l belonging to region r.

y_{il} = number of enterprises in country l applying accounting alternative i as a proportionate part of the number of all European enterprises studied (relative frequency of application of accounting method i in country l).

$y_{i.}$ = relative frequency of application of accounting method i in Europe $= \sum_{l} y_{il}$

$y_{.l}$ = number of enterprises studied in country l as a proportionate part of the number of all European enterprises studied $= \sum_{i} y_{\cdot ie}$

y_{ir} = number of enterprises in region r applying accounting alternative i as a proportionate part of the number of all European enterprises studied (relative frequency of application of accounting method i in region r)

$$= \sum_{l \in M_r} y_{ie}$$

$y_{.r}$ = number of enterprises in region r as a proportionate part of the number of all European enterprises studied

$$= \sum_{l \in M_r} y_{.l}$$

The additive decomposition of the total amount of entropy, which represents a measure for the comparability of specific accounting information between all European enterprises studied, into contributions from individual European countries and groups of countries (regions) is shown in Figure 1 (by analogy to Theil, 1967: 295–303). There are two main parts of the decomposition, namely weighted averages of entropies as well as heterogenities. On the regional level, for each region *r* the corresponding regional entropy:

$$\sum_i \frac{y_{ir}}{y_{.r}} \cdot \ln \frac{y_{.r}}{y_{ir}}$$

is computed as a measure for the degree of comparability of specified accounting information in that region. The respective weighting factor to calculate the average of regional entropies is equal to $y_{.r}$. The weighted

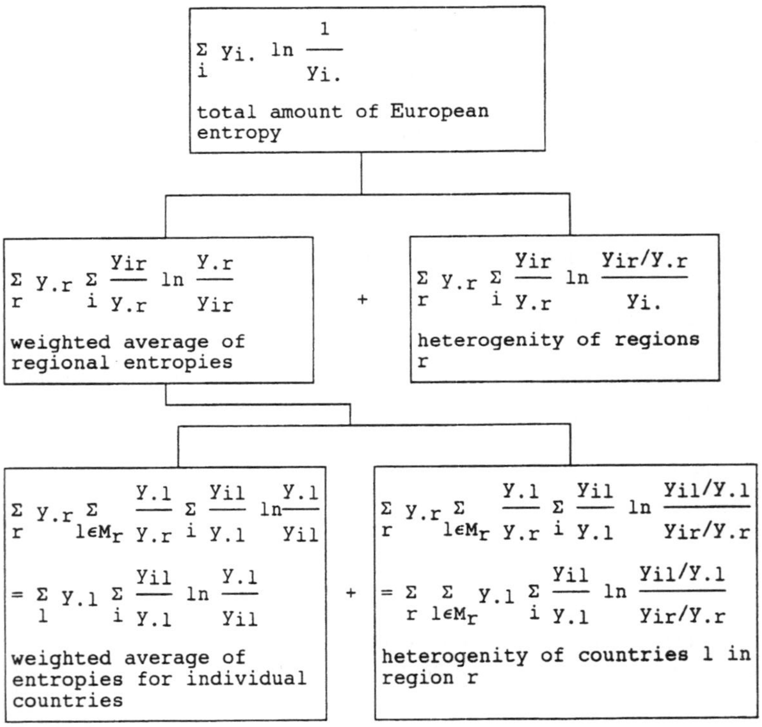

Figure 1 Additive decomposition of entropy into the contributions of individual countries and groups of countries

average of the entropies for the individual countries *l* is computed analogously.

In terms of heterogenity, which shall not be discussed in detail, the distributions of the relative frequencies of application among the alternative accounting methods *i* in the individual countries, in the regions and in all Europe are compared (by analogy to Theil, 1967: 297–8). The terms of heterogenity can be characterized as correcture terms which may not be interpreted as a constituent of the index indicating the degree of comparability in individual countries or regions. Rather, they are added to the weighted averages of entropies for countries or regions to calculate the total amount of entropy for all Europe. In the special case of the relative frequencies of application being equally distributed among the alternative accounting methods on all geographical levels, the entropies take the same value for all countries, regions and for the whole of Europe, and therefore all heterogenities become zero. In this case, the degree of comparability of financial accounting information is judged equally on all geographical levels.

MEASURING THE EFFECTS OF MULTIPLE REPORTING ON THE COMPARABILITY OF FINANCIAL ACCOUNTING INFORMATION

The problem of assignment

In the following, the special difficulties of measuring the comparability of financial accounting information at the occurrence of multiple reporting is treated. These difficulties are caused by the so-called assignment problem. This means that the number of enterprises where multiple reporting is found may not be assigned definitely to one of the accounting alternatives applied with multiple reporting (van der Tas, 1988: 163; 1992a: 73; 1992c: 184). Also multiple reporting may not be treated as a separate accounting method with a frequency of application of its own.

Both of the aforementioned procedures would lead to obvious mistakes while measuring comparability. To begin with, assigning the frequency of application of multiple reporting to the frequency of application of an accounting alternative applied thereby would be quite arbitrary. Furthermore, both procedures would cause the degree of comparability to be underestimated for they do not take into consideration that enterprises where multiple reporting is found are not only mutually comparable, but also with the enterprises applying only one of the accounting alternatives used with multiple reporting. Moreover, any compromise solution distributing the frequency of application of multiple reporting among the accounting alternatives applied thereby would be arbitrary and deficient, too.

Obviously, the effort of measuring comparability of accounting information at the occurrence of multiple reporting by means of entropy seems to fail because the frequencies of application of diverse accounting methods needed as input for the index used may not be specified definitely. However, at least for multiple reporting with two accounting alternatives only, a well-defined situation without multiple reporting may be specified which is equivalent to the situation with multiple reporting regarding the comparability of accounting information. Thus, the use of entropy would become possible. To ascertain this equivalent situation, the so-called *C*-index (van der Tas, 1988: 163–5, 167–8; 1992a: 74–9; 1992c: 185–8; 199–202) is used which will be described briefly in the following.

The *C*-index

The derivation of the *C*-index is based on the idea that the number of pairs of enterprises applying the same accounting alternatives respectively to collect and transform information about like transactions or events be a measure for the comparability of accounting information. The ratio of these pairs of enterprises to the maximum possible number of such pairs of enterprises is computed. This maximum is reached if all enterprises studied are applying the same accounting method. In the case of two accounting alternatives existing, the *C*-index is calculated in the following way (van der Tas, 1988: 163–4, 167–8; 1992a: 74–9; 1992c: 185–202):

$$C = \frac{a_1 \cdot (a_1 - 1) + a_2 \cdot (a_2 - 1) - a_{12} \cdot (a_{12} - 1)}{m \cdot (m - 1)}$$

with C = *C*-index, a_1 = number of enterprises applying accounting method 1 (including multiple reporting), a_2 = number of enterprises applying accounting method 2 (including multiple reporting), a_{12} = number of enterprises applying multiple reporting with accounting methods 1 and 2 simultaneously, and m = total number of enterprises studied with $m = a_1 + a_2 - a_{12}$.

On the grounds of its structure, the *C*-index is in a position to cope with the assignment problem. Nevertheless, the *C*-index may not directly be used as a measure of comparability, since this index does not meet two of the requirements raised above. First, the *C*-index depends on the number of enterprises studied. For instance, in a situation with two alternative accounting methods whose relative frequencies of application are $y_1 = 0.6$ and $y_2 = 0.4$ respectively, for $m = 100$ enterprises the absolute frequencies of application and the *C*-index are $a_1 = 60$, $a_2 = 40$ and $C = 0.516$, whereas for $m = 200$ enterprises $a_1 = 120$, $a_2 = 80$ and $C = 0.51759$. In fact, there is no reason for assuming different degrees of comparability for $m = 100$ and $m = 200$ enterprises.

Furthermore, the *C*-index is not additively decomposable according to geographical criteria. The decomposition of the *C*-index for some larger geographical unit into the contributions of the individual countries forming part of that unit results in multiplicative expressions that may not be assigned definitely to the individual countries since these expressions contain products of frequencies of application of an accounting alternative in two different countries.[2]

Thus, the C-index is suited to cope with the problem of assignment but cannot be decomposed additively, while entropy is fulfilling all the requirements that ought to be met by a measure of comparability but fails at the occurrence of multiple reporting. Subsequently, a combination of C-index and entropy shall be put forward that is appropriate to measure the degree of comparability at the occurrence of multiple reporting.

Applying the entropy index to situations with multiple reporting

A situation (characterized by the frequencies of application of the existing accounting alternatives) with multiple reporting can be transformed by means of the C-index into a so-called 'equivalent situation' without multiple reporting so that the degree of comparability can be measured using the entropy. However, the definite determination of an equivalent situation is only possible for multiple reporting with two accounting alternatives. This case shall be investigated, in the first instance, with the aid of a simple example.

To collect and transform information on a specific kind of transaction in the annual accounts, two alternative accounting methods are available. The number of enterprises studied is $m = 100$ whereof $a_1 = 60$ enterprises are applying accounting alternative 1 and $a_2 = 60$, alternative 2, i.e. multiple reporting with both alternatives is found at $a_{12} = 20$ enterprises. In this situation, entropy is not applicable because of the impossibility of assigning the frequency of application a_{12} definitely to one of the two alternatives. Therefore, an equivalent situation is constructed showing the same degree of comparability as the situation described before, but without multiple reporting. To measure the equivalence of the degrees of comparability, the C-index is used as an auxiliary quantity. The value of the C-index for the situation with multiple reporting described above amounts to:

$$C = \frac{a_1 \cdot (a_1 - 1) + a_2 \cdot (a_2 - 1) - a_{12} \cdot (a_{12} - 1)}{m \cdot (m - 1)}$$

$$= \frac{60 \cdot 59 + 60 \cdot 59 - 20 \cdot 19}{100 \cdot 99} = 0.677$$

Now an equivalent situation is sought characterized by two absolute frequencies of application a_1' and a_2' such as to meet the following equations:

$$a_1' + a_2' = m = 100$$

$$\frac{a_1' \cdot (a_1' - 1) + a_2' \cdot (a_2' - 1)}{m \cdot (m - 1)} = 0.677$$

The first of these two equations ensures that effects resulting from a change in the number of enterprises studied are eliminated from the value of the C-index. In the second equation, the value of the C-index for the equivalent situation is specified. From this system of equations, the values of the frequencies of application a_1' and a_2' can be derived as follows:

$$\begin{aligned} a_1' &= + \sqrt{(C - 1) \cdot m \cdot (m - 1)/2 + m^2/4} + m/2 \\ &= + \sqrt{(0.677\text{-}1) \cdot 100 \cdot (100\text{-}1)/2 + 100^2/4} + 100/2 \\ &= + 30 + 50 \end{aligned}$$

$$\begin{aligned} a_2' &= m - a_1' \\ &= 100 - (+ 30 + 50) \\ &= 50 + 30 \end{aligned}$$

Hence, the set of solutions to the system of equations consist of the pairs $a_1' = 80$, $a_2' = 20$ and $a_1' = 20$, $a_2' = 80$. These two pairs of solutions only differ formally from one another, for obviously they show the same degree of comparability which can now be measured by means of entropy:

$$E = 0.8 \cdot \ln \frac{1}{0.8} + 0.2 \cdot \ln \frac{1}{0.2} = 0.5004$$

In any case of multiple reporting with only two accounting alternatives, a definite equivalent situation can be constructed using the formulae for a_1' and a_2' mentioned above. There are always two pairs of solutions $a_1' \geq 0$, $a_2' \geq 0$. In contrast to the example, these solutions as a rule are not integers. However, since the (ficticious) absolute frequencies of application of the equivalent situation must be transformed into relative quantities before computing entropy, this fact does not argue against the suitability of the approach put forward to quantify the degree of comparability of financial accounting information.

As can be shown by means of the general formulae for a_1' and a_2', both pairs of solutions feature the same degree of comparability and hence the same value of entropy. Thus, at the occurrence of multiple reporting with only two accounting alternatives an equivalent situation without multiple reporting can be constructed which is well-defined in the sense that exactly one value of entropy may be assigned to it.

The approach put forward in this contribution to solve the assignment problem is to link C-index and entropy so that the advantages of these two measures complement one another while any disadvantages are eliminated. The inability of entropy to cope with the assignment problem is offset by the application of the *C*-index, whose dependence on the number *m* of enterprises studied is taken into consideration, by a conditional equation keeping *m* constant. In addition, the problems arising from the fact that the *C*-index is not additively decomposable are also solved since by means of the construction of an equivalent situation the additive decomposition of entropy may be exploited in situations with multiple reporting as well.

If comparability of accounting information is to be measured considering several countries whereby multiple reporting is found with two specified accounting alternatives, the equivalent situations and the entropies for the individual countries and for all countries as a whole are determined as follows:

- For each country where multiple reporting is found an equivalent situation and the pertinent entropy are calculated separately, i.e. disregarding the other countries.
- The frequencies of application observed in each individual country are summed up to a total amount for each accounting alternative. From there, an equivalent situation is constructed for all countries as a whole which is taken as a basis for the calculation of the total entropy.

Summing up the application frequencies in the equivalent situations determined for the individual countries and calculating a total entropy would result in an incorrect measurement of the comparability for all countries as a whole, because this procedure would not consider the effects of multiple reporting on the comparability of accounting information from different countries.

If multiple reporting is found not with two but with three or more accounting alternatives an equivalent situation is no longer definitely determinable. *C* being the value of the *C*-index of a situation with multiple reporting, an equivalent situation is characterized by the following equations which the (fictitious) absolute frequencies of application a_i' of the *n* accounting alternatives applied with multiple reporting have to fulfill:

$$\frac{\sum_{i=1}^{n} a_i' \cdot (a_i' - 1)}{m \cdot (m - 1)} = C'$$

$$\sum_{i=1}^{n} a_i' = m$$

For $n \geq 3$ accounting alternatives applied with multiple reporting, this system of equations has an infinite number of solutions, i.e. there is an infinite set of equivalent situations with different values of entropy meeting the equations. However, a conservative estimate of the degree of comparability can be made determining that equivalent situation with maximum value of entropy. Since entropy is an inverse measure, maximum value of entropy corresponds to minimum degree of comparability. By means of electronic data processing, it is quite easy to determine numerically the extreme values of entropies assigned to the equivalent situations (at least in cases of multiple reporting with three accounting alternatives). Besides, the question remains if multiple reporting with more than two accounting alternatives is of importance in practice.

MEASURING COMPARABILITY: AN EXAMPLE

In a survey for the year 1989, the Fédération des Experts Comptables Européens (FEE – Federation of European Accountants) has analysed the annual accounts of a total of 441 enterprises from 15 countries (FEE, 1991: 1). Each of these countries is assigned to one of the following three groups, respectively (FEE, 1991: 1):

- The group EC I consists of those EC countries where the application of a legislation transforming the 4th EC directive was mandatory in 1989.
- The group EC II is made of those EC countries where there was no legislation transforming the 4th EC directive to be applied mandatorily in 1989.
- The group Non-EC consists of European countries which were not members of EC in 1989.

The FEE survey treats 12 domains in accounting (FEE, 1991: v-vi). For each of these domains, several individual problems of collecting, transforming and reporting accounting information are discussed enumerating the respective accounting alternatives, and their absolute frequencies of application observed. Hence, the FEE survey is basically appropriate to serve as a data base for applying the concept of measuring comparability of accounting information put forward in the previous sections.

The data collected in the FEE survey are not employed there for further calculations. The comments in the survey are restricted to explanations concerning the problems of collecting, transforming and reporting accounting information and the respective alternative accounting methods. Nevertheless, statements are presented which are designated as conclusions drawn from the data collected (FEE, 1991: 5). However, since no reasons are given for these statements, they are hypotheses only. Subsequently, two of these hypotheses (in the following called H 1 and H 2) shall be investigated more closely. In detail, H 1 and H 2 read as follows:

- H 1: Comparing the accounting practice between the country groups EC I, EC II and Non-EC, only minor differences are found.
- H 2: There are major differences between the countries of group EC I regarding the practice of accounting unless the publication and disclosure of information are concerned.

These hypotheses are now tested by considering the recognition of the income effect of foreign currency translation differences. Table 1 shows the data collected in the FEE survey concerning this matter (FEE, 1991: 243, 246, 251) and the calculations needed. In Table 1, for each country, each group of countries and for all countries as a whole, the number of enterprises is given where there is evidence of an income effect resulting from the translation of foreign currency balances and where information is given as to the recognition of this income effect (cf. the line 'number of enterprises').

For each country, each group of countries and for all countries as a whole, the absolute frequencies of application of four recognition alternatives are listed in Table 1. Multiple reporting is not found. From these data, values of entropy are calculated for each country, group of countries and for all countries as a whole. These values of entropy are measures for the degree of comparability of accounting information within the geographical regions for which they are calculated. Within the scope of a more extensive investigation, such calculations may be carried out and compared to one another for several periods of time.

However, this contribution is designed to verify or falsify the two hypotheses H 1 and H 2. To that end, two heterogenities have to be calculated. The heterogenity on the regional level, Het_{total}, has a value of 0.04939459.[3] This amount is a measure of the dissimilarity of the distributions of the application frequencies among the alternative recognition methods in the groups of countries EC I, EC II and Non-EC as well as in all Europe (by analogy to Theil, 1967, 297–8). Computing the ratio V_{total} of Het_{total} to the total entropy E_{total} yields a value of

$$V_{total} = \frac{Het_{total}}{E_{total}} = \frac{0.04939459}{0.96109846} = 5.14\%$$

Now the question arises as to which is the critical share V_{crit} where the hypothesis H 1 is just becoming false. This question is not discussed in the following for this would be beyond the scope of the present contribution which is intended to demonstrate the applicability of the measuring concept put forward. For instance, for $V_{crit} = 10\%$ H 1 would be judged to be correct.

Hypothesis H 2 is tested analogously. The heterogenity $Het_I = 0.58619315$ is a measure of the dissimilarity of the distributions of the application frequencies among the alternative recognition methods in the countries of group EC I and in EC I as a whole (by analogy to Theil, 1967: 268).

Table 1 Comparability of accounting information concerning the recognition of the income effect of translation differences in 15 European countries

	Belgium	*Denmark*	*France*	*Germany*	*Greece*	*Ireland*	*Luxembourg*	*Netherlands*	*UK*	*EC I*
Number of enterprises	12	19	32	43	19	32	9	18	37	221
Recognized:										
all gains and losses	6	17	1	0	1	28	2	16	35	106
realized gains and all losses	6	0	31	43	18	1	6	0	1	106
only realized gains and realized losses	0	2	0	0	0	0	0	0	1	3
other	0	0	0	0	0	3	1	2	0	6
Entropy	0.69314	0.35129	0.13906	0	0.20619	0.44706	0.84868	0.34883	0.24775	0.86107

	Italy	*Spain*	*EC II*	*Finland*	*Norway*	*Sweden*	*Switzerland*	*Non-EC*	*Total*
Number of enterprises	11	7	18	3	6	7	6	22	261
Recognized:									
all gains and losses	1	3	4	2	1	0	2	5	115
realized gains and all losses	9	1	10	1	5	3	1	10	126
only realized gains and realized losses	1	2	3	0	0	0	2	2	8
other	0	1	1	0	0	4	1	5	12
Entropy	0.60016	1.27703	1.11999	0.63651	0.45056	0.68290	1.32966	1.24983	0.96109

Calculating the ratio V_I of Het_I to the value E_I of the entropy for the group of countries EC I yields a share of

$$V_I = \frac{Het_I}{E_I} = \frac{0.58619315}{0.86107907} = 68.08\%$$

For hypothesis H 2 to be verified, the ratio V_I must exceed a critical lower boundary V_{crit}, whose amount will not be discussed in the following for this would be beyond the scope of this paper. For example, H 2 would be correct for $V_{crit} = 40\%$.

The example treated in this section has shown the application of the measuring concept developed previously to a practical problem. However, multiple reporting was excluded from consideration since for most cases of multiple reporting contained in the FEE data the survey does not present enough information to construct equivalent situations. In fact, only the absolute numbers a_i of enterprises applying an alternative accounting method i are given in the survey. If there are more than two accounting alternatives, it is impossible to deduce the absolute numbers a_{ij} of enterprises applying multiple reporting with methods i and j simultaneously. However, the numbers a_{ij} are needed to construct an equivalent situation.

Applying the measuring concept put forward in this contribution to conduct an empirical investigation, a period of several subsequent years should be surveyed so that conclusions as to the development of the degree of comparability can be drawn. Furthermore, statistical problems should be considered such as the critical ranges of acceptance or refusal of a hypothesis with the sample size and level of significance given. It would go far beyond the scope of this contribution to demonstrate these aspects in an extensive empirical example. In any case, collection of a data base which is statistically representative, contains the relevant information to cope with multiple reporting, and covering a period of several years, would be a precondition for further research using the method developed here.

SUMMARY AND OUTLOOK

Initially the present contribution was concerned with the notions of comparability of financial accounting information as well as of accounting methods. In this connection, the influence of different economical, political, social and other environmental conditions on the comparability of accounting information was taken into consideration. The degree of comparability may be raised by so-called multiple reporting.

Subsequently, requirements to be met by a measure of comparability were derived from the notion of comparability of financial accounting information defined previously. Concentration indices were shown to be basically appropriate to solve the measuring problem discussed. However, entropy is the only one of all current concentration indices to fulfill all the requirements mentioned above; in particular, it is additively decomposable according to geographical criteria.

A special problem for the measurement of the degree of comparability results from the occurrence of multiple reporting and the assignment problem related thereto. In the case of two alternative accounting methods, the problem was solved by constructing an equivalent situation and combining entropy with the so-called *C*-index. For multiple reporting with more than two accounting alternatives, an approximate solution was suggested.

The applicability of the measuring concept proposed was demonstrated by means of an example from the FEE report for 1989. In particular, the importance of heterogenities in the context of international investigations was shown.

This simple example without multiple reporting reveals the advantages of entropy resulting from its additive decomposition for international investigations of comparability of financial accounting information. For instance, the harmonization effects of the 4th and 7th EC directives in individual EC countries may be quantified by means of entropy and compared with accounting practice in countries not belonging to the EC. Yet, to this end it would be necessary to collect a data base meeting the statistical requirement of a sufficient sample size.

NOTES

1 In any case, multiple reporting will never cause the degree of comparability to fall. In fact, comparability is not affected by the occurrence of multiple reporting if all enterprises studied are applying the same alternative accounting method to collect and transform information on a specific kind of transaction or event.

2 Archer *et al.* (1995) present a method to decompose the *C*-index into a within-country and a between-country component. However, as can be seen by the examples given in this contribution (Archer *et al.*, 1995: 70–1), the within-country and the between-country components do not sum up to the value of the total index. Hence, the decomposition of the C-index is not an additive one in the sense of this paper.

3 As to the calculation of heterogenities, cf. Figure 1.

REFERENCES

Archer, S., Delvaille, P. and McLeay, S. (1995) 'The measurement of harmonisation and the comparability of financial statement items: within-country and between-country effects', *Accounting and Business Research*, 25: 67–80.

Chandler, R. A. (1992) 'The international harmonization of accounting: in search of influence', *International Journal of Accounting*, 27: 222–33.

Choi, F. D. S. and Mueller, G. G. (1992) *International Accounting*, 2nd edition. Englewood Cliffs: Prentice-Hall.

Curry, B. and George, K. D. (1983) 'Industrial concentration: a survey', *Journal of Industrial Economics*, 31: 203–55.

Fédération des Experts Comptables Européens (FEE) (1991) *FEE European Survey of Published Accounts 1991*. London: Routledge.

Fleming, P. D. (1991) 'The growing importance of international accounting standards', *Journal of Accountancy*, 172 (9): 100–6.

Hall, M. and Tideman, N. (1967) 'Measures of concentration', *Journal of the American Statistical Association*, 62: 162–8.

Hildenbrand, W. and Paschen, H. (1964) 'Ein axiomatisch begründetes Konzentrationsmaβ', *Statistische Informationen, Vierteljahreshefte zur wirtschaftlichen Integration Europas*, 5 (3): 53–61.

Horowitz, A. R. and Horowitz, I. (1968) 'Entropy, Marcov processes and competition in the brewing industry', *Journal of Industrial Economics*, 16: 196–211.

International Accounting Standards Committee (IASC) (1992) *International Accounting Standards 1993 – The Full Text of all International Accounting Standards Extant at 1 January 1993*. London: IASC.

Jacquemin, A. P. and de Jong, H. W. (1977) *European Industrial Organisation*. London and Basingstoke: Macmillan.

Jacquemin, A. P. and Kumps, A. -M. (1971) 'Changes in the size structure of the largest European firms: an entropy measure', *Journal of Industrial Economics*, 19: 59–70.

Marfels, Ch. (1971) 'The consistency of concentration measures: a mathematical evaluation', *Proceedings of the American Statistical Association, Business and Economic Section*, 143–51.

Marfels, Ch. (1972) 'On testing concentration measures', *Zeitschrift für Nationalökonomie*, 32: 461–86.

Münzner, H. (1963) 'Probleme der konzentrationsmessung', *Allgemeines Statistisches Archiv*, 47: 1–9.

Nobes, Ch. W. and Parker, R. H. (1991) 'Introduction, and causes of differences', in Nobes, Ch. W. and Parker, R. H. (eds) *Comparative International Accounting*, 3rd edition. New York: Prentice Hall, pp. 3–22.

Parker, R. H. (1991) 'Financial reporting in the United Kingdom and Australia', in Nobes, Ch. W. and Parker, R. H. (eds) *Comparative International Accounting*, 3rd edition. New York: Prentice Hall, pp 122–58.

Paschen, H. (1969) *Die Messung der Betriebs- und Unternehmenskonzentration*. Freiburg im Breisgau: Rudolf Haufe.

Paschen, H. and Buyse, R. (1971) 'Zur messung der betriebs- und unternehmenskonzentration', *Statistische Hefte*, 12: 2–13.

Radebaugh, L. H. and Gray, S. J. (1993) *International Accounting and Multinational Enterprises*. New York: Wiley.

Rosenbluth, G. (1955) 'Measures of concentration', in *Conference on Business Concentration and Price Policy*, National Bureau of Economic Research, Princeton: NBER, pp. 57–95.

Theil, H. (1967) *Economics and Information Theory*. Amsterdam: North-Holland.

van der Tas, L. G. (1988) 'Measuring harmonisation of financial reporting practice', *Accounting and Business Research*, 18 (70): 157–69.

van der Tas, L. G. (1992a) 'Evidence of EC financial reporting practice harmonization – the case of deferred taxation', *European Accounting Review*, May, 1 (1): 69–104.

van der Tas, L. G. (1992b) 'Harmonisatie van de financiële verslaggeving – Specifiek gericht op de Europese Gemeenschap', *Maandblad voor Accountancy en Bedrijfseconomie*, 66: 407–19.

van der Tas, L. G. (1992c) *Harmonisation of Financial Reporting – With a Special Focus on the European community*. Maastricht: Datawyse.

van Hulle, K. (1992) 'Harmonization of accounting standards – a view from the European Community', *European Accounting Review*, 1 (1) May: 161–72.

Zeff, S. A. (1972) *Forging Accounting Principles in Five Countries: A History and an Analysis of Trends*. Champaign, Illinois: Stipes Publishing.

[6]

Accounting and Business Research, Vol. 29. No. 1. pp. 73-86. Winter Issue

International harmony measures of accounting policy: comparative statistical properties

Richard D. Morris and R. H. Parker*

Abstract—Van der Tas's (1988) I index and the between-country C index introduced by Archer et al. (1995) are competing measures of international harmony. We present comparative statistical properties of these indices, via a simulation study covering three accounting methods in 10 countries, with uniform, bimodal and unimodal distributions of companies across accounting methods. The indices are also adjusted for non-disclosures using techniques developed by Archer and McLeay (1995) and Archer et al. (1995). The I index and the between-country C index are mathematically equivalent in the two-country case even in the presence of non-disclosures. As more countries are compared, the two indices diverge. The means and standard deviations of the I index, with a correction proposed by Archer and McLeay (1995), decrease and there is little skewness or kurtosis. In contrast, as more countries are compared, the between-country C index exhibits more stability in means, lower standard deviations, higher skewness and kurtosis. The between-country C index may be superior to the corrected I index because (i) between-country C index means approximate their 'expected values' (where all observations equal expected values) more closely than do corrected I index means; and (ii) between-country C index means are more stable than corrected I index means where the data come from stable distributions.

1. Introduction

Beginning with van der Tas (1988), a stream of literature[1] has examined national and international harmony[2] of accounting policies using a number of index measures. These measures are van der Tas's H, I and C indices, and two derivatives of the C index—the between-country C index and the within-country C index—identified by Archer et al. (1995). The I index and the between-country C index are measures of international harmony. Little is known about their statistical properties as more countries are compared or as the distribution of companies across accounting methods changes. We examine these properties using a simulation study. Techniques to adjust the C index for non-disclosures, suggested by Archer and McLeay (1995) and Archer et al. (1995), are extended to the I index.

2. Background to harmony measures

Van der Tas (1988) introduced to the accounting literature precise ways of measuring national and international harmony of accounting policies. National harmony is measured by the H or Herfindahl index, used in industrial concentration studies. H is the sum over accounting methods of their squared frequencies of use within a single country, that is:

$$H = \sum_{i=1}^{k} p_i^2$$

where H = the Herfindahl index
k = number of alternative accounting methods
p_i = the relative frequency of accounting method i.

*The authors are, respectively, at the University of New South Wales and the University of Exeter. The financial assistance of the Institute of Chartered Accountants of Scotland is gratefully acknowledged. The authors are grateful for helpful comments from the editor, the referee and S. J. Gray. Correspondence should be addressed to Dr R. D. Morris, School of Accounting, University of New South Wales, Sydney 2052, Australia. E-mail richard.morris@unsw.edu.au. This paper was first submitted in January 1996 and finally accepted in July 1998.

[1] See for example Emenyonu and Gray (1992, 1996), Hermann and Thomas (1995), Archer and McLeay (1995), Archer et al. (1995, 1996).

[2] According to Tay and Parker (1990: 73), harmony is a state indicated by a clustering of companies around one or a few available accounting methods, whereas harmonisation is a process of movement away from total diversity of accounting methods. For simplicity we refer only to harmony measures, but our conclusions apply equally to measures of harmonisation. We cover only de facto or material harmony which refers to what companies actually do, rather than de jure or formal harmony which refers to accounting standards and similar regulations. For measures of formal harmony, see Rahman et al. (1996).

For international comparisons, van der Tas introduced the I index as an analogue of the H index. He defined the I index as:

$$I = \sum_{i=1}^{k} (f_{i1}\, f_{i2} \ldots f_{im})$$

where f_{i1}, f_{i2}, ...f_{im} are the relative frequencies of accounting method i in each of m countries and k is the number of alternative accounting methods. Van der Tas's I index is the sum over accounting methods of the product of the relative frequencies of accounting method i in each of m countries.

The I index tends to zero as more countries are compared, since additional relative frequencies will almost always be fractions, resulting in a skewed distribution for I over the range 0-1. To overcome this skewness, van der Tas suggested applying the (m-1)th root as a correction factor:

$$I^* = I^{1/(m-1)}$$

where I^* = corrected I index

m = number of countries.

Archer and McLeay (1995) have criticised van der Tas's formulation of the I index. They argue that the correction factor 1/(m-1) is not consistent with the I index being an analogue of the H index because 1/(m-1) does not equal 2—the exponent in the H index—and is applied to the sum of cross products and not to individual cross products for each accounting method. To ensure that the I index is an analogue of the H index, Archer and McLeay (1995: 4) suggest that the I index be calculated as:

$$I = \sum_{i=1}^{k} (f_{i1}\, f_{i2} \ldots f_{im})^{2/m}$$

where m is the number of countries and k the number of accounting methods as before. Archer and McLeay's I index is the sum across accounting methods of the squared geometric means of the relative frequencies of accounting method i in each of m countries. In the two country case, the exponent equals 1 and the corrected and uncorrected I indices are equivalent.

Van der Tas (1988) also introduced the comparability or C index as a means of dealing with companies using multiple accounting policies for the same issue (e.g. via footnote disclosures), although the index can be employed as an alternative to the H and I indices. The C index is based on combinatorial mathematics and measures the probability that any pair of randomly selected companies adopts the same accounting method. It is the number of company pairs in which each pair uses the same accounting method, summed over accounting methods and divided by the number of possible pairs if all companies used the same accounting method (Archer and McLeay, 1995: 5–6). Pair members can be from the same or different countries. Algebraically, van der Tas's C index is:

$$C = \frac{\sum_{j=1}^{k} (x_j\,(x_{j-1}))}{n\,(n-1)}$$

where x_j is the number of companies using accounting method j, k the number of accounting methods, and n the total number of companies.

Van der Tas showed that the H index and his C index were related thus (assuming no multiple reporting):

$$C = \frac{H - 1/n}{1 - 1/n} \text{ or } H = \left(\frac{n-1}{n}\right) C + \frac{1}{n}$$

where n is the total number of companies. As $n \rightarrow \infty$, $C \rightarrow H$. The convergence occurs rapidly for even moderate values of n.

When used to measure international harmony, van der Tas's C index does not distinguish between national and international effects. To correct this deficiency, Archer et al. (1995) decomposed van der Tas's C index into a between-country C index and a within-country C index, the former being used for measuring international harmony of accounting policies. The between-country C index is the number of pairs of companies using the same accounting method, where each pair member is from a *different* country, divided by the total number of company pairs if all companies used the same accounting method but each pair member is from a different country. Intuitively, the between-country C index gives the probability that any pair of randomly selected companies, each from a different country, uses the same accounting method. Using Archer et al.'s (1995) notation, the between-country C index is:

$$\frac{\sum_i \sum_j x_{ij}\,(x_{+j} - x_{ij})}{\sum_i x_{i+}\,(x_{++} - x_{i+})}$$

where x_{ij} is the number of companies in country i using accounting method j, x_{+j} is the total number of companies in all countries using method j, x_{++} is the grand total of companies across countries, and x_{i+} is the number of companies in country i.

The within-country C index is the number of pairs of companies using the same accounting method, where each pair member comes from the *same* country, divided by the sum across countries of the number of company pairs in each country if all companies used the same accounting method. Using Archer et al.'s (1995) notation, the within-country C index is:

$$\frac{\sum_i \sum_j x_{ij}(x_{ij}-1)}{\sum_i x_{i+}(x_{i+}-1)}$$

To illustrate, Table 1 shows the I indices, with Archer and McLeay's correction, and the between-country C indices for fixed asset valuation in three countries A, B and C. Samples of 50 companies from each country use historical cost, replacement cost, and net realisable value in the numbers shown. Historical cost and replacement cost are equally popular in country A, net realisable value predominates in country B, while the three methods are used evenly in country C. The I index for countries A/B is low because of the non-use of net realisable value in country A and replacement cost in country B. The I indices for A/C and B/C exceed A/B because the three accounting methods are used evenly in country C and boost the I indices for A/C and B/C. The between-country C index for each two-country comparison equals its corresponding I index, a point which will be returned to later.

Archer and McLeay (1995: 5, 10–11) argue that the between-country C index is a more robust measure of international harmony than the I index. The I index tends to zero if one or more accounting methods have low frequencies in one country. In particular, the contribution of an accounting method to the I index is zero if that method is not used in one country, even if it is widely used in all other countries. The between-country C index avoids these problems. For example, in Table 1, the three country I index, with Archer and McLeay's correction, is only 0.07, yet the corresponding between-country C index is 0.24, because (as already mentioned) net realisable value and replacement cost are not used in countries A and B respectively, and hence contribute nothing to the I index even though these accounting methods are used by 103 companies (69%) in the total sample.

The between-country C index and the Archer and McLeay-corrected I index are competing measures of international harmony with the between-country C index superior to the corrected I index, if Archer and McLeay's criticisms are accepted. Beyond simple examples like Table 1, little is known of the relationship between these indices as more countries are compared. Also little is

Table 1
Numerical example

	Country			
	A	*B*	*C*	*Total*
Historical cost	25	5	17	47
Replacement cost	25	0	16	41
Net realisable value	0	45	17	62
Total	50	50	50	150
	A/B	*B/C*	*A/C*	*A/B/C*
Archer and McLeay I index	0·05	0·34	0·33	0·07
Between-country C Index	0·05	0·34	0·33	0·24

Calculations:

Archer & McLeay I index:
A/B: $(25/50 \times 5/50) + (25/50 \times 0/50) + (0/50 \times 45/45) = 0{\cdot}05$
B/C: $(5/50 \times 17/50) + (0/50 \times 16/50) + (45/50 \times 17/50) = 0{\cdot}34$
A/C: $(25/50 \times 17/50) + (25/50 \times 16/50) + (0/50 \times 17/50) = 0{\cdot}33$
A/B/C: $(25/50 \times 5/50 \times 16/50)^{2/3} + (25/50 \times 0/50 \times 16/50)^{2/3} + (0/50 \times 45/50 \times 17/50)^{2/3} = 0{\cdot}07$

Between-country C index:
A/B: $[25(5) + 25(0) + 0(45)] / (50 \times 50) = {\cdot}05$
B/C: $[5(17) + 0(16) + 45(17)] / (50 \times 50) = {\cdot}34$
A/C: $[25(17) + 25(16) + 0(17)] / (50 \times 50) = {\cdot}33$
A/B/C: $[[25(5) + 25(0) + 0(45)] + [17(25 + 5)] + [16(25 + 0)] + [17(0 + 45)]] / [(50 \times 50) + (50 \times 100)] = 0\ 24$

Table 2
Index Formulae

Panel 1

	Country A	*Country B*	*Country C*	*Country D*
Method 1	a_1	b_1	c_1	d_1
Method 2	a_2	b_2	c_2	d_2
Method 3	a_3	b_3	c_3	d_3
Total	n_a	n_b	n_c	n_d

Panel 2

Countries I Index with Archer and McLeay's correction

A/B $$\frac{a_1b_1 + a_2b_2 + a_3b_3}{n_an_b}$$

A/B/C $$\frac{(a_1b_1c_1)^{2/3} + (a_2b_2c_2)^{2/3} + (a_3b_3c_3)^{2/3}}{(n_an_bn_c)^{2/3}}$$

A/B/C/D $$\frac{(a_1b_1c_1d_1)^{2/4} + (a_2b_2c_2d_2)^{2/4} + (a_3b_3c_3d_3)^{2/4}}{(n_an_bn_cn_d)^{2/4}}$$

Panel 3

Countries between-country C index

A/B $$\frac{a_1b_1 + a_2b_2 + a_3b_3}{n_an_b}$$

A/B/C $$\frac{a_1b_1 + a_2b_2 + a_3b_3 + c_1(a_1+b_1) + c_2(a_2+b_2) + c_3(a_3+b_3)}{n_an_b + n_c(n_a + n_b)}$$

A/B/C/D $$\frac{a_1b_1 + a_2b_2 + a_3b_3 + c_1(a_1+b_1) + c_2(a_2+b_2) + c_3(a_3+b_3) + d_1(a_1+b_1+c_1) + d_2(a_2+b_2+c_2) + d_3(a_3+b_3+c_3)}{n_an_b + n_c(n_a + n_b) + n_d(n_a + n_b + n_c)}$$

known about the indices' sensitivity to variations in the distribution of companies across accounting methods as more countries are compared. Accordingly, further examination of these matters is warranted.

Table 2 contains an algebraic example which shows how the corrected I index and the between-country C index evolve as additional countries are compared. Three accounting methods are used by a1, a2 and a3 companies in country A, by b1, b2 and b3 companies in country B and so on for four countries as shown in panel 1. Applying the formulae described above and rearranging terms, the corrected I index and the between-country C index appear in panels 2 and 3 respectively.

In the two country case, the corrected I index and the between-country C index are identical. The identity can be shown to hold for any number of accounting methods. For more than two countries, the two indices diverge, but each evolves in a systematic pattern. Panel 2 shows that as an additional country D is added to the corrected I index, the marginal change to the numerator is that the number of companies using method i in country D is multiplied by the product of the number of companies using method i in countries A, B and C, while the marginal change to the denominator is that the number of companies in country D is multiplied by the product of the numbers of companies in countries A, B and C. In both numerator and denominator, the exponents equal two divided by the number of countries.

Panel 3 shows that as an additional country D is added to the between-country C index, the marginal change to the numerator is that the number using method i in country D is multiplied by the sum of the numbers using method i in countries A, B and C, while the marginal change to the denominator is that the total number in country D is multiplied by the sum of the totals in other countries. That is, as additional countries are added marginal changes to the indices involve *products*, and a change to the exponents to reflect the number of countries, for the corrected I index and *sums* for the between-country C index.

3. Simulation study

Table 2 does not show the statistical properties of the two indices as more countries are compared. Using a simulation study, we investigate these properties. The study is designed to be similar to Emenyonu and Gray (1992, 1996) and Herrman and Thomas (1995) in sample size, number of accounting methods and number of countries.

Samples of 50 companies were drawn from each of 10 countries, with 250 iterations of the selection process. Within each country, there are three accounting methods covering a particular accounting issue. Companies are assumed to be distributed across accounting methods in three mutually exclusive ways: (a) uniformly[3] so that the probability of companies choosing accounting method i in country m is the same for all i and m; (b) bimodally so that the probability of companies choosing either of two accounting methods—the same two in all countries—is twice that of choosing the third accounting method; (c) unimodally so that the probability of one accounting method being chosen is three times the probability of either of the other methods being chosen.

In the unimodal data set, the dominant accounting method alternates across countries, being the first in countries 1, 4, 7 and 10, the second in countries 2, 5 and 8, and the third in countries 3, 6 and 9. For the uniform data set, there is also a fourth accounting 'method' (dealt with later) representing companies which do not disclose how they account for the particular issue. The expected value of each observation in the uniform data set is 50/4 or 12.5. For the other data sets, companies were assigned to accounting methods using the Poisson distribution with mean values for each dominant accounting method of 20 in the bimodal, and 30 in the unimodal, data set. So expected values of the three accounting methods are 20, 20 and 10 in the bimodal data set and 30 for the dominant accounting method and 10 for each of the other two methods in the unimodal data set.

An important issue is what statistical properties of the corrected I index and the between-country C index to measure. The uniform and the bimodal data sets have stable distributions of companies across accounting methods while the unimodal data set has three different distributions, depending on which accounting method is dominant, the first for countries 1, 4, 7, 10, the second for countries 2, 5, 8 and the third for countries 3, 6, 9. Therefore, it seems reasonable to compare the stability of the I index and the between-country C index across the three data sets. Stability will be measured by examining changes in the means, standard deviations, skewness and kurtosis of each index as more countries are compared. Stability will also be examined by comparing each index's mean with its 'expected value', which is the value of each index where *all* observations in the underlying data set equal their expected values. This comparison is of interest because it indicates how extensively the obtained means have been affected by variability in the data sets.

3.1. Simulation results—the I index

Table 3, panel 1 shows the means, standard deviations, skewness and kurtosis for the I index with Archer and McLeay's correction where the underlying data are uniformly distributed. Panels 2 and 3 show these results for the bimodal and unimodal data sets respectively. In each panel, the final row shows the index's 'expected value'.

For the uniform data set in panel 1, the means and standard deviations for Archer and McLeay's I index[4] both decline, but at a decreasing rate, as more countries are compared. There is no pronounced skewness or kurtosis. Similar results occur for the bimodal data set in panel 2, except that

[3] Tay and Parker (1990: 85) suggested the uniform distribution as a benchmark against which to judge actual practices. SPSS for Windows 95 was used to randomly allocate companies to accounting methods in each country. An unavoidable imperfection in the simulation with the uniform distribution is that SPSS gives numbers for each accounting method i in country m which are not whole numbers, but are correct to 14 decimal places. The problem also occurs with other packages such as Excel. It is unlikely that the imperfection biases our results. The problem does not occur with the bimodal and unimodal data sets.

[4] By way of comparison, for each data set, the mean of the unadjusted I index declines sharply as the number of countries increases, the mean index for m countries being approximately one third of the mean index for m-1 countries. The standard deviation also declines sharply. The distribution of the index becomes markedly positively skewed and leptokurtic for the uniform and unimodal data sets. These results demonstrate the tendency, noted originally by van der Tas (1988), for the uncorrected I index to tend to zero as more countries are compared. Like Archer and McLeay's correction, van der Tas's correction to the I index arrests the decline in the unadjusted I index. For the uniform data set, the mean I index with van der Tas's correction declines steadily as more countries are compared from 0.329 for 2 countries to 0.287 for 10 countries, and the standard deviation declines. For the bimodal data set, the means for the van der Tas I index increase from 0.354 for 2 countries to 0.378 for 10 countries, and the standard deviation declines. Neither index exhibits pronounced skewness. For the unimodal data set in panel 3, the means for the van der Tas I index fluctuate in a narrow band between 0.270 and 0.287, while the standard deviation declines, and there is no pronounced skewness or kurtosis. In each data set, for three or more countries, the mean van der Tas I index is always greater than the corresponding mean Archer and McLeay I index, which in turn is always greater than the mean unadjusted I index. As more countries are compared, the means of the unadjusted I index converge on the 'expected values'. In contrast, the van der Tas I index, like the Archer and McLeay I index, systematically tracks below its 'expected value'.

Table 3
Simulation results — the I index with Archer and McLeay's correction

Panel 1: Uniform data set

	Number of countries								
	2	*3*	*4*	*5*	*6*	*7*	*8*	*9*	*10*
mean	0·329	0·280	0·250	0·226	0·215	0·206	0·197	0·193	0·189
s.d.	0·115	0·093	0·074	0·063	0·056	0·053	0·049	0·045	0·043
skewness	0·097	0·379	0·241	0·296	0·223	0·301	0·283	0·235	0·229
kurtosis	0·199	0·187	0·093	−0·315	0·004	−0·054	0·041	−0·053	0·064
expected value	0·333	0·333	0·333	0·333	0·333	0·333	0·333	0·333	0·333

Panel 2: Bimodal data set

	Number of countries								
	2	*3*	*4*	*5*	*6*	*7*	*8*	*9*	*10*
mean	0·354	0·345	0·339	0·336	0·334	0·332	0·330	0·329	0·328
s.d.	0·033	0·029	0·026	0·024	0·023	0·021	0·020	0·019	0·019
skewness	0·693	0·590	0·376	0·162	−0·103	−0·384	−0·633	−0·383	−0·460
kurtosis	1·461	0·562	0·563	0·494	0·746	2·033	2·472	1·638	1·513
expected value	0·360	0·360	0·360	0·360	0·360	0·360	0·360	0·360	0·360

Panel 3: Unimodal data set

	Number of countries								
	2	*3*	*4*	*5*	*6*	*7*	*8*	*9*	*10*
mean	0·277	0·240	0·240	0·231	0·220	0·220	0·218	0·213	0·212
s.d.	0·038	0·037	0·039	0·032	0·039	0·040	0·036	0·039	0·040
skewness	0·138	−0·428	−0·445	−0·903	−0·822	−1·113	−1·174	−1·079	−1·101
kurtosis	0·195	0·051	0·225	1·006	0.558	1·502	1·473	0·820	0·812
expected value	0·280	0·250	0·259	0·255	0·250	0·252	0·252	0·250	0·251

the index is leptokurtic for 7 or more countries. For the unimodal data set in panel 3, the Archer and McLeay I index means decline as more countries are compared, the rate of decline increasing for three, six and nine country comparisons when the three distributions of accounting methods occur in equal numbers. Standard deviations remain steady; there is negative skewness but no pronounced kurtosis.

In panels 1 and 2, the 'expected values' of the Archer and McLeay I index are 0.333 and 0.36 respectively for all countries. However, the obtained means fall increasingly below these amounts, by more than two standard deviations for six or more countries (panel 1) or for three or more countries (panel 2). In panel 3, the means also fall by increasing amounts below the corresponding 'expected values', but in each case by less than one standard deviation.

3.2. Simulation results—the between-country C index

Table 4 shows the means, standard deviations, skewness, kurtosis and 'expected values' of the between-country C index for the uniform data set (panel 1), bimodal data set (panel 2) and unimodal data set (panel 3).

In panels 1–3, the two country columns are identical to the equivalent columns for the I indices in panels 1–3 of Table 3. As more countries are compared, the mean between-country C index is stable for the uniform and bimodal data sets, but increases steadily for the unimodal data set. In all three panels, the standard deviation declines. As more countries are compared, the index becomes increasingly positively skewed for the uniform data set, and leptokurtic for the uniform and unimodal data sets.

Table 4
Simulation results — between-country C index

Panel 1: Uniform data set

	Number of countries								
	2	*3*	*4*	*5*	*6*	*7*	*8*	*9*	*10*
mean	0·329	0·335	0·336	0·333	0·334	0·333	0·333	0·333	0·333
s.d.	0·115	0·074	0·048	0·037	0·03	0·026	0·023	0·021	0·018
skewness	0·097	0·904	1·048	1·027	1·018	1·131	1·311	1·457	1·559
kurtosis	0·199	1·363	1·608	1·656	1·392	1·511	2·269	3·038	3·398
expected value	0·333	0·333	0·333	0·333	0·333	0·333	0·333	0·333	0·333

Panel 2: Bimodal data set

	Number of countries								
	2	*3*	*4*	*5*	*6*	*7*	*8*	*9*	*10*
mean	0·354	0·355	0·354	0·354	0·354	0·354	0·354	0·354	0·354
s.d.	0·033	0·026	0·021	0·019	0·017	0·015	0·013	0·013	0·012
skewness	0·693	0·983	0·831	0·788	0·727	0·681	0·502	0·670	0·557
kurtosis	1·461	0·807	0·428	−0·024	−0·047	0·229	−0·236	0·328	−0·111
expected value	0·360	0·360	0·360	0·360	0·360	0·360	0·360	0·360	0·360

Panel 3: Unimodal data set

	Number of countries								
	2	*3*	*4*	*5*	*6*	*7*	*8*	*9*	*10*
mean	0·277	0·284	0·309	0·312	0·314	0·319	0·320	0·321	0·324
s.d.	0·038	0·023	0·017	0·010	0·009	0·008	0·006	0·005	0·005
skewness	0·138	−0·241	0·460	0·593	0·804	0·507	0·524	0·324	0·375
kurtosis	0·195	−0·383	0·522	0·906	2·958	0·910	1·164	1·149	0·904
expected value	0·280	0·280	0·307	0·312	0·312	0·318	0·320	0·320	0·323

The C index mean values closely track their 'expected values' in panel 1, and fall just below their 'expected values', on average by 0.006 in panel 2. In both cases, the differences are all less than one standard deviation. Interestingly, the 'expected values' for the between-country C index in panels 1 and 2 are constant for all countries and are the same as for the Archer and McLeay I indices in panels 1 and 2 of Table 3. In panel 3 of Table 4, the 'expected value' rises from 0.28 for two countries to 0.323 for 10 countries, and the obtained means closely track above the 'expected values', again by less than one standard deviation in all cases.

The between-country C index means from the simulation always exceed their I index counterparts for three or more country comparisons. Figure 1 shows index means for the uniform data set.

4. Adjusting indices for non-disclosures

Failure to disclose the use (or non-use) of a particular accounting method can be a confounding factor in studies of national or international harmony. The impact of non-disclosures increases with their relative frequency. Archer and McLeay (1995) and Archer et al. (1995) suggest three alternative ways to handle non-disclosures[5]—they can be omitted from all statistical analyses, treated as

[5] They also state that sometimes a 'default' assumption may be made whereby non-disclosers can be assumed, from the surrounding circumstances, to use a particular method, such as one required by an accounting standard. In that case non-disclosers can simply be added to companies disclosing that they do use the method. Archer et al. (1996), in their statistical modelling of harmonisation, also treat non-disclosures as if they were a separate accounting method.

Figure 1
Corrected I index and between-country C index (uniform data set)

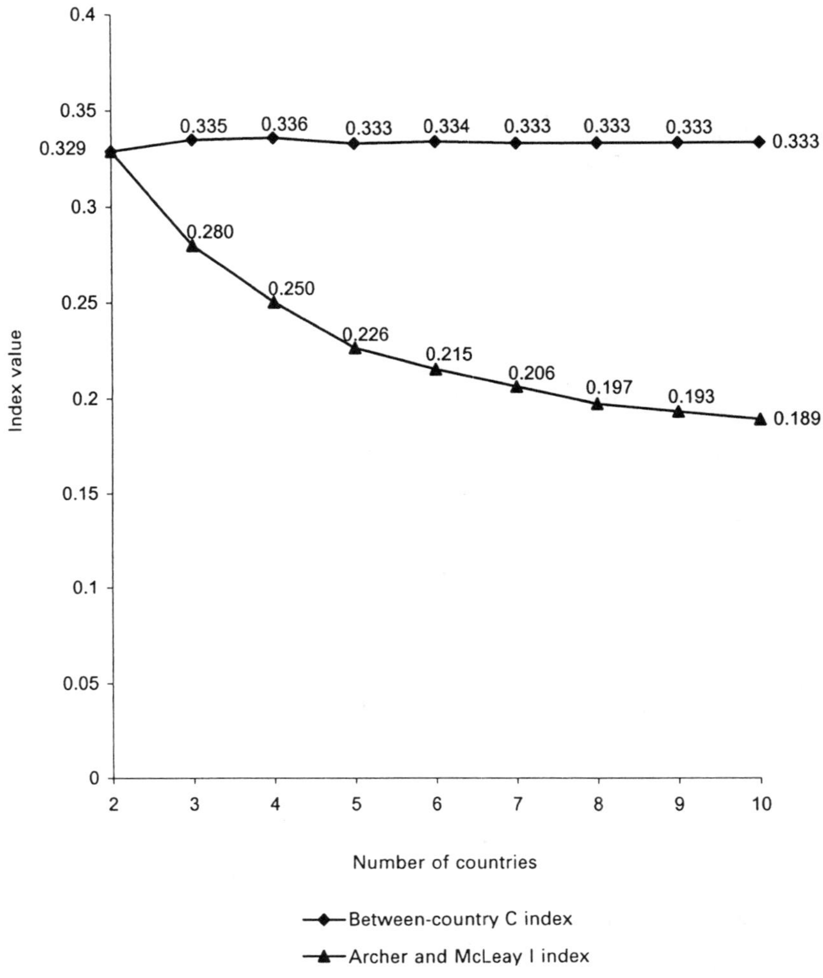

not applicable, or treated as if the item exists but is not disclosed. Their suggestions were made in the context of the C index. Treating non-disclosures as not applicable means that each non-disclosing firm is comparable with all other non-disclosers and with every disclosing firm for the item in question. The C index must be adjusted upwards accordingly to give a disclosure-adjusted comparability index. In contrast, if the item exists but is not disclosed, the denominator, but not the numerator, of the C index is adjusted for non-disclosures to give a raw comparability index. For any accounting issue, the disclosure-adjusted C index will usually produce higher scores, and the raw C index lower scores, than the C index calculated by omitting non-disclosures entirely.

Archer and McLeay (1995) define the disclosure-adjusted comparability index as: 'Pairwise comparisons between companies using the same method and with and between (non-disclosing) companies/Maximum pairwise comparisons between all companies'. They define the raw comparability index as: 'Pairwise comparisons between companies using the same method/Maximum pairwise comparisons between all companies'.

We illustrate their rules with the between-country C index,[6] and extend them to the I index. In an Appendix, we suggest a rule for adjusting the H index for non-disclosures and indicate its relationship to van der Tas's C index.

In the algebraic example in Table 2, let $ø_a,..,ø_d$ be the non-disclosers in countries A,..,D respectively. The formulae for disclosure-adjusted and raw between-country C indices for 2, 3 and 4 country comparisons appear in Table 5, panels 1 and 2.

4.1. Simulation results—between-country C index with non-disclosures

For brevity, we restrict our simulation results for the non-disclosure case to the uniform data set. We simulated the disclosure-adjusted C index and the raw C index for two to 10 country comparisons, using the fourth accounting 'method' to represent non-disclosures. The results appear in Table 6, panels 1 and 2.

Like the unadjusted between-country C index in Table 4, both disclosure-adjusted and raw between-country C indices exhibit pronounced stability in their mean values and declining standard deviations as the number of countries compared increases. The disclosure-adjusted index tracks 0.625 and the raw index tracks 0.187, which are their 'expected values' if the number of companies choosing accounting method i (including the non-disclosers) in country m always equalled the expected value of 12.5. Unlike the unadjusted between-country C index, both disclosure-adjusted and raw indices exhibit little skewness and tend to be platykurtic. Comparing Tables 4 and 6, the ranking of the between-country C indices means is (i) disclosure-adjusted; (ii) unadjusted index; (iii) raw index, regardless of the number of countries compared.

4.2. Disclosure-adjusted I index

A disclosure-adjusted I index can be computed by modifying the formula for the unadjusted I index. The number of non-disclosers for country m are added to scores for each accounting method in country m in the numerator of the I index, and are

[6] We thank Stuart McLeay for his assistance in calculating the disclosure-adjusted and raw C indices and their derivatives.

Table 5
Between-country C index with non-disclosures: formulae

Panel 1

Countries	*Disclosure-adjusted between-country C index*
A/B	$\dfrac{a_1b_1 + a_2b_2 + a_3b_3 + ø_an_b + ø_bn_a + ø_aø_b}{(n_a + ø_a)(n_b+ø_b)}$
A/B/C	$\dfrac{[a_1b_1 + a_2b_2 + a_3b_3 + c_1(a_1+b_1) + c_2(a_2+b_2) + c_3(a_3+b_3) + ø_a(n_b + n_c) + ø_b(n_a + n_c) + ø_c(n_a + n_b) + ø_aø_b + ø_c(ø_a+ø_b)]}{[(n_a+ø_a)(n_b+ø_b) + (n_c + ø_c)(n_a + ø_a + n_b + ø_b)]}$
A/B/C/D	$\dfrac{[a_1b_1 + a_2b_2 + a_3b_3 + c_1(a_1+b_1) + c_2(a_2+b_2) + c_3(a_3+b_3) + d_1(a_1+b_1+c_1) + d_2(a_2+b_2+c_2) + d_3(a_3+b_3+c_3) + ø_a(n_b + n_c + n_d) + ø_b(n_a + n_c+ n_d) + ø_c(n_a + n_b + n_d) + ø_d(n_a + n_b+ n_c) + ø_aø_b + ø_c(ø_a+ø_b) + ø_d(ø_a+ø_b+ø_c)]}{[(n_a+ø_a)(n_b+ø_b) + (n_c + ø_c)(n_a + ø_a + n_b + ø_b) + (n_d + ø_d)(n_a + ø_a + n_b + ø_b + n_c + ø_c)]}$

Panel 2

Countries	*Raw between-country C index*
A/B	$\dfrac{a_1b_1 + a_2b_2 + a_3b_3}{(n_a + ø_a)(n_b+ø_b)}$
A/B/C	$\dfrac{a_1b_1 + a_2b_2 + a_3b_3 + c_1(a_1+b_1) + c_2(a_2+b_2) + c_3(a_3+b_3)}{[(n_a + ø_a)(n_b + ø_b)] + [(n_c + ø_c)(n_a + ø_a + n_b + ø_b)]}$
A/B/C/D	$\dfrac{[a_1b_1 + a_2b_2 + a_3b_3 + c_1(a_1+b_1) + c_2(a_2+b_2) + c_3(a_3+b_3) + d_1(a_1+b_1+c_1) + d_2(a_2+b_2+c_2) + d_3(a_3+b_3+c_3)]}{[(n_a+ø_a)(n_b+ø_b) + (n_c + ø_c)(n_a + ø_a + n_b + ø_b) + (n_d + ø_d)(n_a + ø_a + n_b + ø_b + n_c + ø_c)]}$

Table 6
Between-country C index with non-disclosures (uniform data set)

Panel 1
Disclosure-adjusted between-country C index

	Number of countries								
	2	*3*	*4*	*5*	*6*	*7*	*8*	*9*	*10*
mean	0·623	0·632	0·633	0·629	0·627	0·627	0·627	0·626	0·625
s.d.	0·160	0·118	0·097	0·091	0·082	0·072	0·069	0·064	0·062
skewness	−0·489	−0·112	−0·013	0·039	0·068	−0·106	−0·146	−0·125	−0·173
kurtosis	0·051	0·015	−0·384	−0·649	−0·591	−0·442	0·463	−0·313	0·478
expected value	0·625	0·625	0·625	0·625	0·625	0·625	0·625	0·625	0·625

Panel 2
Raw between-country C index

	Number of countries								
	2	*3*	*4*	*5*	*6*	*7*	*8*	*9*	*10*
mean	0·182	0·187	0·187	0·186	0·187	0·187	0·186	0·186	0·187
s.d.	0·094	0·073	0·058	0·050	0·042	0·038	0·035	0·033	0·032
skewness	0·653	0·560	0·334	0·173	0·177	0·283	0·157	0·215	0·252
kurtosis	0·254	0·324	−0·185	−0·212	−0·285	−0·233	−0·305	−0·372	−0·576
expected value	0·187	0·187	0·187	0·187	0·187	0·187	0·187	0·187	0·187

added to the total number of companies in country m in the denominator. It is necessary to deduct a correction factor for double-counting non-disclosers in the numerator, because non-disclosers are added to the frequencies of each accounting method. The severity of double-counting increases with the number of accounting methods. The correction factor should reduce the numerator of the I index, be related to the number of accounting methods and the number of countries. For m countries, n accounting methods, the correction factor is $-(n\text{-}1)(\Pi \o_m)$. The disclosure-adjusted I index for two countries based on Table 2, panel 1 would be:

$$\frac{[(a_1+\phi_a)(b_1+\phi_b)+(a_2+\phi_a)(b_2+\phi_b)+(a_3+\phi_a)(b_3+\phi_b)-2(\phi_a\phi_b)]}{(n_a+\phi_a)(n_b+\phi_b)}$$

which simplifies to:

$$\frac{a_1b_1+a_2b_2+a_3b_3+\phi_an_b+\phi_bn_a+\phi_a\phi_b}{(n_a+\phi_a)(n_b+\phi_b)}$$

and is the same as the two country disclosure-adjusted between-country C index.

Unfortunately, for more than two countries, Archer and McLeay's correction cannot be made to the disclosure-adjusted I index,[7] because the presence of the correction factor for non-disclosers in the numerator violates Archer and McLeay's condition that the I index should be the sum across accounting methods of their squared geometric means of the relative frequencies of each accounting method i across m countries. The correction factor is not a geometric mean. Mechanically applying Archer and McLeay's correction to the disclosure-adjusted I index can produce index values greater than 1. Consequently, we do not investigate the disclosure-adjusted I index further.

4.3. *Raw I index*

By analogy with the raw between-country C index, the raw I index for m countries is the numerator of the unadjusted I index for m countries divided by the product of the number of companies plus non-disclosers in each country 1, 2, ..., m. Using the example from Table 2, the raw I index for 2, 3 and 4 countries, with Archer and McLeay's correction, is shown in Table 7. The index in the two country case is the same as the raw between-country C index.

[7] Van der Tas's correction can be made to the disclosure-adjusted I index.

Table 7
Raw I index with Archer and McLeay's correction

Countries	*Formulae*
A/B	$\frac{a_1b_1 + a_2b_2 + a_3b_3}{(n_a + ø_a)(n_b + ø_b)}$
A/B/C	$\frac{(a_1b_1c_1)^{2/3} + (a_2b_2c_2)^{2/3} + (a_3b_3c_3)^{2/3}}{[(n_a + ø_a)(n_b + ø_b)(n_c + ø_c)]^{2/3}}$
A/B/C/D	$\frac{(a_1b_1c_1d_1)^{2/4} + (a_2b_2c_2d_2)^{2/4} + c\,(a_3b_3c_3d_3)^{2/4}}{[(n_a + ø_a)(n_b + ø_b)(n_c + ø_c)(n_d + ø_d)]^{2/4}}$

4.4. Simulation results—the I index with non-disclosures

Table 8 shows simulation results for the raw I index with Archer and McLeay's correction. The means and standard deviations of the raw I index decline as more countries are compared, and there is no pronounced skewness or kurtosis. The means fall increasingly below the constant 'expected value' of 0.187.[8]

Figure 2 shows the means for the disclosure-adjusted and raw between-country C indices and the raw I index with Archer and McLeay's correction. For two-country comparisons the two raw indices are equal. If more than two countries are compared, the ranking of the indices is always (i) disclosure-adjusted between-country C index, (ii) raw between-country C index, (iii) raw between-country I index with Archer and McLeay's correction.

[8] In contrast, the means and standard deviations for the raw I indices *without* Archer and McLeay's correction, converge on zero as more countries are compared, and the means closely track their 'expected values'. Compared to the unadjusted I index in footnote 4, the rate of convergence for the means is faster for the raw I index. The mean raw I index without Archer and McLeay's correction commences from 0.182 for two countries and the mean for m countries is about 25% of the mean for m-1 countries. The raw I index without Archer and McLeay's correction tends to be increasingly positively skewed and leptokurtic as more countries are compared.

5. Discussion

This paper has demonstrated some comparative statistical properties of the I index and the between-country C index. In two country comparisons, the I index and the between-country C index are always equal, even when adjustment is made for non-disclosures. The result holds irrespective of the number of accounting methods in each country and the underlying distribution of companies across accounting methods.

For comparisons involving more than two countries, the corrected I index and the between-country C index diverge. Archer and McLeay's (1995), and not van der Tas's (1988), correction to the I index has been used because it is more consistent with van der Tas's original idea that the I index should be an analogue of the H index. Our simulation results, based on uniformly, bimodally and unimodally distributed data sets show that the means of Archer and McLeay's I index decrease for all data sets as more countries are compared. Standard deviations also fall for the uniform and bimodal data sets. There is pronounced skewness for seven or more countries with the unimodal data set, and pronounced kurtosis in the bimodal data set for seven or more countries, and in the unimodal data set for seven or eight countries. For all data sets, the index means fall increasingly be-

Table 8
Simulation results: raw I index with Archer and McLeay's correction (uniform data set)

	Number of countries								
	2	*3*	*4*	*5*	*6*	*7*	*8*	*9*	*10*
mean	0·182	0·152	0·134	0·120	0·113	0·109	0·103	0·101	0·099
s.d.	0·094	0·075	0·058	0·049	0·042	0·038	0·035	0·033	0·032
skewness	0·653	0·788	0·576	0·627	0·604	0·766	0·675	0·601	0·600
kurtosis	0·254	0·616	0·222	0·295	0·113	0·400	0·503	0·199	0·326
expected value	0·187	0·187	0·187	0·187	0·187	0·187	0·187	0·187	0·187

Figure 2
Corrected I index and between-country C index with non-disclosures (uniform data set)

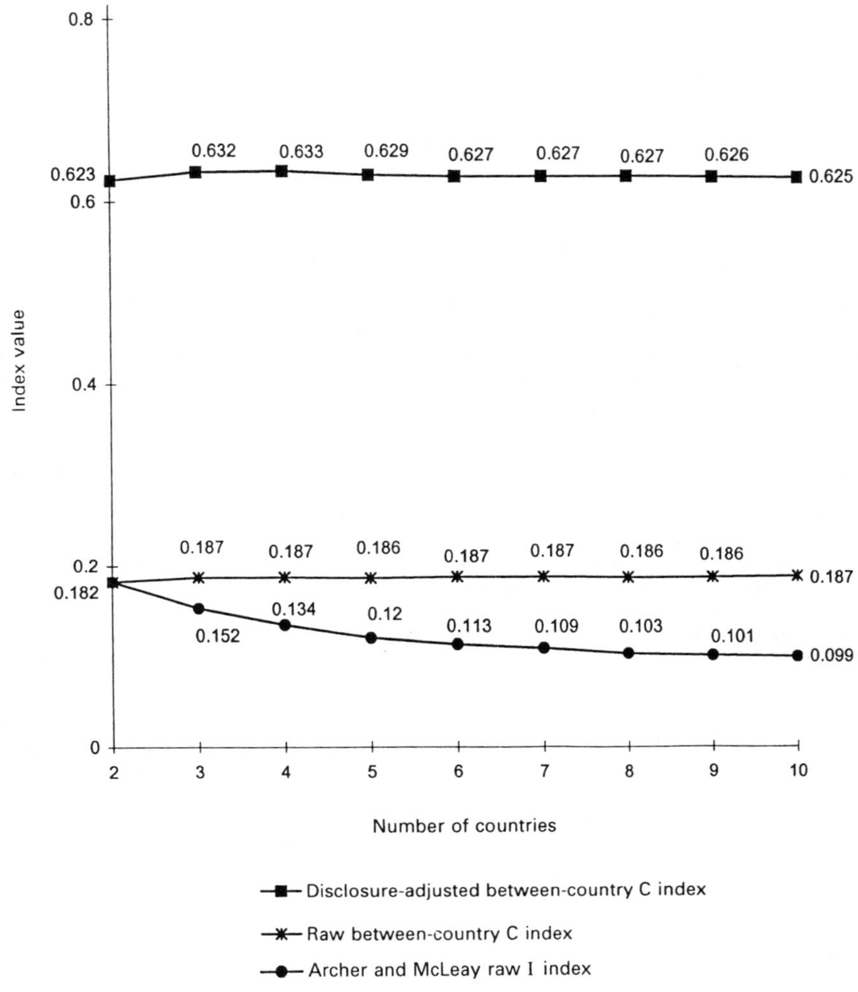

low their 'expected values' (where all observations equal their expected values).

The means of the between-country C index closely approximate their 'expected values' for all country comparisons and usually exceed the corresponding mean I index with Archer and McLeay's correction. The between-country C index's 'expected value' is a constant for the uniform and bimodal data sets and slowly rises for the unimodal data set. Standard deviations fall as the number of countries increases. Skewness and kurtosis vary across data sets but tend to be greater than for the corrected I index as more countries are compared.

For the non-disclosure case, our results are only for the uniform data set. Techniques of dealing with non-disclosures developed by Archer and McLeay (1995) and Archer et al. (1995) for the C index and its derivatives are used. Two variants of the between-country C index are calculated: a disclosure-adjusted version used when non-disclosures are 'not applicable'; and a raw version used when the missing item is applicable to a firm but is not disclosed. Adjusting the between-country C index for non-disclosures tends to shift the mean by a constant, upwards for the disclosure-adjusted, and downwards for the raw, between-country C index. Both adjustments for non-disclosures remove the skewness and kurtosis exhibited by the unadjusted index. The disclosure-adjusted and raw between-country C indices closely track their 'expected values' which are constant for all countries.

We propose disclosure-adjusted and raw versions of the I index (and show in the Appendix the relationship between the H index and van der Tas's C index with non-disclosures). Unfortunately, Archer and McLeay's correction cannot be applied validly to the disclosure-adjusted I index, except in the two-country case. For this reason, the between-country C index is preferable if a disclosure-adjusted index is required. Adjusting for non-disclosures in the case of the raw I index tends to shift its distribution downwards. The means of the raw I index with Archer and McLeay's correction converge on zero as the number of countries increases, and fall increasingly below a constant 'expected value'. Standard deviations also fall and there is no marked skewness or kurtosis.

As Archer and McLeay (1995) noted and our results demonstrate, the assumption made about non-disclosures can have a substantial impact on the resultant harmony measures, especially if the number of non-disclosers is large. Deciding how to handle non-disclosures depends on the underlying facts and requires careful judgement. Using unadjusted indices, that is ignoring non-disclosures, would be reasonable if non-disclosures were relatively infrequent. If non-disclosures are 'not applicable', a dilemma can occur. Usually, the disclosure-adjusted between-country C index should be used. However, if the number of non-disclosers is very much larger than the number of disclosing firms, non-disclosers will dominate the index, which then approaches 1 and may mask the fact that considerable variation exists among disclosing firms. In that case, ignoring non-disclosures may be preferable in order to bring out variation among the disclosing firms. The raw indices should be used if the accounting policy applies to non-disclosers but they have not disclosed their accounting method.

In short, for the three data sets employed, the between-country C index exhibits more stability, either absolutely or in relation to its 'expected values', than does the corrected I index, even when both indices are adjusted for non-disclosures. The stability of the between-country C index is more consistent with the stability in the uniform and bimodal data sets, which each assigns an unchanging distribution of companies to accounting methods across countries. The unimodal data set is less stable than the other data sets, as the dominant accounting method changes across countries. Yet even here the between-country C index tracks its 'expected values' more closely than does the corrected I index. Where all countries have identical data distributions, it seems counterintuitive that the corrected I index shows decreasing harmony as the number of countries increases. For these reasons, the between-country C index may be superior to the I index.

An implication of the findings is that it would be a mistake to apply identical benchmarks to both indices, for example to say that 'considerable harmony' exists if the value of either index exceeds 0.85. For the same data set, the between-country C index is likely to indicate a higher level of harmony than the Archer and McLeay I index as the number of countries increases. Lower benchmarks should be set for the corrected I index if it is used.

Appendix

The H index and van der Tas's C index with non-disclosures

Let a_1, a_2 and a_3 be three accounting methods in a country,

$n = a_1 + a_2 + a_3$

ϕ = the number of non-disclosers

Disclosure-adjusted H index is:

$$\frac{(a_1+\phi)^2+(a_2+\phi)^2+(a_3+\phi)^2-2\phi^2}{(n+\phi)^2}$$

$$=\frac{a_1{}^2+a_2{}^2+a_3{}^2+\phi^2+2\phi n}{(n+\phi)^2}$$

An adjustment must be made for double-counting non-disclosers. In any country with n accounting methods and ϕ non-disclosers, the correction for double counting in the numerator is $-(n-1)\phi^2$.

The disclosure-adjusted van der Tas C index[9] is:

[9] The number of pairs which can be chosen from n objects is 0.5n(n-1). Because van der Tas's C index is the ratio of pairs of comparable companies, the numerator and denominator of the index contains weightings of 0.5 which cancel out and for simplicity have been omitted earlier in the text. The cancellation cannot occur with the disclosure-adjusted van der Tas C index because its numerator contains $\phi(a_1 + a_2 + a_3)$, the number of pairs formed between non-disclosers and all other companies, which does not require a 0.5 weighting. No 0.5 weightings are necessary with between-country C indices because of the condition that each pair member comes from a different country.

$$\frac{0.5[a^1 (a^1 - 1) + a^2 (a^2 - 1) + a^3 (a^3 - 1) + \phi (\phi - 1)] + \phi (a^1 + a^2 + a^3)}{0.5 (n + \phi) (n + \phi - 1)}$$

$$= \frac{a_1^2 + a_2^2 + a_3^2 + \phi^2 - (n + \phi) + 2\phi n}{(n + \phi) (n + \phi - 1)}$$

The relationship between the disclosure-adjusted H and van der Tas C indices is:

$$(n + \phi)^2 H = (n + \phi) (n + \phi - 1) C + (n + \phi)$$

$$H = \left(\frac{n + \phi - 1}{n + \phi}\right) C + \frac{1}{n + \phi}$$

The raw H index is

$$\frac{a_1^2 + a_2^2 + a_3^2}{(n + \phi)^2}$$

while the raw van der Tas C index is:

$$\frac{a_1 (a_1 - 1) + a_2(a_2 - 1) + a_3 (a_3 - 1)}{(n + \phi) (n + \phi - 1)}$$

$$= \frac{a_1^2 + a_2^2 + a_3^2 - n}{(n + \phi) (n + \phi - 1)}$$

The relationship between the two raw indices is:

$$H = \left(\frac{n + \phi - 1}{n + \phi}\right) C + \frac{n}{(n + \phi)^2}$$

In both disclosure-adjusted and raw cases, the H and C indices converge as $n \to \infty$. If $ø = 0$, the relationship between H and C becomes that proposed originally by van der Tas (1988) for the unadjusted case, stated earlier.

References

Archer, S. and McLeay, S. (1995). 'On Measuring the Harmonisation of Accounting Practices'. Paper presented at Workshop on International Accounting, Geneva.

Archer, S., Delvaille, P. and McLeay, S. (1995). 'The measurement of harmonisation and the comparability of financial statement items: within-country and between-country effects'. *Accounting and Business Research*, 25 (Spring): 67–80.

Archer, S., Delvaille, P. and McLeay, S. (1996). 'A statistical model of international accounting harmonization'. *Abacus*, 32 (March): 1–29.

Emenyonu, E. and Gray, S. (1992). 'EC Accounting harmonisation: an empirical study of measurement practices in France, Germany, and the UK'. *Accounting and Business Research*, 23 (Winter): 49–58.

Emenyonu, E. and Gray, S. (1996). 'International accounting harmonization and the major developed stock market countries: an empirical study'. *International Journal of Accounting*, 31 (3) 269–280.

Herrmann, D. and Thomas W. (1995). 'Harmonisation of accounting measurement practices in the European Community'. *Accounting and Business Research* (Autumn): 253–265.

Rahman, A., Perera, P. and Ganeshanandam, S. (1996) 'Measurement of formal harmonisation in accounting: an exploratory study'. *Accounting and Business Research*, 26 (Autumn): 325–339.

Tay, J. S. W. and Parker, R. H. (1990). 'Measuring international harmonization and standardization'. *Abacus*, 26 (March): 71–88.

van der Tas, L. G., (1988). 'Measuring harmonisation of financial reporting practice'. *Accounting and Business Research*, 18 (Spring): 157–169.

[7]

The European Accounting Review 2000, **9:3**, 349–369

Evaluating the statistical significance of *de facto* accounting harmonization: a study of European global players

Leandro Cañibano
Universidad Autónoma de Madrid, Spain
Araceli Mora
Universidad de Valencia, Spain

ABSTRACT

Two different forces are involved in the international harmonization of accounting: institutional endeavours to harmonize accounting internationally by developing common accounting rules and reporting standards, and spontaneous efforts by 'global players' to adopt accounting methods that will improve communication with users in other countries. These two developments are proceeding side by side, generally reinforcing one another but occasionally moving independently.

This paper is primarily concerned with the process of harmonization of financial accounting within the European Union. The hypothesis we want to test is that, in spite of the obstacles to the harmonization of regulations in the European Union, there has been greater conformity in recent years in the accounting practices of companies which operate on the international stage. If so, the implications for the harmonization strategies of the international bodies are important.

In this study, we first carry out a critical analysis of previous research on accounting harmonization, summarizing the methods used in empirical studies of *de facto* harmonization and the results obtained. We note that the major deficiency in the index-based methods of measuring harmonization is that no test of significance has been included in prior research. In this paper, we propose a bootstrapping test of the C index as a way of measuring the significance of the change in its value. We consider a sample of eighty-five 'global players' from thirteen countries and we analyse their financial statements with regard to four accounting issues (deferred taxation, goodwill, leasing and foreign currency translation), providing estimates of the significance of *de facto* accounting harmonization for the periods from 1991–2 to 1996–7.

1. INTRODUCTION

The free flow of comparable financial information resulting from the harmonization of accounting is a necessary condition for achieving a common

Address for correspondence
Araceli Mora, Departamento de Contabilidad, Facultad de Economía, Campus El Tarongers, Avenida de los naranjos s/n, Valencia 46022, Spain.

ISSN 0963-8180 print/1468-4497 online DOI: 10.1080/09638180020017113
Published by Routledge Journals, Taylor & Francis Ltd on behalf of the EAA

market in the European Union. However, the development of global capital markets has created another force for the international harmonization of accounting amongst the companies whose shares are traded on those markets and who have to satisfy the information needs of investors in different countries. This second force, as Thorell and Whittington (1994) point out, is, in one sense, broader, because it extends across the world, but it is, in another sense, narrower, because it is confined substantially to a limited number of international corporations whose securities are traded on global markets.

The European Union strategy with respect to the accounting harmonization of rules has been to use directives, to which all the member states have adapted their legislation. But there appear to be some problems involved in this process. The EU has undoubtedly made progress towards harmonization of accounting law, but the requirements of the EU directives are minimal and do not appear to be sufficient to achieve the desired comparability of financial statements. The inclusion of stricter rules in the directives would not seem to be an acceptable strategy (European Commission, 1995). Regulated international harmonization is difficult to achieve in a business world of cultural, legal, political and economic differences among countries. Now, requiring the use of International Accounting Standards (IASs) for consolidated financial statements would seem to be the strategy adopted by the European Commission (European Commission, 1995). In fact, certain countries (e.g., France, Germany, Italy and Belgium) have already brought their legislation into line with this strategy. However, the use of IASs by 'global players' does not guarantee the comparability of their financial statements because IASs still provide for alternative accounting procedures in some areas.

On the other hand, firms adopting an international competitive strategy are operating in a culture that depends upon global resources. To obtain foreign customers and enhance public image, firms may choose to disclose at least as much as their competitors, which may or may not be 'more' than they are already disclosing in their home country (Thorell and Whittington, 1994). This could be another driving force behind greater comparability that is independent from the institutional efforts previously mentioned.

Therefore, as Meek and Saudagaran (1990) pointed out:

> two significant outgrowths of the transnational financial reporting problem are: institutional endeavors to harmonize accounting internationally by developing accounting and reporting standards, and voluntary efforts by MNCs themselves to improve communication with users in other countries. These two developments are proceeding side by side, generally reinforcing one another but occasionally moving independently.

This paper is primarily concerned with the process of harmonization of the financial accounting practices of European 'global players'. The aim of this study is therefore to ascertain whether the level of comparability in practice among 'global players' has increased in recent years, despite the problems and obstacles involved in the harmonization of rules. Accordingly, we wish to test whether there has been such a 'spontaneous harmonization' in recent years among the accounting practices of companies that operate on the international stage, independently from the harmonization of laws. If so, the implications for the harmonization strategies of international bodies are important.

In this study we carry out a critical analysis of previous research on accounting harmonization, summarizing the methods used in empirical studies of *de facto* harmonization and the results obtained. We note that the major deficiency in the index-based methods of measuring harmonization is that no test of significance has been included in prior research. In this paper, we propose a bootstrapping test of the C index as a way of measuring the significance of the change in its value. We consider a sample of 'global players' from thirteen countries, and we analyse their financial statements with regard to four accounting issues which are considered by previous literature as being among the most controversial in terms of comparability (deferred taxation, goodwill, leasing and foreign currency translation). Then, we provide estimates of the significance of *de facto* harmonization for the periods from 1991–2 to 1996–7.

The remainder of this paper is organized as follows: the second section presents the different concepts of accounting harmonization to be found in the international accounting literature. The third section analyses previous empirical research. The fourth section discusses the proposed research methodology, together with data selection, statistical analysis and results. Lastly, the fifth section concludes with an analysis of the results, a summary of the findings and a description of the limitations and implications of the results.

2. THE CONCEPT OF ACCOUNTING HARMONIZATION

We consider it is important to clarify the different uses of the term 'accounting harmonization' in the literature and previous research in order to understand the aim, the proposal of the methodology and the conclusions of this study. First of all, it is important to distinguish between two terms as used in the international accounting context: 'standardization' and 'harmonization'. *Standardization* implies uniform standards in all countries that participate in the effort. *Harmonization*, however, implies a reconciliation of different points of view and permits different requirements in individual countries provided that there is no logical conflict. *Harmonization* is a process, a movement towards *harmony*, which is a state. *Standardization* is also a process, a movement towards *uniformity*, which is also a state (see Tay and Parker, 1990; Nobes and Parker, 2000). *Harmonization* is a more realistic and conciliatory approach and seems more attainable than rigid *standardization*.

As Van der Tas (1988: 157) points out:

> harmonization is a coordination, a tuning of two or more objects. Users are confronted with several financial reports. It would be useful for them if these financial reports were more in harmony. Therefore financial reports are a target of

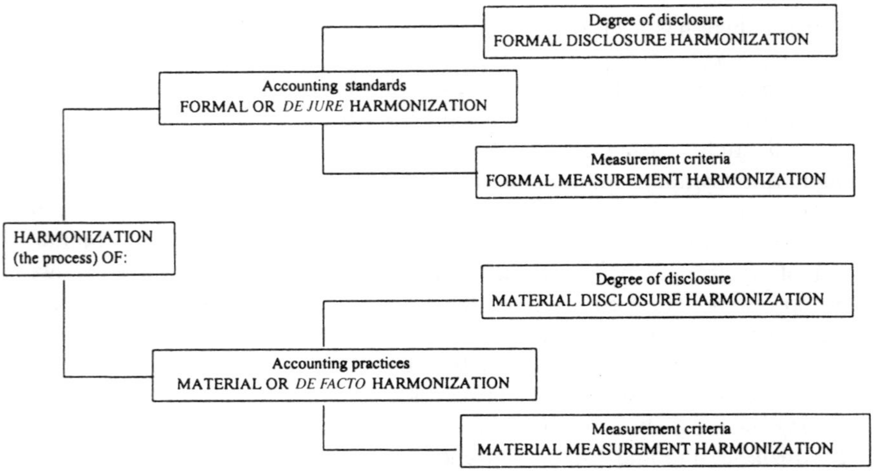

Figure 1 The concept of harmonization

> harmonization. One way to harmonize financial reports is to formulate standards, thus setting limits to the difference between financial reports. They are also an object of harmonization themselves.

Accordingly, a distinction can be drawn between two types of harmonization, namely, '*de facto*' or material harmonization and '*de jure*' or formal harmonization. The former refers to the increase in comparability that arises from greater conformity in practices, and the latter to harmonization of regulations. Formal harmonization would normally lead to material harmonization, but this is not necessarily the case. Formal harmonization may be accompanied by disharmonization if the standards allow for more options for companies. At the same time, material harmonization might take place without being increased by formal harmonization. This will be referred to as *spontaneous harmonization*.

Both formal and material harmonization may refer to the degree of disclosure or to the accounting method selected. The former is called *disclosure harmonization* and the latter *measurement harmonization*. Figure 1 illustrates the different meanings of the term harmonization. As Tay and Parker (1990: 75) say,

> taking account of both the desirability of international comparability of financial statements and the operational difficulties involved in measuring processes rather than states, the most suitable concept for measurement appears to be *de facto* harmonization, in the form of studies of *de facto* harmony over time.

Following Tay and Parker (1990), for the purposes of this paper, we will focus on ***de facto* measurement harmonization**. It can be said that two financial reports are comparable in respect of one specific event if under the same circumstances this event is accounted for in the same way in both reports or if multiple reporting takes place. Multiple reporting means that a company gives additional information based on an accounting method other than its primary accounting method. *De facto* measurement harmonization is an increase in the degree of comparability and means that more companies in the same circumstances apply the same method to an event or give additional information in such a way that the financial reports of more companies can be made comparable.

The notion of harmony, under these circumstances, is such that the process of harmonization will lead to a situation of maximum harmony with respect to a particular financial statement item when all companies in all countries use the same accounting method. Although, as Herrmann and Thomas (1995) point out, this notion ignores the possibility that companies may be subject to different circumstances which arguably justify the use of correspondingly different accounting methods in respect of that item. For Archer *et al.* (1996), this implies an alternative notion of international harmony. According to this notion, a state of international harmony exists when, all other things being equal, the odds of selecting a given accounting method are identical in each group.

The existence of different notions of material harmony implies, in our opinion, the use of different methods of measuring such harmony depending on the concept used by the researcher in question, as discussed in a later section.

3. PREVIOUS LITERATURE

In the field of the measurement of harmonization, some researchers have investigated formal harmonization using different statistical methodologies (e.g., Nair and Frank, 1981; Garrod and Sieringhaus, 1995; Rahman *et al.*, 1996; Laínez *et al.*, 1996). But most of the empirical studies have measured *de facto* harmonization or *de facto* harmony at a point in time (e.g., Van der Tas, 1988, 1992a, 1992b; Walton, 1992; Emenyonu and Gray, 1992; Archer *et al.*, 1995, 1996; Herrmann and Thomas, 1995; García-Benau, 1994;[1] Krisement, 1997; Laínez *et al.*, 1997; McLeay *et al.*, 1999; Pierce and Weetman, 2000).

We will now focus our attention on the studies whose main aim has been to evaluate either the *de facto* harmonization process or the state of *de facto* harmony in Europe. In Table 1 representative studies in this field are shown, indicating their objectives, data source, methodology and main conclusions.

According to Rahman *et al.* (1996: 326):

> accounting harmonization studies are very much at an experimental stage, where methodology and analytical techniques are still being proposed and tested on particular samples of accounting issues and countries. Despite similarities in their purpose, they varied in their results. This is attributable to the differences in the issues selected, countries examined and the analytical techniques used.

Table 1 Material harmonization studies

	Van der Tas (1988)	*Van der Tas (1992a, 1992b)*	*Emenyonu and Gray (1992)*	*Archer et al. (1995)*	*Herrmann and Thomas (1995)*	*Garcia Benau (1994)*	*Archer et al. (1996)*	*Krisement (1997)*	*McLeay et al. (1999)*
Objective (European material harmonization or harmony)	*The proposal of a methodology* • C index • Examples of national and international harmonization	*Harmonization* • Deferred taxation	*Harmony* • Inventory valuation • Depreciation • Goodwill • R&D • Fixed assets • Ext. items	*Harmonization* • Deferred taxation • Goodwill	*Harmony* • Fixed asset valuation • Depreciation methods • Goodwill • R&D • Inventories • Foreign currency	*Harmony* • Foreign currency • R&D • Leasing	*Harmonization* • Deferred taxation • Goodwill	*Proposal of a methodology* • Foreign currency as an example	*Proposal of a methodology* • Goodwill as example
Data source	Annual Reports (1978–84) *National* • UK, Netherlands and USA *International* • USA and Netherlands	Annual Reports (1978–88) 154 companies • Belgium • Denmark • France • Germany • Greece • Ireland • Luxembourg • UK • Netherlands	Annual Reports (1989) 78 companies • France • Germany • UK	Annual Reports (1986–7 and 1990–2) 89 companies • Belgium • France • Germany • Ireland • Netherlands • Sweden • Switzerland • UK	Annual Reports (1992–3) 20 companies • Belgium • Denmark • France • Germany • Ireland • Netherlands • Portugal • UK	Survey Data (FEE report for 1989) • Belgium • France • Denmark • Germany • Greece • Ireland • Luxembourg • Netherlands • UK	Annual Reports (1986–7 and 1990–1) 89 companies • Belgium • France • Germany • Ireland • Netherlands • Sweden • Switzerland	Survey Data (FEE Report 1989) • Belgium • France • Denmark • Germany • Greece • Ireland • Luxembourg • Netherlands • UK	Annual Reports (1987–93) 286 companies • Austria • Belgium • Denmark • Finland • France • Germany • Ireland • Luxembourg • Netherlands • Spain • Sweden • Switzerland • UK
Methodology	• H index • C index	• C index • Chi-square	• I index	• C index	• I index • Adjusted I index • Chi-square	• I index • Adjusted I index (IC) • Chi-square	• Nested hierarchy of log-linear models	• V ratio (heterogeneity + entropy)	• Nested statistical models
Main conclusions	C index is a good method for measuring harmony	The degree of harmony increases considering the 'notes to the accounts' for individual and consolidated accounts. Positive impact of Fourth Directive on individual accounts and no significant impact on consolidated accounts	Relative lack of harmony	C index is an imperfect measure. Little progress in the period. This could be due to small or negative within-country comparability	High level of harmony in • FCT • Inventory value • Depreciation Low level of harmony in • R&D • Fixed assets • Goodwill	Certain progress has been made. FCT has the higher index	Little progress in the period. This could be due to small or negative within-country comparability	Entropy helps to measure harmonization	Harmony does not depend on there being a uniform method but in adopting the same method under the same circumstances. Increase in disharmony in goodwill

In this section we briefly analyse the different data sources and methodologies used in the studies shown in Table 1. First, we want to point out that, though most of these authors say they have measured the 'level of harmonization', some of them do not compare two periods of time and, accordingly, they are actually measuring the 'level of harmony' at that date. Only in the cases of Van der Tas (1992a, 1992b), Archer *et al.* (1995, 1996) and McLeay *et al.* (1999) is a measurement of the process carried out.

Data sources

Data instruments or sources of data which can be used in *de facto* harmonization studies are mainly of five types: annual reports, accounting regulations, public databases, questionnaires and laboratory techniques. The choice of data source has important repercussions for the overall research design, since there are advantages and difficulties involved with using each of them. We will focus on the two data sources used in the studies shown in Table 1, survey data and annual accounts.

There are obvious advantages involved in using questionnaires. As Tay and Parker (1990) say, someone else has already done all the difficult and tedious work of collecting data, which relate to a large number of countries and/or companies, cover a wide range of accounting topics and are available in a language which the researcher can understand. The difficulties with using survey data are well summarized by Nobes (1981). The validity of data, the way the data are presented, inaccuracies which the researcher may not be aware of due to his/her unfamiliarity with different accounting systems and the time lag between publication of the survey and the period surveyed are some of the limitations.

The use of annual reports obviously has great advantages, but also difficulties. It does not have the disadvantages mentioned above, but the collection of data is tedious, companies sometimes do not send the financial information and the reports may not be available in a language the researcher can understand.

Methodologies

Until now, two different methodologies for measuring the level of harmony have been developed: indices and statistical models.

Van der Tas (1988) promotes the idea of **indices**, and meticulously develops the H, C and I indices. The H index from which the I index is developed permits quantification of industrial concentration. Its use in the context of financial reporting harmonization implies an analogy between accounting harmonization and industrial concentration. The idea is that comparability increases when the result of the choice that companies make between alternative accounting methods becomes concentrated on one or only a limited number of methods. The H index adds the square of the relative frequencies of each of the applied methods. But, according to Tay and Parker (1990), this use of the H index 'is worthy of some discussion'. In any case, the main problem of this index is coping with multiple reporting or additional data in the notes regarding the results of alternative measurement methods. Each company (or financial report) must be assigned to one, and only one, alternative measurement method. This problem was solved with the C index developed by Van der Tas (1988). The C index is able to take into account multiple reporting and reconciliation data in the notes to financial statements. Some other adjusted indices based on these two indices have been subsequently developed to try to avoid some of the above limitations. Thus, for example, Krisement (1997) recently proposed a methodology that links the C index and entropy so that, in her opinion, 'the advantages of these two measures complement one another while any disadvantages are eliminated'.

The possibility of using a **statistical modelling approach** was hinted at by Tay and Parker (1990). They suggest that the level of harmony in the accounting practices adopted by companies in different countries may be assessed for a particular financial statement item by comparing 'the observed distribution of companies between different methods with either a random distribution or some expected distribution' and that a suitable representation of a random distribution could be 'a distribution in which equal numbers of companies would be expected to use each of the available alternatives'. Given this approach, Tay and Parker propose the 'evidence of harmony would then be the existence of a significant difference between the observed and expected distributions, as measured by some appropriate significance test, for example chi-square'. Other authors such as Archer *et al.* (1996) developed statistical models which allowed them to measure the level of harmony between countries in a period and the variations in the level of harmony (harmonization) between two periods. McLeay *et al.* (1999) recently developed a new statistical measurement technique. It is important to note that, despite the fact that certain authors used both techniques (indices and statistical models), as alternatives, they are not. The concept of harmonization is different in the two cases. In the case of the statistical model of McLeay *et al.* (1999), these researchers provide a measure of harmonization for which the comparability 'would depend on the use of accounting methods appropriate to a firm's circumstances, and not on the use of the same method by all firms'.

It is important to note that all the methodologies are applied to measure accounting issues separately. Measuring separately gives more refined results because one is able to measure the degree of material measurement harmony for each sort of transaction or event accounted for in the financial report, whereas measuring harmony of the aggregate of all sorts of transactions or events gives only aggregate results, making it difficult to draw policy conclusions on the basis of these measurements. At the same time, measuring harmony of the aggregate of all sorts of transactions or events would require

Table 2 Sample of companies

Company	*Country*	*Company*	*Country*
Abbey PLC	Eire	Kvaerner AS	Norway
Accor	France	LVMH	France
Addeco SA	Switzerland	Man AG	Germany
Akzo Nobel	Netherlands	Movenpick Holding	Switzerland
Alusuissel-Lonza Holding	Switzerland	Norsk Hydro	Norway
Arbed SA/Ares Group	Luxembourg	Oce van den Grinten	Netherlands
Asea AB/ABB Group	Sweden	P&C PLC	England
Astra AB	Sweden	Perkins Foods PLC	England
Audiofina SA	Luxembourg	Pernod Ricard SA	France
Bayer AG	Germany	Philips NV	Netherlands
Benetton Group SA	Italy	Pilkington PLC	England
Bilspedition Transport & Logistics	Sweden	Pirelli SPA	Italy
		PSA Peugeot Citroën SA	France
Body Shop International PLC	England	Remy Cointreau	France
		Rentokil Initial PLC	England
Bridgen Group PLC	England	Repsol	Spain
British Petroleum PLC	England	Rexam PLC/Bowater PLC	England
BSN Groupe	France	Rio Tinto/RTZ PLC	England
Caradon PLC	England	Royal Dutch Petroleum	Netherlands
Clondalkin Group PLC	Eire	Royal Nedlloyd Group	Netherlands
CMB Packaging	Belgium	Royal Pakhoed NV	Netherlands
Compagnie des Machines Bull	France	RWE AG	Germany
		Ryan Hotels	Eire
Computer 2000	Germany	Saipem SPA	Italy
Continental AG	Germany	Sandvik	Sweden
Daimler Benz AG	Germany	SCA	Sweden
Danisco A/S	Denmark	Schering AG	Germany
Degussa AG	Germany	Shell Trading and Transport PLC	England
Deutsche Babcock AK	Germany		
Electrolux	Sweden	Siemens AG	Germany
Elf Sanofi	France	SKF	Sweden
Elsevier	Netherlands	Société Générale de Belgique	Belgium
Emess PLC	England		
Endesa	Spain	Stora Kopparbergs Bergslags	Sweden
Ericsson	Sweden		
Esselte	Sweden	Stork NV	Netherlands
GN Great Nordic	Denmark	Telefonica	Spain
Grand Metropolitan PLC/Guinness	England	Total SA	France
		Unilever NV	Netherlands
Great Universal Stores PLC	England	Veba AG	Germany
Hafslund Nycomed	Norway	Vew/Vereinigte Elektrizitatswer	Germany
Heineken NV	Netherlands		
Hunter Douglas NV	Netherlands	Volkswagen AG	Germany
ICI PLC	England	Volvo AB	Sweden
Independent Newspapers PLC	Eire	Wella AG	Germany
		Woodchester Investment PLC	Eire
Jefferson Smurfit Group	Eire		
KNP BT	Netherlands		

a complete list of the types of transaction and event. It would be very difficult to make an exhaustive list because of the tremendous number of types of transaction and event and of the fact that such a list would change in the course of time. Accordingly, measuring *de facto* measurement harmony separately for each sort of transaction or event is more practical.

Lastly, we want to point out that, in order to measure the 'process of harmonization', most studies compare the value of the indices in the two periods to ascertain whether it has increased, or compare the statistical distribution of the two periods to see if the probability of being a non-random distribution has increased. Until now, only Archer *et al.* (1996) have analysed whether the difference between the two periods is statistically significant using their statistical model approach, but nobody has analysed whether the differences obtained with indices were statistically significant, which is one of the main aims of the present study.

4. THE EMPIRICAL ANALYSIS

Methodology

The C index

From among the different models for measuring the level of harmonization proposed in previous studies we have selected the C index. Although in some of the studies shown in Table 1 the authors used indices and statistical models as alternatives, as we have already mentioned, they are not. The suitability of each method depends, in our opinion, on the concept of harmonization used and the objectives of the study. As we mentioned before, the use of a statistical model implies a concept of the term 'harmony' that supposes that the distribution of companies between the different alternatives is the same in all countries. On the other hand, the use of an index implies that maximum harmony is reached when all the companies in the sample select the same alternative (or give information to reconciliate). For the purpose of this study we consider a sample of companies with very similar characteristics, aiming to test whether they concentrate on certain alternatives regardless of their countries of origin. We assume that 'global players' operate in an international context and the characteristics of the users of their financial statements are similar independently of their national context. Our aim is not then to measure the level of harmony between the countries but the level of harmony of these kind of companies, the 'global players', which are supposed to operate under similar circumstances. For this purpose we have considered the C index as the most suitable method for our analysis. The reason is that it allows us to measure the concentration of companies on one or some alternatives, while a statistical model would be more suitable if we wanted to test the level of harmony between the countries. This would be the case if the sample consisted of companies with a variety of characteristics, and was big enough to obtain significant results for every country. For the same reason, we have not broken down the index in the within-country and between-country comparability indices as other authors have done (see Archer *et al.*, 1995), as we are not interested in measuring the level of harmony between countries but between specific companies, the so-called global players. But, in spite of this, these companies belong to different national regulatory systems, so this could not simply be ignored. Indeed, the results in Tables 3 to 6 are expressed per countries.

We calculate the index in the following way:

$$\text{Total comparability index} = \Sigma(x_{+j}(x_{+j} - 1)/x_{++}(x_{++} - 1))$$

where x_{+j} is the number of cases in which the accounting method j is selected. The value of the index would be 1 when all the companies select the same accounting method.

The bootstrapping test and the chi-square test

Having calculated the value of the C index for the four accounting issues (income tax, financial leases, goodwill and foreign currency translation) in the two periods (1991–2 and 1996–7), we analysed whether the change between the two periods was statistically significant by using a simple bootstrapping procedure. No straightforward method has been developed to test the statistical significance of changes in the index until now.

The bootstrapping procedure is a method for estimating the distribution of an estimator or test statistic by resampling one's data. This technique was developed by Efron in 1979 (quoted in Greene, 1997) and has been appearing with increasing frequency in applied econometrics literature. However, as Horowitz (1995) points out, 'the theory of the bootstrap for many semi-parametric estimators of interest in econometrics (e.g. single-index models, sample-selection models, partially linear models) is still largely undeveloped'.

We consider that the characteristics of the bootstrapping test could make it an appropriate method if the value of a change in the C index from one period to another is considered significant in order to conclude whether there is (or not) a process of harmonization. Our hypothesis in its null form is:

H_0: The observed change in the value of the index is not different from the changes we obtain with a randomly generated distribution.

If we find that the observed change is unlikely to come from the generated distribution, we conclude that the initial assumption is rejected. The distribution is generated by 1,000 interactions, where the accounting choices are randomly allocated using the binomial distribution, with the number of trials set to the sample size and the probability of success determined by the number of occurrences of that accounting method in the sample. The index is then

Table 3 Income tax index

	Period 1991–2						*Period 1996–7*					
	A1	*A2*	*A3*	*A4*	*A5*	*Total*	*A1*	*A2*	*A3*	*A4*	*A5*	*Total*
Belgium	0	2	0	0	0	**2**	0	2	0	0	0	**2**
Denmark	0	1	1	0	0	**2**	0	2	0	0	0	**2**
Ireland	0	0	5	0	1	**6**	0	0	5	0	1	**6**
France	0	7	0	2	0	**9**	0	9	0	0	0	**9**
Germany	8	4	0	2	0	**14**	4	8	0	2	0	**14**
Italy	1	1	1	0	0	**3**	0	3	0	0	0	**3**
Luxembourg	0	0	2	0	0	**2**	0	2	0	0	0	**2**
Netherlands	1	10	0	1	0	**12**	1	10	0	1	0	**12**
Norway	3	0	0	0	0	**3**	0	3	0	0	0	**3**
Spain	0	3	0	0	0	**3**	0	3	0	0	0	**3**
Sweden	8	1	1	1	0	**11**	3	7	1	0	0	**11**
Switzerland	0	1	1	1	0	**3**	0	3	0	0	0	**3**
UK	0	0	14	1	0	**15**	0	1	14	0	0	**15**
Total	**21**	**30**	**25**	**8**	**1**	**85**	**8**	**53**	**20**	**3**	**1**	**85**
Total comparability			**0.27**						**0.41**			

Table 4 Financial leases index

	Period 1991–2						*Period 1996–7*					
	A1	*A2*	*A3*	*A4*	*A5*	*Total*	*A1*	*A2*	*A3*	*A4*	*A5*	*Total*
Belgium	0	1	0	1	0	**2**	0	1	0	1	0	**2**
Denmark	0	2	0	0	0	**2**	0	2	0	0	0	**2**
Ireland	0	5	1	0	0	**6**	0	5	1	0	0	**6**
France	0	6	3	0	0	**9**	0	8	0	1	0	**9**
Germany	0	1	9	3	1	**14**	0	3	7	4	0	**14**
Italy	0	2	0	0	1	**3**	0	3	0	0	0	**3**
Luxembourg	0	2	0	0	0	**2**	0	2	0	0	0	**2**
Netherlands	0	4	2	6	0	**12**	0	4	1	7	0	**12**
Norway	0	1	0	2	0	**3**	0	2	0	1	0	**3**
Spain	1	0	0	2	0	**3**	1	0	0	2	0	**3**
Sweden	0	1	4	6	0	**11**	0	6	2	4	0	**12**
Switzerland	0	1	1	0	1	**3**	0	1	1	0	1	**3**
UK	0	14	0	1	0	**15**	0	15	0	0	0	**15**
Total	**1**	**40**	**20**	**21**	**3**	**85**	**1**	**52**	**12**	**20**	**1**	**86**
Total comparability			**0.33**						**0.46**			

calculated for each of the 1,000 interactions and 999 changes in the index are subsequently derived. The observed change in the index is then compared with this generated distribution. The probability of the observed change not being greater than zero is given by the rank of the observed change when contrasted with the generated distribution (see Noreen, 1992; Bradley and Tibshirani, 1993).

Table 5 Goodwill index

	Period 1991–2						*Period 1996–7*					
	A1	*A2*	*A3*	*A4*	*A5*	*Total*	*A1*	*A2*	*A3*	*A4*	*A5*	*Total*
Belgium	0	0	2	0	0	**2**	0	0	2	0	0	**2**
Denmark	0	1	0	1	0	**2**	0	2	0	0	0	**2**
Ireland	0	4	1	0	2	**7**	0	2	2	0	2	**6**
France	0	0	9	0	0	**9**	0	1	8	0	0	**9**
Germany	2	7	3	1	1	**14**	0	2	8	1	3	**14**
Italy	0	0	1	0	2	**3**	0	0	1	2	0	**3**
Luxembourg	0	0	1	1	0	**2**	0	0	1	1	0	**2**
Netherlands	0	9	0	0	3	**12**	0	8	3	0	1	**12**
Norway	0	0	3	0	0	**3**	0	0	3	0	0	**3**
Spain	0	0	3	0	0	**3**	0	0	3	0	0	**3**
Sweden	2	0	9	0	0	**11**	0	0	11	0	0	**11**
Switzerland	2	0	0	1	0	**3**	0	0	2	1	0	**3**
UK	0	12	1	0	2	**15**	0	11	1	0	3	**15**
Total	**6**	**33**	**33**	**4**	**10**	**86**	**0**	**26**	**45**	**5**	**9**	**85**
Total comparability			**0.31**							**0.38**		

Table 6 Foreign currency index

	Period 1991–2						*Period 1996–7*					
	A1	*A2*	*A3*	*A4*	*A5*	*Total*	*A1*	*A2*	*A3*	*A4*	*A5*	*Total*
Belgium	1	0	1	0	0	**2**	1	0	1	0	0	**2**
Denmark	2	0	0	0	0	**2**	2	0	0	0	0	**2**
Ireland	6	0	0	0	0	**6**	6	0	0	0	0	**6**
France	5	0	0	1	3	**9**	8	0	0	1	0	**9**
Germany	2	7	1	1	3	**14**	5	7	0	1	1	**14**
Italy	0	0	0	1	2	**3**	1	1	0	0	1	**3**
Luxembourg	2	0	0	0	0	**2**	2	0	0	0	0	**2**
Netherlands	9	1	1	0	1	**12**	10	0	2	0	0	**12**
Norway	1	0	3	0	0	**4**	2	2	1	0	0	**5**
Spain	1	0	1	2	0	**4**	1	0	2	0	0	**3**
Sweden	5	1	2	1	2	**11**	8	0	1	2	0	**11**
Switzerland	1	0	0	0	2	**3**	1	0	0	0	2	**3**
UK	12	1	0	0	2	**15**	15	0	0	0	0	**15**
Total	**47**	**10**	**9**	**6**	**15**	**87**	**62**	**10**	7	**4**	**4**	**87**
Total comparability				**0.34**						**0.53**		

Besides the previously described methodology for measuring the harmonization process, we have also calculated the chi-square test, but not to ascertain whether there is a significant difference between the countries in one period, as in the case of previous studies, but rather to see whether there is a significant difference in the distribution of companies between alternative accounting methods in the two periods.[2]

In fact, the chi-square test has not been used in previous research to test the significance but it is important to notice that its application in this case has a lot of limitations. One of the assumptions to apply this test is the independence between the two groups (in our case the same sample of companies in two different periods), so the probability of a company to select one alternative in the second period is independent from its selection in the first period. We are aware that it is not easy to assume independence between the two periods when selecting the alternatives, since companies cannot easily shift from one method to another every year. Another limitation to apply the test is the requirement of at least one specific frequency for each of the alternatives.[3] At any rate, and in spite of these limitations, we have considered it could be interesting to compare the results obtained from this further test with those deriving from the bootstrapping test.

The data and the sample

The sample comprises 85 companies[4] from thirteen European countries whose shares are traded internationally ('global players') (see Table 2). The financial statements of the European companies from those countries whose shares were listed in more than one stock exchange market (the national and at least one foreign market) were required by mail. The whole required information was sent by 85 companies which formed the final sample. Therefore there are certain companies that may be global players that are not included in this sample, and there is also a non-response bias relating to companies that did not provide the report requested. This is a common limitation of this kind of study and is quite difficult to solve (see McLeay *et al.*, 1999, for a further description).

We have analysed their financial statements for the accounting periods 1991–2 and 1996–7 to ascertain which alternative is used by each company for each accounting issue we have considered. The selection of this period has been due to several reasons. First, it has not been analysed in prior research. Second, it has been a recent period in which not many changes in the formal harmonization process have occurred, so that it allows us to test our hypothesis of 'spontaneous harmonization'. It is important to note that in the most recent years changes in laws and rules have been undertaken in some European countries to adapt to the new strategy of harmonization for consolidated accounts of the European Commission.

The accounting issues selected are:

- income tax;
- financial leases;
- goodwill;
- foreign currency translation.

The reason for selecting these specific issues is largely that they have all been considered as among the most controversial in terms of comparability. A very good example of this is the attention that the IASC has given to these issues revising the standards and even the exposure drafts, several times in some cases. Although we could have introduced even more controversial issues, such as asset revaluation and depreciation, among others, we have considered that for the purpose of our analysis these four aspects were sufficient to test our hypothesis and to apply our proposed methodology. For each of these issues we considered five alternatives, as follows:

(a) *Income tax*

A1: Nil provision or 'taxes payable' approach.
A2: Full provision.
A3: Partial provision.
A4: Deferred tax recognized but method used not specified.
A5: No recognition of deferred tax and it is not known whether or not deferred tax accounting is applicable.

(b) *Financial leases*

A1: Capitalization as intangible assets.
A2: Capitalization as tangible fixed assets.
A3: Non-capitalization.
A4: The method used and whether it is applicable or not are not specified.
A5: Capitalization as other assets.

(c) *Goodwill*

A1: Credited to income in the year of acquisition.
A2: Written off against reserves in the year of acquisition.
A3: Shown as an asset and amortized in more than five years.
A4: Shown as an asset and amortized in less than five years.
A5: The method used and whether it is applicable or not are not specified.

(d) *Foreign currency translation*

For this issue we considered only the accounting treatment of the differences arising from the foreign currency translation of monetary items and transactions in foreign currency, and not that of the differences in the translation of subsidiaries' accounts.

A1: Exchange gains and losses as income/loss for the year.
A2: Exchange losses as period expenses and no recognition of unrealized gains.
A3: Exchange losses as period expenses and unrealized gains deferred.
A4: No recognition of unrealized exchange differences.
A5: The method used and whether it is applicable or not are not specified.

Results

In this section we show our results of the selected accounting issues.

The indices

(a) *Deferred taxation*
The number of companies which select the stated alternatives in each country and the values of the C index for the two periods considered are shown in Table 3. A clear increase can be observed in the value of the total comparability index. The companies clearly concentrate their selection on alternative A2 in 1996–7 (the full provision), due mainly to the large number of companies which depart from the nil-provision approach and to the companies which used a deferred tax method but without specifying which was, although they do know.

(b) *Financial leases*
The results are shown in Table 4. There is a clear increase in the value of the total index. There is a concentration on the alternative of capitalization as tangible fixed assets in the second period, clearly due to the considerable number of companies which changed from the alternative of non-capitalization (A3) to capitalization as tangible fixed assets (A2). It can be observed that, in this case, the number of companies for which the method used is unknown (A4) is high and does not decrease in the later period considered.

Non-capitalization prevails mainly in German companies, which is normal, taking into account that in the considered period consolidated accounts had to comply with the principles used in individual accounts, which are greatly influenced by tax rules.

(c) *Goodwill*
The results are shown in Table 5. The increase in the total index is due mainly to the companies which passed from writing off the goodwill in the year of acquisition against income or reserves (alternatives A1 and A2), to the alternative A3, i.e. to amortize the goodwill in more than five years. However, many companies (mainly in the UK and the Netherlands) still use alternative A2 (written off against reserves in the year of acquisition).

(d) *Foreign currency translation*
The results are shown in Table 6. A large increase in the total index can be observed in this case, due mainly to a concentration on A1 implying the recognition of the realized and unrealized gains and losses in the income statement. This was due mainly to the fact that many companies did not provide any information on the method used in 1991–2, whereas they did in 1996–7. Accordingly, the increase in the index may be due not to a har-

Table 7 Bootstrapping test

Accounting issue	*Total index 1991–2*	*Total index 1996–7*	*Bootstrapping ranking out of 1000*
Deferred taxation	0.27	0.41	9
Leasing	0.33	0.46	23
Goodwill	0.30	0.38	10
Foreign currency translation	0.34	0.53	1

Table 8 Chi-square test

Accounting issue	χ^2 *test*	*Significance level*
Deferred taxation	15.03	0.004
Leasing	6.10	0.047
Goodwill	4.39	0.222
Foreign currency translation	9.08	0.059

monization in the measurement criteria but simply to the disclosure of the method used.

Statistical analysis of the significance

After calculating the value of the indices in the two periods, we used the bootstrapping test to see whether the observed increase in the value of the total index for the four accounting issues is statistically significant. There is not a statistical rule to determine the limits to consider a result as significant. In this case we have to consider that a difference which is between the first ten differences of 1,000 could be regarded as a significant change in the value of the index, and not a random difference. The results are shown in Table 7.

It can be observed that the difference between the two values of the indices we obtained for the two periods could be considered higher than a random difference in all cases. Just as in the case of leasing, the result seems to be less significant but considering the 999 random differences the twenty-third can also be considered, in our opinion, as a non-random difference.

On the other hand, the results of testing the significance of the differences between the indices using the chi-square test are shown in Table 8. It can be observed that the different distribution of companies among the alternatives seems to be statistically significant (at the 0.05% level) in the case of deferred taxation, leasing. In the case of foreign currency translation the results are significant at the 0.1% level, and they are not significant in the case of goodwill. It should be noted that in the case of lease transactions and goodwill the criteria of the frequencies of the chi-square test were not followed (see note

3). Accordingly, we had to consider only two alternatives in the case of leasing (the most widely used and the others) and three alternatives in the case of goodwill (the two most widely used and the others) and, therefore, the results must be examined with caution.

5. SUMMARY, CONCLUSIONS AND IMPLICATIONS

The main objectives of this paper are, on the one hand, to test whether there has been a 'spontaneous harmonization' process in the accounting practices of European 'global players', focusing on certain measurement criteria relating to specific controversial accounting issues. On the other hand, we want to propose a methodology for testing the significance of the results obtained. With these purposes in mind, we have first described the situation of the research in the field of harmonization by making a classification of the studies and a critical analysis of previous studies on material harmonization (their data sources, methodologies and results).

We consider one of the major deficiencies in the index-based methods of measuring harmonization is that no test of significance has been included in previous research. In this paper, we propose a bootstrapping test of the C index as a way of measuring the significance of the change in its value.

For the empirical analysis, we consider a sample of 'global players' from thirteen European countries and analyse their financial statements. Taking into account four accounting issues (deferred taxation, goodwill, leasing and foreign currency translation) we calculate the C index for the periods 1991–2 and 1996–7. Then, besides comparing the value of the index in the two periods for the four accounting issues, we analyse whether there is a statistically significant increase in the level of harmony between the two periods, firstly by analysing the difference in the value of the index using a bootstrapping procedure, and second by using the chi-square test. The main conclusions we obtained from this study can be summarized as follows.

The concept of harmonization used in research is important for knowing which methodology is more suitable to empirical analysis. Indices and statistical models are not alternative methods because the implicit concept of harmonization is different. We consider that the C index is an adequate method for testing our hypothesis and the bootstrapping test seems to be an appropriate way of measuring the significance in the increase in the value of the indices.

In relation to the process of harmonization, previous empirical studies showed there has been an increase in the level of harmony of European accounting practices. Since the end of the 1980s 'global players' seemed to be involved in a process of 'spontaneous' *de facto* measurement harmonization, which was occurring independently from the formal harmonization of accounting standards. In our empirical analysis we have obtained a higher value for the index in the second period and, using the bootstrapping procedure, we have concluded that this increase is significant in all the cases we have considered. So our results corroborate the evidence that this process of spontaneous harmonization of European 'global players' went on in the 1990s.

In our opinion, the implications of this empirical evidence of spontaneous harmonization of 'global players' is that the formal harmonization process carried out by the adaptation of national accounting rules to the EU directives does not seem to be sufficient for the international players. The problems involved in the comparability of financial statements still constitute a barrier in an international context and 'global players' and financial analysts which operate in a global market are pressuring the institutional regulatory bodies, in particular the European Commission.

The implications for regulatory bodies of results of this kind are important. The existence of a *de facto* harmonization process creates pressure to achieve formal harmony, at least for these specific companies whose characteristics make them less easily influenced by specific national factors. In fact, the national regulatory bodies of certain European countries have adopted the strategy of allowing certain companies to use international standards for consolidated accounts following the 'new strategy for international harmonization' of the European Commission (European Commission, 1995). The last Communication of the European Commission (European Commission, 2000) in which the inclusion of IASs in the directives for consolidated accounts of listed companies is proposed, is a good example of the reaction of the institutional bodies to this evidence.

ACKNOWLEDGEMENTS

The authors are grateful to the Departamento Dirección y Gestión de Empresas (Corporate Management and Administration Department) of Universidad de Almería, where the financial statements were collected, and especially to Professor Bill Rees from Glasgow University and Professor Stuart McLeay from the University of Wales for their help and useful comments. We are also grateful to the participants in the British Accounting Association Congress 1999 and the European Accounting Association Congress 1999 and to the two anonymous reviewers for their effort and their comments and suggestions to improve the paper.

This study forms part of a research project financed by the Directorate-General of Higher Education (DGES) of the Spanish Ministry of Education and Culture (PB96-0022) and the project Harmonia (Accounting Harmonisation and Standardisation in Europe: Enforcement, Comparability and Capital Market Effects) financed by the European Commission under the Potential Human Program.

NOTES

1 There is an English version of this study in Socías (1996).
2 This test assumes independence between the two groups considered. In the case at hand, the results must be taken with caution because the selection of one accounting alternative in one period could not be considered independent from the selection made in previous years.
3 At least 20% of the alternatives must have a frequency of five and none less than one. In case it does not happen, some of the alternatives must combine in order to comply with the requirement.
4 Although the sample consists of 85 companies, the total number of cases will be higher for some specific issues because certain companies use two alternative accounting methods at the same time.

REFERENCES

Archer, S., Delvaille, P. and McLeay, S. (1995) 'The measurement of harmonisation and the comparability of financial statement items: within-country and between-country effects', *Accounting and Business Research*, 25(98): 67–80.
Archer, S., Delvaille, P. and McLeay, S. (1996) 'A statistical model of international accounting harmonization', *Abacus*, 32(1): 1–29.
Bradley, E. and Tibshirani, K. J. (1993) *An Introduction to the Bootstrap*. London: Chapman & Hall.
Emenyonu, E. N. and Gray, S. J. (1992) 'EC accounting harmonisation: an empirical study of measurement practices in France, Germany and UK', *Accounting and Business Research*, 23(89): 49–58.
European Commission (1995) 'Accounting harmonisation: a new strategy *vis-à-vis* international harmonisation', COM 95 (508).
European Commission (2000) 'EU financial reporting strategy: the way forward', COM (2000)-359-Final.
García Benau, M. A. (1994) *Armonización de la información financiera en Europa*. Madrid: ICAC.
Garrod, N. and Sieringhaus, I. (1995) 'European Union accounting harmonization: the case of leased assets in the United Kingdom and Germany', *European Accounting Review*, 4(1): 155–64.
Greene, W. H. (1997) *Econometric Analysis*. Englewood Cliffs, NJ: Prentice-Hall.
Herrmann, D. and Thomas, W. (1995) 'Harmonisation of accounting measurement practices in the European Community', *Accounting and Business Research*, 25(100): 253–65.
Horowitz, J. L. (1995) 'Bootstrap methods in econometrics: theory and numerical performance', Paper presented at the 7th World Congress of the Econometric Society, Tokyo, August.
Krisement, V. (1997) 'An approach for measuring the degree of comparability of financial accounting information', *European Accounting Review*, 6(3): 465–85.
Laínez Gadea, J. A., Callao Gastón, S. and Jarne Jarne, J. I. (1996) 'Información exigida por las bolsas de valores: análisis empírico de la armonización internacional', *Revista Española de Financiación y Contabilidad*, 25(86): 35–56.
Laínez Gadea, J. A., Callao Gastón, S. and Jarne Jarne, J. I. (1997) 'Accounting diversity versus international accounting harmonization. Empirical evidence', Paper presented at the Annual Congress of the European Accounting Association, Graz, April.
McLeay, S., Neal, D. and Tollington, T. (1999) 'International standardization and

harmonization: a new measurement technique', *Journal of International Financial Management and Accounting*, 10(1): 42–70.
Meek, G. K. and Saudagaran, S. M. (1990) 'A survey of research of financial reporting in a transnational context', *Journal of Accounting Literature*, 9: 145–82.
Nair, R. D. and Frank, W. G. (1981) 'The harmonization of International Accounting Standards', *International Journal of Accounting*, Fall.
Nobes, C. W. (1981) 'An empirical investigation of international accounting principles: a comment', *Journal of Accounting Research*, Spring: 268–80.
Nobes, C. W. and Parker, R. (2000) *Comparative International Accounting*, 6th edn. London: Financial Times/Prentice-Hall.
Noreen, E. (1992) *Computer Intensive Methods for Testing Hypothesis: An Introduction*. London: John Wiley.
Pierce, A. and Weetman, P. (2000) 'The impact of non-disclosure on measurement of de facto harmonisation: a two country comparison', Paper presented at the 23rd Annual Congress of the European Accounting Association, Munich.
Rahman, A., Perera, H. and Ganeshanandam, S. (1996) 'Measurement of formal harmonisation in accounting: an exploratory study', *Accounting and Business Research*, 26(4): 325–39.
Socías, A. (ed.) (1996) *Readings in Accounting in the European Union*. Palma.
Tay, J. S. W. and Parker, R. H. (1990) 'Measuring international harmonization and standardization', *Abacus*, 26(1): 71–88.
Tay, J. S. W. and Parker, R. H. (1992) 'Measuring international harmonization and standardization: a reply', *Abacus*, 28(2): 217–20.
Thorell, P. and Whittington, G. (1994) 'The harmonization of accounting within the EU: problems, perspectives and strategies', *European Accounting Review* 2: 215–39.
Van der Tas, L. G. (1988) 'Measuring harmonisation of financial reporting practice', *Accounting and Business Research*, 18(70): 157–69.
Van der Tas, L. G. (1992a) 'Evidence of EC financial reporting practice harmonization', *European Accounting Review*, 1(1): 69–104.
Van der Tas, L. G. (1992b) 'Measuring international harmonization and standardization: a comment', *Abacus*, 28(2): 211–16.
Walton, P. (1992) 'Harmonization of accounting in France and Britain: some evidence', *Abacus*, 28(2): 186–99.

[8]

The European Accounting Review 2001, **10:1**, 51–72

Measurement of harmony of financial reporting within and between countries: the case of the Nordic countries

Sally Aisbitt
Open University Business School, Milton Keynes, UK

Manuscript first received: June 2000. Manuscript accepted: January 2001.

ABSTRACT

This article aims to examine the usefulness of Archer *et al.*'s (1995) decomposed C-index in measuring harmony and hence harmonization. Financial reporting in the Nordic countries (Denmark, Finland, Norway and Sweden) at four dates in the period between 1981 and 1998 is used as a case study to demonstrate the method and to generate debate about the methodology. The discussion of the results of the analysis leads to the identification of a number of problems that arise in the interpretation of the indices. The difficulties have been divided into two main groups: (1) problems relating to causal inference; and (2) problems relating to properties of the indices. It is argued that the inter-play between these difficulties means that the use and interpretation of the indices is very complicated. Overcoming these obstacles would require a far more intricate model, which might prove less satisfactory than a qualitative analysis based on closer examination of the base data.

1. INTRODUCTION

Over the last twenty-five years there have been a number of efforts made by legislators and accounting standard setters to reduce the number of different accounting treatments used to account for particular transactions or balances (harmonization). To some extent this has been in response to perceived needs of the capital markets. This was intended to facilitate comparison of financial statements of different enterprises within a country and between countries. To assess the success of these harmonization efforts a number of indices have been devised to measure the extent of *de facto* harmony of financial reporting within and between countries at a particular date. By comparing the values of the indices longitudinally it should be possible to quantify harmonization.

Early attempts to measure harmonization (e.g. Nair and Frank, 1981; Doupnik and Taylor, 1985; McKinnon and Janell, 1984) used descriptive statistics and

Address for correspondence
Accounting and Finance Research Unit, The Open University Business School, Walton Hall, Milton Keynes, MK7 6AA, UK. E-mail: S.A.Aisbitt@open.ac.uk

ISSN 0963-8180 print/1468-4497 online DOI: 10.1080/09638180120052249
Published by Routledge Journals, Taylor & Francis Ltd on behalf of the EAA

variance analysis to assess the success of the standards produced by the International Accounting Standards Committee. The limitations of these studies have been discussed in some detail (e.g. Nobes, 1987; Tay and Parker, 1990; van der Tas, 1992a). More recent research has developed from the work of van der Tas (1988) that looked at the way in which accounting practices reported a particular transaction or event and developed three indices for measuring harmonization:

1 *H*-index to measure harmonization within countries;
2 *C*-index to measure harmonization within countries where there is multiple reporting;
3 *I*-index to measure harmonization between countries.

These indices have been used by van der Tas in subsequent work (1992b, 1992c) and by other researchers in conjunction with χ^2 (e.g. Emenyonu and Gray, 1992, 1996; Herrmann and Thomas, 1995; Emenyonu and Adhikari, 1998).

Archer *et al.* (1995) recognized the need to decompose the *C*-index into within-country and between-country components to highlight the dangers of assuming that all companies within a country report similar items in the same way. In 1996, Archer *et al.* developed their methodology further by using a nested hierarchy of log–linear models. This captured the extent to which changes in harmony could be attributed to efforts towards international harmonization or national standardization. The methodology is extremely complex but Archer *et al.* (1996) reconcile their results with the indices of van der Tas (1988) and Archer *et al.* (1995). It could be argued that the same conclusions could be derived from the Archer *et al.* (1995) methodology and close scrutiny of the original data.

These indices have not gone unchallenged. Krisement (1997) criticized van der Tas's (1988) *C*-index on the grounds that it was affected by the number of observations in the calculations, and Archer *et al.*'s (1995) model because the within- and between-country components do not sum to the total value of the index. Morris and Parker (1998) presented the statistical properties of van der Tas's (1988) *I*-index and Archer *et al.*'s (1995) between-country *C*-index. The latter was found to be more stable when the number of countries increased. On the basis that Archer *et al.*'s (1995) methodology seems to combine reliability with simplicity, it seems an attractive means of assessing harmony and harmonization.

This paper aims to examine the usefulness of Archer *et al.*'s (1995) indices by applying them to data obtained from annual reports in the Nordic countries. Analysis of the results reveals a number of problems of interpretation, which bring the helpfulness of the indices into question.

2. MEASUREMENT OF HARMONIZATION OF ACCOUNTING PRACTICE WITHIN AND BETWEEN THE NORDIC COUNTRIES: RATIONALE

This paper examines the Nordic countries in detail by examining harmony within and between Denmark, Finland, Sweden and Norway. Accounting practices in the

Nordic countries have often been classified as a single group (e.g. Doupnik and Salter, 1995) and accounting legislation that was in force in the 1980s had a common source, but the four countries have developed interpretations of that legislation, subsequent legislation and accounting standards separately. Quantifying the extent of harmony of financial reporting within and between these countries could be useful to test classifications or to assess the effect of regulations or other factors on financial reporting.

The dates chosen for this study (1981/2,[1] 1992, 1994 and 1998) were selected to represent periods when different combinations of accounting legislation and standards were in force. The varying regulatory positions might be expected to contribute to varying levels of harmony.

The data for this study were obtained from the annual reports (published financial statements) of the companies listed in Appendix A. Annual reports were requested directly from companies listed on the stock exchange of each of the Nordic countries. From the replies, twelve companies were selected from each country for inclusion in the study. Selection aimed to include companies from a range of industries and exclude those likely to have idiosyncratic financial reporting, e.g. banking, financial services, co-operatives and gaming. The sample size chosen was intended to be large enough to have some expectation of being representative but small enough to allow intimate knowledge of the annual reports.

Where companies had published more than one language version of the annual report, they were asked to furnish copies of each version, which were compared.[2] If they were found to be direct translations, i.e. there was no difference in the information provided, then, for convenience, English-language (or Swedish-language in the case of some Finnish companies[3]) editions were used when they were available. In the case of companies that provided only Finnish-language reports, the accounts were examined with the assistance of a native speaker.

As the number of observations affects the indices, every effort was made to ensure equal numbers of observations in each country and in each year. However, where this was not possible[4] total scores were 'grossed up' to give a total of twelve observations, with 'dummy' observations exhibiting characteristics mirroring those of the actual observations.[5]

To obtain an overall picture of financial reporting, twenty items were identified as representing the essence of financial reporting. The starting point for determining these issues was Nobes (1983). This was then augmented for items that might be of particular interest to a multinational investor, such as disclosures regarding US accounting or International Accounting Standards (IASs). The items involved a mixture of measurement and disclosure issues. The choice of these 'essential elements of accounting' is discussed further under limitations of the methodology below.

The aspects of financial statements examined and the indices calculated are summarized in Table 1. Details of the different accounting treatments used in the classification of observations are set out in Appendix B.

Table 1 Indices of harmony

Aspect of financial statements	*No. of possible treatments*[a]	*Within-country index*				*Between-country index*				*Total index*			
		1981/2	*1992*	*1994*	*1998*	*1981/2*	*1992*	*1994*	*1998*	*1981/2*	*1992*	*1994*	*1998*
1. Valuation of tangible fixed assets	3	67.8	47.8	51.1	56.4	36.6	49.3	49.3	47.7	43.9	49.0	49.7	49.7
2. Valuation of listed investments (held short term)	4	70.2	62.2	47.7	40.2	12.5	27.7	32.8	38.2	26.0	35.8	36.3	38.7
3. Unsettled gains on foreign exchange	3	56.3	50.5	57.6	66.3	31.3	36.3	37.0	60.4	37.1	39.6	41.8	61.8
4. Publication of group accounts	4	84.7	100.0	100.0	100.0	81.3	100.0	100.0	100.0	82.0	100.0	100.0	100.0
5. Goodwill on acquisition in consolidated accounts	5	40.3	49.8	48.1	54.9	27.9	19.4	22.1	37.6	30.8	26.5	28.2	41.7
6. Method of preparing funds flow or cash flow statement	5	69.2	76.4	76.9	91.7	49.6	47.7	76.9	91.8	54.2	54.4	76.9	91.8
7. Use of legal reserves	3	79.5	67.1	58.7	64.8	36.2	21.6	28.0	27.9	46.3	32.2	35.2	36.5
8. Method of depreciation (e.g. straight line)	5	52.7	55.2	51.9	70.8	37.1	21.9	44.2	66.7	40.7	29.7	46.0	67.6
9. Method of stock valuation (e.g. FIFO)	5	62.8	46.4	49.2	42.0	54.7	46.9	42.9	41.9	56.6	46.8	44.4	41.9
10. Review of past and future performance	2	100.0	100.0	100.0	100.0	100.0	100.0	100.0	100.0	100.0	100.0	100.0	100.0
11. Disclosure of segmental turnover	2	81.5	88.3	95.8	100.0	71.7	88.0	95.8	100.0	74.0	88.0	95.8	100.0
12. Disclosure of segmental profit	2	59.5	58.4	62.5	77.7	46.5	55.2	64.4	73.6	49.5	56.0	63.9	74.6
13. Disclosure of number of employees	2	94.0	100.0	100.0	100.0	93.8	100.0	100.0	100.0	93.8	100.0	100.0	100.0

continued overleaf

14. Disclosure of directors' remuneration	2	68.2	91.3	83.3	100.0	67.6	91.5	84.7	100.0	67.7	91.5	84.4	100.0
15. Disclosure of directors' interests in shares	2	86.4	79.2	82.2	95.8	57.7	43.7	80.6	48.6	64.4	52.0	80.9	59.7
16. Disclosure of accounting policies	2	94.6	95.8	100.0	100.0	94.4	95.8	100.0	100.0	94.5	95.8	100.0	100.0
17. Disclosure of earnings per share	2	60.1	92.4	91.7	95.8	47.5	91.7	91.9	95.8	50.4	91.8	91.8	95.8
18. Disclosures about share ownership	2	51.6	81.4	80.7	100.0	48.5	80.8	81.0	100.0	49.2	80.9	80.9	100.0
19. US GAAP reconciliations	3	95.1	78.2	68.2	74.2	95.0	68.9	58.4	66.3	95.0	71.1	60.7	68.2
20. IAS reconciliations	3	89.7	73.9	72.3	95.8	89.8	62.6	62.6	95.8	89.8	65.3	64.9	95.8
Median		**69.7**	**77.3**	**74.6**	**93.8**	**52.2**	**58.9**	**70.7**	**82.7**	**55.4**	**60.7**	**70.9**	**83.2**

Note:
[a]The number of treatments has been shown to give an indication of the minimum value of the index. Within countries, the minimum value of the index would occur when the choice of treatments was split equally in each country (e.g. 50% choose treatment A and 50% choose treatment B, when there are two treatments available). On this basis the minimum values of the indices would be as shown in the following table:

Minimum value of *C*-index when equal choices between methods are made in each country

Number of possible treatments	*Within-country index*	*Between-country index*	*Total index*
2	45.5	50.0	48.9
3	27.3	33.3	31.9
4	18.2	25.0	23.4
5	12.7	20.0	18.3

Minimum values of the between-country index could be as low as zero for financial statement items with four (or more) possible treatments, because all companies in a particular country could adopt the same treatment, but the treatment could be different in each country.

3. DISCUSSION OF HARMONIZATION INDICES

General

This section deals with the harmonization indices calculated for the Nordic countries as shown in Table 1. Direct comparison of these results with previous studies is not possible as this paper deals with different accounting items in different countries at different times.

The median provides a crude summary of the level of harmony. Perhaps unsurprisingly, given the different regulations in each country, the level of harmony within countries was higher than the level of harmony between countries and hence the total level of harmony. The level of harmony (within-countries, between-countries and total) was higher in 1998 than in 1981. Harmony did not increase between each period: harmony within countries decreased between 1992 and 1994.

The Wilcoxon signed ranks test was used to evaluate whether the changes in harmony were significant. Sets of indices were compared for successive dates. The test statistics are shown in Table 2. The null hypothesis was that the level of harmony would be the same at successive dates. From the statistics, it can be seen that the null hypothesis was rejected in the comparisons between 1994 and 1998 and accepted for all other pairs.

To explore the reasons for the (lack of) harmonization, the changes in the values of the indices will be examined on an item-by-item basis. The chances in harmony between 1981/2 and 1998 are summarized in Tables 3–5. While there were some decreases in harmony between the dates subjected to statistical analysis, there were more increases in harmony. This leads to the question of

Table 2 Wilcoxon signed ranks test statistics

Details of Pairs	*Z*	*Asymp. sig. (2-tailed)*
1981/2 and 1992		
Within-country	−0.181[a]	0.856
Between-country	−0.745[a]	0.457
Total	−0.624[a]	0.533
1992 and 1994		
Within-country	−0.379[b]	0.705
Between-country	−1.931[a]	0.053
Total	−1.817[a]	0.069
1994 and 1998		
Within-country	−2.741[a]	0.006
Between-country	−2.430[a]	0.015
Total	−2.499[a]	0.012

Notes:
[a]Based on negative ranks.
[b]Based on positive ranks.

Table 3 Changes in harmony between countries between 1981/2 and 1992

Increase in harmony	*Decrease in harmony*	*No change in harmony*
Valuation of tangible fixed assets	Consolidation goodwill	Performance review[a]
Valuation of listed investments	Cash flow statement	
Unsettled gains on foreign exchange	Legal reserves	
Publication of group accounts	Depreciation method	
Disclosure of segmental turnover	Stock valuation method	
Disclosure of segmental profit	Disclosure of directors' interests in shares	
Disclosure of number of employees	US GAAP reconciliations	
Disclosure of directors' remuneration	IAS reconciliations	
Disclosure of accounting policies		
Disclosure of earnings per share		
Disclosures about share ownership		

Note:
[a]100% harmony was measured at both dates.

Table 4 Changes in harmony between countries between 1992 and 1994

Increase in harmony	*Decrease in harmony*	*No change in harmony*
Valuation of listed investments	Method of stock valuation	Valuation of tangible fixed assets
Unsettled gains on foreign exchange	Disclosure of directors' remuneration	Publication of group accounts[a]
Consolidation goodwill	US GAAP reconciliations	Performance review[a]
Cash flow statement		Disclosure of number of employees[a]
Legal reserves		IAS reconciliations
Depreciation method		
Disclosure of segmental turnover		
Disclosure of segmental profit		
Disclosure of directors' interests in shares		
Disclosure of accounting policies		
Disclosure of earnings per share		
Disclosures about share ownership		

Note:
[a]100% harmony was measured at both dates.

Table 5 Changes in harmony between countries between 1994 and 1998

Increase in harmony	*Decrease in harmony*	*No change in harmony*
Valuation of listed investments	Valuation of tangible fixed assets	Publication of group accounts[a]
Unsettled gains on foreign exchange	Legal reserves	Performance review[a]
Consolidation goodwill	Method of stock valuation	Disclosure of number of employees[a]
Cash flow statement	Disclosure of directors' interests in shares	Disclosure of accounting policies[a]
Depreciation method		
Disclosure of segmental turnover		
Disclosure of segmental profit		
Disclosure of directors' remuneration		
Disclosure of earnings per share		
Disclosures about share ownership		
US GAAP reconciliations		
IAS reconciliations		

Note:
[a]100% harmony was measured at both dates.

what is driving the changes in levels of harmony. The European Company Law harmonization programme set (and sets) great store by the use of legislation to promote harmony. This section examines the role that legislation might have played in the harmonization (and de-harmonization) observed in this study. It appears that the increases in harmony were not restricted to periods where harmonizing legislation had been implemented. It is therefore impossible to draw the conclusion that changes in legislation have contributed to or detracted from harmonization on a general level. Consequently, it will be necessary to examine items in greater detail in the context of factors other than legislation that might have influenced practice. Anomalies specific to the data and the methodology will be highlighted in the course of the discussion.

Areas where there seems to be some evidence that legislation contributed to harmonization

The publication of group accounts was a requirement of the proposed Nordic Companies Act[6] and this was incorporated in consequent legislation of the 1970s (effective in 1981/2) in all countries except Denmark as an obligation to publish both a consolidated balance sheet and a consolidated profit and loss account. The publication of a consolidated profit and loss account did not become necessary in

Denmark until the 1981 Companies Act. Practice seems to reflect the legislation: in Finland, Norway and Sweden consolidated balance sheets and profit and loss accounts were published by all sample companies from 1981 onwards. In Denmark, all companies published full group accounts from the 1992 survey onwards. However, in 1981, five Danish companies provided full consolidated accounts, one published an abbreviated consolidated profit and loss account and balance sheet, one gave only a consolidated balance sheet and one provided no consolidated information.[7]

The proposed Nordic Act also included an annual report in its definition of the annual financial statements. This was incorporated in all the Nordic implementations and was followed by all companies in the sample. All companies provided a review of the year's activities, but the breadth and depth of information presented varied between companies and over time. It was not possible to quantify this variation within the model.

Segmental reporting is an area where most companies seem to need to be forced to disclose information. The analysis shows that segmental turnover and profit were only generally published when there was a legal requirement. The proposed Nordic Act did not deal with this area, but Finland, Sweden and Norway included a requirement for disclosure of segmental turnover in the legislation effective in the 1980s. This, combined with subsequent implementations of the Fourth Directive, meant that there was greater harmony in disclosure of segmental turnover between the countries than in disclosure of segmental profit, where there were and are fewer legal requirements.

A similar picture emerges with disclosures about accounting policies, numbers of employees, directors' remuneration and directors' interests in shares in the company. The proposed Nordic Act dealt with disclosures of accounting policies, numbers of employees and directors' remuneration. Companies were making high levels of disclosures in these areas in 1981/2 and there was 100% harmony between countries by the 1992 data for number of employees and by 1994 for accounting policies. Differing national requirements with respect to directors' interests in shares in the company ensured that, while the within-country index was high (reaching a maximum of 95.8 in 1998), the between-country index was lower (48.6 in 1998).

Areas where harmonization seems to have occurred independently of legislation

The publication of a funds flow or cash flow statement was required by legislation in Finland, Norway and Sweden from the 1970s (although it was not mentioned in the proposed Nordic Act). Although it is still not a legal requirement in Denmark, by 1992 all Danish companies in the sample were producing some form of cash flow statement. Even where there was a legal requirement for this statement, there was no guidance in law regarding format and computation. Consequently, accounting standards were important in this area. Initial standards on funds flow statements were issued in 1976 (Norway), 1983 (Finland), 1984 (Sweden) and IAS 7 (1979) was applicable in Denmark. This explains the high within-country indices throughout the period. However, it was only as standards were revised, into line with IASs, that the high within-country indices were matched by high between-country indices.

None of the financial reporting legislation specifies a depreciation method that is to be applied, yet an increase in harmony was observed in this area in later years. This may reflect the change in the relationship between tax and financial accounting as the trend was away from reducing balance and maximum permitted for tax purposes towards straight line. However, this item is one where the limitations of the methodology are particularly apparent, so the results need to be viewed with some caution. This is discussed in more detail below.

Disclosures about share ownership and earnings per share seem to have been driven more by market forces or regulations associated with the stock exchange than by legislation intended to harmonize financial reporting. Nevertheless, the result has been to increase harmony in financial reporting in these areas within and between countries.

Areas where harmony has decreased in spite of legislation

It is noticeable that the areas where harmony has decreased are not covered in detail in the legislation. This provides some comfort for those seeking to legislate for harmony in so far as it may be concluded that, had the legislation been more detailed, the de-harmonization may not have occurred. It should also be pointed out that some of the decreases in harmony recorded (e.g. with respect to US GAAP and IAS reconciliations) do not actually represent a movement away from presenting information in a way that allows comparison within and between countries. This limitation is discussed further below.

4. LIMITATIONS OF THE METHODOLOGY

The discussion above has started to illustrate some difficulties experienced with the methodology. These will be debated further in this section along with the implications for previous and future research. For convenience the limitations of the methodology have been divided into two main groups:

1 problems relating to causal inference; and
2 problems relating to properties of the indices.

Problems relating to causal inference

The discussion above attempted to associate changes in harmony with a single factor, i.e. legislation. This was clearly not entirely successful. The reason for this is that companies are not preparing their annual reports in a vacuum. They are influenced by a range of factors including changes in non-legislative regulations, developments in accounting practice and thought, industry factors and (perceived) demands of the market. It is not possible to control for other factors such that the index of harmony can be deemed to reflect only the effect of one cause, e.g. legislation. Cross-checking of indices calculated by reference to different criteria has been carried out by other researchers. For example, Peill (2000) compared the results of indices computed by industry with indices computed by country to obtain an indication of industry effects. Such an exercise could be repeated to try to account for a number of factors, but it is unlikely that all possible causes could be identified and/or controlled for. The dangers of false causal inference have been pointed out elsewhere (e.g. Nobes, 1987: 79). While possible causes of changes in harmony can be identified, it is important to exercise caution in attempting to attribute changes to a single cause.

Problems relating to properties of the indices

There are a number of difficulties in the methodology associated with the properties of the indices. These can be further divided into reliability and validity problems.

(a) Reliability problems

Reliability problems are concerned with the technical constructs of the indices and their application.

Disclosure (or non-disclosure) and its interpretation The analysis is dependent on the disclosures provided in the annual reports, so to that extent all the indices are measuring harmony of disclosure. Non-disclosure of an item is problematic, as it is not always clear whether the item is applicable to the company but it has failed to disclose, or whether the item is not applicable. In the analysis presented here, non-disclosure is regarded as an accounting treatment. This is justified below under Archer *et al.*'s (1995: 70–1) three headings regarding non-disclosure and the comparability index.

(i) *Problems of non-disclosure.* One approach to non-disclosure is to simply omit items from the analysis where there is insufficient information disclosed. Certain items, e.g. long-term contract work in progress, were omitted from this analysis as so few of the companies examined had disclosures of such items. The items in Table 1 were analysed, in spite of the relatively high number of non-disclosures and hence the potential significance for measuring harmony. The effect of this is discussed below.

(ii) *Non-disclosure of method.* In some cases, it might be assumed that the disclosure is not necessary because the company has used the policy required by law or standards. Given the importance of practice, in addition to written requirements in the Nordic countries, it was not possible to make such assumptions for the non-disclosures in the sample, without risking distortion of the results. Therefore, this approach was not adopted.

(iii) *Non-disclosure of item.* It might be assumed that the item has not been disclosed because it does not apply to the company. It could therefore be assumed that the company is comparable with others that have disclosed the item, regardless of the method used and adjusted indices could be calculated. Further research on the effects of such adjustments was reported by Pierce and Weetman (2000). On the face of it, this approach seems reasonable for measurement items (e.g. valuation of listed investments – a company may not have any, so there is no need to disclose an accounting policy for their valuation), but cannot be justified for some of the disclosure items (e.g. disclosure of number of employees – all the companies in the sample would have had employees). The calculation of adjusted indices was rejected as it was clear from many of the annual reports that the item was applicable, but that the company had chosen not to make disclosures. The adjusted indices would therefore have presented a level of harmony that was higher than the true level of harmony.

While treating non-disclosure as a specific treatment highlights the issue, where there are high levels of non-disclosure, a false impression of harmony may be created. For example, very few of the Finnish companies disclosed any information about the valuation of listed investments, so this contributed to high within-country indices. Although the Finnish reports are directly comparable, they do not provide information which allows a user greater understanding of the figures.

The terminology used by companies varies and it is not always clear to what extent the terms are synonymous. This was particularly problematic in the area of legal reserves. Some companies had balances labelled as 'legal reserves' or 'statutory reserves' while others referred to 'restricted reserves'. In some cases it was clear that the 'restricted reserves' were simply non-distributable reserves, and the reasons for their existence were not related to a requirement for legal reserves. In other cases, it was not clear what the nature of the restricted reserves was. As another example of wording problems, Rautakirja reported that 1982 depreciation was 6.8% of wages costs. It was assumed that the company was attempting to put the depreciation charge in context, rather than explaining the depreciation method.

The way in which information was disclosed varied between companies. For example, the number of employees could be given as a 'key figure' on the inside cover of the report, in the directors' report or in the notes to the profit and loss account. It has been assumed here that users are indifferent to the location of the information, so disclosure is dealt with purely on a yes/no basis. Admittedly, this means that not all of the information will have been subject to the same audit procedures, but it is assumed that un-audited information is better than no information, so has been treated as full disclosure. The model does not recognize variations in the extent of disclosures, so a report giving the average number of employees in the year for the group as a whole is regarded as comparable to a report that analyses the employees between male and female and indicates the business segments to which they contributed.

Previous authors have not raised the matter of interpreting information published in annual reports. It may be difficult to establish a range of accounting treatments that are mutually exclusive. In the case of depreciation, companies might explain that they use one of three methods:

A Straight line
B Reducing balance
C Maximum permitted for tax purposes.

Method C could well be the same as A or B, but it is impossible to glean this information from the annual report. Three categories would be used for the avoidance of doubt, but this provides the potential for an artificially lower index. Where data were obtained from a database, some categorization of accounting practices could have already taken place, but in other studies, this would have been carried out by the authors. Although this could have an important effect on the analysis, the only author to mention it was Christiansen (1995).

Effect on index of possible number of treatments The determination of the number of possible treatments to be incorporated in the model for calculating the indices was highly judgemental. As indicated above, for most of the disclosure items only two possible treatments were considered: disclosed or not disclosed. In other areas, e.g. the method of preparing the cash flow or funds flow statement, it was clear that there was a very wide range of possible treatments. To make the data analysis manageable, it was decided to limit the number to five:

1 indirect method reconciled to change in working capital;
2 indirect method reconciled to change in cash/liquid funds;
3 reconciliation of sources to application of funds;
4 direct method reconciled to change in cash/liquid funds;
5 no cash flow or funds flow statement published.

However, there was clearly scope for further variation within each of these treatments, e.g. there was variation in the definition of cash/liquid funds. As a result, the indices present a somewhat false picture of harmony.

If there are, say, two possible treatments the index that is calculated would be different from if there were, say, five possible treatments. For example, accounting policies in ten companies in each of four countries could be classified as shown in Panel A or B of Table 6. The resultant *C*-indices would be as shown in Panel C of Table 6.

As the example demonstrates, the smaller the number of possible accounting treatments, the easier it is to demonstrate a high level of harmony. Van der Tas

Table 6 Example illustrating the effect of the number of possible accounting treatments on the indices

Panel A: Five possible accounting treatments

Accounting treatment	*Country*			
	1	*2*	*3*	*4*
A. All assets at strict historical cost	2	1	2	6
B. All assets except land at strict historical cost	2	1	1	2
C. All assets except buildings at strict historical cost	2	1	2	2
D. All assets except land and buildings at strict historical cost	2	1	1	0
E. All assets at current values	2	6	4	0
Total	**10**	**10**	**10**	**10**

Panel B: Two possible accounting treatments

Accounting treatment	*Country*			
	1	*2*	*3*	*4*
A. All assets at strict historical cost	2	1	2	6
B. Some or all assets at market value	8	9	8	4
Total	**10**	**10**	**10**	**10**

Panel C: Indices of harmony

Basis of classification of accounting practices	*Within-country index*	*Between-country index*	*Total index*
Panel A	25.0	19.7	20.9
Panel B	63.9	57.7	59.1

(1988, 1992b, 1992c) and Archer *et al.* (1995, 1996) tend to use larger numbers of possible treatments than Herrmann and Thomas (1995) and Emenyonu and Gray (1992, 1996). This makes comparison of indices between the different researchers invalid. There is also the possibility that, within a single piece of research, different numbers of accounting treatments might be used for processing data on different items, e.g. there could be six possible treatments for deferred tax, but only three possible treatments for goodwill, so the indices might suggest that the harmony was much greater for goodwill than for deferred tax, although the goodwill treatments could be further subdivided. This would make comparisons of harmony difficult between items. That problem exists for the interpretation of van der Tas (1988), Emenyonu and Gray (1992), Herrmann and Thomas (1995), Archer *et al.* (1995) and Emenyonu and Adhikari (1998). Emonyonu and

Gray (1996) do not provide sufficient information to determine the number of possible accounting treatments for each item.

Classification of treatments Having decided on possible treatments that would cover all eventualities, it was not always easy to classify the practices of particular companies. Companies may amortize goodwill on consolidation over different periods, depending on the nature of the acquisition, e.g. a company might generally amortize goodwill over five years, but may decide to amortize the goodwill on a particular acquisition over twenty years. In such cases, the company was treated as using the longest period. Consequently, the harmony indices for the treatment of goodwill have probably been understated, i.e. they show a lower level of harmony than is probably the case. For some items, e.g. depreciation, it was apparent that different methods were applied in the case of foreign subsidiaries, so the method used in the accounts of the domestic companies was taken to be the main method. On the other hand, in the case of revaluing fixed assets, while it was suspected that revaluations may only have been used in the accounts of foreign subsidiaries, this was seldom made clear. Therefore, companies with revaluations were classed as having some or all assets revalued, regardless of whether this seemed to be domestic or foreign practice.

Choice of financial statement items Although a justification has been provided for the financial statement items chosen here, the 'essential elements of financial statements' are still subjective. Another combination of financial statement items could lead to quite different results. It is therefore important to be clear about the purpose of the analysis and to select items accordingly.

(b) Validity problems

Validity problems relate to the (in)ability of the indices to capture increases or decreases in harmony. Taking the indices at face value without examining the underlying data is dangerous. As discussed above with respect to non-disclosures, a high index does not necessarily mean that financial statements are comparable. The decreases over time in the between-country indices for US GAAP and IAS reconciliations disguise the fact that more companies were providing information in this area. It is perhaps worth noting that the within-country indices in this area were higher than between-country indices, suggesting that the countries seem to have different attitudes to this form of harmonization. While few companies provided IAS reconciliations, it should be pointed out that in the period under statistical review, there was a somewhat erroneous perception that there were few major differences between practices in the Nordic countries and those permitted under IASs. Companies may therefore have decided that additional disclosures regarding IASs were unnecessary.

Increase in the index does not necessarily mean increase in harmony All authors who have used harmonization indices have recognized that companies might be using a mixture of more than one method; e.g. depreciation could be calculated on the basis of straight line, reducing balance or a mixture. Where harmony seems high because a high number of companies use the method 'mixture of methods', this does not necessarily mean that the financial reports are comparable. In the case of stock valuation, it could be that all US-based companies within multinational groups use LIFO and all other subsidiaries use FIFO. It could be that all groups of companies in the sample took this approach, which would mean that the financial statements were comparable, although a mixture of methods had been used. However, the mixture of methods could be more diverse. In this case, all financial statements using a mixture of LIFO and FIFO would not be comparable (although a high *C*-index would be calculated).

Van der Tas (1988) discussed harmony in terms of the comparability of financial reports containing similar transactions. He identified the following accounting treatments for the valuation of tangible fixed assets:

A historical cost
B current value
C land at current value, buildings at historical cost
D land at historical cost, buildings at current value
E both A and B
F both A and C
G both B and D
H both [*sic*] A, B and D

If all companies moved towards treatment A, there would be an increase in the *C*-index, but this would not necessarily be an increase in harmony, as there would not necessarily be an increase in comparability because costs would relate to different dates. It could be argued that an increase in comparability would only be achieved if all companies moved towards a treatment that involved B. A similar argument could be made in respect of Emenyonu and Gray's (1992) and Herrmann and Thomas's (1995) analysis of stock valuations. If all companies tended towards 'cost', then the harmonization index would increase, although the increase in comparability would not necessarily be as great as if the companies had all moved towards market value. For some assets the level of comparability would be dependent on how 'cost' had been determined (e.g. FIFO or LIFO) as discussed above.

Where 'not disclosed' is regarded as a specific treatment (e.g. Herrmann and Thomas, 1995) an increase in the harmonization index could be caused by an increase in the number of companies not disclosing. This does not automatically mean a lack of harmony of measurement practices: it may simply be a lack of information on which to base an opinion. As discussed above, the reason for the non-disclosure will determine whether this is really an increase in harmony.

Decrease in index does not necessarily mean decrease in harmony Just as an increase in the index does not necessarily mean an increase in harmony, a decrease in the index does not necessarily mean a decrease in harmony. Had earlier researchers extended their studies to deal with disclosure as well as measurement issues, they might have encountered difficulties similar to those described above regarding disclosure of information regarding IASs, where a decrease in the indices reflected the increase in information being provided by some companies, which was clearly intended to increase the comparability.

Some suggestions for the future

This discussion has highlighted areas where caution may be necessary in the interpretation of previous studies. It has also put forward suggestions that future researchers may be able to embrace to reduce the limitations of harmonization measurement exercises. These may be summarized as follows:

1. To avoid losing the richness of the data, the number of possible accounting treatments should probably be closer to those used by van der Tas (1988, 1992b, 1992c) and Archer *et al.* (1995, 1996) than to those used by Emenyonu and Gray (1992, 1996) and Herrmann and Thomas (1995).
2. Where the number of possible accounting treatments varies between items, this should be drawn to the attention of the reader, with some indication of the likely effect on the harmonization indices.
3. Every effort should be made to ensure that categories and/or the way accounting treatments are allocated to them are mutually exclusive.
4. To improve the understanding of information in the annual reports and its classification, either more information could be obtained from the preparers of the financial statements, or (perhaps more practically) analysis could be restricted to companies with clear disclosure. However, this would introduce further bias to the sample and hence the results.

Finally, it is important to keep the use of harmonization measurement techniques in perspective. There is a danger that they become an end in themselves. The aim of all these methods is to assess the progress of harmonization, so measures may become less helpful as harmonization increases. Nevertheless, as absolute harmony seems unachievable, indices might provide some indication of when 'maximum harmony' has been achieved or the extent to which 'minimum harmony' has been exceeded.

5. CONCLUSION

This article has illustrated the use of quantitative methods to assess the extent of harmonization of financial reporting practices within and between the Nordic countries. This has provided some evidence of harmonization in the period from 1981/2 to 1998. However, there were also instances of de-harmonization in the period. The limitations in the methodology discussed above mean that any conclusions need to be regarded with caution. Problems of reliability and validity of the indices of harmony mean that the results can only be fully understood in the context of the details of the raw data. While it is disappointing that the analysis was not more conclusive, it has provided the opportunity to examine and document the limitations of statistical measures from a new perspective. Previous criticisms have concentrated on mathematical issues and the difficulties of identifying the object of measurement. This article has demonstrated more of the problems of obtaining data and processing them in the model.

While the dangers of false causal inference have been pointed out, the results provide some encouragement to bodies promoting harmonization. This is to the extent that there is some correspondence between increases and decreases in harmony and changes in legislation and non-statutory regulations. Nevertheless, many of the changes in harmony cannot be explained by amendments to regulations. Although the volume of legislation governing the form and content of financial statements in the Nordic countries has increased over the last twenty-five years, it is still far from detailed. This means that there is scope for choice, unless it is restricted by other legislation (e.g. relating to taxation), accounting standards or what is considered to be Good Accounting Practice. The relationship between statute, standards and practice is one that varies over time and between countries and requires further investigation.

APPENDIX A: ANNUAL REPORTS EXAMINED

Denmark	*Finland*	*Norway*	*Sweden*
Aarhus Olie	Enso (Stora Enso)	Aker	AGA
Carlsberg	Espoon Sähkö	Bergesen[a]	Astra
Cheminova	Finnair[a]	Dyno[a]	Bilspedition
Christian Hansen	Huhtamäki	Elkem[a]	Celsius[a]
Coloplast[a]	Kymmene	Elkjøp[a]	Electrolux
Danisco[a]	Lemminkäinen[a]	Fesil[a]	Ericsson
H&H[a]	Metsä-Serlä[a]	Hafslund Nycomed	Gambro
Korn & Folderstoff	Neste (Fortum)	Kværner	NCC[a]
Monberg & Thorsen	Nokia	Norskeskog	Sandvik
Motortramp[a]	Outokumpu	Norsk Hydro	SKF
NKT Holdings	Rauma Repola	Orkla[a]	Stora
Sophus Berendsen	Rautakirja	Schibsted[a]	Skanska[b]
			Volvo

Notes:
[a]One or more reports missing.
[b]Analysed only in 1998 as a replacement for Stora, which was analysed under Finland as Stora Enso.

APPENDIX B: POSSIBLE TREATMENTS USED IN ASPECTS OF FINANCIAL STATEMENTS EXAMINED

Aspect of financial statements	*Possible treatments*
1. Valuation of tangible fixed assets	Some or all assets revalued All assets at strict historical cost or lower (i.e. cost minus depreciation or net realizable value) Method not disclosed
2. Valuation of listed investments (held short term)	Fair value Lower of cost and market Lower of cost and written-down value Method not disclosed
3. Unsettled gains on foreign exchange	Some or all gains taken to income Gains recognized in the balance sheet only Method not disclosed
4. Publication of group accounts	Full consolidated P&L and balance sheet published Abbreviated consolidated P&L and balance sheet published Consolidated balance sheet only No group accounts
5. Goodwill on acquisition in consolidated accounts	Goodwill written off to reserves immediately Goodwill written off over 10 years or less Goodwill written off over 20 years or less Goodwill written off over 40 years or less Method not disclosed
6. Method of preparing funds flow or cash flow statements	Indirect method reconciled to change in working capital Indirect method reconciled to change in cash/liquid funds Reconciliation of sources to application of funds No cash flow or funds flow statement published
7. Use of legal reserves	Legal reserves evident 'Restricted reserves' evident Neither of the above evident
8. Method of depreciation (e.g. straight line)	Straight line only Reducing balance only Mixture of methods Maximum permitted for tax purposes Method not disclosed
9. Method of stock valuation (e.g. FIFO)	FIFO LIFO AVCO Mixed methods Method not disclosed
10. Review of past and future performance	Disclosed Not disclosed
11. Disclosure of segmental turnover	Disclosed Not disclosed
12. Disclosure of segmental profit	Disclosed Not disclosed

(*continued*)

APPENDIX B: (*continued*)

Aspect of financial statements	*Possible treatments*
13. Disclosure of number of employees	Disclosed Not disclosed
14. Disclosure of directors' remuneration	Disclosed Not disclosed
15. Disclosure of directors' interests in shares	Disclosed Not disclosed
16. Disclosure of accounting policies	Disclosed Not disclosed
17. Disclosure of earnings per share	Disclosed Not disclosed
18. Disclosures about share ownership	Disclosed Not disclosed
19. US GAAP reconciliations	Full reconciliation to US GAAP presented Explanation of principal differences from US GAAP No disclosures about US GAAP
20. IAS reconciliations	Full reconciliation to IASs presented Explanation of principal differences from IASs No disclosures about IASs

ACKNOWLEDGEMENTS

The author is grateful for advice and suggestions from Professor Christopher Nobes (University of Reading), participants at the European Accounting Association Congress in Munich and three anonymous referees. Finnish language assistance was provided by Mr Timmy McLellan. The paper is part of a larger project that has received generous funding from the Institute of Chartered Accountants in England and Wales.

NOTES

1 The year 1981 for Denmark, Norway and Sweden; 1982 for Finland.

2 Due to the length of time since (particularly the earlier) reports were published, companies were not always able to provide all editions and in some instances (e.g. some Danish companies in 1981) only English editions were available. It is therefore possible that these versions contained more (or less) information than the domestic editions.

3 The author is able to read Danish, Norwegian and Swedish, but not Finnish.

4 Denmark: 1981; Finland: 1982; Norway: 1992, 1981 Sweden: 1981.

5 For example, supposing only ten reports were available in a country in a particular year and in these reports eight companies had applied method A and two companies had applied method B for a particular financial statement item. Then 'dummy' observations would be entered: method A: 1.6 companies; method B: 0.4 companies. For the sake of completeness, the indices were also calculated based on the actual number of observa-

tions. Although the values of the indices were different in 1981/2 and 1992 from those using the dummy variables, the conclusions that would be drawn from them would be qualitatively the same.

6 For further discussion of the proposed Nordic Companies Act, see, for example, Monsen and Wallace (1995).

7 Three of the companies providing full consolidated accounts had only supplied English editions of their annual reports, so it is possible that this edition provided additional information to that provided for Danish users.

REFERENCES

Archer, S., Delvaille, P. and McLeay, S. (1995) 'The measurement of harmonisation and the comparability of financial statement items: within-country and between-country effects', *Accounting and Business Research*, 25(98): 67–80.

Archer, S., Delvaille, P. and McLeay, S. (1996) 'A statistical model of international accounting harmonization', *Abacus*, 32(1): 1–29.

Christiansen, M. (1995) *The Measurement of International Accounting Comparability – Some Considerations*, Birmingham: EAA.

Doupnik, S. and Taylor, M. E. (1985) 'An empirical investigation of the observance of IASC standards in Western Europe', *Management International Review*, 25(1): 27–33.

Doupnik, T. S. and Salter, S. B. (1995) 'External environment, culture, and accounting practice: a preliminary test of a general model of international accounting development', *International Journal of Accounting*, 30: 189–207.

Emenyonu, E. N. and Adhikari, A. (1998) 'Measuring the degree of international harmony in selected accounting measurement practices', *Australian Accounting Review*, 8(2): 24–32.

Emenyonu, E. N. and Gray, S. J. (1992) 'EC accounting harmonisation: an empirical study of measurement practices in France, Germany and the UK', *Accounting and Business Research*, 89: 49–58.

Emenyonu, E. N. and Gray, S. J. (1996) 'International accounting harmonization and the major developed stock market countries: an empirical study', *International Journal of Accounting*, 31(3): 269–79.

Herrmann, D. and Thomas, W. (1995) 'Harmonisation of accounting measurement practices in the European Community', *Accounting and Business Research*, 25(100): 253–65.

Krisement, V. M. (1997) 'An approach for measuring the degree of comparability of financial accounting information', *European Accounting Review*, 6(3): 465–85.

McKinnon, S. M. and Janell, P. (1984) 'The International Accounting Standards Committee: a performance evaluation', *International Journal of Accounting*, Spring: 19–34.

Monsen, N. and Wallace, W. A. (1995) 'Evolving financial reporting practices: a comparative study of the Nordic countries' harmonization efforts', *Contemporary Accounting Research*, 11(2): 973–97.

Morris, R. D. and Parker, R. H. (1998) 'International harmony measures of accounting policy: comparative statistical properties', *Accounting and Business Research*, 29(1): 73–86.

Nair, R. D. and Frank, W. G. (1981) 'The harmonization of International Accounting Standards, 1973–1979', *International Journal of Accounting*, Fall: 61–77.

Nobes, C. W. (1983) 'A judgmental international classification of financial reporting practices', *Journal of Business Finance and Accounting*, Spring: 1–19.

Nobes, C. W. (1987) 'An empirical investigation of the observance of IASC standards in Western Europe: a comment', *Management International Review*, 27(4): 78–9.

Peill, E. (2000) 'Harmonization of accounting measurement practices across industries in the European Union', European Accounting Association Congress, Munich.

Pierce, A. and Weetman, P. (2000) 'The impact of non-disclosure on measurement of *de facto* harmonisation: a two-country comparison', European Accounting Association Congress, Munich.

Tay, J. S. W. and Parker, R. H. (1990) 'Measuring international harmonization and standardization', *Abacus*, 26(1): 71–88.

van der Tas, L. G. (1988) 'Measuring harmonisation of financial reporting practice', *Accounting and Business Research*, 18(70): 157–69.

van der Tas, L. G. (1992a) 'Measuring international harmonization and standardization: a comment', *Abacus*, 28(2): 211–16.

van der Tas, L. G. (1992b) 'Evidence of EC financial reporting practice harmonization: the case of deferred taxation', *European Accounting Review*, 1(1): 69–104.

van der Tas, L. G. (1992c) *Harmonisation of Financial Reporting with a Special Focus on the European Community*. Maastricht: Datawyse.

ABACUS, Vol. 37, No. 3, 2001

ROBERT H. PARKER AND RICHARD D. MORRIS

The Influence of U.S. GAAP on the Harmony of Accounting Measurement Policies of Large Companies in the U.K. and Australia

U.S. GAAP has increasingly become an influence on accounting practices in other countries, even aside from those traditionally considered under direct U.S. influence. The change arises from the large number of U.S. accounting standards, non-U.S. companies listing on U.S. stock exchanges, and the amount of U.S. direct investment abroad. As the impact of U.S. GAAP varies across countries, it may affect international accounting harmony. This idea is tested by examining the level of international harmony for eleven accounting measurement policies in matched pairs of large companies from Australia and the U.K., two countries with historically strong cultural and economic links. It is argued that, in recent decades, accounting practice in Australia, more so than in the U.K., has become increasingly U.S.-oriented. The concepts of harmony of Tay and Parker (1990) and Archer *et al.* (1996) are employed. International harmony is measured by the between-country C index and chi-square test; national harmony by van der Tas's (1988) H index. While considerable national harmony is found in the U.K. for seven and in Australia for five accounting policies, there is considerable or complete international harmony for only three policies. Evidence is presented of the influence of U.S. GAAP as one factor explaining the poor degree of U.K./Australia international harmony. Australian companies appear to follow U.S. GAAP to a greater extent than do U.K. companies. The state of partial harmony thus existing restricts international comparability of accounting reports and may cause problems for regulators.

Key words: Accounting policies; Comparability; Harmonization; Harmony; Standardization; U.S. GAAP, U.K., Australia.

INTRODUCTION

This article examines the influence of U.S. GAAP as an impediment to the international harmony of accounting measurement policies between other countries. The

---

Robert H. Parker is Emeritus Professor, University of Exeter, and Richard D. Morris is a Senior Lecturer in the School of Accounting, University of New South Wales.
The financial assistance of the Institute of Chartered Accountants of Scotland is gratefully acknowledged. We acknowledge use of the Australian Stock Exchange's Statex database in selecting the Australian sample. We have benefited from the comments of T. E. Cooke, S. J. Gray, C. W. Nobes, C. B. Roberts, R. S. O. Wallace, S. A. Zeff, the editor and two anonymous referees.

study is prompted by the current widespread interest in international harmonization of accounting standards. It is also prompted by the international influence of U.S. GAAP flowing from that country's major contribution (via accounting standards and similar pronouncements) to solutions for financial reporting issues, its capital markets as a source of finance for non-U.S. corporations, and its substantial direct investments abroad. U.S. GAAP can impede international harmony by creating partial harmony whereby some but not all countries follow U.S. GAAP. Partial harmony restricts international comparability of accounting reports, thereby causing problems for regulators seeking to increase international harmony of accounting standards and practices. This influence of U.S. GAAP is examined by studying the harmony of accounting measurement policies of large companies in the U.K. and Australia in 1993. Although traditionally considered close because of historical, cultural, legal and economic links, the two countries have in fact diverged for some years due to the U.K.'s entry into the EU and an increasing U.S. influence on Australian accounting. The year 1993 falls in a period where differences between U.S. GAAP and that of other countries were receiving publicity, as illustrated by the large discrepancy between Daimler-Benz's 1993 earnings in U.S. GAAP versus German GAAP, revealed after the company listed on the New York Stock Exchange (Mueller *et al.*, 1997, p. 28). The International Accounting Standards Committee (IASC) agreed in 1993 on the first ten revised standards of its Comparability/Improvements Project, but the lengthy process of obtaining endorsement of International Accounting Standards (IASs) for cross-border securities' listings had not then progressed far enough for IASs to be a serious confounding factor in our study. Considerable national harmony is found within the U.K. and Australia for most of the accounting policies examined. However, there is only minimal international harmony between these countries, due apparently to a greater tendency in Australia than in the U.K. for companies to conform broadly to U.S. GAAP.

Background

International Harmonization Recently, increasing interest has emerged in international harmonization of accounting standards. Well-known examples are the European Union's (EU's) company law harmonization program, standards issued by the IASC, and the work of the International Organization of Securities Commissions (IOSCO). The EU's programme produced a series of directives to be implemented by each member state. The Fourth and Seventh Directives contained wide-ranging and, for some countries, radical accounting proposals. The IASC has, as one of its objectives, increasing harmony of accounting standards internationally (Wyatt, 1989, p. 106). It has long sought international acceptance of IASs, particularly for cross-border securities listings. IOSCO, with members from the securities commissions of many countries including the U.S., the U.K. and Australia, has encouraged, but has also been a demanding critic of, the IASC's harmonization efforts.

The IASC's harmonization efforts have borne fruit slowly. Early IASs were criticized for their permissiveness (for example, see Walker, 1978). The Comparability and Improvements Project (1989–93) aimed at reducing flexibility in IASs

(Salter and Roberts, 1996, p. 24; Ma *et al.*, 1997, p. 493) resulted in a set of revised, tighter IASs. Flexibility remained. IOSCO refused to endorse all the revised IASs for cross-border securities listings. In 1994, IOSCO identified a set of 'core' IASs, further work on which it wished to see satisfactorily completed (Schweikart *et al.*, 1996, p. 113; Zeff, 1998). An agreement between IOSCO and the IASC in July 1995 was to allow these core IASs, if endorsed by IOSCO, to be accepted in place of domestic standards for cross-border securities listings (Ma *et al.*, 1997, p. 495). This agreement was followed by the EU signalling that large European multinational corporations should be able to use IASs provided that these are consistent with the Fourth and Seventh Directives (Commission of the European Communities, 1995, paras 1.4, 5.1–5.9; Flower, 1997). In April 1996, the U.S. Securities and Exchange Commission (SEC) stated that it would consider recognizing the core IASs for foreign corporations issuing securities in the U.S., provided certain conditions were met (Levitt, 1997). The IASC substantially completed the key components of its core standards work program in March 1999 with the publication of an interim standard on financial instruments. And in May 2000, IOSCO finally announced that it would endorse these standards for cross-border securities' offerings. However, countries can still require 'supplementary treatments' including reconciliation of IAS GAAP with domestic GAAP (IOSCO Report on IAS, 2000). An EU policy document issued in June 2000 proposed that all EU countries should require their listed companies to adopt IASs in consolidated accounts by 2005 at the latest (EU Financial Reporting Strategy, 2000).

International harmonization of accounting standards, *via its impact on practice*, is said to improve the allocation of goods, labour and capital in international markets, to reduce firms' costs of capital and operating expenses, and to facilitate social control of multinational corporations (Most, 1994).[1] These advantages purportedly arise because harmonization will, among other things, increase the comparability of accounting reports between countries (Wyatt, 1989, p. 107; Meek and Saudagaran, 1990, p. 167; Saudagaran and Meek, 1997, p. 10). Comparability is one of the qualitative characteristics of accounting information in Conceptual Framework documents (see Belkaoui and Jones, 1996, ch. 7). *Ceteris paribus*, the greater the level of harmony in accounting standards, the greater should be the level of comparability between accounting reports.

Ironically, the EU's and the IASC's efforts can also impede harmonization because they influence some but not all countries. Partial harmony is thus created, whereby harmony between two or more countries may result in disharmony with other countries. After the Fourth and Seventh Directives, accounting regulations of EU countries may be in harmony but not with non-EU countries. Countries that adopt IASs as domestic GAAP (there were twenty-nine such countries in early 2001, IASC, 5 March 2001) have their accounting standards in harmony but not necessarily with those of other countries. U.S. GAAP can likewise impede international harmonization and thus create another instance of partial harmony.

[1] These alleged benefits have not gone unchallenged. Criticisms of harmonization are reviewed in Meek and Saudagaran, (1990, p. 168), Most (1994), Saudagaran and Meek (1997, p. 11).

U.S. GAAP as an Intervening Variable U.S. GAAP has long been a major source of authority on financial accounting issues internationally, as even the most casual glance at English-language non-U.S. financial accounting textbooks will attest. With the work of the Financial Accounting Standards Board (FASB) and the proliferation of its Statements of Financial Accounting Standards, this influence is growing and is twofold. First, U.S. GAAP influences other countries' accounting standards. Because of historical and/or geographical factors, accounting standards in countries such as Canada, Indonesia, Japan, Mexico, Panama, the Philippines and Taiwan are or have been strongly influenced by U.S. GAAP (Nair and Frank, 1980, p. 429; Diga, 1997, ch. 9; Wu *et al.*, 1997, ch. 11; Nobes, 1998a, pp. 58, 61; Rahman, 1998, table 2). However, even in countries outside this sphere, U.S. GAAP has an impact. For example, current standards on translation of foreign subsidiaries' balance sheets in Britain and Australia are based on SFAS 52 (Eddey, 1995, pp. 386–7; Flower, 1998). Second, U.S. GAAP, via its aforementioned impact on foreign accounting standards, influences the *practices* of non-U.S. corporations. But U.S. GAAP also has more direct influences on non-U.S. practices. For example, the Securities and Exchange Commission (SEC) requires non-U.S. corporations with securities listed on U.S. stock exchanges to provide a reconciliation between their own reported earnings and those that would have been reported if they had followed U.S. GAAP (the Form 20-F filings). In 1994, there were 217 such corporations listed on the New York Stock Exchange, 325 on Nasdaq and 74 on the American Stock Exchange (Gray and Roberts, 1997, p. 194). The requirement provides an incentive for these corporations to comply if possible with U.S. GAAP to minimize costs. The U.S. is a very large investor in other countries. Of OECD countries, the U.S. had the largest direct investment outflow from 1990–8 (OECD 2000, chart 2); and in 1998 twenty-six of the world's top hundred transnational corporations (ranked by foreign assets) were American (UNCTAD, 2000). U.S. foreign investment creates a demand in host countries for U.S. GAAP in reporting to U.S. investors. Finally, foreign companies not contemplating listing in the U.S. may adopt U.S. GAAP because it is perceived to be more comprehensive, more conservative, less flexible, or in some other way better, than either domestic standards or the IASs.

The Influence of U.S. GAAP in Australia Traditionally, accounting in Australia and in the U.K. have been considered similar because of the historical, legal, cultural and other links between the two countries. Until 1961, most Companies Acts in Australia were based on U.K. precedents (Morris and Barbera, 1990). Recommendations issued by the Institute of Chartered Accountants in Australia between 1946 and 1963 were very closely based on those issued by the Institute of Chartered Accountants in England and Wales (Zeff, 1973, p. 3). In a classification based on 1973 measurement practices data, Nair and Frank (1980, p. 429) placed the U.K. and Australia, but not the U.S., in the same group, as did Nobes (1998a, p. 58) in a classification albeit based on 1980 data.

Over the past twenty to thirty years, however, Australian accountants have been perceived as moving away from the U.K. and towards the U.S. (Morris and Barbera,

1990, p. 238), at the same time that the U.K. has been increasingly influenced by its fellow member states of the EU. Gibson (1979, p. 33) noted the 'change in orientation':

> The first recommendations of the [Australian] accounting profession [were], in essence, the English equivalents with Australia substituted where necessary for England and Wales. In more recent times there has been, however, a noticeable turn towards the American profession and the influence of American thinking is found readily in the more recently issued [i.e. late 1970s] standards.

Philp (1993, p. 19), an Australian accounting practitioner, stated: 'Australia has made good progress in developing standards very much in accord with those of the United States'. Miller (1994, p. 340) observed that the U.S. is the most important external influence on accounting and auditing in Australia, although Australia is eclectic in following overseas initiatives and has itself taken an important role in the IASC.

Furthermore, from the late 1960s onwards formal links were established 'between existing local firms and the big international accounting firms most of which, regardless of their historical origins, are perceived to be directed principally from their American offices' (Gibson and Arnold, 1981, p. 58). The setting of formal auditing standards, developed first in the U.S., was taken up in Australia before it was in the U.K. Australian standard setters followed U.S. rather than U.K. precedents on tax effect accounting even to the extent of providing a rule appropriate to the treatment of future tax benefits of tax losses in the U.S. which was not relevant in Australia (Gibson, 1984). Goodwill and accounting for the extractive industries are other cases where Australia has been aligned more with U.S. than with U.K. regulations (Brunovs and Kirsch, 1991, p. 155; Luther, 1996, p. 76).

One possible reason for this change in orientation has been the increase in foreign direct investment (FDI) from the U.S. and a decline in FDI from the U.K.: 'For most of Australia's recent history, the United Kingdom and the United States have been major sources of FDI. However . . . Australia's reliance on the United Kingdom as a source of FDI has fallen considerably since 1984–85' (Bureau of Industry Economics, 1996, pp. 7–8). From 1985 to 1998, FDI inflow to Australia from the U.S. amounted to A$29,404m, about double that from the U.K. which at A$14,508m was the second largest source (OECD, 1997, p. 25; OECD, 2000, pp. 41–2).

The influence of U.S. GAAP on Australian versus U.K. accounting *practices* has not been previously studied. Glimpses are discernible from three studies which examined the Form 20-F filings of U.K. and Australian companies listed on U.S. stock exchanges. Weetman and Gray (1991) showed that, for forty-one such U.K. companies, profits from 1986–8 calculated using U.K. accounting standards significantly exceeded profits using U.S. GAAP. Weetman *et al.* (1998) found that, for twenty-five of these U.K. companies, the gap between the two sets of profits had increased by 1994. Norton (1995) conducted a similar study for thirteen U.S.-listed Australian companies for 1985–93. She found that reported profits using Australian accounting standards did not on average differ significantly from profits using U.S. GAAP, although there was wide variation across companies. She did find some significant differences for shareholders' equity. In sum, for these U.S.-listed companies, Australian practice appears closer to U.S. GAAP than does U.K. practice.

Therefore, it is worth examining the extent to which in the 1990s there was greater influence of U.S. GAAP on the accounting measurement policies[2] of Australian companies than on U.K. companies. This is done by measuring between-country or international harmony in a selection of large U.K. and large Australian companies. The proposition tested is that such harmony is relatively low and that this can be explained, at least in part, by the greater influence of U.S. GAAP on large Australian companies than on large U.K. companies. It is further posited that the influence is not restricted to Australian companies listed on U.S. stock exchanges but extends to large Australian companies generally. In order to test these propositions, use is made of some of the measures of harmony developed by, among others, van der Tas (1988, 1992a, 1992b) and Archer *et al.* (1995). Data are drawn from 1993 annual reports of U.K. and Australian companies.

HARMONY AND HARMONIZATION

Before proceeding, the terms 'harmony' and 'harmonization' of accounting measurement policies are defined, and their relationship to 'comparability', 'standardization' and 'uniformity' is clarified. There are many definitions of harmony and harmonization in the literature.[3] Tay and Parker (1990, p. 73) defined harmony as a clustering of companies around one or a few available accounting methods, and harmonization as a movement away from total diversity of accounting methods. Harmony is a state measured at a point of time, whereas harmonization is a process measured by comparing harmony at different times (as in Emenyonu and Gray 1996).

2 It would be also possible to examine accounting disclosure policies. Both measurement and disclosure policies are subject to U.S. GAAP and have been the subjects of international harmonization. Nair and Frank (1980) have shown the importance of distinguishing between measurement and disclosure when classifying national financial reporting systems. Van der Tas (1992a) provides schema for classifying levels of disclosure and measurement harmony. However, the present article follows previous studies (e.g., van der Tas, 1988; Emenyonu and Gray, 1992, 1996; Tay, 1994; Archer *et al.*, 1995; Hermann and Thomas, 1995; Tarca, 1998) in being restricted to measurement policies, which arguably are more interesting in that they affect earnings per share and other important ratios.

3 As summarised in Falk (1994, p. 600), harmony has been described as a state in which 'many member bodies share a sufficient level of individual needs and grievance to produce a common purpose' (Wallace, 1990, p. 10); standards and practices 'do not logically conflict' (Choi and Mueller (1992, p. 257) or accounting 'choices are permitted under very special circumstances' (Wolk and Heaston, 1992, p. 96), while harmonization is a 'process of setting boundaries to the degree of variation among accounting practices' (Arpan and Radebaugh, 1985). Van der Tas (1988, p. 157; 1992a, p. i) defined harmony as the correspondence between two or more objects at a particular point in time; and harmonization as an increase in harmony, that is a coordination or tuning of two or more objects. To Meek and Saudagaran (1990, p. 169), harmonization 'implies a reconciliation of different points of view and permits different requirements in individual countries as long as there is no logical conflict', while Nobes (1998b, p. 117) defined harmonization as 'a process of increasing the compatibility of accounting practices by setting bounds to their degree of variation'.

Tay and Parker (1990) distinguished between de jure and de facto harmony. De jure harmony refers to the extent that regulations in companies acts, accounting standards, etc. are aligned. De facto harmony refers to what companies actually do, that is to their disclosed accounting practices (Parker 1996, p. 317). Alternatively, van der Tas (1988, p. 158; 1992a, chs 2, 3) distinguished between *formal*, *material* and *spontaneous* harmonization; and this can also apply to harmony. Formal harmonization is the harmonization of regulations (see Rahman *et al.*, 1996); material harmonization refers to accounting practices as influenced by regulations or by market forces; while spontaneous harmonization arises from market forces and not from regulations. De jure harmony and formal harmony are equivalent terms, as are material harmony and de facto harmony, while spontaneous harmony is a subset of material harmony. Both regulations and market forces influence the accounting policies examined, so, consequently, the current study entails consideration of de facto or material harmony.

Tay and Parker's harmony is on a continuum. At one end zero de facto harmony or complete diversity means each company uses a different method to account for a given item; at the other end complete de facto harmony—also called uniformity—means that every company uses the same accounting method. Similarly, there is zero de jure harmony if different rules apply across countries, and complete de jure harmony if the same rules apply. However, complete de jure harmony does not imply complete de facto harmony, either because the uniform rules may permit several accounting methods or the rules may not be rigorously enforced.

Tay and Parker (1990, pp. 73–4) also distinguish between harmonization and standardization. Standardization is an analogous process to harmonization but applies to situations where regulations and practices are, or are becoming, increasingly strict or rigid. Standardization 'generally means the imposition of a rigid and narrow set of rules, and may even apply a single standard or rule to all situations' (Choi *et al.*, 1999, p. 248). Van der Tas (1992a, pp. 31–2) considers standardization as part of the harmonization process rather than a separate concept.

De jure and de facto harmonization and standardization are usually measured between countries, but can also occur over time *within* a single country.[4] A high level of within-country de facto harmony is a necessary but not sufficient condition for between-country de facto harmony, as there can be little between-country harmony if there is low within-country harmony. De facto uniformity between countries implies de facto uniformity within them. However, de facto uniformity within countries and zero international harmony are possible on, say, depreciation accounting because all companies in country 1 use straight line, all in country 2 reducing balance, all in country 3 sum of digits depreciation, and so on.

Tay and Parker's view of harmony can conflict with comparability. International differences in economic circumstances, financing arrangements, legal structures,

[4] De jure harmonization can occur within a country where conflicts among that country's different rules, for example, in its companies acts, stock exchange listing rules and accounting standards, are removed. In Australia, a good example of de jure harmonization is the various attempts since 1901 to make uniform the Companies Acts of the different states (see Morris and Barbera, 1990).

cultures and the like can lead to different accounting choices. For example, one firm might choose FIFO, another LIFO for valuing inventory because each has physical flows of goods corresponding to the flow assumption in the method chosen. These firms are not in complete harmony (by Tay and Parker's definition) but arguably their accounts are still comparable. Different economic circumstances of firms are allowed for by standards permitting several inventory accounting methods. Consequently there could be a high level of de jure harmony between countries (van der Tas's, 1992a, p. 47 'identity with options') but a low level of de facto harmony.

The difficulty has been addressed by Archer *et al.* (1996) and McLeay *et al.* (1999). They propose an alternative approach to harmony, harmonization and standardization which simultaneously allows for within-country, between-country, inter-temporal, and firm-specific differences in accounting policy choice (hereafter, Archer *et al.*'s 1996 view). They define harmony as a state where *ceteris paribus* 'the odds of selecting a given accounting method are identical in each country', that is 'accounting policy frequency distributions are identical across countries' and harmonization occurs when those distributions become aligned over time (Archer *et al.*, 1996, pp. 1, 8, 9). Standardization is defined as a process 'which constrains choice and results ultimately in the adoption of the same accounting method by all firms in all countries . . . International standardization . . . is an increase in the unconditional probability that a particular accounting method will be adopted by firms' (McLeay *et al.*, 1999, p. 43).

Tay and Parker's view of harmony and that of Archer *et al.* (1996) are conceptually different. The case where N firms from each of X countries each used one of N different methods to depreciate fixed assets would be zero international harmony to Tay and Parker (strictly, as $N \to \infty$) but could be perfect international harmony to Archer *et al.* The latter's view of harmony assumes that diversity in accounting choices reflects real underlying differences, and opportunistic policy choices ('creative accounting') are random events. McLeay *et al.*'s (1999) view of standardization allows for regulatory attempts to narrow choice for whatever reason, including curbing creative accounting. Tay and Parker's view of standardization (and harmonization) assumes that less diversity is better. So, Archer *et al.*'s and Tay and Parker's views of standardization may be compatible, but their views of harmonization are not.

Fortunately, the incompatibility between the two views of harmonization can be reconciled, not conceptually but for practical purposes. Van der Tas (1992a, pp. 83–4) argues that harmonization (in Tay and Parker's sense) of financial reporting is a necessary but not sufficient condition for comparability. Harmonization makes comparability easier by reducing financial reporting diversity allowing real underlying differences to be pinpointed better. However, 'we must for each case seek an optimal trade-off between the abolition of differences in measurement methods on the one hand and the need on the other hand to avoid rigidity which would work against other qualitative characteristics of accounting information' (van der Tas, 1992a, p. 84). Accordingly, as detailed shortly, a scheme is introduced for classifying less than complete de facto harmony (in Tay and Parker's sense). In this article measurement methods that reflect both competing views of harmony are also used. And, as differences in, say, economic circumstances, legal frameworks can cause problems in measuring accounting harmony, these are controlled for in our sampling procedures.

RESEARCH DESIGN

Choice of Countries
Australia and the U.K. were chosen because they are two countries with strong historical and cultural links, similar accounting professions, legal systems and capital market structures. By comparing accounting practices from both countries, these factors are controlled for.

Choice of Companies
Large companies were chosen because international harmonization is much more important for them since they are more likely to attract foreign investors, to borrow or to operate abroad. Large companies are thus more likely to experience an international capital market demand for information above that from their domestic capital market. Hence they are more likely to use internationally recognized standards such as IASs or U.S. GAAP.

Sampling Procedure
Data from 1993 published accounts were collected. At the time differences between U.S. and other GAAPs were being publicized, and IASs were still not rigorous enough to constitute a major confounding factor in the analysis. The sampling procedure began by choosing U.K. companies from the top 60 in *The Times 1000*, 1994 edition, which excludes financial institutions and measures size by turnover based on 1993 data. Turnover has the advantage of producing less volatile rankings than does, for example, market capitalization. Excluded from the U.K. top 60 were private companies, the fully owned subsidiaries of North American and Japanese companies, and state-owned enterprises (the Post Office, British Coal, British Rail) because their accounting policies may have been influenced by lack of public interest in their accounts, overseas parent's policies or government policies, respectively. Five privatized companies (British Airways, British Telecom, National Power, PowerGen and Rolls-Royce) were also excluded because of the difficulty of matching them with non state-owned Australian companies. Finally, the retail group Isoceles was excluded—it was in the process of reconstruction and thus may have had accounting policies influenced by these unusual circumstances. This left forty companies.

The forty U.K. companies were matched with forty Australian companies on the basis of industry and size, the latter measured by 1993 turnover using the Statex database supplied by the Australian Stock Exchange and held by the Schools of Accounting and Banking and Finance at the University of New South Wales. Industry affects accounting measurement practices; for example, Foster (1986, p. 144) reported strong differences in the use of FIFO, LIFO and average cost inventory valuation methods across U.S. industries. Therefore, pairing by industry controls for factors that might drive such differences. Wherever possible, matching subsidiaries with their U.K. parent companies was avoided since the latter's accounting policies might unduly influence those of the former. For ICI, however, such a match was unavoidable.

As far as possible, listed companies were chosen. All forty of the U.K. companies were listed on the London Stock Exchange; thirty-eight of the forty Australian companies were listed on the Australian Stock Exchange. Of the two unlisted Australian companies, Davids Ltd was listed in 1994 so its 1993 accounting policies may have reflected that intention. The other unlisted company was Optus Communications, Australia's second telephone company, and one very much in the public eye, which did list in 1998. Many of our companies were multi-listed. Ten of the Australian companies were listed on the London Stock Exchange. Seventeen of the U.K. companies and seven of the Australian companies were listed or traded on a U.S. stock exchange. Three of the U.K. companies were listed on the Australian exchange. All but one of the Australian companies listed or traded in the U.S. were also listed in London. It will be observed that more Australian companies were listed in the U.K. than were listed or traded in the U.S., but that more U.K. companies were listed or traded in the U.S. than were listed in Australia. Thus, the regulations of the U.S. SEC were likely to be influential for the U.K. and Australian companies listed in the U.S. However, our hypothesis is that U.S. GAAP's influence is stronger in Australia than in the U.K., and that it applies to all large Australian companies.

Four problems were encountered when matching. First, given the smaller size of the Australian economy, the Australian companies were inevitably smaller than their U.K. counterparts. Hence Australian companies should be less concerned with international capital market pressures, as shown by the larger number of U.K. companies listed in the U.S. The size difference is a bias *against* our hypothesis about the influence of U.S. GAAP. Second, differences in industrial structure mean that some large Australian companies are not in the sample, given that the U.K. companies were used as the starting point. The absentees include BTR Nylex, Pioneer International and Amcor. Third, most companies selected operate in more than one industry, making matching by industry difficult. Matched companies were aligned using each one's most important industry or industries (by contribution to overall sales or profits). Fourth, thirty-five of the Australian companies were in the top 120 listed companies ranked by sales in 1993. Both unlisted companies (Davids Ltd and Optus Communications) would have been in the top 120 had they been listed. The other three companies (Mildara Blass, Village Roadshow and Blackmores) ranked 181, 219 and 230 respectively by sales in 1993. They were included because we could find no better matches for the comparable U.K. companies. Mildara Blass and Village Roadshow were in the top 150 Australian companies by market capitalization in June 1993.

Choice of Accounting Measurement Policies

Accounting measurement policies are conveniently listed in the accounting policies sections of company annual reports. Managers choose accounting policies but this is constrained by regulation. Only some companies' accounting policies were written with admirable clarity. All accounting policies were read and agreed upon by both authors. 'Accounting policies' statements of companies in one country sometimes take for granted what needs to be spelt out in other countries. For example, Australian companies seldom make it plain that they account for deferred taxation liabilities on a full provision (comprehensive allocation) rather than a partial provision basis, and U.K. companies do not always state clearly that they are using the liability rather than the deferral method. Thus, stated accounting policies were interpreted in the light of the authors' knowledge of prevailing accounting laws and standards. Care was taken, however, to do this in such a way as not to substitute a de jure harmony for a possible de facto disharmony.

A few companies explicitly disclosed the influence of U.S. GAAP and the IASs. For example, Shell and Unilever, treated here as U.K. companies, stated that they took account of Dutch and U.S., as well as U.K., accounting principles. Australian company Coles Myer stated that its financial statements conformed in all material respects with IASs on topics that had corresponding Australian accounting standards.

Excluding those measurement policies where it was not possible clearly to distinguish a number of alternative methods, or which were applicable only to a very small number of companies, data on eleven accounting policies were collected:

1. valuation of tangible fixed assets;
2. depreciation of tangible fixed assets;
3. method of inventory valuation;
4. research and development;
5. goodwill on consolidation;
6. foreign exchange translation;
7. capitalization of interest on construction;
8. capitalization of other identifiable intangibles;
9. capitalization of finance leases;
10. deferred taxation liabilities; and
11. method of depreciation.

It is not possible to assess the relative importance of accounting policies. Each policy is therefore given an equal weight in the results presented below.

Broad Conformity With U.S. GAAP

U.S. GAAP can influence practice overtly or covertly in another country: overtly, where companies outside the U.S. explicitly adopt U.S. GAAP; covertly, where non-U.S. accounting standards have rules the same as, or consistent with, U.S. GAAP and a clear link can be established between the two. U.S. GAAP comprises a vast body of rules that in general are less permissive and more detailed than those of U.K. GAAP and Australian GAAP (Biddle and Saudagaran, 1991; Adhikari and Tondkar, 1992). The greater amount of detailed prescription in U.S. GAAP compared with U.K. GAAP is comprehensively illustrated in Pereira *et al.* (1994). No equivalent comparison of U.S. GAAP and Australian GAAP has been published but the main differences appear in Miller (1994) and Norton (1995). Many differences between U.S. GAAP and the other GAAPs are trivial.

Of concern in the present paper is the extent to which the accounting measurement policies selected by large U.K. and Australian companies broadly conform with U.S. GAAP. For the accounting measurement policies selected, broad conformity with U.S. GAAP is defined as follows: all tangible fixed assets to be valued at historical cost and depreciated; inventories to be valued at the lower of cost and the mid-point of net realizable value (NRV), replacement cost and NRV less a normal profit margin (assumed to be not materially different in practice from lower of cost and NRV); research and development costs to be expensed; goodwill on consolidation to be capitalized and amortized; foreign balance sheets to be translated at closing exchange rates, foreign profit and loss accounts at average exchange rates, except in certain circumstances where the temporal method is to be used instead; interest on construction normally to be capitalized; other identifiable intangibles to be capitalized and amortized; finance (capital) leases to be capitalized and amortized; full provision (comprehensive allocation) of deferred taxation liabilities and the liability method; both straight line and reducing balance methods of depreciation permitted.

In 1993 Australian accounting standards broadly conformed with U.S. GAAP on all the above accounting policies, except the valuation of tangible fixed assets (cost or revaluation permitted), research and development (expensed or capitalized), while there were no Australian standards for interest on construction or identifiable intangibles. Australia's goodwill standard AASB 1013 requires capitalization and amortization of purchased goodwill over a maximum of twenty years; the comparable U.S. standard APB Opinion 17 has a maximum amortization period of forty years.[5] Thus, compliance with AASB 1013 would also mean compliance with APB 17. U.K. accounting standards did not conform with U.S. GAAP on goodwill (allowing either capitalization and amortization or write off to reserves) and deferred tax (partial allocation), but were otherwise broadly the same as Australian standards. Thus, Australian standards were more aligned with U.S. GAAP than were U.K. standards, although the difference is not statistically significant ($\chi^2_2 = 1.0$). U.S. standards normally precede U.K. and Australian standards chronologically and it is often possible to observe to what extent U.K. and Australian standard setters have, or have not, followed U.S. precedents. On all issues where Australian and U.K. standards broadly conformed to U.S. GAAP, the U.S. standards were issued first.

[5] See Gibson (1984) for deferred tax; Eddey (1995) for foreign currency translation; Leo *et al.* (1995) for goodwill and identifiable intangibles. Since 1993, no significant changes in the relationship between U.S. GAAP and Australian GAAP have occurred for most of the policies listed. Both countries have adopted the balance sheet method of deferred tax. The U.S. has recently moved to abolish amortization of goodwill and instead require that goodwill be periodically reviewed for impairment (FASB, 2001).

MEASURES OF HARMONY

Analysing the results of a survey of the use of industrial concentration measures, Curry and George (1983, p. 215) note that 'The literature which considers the mathematical properties of concentration measures has not resolved the question of which is the best measure to use'. It is not surprising that the comment also applies to the much more recent literature on measures of accounting harmony. Since two different concepts of harmony are examined—Tay and Parker's (1990) and Archer *et al.'s* (1996)—measures appropriate to each are used. In the main they give similar signals.

Tay and Parker's (1990) View of Harmony

The H Index and the I Index The H or Herfindahl index is used in industrial concentration studies and was first proposed as a measure of harmony by van der Tas (1988). For any country, H is the sum over accounting methods of their squared frequencies of use:

$$H = \sum_{i=1}^{n} p_i^2$$

where H = the Herfindahl index,
n = number of alternative accounting methods, and
p_i = the relative frequency of accounting method i.

H has a maximum value of 1 (uniformity) and a minimum value of 1/n (where n accounting methods are adopted in equal proportions, Hermann and Thomas, 1995, p. 256). As less than complete harmony can occur because of different economic circumstances among firms, the following scheme is used here for judging the level of harmony. An H index of 0.75 to 0.89 is regarded as evidence of 'some' harmony and an H index of 0.90 to 0.99 as evidence of 'considerable' harmony. An index of 1.00 is 'complete' harmony, of less than 0.75 'little' harmony.

To measure international harmony, van der Tas (1988) suggested the I index, as an analogue of the H index. The I index is the sum over accounting methods of the product of the relative frequencies of accounting method i in each of n countries:

$$I = \sum_{i=1}^{n} (f_{i1}\, f_{i2} \ldots f_{im})$$

where $f_{i1}, f_{i2}, \ldots f_{im}$ are the relative frequencies of method i in countries 1, 2 . . . m, and n is the number of alternative accounting methods.

Because I tends rapidly to zero if m exceeds two, van der Tas (1988) suggested that the I index be raised to the power 1/(m – 1). The I index thus corrected has been used in many studies.[6] However, it is a flawed construct. Archer and McLeay (1995) have argued that taking the (m – 1)th root of the I index destroys its analogue

[6] See van der Tas (1988, 1992a), Emenyonu and Adhikara (1998); Emenyonu and Gray (1992, 1996), Hermann and Thomas (1995), Tarca (1998).

nature with the H index, because 1/(m – 1) does not equal 2—the exponent in the H index. They suggest that the I index be reformulated as:

$$I = \sum_{i=1}^{n} (f_{i1}\ f_{i2} \ldots f_{im})^{2/m}$$

where

f_{i1} = the relative frequency of accounting method i in country 1,
n = the number of alternative accounting methods, and
m = the number of countries.

Their corrected I index is the sum across accounting methods of the squared geometric means of the relative frequencies of accounting method i in each of m countries. So formulated, it becomes a multi-country analogue of the H index (Morris and Parker, 1998, p. 74).

The Between-Country C Index

For international comparisons, Archer *et al.* (1995), building on a comparability index of van der Tas (1988), suggest the use of a between-country comparability index. Using Archer *et al.'s* (1995) notation, the formula for this index is:

$$\sum_i \sum_j x_{ij}\,(x_{+j} - x_{ij}) \,/\, \sum_i x_{i+}\,(x_{++} - x_{i+})$$

where

i refers to countries,
j to accounting methods,
x_{+j} to accounting method totals,
x_{i+} to country totals, and
x_{++} to the overall total (number of countries by number of accounting methods).

The between-country C index gives the probability that any pair of randomly selected companies, each from a different country, use the same accounting method.

Morris and Parker (1998) show that the between-country C index and the I index are mathematically equivalent for two country comparisons, but diverge when the number of countries exceeds two. Based on a simulation study, they conclude that the between-country C index is the better measure because it reflects more closely than does the I index (with Archer and McLeay's 1995 correction) the underlying distributions of accounting methods across countries. Archer *et al.* (1996) report that when measuring harmonization, the between-country C index gives signals consistent with their nested linear model approach, discussed next. International comparisons for the current study are reported using the between-country C index, because of its general superiority to the I index. Since the value of the between-country C index is in part a function of the amount of national harmony, the same cut-off points will be used in assessing international harmony as for national harmony.

To illustrate, suppose in matched samples of forty U.K. companies and forty Australian companies, tangible fixed assets are stated at historical cost or are revalued as shown:

INFLUENCE OF U.S. GAAP IN U.K., AUSTRALIA

	U.K.	Australia	Total
Historical cost	14	3	17
Revalued	26	37	63
Total	40	40	80

The H index for the U.K. is

$$(14/40)^2 + (26/40)^2 = 0.55$$

while the H index for Australia is

$$(3/40)^2 + (37/40)^2 = 0.86$$

indicating little national harmony in the U.K. but some in Australia.

The between-country C index is:

$$[14(17 - 14) + 3(17 - 3) + 26(63 - 26) + 37(63 - 37)]/$$
$$[40(80 - 40) + 40(80 - 40)] = 0.63$$

and indicates little international harmony.

Archer et al.'s (1996) View of Harmony

Archer *et al.* (1996) and McLeay *et al.* (1999) use a series of nested linear models to measure within-country, between-country, inter-temporal and firm-specific effects on accounting policy choices. In any setting, the existence of each effect is measured by whether the additional layer, appropriate to that effect, of the nested models yields significant increases in explanatory power over its predecessor. International harmonization occurs when the distributions of firms across accounting methods in two or more countries become aligned over time. Standardization occurs when the distribution of accounting methods across firms changes over time so that the absolute frequency of one accounting method significantly increases.

The Chi-Square Test

To use Archer *et al.*'s (1996) and McLeay *et al.*'s (1999) methodology, at least two years of data are necessary. We have only one year. Accordingly, we use the chi-square test, which is equivalent to Archer *et al.*'s (1996) static model of harmony (Archer *et al.*, 1996, p. 7, fn 7). The chi-square test was suggested by Tay and Parker (1990) and used by Emenyonu and Gray (1992, 1996) and Hermann and Thomas (1995). This statistic tests observed patterns of use against the null hypothesis of no significant difference across countries in the distributions of companies using accounting alternatives A, B, C, etc. International harmony is indicated when chi-square is not significantly different from zero. In the tangible fixed assets illustration, $\chi_1^2 = 9.04$, which is significantly different from zero at the 1% level, and shows that the distributions of accounting policies are different in the two countries.[7]

Harmonization has also been measured using multiple discriminant analysis (see Rahman *et al.*, 1996). However, the technique is more suited to measuring de jure or formal, rather than de facto or material, harmonization.

The chi-square test can be unreliable when expected cell frequencies are small. Statistics textbooks usually state that the minimum acceptable expected cell size for the chi-square test is 5. The data in the current study frequently violate that condition. However, combining categories to attain a minimum expected size of 5—the remedy usually suggested—would mean losing some fineness in data and much intrinsically interesting variation across countries. Combining categories can also affect randomness in samples and the inferences that can be drawn from the data (Everitt, 1977, p. 40). In any event, the minimum expected cell size of 5 is actually an arbitrary rule (Cochran 1952, p. 328), and statisticians have suggested other solutions to the problem. Cochran (1954, p. 420), a frequently cited authority, thought that the minimum expected cell size could be 1 if the degrees of freedom were greater than 1 and no more than about 20 per cent of cells had expected frequencies less than 5.[8] For the current study, chi square statistics were computed without combining categories, and then recomputed after combining categories so that Cochran's (1954) rule was satisfied. Whether the two chi-square statistics gave the same accept/reject decision at the 5% significance level for the null hypothesis was then checked. Fisher's exact test was used for 2 × 2 comparisons if Cochran's rule could not be satisfied. The first chi-square (unadjusted) is reported but cases are flagged where the chi square may be unreliable because it conflicted either with the Cochran chi-square or with Fisher's exact test.

Some Practical Problems

A number of practical problems arose in analysing the data:

1. How sensitive are the results to the degree of fineness used in distinguishing one accounting method from another?
2. How should the use of more than one accounting method by the same company be treated?
3. How should the non-disclosure of an accounting method be treated?

Classifying accounting policies is difficult. Here, what were perceived as sensible categories were adopted. However, notably the degree of fineness in classifying

[8] Later research indicates Cochran's rules are too conservative. Let r be the number of rows in a contingency table, c the number of columns, k the number of cells with expected frequency less than 5, and n the sample size. Lewontin and Felsenstein (1965) thought that the conservative minimum expected frequency in 2 × c tables was 1, but also the expected frequency could safely be as low as 0.5. Snedecor and Cochran (1967, p. 235) stated that for 1 × c tables, a minimum expected frequency of 1 was sufficient. Yarnold (1970, p. 865) suggested that where r × c was at least 3, the minimum expected cell size was 5k/(r × c). Roscoe and Byars (1971, p. 759) thought that, where the 5% significance level is used for hypothesis testing, the minimum average expected frequency n/(r × c) should be at least 2 with data from uniform distributions, 4 with data from moderately skewed distributions, and 6 with data from extremely skewed distributions. Conover (1980, p. 156) stated that the minimum expected cell size could be as small as 1 provided r and c were 'not too small'. Agresti (1990, pp. 246–7) stated that the chi-square statistic is adequate when the minimum average expected frequency n/(r × c) exceeds 1, and in general the required minimum average falls as r × c increases; however, the chi square statistic becomes unreliable in tables with both small and moderately large expected frequencies. In our study, the average expected frequency always exceeds 1, and usually exceeds Roscoe and Byars' minimum of 6. Therefore, the use of chi-square is done with confidence.

accounting policies can influence national and international harmony measures. For example, the classification of foreign exchange translation methods (discussed later in Table 1) distinguishes four separate methods:

1. Closing (current) rate method (average rate in the profit and loss account), chosen by thirty-two U.K. companies and twenty-three Australian companies.
2. Closing (current) rate method (closing rate in the profit and loss account)—six U.K. companies, two Australian companies.
3. Temporal method—no U.K. companies, two Australian companies.
4. Closing rate method plus temporal method—no U.K. companies, seven Australian companies.

Apparent harmony can be increased by merging methods, for example, by regarding the closing (current) rate approach as one method, irrespective of the rate used to translate the profit and loss account, and the temporal approach as one method irrespective of its coupling with the closing rate approach. Having a large number of separate accounting methods can produce very low between-country C index values, which indicates little international harmony.

Where a company uses more than one accounting method, the combination has been treated as one method, as illustrated by the case of foreign exchange translation.

Where accounting policies are not fully disclosed by all companies, the data have a 'not-disclosed' category. Careful reading of the full annual report, and in many cases direct communication with the company, reduced the number of non-disclosures. Of the eleven accounting policies looked at, there were no non-disclosures in three (valuation of tangible fixed assets, depreciation of tangible fixed assets, deferred taxation liabilities). There were relatively few non-disclosures in four policies (inventory valuation, goodwill on consolidation, foreign exchange translation, depreciation method). This leaves only four policies (research and development costs, interest on construction, other identifiable intangibles, finance leases) where the number of non-disclosures was large and their impact rather uncertain.

Archer and McLeay (1995) and Archer *et al.* (1995, 1996) suggest three alternative ways to handle non-disclosures: they can be omitted from all statistical analyses, treated as not applicable, or treated as if the item exists but the method is not disclosed.[9] Their suggestions are in the context of the C index. Treating non-disclosures as not applicable means that, for the item in question, each non-disclosing company is comparable with all other non-disclosers and with every disclosing company. Consequently, the numerator and denominator of the C index are increased to allow for the impact of non-disclosures, giving a disclosure-adjusted comparability index. In contrast, if the item exists but the method is not disclosed, the C index denominator, but not the numerator, is increased to allow for non-disclosures, giving a raw comparability index. The disclosure-adjusted C index will

[9] They also state that sometimes a 'default' assumption may be made whereby non-disclosers can be assumed, from the surrounding circumstances, to use a particular method, such as one required by an accounting standard. In that case, non-disclosers can simply be added to companies disclosing that they do use the method. In their statistical model, Archer *et al.* (1996, p. 13) alternately treat non-disclosures as equivalent to an additional accounting method or ignore them.

usually produce higher scores, and the raw C index always lower scores, than the C index which omits non-disclosures entirely. Morris and Parker (1998) present formulae for, and simulations of, disclosure-adjusted and raw versions of the between-country C index (and an extension to the H and I indices).

To illustrate Archer and McLeay's (1995) and Archer *et al.*'s (1995, 1996) rules, suppose that, in the fixed asset valuation example, non-disclosers are U.K. 5, and Australia 10. The matrix will now be:

	U.K.	Australia	Total
Historical cost	14	3	17
Revalued	26	37	63
Not disclosed	5	10	15
	45	50	95
H Index			
Disclosure adjusted	0.64	0.91	
Unadjusted	0.55	0.86	
Raw	0.43	0.55	
Between-country C index			
Disclosure adjusted	0.78		
Unadjusted	0.63		
Raw	0.45		

Disclosure-adjusted and raw indices are based on formulae in Morris and Parker (1998, p. 81); the unadjusted indices ignore non-disclosures. In each case, the disclosure-adjusted index values exceed the unadjusted index values, which in turn exceed the raw index values. The effect of non-disclosures increases with their relative frequency—for example, the gap between disclosure-adjusted and raw H indexes is greater for Australia, because it has the larger proportion of non-disclosers.

Deciding how to handle non-disclosures depends on the underlying facts. Using unadjusted indices, that is, ignoring non-disclosures, would be reasonable if non-disclosures were infrequent. Disclosure-adjusted indices should be used if it is known that non-disclosers are 'not applicable' because these companies had no fixed assets. Raw indices should be used if the non-disclosers are known to have fixed assets but have not disclosed the accounting method.

RESULTS

Analysis of Accounting Policies

Table 1 summarizes the data for each accounting policy.

Valuation of tangible fixed assets. There was some national harmony in Australia but little harmony in the U.K. There was little international harmony as shown by the low between-country C index value and the significant chi-square.

Depreciation of tangible fixed assets. There was complete national harmony in Australia but little national harmony in the U.K. About one-third of British

INFLUENCE OF U.S. GAAP IN U.K., AUSTRALIA

TABLE 1

RESULTS: INDIVIDUAL ACCOUNTING POLICIES

	U.K.	Australia	Total	Between-country C index	χ^2	d.f.
Valuation of tangible fixed assets						
Historical Cost	14	3	17			
Current cost	1	0	1			
Revaluation	25	37	62			
	40	40	80	0.60	10.44*	2
H	0.51	0.86				
Depreciation of tangible fixed assets						
All tangible assets (except freehold land and investment properties) depreciated	27	40	67			
Some land and buildings not depreciated	13	0	13			
	40	40	80	0.68	15.52*	1
H	0.56	1.00				
Inventory valuation						
Lower of cost and net realizable value	40	40	80	1.00	0	1
H	1.00	1.00				
Research and development costs						
Written off to P&L a/c	24	17	41			
Both capitalized and written off	1	15	16			
	25	32	57			
Not disclosed	15	8	23			
	40	40	80	discl. adj. 0.76 unadj. 0.53 raw 0.26	12.79*	1
H—Discl. adj.	0.97	0.68				
—Unadj.	0.92	0.50				
—Raw	0.36	0.32				
Goodwill on consolidation						
Written off to reserves	37	0	37			
Amortized	1	33	34			
Written off and amortized	1	0	1			
	39	33	72			
Not disclosed	1	7	8			
	40	40	80	discl. adj. 0.22 unadj. 0.03 raw 0.02	68.12*	2
H—Discl. adj.	0.91	1.00				
—Unadj.	0.90	1.00				
—Raw	0.86	0.68				
Foreign exchange translation of subsidiaries						
Closing (current) rate method (average rate in P&L)	32	23	55			
Closing (current) rate method (closing rate in P&L)	6	2	8			
Temporal method	0	2	2			

TABLE 1 (Continuted)

	U.K.	Australia	Total	Between-country C index	χ^2	d.f.
Closing (current) rate method plus temporal method	0	7	7			
	38	34	72			
Not disclosed	2	6	8			
	40	40	80	discl. adj. 0.66 unadj. 0.58 raw 0.47	12.29*	3
H—Discl. adj.	0.76	0.64				
—Unadj.	0.73	0.51				
—Raw	0.66	0.37				
Interest on construction						
Capitalized	18	15	33			
Not capitalized	3	6	9			
	21	21	42			
Not disclosed	19	19	38			
	40	40	80	discl. adj. 0.90 unadj. 0.65 raw 0.18	1.27	1
H—Discl. adj.	0.93	0.89				
—Unadj.	0.76	0.59				
—Raw	0.21	0.16				
Other identifiable intangibles						
Written off to reserves	4	0	4			
Capitalized and amortized	3	19	22			
Capitalized and not amortized	6	14	20			
	13	33	46			
Not disclosed	27	7	34			
	40	40	80	discl. adj. 0.82 unadj. 0.33 raw 0.09	12.51*	2
H—Discl. adj.	0.93	0.67				
—Unadj.	0.36	0.51				
—Raw	0.04	0.35				
Finance leases						
Capitalized	31	33	64			
Not capitalized	1	0	1			
	32	33	65			
Not disclosed	8	7	15			
	40	40	80	discl. adj. 0.98 unadj. 0.97 raw 0.64	1.06	1
H—Discl. adj.	0.96	1.00				
—Unadj.	0.94	1.00				
—Raw	0.60	0.68				
Deferred taxation liabilities						
Full provision, liability method	2	40	42			
Partial provision, liability method	38	0	38			
	40	40	80	.05	72.38*	1
H	0.91	1.00				

continued overleaf

Table 1 (Continued)

	U.K.	Australia	Total	Between-country C index	χ^2	d.f.
Depreciation method						
Mainly straight line	33	24	57			
Mainly reducing balance	0	1	1			
Both straight line and reducing balance	4	10	14			
Other	3	4	7			
	40	39	79			
Not disclosed	0	1	1			
	40	40	80	discl. adj. 0.55 unadj. 0.54 raw 0.53	5.14[a]	3
H—Discl. adj.	0.70	0.48				
—Unadj.	0.70	0.46				
—Raw	0.70	0.43				

* Significant at 5% level.
[a] May not be reliable.
Discl. adj. = disclosure-adjusted index—assumes non-disclosures are of items not applicable to firms.
Unadj. = index ignores non-disclosures.
Raw = raw index—assumes non disclosures are of items relevant to firms.

companies did not depreciate buildings in 1993. None of them depreciated investment properties and freehold land. Two Australian retail companies (Coles Myer and Foodland) did not depreciate investment properties. There was little international harmony between the U.K. and Australia, as indicated by the between-country C index and chi-square.

Inventory valuation. The lower of cost and net realizable value was the predominant practice and there was complete national harmony in both the U.K. and Australia. There was therefore also complete international harmony as indicated by the between-country C index and chi-square.

Research and development costs. Not all large companies have a research and development function so there were many non-disclosures. Their treatment influences the extent of national and international harmony for this item. If non-disclosures are 'not applicable' (i.e., if the disclosure adjusted indices are used), there was considerable national harmony in the U.K., little in Australia, and some international harmony. If non-disclosures are treated as 'existing but not disclosed' (i.e., if the raw indices are used), the H and between-country C indices indicate little national or international harmony. Similarly, the chi-square tests show little international harmony although these ignore non-disclosures.

Goodwill on consolidation. There was complete or considerable national harmony in both countries but little international harmony between the U.K. and Australia. This reflects the fact that whereas the capitalization and amortization of goodwill on consolidation was the predominant practice in Australia, in the U.K. almost all companies wrote it off against reserves. These conclusions are minimally altered if the indices are adjusted for non-disclosures.

Foreign exchange translation. Subject to the comments above about fineness of classification, there was little national harmony in either country. There was little international harmony according to the between-country C index. Nor does the chi-square statistic indicate international harmony. If the indices are adjusted upwards for non-disclosures there was some national harmony in the U.K. In both countries there was a preference for the closing (current) rate of foreign exchange translation, with most companies using average rather than closing rates in the profit and loss account. U.K. companies did not use the temporal method. The temporal method was, however, used in Australia, sometimes in conjunction with the closing rate method. This may be the result of different interpretations of similar rules rather than a lack in the U.K., compared with Australia, of subsidiaries 'integrated' with their parents.

Interest on construction. The extent of national and international harmony depends on the treatment of non-disclosures. If these are 'not applicable' (i.e., if the disclosure adjusted indices are used), there was considerable national harmony in the U.K., some harmony in Australia, and considerable international harmony between the U.K. and Australia as measured by the between-country C index. If non-disclosures are treated as 'existing but not disclosed' (i.e., if the raw indices are used), there was little national or international harmony. A similar finding emerges from the unadjusted indices, although there was some national harmony in the U.K. The chi square test, which ignores non-disclosures, indicates harmony across both countries, so that it and the between-country C index conflict.

Other identifiable intangibles. Other identifiable intangibles in general exhibited little national or international harmony under H or between-country C indices, with and without adjustment for non-disclosures, and are consistent with the chi-square test. The high disclosure adjusted H index for the U.K. and disclosure adjusted between-country C index are the result of the very high degree of non-disclosure (over two-thirds) by U.K. companies.

Finance leases. The extent of harmony depends on the treatment of non-disclosures. If the disclosure-adjusted indices are used, there was considerable or complete national harmony within each country, and considerable international harmony. A similar picture emerges if non-disclosures are ignored. However, if the raw indices are used, there was little national or international harmony using the index measures. The chi-square and Fisher exact tests reinforce the results for the index measures that ignore non-disclosures or treat them as 'not applicable'. U.K. and Australian accounting standards require the capitalization of finance leases. With one exception, all the U.K. companies which disclosed finance leases capitalized them. The exception was Unilever which stated (our italics) that lease rental payments 'which are *principally* in respect of operating leases, are charged to profit and loss account'. It is highly probable that the non-disclosing U.K. and Australian companies did not have finance leases, and that therefore the raw indices can be ignored.

Deferred taxation liabilities. There was considerable national harmony in both countries, but there is little harmony between the U.K. and Australia. All the Australian companies chose full provision plus the liability method whereas all but two of the U.K. companies chose partial provision and the liability method. The companies that practised full provision instead were the Anglo-Dutch multinationals Shell and Unilever.

Depreciation Method. There was little national harmony in either country. The between-country C index, but not the chi-square, indicates little international harmony. Straight line depreciation was more common than reducing balance in both countries. These results are influenced by classifying as a separate category fourteen firms that used both methods. Merging these firms with those that used straight line only would increase the level of harmony.

The above results show little international harmony between the U.K. and Australia using the between-country C index and the chi-square test. Even with disclosure-adjusted indices there was considerable international harmony on only three policies (inventory valuation, interest on construction, finance leases), some harmony on two policies (identifiable intangibles, research and development) and little harmony on six policies (valuation of tangible fixed assets, depreciation of tangible fixed assets, goodwill on consolidation, foreign exchange translation, deferred taxation liabilities, depreciation method).

U.S. GAAP as an Intervening Factor

Tables 2, 3, 4 and 5 rearrange these results in the light of our hypotheses regarding the influence of U.S. GAAP.

Table 2 shows, for each accounting policy, the number of companies in the U.K. and Australia that either did or did not conform to U.S. GAAP (ignoring non-disclosures). One country is more in conformity with U.S. GAAP if its relative frequency of companies complying with U.S. GAAP significantly exceeds that of the other country. The table suggests that large companies in both countries were either broadly or completely in conformity with U.S. GAAP on five policies: inventory valuation, foreign exchange translation of subsidiaries, interest on construction,

TABLE 2

BROAD CONFORMITY WITH U.S. GAAP

Accounting policy	U.K. Yes	U.K. No	Australia Yes	Australia No	χ^2
Valuation of tangible fixed assets	14	26	3	37	9.04*
Depreciation of tangible fixed assets	27	13	40	0	15.52*
Inventory valuation	40	0	40	0	0
Research and development costs	24	1	17	15	12.79*
Goodwill on consolidation	1	38	33	0	68.12*
Foreign exchange translation of subsidiaries	32	6	32	2	1.79
Interest on construction	18	3	15	6	1.27
Other identifiable intangibles	3	10	19	14	4.46*
Finance leases	31	1	33	0	1.06
Deferred taxation liabilities	2	38	40	0	72.38*
Depreciation method	40	0	40	0	0

* Significant at 5% level.

finance leases, and depreciation method. However, on the other six policies, large U.K. and Australian companies differed significantly on compliance with U.S. GAAP, as shown by the chi-square statistics. Australian companies were more in conformity with U.S. GAAP on four policies: depreciation of tangible fixed assets, goodwill on consolidation, other identifiable intangible assets, and deferred taxation liabilities. U.K. companies were more in conformity with U.S. GAAP on two policies: valuation of tangible fixed assets and research and development costs. Overall, Australian companies were in conformity with U.S. GAAP on more accounting policies than were U.K. companies.

Then examined was whether the level of international harmony was higher when both countries conformed to U.S. GAAP, and lower when only one or neither did. Table 3 ranks the eleven policies in descending order of the between-country C index. Here, broad conformity with U.S. GAAP is defined as any case where at least two-thirds of a country's sample broadly conformed to U.S. GAAP. Both U.K. and Australian companies did so for the first three policies (inventory valuation, finance leases, interest on construction) and the sixth, seventh and ninth policies (depreciation of tangible fixed assets, foreign exchange translation, depreciation method). For the other five policies, one or none of the two sets of companies complied with U.S. GAAP. The probability of observing the foregoing pattern by chance is 0.089 (Mann-Whitney U test) which is not significant at conventional levels. However, foreign exchange translation and depreciation method are the only policies in our study in which U.S. GAAP allows some choice. Conformity with U.S. GAAP for foreign exchange translation and depreciation method will not promote harmony in the way that conformity with U.S. GAAP might for other policies. Omitting the two policies produces a significant result (Mann-Whitney probability = .028). Therefore, international harmony between U.K. and Australian companies is higher when both countries broadly conform to U.S. GAAP and lower when only one or neither of them does.

The above result depends on how 'broad conformity with U.S. GAAP' is defined. If the term is taken to mean a simple majority of companies in a country, then the between-country C index finding is strengthened; if a three-quarters majority, the finding is not statistically significant. On the other hand, if foreign exchange translation and depreciation method are omitted, the finding is significant for all three definitions of 'broad conformity with U.S. GAAP'. A two-thirds majority is thought to be a reasonable middle path for presentation purposes.

Ignoring depreciation method and foreign exchange translation, the chi-squares in Table 3 (taken from Table 1) show that there is harmony for the first three policies but not the others. The chi-squares also show international disharmony in all cases where one or neither country conforms to U.S. GAAP, but only in one case, depreciation of tangible fixed assets, where both countries conform to U.S. GAAP. The finding is consistent with that for the between-country C index.

The two accounting policies where U.K. and Australian companies were furthest apart were goodwill and deferred tax. Both are cases where U.K. GAAP, but not

INFLUENCE OF U.S. GAAP IN U.K., AUSTRALIA

TABLE 3

ACCOUNTING POLICIES: NATIONAL VS. INTERNATIONAL HARMONY

Accounting policy	Between-country C index	H indexes U.K.	H indexes Australia	$\chi 2$	Broad conformity with U.S. GAAP
	Considerable international harmony				
Inventory valuation	1.00	1.00	1.00	0	U.K. and Australia
Finance leases	0.98	0.96	1.00	1.06	U.K. and Australia
Interest on construction	0.90	0.93	0.89	1.27	U.K. and Australia
	Some international harmony				
Other identifiable intangibles	0.82	0.93	0.67	12.51*	Neither
Research and development	0.76	0.97	0.68	12.79*	U.K.
	Little international harmony				
Depreciation of tangible fixed assets	0.68	0.56	1.00	15.52*	U.K. and Australia
Foreign exchange translation	0.66	0.76	0.64	12.29*	U.K. and Australia
Valuation of tangible fixed assets	0.60	0.51	0.86	10.44*	Neither
Depreciation method	0.55	0.70	0.48	5.14	U.K. and Australia
Goodwill	0.22	0.91	1.00	68.12*	Australia
Deferred tax	0.05	0.91	1.00	72.38*	Australia

* Significant at 5% level.
Broad Conformity with U.S. GAAP = at least a two-thirds majority of companies in the country conform with U.S. GAAP.

Australian GAAP, differed substantially from U.S. GAAP. On deferred tax the Australian standard, like the U.S., requires full provision whereas the U.K. standard requires partial provision. (The two companies not complying with the U.K. standard were the Anglo-Dutch multinationals Shell and Unilever.) On goodwill, the U.K. standard in 1993 was more permissive: U.K. companies, unlike Australian and U.S. companies, had the option to amortize goodwill or to write if off immediately to reserves. No U.K. company chose to amortize except Unilever.

TABLE 4

IMPACT OF INTERACTION BETWEEN U.S. GAAP AND AUSTRALIAN/ U.K. STANDARDS ON BROAD CONFORMITY WITH U.S. GAAP

	Standard aligned with U.S. GAAP	Standard not aligned with U.S. GAAP	No standard
Panel A: Australia			
Sample companies broadly conform to U.S. GAAP	7	0	1
Do not broadly conform	0	2	1
		$\chi^2_2 = 8.44$*	
Panel B: U.K.			
Sample companies broadly conform to U.S. GAAP	5	1	1
Do not broadly conform	0	3	1
		$\chi^2_2 = 5.62$	

Broad Conformity with U.S. GAAP = at least a two-thirds majority of companies in the country conform with U.S. GAAP.
* Significant at 5% level.

The results in Tables 2 and 3 can be reinforced by considering the interaction between U.S. GAAP and Australian or U.K. standards on broad conformity of practice with U.S. GAAP. Where Australian or U.K. standards are aligned with U.S. GAAP, practice should exhibit more conformity with U.S. GAAP and, if our hypothesis is correct, the tendency should be greater in Australia. Table 4 shows the results of this analysis, Panel A for Australia, Panel B for the U.K. Again, broad conformity with U.S. GAAP means at least a two-thirds majority of sample companies complying with U.S. GAAP.

In all seven cases where Australian standards were aligned with U.S. GAAP, the Australian sample broadly conformed with U.S. GAAP; in the two cases (valuation of fixed assets, research and development) where standards did not align with U.S. GAAP practice did not broadly conform with U.S. GAAP. In the two cases where there were no Australian standards (interest on construction, identifiable intangibles) practice broadly conformed with U.S. GAAP in one but not both. The pattern in Panel A is statistically significant and is consistent with our hypothesis.

In all cases where U.K. standards were aligned with U.S. GAAP the U.K. sample broadly conformed with U.S. GAAP. Where the U.K. standard conflicted with U.S. GAAP, practice tends not to comply with U.S. GAAP, and broadly conforms with U.S. GAAP on one issue but not both where there were no U.K. standards. Unlike Panel A, the pattern in Panel B is not statistically significant, and this is also consistent with our hypothesis.

TABLE 5

IMPACT OF U.S. LISTING ON BROAD CONFORMITY WITH U.S. GAAP

Accounting policy	U.K.					Australia				
	U.S. listed		Not U.S. listed			U.S. listed		Not U.S. listed		
	Yes	No	Yes	No	χ^2	Yes	No	Yes	No	χ^2
Valuation of tangible fixed assets	9	8	5	18	4.18*	0	7	3	30	0.7
Depreciation of tangible fixed assets	15	2	12	11	5.81*	7	0	33	0	0
Inventory valuation	17	0	23	0	0	7	0	33	0	0
Research and development costs	13	0	11	1	1.13	3	3	14	12	0.03
Goodwill on consolidation	1	15	0	23	1.48	7	0	26	0	0
Foreign exchange translation of subsidiaries	16	1	16	5	2.26	7	0	25	2	0.55
Interest on construction	7	1	11	2	0.03	6	1	9	5	1.05
Other identifiable intangibles	1	6	2	4	0.67	4	3	15	11	0.001
Finance leases	13	1	18	0	1.31	6	0	27	0	0
Deferred taxation liabilities	2	15	0	23	2.85	7	0	33	0	0
Depreciation method	17	0	23	0	0	7	0	33	0	0

* Significant at 5% level.

In Panels A and B, similar patterns and statistical significance to those reported are found if broad conformity with U.S. GAAP means at least a simple majority, a three-quarters majority, or full compliance.[10] The results are also unchanged if depreciation method and foreign exchange translation, where U.S. GAAP is more flexible, are omitted from Table 4. As mentioned, in each case of conformity, the U.K. or Australian standard was issued after the U.S. standard and in many cases it is possible to see a transfer of ideas in the standards between the U.S. and the other countries. In short, there appears to be an interaction effect between U.S. GAAP and Australian or U.K. standards, but the effect is marginally stronger in Australia.

It was hypothesized that the influence of U.S. GAAP in Australia would not be restricted to those Australian companies listed in the U.S. Table 5 decomposes

[10] All chi square tests were compared with the Fisher exact test, the latter conducted after collapsing the not aligned and no standard columns. Results for Panel A are the same under both tests for all definitions of 'broad conformity with U.S. GAAP'. For Panel B both tests give the same results where 'broad conformity with U.S. GAAP' means at least a three-quarter majority or full compliance, but conflict where broad conformity means either a simple majority or a two-thirds majority. On balance, the chi square test is believed by the authors to be more informative as it does not result in any loss of information from aggregating categories.

Table 2 into firms which were/were not listed in the U.S. Inspection of this table suggests that U.K. companies listed in the U.S. were more likely to conform broadly with U.S. GAAP in the case of valuation of tangible fixed assets and depreciation of tangible fixed assets, but on other policies were no more likely to conform with U.S. GAAP than were U.K. companies not listed in the U.S. On all policies U.S.-listed Australian companies were no more likely to conform with U.S. GAAP than their non-U.S.-listed counterparts. These results suggest that U.S.-listing status had a limited effect on conformity with U.S. GAAP for both samples. Therefore, the greater tendency of large Australian companies in general to follow U.S. GAAP than do large U.K. companies, in Tables 2, 3 and 4 appears to be an intervening factor reducing the degree of international harmony between large U.K. and Australian companies. U.S.-listing status does not have a similar impact.

CONCLUSIONS

The hypothesis was that U.S. GAAP could act as an impediment to international harmony of accounting measurement policies in other countries by creating a situation of partial harmony in which some but not all countries harmonized with U.S. GAAP. This idea was tested by examining eleven accounting measurement policies of forty matched pairs of large companies from Australia and the U.K. using data from 1993 annual reports. The hypothesis was that, despite the traditional links between the two countries, U.S. GAAP would have a greater influence on Australian than on U.K. practices at the time, because of the increasing U.S. influence on Australian accounting standards, its accounting profession and increasing direct U.S. investment in Australia. The companies sampled display little international harmony on most accounting policies studied, although they do display considerable or complete *national* harmony on some policies (seven for the U.K. and five for Australia). Australian companies appear to conform more to U.S. GAAP than do U.K. companies. U.K./Australian international harmony is higher when both countries conform to U.S. GAAP, and lower when only one or neither does; while U.S.-listing status seems to have no influence.

The conformity of Australian companies with U.S. GAAP is an example of partial harmonization, which hinders international comparability of accounts and may cause problems for regulators seeking to improve harmonization internationally. The finding may be of interest to national standard setters trying to impose new standards that do not conform to U.S. GAAP.

Although differing levels of conformity with U.S. GAAP is a plausible reason for the lack of international harmony between the U.K. and Australia, it is not a complete explanation. More research, perhaps by examining changes in international harmony across time, is necessary to further explore why these countries, despite their strong historical links, now differ in terms of international harmony of accounting policy measures. Further insight could be obtained by comparing the U.K. and Australian companies individually with large U.S. companies, or U.K. companies with companies in other countries (such as France) whose large companies are known to be influenced by U.S. GAAP. Also, U.K. practices may have moved away from Australian practices because of EU harmonization, as could be shown by comparing U.K. practice with that of other EU countries.

Since 1996, Australia has had a program of harmonizing its accounting standards with those of the IASC (Parker and Porter 2000, p. 39). The revised IASs endorsed by IOSCO in May 2000 have brought IAS GAAP and U.S. GAAP closer together but some differences still remain between the two GAAPs. Therefore, the impact of the Australian/IASC harmonization program on broad conformity with U.S. GAAP among Australian companies is uncertain and requires investigation.

REFERENCES

Adhikari, A., and R. H. Tondkar, 'Environmental Factors Influencing Accounting Disclosure Requirements of Global Stock Exchanges', *Journal of International Financial Management and Accounting*, Summer 1992.

Agresti, A., *Categorical Data Analysis*, John Wiley, 1990.

Archer, S., and S. McLeay, 'On Measuring the Harmonization of Accounting Practices', Paper presented at Workshop on Accounting in Europe, Geneva, 1995.

Archer, S., P. Delvaille and S. McLeay, 'The Measurement of Harmonisation and the Comparability of Financial Statement Items: Within-Country and Between-Country Effects', *Accounting and Business Research*, Spring 1995.

——, 'A Statistical Model of International Accounting Harmonization', *Abacus*, March 1996.

Arpan, J. S., and L. H. Radebaugh, *International Accounting and Multinational Enterprises*, John Wiley, 1985.

Belkaoui, A. R., and S. Jones, *Accounting Theory*, Australian edition, Harcourt Brace, 1996.

Biddle, G. C., and S. M. Saudagaran, 'Foreign Stock Listings: Benefits, Costs and the Accounting Policy Dilemma', *Accounting Horizons*, September 1991.

Brunovs, R., and R. J. Kirsch, 'Goodwill Accounting in Selected Countries and the Harmonization of International Accounting Standards', *Abacus*, September 1991.

Bureau of Industry Economics, *Evaluation of the Investment Promotion and Facilitation Program*, Australian Government Publishing Service, 1996.

Choi, F. D. S., C. A. Frost and G. K. Meek, *International Accounting* 3rd ed., Prentice-Hall, 1999.

Choi, F. D. S., and G. G. Mueller, *International Accounting*, 2nd ed., Prentice-Hall, 1992.

Cochran, W. G., 'The χ^2 Test of Goodness of Fit', *Annals of Mathematical Statistics*, Vol. 23, 1952.

——, 'Some Methods for Strengthening the Common χ^2 Tests', *Biometrics*, December 1954.

Commission of the European Communities, *Accounting Harmonisation: A New Strategy Vis-à-vis International Harmonisation*', 14 November 1995.

Conover, W. J., *Practical Nonparametric Statistics*, 2nd ed., John Wiley, 1980.

Curry, B., and K. D. George, 'Industrial Concentration: A Survey', *Journal of Industrial Economics*, March 1983.

Diga, J., 'Accounting in the Philippines', in N. Baydoun, A. Nishimura and R. Willet (eds), *Accounting in the Asia-Pacific Region*, John Wiley, 1997.

Eddey, P. H., *Accounting for Corporate Combinations and Associations*, 4th ed., Prentice-Hall, 1995.

Emenyonu, E. N., and A. Adhikari, 'Measuring the Degree of International Harmony in Selected Accounting Measurement Practices', *Australian Accounting Review*, Vol. 8, No. 1, 1998.

Emenyonu, E. N., and S. J. Gray, 'EC Accounting Harmonization: An Empirical Study of Measurement Practices in France, Germany, and the UK', *Accounting and Business Research*, Winter 1992.

——, 'International Accounting Harmonization and the Major Developed Stock Market Countries: An Empirical Study', *International Journal of Accounting*, Vol. 31, No. 3, 1996.

'EU Financial Reporting Strategy', *IASC Insight*, June 2000.

Everitt, B. S., *The Analysis of Contingency Tables*, Chapman & Hall, 1977.

Falk, H., 'International Accounting: A Quest for Research', *Contemporary Accounting Research*, Fall 1994.

Financial Accounting Standards Board [FASB], 'Business Combinations' Project Summary, Update 26 January 2001 (from http://www.fasb.org).

Flower, J., 'The Future Shape of Harmonization: The EU versus the IASC versus the SEC', *The European Accounting Review*, Vol. 6, No. 2, 1997.

——, 'Foreign Currency Translation', in C. W. Nobes and R. H. Parker (eds), *Comparative International Accounting*, 5th ed., Prentice-Hall, 1998.

Foster, G., *Financial Statement Analysis*, 2nd ed., Prentice-Hall, 1986.

Gibson, R. W., 'Development of Corporate Accounting in Australia', *Accounting Historians Journal*, Fall 1979, reprinted in Parker (1990).

——, 'Episodes in the Australian Tax Accounting Saga', *Accounting Historians Journal*, Fall 1984, reprinted in Parker (1990).

Gibson, R. W., and Arnold, R., 'The Development of Auditing Standards in Australia', *Accounting Historians Journal*, Spring 1981, reprinted in Parker (1990).

Gray, S. J., and C. B. Roberts, 'Foreign Company Listings on the London Stock Exchange: Listing Patterns and Influential Factors', in T. E. Cooke and C. W. Nobes (eds), *The Development of Accounting in an International Context: A Festschrift in Honour of R. H. Parker*, Routledge, 1997.

Hermann, D., and W. Thomas, 'Harmonisation of Accounting Measurement Practices in the European Community', *Accounting and Business Research*, Autumn 1995.

International Accounting Standards Committee, 'Use of IAS in Countries Around the World', http://www.iasc.org.uk/frame/cen1-12a-d.htm: Internet accessed 5 March 2001.

'IOSCO Report on IAS', *IASC Insight*, June 2000.

Leo, K. J., J. R. Hoggett and J. Radford, *Accounting for Identifiable Intangibles and Goodwill*, Australian Society of Certified Practising Accountants, 1995.

Levitt, A., 'US SEC Makes No Promises', *Accountancy International Edition*, February 1997.

Lewontin, R. C., and J. Felsenstein, 'The Robustness of Homogeneity Tests in 2 × N Tables', *Biometrics*, Vol. 21, 1965.

Luther, R., 'The Development of Accounting Regulation in the Extractive Industries: An International Review', *The International Journal of Accounting*, Vol. 31, No. 1, 1996.

Ma, R., C. Lambert and R. Hopkins, 'International Harmonisation and the Pacific Asia Region', in R. Ma (ed.), *Financial Reporting in the Pacific Asia Region*, World Scientific, 1997.

McLeay, S., D. Neal and T. Tollington, 'International Standardisation and Harmonisation: A New Measurement Technique', *Journal of International Financial Management and Accounting*, Vol. 10, No. 1, 1999.

Meek, G. K., and S. M. Saudagaran, 'A Survey of Research on Financial Reporting in a Transnational Context', *Journal of Accounting Literature*, Vol. 9, 1990.

Miller, M. C., 'Australia', in T. E. Cooke and R. H. Parker (eds), *Financial Reporting in the West Pacific Rim*, Routledge, 1994.

Morris, R. D., and M. R. Barbera, 'A Chronology of the Development of Corporate Financial Reporting in Australia: 1817 to 1988', in Parker (1990).

Morris, R. D., and R. H. Parker, 'International Harmony Measures of Accounting Policy: Comparative Statistical Properties', *Accounting and Business Research*, December 1998.

Most, K. S., 'Toward the International Harmonization of Accounting', *Advances in International Accounting*', Vol. 6, 1994.

Mueller, G. G., H. Gernon and G. K. Meek, *Accounting: An International Perspective*, 4th ed., Irwin, 1997.

Nair, R. D., and W. G. Frank, 'The Impact of Disclosure and Measurement Practices on International Accounting Classifications', *The Accounting Review*, July 1980.

Nobes, C. W., 'International Classification of Financial Reporting', in C. W. Nobes and R. H. Parker, *Comparative International Accounting*, 4th ed., Prentice-Hall, 1998a.

——, 'Harmonization of Financial Reporting', in C. W. Nobes, and R. H. Parker, *Comparative International Accounting*, 4th ed., Prentice-Hall, 1998b.

Norton, J., 'The Impact of Financial Accounting Practices on the Measurement of Profit and Equity: Australia versus the United States', *Abacus*, September 1995.

Organisation for Economic Co-Operation and Development [OECD], *International Direct Investment Statistics Yearbook 1997*, OECD, 1997.

——, *International Direct Investment Statistics Yearbook 1999*, OECD 2000.

Parker, C., and B. Porter, *The CPA Summary of Australian GAAP 2000*, Accountnet, 2000.

Parker, R. H. (ed.), *Accounting in Australia: Historical Essays*, Garland, 1990.

——, 'Harmonizing the Notes in the UK and France: A Case Study in *De Jure* Harmonization', *The European Accounting Review*, Vol. 5, No. 2, 1996.

Pereira, V., R. Paterson, and A. Wilson, *UK/US GAAP Comparison*, 3rd ed., Kogan Page for Ernst & Young, 1994.

Philp, R., 'Comment: Out of Step', *Australian Accounting Review*, May 1993.

Rahman, A., 'Accounting Harmonisation in the Asia-Pacific Region—Outlook and Concerns', *Singapore Accountant,* January/February 1998.

Rahman, A., H. Perera and S. Ganeshanandam, 'Measurement of Formal Harmonisation in Accounting: An Exploratory Study', *Accounting and Business Research*, Autumn 1996.

Roscoe, J. T., and J. A. Byars, 'An Investigation of the Restraints with Respect to Sample Size Commonly Imposed on the Use of the Chi-Square Statistic', *Journal of the American Statistical Association*, December 1971.

Salter, S. B., and C. B. Roberts, 'The IASC Comparability Project: Examining the Outcomes Using Two Theoretical Models', *Advances in International Accounting*, Vol. 9, 1996.

Saudagaran, S. M., and G. K. Meek, 'A Review of Research on the Relationship Between International Capital Markets and Financial Reporting by Multinational Firms', *Journal of Accounting Literature*, Vol. 16, 1997.

Schweikart, J. A., S. J. Gray and S. B. Salter, 'An Interview with Sir Bryan Carsberg, Secretary-General of the International Accounting Standards Committee', *Accounting Horizons*, March 1996.

Snedecor, G. W., and W. G. Cochran, *Statistical Methods*, 6th ed., Iowa State University Press, 1967.

Tarca, A., 'The Measurement of International Harmonisation in Financial Reporting', *Australian Accounting Review*, Vol. 8, No. 1, 1998.

Tay, J. S. W., 'Financial Reporting in the UK and the Netherlands Before and After the Implementation of the Fourth Directive: Evidence on Harmony, Harmonization and Quality of Information', Paper presented at the 17th Annual Congress of the European Accounting Association, Venice, April 1994.

Tay, J. S. W., and R. H. Parker, 'Measuring International Harmonization and Standardization', *Abacus*, March 1990.

United Nations Conference on Trade and Development (UNCTAD), *World Investment Report 2000: Cross-border Mergers and Acquisitions and Development*, United Nations, 2000.

van der Tas, L. G., 'Measuring Harmonisation of Financial Reporting Practice', *Accounting and Business Research*, Spring 1988.

——, *Harmonization of Financial Reporting*, Datawyse, 1992a.

——, 'Measuring International Harmonization and Standardization: A Comment', *Abacus*, September 1992b.

Walker, R. G., 'International Accounting Compromises: The Case of Consolidation Accounting', *Abacus*, December 1978.

Wallace, R. S. O., 'Survival Strategies of Global Organization: The Case of the International Accounting Standards Committee', *Accounting Horizons*, June 1990.

Weetman, P., and S. J. Gray, 'A Comparative International Analysis of the Impact of Accounting Principles on Profits: The USA versus the UK, Sweden and The Netherlands', *Accounting and Business Research*, Autumn 1991.

Weetman, P., E. A. E. Jones, C. A. Adams and S. J. Gray, 'Profit Measurement and UK Accounting Standards: A Case of Increasing Disharmony in Relation to US GAAP and IASs', *Accounting and Business Research*, Summer 1998.

Wolk, H. I., and P. H. Heaston, 'Toward the Harmonization of Accounting Standards: An Analytical Framework', *The International Journal of Accounting*, September 1992.

Wu, F. H., J. Kang, C.-C. Yeh and S.-H. Lin, 'Financial and Management Practices in Taiwan', in N. Baydoun, A. Nishimura and R. Willet (eds), *Accounting in the Asia-Pacific Region*, John Wiley, 1997

Wyatt, A., 'International Accounting Standards: A New Perspective', *Accounting Horizons*, September 1989.

Yarnold, J. K., 'The Minimum Expectation in χ^2 Goodness of Fit Tests and the Accuracy of Approximations for the Null Hypothesis', *Journal of the American Statistical Association*, June 1970.

Zeff, S. A. 'Forging Accounting Principles in Australia', Australian Society of Accountants Bulletin No. 14, March 1973. Reprinted in Parker (1990).

——, 'The Coming Confrontation on International Accounting Standards', Research Seminar, School of Accounting, University of New South Wales, March 1998.

[10]

Accounting and Business Research. Vol. 26, No. 4, pp. 325–339, 1996

Measurement of Formal Harmonisation in Accounting: An Exploratory Study

Asheq Rahman, Hector Perera and Siva Ganeshanandam*

Abstract—Extant research in evaluation of accounting harmonisation has mainly focused on measurement of harmonisation and evaluation of its impact on share market indicators. Within these themes, however, researchers have been studying the impact of formal harmonisation on material harmonisation, and share prices and returns. Given the important role formal harmonisation plays in accounting harmonisation, this study introduces a methodology for the measurement of formal accounting harmony between countries. The methodology introduced in this paper can be used to identify areas of harmony or disharmony for policy-making purposes. It also provides means of gaining valuable insights into the nature of harmony or disharmony between different countries' accounting rules. Finally, it creates new grounds for examining various other aspects of accounting harmonisation.

1. Introduction

Growing economic cooperation between countries at both global and regional levels has led to greater attention being paid to empirical evaluation of international accounting harmonisation (e.g., see Nobes, 1992). In the accounting literature, the concept of harmonisation has been interpreted in a number of different ways. Tay and Parker (1990) identified two types of harmonisation, namely, de facto harmonisation and de jure harmonisation. The former refers to harmonisation between practices and the latter to harmonisation between regulations. They also differentiated between harmonisation and standardisation, explaining that harmonisation meant clustering of accounting practice around a few available methods with a view to achieving harmony between accounting practices; and standardisation meant strict adherence to one set of rules to achieve uniformity in practices. Van der Tas (1988 and 1992b) provided an alternative terminology for describing harmonisation. He called de jure harmonisation 'formal harmonisation' and de facto harmonisation, irrespective of whether the practices were influenced by regulations or not, 'material harmonisation'.

Extant studies on the evaluation of accounting harmonisation have focused on the investigation of material harmonisation or its effects, rather than researching formal harmonisation. However, practically every study evaluating material harmonisation has measured the effects of the state of formal harmony on practice. For example, Nair and Frank (1981), Evans and Taylor (1982), Doupnik and Taylor (1985) and Yang and Lee (1994) explore the effects of International Accounting Standards Committee standards; Emenyonu and Gray (1992), van der Tas (1992b) and Walton (1992) study the impact of the EU Fourth Directive; and Alford et al. (1993), Amir et al. (1993) and Barth and Clinch (1994) examine the effects of certain countries' accounting standards on share prices, through the standards' effects on accounting numbers. It is, therefore, well recognised that a primary factor driving material harmonisation is formal harmonisation. This view is also evident from the findings of Alford et al. (1993), Amir et al. (1993) and Barth and Clinch (1994), that differences between generally accepted accounting principles of different countries lead to share price and return variations. This, they found, was due to the variations in value relevance of different countries' GAAPs. Consequently, this study proposes to demonstrate the use of a research de-

*The authors are at Massey University, New Zealand. They gratefully acknowledge: the New Zealand Society of Accountants Coopers & Lybrand Peter Barr Fellowship and the Massey University Research Fund for funding the project; Kevin Simpkins of Ernst and Young, associate professor Lindsay Trotman of the Department of Business Law, Massey University, and April McKenzie and Robert Lowe of the New Zealand Society of Accountants, for providing necessary information; and Janice Loftus, Mike Adams, Joanne Locke, and participants of the Massey University Department of Accountancy Seminar Series, Centre for Accounting and Auditing Seminar Series, Nanyang Technological University and the 1994 Annual Conference of the Accounting Association of Australia and New Zealand for their comments and support. Correspondence should be addressed to Dr Rahman, Department of Accountancy, Massey University, Palmerston North, New Zealand. This paper was received in June 1994 and accepted in January 1996.

sign for evaluating the state of formal harmony across countries.

The remainder of the paper is organised into five sections. Section 2 reviews the literature on accounting harmonisation evaluation and establishes the purposes of this study. Section 3 sets out the research design used for making the necessary comparisons. Section 4 describes the data. The results of the comparisons are analysed in Section 5, with some conclusions reported in the final section.

2. Extant literature

The reviews of international financial accounting research, e.g. Meek and Saudagaran (1990), Wallace and Gernon (1991), Choi and Mueller (1992), Wallace (1992) and Radebaugh and Gray (1993), identify a group of studies that have statistically clustered countries based on accounting and environmental parameters. Within these studies, Wallace and Gernon (1991) explain, accounting practices are compared and contrasted to identify the relative similarity or dissimilarity between different countries. The primary aim of these studies was to broadly categorise the countries or to evaluate the influence of the environmental factors on the general level of disclosure practices or requirements in different countries.

The cluster studies may be seen as a first major step towards examining international accounting harmonisation empirically. Tay and Parker (1990) and Emenyonu and Gray (1992) have identified several studies that empirically measure accounting harmonisation between different countries.[1] Other studies, such as Walton (1992) and van der Tas (1992b), have followed since these reviews.

Measurement studies mainly investigate material harmony at a point in time (e.g., van der Tas, 1988; Walton, 1992; Emenyonu and Gray, 1992) or movements in harmony (e.g., Nair and Frank, 1981; Evans and Taylor, 1982; van der Tas 1992b; and Yang and Lee, 1994). In addition, there have been studies that used other methods for evaluating harmonisation or the need for harmonisation. For example, Adhikari and Tondkar (1992) examined the reasons for the variation between accounting regulations. More recently, a new dimension has been added to research in accounting harmonisation by studying the effects of accounting practice and regulations on share price and return movements. The objective of this type of research is to examine the justification for accounting harmonisation (e.g., Alford et al., 1993; Amir, Trevor and Venuti, 1993; Barth and Clinch, 1994). However, one caveat here is that they do not ascertain whether the accounting numbers are actually being used by investors or how they are being used in share trading decisions.

In short, empirical studies on accounting harmonisation have focused on the state of accounting harmony by measuring the level of material harmony, identifying the reasons for formal harmony and disharmony or examining the impact of the state of harmony on share prices and returns. Therefore, they may be broadly classified as evaluation studies.

From a contextual viewpoint, two groups of studies can be identified in the extant literature on evaluation of harmonisation, i.e., those with a global perspective (e.g., Nair and Frank, 1981; Evans and Taylor, 1982; Alford et al., 1993; Amir et al., 1993 and Barth and Clinch, 1994) and those with a regional perspective (e.g., Doupnik and Taylor, 1985; Walton, 1992; Emenyonu and Gray, 1992; van der Tas, 1992b; Yang and Lee, 1994). The first group uses sample countries (employing Price Waterhouse International indices) or companies from sample countries (using other databases or annual reports) to study the variation in accounting rules and practices between countries at a global level. The second group focuses on evaluating harmonisation within particular clusters of countries.

Accounting harmonisation studies are very much at an experimental stage, where methodology and analytical techniques are still being proposed and tested on particular samples of accounting issues and countries. The accounting issues and countries, in most cases, are to a certain extent purposively selected. For example, global studies of Nair and Frank (1981) and Evans and Taylor (1982) have selected certain basic issues covered by early IASC standards to study the impact of IASC initiatives on global accounting practices. Despite similarities in their purpose, they varied in their results. This is attributable to the differences in the issues selected, countries examined and the analytical techniques used.

Similarly, regional studies have been primarily motivated by regional initiatives to harmonise accounting practice. For example, Walton (1992), Emenyonu and Gray (1992) and van der Tas (1992b), have studied the impact of the EU Fourth Directive on material harmonisation. Some regional studies have, however, investigated the impact of global initiatives. For example, Doupnik and Taylor (1985) and Yang and Lee (1994) studied the movement towards harmonisation by western European and pan Pacific countries, respectively, in response to IASC standards. Again, results of regional studies vary because of variations in the analytical techniques adopted and samples of issues and countries selected.

[1] Van der Tas (1992a) has argued that not all of the six studies Tay and Parker (1990) reviewed were studies specifically dealing with harmonisation. Tay and Parker (1992) have contended that all six studies were 'more or less' (p. 217) linked with harmonisation.

The market-based studies, such as Alford et al. (1993), Amir, Trevor and Venuti (1993) and Barth and Clinch (1994), have been more purposive in that they examined a particular regulatory measure — the need for Securities and Exchange Commission US GAAP reconciliation requirement for overseas firms listed on US stock exchanges. However, these studies have special experimental features; for example, they look at the effects of only some of the accounting standards or accounting numbers. Moreover, the causal relationship between GAAP and share prices has yet to be clearly established, especially for countries where accounting standards do not necessarily reflect GAAP due to weaker forms of enforcement than that of the US.

Data instruments or sources of data used in harmonisation studies have been mainly of five types: annual reports, accounting regulations, public databases, questionnaires and laboratory techniques. All those using annual reports, public databases, questionnaires and laboratory techniques studied material harmonisation. The only formal harmonisation study, Adhikari and Tondkar (1992), used stock exchanges' listing requirements as the source for accounting regulations. All annual report studies have small samples (between nine to 26 firms from each country surveyed) of mainly large firms. However, in making this observation one should appreciate the difficulties involved in collecting information from annual reports.

The use of public databases, such as Price Waterhouse International indices (PWI 1973, 1975 and 1979), in some of the studies created complications. PWI (1973, 1975 and 1979) seem to mix de jure and de facto aspects in a perplexing way. For example, they rank required and insisted upon methods higher than predominant practice. Required methods and, more specifically, insisted upon methods cannot always ensure greater adherence to a practice; especially if prescriptions are issued without government backing, they may at times be minority practice. The adoption of current cost accounting and investment property accounting standards in New Zealand highlighted this issue. In the case of current cost accounting, the standard had to be reduced to the status of a recommendation in 1986 due to non-compliance and, for investment property accounting, the standard had to be changed in 1989 to accommodate the predominant practices. Accounting standards in New Zealand had no government backing until July 1994. Therefore, they did not attract 100% compliance, as is assumed by PWI indices. A similar situation prevailed in most countries at the time of the PWI surveys. Consequently, the PWI indices' mixing of regulations with practices to reflect prevailing practices is misleading. In addition to this, Nobes (1981) identified several other problems associated with PWI indices.

For their study of formal harmonisation, Adhikari and Tondkar (1992) surveyed the reporting requirements of 35 stock exchanges from different countries. Although this is commendable, their study did not include other more influential sources of regulation, i.e., statutory requirements and accounting standards. In countries such as the UK, US, Australia and New Zealand, both company law and accounting standards are more prescriptive than stock exchange requirements in financial reporting. They not only influence the stock exchange requirements for financial disclosure, but also directly influence the listed firms on many issues not included in the stock exchange requirements.

Those measuring harmony at a point in time, or changes between the state of harmony between two points in time, use some form of frequency analysis. Van der Tas (1988 and 1992b) propagates the idea of indices, and meticulously develops the indices, H, C and I. These indices are mainly useful to measure material harmony. Tay and Parker (1990) favour the idea of statistical analyses, such as chi-square tests. More recently, Emenyonu and Gray (1992), appreciating the usefulness of both statistical analyses and indices, adopted both types of techniques. Their analyses clearly show that the two sets of techniques are complementary for the purpose of measuring material harmonisation.

Studies explaining the differences between accounting practices or regulations, or the influence of accounting variations on share prices and returns, adopt causal models such as regression. In the studies dealing with explaining the differences between practices or regulations, the aim is to identify the determinants of the variations in practice or regulations. In the case of the studies dealing with share price and return fluctuations, accounting practice and regulations are seen as the determinants of the observed phenomenon.

Judging from the important findings, strengths and weaknesses of the harmonisation studies, it is clear that harmonisation research has several dimensions. There are those studies that measure material harmony as an outcome of formal harmonisation; and those that explain the reasons for the state of formal harmony, and, more recently, market-based studies have extended research to understand the effects of material harmony on stock market indicators. Although harmonisation researchers should be commended for their ingenuity and resourcefulness, there are still many issues that need attention, one of which is the measurement of formal harmony — the theme of this research.

Tay and Parker (1990) observed that insufficient research had been done to date on the measurement of harmonisation. Walton (1992) and Emenyonu and Gray (1992) made observations that measurement studies have only been exploratory in nature. Emenyonu and Gray (1992) felt the need for comprehensive studies covering several accounting issues in all countries of a region or economic grouping. In this respect, this study is aimed at providing a means of comprehensively evaluating formal accounting harmony. The motivation of this study is also tuned within the objectives of a regional economic initiative, in that it exemplifies the manner in which formal harmony could be evaluated within the context of a particular setting.

This study provides for the measurement of differences between the requirements of two countries by accounting categories, generally specified by the countries being examined. Since in each category there are normally several subsets of requirements, the study illustrates the use of a multivariate statistical technique, the multiple discriminant analysis, to identify categories where similarities and dissimilarities exist. This technique allows for composite measures for each category.

3. Research design

The research design adopted in this study demonstrates the application of empirical analyses to measure formal accounting harmony. An attempt is made to conduct a detailed analysis of the state of formal harmony between two neighbouring countries, Australia and New Zealand.

There are two reasons for the choice of Australia and New Zealand for this study. First, cluster studies based on broad environmental or accounting practice variables have identified the two countries as members of the same country cluster (da Costa, Bourgeois and Lawson, 1978; Frank, 1979; Nair and Frank, 1980; Nobes, 1992). Broad comparisons of the accounting standards (Sharpe and McGregor, 1993a; 1993b) and detailed comparison of accounting regulatory mechanisms (Rahman, Perera and Tower, 1994) also confirm the view that, in general, the two countries' accounting regulatory environments are similar. The broad similarities between them will allow the results of the comparisons to be meaningfully interpreted. For example, since the two countries' regulatory systems are alike, similar requirements in an area would mean that the reporting entities in both countries are faced with analogous rules. In other words, similar requirements would indeed mean greater harmony. However, if the regulatory systems were very different, for instance if one country had government-backed standards and the other had non-binding professional guidelines, similar requirements in an area would not mean that material harmony is high, because variations in practice may still exist despite such formal harmony.

Second, growing business relations between Australia and New Zealand through the Closer Economic Relations (CER) efforts, strengthened by the similarities in their economic, legal and accounting infrastructures, have led to demands for uniformity in the two countries' regulations and regulatory mechanisms (Holmes et al., 1986; Lloyd, 1991). In the accounting domain, Australia's and New Zealand's professional bodies have shown great interest in recent years in harmonising their standards and practices. Increased participation in each other's activities, such as setting accounting standards and competency standards for professional accountants, clearly indicates their willingness to cooperate in achieving common objectives (Birkett, 1993; *New Zealand Herald*, 8 March 1989; Sharpe and McGregor, 1993a, 1993b; Hill, 1993). Such signals of close relations indicate that this study's results will be of use to policy-makers.

This study involves a comparison of all accounting requirements applicable to listed companies. These companies are important players in the international capital markets, and they are of immediate concern for the purposes of business regulation harmonisation under the CER Agreement (1993) between Australia and New Zealand (Reports to Governments by Steering Committee of Officials, 1992). However, the same analysis can be extended to include other types of business and non-business entities.

To make the comparison exhaustive, the disclosure and measurement requirements are matched separately. Another reason for the separation between the two types of requirement is that, of late, accounting policy-makers in Australia and New Zealand, like those of other Anglo-American countries, have seen more criticism in measurement areas than in disclosure. The separate comparisons would allow a clear exposure of measurement requirement differences.

The typology used for identifying the nature of the requirements is as follows:

Type 1. **Required** for all listed companies, i.e., requirements of the statutes, stock exchange listing requirements and accounting standards.

Type 2. **Recommended or suggested** by the statutes, stock exchange listing requirements, accounting standards, accounting guidelines (Australia) and technical practice aids (New Zealand).

Type 3. **Allowed or not required or not prohibited** by the above requirements.

Type 4. **Not permitted** by the statutes, stock exchange listing requirements or accounting standards.

A similar typology was used by Gray, Campbell and Shaw (1984) to identify the different types of requirement for disclosure and measurement. In this scheme all items of disclosure and measurement are given equal weight. There are certain categories of requirement (e.g., consolidation and fixed assets) that can be regarded as more important than others. These areas generally have a larger number of requirements. Therefore, for the purposes of analyses in this study, the weight of the importance of an issue is reflected through the number of items in a category of requirements.

The requirement for each item of disclosure and measurement using the above typology is considered to be providing discrete data. This is because the types of requirement identified do not represent a particular order of intensity in regard to accounting harmonisation. Although Types 1 and 4 requirements are coercive enough to create definite patterns of accounting practice, Types 2 and 3 requirements lack the strength to create such an impact. From the harmonisation viewpoint, if one country chooses to use Type 1 requirement for an accounting issue and the other chooses Type 4 requirement for the same accounting issue, then the outcome will invariably be disharmony for that issue. Conversely, if both countries choose either Type 1 or Type 4 requirement for an accounting issue, then the most likely outcome will be harmony. However, since both Types 2 and 3 requirements are of insufficient coercive influence for standardising practice, if the two countries choose to adopt any of these two types of requirements for an accounting issue, there will be ample room for disharmony in practice for that issue. The numbering of requirements does not imply that the data are ordinal in form in the sense of harmony. In other words, the data could be treated as discrete data, i.e., no particular strength attached to the difference between the two countries' observed requirements. Given that Types 1 and 4 requirements are of greater strength than Types 2 and 3 requirements, one could suggest that some form of weighting could be used to reflect this. However, no weighting procedure was used because such procedures themselves introduce subjectivity. Introduction of such subjectivity is evident from the multifarious interpretations of the Price Waterhouse International (1979) typology by Nobes (1981), Belkaoui (1983) and Cooke and Wallace (1990). Therefore, the requirements (the observations of this study) have been treated as discrete data of equal weight.

Tay and Parker (1990 and 1992) and van der Tas (1988 and 1992b) suggested the use of international harmonisation indices (C and I indices) for measuring the degree of accounting harmonisation between countries. These indices were meant for measuring de facto or material harmonisation, not de jure or formal harmonisation. The calculations of the indices require the information regarding the adoption of different accounting methods by different firms. This study, however, proposes to measure the similarities or differences in the two countries' disclosure and measurement requirements under the various categories mentioned above. In other words, it is an attempt to make an item by item comparison by relevant categories. This was achieved by applying the following statistical procedure.

Multiple discriminant analysis (MDA) was conducted to measure the level of harmony between the two countries' disclosure and measurement requirements, according to the categories in Table 1. For this analysis, the specific requirements under each category were seen as observations, and the categories as groups of observations. The concept of distance between groups of observations is often used as a measure of discrimination. The generalised distance analogous to the Mahalanobis distance, which has been shown to be fairly robust with discrete variables (Krzanowiski, 1988), was considered appropriate for this study because it focuses on identifying the varying differences between categories of attributes (i.e., measurement and disclosure requirements in this case). Krzanowiski (1988) points out that, since Mahalanobis distance is primarily defined for continuous variables, the use of the distance on discrete data should be treated purely in a descriptive fashion. In other words, all significance tests applied to this data must be treated with caution. Nevertheless, the Mahalanobis distance procedure computes distance measures between objects that are comparable to the R^2 in regression analysis (Hair et al., 1992).

Every observation within the categories has been re-expressed as a set of binary variables (with an abitrary scoring of 0 or 1) because it is easier to work with binary variables while applying Mahalanobis analysis on discrete variables (Krzanowiski, 1988). This conversion was performed on the data and then the Mahalanobis-like distances were calculated. It was decided to compute these distances between Australia and New Zealand for each category of requirements separately, so that discrimination for the different categories could be ranked accordingly.

To amplify the discrimination, the distances were supplemented by data regarding the number of exact matches between the two countries' requirements within each category. This matching process took into consideration what the requirements stated and their strength. The number of requirements in the different types of prescriptions for each category was also computed, to understand whether the strength of the requirements was a contributing factor in the variances.

In short, the research design is set up in a sequence that allows for the identification of (a) categories of requirement with variances between two countries, and (b) the degree of uniformity within each category to see if the variance is due to any mismatch of requirements. This is followed by an examination of whether the strength of the requirements was a contributing factor for the variance between the two countries. However, a detailed examination of the reasons for the differences between the requirements is outside the scope of this study.

4. Data

As a measure of comprehensiveness, the study includes all the three main sources of accounting regulation that affect listed firms, i.e., statutory requirements, stock exchange listing requirements and accounting standards. It is expected that this will provide for a more robust inquiry into the measurement of formal harmony between countries. The following sources of information were used to collect the necessary data for the two countries.

Australia:

1. CCH *Australian Corporations Law Guide*, 1993.
2. *Listing Rules* of the Australian Stock Exchange as at July 1993.
3. *1993 Model Financial Accounts* of the Centre for Professional Development (Australia).
4. *Members' Handbook*, as at December 1993, of the Australian Society of Certified Practising Accountants.

New Zealand:

1. Companies Act 1993.
2. Financial Reporting Act 1993.
3. CCH *Guide Book to New Zealand Companies and Securities Law*, 1990.
4. *New Zealand Stock Exchange Listing Requirements* as at May 1993.
5. *1993 Model Financial Statements* of the Centre for Professional Development (NZ) Ltd.
6. *New Zealand Accounting Standards* as at December 1993.

The categories of disclosure and measurement requirements are shown in Table 1. In preparing Table 1, an attempt has been made to maintain the same disclosure and measurement categories used in the three main sources of regulation.

In both New Zealand and Australia, the companies/corporations statutes and listing requirements provide only disclosure requirements, and accounting standards provide disclosure and measurement rules. Therefore, for disclosure categories, all relevant items as required by the companies/corporations statutes, listing requirements and accounting standards and their respective schedules were collected. For measurement categories, the accounting treatments of major items as laid out in the accounting standards were collected. Most items of information were clearly identifiable, and were categorised in a similar manner in the two countries. Nevertheless, there were some items that could not be matched directly. An effort was made to include such requirements of both countries under a representative category. For example, in classifying assets, a very broad category, i.e., non-current assets, is used in Australia. This category has been covered by several accounting standards in New Zealand. Therefore, the Australian category was broken down to match with the various categories identified in the New Zealand accounting standards, such as fixed assets and investment properties.

Furthermore, some refinements had to be made by creating a few additional categories for both countries, and eliminating duplication between categories that arose from some requirements being stated differently in different sources of regulation. The refinement process also included interviewing the financial accounts controllers of some of the New Zealand companies that were listed in both Australia and New Zealand to identify subtle differences between the two countries' requirements that the researchers could have overlooked. A total of 12 companies are currently listed on both New Zealand and Australian stock exchanges.[2] Nine of the 12 companies responded to the request for interviews. Two out of the nine that responded could not participate in the research because of their own time pressures, and one could not be scheduled for an interview because of the researchers' time constraints. Therefore, only six controllers could be interviewed.[3] The interviews were semi-structured, focusing on the issues of this research. This allowed the executives to bring in matters of concern that were initially not included in the research design.

With these refinements, 518 disclosure items spread over 31 categories and 469 measurement items spread over 28 categories were established.

5. Analysis and results

The following comparisons were conducted to identify and explain the similarities and differences between Australian and New Zealand disclosure and measurement requirements:

a) Disclosure requirements of:
 (i) accounting standards as at 30 October 1993;
 (ii) legislations as at 30 October 1993;

---

[2] Although only 12 firms are listed in both countries, the number of firms that operate or are incorporated on both sides of the Tasman is much larger.

[3] The companies whose executives were interviewed are: Carter Holt Harvey Ltd.; Fletcher Challenge Ltd.; Heritage Mining; Lion Nathan Ltd.; New Zealand Oil and Gas; and Telecom New Zealand Ltd.

Table 1
Schedule of Disclosure and Measurement Categories

	Disclosure requirements		*Measurement requirements*
D1	General issues	M1	Fixed assets (New Zealand)/non-current Assets (Australia)
D2	Profit and loss disclosures	M2	Depreciation of fixed/non-current assets
D3	Other profit and loss items, i.e., to be disclosed through notes or as supplementary information	M3	Leases
D4	Format of statements	M4	Inventories
	Balance sheet disclosures:	M5	Investment properties
D5	Receivables	M6	Properties intended for sale
D6	Inventories	M7	Joint ventures
D7	Investments	M8	Partnerships
D8	Property, plant and equipment	M9	Debt defeasance
D9	Leases	M10	Set-off of debt
D10	Intangibles	M11	Subsequent events
D11	Liabilities (current and non-current)	M12	Contingencies
D12	Other disclosures with respect to liabilities	M13	Research and development
D13	Provisions	M14	Expenditure carried forward
D14	Share capital	M15	Accounting for tax
D15	Reserves	M16	Extraordinary items and prior period adjustments
D16	Other supplementary disclosure with respect to assets and liabilities	M17	Cash flow information
D17	Accounting policy	M18	Consolidation
D18	Foreign currency	M19	Foreign currency
D19	Segments	M20	Segments
D20	Construction contracts	M21	Related party Disclosure
D21	Extractive industry	M22	Construction contracts
D22	Earnings per share	M23	Extractive industry
D23	Miscellaneous disclosure	M24	Marketable securities
	Group accounts	M25	Pensions
D24	Consolidated statements	M26	Livestock
D25	Equity accounting	M27	Bloodstock
D26	Joint ventures	M28	Earnings per share
D27	Partnerships		
D28	Related party disclosures		
	Cash flow information		
D29	Cash flows related to operating activities		
D30	Cash flows related to investing activities activities		
D31	Cash flows related to financing activities		

(iii) stock exchange listing requirements as at 30 October 1993;

(iv) accounting standards[4], legislative requirements and stock exchange listing requirements as at 30 October 1993, combined together.

b) Measurement requirements of accounting standards as at 30 October 1993.

Tables 2 to 6 provide the distance measures, the percentage of exact matches and items in each prescription type for Australia and New Zealand for the various requirements categories. The categories are listed in ascending order of distance between the two countries. Distance measures range from zero to infinity. The distance measures mean the extent of dissimilarity or likeness between Australia and New Zealand for each category of requirement. For example, a zero difference indicates that the two countries have uniform requi-

[4] For the purpose of this study, the Australian accounting standards included standards approved by the Australian Accounting Standards Board, the standards endorsed by the Institute of Chartered Accountants of Australia and the Australian Society of Certified Practising Accountants, and the Australian Accounting Research Foundation's accounting guidelines. In terms of their strength, standards were seen as prescriptive and the guidelines as suggestive. The New Zealand accounting standards included all accounting standards and Technical Practice Aids of the New Zealand Society of Accountants. In terms of their strength, standards were seen as prescriptive and the practice aids as suggestive.

Table 2
Comparison of combined disclosure requirements of Australia and New Zealand

Disclosure requirements		*Items in each type of prescription*								*% of exact matches*	*Distance*
		New Zealand				*Australia*					
Category	*No. of items*	*1*	*2*	*3*	*4*	*1*	*2*	*3*	*4*		
D17	9	9	-	-	-	9	-	-	-	100.0	0.0000
D20	2	2	-	-	-	2	-	-	-	100.0	0.0000
D29	9	9	-	-	-	9	-	-	-	100.0	0.0000
D30	10	10	-	-	-	10	-	-	-	100.0	0.0000
D9	12	10	-	1	1	10	-	1	1	83.3	0.0000
D18	7	4	-	3	-	4	-	3	-	71.4	0.0000
D7	33	20	-	13	-	23	-	10	-	48.5	0.0356
D3	61	46	1	14	-	42	-	19	-	47.5	0.0635
D25	11	8	2	1	-	9	1	1	-	54.5	0.0660
D31	9	7	-	2	-	8	-	1	-	88.9	0.0808
D8	20	17	-	3	-	19	-	1	-	80.0	0.1086
D11	22	19	-	3	-	16	-	6	-	68.2	0.1123
D1	31	24	-	7	-	28	-	3	-	67.7	0.1229
D24	31	23	-	5	3	16	2	10	3	32.3	0.1229
D13	7	2	-	5	-	4	-	3	-	14.3	0.3117
D19	10	9	-	1	-	9	1	-	-	80.0	0.4000
D5	23	15	-	8	-	21	-	2	-	56.5	0.4251
D28	33	24	-	9	-	33	-	-	-	72.7	0.7273
D4	16	5	1	6	4	6	-	10	-	50.0	0.8784
D6	15	10	-	5	-	15	-	-	-	66.7	0.9333
D2	24	17	6	1	-	18	-	6	-	62.5	0.9583
D26	8	8	-	-	-	5	-	3	-	62.5	1.0500
D10	11	10	-	1	-	5	-	4	2	45.5	1.2024
D14	19	18	-	1	-	9	-	10	-	52.6	1.4211
D16	10	3	-	7	-	9	-	1	-	20.0	2.1600
D2	21	20	-	1	-	8	-	13	-	42.9	2.2120
D15	9	9	-	-	-	4	-	5	-	44.4	2.2222
D23	14	8	3	3	-	-	7	7	-	0.0	2.4762
D22	5	1	4	-	-	3	-	2	-	20.0	7.4667
D27	13	10	-	1	2	-	-	13	-	7.7	22.1539
D21	13	-	7	6	-	12	-	1	-	0.0	24.3077

Key
Type of prescription:
1. Required
2. Recommended or suggested
3. Allowed/permitted or not required
4. Not permitted

rements for the category concerned, whereas a very high distance figure represents a category that has two very different sets of requirements or an instance where one country has a set of requirements and the other has none. However, extremely large distance figures may also be unreliable. In such cases the covariances of the two sets of requirements, which were used as a denominator in the calculation of Mahalanobis distances, were too small to provide a precise measure. Distance figures greater than 99 have been stated as 99.0000 to keep the table columns up to six digits.

In the case of percentage of matches within each category (see '% of exact matches' column, Tables 2 to 6) the higher the percentage, the greater the level of uniformity for a category. However, exact matches do not, in all instances, mean that the two countries have the same requirements. The two countries' requirements are not always stated in the same manner or in the same parts of the corresponding documents stating the requirements. Many of the matches were observed only after the data were carefully refined to fit under the different items and categories of requirements. The matches, therefore, represent only the congruence between the two countries' requirements. Moreover, not all matches of requirements may lead to uniformity in practice. As mentioned earlier, only Types 1 and 4 requirements are coercive enough to have a definite influence on practice. Therefore, only if the requirements fall into these two types is there going to be a definite impact on material harmony. As already pointed out, weighting the requirements for their impact on actual practice is a subjective procedure, and has not been introduced into the computations. In this regard, as pointed out in the research design, the strengths of the requirements within a category for each coun-

Table 3
Comparison of Accounting Standards Disclosure Requirements

Disclosure requirements		*Items in each type of prescription*								*% of exact matches*	*Distance*
		New Zealand				*Australia*					
Category	*No. of items*	*1*	*2*	*3*	*4*	*1*	*2*	*3*	*4*		
D6	15	9	-	6	-	9	-	6	-	100.0	0.0000
D17	9	9	-	-	-	9	-	-	-	100.0	0.0000
D20	2	2	-	-	-	2	-	-	-	100.0	0.0000
D29	9	9	-	-	-	9	-	-	-	100.0	0.0000
D30	10	10	-	-	-	10	-	-	-	100.0	0.0000
D9	12	10	-	1	1	10	-	1	1	83.3	0.0000
D18	7	4	-	3	-	4	-	3	-	71.4	0.0000
D8	20	15	-	5	-	14	-	6	-	75.0	0.0120
D25	11	8	2	1	-	9	1	1	-	54.5	0.0660
D1	31	9	1	21	-	8	-	23	-	93.5	0.0731
D31	9	7	-	2	-	8	-	1	-	88.9	0.0808
D4	16	3	1	12	-	3	-	13	-	81.2	0.1260
D24	31	21	-	7	3	11	2	16	2	29.0	0.2790
D3	61	33	2	26	-	18	-	43	-	57.4	0.3744
D19	10	9	-	1	-	9	1	-	-	80.0	0.4000
D13	7	2	-	5	-	-	-	7	-	71.4	0.6857
D2	24	14	7	3	-	14	1	9	-	58.3	0.7099
D16	10	3	-	7	-	-	-	10	-	70.0	0.7714
D26	8	8	-	-	-	5	-	3	-	62.5	1.0500
D7	33	15	-	18	-	1	-	32	-	57.6	1.2587
D11	22	14	-	8	-	2	-	20	-	45.5	1.8086
D28	33	17	-	16	-	33	-	-	-	51.5	1.8253
D5	23	14	-	9	-	1	-	22	-	43.5	2.1845
D23	14	8	3	3	-	-	7	7	-	0.0	2.4762
D10	11	10	-	1	-	2	-	8	1	18.2	4.1897
D21	13	-	7	6	-	8	-	5	-	30.8	5.1077
D14	19	15	-	4	-	-	-	19	-	21.1	7.1053
D12	21	20	-	1	-	3	-	18	-	19.0	7.4389
D27	13	10	-	1	2	-	-	13	-	7.7	22.1539
D15	9	9	-	-	-	-	-	9	-	0.0	99.0000
D22	5	-	5	-	-	3	-	2	-	0.0	99.0000

try (see 'Items in each type of prescription' column of Tables 2 to 6) should be noted in examining the results of the matching procedure used in this study.

Table 7 summarises the more important aspects of the information in Tables 2 to 6. It provides the frequencies (by categories) of distances and exact matches between the disclosure and measurement requirements of the two countries.

The remaining discussion in this section shows how the statistics of the above analyses can be interpreted.

5.1. Overall Disclosure Requirements

The results of the comparison of the combined disclosure requirements of Australia and the combined disclosure requirements of New Zealand are shown in Tables 2 and 7. Of the 31 categories of disclosure, six categories indicated a 0.00 distance between the two countries. For 15 categories the distance was between 0.01 and 0.99, for eight categories it was between 1.00 and 19.99, and for the remaining two it was greater than 20.

The categories with large distances of over 20 were extractive industry accounting (D21)[5] and partnership accounting (D27). For extractive industries, Australia on the whole has more requirements, with an accounting standard supported by additional stock exchange requirements, while New Zealand does not have firm guidelines specifically aimed at the industry. Table 2 confirms this by showing that there are no matches between Australian and New Zealand requirements. There are 12 requirements in Australia on this matter, whereas New Zealand has only seven guidelines. This can be explained, at least partly, in terms of top companies' industrial characteristics in the two countries. As identified in Ryan (1992) and Ryan et al. (1991), in 1990 26% of the top Australian companies were engaged in mining and exploration activities, whereas the relevant figure for New Zealand was only 9%.

For partnership accounting, Australia has no requirements comparable to those of the New Zea-

[5] Refers to the category serial number as itemised in Table 1.

Table 4
Comparison of Legislative Disclosure Requirements

Disclosure requirements		*Items in each type of prescription*								*% of exact matches*	*Distance*
		New Zealand				*Australia*					
Category	*No. of items*	*1*	*2*	*3*	*4*	*1*	*2*	*3*	*4*		
D17	9	-	-	9	-	-	-	9	-	100.0	0.0000
D18	7	-	-	7	-	-	-	7	-	100.0	0.0000
D19	10	-	-	10	-	-	-	10	-	100.0	0.0000
D20	2	-	-	2	-	-	-	2	-	100.0	0.0000
D21	13	-	-	13	-	-	-	13	-	100.0	0.0000
D22	5	-	-	5	-	-	-	5	-	100.0	0.0000
D23	14	-	-	14	-	-	-	14	-	100.0	0.0000
D25	11	-	-	11	-	-	-	11	-	100.0	0.0000
D26	8	-	-	8	-	-	-	8	-	100.0	0.0000
D27	13	-	-	13	-	-	-	13	-	100.0	0.0000
D29	9	-	-	9	-	-	-	9	-	100.0	0.0000
D30	10	-	-	10	-	-	-	10	-	100.0	0.0000
D31	9	-	-	9	-	-	-	9	-	100.0	0.0000
D1	31	12	-	19	-	11	-	20	-	77.4	0.0043
D9	12	-	-	12	-	1	-	11	-	91.7	0.1567
D28	33	9	-	24	-	16	-	17	-	78.8	0.1947
D24	31	1	1	29	-	6	1	23	1	74.2	0.2141
D3	61	4	-	57	-	15	-	46	-	75.4	0.2593
D12	21	-	-	21	-	5	-	16	-	76.2	0.5952
D14	19	-	-	19	-	6	-	13	-	68.4	0.8745
D15	9	-	-	9	-	3	-	6	-	66.7	0.8389
D4	16	1	1	10	4	4	-	12	-	50.0	1.0135
D10	11	-	-	11	-	4	-	6	1	54.5	1.5152
D8	20	-	-	20	-	10	-	10	-	50.0	1.9000
D2	24	-	-	24	-	13	-	11	-	45.8	2.2552
D13	7	-	-	7	-	4	-	3	-	42.9	2.2857
D11	22	-	-	22	-	12	-	1	-	45.5	2.2909
D7	33	-	-	33	-	19	-	14	-	42.4	2.6320
D16	10	-	-	10	-	8	-	2	-	20.0	7.2000
D5	23	-	-	23	-	20	-	3	-	13.0	12.7536
D6	15	-	-	15	-	14	-	1	-	6.7	26.1333

land accounting standard. This is also reflected in the fact that the percentage of exact matches was a mere 7.7. Another item where there is a large distance is earnings per share (D22). Here, New Zealand lags behind Australia by having only a technical practice aid instead of a standard, and with only one stock exchange disclosure requirement.

An interesting item to note is miscellaneous disclosures (D23). This is basically a group of items of lesser importance where both countries mainly have guidelines, practice aids or short standards. The fourth highest distance (2.4762; Table 2) is in this area. This is because the two countries seem to have variations in these, presumably, fringe areas which in most cases reflect the individual country's traits. For example, New Zealand has requirements on goods and services tax because of its regime on that issue (whereas Australia has no such requirements), and Australia has guidelines on capital gains accounting because of its capital gains tax regime (whereas New Zealand has no such guidelines).

5.2. Disclosure Requirements in Accounting Standards

The greatest amount of variation in distances seems to exist in the case of accounting standards (see Table 7). For accounting standards among the 31 categories of requirements only seven had zero distances; 11 had between 0.01 and 0.99 distances; 10 had between one and 19.99 distances; and three had above 20 distances.

Among the accounting standards' disclosure requirements, the greatest differences were found in earnings per share (D22), reserves (D15) and accounting for partnerships (D27) (Table 3). For both reserves and partnerships, New Zealand has standards covering them, with nine and 10 requirements, respectively, whereas Australian standards are silent on these issues. For earnings per share, the difference is because Australia has a standard with three requirements, whereas New Zealand has a technical practice aid with five guidelines, indicating that one has stricter requirements than the other.

Table 5
Comparison of Stock Exchange Disclosure Requirements

Disclosure requirements		*Items in each type of prescription*								*% of exact matches*	*Distance*
		New Zealand				*Australia*					
Category	*No. of items*	*1*	*2*	*3*	*4*	*1*	*2*	*3*	*4*		
D2	24	15	-	9	-	15	-	9	-	100.0	0.0000
D4	16	4	-	12	-	4	-	12	-	100.0	0.0000
D5	23	3	-	20	-	3	-	20	-	100.0	0.0000
D6	15	1	-	14	-	1	-	14	-	100.0	0.0000
D7	33	11	-	22	-	11	-	22	-	100.0	0.0000
D8	20	3	-	17	-	3	-	17	-	100.0	0.0000
D9	12	-	-	12	-	-	-	12	-	100.0	0.0000
D10	11	-	-	11	-	-	-	11	-	100.0	0.0000
D11	22	6	-	16	-	6	-	16	-	100.0	0.0000
D12	21	-	-	21	-	-	-	21	-	100.0	0.0000
D13	7	-	-	7	-	-	-	7	-	100.0	0.0000
D14	19	9	-	10	-	9	-	10	-	100.0	0.0000
D15	9	1	-	8	-	1	-	8	-	100.0	0.0000
D17	9	3	-	6	-	3	-	6	-	100.0	0.0000
D18	7	-	-	7	-	-	-	7	-	100.0	0.0000
D19	10	1	-	9	-	1	-	9	-	100.0	0.0000
D20	2	-	-	2	-	-	-	2	-	100.0	0.0000
D23	14	-	-	14	-	-	-	14	-	100.0	0.0000
D24	31	6	-	25	-	6	-	25	-	100.0	0.0000
D25	11	-	-	11	-	-	-	11	-	100.0	0.0000
D26	8	-	-	8	-	-	-	8	-	100.0	0.0000
D27	13	-	-	13	-	-	-	13	-	100.0	0.0000
D28	33	-	-	33	-	-	-	33	-	100.0	0.0000
D29	9	91	-	-	-	9	-	-	-	100.0	0.0000
D30	10	0	-	-	-	10	-	-	-	100.0	0.0000
D3	61	15	-	46	-	16	-	45	-	95.1	0.0014
D31	9	7	-	2	-	8	-	1	-	88.9	0.0808
D1	31	19	-	12	-	24	-	7	-	71.0	0.1222
D16	10	-	-	10	-	1	-	9	-	90.0	0.2000
D22	5	1	-	4	-	-	-	5	-	80.0	0.4000
D21	13	-	-	13	-	5	-	8	-	61.5	1.1539

Distances also seem to be high for share capital (D14), extractive industries (D21), intangibles (D10) and other disclosures with respect to liabilities (D12). Except for extractive industries, in the other three categories New Zealand standards seem to have a higher number of requirements than Australian standards (Table 3). However, the legislative requirements and/or the stock exchange requirements in Australia seem to fill in, to some extent, for the lack of accounting standards in these areas. For extractive industries, Australia not only has a standard as compared to a weaker technical practice aid in New Zealand, it has more requirements as well.

5.3. Legislative Requirements for Disclosure

For legislative requirements, 13 categories had zero distances; eight had between 0.01 and 0.99 distances; nine had one to 19.99 distances; and only one had above 20 distance (Table 7). Inventories (D6), receivables (D5) and other supplementary disclosures with respect to assets and liabilities (D16) seemed to be the areas of high difference (Table 4). In all these cases, Australia had more requirements than New Zealand. Closer scrutiny of observations indicated that for inventories and receivables, New Zealand's void in legislative requirements was filled by its accounting standards. In the case of other disclosure requirements, Australia had provisions for additional disclosure with respect to expenditure commitments, leases and contingencies. These items were, however, covered in New Zealand by the accounting standards.

5.4. Stock Exchange Listing Requirements for Disclosure

The stock exchange requirements seemed to have the least variances, with 25 out of 31 categories having 0.00 distances, and the highest distance being only 1.15385 (Table 5). The number of categories with 100% matching between the stock exchange requirements of the two countries is 25 and not less than 60% matching in any of the other six categories. In effect, the two countries' stock exchange requirements were almost identical.

Table 5 shows that extractive industries is the area with the highest amount of variance among

Table 6
Comparison of Accounting Standard Measurement Requirements

Disclosure requirements		*Items in each type of prescription*								*% of exact matches*	*Distance*
		New Zealand				*Australia*					
Category	*No. of items*	*1*	*2*	*3*	*4*	*1*	*2*	*3*	*4*		
M7	10	8	-	-	2	8	-	-	2	100.0	0.0000
M20	18	10	3	-	5	10	3	-	5	100.0	0.0000
M17	24	20	-	2	2	19	1	3	1	87.5	0.0000
M22	9	6	-	3	-	6	-	5	-	33.3	0.0000
M4	30	4	12	8	6	8	9	5	8	66.7	0.0100
M18	51	41	3	2	5	40	3	-	8	80.4	0.0300
M2	28	9	3	10	6	11	2	10	5	67.9	0.0300
M11	9	7	1	-	1	5	2	2	-	44.4	0.0800
M3	26	20	2	4	-	22	-	4	-	69.2	0.1600
M9	18	17	-	1	-	14	2	2	-	83.3	0.3000
M19	30	21	-	3	6	20	2	-	8	66.7	0.3700
M14	14	4	-	8	2	5	1	4	4	71.4	0.4600
M23	21	-	14	6	1	11	3	2	5	19.0	0.5000
M15	14	11	-	2	1	8	-	6	-	71.4	0.5300
M13	14	9	1	-	4	9	4	-	1	64.3	0.5500
M1	46	27	5	9	5	17	1	24	4	43.5	0.5800
M10	10	10	-	-	-	7	1	2	-	70.0	0.7700
M21	5	5	-	-	-	3	2	-	-	60.0	1.0700
M12	12	4	-	7	1	-	-	12	-	58.3	1.3100
M16	11	10	-	-	1	5	-	5	1	54.5	1.5800
M24	10	1	-	3	6	-	5	-	5	40.0	2.5800
M8	10	5	-	3	2	-	-	10	-	30.0	2.5800
M26	7	-	5	2	-	-	-	7	-	28.6	4.2000
M6	9	9	-	-	-	2	-	7	-	22.2	4.2900
M5	12	10	2	-	-	1	-	11	-	8.3	20.5300
M25	7	-	-	7	-	7	-	-	-	0.0	99.0000
M28	10	-	10	-	-	-	-	10	-	0.0	99.0000
M27	4	-	4	-	-	2	-	2	-	0.0	99.0000

Table 7
Distance Intervals and Proportionate Number of Matches Between the Disclosure and Measurement Requirements of Australia and New Zealand

	Disclosure requirements (number of categories)				*Measurement Requirements (number of categories)*
	Combined	*Accounting standards*	*Legislative*	*Stock exchange*	
Distance intervals					
00	6	7	13	25	4
0.01-0.99	15	11	8	5	13
1.00-19.99	8	10	9	1	7
>20	2	3	1	0	4
Proportionate number of matches					
>50% of the items	18	20	22	31	16
<50% of the items	13	11	9	0	12

all stock exchange rules. However, Table 5 also shows that the two countries' stock exchanges do not provide requirements for many items of disclosure under several categories, thereby contributing very little towards harmonisation.

Tables 3, 4 and 5 reveal that the legislatures and the stock exchanges prescribe requirements in fewer categories than accounting standards. The variance in the range of distances for the three sources of regulation seems to be positively associated with the extent of coverage of the categories by each of the sources.

5.5. Measurement Requirements

The analysis of the measurement requirements (see Table 6) shows that out of the 28 categories of requirement, four indicate no or very little difference between Australia and New Zealand; 13 indicate a distance of 0.01 to 0.99; seven indicate a distance of one to 19.99; and only four exceed a distance of 20.

The categories with high distances were bloodstock (M27), earnings per share (M28), pensions (M25) and investment properties (M5). For bloodstock accounting, Australia has a complete void, with New Zealand having a technical practice aid to cover the issue. As indicated in Ryan (1992) and Ryan et al. (1991), in 1990 7% of top New Zealand companies were engaged in frozen meat and by-products, whereas none of the top Australian companies had this as their area of business. For earnings per share, Australia has a standard with more specific requirements, while New Zealand has a technical practice aid that only provides broad guidance. For pension accounting, New Zealand has yet to make a move to provide some guidance, whereas Australia has already issued a standard. For investment properties, New Zealand has a standard but Australia has not made any serious attempt at one. A similar situation exists for properties intended for sale, as indicated by a distance of 6.22. In both these cases, Australia has made only broader guidelines within its non-current assets standard. This again is reflected in the industrial characteristics of the two countries' large companies. Proportionately more New Zealand top companies were in property business (7%) compared with their Australian counterparts (4%) (Ryan, 1992; Ryan et al., 1991).

Table 7 shows that 50% or less exact matching of the regulatory provisions within each category of disclosure and measurement rules is quite common. For the comparison of the two countries' combined disclosure requirements, in 13 out of 31 categories there is 50% or less exact matches. For accounting standard disclosure requirements, matches of 50% or less exists for 11 out of the 31 categories. For legislative requirements, there are nine such categories, with the stock exchange requirements having no such categories. For measurement requirements such mismatches exist for 12 out of 28 categories.

Further scrutiny of the 'Items in each type of prescription' column of Tables 2 and 6 reveals that a lot of the matches between the requirements could have arisen due to the presence of Types 2 and 3 requirements. This is especially evident in Table 5 for stock exchange requirements. This leaves room for diversity in reporting practices.

6. Conclusions

This paper proposed to demonstrate the use of a research design that allows for the measurement of formal accounting harmonisation across countries. This has been achieved by a statistical-empirical comparison between the measurement and disclosure requirements for Australian and New Zealand listed companies.

The methodology adopted here provides several benefits. It allows for the identification of accounting areas where formal disharmony exists. The logic behind the calculations is fairly simple because it only involves calculation of distances between the countries for each category of requirement, through a process of matching the individual items of requirement under each category. The matching of items also provides an insight into the nature of variances between the rules of two countries. For instance, it identifies the extent of uniformity (exact matches) between the requirements of two countries. It allows for the discovery of possible material disharmony despite the existence of similar rules, which can occur due to rules of dissimilar strengths. Such an appraisal of accounting rules can assist accounting policy-makers at both regional and global levels in targeting areas needing greater attention for harmonisation purposes. For example, an application of a similar type would be useful for the IASC's comparability project or the European Union's harmonisation project. The discrimination between different countries' rules can also be correlated with other environmental characteristics to identify the reasons for the variations in specific categories of rules. This may help in determining appropriate courses of action to achieve formal harmonisation in targeted areas.

The research methodology presented here opens up several research directions. For example, the distances computed in this study can be correlated with the differences in actual practice to see how much of the material harmony is explained by regulatory arrangements. For instance, if no significant correlation is found between the two, then achievement of formal harmonisation may not lead to material harmonisation. Similar tests may also be conducted to understand the association between share price variations and formal harmonisation.

In addition to the type of research demonstrated here, other forms of research, such as those involving interviews, case studies or surveys, may be necessary to fully understand the underlying or subtle issues surrounding formal accounting harmonisation. Presence of such issues was encountered in the brief interviewing process used in this study. The interviews showed that, apart from the variations in the rules, there were variations in the format and language in which the rules are presented, and the frequency of reporting required by certain authorities within the two countries for certain qualitative information. These, the interviewees felt, affected material harmonisation.

Finally, because of the growing influence of accounting regulations on accounting practice and market indicators, it is essential that formal accounting harmonisation be more carefully and extensively examined to make material harmonisation effective. The rapid expansion of global and regional market systems is making research in this area more pertinent. The need for such research is also becoming more critical as a result of the proliferation of national accounting regulatory systems. In this respect, this study has only touched a vast area of research. Although it has covered only two countries and listed companies, similar studies using the multiple discriminant analysis methodology can be conducted on more than two countries at a time and on other forms of organisations.

References

Adhikari, A. and Tondkar, R.H. (1992), 'Environmental Factors Influencing Accounting Disclosure Requirements of Global Stock Exchanges', *Journal of International Management and Accounting*, Vol. 4, No. 2, pp. 75–105.

Alford, A., Jones, J., Leftwich, R. and Zmijewski, M. (1993), 'The Relative Informativeness of Accounting Disclosures in Different Countries', *Journal of Accounting Research*, 31, Supplement, pp. 183–229.

Amir, E., Harris, T. and Venuti, E. (1993), 'A Comparison of the Value Relevance of US versus non-US GAAP Accounting Measures using Form 20-f Reconciliations, *Journal of Accounting Research*, 31, Supplement, pp. 230–264.

Barth, M.E. and Clinch, G. (1994), 'International Accounting Differences and their Relation to Share Prices: Evidence for UK, Australian and Canadian Firms', a Harvard Business School and working paper, May.

Belkaoui, A. (1983), 'Economic, Political and Civil Indicators and Reporting and Disclosure Adequacy: Empirical Investigation', *Journal of Accounting and Public Policy*, Vol. 2, No. 3, pp. 207–219.

Birkett, W.P. (1993), 'Competency Based Standards for Professional Accountants in Australia and New Zealand', a Discussion Paper (Melbourne: Australian Society of CPAs).

Choi, F.D.S. and Mueller, G.G. (1992), *International Accounting* (Englewood Cliffs, NJ: Prentice-Hall Inc.).

Cooke, T.E. and Wallace, O. (1990), 'Financial Disclosure Regulation and its Environment, *Journal of Accounting and Public Policy*, 9, pp. 79–110.

da Costa, R.C., Bourgeois, J.C. and Lawson, W.M. (1978), 'A Classification of International Financial Accounting Practices, *International Journal of Accounting Education and Research*, Vol. 13, No. 2, Spring, pp. 73–85.

Doupnik, S. and Taylor, M.E. (1985), 'An Empirical Investigation of the Observance of IASC Standards in Western Europe', *Management International Review*, Vol. 25, No. 1, pp. 27–33.

Emenyonu, E.N. and Gray, S.J. (1992), 'EC Harmonisation: An Empirical Study of Measurement Practices in France, Germany and the UK, *Accounting and Business Research*, Vol. 23, No. 89, pp. 49–58.

Evans, T.G. and Taylor, M.E. (1982), 'Bottom-line Compliance with the IASC: A Comparative Analysis', *International Journal of Accounting*, Vol. 18, No. 1, Fall, pp. 115–128.

Frank, W.G. (1979), 'An Empirical Analysis of International Accounting Principles, *Journal of Accounting Research*, Vol. 17, No. 2, Spring, pp. 593–605.

Gray, S.J., Campbell, S.G. and Shaw, J.C. (1984), *International Financial Reporting: A Comparative Survey of Accounting Requirements and Practices in 30 Countries* (London: Macmillan).

Hair, J., Anderson, R., Tatham, R. and Black, W. (1992), *Multivariate Data Analysis* (NJ: Prentice-Hall).

Hill, M. (1993), 'New Zealand Endorsement', *Accountants Journal*, Vol. 72, No. 5 pp. 40–41.

Holmes, F. with Harvey, M., Mason, G. and Garcia, M. (1986), *Closer Economic Relations with Australia* (Wellington: Institute of Policy Studies).

International Accounting Standards Committee (1989), *Comparability of Financial Statements* (London: IASC).

Krzanowski, W.J. (1988), *Principles of Multivariate Analysis* (London: Oxford University Press).

Lloyd, P.J. (1991), *The Future of CER—A Single Market for Australia and New Zealand* (Wellington: Institute of Policy Studies).

Meek, G. and Saudagaran, S. (1990), 'A Survey of Research on Financial Reporting in a Transnational Context', *Journal of Accounting Literature*, 9, pp. 145–182.

Nair, R.D. and Frank, W.G. (1980) 'The Impact of Disclosure and Measurement Practices on International Accounting Classifications', *Accounting Review*, Vol. 55, No. 3, July, pp. 426–450.

Nair, R.D. and Frank, W.G. (1981) 'The Harmonization of International Accounting Standards 1973–1979', *International Journal of Accounting*, Vol. 17, No. 1, Fall, pp. 61–77.

Nobes, C.W. (1981), 'An Empirical Analysis of International Accounting Principles: A Comment', *Journal of Accounting Literature* Vol. 19, No. 1, pp. 268–270.

Nobes, C.W. (1992), *International Classification of Financial Reporting* (London: Routledge).

Price Waterhouse International (1973), *Accounting Principles and Reporting Practices* (New York: Price Waterhouse International).

PWI (1975), *Accounting Principles and Reporting Practices* (New York: Price Waterhouse International).

PWI (1979), *International Survey of Accounting Principles and Reporting Practices* (London: Butterworths).

Radebaugh, L.H. and Gray, S.J. (1993), *International Accounting and Multinational Enterprises* (New York: John Wiley and Sons Inc.).

Rahman, A.R., Perera, M.H.B. and Tower, G. (1994), 'Accounting Harmonization between Australia and New Zealand: Towards a Regulatory Union', *International Journal of Accounting*, Vol. 29, No. 3, pp. 316–333.

Ryan, J.B. (ed.) (1992), *New Zealand Company Financial Reporting* (Auckland: University of Auckland).

Ryan, J.B. Andrew, B.H., Gaffikin, M.J. and Heazlewood, T. (1991), *Australian Company Financial Reporting 1990* (Melbourne: Australian Accounting Research Foundation).

Reports to Governments by Steering Committees of Officials (1992), *The Harmonization of Australian and New Zealand*

Business Law: Closer Economic Relations—Trade Agreement, unpublished report, July.
Sharpe, M. and McGregor, W. (1993a), Australia New Zealand Closer Economic Relationship: Harmonisation of Accounting Standards, Unpublished paper.
Sharpe, M. and McGregor, W. (1993b), 'Trans-Tasman Harmonisation of Accounting Standards—Conquering the Constraints', *Accountants Journal*, Vol. 72, No. 5, pp. 38–40.
Tay, J.S.W. and Parker, R.H. (1990), 'Measuring International Harmonisation and Standardisation', *Abacus*, Vol. 26, No. 1 pp. 71–88.
Tay, J.S.W. and Parker, R.H. (1992), 'Measuring International Harmonisation and Standardisation: A Reply', *Abacus* Vol. 28, No. 2, pp. 217–221.
Wallace, R.S.O. and Gernon, H. (1991), 'Frameworks of International Comparative Financial Accounting', *Journal of Accounting Literature*, 10, pp. 209–264.
Wallace, R.S.O. (1992), 'The Contingency Approach to Cross-national Financial Accounting Research, *Proceedings*, British Accounting Association Annual Conference, Warwick University, 13–15 April.
Walton, P. (1992), 'Harmonization of Accounting in France and Britain: Some Evidence', *Abacus*, Vol. 28, No. 2 pp. 186–199.
van der Tas, L.G. (1988), 'Measuring Harmonization of Financial Reporting Practice', *Accounting and Business Research*, Vol. 18, No. 70, pp. 157–169.
van der Tas, L.G. (1992a), 'Measuring International Harmonization and Standardization: A Comment', *Abacus*, Vol. 28, No. 2 pp. 211–215.
van der Tas, L.G. (1992b), 'Evidence of EC Financial Reporting Practice Harmonisation: The Case of Deferred Taxation, *European Accounting Review*, Vol. 1, No. 1, pp. 69–104.
Yang, D.C. and Lee, C.M. (1994), 'An Empirical Analysis of Pan-Pacific Accounting Practices in the 1970s, *Advances in International Accounting*, 6, pp. 133–145.

[11]

Accounting and Business Research, Vol. 28. No. 3. pp. 189–208. Summer 1998

Profit Measurement and UK Accounting Standards: A Case of Increasing Disharmony in Relation to US GAAP and IASs

P. Weetman, E. A. E. Jones, C. A. Adams and S. J. Gray*

Abstract—UK accounting practice differs from International Accounting Standards (IASs) particularly with regard to amortisation of goodwill, provision for deferred taxation and the accounting treatment of pension costs. Under the core standards programme of the IASC the IASs have emerged closer to US practice. This paper evaluates the profit of those UK companies reporting to the Securities and Exchange Commission (SEC) in 1988 and 1994, spanning a period which saw the establishment of the ASB and the implementation of the IASC's comparability project. An increasing gap was found between the reported profit under UK accounting principles and that restated under US GAAP. The difference lay most frequently in accounting for goodwill, provision for deferred tax, and the accounting treatment of pension costs, with accounting for goodwill showing a particularly significant impact in 1994. Notwithstanding the introduction of FRS 10, an overall impression of increasing disharmony could continue to cause reconciliations to be required of UK companies seeking full listing on a US stock exchange, with consequent disadvantage relative to companies in other European countries seeking international capital in the US.

1. Introduction

A practical instance of the demand for harmonisation of accounting practices has been provided in the consultation between the International Accounting Standards Committee (IASC) and the International Organisation of Securities Commissions (IOSCO). This has resulted in a target of revising the priority standards to IOSCO satisfaction by mid-1998, a project commonly referred to as 'the core standards programme' (IASC 1993a: 4). The divergence between UK accounting practice and International Accounting Standards (IASs) is noted in a number of areas (Keegan and King, 1996) but particularly with regard to the amortisation of goodwill, accounting for deferred taxation and the accounting treatment of pension costs and employee benefits.

A key element to gaining acceptance of the IASC core standards by IOSCO is participation by the US Securities and Exchange Commission (SEC), as a member body of IOSCO (IASC 1996b). The SEC imposes strict accounting requirements on foreign companies seeking a full listing on a US stock exchange. In particular, the SEC requires a report on form 20-F, a lengthy document which, in the case of UK companies as foreign registrants, includes a reconciliation of profit reported under UK accounting principles[1] to the profit figure which would have been reported under US GAAP. If in future the SEC accepts financial statements prepared under IASs then reconciliations will no longer be required where IASs are applied in full. However, if UK accounting standards remain different from IASs, there may well be a continuing requirement for reconciliations to be reported by UK companies while other companies enjoy exemption because they apply IASs in full.

*The authors are, respectively: professor of accounting, Heriot-Watt University; research associate, Heriot-Watt University; senior lecturer, University of Glasgow; and professor, University of New South Wales. They are grateful to the anonymous referees, conference participants at the Financial Accounting and Auditing Research Conference, London, July 1997 and at the British Accounting Association Scottish Conference, Edinburgh, September 1997, and to Bob Parker, Neil Garrod and Bill Rees. Correspondence or enquiries should be addressed to Professor Pauline Weetman, Department of Accountancy and Finance, Heriot-Watt University, Edinburgh, EH14 4AS. Telephone 0131 451 3293; Fax 0131 451 3008; email P. Weetman@hw.ac.uk. The first version of this paper was submitted October 1997, and the final version accepted in March 1998.

[1] This paper avoids the abbreviation 'UK GAAP' which is more broadly expressed as the all-encompassing 'generally accepted accounting principles' mentioned in UK company law (Companies Act 1985 s262 (3) and Coopers and Lybrand 1988: 2001) but which has been espoused as 'generally accepted accounting practice' in a popular text from the firm of Ernst & Young (Davies et al, 1997).

In this context it is relevant to investigate the materiality of the differences in reported profit, as perceived by the US reader, of the profit and loss account stated under both US GAAP and UK accounting principles. Information is deemed to be material if it could influence users' decisions taken on the basis of the financial statements (ASB 1995: para. 2.7). The relative materiality of adjustments, indicated by this research, provides a benchmark against which to assess the likely impact of a continuing requirement to prepare reconciliations where there is a lack of compatibility with IASs. It is also relevant to consider relative magnitudes of material differences over the period in the early 1990s during which UK standards were being set under a new regime and the IASC was revising its standards.

A direct question regarding the future impact of non-compliance with IASs would be to seek quantification of *de facto* differences between profit reported under UK accounting principles and that reported under IASs. As UK companies do not provide such reconciliations, that would require a simulation or a speculative recalculation using information in the public domain. The reconciliations contained in form 20-F allow quantification of *de facto* differences between UK practices and US GAAP. The impact of UK practices which depart from IASs may be derived by comparing details of the various regulations.

Accordingly, the questions addressed in the paper are:

- what were the *de jure* differences between measurement practices under UK accounting principles as compared to those under US GAAP, during the period 1988 to 1994?
- what were the *de facto* differences in reported profits under UK accounting principles and US GAAP in 1988 and 1994, and what were the relative magnitudes of those differences?
- what implications do the quantified differences have for policy makers in setting UK standards, with particular regard to alignment with the IASs?

This paper evaluates the differences in profit measurement arising from reporting under both UK accounting principles and US GAAP at two points in time, namely 1988 and 1994. These dates have been chosen because the intervening period encompasses the change from the Accounting Standards Committee (ASC) to the Accounting Standards Board (ASB) in the UK and the implementation of the IASC's comparability project, but it predates the start of the IASC's core standards project. The paper estimates the extent to which the reported differences would remain if the core standards were accepted by the SEC but, at the same time, some UK standards were not aligned with the core standards. The paper also offers an evaluation of the extent of differences in reported profit during the early years of operation of the ASB.

Previous research analysing reports on form 20-F issued by companies, prior to the start of the IASC's comparability project (Weetman and Gray 1991), showed substantial differences when profit reported under UK accounting principles was compared with that under US GAAP. Since that time the pressures for international harmonisation have grown, most importantly across the major capital markets of the world. It is a matter for continuing debate as to whether investors can cope with accounting diversity. Choi and Levich (1991), interviewing stock market participants in the UK, US, Japan, Switzerland and Germany, found that about half the respondents felt that accounting diversity affected their decisions. Bhushan and Lessard (1992) found that, among US and UK-based international investment managers, uniform disclosure or harmonisation was seen as more important than quantitative reconciliation to US GAAP.

The purpose of this paper is to explore the extent to which there is greater or lesser diversity due to differences in reported profit as a result of differences between UK accounting principles and US GAAP. The next section draws on prior literature for factors creating pressure for international harmonisation of the paper. There follows in Section 3 a brief analysis of *de jure* differences in comparisons of UK accounting principles with US GAAP and with IASs. *De facto* differences between accounting practices under UK accounting principles and US GAAP are quantified using the 'index of comparability' measure described in Section 4 and applied to the sample as outlined in Section 5. The results are discussed in some detail in Section 6. Section 7 draws conclusions regarding the quantified differences and the policy implications.

2. Pressures for international harmonisation

International pressures for improvement in the comparability of accounting and information disclosure arise from the diverse interests and concerns of a wide range of participant groups and organisations around the world. Since the early 1970s, when the IASC was established, these pressures have grown at a rapid pace along with the development of stock markets internationally and especially those in emerging economies (IASC 1996b). While IASs issued during the 1970s and 1980s were recognised to have made a contribution towards international harmonisation, by the late 1980s the performance of the IASC was increasingly being questioned on account of the flexibility of the standards and continuing lack of comparability of financial statements across borders.

2.1. Involvement of IOSCO

An important development at this time was the interest of the IOSCO in the IASC's provision of mutually acceptable international accounting standards for use in multinational company security offerings and listings. IASC invited IOSCO to join its consultative group in 1987 (Wallace, 1990: 18–19). In 1988 a report of the Technical Committee of IOSCO concluded that differences in national accounting requirements presented a major impediment to multinational securities offerings and other foreign listings. The IASC and IOSCO agreed to work together to find a solution that would allow a company to list its securities in any foreign stock market on the basis of one set of financial statements conforming to IASs (Cairns, 1995: 57). The IASC responded in 1989 with the comparability project set out in the exposure draft E 32 *Comparability of Financial Statements* (IASC 1989). The proposals in E 32 were designed to eliminate most of the choices of accounting treatment then permitted under International Accounting Standards. IOSCO indicated that being seen to adopt a more uniform approach, as E 32 advocated, would enhance the credibility and acceptability of IASs by the international investment community.

The outcome of the comparability project proposals, refined by the *Statement of Intent* (IASC 1993b), was that 10 IASs were revised. These revisions included the elimination of some 20 permitted accounting treatments. Of relevance to this paper were the elimination of: the use of closing exchange rates when translating income statements; the expensing of development costs where specified criteria were met; and the immediate write-off to shareholders' interests of positive goodwill.

Subsequent to completion of the IASC's comparability project, IOSCO indicated that more work would be required (Cairns, 1995: 41) and presented a list of core standards which it might be willing to accept provided the full programme of core standards could be completed successfully within a specified limit of time (IASC 1994: 13). In 1995 the Technical Committee of IOSCO agreed that successful completion of the IASC's work plan by the end of 1999 would mean that IASs would form a comprehensive set of core standards. The Technical Committee would then be in a position to recommend endorsement of IASs for cross-border raising of capital and for listings in stock markets around the world. At the urging of multinational companies and members of IOSCO, the Board of IASC brought forward the target date to March 1998 (IASC 1996a:1, 9–12).

2.2. US approach to IASs

A key player in the success of the IASC endeavour is the US. Both the SEC and the Financial Accounting Standards Board (FASB) have expressed support for the objectives of the IASC's core standards programme. However, they have qualified this by stating that acceptance is dependent on IAS's constituting a comprehensive set of generally accepted accounting principles. The standards must also be of high quality and be rigorously interpreted and applied. The chairman of the FASB has been critical of the speed with which the IASC has carried out the core standards programme, questioning whether this is compatible with high quality standards (IASC 1996b). The FASB has also identified more than 250 differences between IASs and FASB standards (FASB 1996, IASC 1996b). The IASC has pointed out that not all these differences relate to the core standards identified as priority matters but has confirmed that it will refer to the FASB's analysis as these standards are developed (IASC 1996b).

2.3. UK approach to IASs

Since 1990 the ASB, working within the European Directives, has refined and extended UK financial reporting requirements in ways which, in some measurement respects, have moved UK practice towards that of the US. At the same time measurement practices in the US have been developing further. Some of the most difficult and internationally contentious issues have only recently begun to be tackled by the ASB. In particular there are the issues of accounting for goodwill, deferred taxation and pension costs. This paper shows that in 1994 these remained the most frequent causes of reported difference in profit between UK accounting principles and US GAAP. By the end of 1994 Financial Reporting Standards (FRSs) numbers one to six were in operation as mandatory requirements.

The chairman of the ASB has articulated the fear that if the IASC did not deliver the core standards within the agreed time scale then companies seeking US funding would switch to US GAAP and would probably not be interested thereafter in further changing to IASC standards (FRC 1996). Three possible strategies have been analysed by the chairman as a basis for reacting to the mounting pressure for harmonisation:

- adopt international standards for domestic purposes;
- develop domestic requirements without regard to international standards; or
- harmonise domestic requirements with international standards where possible.

Analysis of limitations and benefits lent support to the third of these and to the view that the ASB should depart from international consensus only when:

- there were particular legal or fiscal problems that dictated such a course; or
- the Board genuinely believed that the international approach was wrong and that an independent UK standard might point the way to an eventual improvement in international practice.

It was noted that the ASB had taken an independent course with regard to accounting for goodwill, and indicated the need for debate on accounting for deferred tax and accounting for pension costs (FRC, 1996: 42–46). This paper offers a contribution to that debate.

3. UK/US/IAS accounting differences

Accounting differences may be classified *de jure* by examining the regulations, or *de facto* by examining the practice.

3.1. De jure differences

Measurement practices of UK accounting which are not compatible with those of US GAAP are listed in Table 1. Panel (a) of Table 1 indicates the UK measurement practices which differ from both US GAAP and IASs. Panel (b) of Table 1 indicates the UK measurement practices which differ from US GAAP but are compatible with those of the IASs.

We provide later an evaluation of the UK/US differences in reported profit arising in total and for each item of Table 1 separately. If in future the SEC accepts financial statements prepared under IASs then, in principle, reconciliations will no longer be required of any company reporting under IASs. If, however, UK accounting standards remain different from IASs, there may well be a continuing requirement for reconciliations to be reported by UK companies in respect of those items in panel (a) of Table 1 (with the possible exception of accounting for goodwill under the new UK standard on intangibles). However the items in panel (b) of Table 1 would probably no longer be required.

An important change during the period which brought UK accounting closer to US GAAP was in respect of reporting extraordinary items, common in 1988 but virtually non-existent in 1994 as a result of the implementation of FRS 3 *Reporting financial performance* (ASB 1992a). Other evidence of movement towards US GAAP may be seen in aspects of UITF 6 *Accounting for post-retirement benefits other than pensions* (ASB 1992b) and in FRS 4 *Capital instruments* (ASB 1993), FRS 5 *Reporting the substances of transactions* (ASB 1994a) and FRS 6 *Acquisitions and mergers* (ASB 1994b). However, the US regulations on all these matters are more detailed. Situations remain where the UK practice under the new standards may not satisfy the US requirements entirely.

While these UK changes were bringing UK practices closer to US GAAP, new and amended US standards were widening the gap. In particular, the accounting treatment of deferred taxation was finally agreed in the form of SFAS 109; further SFASs appeared in relation to specific aspects of financial instruments; EITF guidance was issued on restructuring costs; and SFAS 115 provided a stricter approach to investments in marketable equity securities and debt securities.

Overall, from the detailed comparisons contained in Appendix A, it would appear that there was no significant *de jure* harmonisation of accounting measurement practices between UK accounting principles and US GAAP over the period 1988 to 1994 in the main areas of difference in policy and practice.

Analysis of differences in legislation gives no indication of how frequently such differences will be encountered in practice or how significant the differences may be in their impact on profit. The next section of the paper turns to the empirical evidence based on UK companies which report under US GAAP as well as under UK accounting principles.

3.2. De facto differences

De facto differences in UK and US accounting practices over the period 1986–1988 inclusive were analysed by Weetman and Gray (1991) using the reports of UK companies to the SEC on form 20-F. The availability of such data is confined to those UK companies which have a full listing on a US stock exchange. The advantage of the data lies in the detail of the reconciliation and the quality, being audited information prepared by the company. From a research perspective, each company provides a 'matched' set of data showing how the company's reported profit compares under each set of GAAP. This paper extends that matching by taking companies whose accounting information was available in both 1988 and 1994 (Appendix B).

4. The index of comparability as an indicator of harmonisation

Gray (1980) first used the 'index of conservatism' in comparing profit measurement practices of several countries. However, for the purposes of this paper, renaming the index as a measure of 'comparability' places clearer emphasis on relative accounting treatment without requiring a judgment as to which is more or less conservative. The index of comparability indicates the measurement impact of accounting differences and may therefore be distinguished from other indicators of harmon-

Table 1
Incompatibility of UK measurement practices with US GAAP and relation to IASs

(a) Measurement practices where UK is not compatible with either US GAAP or IAS	
Goodwill	UK SSAP 22 not compatible with either IAS 22 or US GAAP
Deferred taxation	UK SSAP 15 (revised) not compatible with either IAS 12 or US GAAP
Pension costs and post-retirement benefits other than pensions	SSAP 24 is not currently compatible with US GAAP and will not be compatible with the revised IAS (1998) which is closer to US GAAP
Capitalisation of development costs	SSAP 13 is permissive on capitalisation of development costs; IAS 21 is closer to US GAAP in prescribing conditions for capitalisation
Financial instruments	FRS 4 prohibits split accounting for mixed capital instruments
Consolidation policy	FRS 2 leaves little scope for exclusion of a subsidiary. IAS 27 allows exclusion. US definition of control is close to that of UK
Discontinued operations	FRS 3 differs from US definition. IAS policy remains under consideration
(b) Measurement practices where UK differs from US GAAP but is compatible with IAS	
Valuation of property, plant and equipment	UK compatible with IAS 16. US GAAP does not permit revaluation
Borrowing costs	UK compatible with IAS 23. US GAAP has more specific rules
Foreign currency translation	UK compatible with IAS 21 where UK companies choose average rate for translating P&L account, but not compatible with US GAAP
Dividends payable	Dividends proposed may be accrued in UK or under IASs, not under US GAAP
Correction of fundamental errors resulting from accounting policy change	UK compatible with IAS 8 on fundamental errors; US GAAP requires effect of change in profit and loss account
Business combinations	UK compatible with IAS 22. US GAAP under APB 16 dictates that pooling of interest must be used where specific conditions are met. These conditions are not identical to those of FRS 6
Restructuring costs	Not dealt with in either UK standards or IAS. US GAAP has specific requirements
Revenue recognition	UK meets IAS 18 principles. US GAAP has more specific rules
Investments in marketable equity securities and debt securities	SSAP 19 consistent with IAS 25. US GAAP uses different classifications

(*Sources:* See Appendix A)

isation, such as H, I or C indices which quantify the incidence of accounting differences (van der Tas, 1988).

Gray's index has featured in a number of studies of comparative reported profit (Weetman and Gray 1990 and 1991, Adams et al, 1993, Cooke, 1993, Hellman, 1993, Weetman et al, 1993, Norton, 1995).

4.1. Formula for the index of comparability

Where UK reported profit is being compared to that reported under US GAAP, the index may be expressed by the formula:

$$1-\left(\frac{\text{Profits}_{\text{USA}}-\text{Profits}_{\text{UK}}}{|\text{Profits}_{\text{USA}}|}\right)$$

The measure of profit used is the earnings for ordinary shareholders, after tax and after extraordinary items. The numerical value of the profit or loss in the US is chosen as the denominator because the reconciliation is a report addressed to investors who, it may be assumed, are accustomed to US GAAP and consequently will view the differences as departures from US profit or loss rather than departures from UK profit or loss. The use of US profit in the denominator also allows the index values to be used in inter-country comparisons. Profit is chosen for the denominator rather than a scale factor such as sales or market value, because the paper seeks to evaluate materiality as defined earlier.

Although there is no agreed guidance on materiality, auditors assessing materiality in relation to impact on users will make reference in their work to percentages. Audit practice (Grant Thornton,

1990, para 7.59) indicates a helpful guideline as being 5–10% of profit before taxation, and warns that a judgment based on turnover would not be appropriate in relation to, say, stock valuation. There is also a warning (para 7.63) that items should not be judged material by reasons of value where a small profit is turned into a small loss, or vice versa. This study provides information based on bands at 5% and 10% of profit.

The neutral value of 1.0 is used for consistency with prior literature. An index value greater than 1 means that the UK reported profit is greater than that reported under US GAAP (or a UK loss is not as large as a US loss). An index value less than 1 means that the UK reported profit is less than that reported under US GAAP (or a UK loss is larger than a US loss).

Because the reconciliations reported to the SEC contain considerable detail, it is also possible to present partial index values using the formula:

$$1 - \left(\frac{\text{partial adjustment}}{|\text{Profits}_{\text{USA}}|} \right)$$

These provide a relative measure of the contribution of each reconciling item. The neutral value is retained as 1.0 for consistency of interpretation. The indexes of partial adjustments add to the total index by the formula:

$$\text{Total index} = \sum_{1}^{n} adjustment_n - (n\text{-}1)$$

4.2. Evaluation of the use of the index

It should be noted that the formula carries a disadvantage of reporting extreme index values if the US profit or loss is close to zero. Such occurrences are relatively rare in the data examined and do not seriously inhibit interpretation. The presence of such outliers has to be weighed against the attractiveness of the formula in having parallels in the accounting concept of 'materiality' which is usually judged in relation to profit. Such outliers cause comparable problems in practical interpretation of their impact on users of financial statements, and it has been suggested that materiality may not be judged on a relative value basis when profit is small or the item causes a change from a small profit to a small loss (Grant Thornton, 1990).

Use of the index to evaluate annual data may carry the risk of including in any particular year a short-term timing difference which reverses in the following year due to a difference in recognition criteria. An example might be a provision for a loss, where the timing of loss recognition follows different GAAP rules but the amount of the anticipated loss is the same under both systems. Each form 20-F gives scope for consideration of this aspect because it carries not only the results of the current year but also those of each of the two previous years for comparison. Scrutiny of the three-year comparisons within each 20-F reconciliation showed that only two specific reversals in reconciling items were observable in all the separate adjustments analysed.

As a further check, the data available over three years within each 20-F was aggregated in an attempt to provide a three-year total which would eliminate the potential influence of short-term reversals. The three-year aggregation indicated little evidence of matching items being eliminated in one year against another. It is not reported here in detail because there are difficulties in interpreting aggregation of a current year's profit with comparative data of previous periods. In particular, where a large adjusting item appears in one accounting period, with no reported figure for that line item in the other two years, aggregation of profit over the three-year period will effectively apply income smoothing to that item, leading to conclusions which would not be compatible with the principles of UK and US accounting. Furthermore, where there is a positive adjustment in one year and a negative adjustment in another year, these not being reversals of the same item, the resulting cancellation will again lead to misinterpretation of the significance of those reconciling items for reported annual profit.

One justification for concentrating on the annual result only is that this is the common practice of those who evaluate accounting information. Comments in analysts' reports and the press are largely based on annual results. The general consistency of results from one year to the next over a three-year analysis was shown previously for data in the 1980s (Weetman and Gray, 1991). In the course of the current analysis it was noted that, both at 1988 and 1994, a comparable number of adjusting items was reported for each of the two previous years, as compared with those reported for the current year at the date of the 20-F. This suggests that any one year may be taken as representative of the frequency and magnitude of adjustments.

5. Sample

The total number of UK companies providing a 20-F reconciliation was approximately 45 in each of 1994 and 1988. (There is no authoritative list available on a systematic basis; the information is deduced from listings provided by search agencies and from such sources as the web pages of the New York Stock Exchange.) This group is a sub set of a larger group of UK listed companies[2] (over 220 in 1994 compared with 162 reported by Weetman and Gray for 1988) whose shares are traded in the form of American Depositary Receipts (ADRs) in the US. The companies making use of the ADR facility are exempt from the 20-F filing requirement,[3] which is aimed primarily at those seeking to raise new capital on the US stock market.

Of the 41 UK companies listed in the Appendix to Weetman and Gray (1991) as reporting to the SEC in 1988, 25 reported to the SEC at December 1994, the remainder being unavailable because of intervening takeover or merger, cessation of the US listing and, in one case, a major change of activity, from manufacturing to licensing, in process during 1994 (Appendix B). In order to achieve a matching over the period of transition from Accounting Standards Committee to Accounting Standards Board, only those 25 are the subject of this analysis. The benefit of having a matched sample, albeit relatively small, lies in holding constant the nature of the business over the period of comparison.

As a further check on the constancy of the nature of the business, there was scrutiny of the section of each 20-F report containing the description of the business and the main business segments. None of these companies experienced a fundamental restructuring between the two dates used for the analysis. Three of the utilities had major plans in train but these had not become operational to a significant extent at the end of 1994. All companies reported sales to US customers which were, in the main, proportionately greater in 1994 than in 1988. This group of companies was active in expanding by acquisition rather than by organic growth.

There were changes in key financial indicators (taken from the UK information available on *Datastream*). For the group as a whole, the average level of gearing was higher in 1994, the average debt to equity ratio being 34.8% in 1988 and 44.1% in 1994. A higher level of gearing might be expected where companies active in acquisition were writing off goodwill against reserves, at a rate greater than the rate of expansion of net assets. However the average was distorted by extreme values and there were more companies by number having lower gearing in 1994. Net profit as a percentage of sales (10.0% in 1988 and 8.8% in 1994) and gross profit margin on sales (15.5% in 1988 and 13.7% in 1994) were both lower in 1994, and return on capital employed (18.7% in 1988 and 12.8% in 1994) was also lower. The gross profit margin was the only ratio showing a significant difference based on a Wilcoxon matched-pairs test. The paper does not claim to relate the impact of accounting policy differences to changes indicated by financial ratios. It is a matter for conjecture as to whether users of accounts would remember the financial condition of the company at an earlier period when noting the difference in reported profit under two different sets of accounting principles.

The years ended 31 December 1988 and 1994 are described in the paper as '1988' and '1994' for convenience. Where a company had a year-end other than 31 December, the closest year-end within six months either side was selected. Each company published a detailed quantitative reconciliation and also supporting narrative explanations of the accounting policy differences.

A technical detail relates to the number of adjustments labelled 'miscellaneous'. There was an increase in the number of items recorded in this category between 1988 and 1994. Although the average index value is closer to 1.0, reconciliations described as 'miscellaneous' or 'other' may have been a combination of larger adjustments which were offset against each other. Such items limit the refinement of the analysis of partial adjustments.

6. Results

This section presents the main causes of adjustment in the context of Table 1.

6.1. Main causes of adjustment

The numbers of reconciling adjustments made to reported profit are shown in Table 2, together with the relevant index of comparability measured as a mean and a median over the group as a whole. Each category in Table 2 represents a grouping of more than one type of adjustment or description within the category, so that the total adjustments presented by companies in their reconciliations (approximately 150 adjustments in each year) were significantly greater than the number of line items indicated in Table 2.

The overall index of comparability shows that in 1988 the adjustment to profit under UK accounting principles represented 16.8% of profit under US GAAP (index 1.1679), and by 1994 the difference had risen to 25.3% (index 1.2534). The skewness of the data is indicated by the median

[2]Weetman and Gray (1991) reported 162 in 1988. The *Depositary Receipts Universal Issuance Guide* 1997, available from Citibank, indicates a doubling of the total number of depositary receipt programmes between 1988 and 1994. The listings provided by Citibank include some 220 UK companies, covering most of the FTSE 100 and other major UK companies.

[3]There are three levels of publicly traded ADR programmes. Levels One and Two expand an issuer's share base through broader distribution of existing shares, while Level Three facilitates raising capital by issuing new shares. At Level Three the issuers must comply with full SEC registration and reporting requirements for foreign registrants. (Source: Citibank, *Depositary Receipts Universal Issuance Guide 1997*).

Table 2
Number of companies making each category of adjustment to profit, together with mean and median index of comparability for 1988 and 1994

Nature of adjustment to profit	**1988** *Count*	**1988** *Mean*	**1988** *Median*	**1994** *Count*	**1994** *Mean*	**1994** *Median*
Overall	25	1.17	1.10	25	1.25	1.18
Goodwill	24	1.13	1.06.	23	1.21	1.15
Deferred tax	22	1.06	1.01	23	1.00	1.00
Pensions/post-retirement benefits/ insurance	10	1.01	1.01	19	1.02	1.02
Asset/expense	14	0.98	0.99	14	1.12	1.01
Historic cost/revalued asset	13	0.95	0.98	18	0.98	0.99
Intangibles	3	1.08	1.07	5	1.34	1.06
Restructuring	—	—	—	5	0.80	0.88
Foreign currency translation	5	1.00	1.01	4	0.94	0.99
Financial instruments	2	1.26	1.26	4	0.98	1.04
Leasing	2	1.05	1.05	4	1.16	1.15
Revenue recognition	3	1.02	1.00	3	0.95	0.99
Extraordinary items	12	0.95	1.05	—	—	—
Miscellaneous	5	1.01	1.03	13	0.98	1.01

The following outliers were excluded from calculation of the mean values of profit in respect of the 1994 data:
1. ICI Group plc (Overall index of comparability and partial index of comparability for pension costs and retirement benefits)
2. WPP Group plc (Overall index of comparability and partial index of comparability for amortisation of goodwill)

values, showing corresponding adjustments of 10.1% (index 1.013) in 1988 and 18.2% (index 1.819) in 1994. There is an apparently strong indication, under either the mean or the median, that harmonisation of measurement had moved in a negative direction over the period.

From Table 2 it may be seen that at both dates under consideration, four accounting issues (amortisation of goodwill, provision for deferred taxation, pension costs and the effect of fixed asset revaluation) caused the most frequent reporting of UK/US differences. Other items in those tables confirm the *de jure* differences itemised in Appendix A but their occurrence is less frequent.

The reason for a change in the number of companies showing an adjustment in Table 2 could be:

• the accounting policy difference did not exist in that year;

• the accounting policy difference existed but did not affect the company.

It would be desirable to eliminate the second explanation by reference to the company documentation but this is only occasionally achievable because the company may use the 'miscellaneous' category or may aggregate some groups of adjustments. Notwithstanding this limitation, the initial impression from Table 2 is that the differences which existed in 1988 remained in existence in 1994, augmented by new items such as the accounting treatment of restructuring costs. The adjustments for pension costs in 1988 were increased in 1994 primarily because of additional adjustments for post-retirement benefits. In some cases these are identified separately but in other cases they are aggregated. The only item to disappear between the two dates was extraordinary items.

6.2. Overall materiality of adjustments

The mean and median present convenient summary data for the group as a whole, but investors are more interested in the separate companies when they make investment decisions. Accordingly the findings are presented as distributions of adjustments in bands of materiality, shown in Tables 3 to 6. Comments are made in terms of adjustment to profit but could apply equally to adjustments to net loss. The results of tests of statistical significance relating to Tables 2 to 6 are set out in Table 7.

Turning first to the overall profit, Table 3 shows the distribution according to bands of profit difference which an accountant might describe as 'immaterial' or 'material' or 'potentially material' (i.e. differences less than 5%, more than 10% and a grey area between 5% and 10%). In the majority of cases for both years, UK profit was greater than US profit, with 13 companies in 1988 and 17 companies in 1994 showing differences greater than 10%.

Intuitively, Table 3 gives the impression of significant and growing differences in reported profit due to accounting policy differences. A single-sample t-test and a Wilcoxon test (Table 7a and Table 7b) confirmed that the overall index values for both 1988 and 1994 were significantly greater than 1.0. Two large outliers in 1994 were eliminated from the calculation of the t-statistic but not from the Wilcoxon test. A nonparametric paired test on the index values, comparing 1988 and 1994, indicated that the difference was statistically significant (Table 7c). Out of 25 companies, 16 had an index value in 1994 greater than that of 1988.

The principal factors contributing to the profit differences are now analysed in detail, using the classification of causes set out in Table 1, in order to quantify more specifically the causes of the differences.

6.3. Measurement practices where UK is not compatible with IAS or US GAAP

From Panel (a) of Table 1 there were seven items where UK measurement practices differed from those of US GAAP and IASs at the relevant dates. Comparing these with Table 2 only three occurred frequently (accounting for goodwill, deferred taxation and pension costs), two were found infrequently (capitalisation of development costs and financial instruments) and the other two were either not found (consolidation policy) or were not relevant to measurement of overall profit (discontinued operations). Accordingly the first three are presented here.

Accounting for goodwill

Table 2 reports in one line all the accounting consequences of the UK policy on accounting for goodwill being different from that of the US. This covers adjustments related to annual amortisation of goodwill and also adjustments on the sale of a business where a write-off may be necessary.

Table 4 shows the distribution of values of the partial index of comparability. The number of cases where the adjustment to UK profit was 10% or more of the value of US profit increased from 10 to 14 when comparing 1988 with 1994.

Tables 7a and 7b show that for each of the years 1988 and 1994 the index value was significantly greater than 1.0. The pairwise comparison of reported profits in 1988 and 1994 (Table 7c) showed a significant difference over the period, as would be expected intuitively from the increase in the mean and median values of the index. Of the 23 pairs examined, there were 16 companies where the partial index of comparability in 1994 was greater than in 1988, and seven companies where the partial index was less in 1994. However in the latter cases the index was relatively close to 1.0.

Table 3
Frequency table of distribution of values of index of comparability for profit

Level of materiality	*Index values*	*1988*	*1994*
Adjustment to UK profit is −10% or more of the amount of US profit	≤0.90	5	4
Adjustment to UK profit between −5% and −10% of the amount of US profit	0.91 - 0.94	1	1
Adjustment to UK profit within +/− 5% of US profit	0.95 - 1.04	3	2
Adjustment to UK profit is between +5% and +10% of the amount of US profit	1.05 - 1.09	3	1
Adjustment to UK profit is +10% or more of the amount of the US profit	≥1.10	13	17
Total		25	25
Range (excluding outliers): lowest value		0.65	0.75
highest value		1.79	2.76

The following outlying index values were eliminated before calculating the t-statistic presented in Table 7

Name:	Index value eliminated	Year	Cause
ICI Group plc	3.36	1994	Large pension expense adjustment
WPP Group plc	10.77	1994	Low US profit figure

Table 4
Frequency table of distribution of values of partial index of comparability for amortisation of goodwill

Level of materiality	*Index values*	*1988*	*1994*
Adjustment to UK profit is −10% or more of the amount of US profit	≤0.90	0	0
Adjustment to UK profit is between −5% and −10% of the amount of US profit	0.91 - 0.94	0	0
Adjustment to UK profit within +/− 5% of US profit	0.95 - 1.04	12	8
Adjustment to UK profit is between +5% and +10% of the amount of US profit	1.05 - 1.09	2	1
Adjustment to UK profit is +10% or more of the amount of the US profit	≥1.10	10	14
Total		24	23
Range (excluding outliers): lowest value		1.00	0.95
highest value		1.78	2.30

The following outlying index values were eliminated before calculating the t-statistic presented in Table 7

Name:	Index value eliminated	Year	Cause
WPP Group plc	9.02	1994	Low US profit figure

The increase in the index is not a surprise given the acquisitive nature of these companies, but it does indicate that for companies active in the takeover market there will be an increasing perception of penalty related to amortisation rather than writing-off to reserves. It is possible to see, in this increasingly material impact of the effect of amortisation of goodwill, a cause for the concern expressed among UK companies when it was proposed that amortisation should become the normal practice. (Such concerns are documented in the letters of comment received by the ASB on various discussion papers relating to the subject of accounting for goodwill and intangibles.) The adjustment for intangible fixed assets, where disclosed separately, appeared less frequently. In some cases there were indications that the goodwill adjustment included an element of amortisation of other intangibles.

Accounting for deferred taxation

The frequency table showing distribution of the partial index values (Table 5) confirms a clustering around the neutral value of 1.0 in both years.

From Table 2 it may be seen that the mean value of the partial index for 1988 was 1.06. The t test (Table 7) indicated this was significant at the 5% level, but the Wilcoxon test indicated significance only at the 10% level. In 1994 the partial index was close to 1.0 and not statistically significant. The deferred taxation adjustment was the second most frequently occurring but by 1994 had become, on the average, of insignificant impact on reported profit. From the 21 companies that permitted pairwise comparisons (Table 7c) there were 15 companies for which the index value for 1994 was less than that for 1988. Overall the decrease was significant at the 10% level but not at 5%.

Pension costs and post-retirement benefits

The frequency distribution (Table 6) confirms a clustering around the central value of 1.0. The index values for adjustments relating to pension costs and post retirement benefits ranged from 0.94 to 1.12. In 1994, excluding the outlier, the range had spread further with index values ranging from 0.72 to 1.22 and there were nine companies in the zones of plus or minus 10% or more.

Table 7a shows that even in 1994, where the costs of post-retirement benefits had an effect in addition to pension costs, the mean value of the partial index was not significantly greater than 1.0. This was confirmed by the Wilcoxon test (Table 7b). Although pension costs and post-retirement benefits are a frequent cause of difference, there is no evidence of a material quantifiable difference overall. Investors would focus interest on the relatively infrequent large adjustments.

6.4. Measurement practices where the UK differs from US GAAP but is compatible with IASs

Panel (b) of Table 1 reveals nine items where UK measurement practices differ from US GAAP but are compatible with IASs. Comparing this list with Table 2 it may be seen that the most fre-

Table 5
Frequency table of distribution of values of partial index of comparability for deferred taxation adjustments

Level of materiality	*Index values*	*1988*	*1994*
Adjustment to UK profit is −10% or more of the amount of US profit	≤0.90	1	5
Adjustment to UK profit is between −5% and −10% of the amount of US profit	0.91 - 0.94	1	2
Adjustment to UK profit within +/− 5% of US profit	0.95 - 1.04	12	10
Adjustment to UK profit is between +5% and +10% of the amount of US profit	1.05 - 1.09	4	2
Adjustment to UK profit is +10% or more of the amount of the US profit	≥1.10	4	4
Total		22	23
Range lowest value		0.90	0.73
highest value		1.43	1.34

quently occurring relates to valuation of tangible fixed assets. Accruing dividends payable has no impact on profit measurement and the remaining seven items are found relatively infrequently.

Valuation of property, plant and equipment (Table 2)

The additional depreciation due to asset revaluation caused UK reported profit to be lower than the US figure. There were 14 companies making this adjustment in each year. The partial index of comparability was 0.95 for 1988 and 0.98 for 1994. In neither year was the index significantly less than 1.0. The IASC permits revaluation of fixed assets as an allowed alternative. Accordingly, if the SEC were in future to accept accounting statements consistent with IASs, UK companies could continue to revalue fixed assets and yet not be required to report the difference.

Other items from Table 1, panel (b)

Compulsory capitalisation of interest under US GAAP (borrowing costs—Table 8) caused five companies to make adjustments in 1988 and six in 1994. Since the existing UK practice is compatible with the benchmark treatment of IAS 23, there would be no requirement for a reconciliation in this respect if the SEC accepted practices compatible with IASs.

In the case of foreign currency translation (Table 2), five companies made adjustments in 1998 and four in 1994. Of these, two companies at each date used the year end rate for revenues and expense. Other adjustments (three in 1988 and two in 1994) related to reversal of translation differences on disposal of a foreign currency investment. The impact was not material overall.

Restructuring as an adjustment (Table 2) appeared in 1994 but not in 1988. The five companies reporting this adjustment in 1994 showed that in all cases the UK profit was lower than the US profit because the US rule did not permit the expense which had been reported in the UK.

For revenue recognition (Table 2), the three cases encountered in each year comprised one case of the amortisation of a capital grant, when the US rule allowed a revenue item not reported in the UK, and two cases of sale and leaseback transactions when the US rule did not allow a revenue item recorded in the UK.

6.5. Items not dealt with specifically by IASs

Some adjustments between UK accounting principles and US GAAP were reported which are not covered by a specific IAS. These were lessor accounting and a collection of items related by issues of recognition as an asset or an expense. Lessor accounting differences caused two adjustments in 1988 and four adjustments in 1994. These are quite technical issues which have not yet been developed by the IASC. Table 8 summarises all situations encountered in the reconciliations where an item may be recognised as an asset in one country but as an expense in the other. Relatively few of these are covered by a specific IAS.

Three categories of recognition practice may be identified. One is that the UK reports an asset with amortisation while the US reports an expense. The second is that the UK reports an expense while the US reports an asset with amortisation. The third is that the UK reports a write-off against reserves while the US reports an asset with amortisation. What is perhaps surprising is the number of items where the US approach appears less prudent by reporting an asset and spreading the cost, rather

Table 6
Frequency table of distribution of values of partial index of comparability for pension costs and retirement benefits

Level of materiality	*Index values*	*1988*	*1994*
Adjustment to UK profit is −10% or more of the amount of US profit	≤0.90	0	3
Adjustment to UK profit is between −5% and −10% of the amount of US profit	0.91 - 0.94	1	1
Adjustment to UK profit within +/−5% of US profit	0.95 - 1.04	7	8
Adjustment to UK profit is between +5% and +10% of the amount of US profit	1.05 - 1.09	1	1
Adjustment to UK profit is +10% or more of the amount of the US profit	≥1.10	1	6
Total		10	19
Range (excluding outliers): lowest value		0.94	0.72
highest value		1.12	1.22

The following outlying index values were eliminated before calculating the t-statistic presented in Table 7

Name:	Index value eliminated	Year	Cause
ICI Group plc	3.07	1994	Large pension expense adjustment

than taking the approach of reporting an immediate expense. The quantified impact and direction of the adjustment depends on the date on which the expenditure was incurred. Accordingly there is no systematic direction of the quantified impact of the policy differences. The table gives some support to the proposition that income smoothing is a stronger feature of US accounting.

7. Summary and conclusions

Three questions were asked at the start of the paper:

- What were the *de jure* differences between measurement practices under UK accounting principles as compared to those under US GAAP, during the period 1988 to 1994?
- What were the *de facto* differences in reported profits under UK accounting principles and US GAAP in 1988 and 1994, and what were the relative magnitudes of those differences?
- What implications do the quantified differences have for policy makers in setting UK standards, with particular regard to alignment with the IASs?

The key findings of the study are as follows:

1. Between 1988 and 1994 the most significant element of *de jure* harmonisation was the virtual elimination of extraordinary items in UK reported profits, moving closer to the US position.

2. Between 1988 and 1994 the issue of new US standards increased the level of *de jure* disharmony in terms of the number of potential causes of difference. This was evidenced by the summaries of changes in regulation and by the increased number of categories of adjustments reported by the companies surveyed.

3. As regards *de facto* disharmony, in both 1988 and 1994 the UK reported profit was significantly greater than that under US GAAP. Between 1988 and 1994 the difference between UK and US reported profit increased and the change was statistically significant.

4. In respect of those situations where measurement practices in the UK are not compatible with either US GAAP or IASs (Panel (a) of Table 1), the partial index of comparability indicated that the impact of goodwill amortisation was significantly greater in 1994 than in 1988. The impact of deferred taxation was statistically significant in 1988, but not in 1994. The impact of pension costs and retirement benefit costs, although frequently occurring, was not statistically significant in either year. Capitalisation of development costs, adjustments in respect of financial instruments and matters related to consolidation policy and discontinued operations occurred relatively infrequently.

5. Other adjustments of interest in relation to the gap between UK and US reported profit were related to asset revaluation and to the distinction between assets and expenses. Both indicate a

Table 7
Index of comparability for profit

7a. Mean value and t-statistic

Year	*N*	*Mean*	*St Dev*	*SE mean*	*t*	*P value*
Profit 1988	25	1.17	0.33	0.07	2.55	*0.01
Profit 1994	†23	1.25	0.47	0.10	2.61	*0.01
Partial adjustments						
Goodwill 1988	24	1.13	0.18	0.04	3.57	*0.01
Goodwill 1994	††22	1.21	0.30	0.06	3.36	*0.00
Deferred tax 1988	22	1.06	0.14	0.03	2.17	*0.04
Deferred tax 1994	23	1.00	0.13	0.03	0.11	0.91
Pension costs 1988	10	1.01	0.05	0.02	0.79	0.45
Pension costs 1994	†††18	1.02	0.13	0.03	0.52	0.61

**Significant at 5% (1-tail test for profit and goodwill, 2-tail test for deferred tax and pension costs)*
† For information on 2 outliers excluded from t-test, see Table 3
†† For information on the outlier excluded from t-test, see Table 4
†††For outlier excluded from t-test, see Table 6

7b. Actual median, Wilcoxon statistic and estimated median

Year			*1988*				*1994*	
	N	*Median*	*Wilcoxon statistic*	*P value*	*N*	*Median*	*Wilcoxon statistic*	*P value*
Profit	*25*	*1.10*	*244.0*	*0.02*	*25*	*1.18*	*268.0*	**0.00*
Goodwill	*24*	*1.06*	*300.0*	*0.00*	*23*	*1.15*	*268.0*	**0.00*
Deferred tax	*22*	*1.01*	*184.5*	*0.06*	*23*	*1.00*	*135.0*	*0.94*
Pension costs	*10*	*1.01*	*33.0*	*0.61*	*18*	*1.02*	*106.0*	*0.38*

(No outliers excluded)
**Significant at 5% (1-tail test for profit and goodwill, 2-tail test for deferred tax and pension costs)*

7c. Wilcoxon matched-pairs signed-ranks test

Adjustment (94 vs 88 in pairs)	*N*	*Mean rank +ve ranks*	*Mean rank +ve ranks*	*Cases with +ve ranks*	*Cases with −ve ranks*	*Ties*	*Z*	*2-tailed P*
Total	25	14.81	9.78	16	9	0	−2.00	*0.05
Goodwill	23	13.94	7.57	16	7	0	−2.59	*0.01
Deferred tax	21	10.17	11.33	6	15	0	−1.89	0.06

**Significant at 5%*

relative lack of conservatism in US income measurement, in terms of the lower depreciation charge under historical cost and of the instances where an item is amortised over a period, having been treated as an expense when incurred in the UK. Income smoothing is the most obvious explanation of the second observation. It would be possible for many of these UK practices to continue as acceptable within the bounds of IASC standards. The detail provided in this paper indicates the flexibility of measurement which may survive within a programme of global standard setting.

These research findings have relevance for both the FASB and the ASB in relation to accounting standards. However, generalisation from these results is limited because the companies included are all multinational companies of relatively large market capitalisation. Nevertheless, the financial statements presented by these companies in the UK purported to represent, at each date, a true and fair view of commercial reality. If the divergence from US GAAP increases there may be a perception for US readers that there is an increasing question mark over what represents that commercial reality. UK readers of the 20-F may also question the extent of the difference. The companies undertook essentially the same business at both dates, and so observers might question the credibility of accounting as a means of representing the activities of a business. It is pertinent to note that the UK companies listed in Appendix B are all high-profile organisations having an international presence commercially, and of necessity

Table 8
Recognition of assets

*Nature of adjustment (*indicates that one or more of the adjustments reported has an index number less than 1.0)*	*1988*	*1994*
UK asset with amortisation; US expense when incurred		
Deferred expenditure	–	1
Development costs	1	1*
Purchased R&D expenditure†	–	1
UK expense when incurred; US asset with amortisation		
Acquisition related items (UK debit may to P&L or to reserves)	1*	1
Amortisation of software development costs	1*	1
Program production and development	–	1*
Amortisation of favourable leaseback terms	1	1
Natural resources depletion	–	1
Timberlands depletion and reforestation	–	1
Replacement expenditure (infrastructure assets)	1*	1*
Interest capitalisation†	5*	6*
Loan origination fees and costs	2	2*
UK write-off against reserves; US asset with amortisation		
Amortisation of capital restructuring costs	–	1
Amortisation of convertible bond expenses	1	–
Amortisation of debt issue expenses	1	–
Amortisation of preference share issue costs	–	1
Convertible redeemable preference share issue costs	1	1

†Issues on which there is a specific IAS

feature prominently in relation to the campaign to persuade the SEC to allow foreign registrants to follow IASs rather than FASB standards.

The FASB has pointed to an apparently alarming number of differences between US standards and IASs. This paper has shown that in terms of the concept of materiality it seems unlikely that many of these differences will have an impact on the reported profit of UK multinational companies. The FASB should perhaps distinguish materiality of impact on measurement from detailed aspects of disclosure.

In the UK context, the early years of the work of the ASB concentrated on domestic-oriented issues and by the 1994 reporting period had not significantly reduced the differences between UK and US reporting practices. In the same time period the FASB was issuing standards which were taking US practice further from UK practice. The consequence for UK companies seeking finance in the US market is that they have reported increasingly different profit figures under the two reporting regimes.

The findings of this paper contain a message for the work of the ASB in relation to the IASC work programme and in relation to the ASB's stated aim of ensuring that, through a process of regular communication, accounting standards are produced with due regard to international developments. The subject areas causing greatest difficulty are those where there is the most frequent need for an item of reconciliation and the differences are material in sufficient cases to attract continued interest. Furthermore, the differences (taken as a whole) are increasing over time. It is a matter for further investigation as to whether investors do in fact have 'coping mechanisms', in relation to accounting differences, which can cope with growing disparity.

With the introduction of the accounting standard FRS 10 (ASB 1997) relating to intangible fixed assets, it appears that the ASB may have overcome difficulties with the most significant item, namely accounting for goodwill. It is not yet clear though that US regulators would accept impairment reviews of long-lived intangibles if the impairment test of the UK and the IASs differs from that of the US. Irrespective of the goodwill debate, it seems possible however that if the ASB bows to national pressure rather than moving towards international practice in the particular topics of accounting for deferred taxation and pension costs, reconciliations will continue to be required by the SEC of UK companies.

The research findings also raise a question as to the relationship between UK companies and the standard setters. It may be that the approach most suited after completion and acceptance of the IASC core standards project will be:

- International companies — Apply IASs
- Listed national companies — Potentially facing choice between IASs and UK standards
- Large unlisted national companies — Apply UK standards
- Small national companies — Apply FRSSE (Financial Reporting Standards for Smaller Enterprises).

Such a solution would mean that only multinational and listed national companies would be likely to have a direct interest in matters of harmony or disharmony, while companies essentially having a domestic base would continue to take the guidance of standard setters in a national context.

References

Accounting Standards Board (1992a). *FRS 3 Reporting financial performance.* London: ASB.

Accounting Standards Board (1992b). *UITF 6 Accounting for post-retirement benefits other than pensions.* London: ASB.

Accounting Standards Board (1993). *FRS 4 Capital instruments.* London: ASB.

Accounting Standards Board (1994a). *FRS 5 Reporting the substance of transactions.* London: ASB.

Accounting Standards Board (1994b). *FRS 6 Acquisitions and mergers.* London: ASB.

Accounting Standards Board (1995). *Exposure Draft: Statement of Principles.* London: ASB.

Accounting Standards Board (1997). *FRS 10 Goodwill and Intangible Assets.* London: ASB.

Adams, C. A., Weetman, P. and Gray, S. J. (1993). 'Reconciling national with international accounting standards'. *European Accounting Review*, 2(3): 471–494.

Bhushan, R. and Lessard, D. R. (1992). 'Coping with international accounting diversity: fund managers' views on disclosure, reconciliation and harmonization'. *Journal of International Financial Management and Accounting*, 4(2): 55–87.

Cairns, D. (1995). *A Guide to Applying International Accounting Standards.* London: Accountancy Books.

Choi, F. D. S. and Levich, R. M. (1991). 'Behavioural effects of international accounting diversity'. *Accounting Horizons*, (June): 1–13.

Cooke, T. E. (1993). 'The impact of accounting principles on profits: the US versus Japan'. *Accounting and Business Research* (Autumn): 460–476.

Coopers & Lybrand (1998). *The Coopers and Lybrand Manual of Accounting: The Guide to UK Accounting Law and Practice.* London: Accountancy Books.

Davies, M., Paterson, P. and Wilson, A. (1997). *UK GAAP* (fifth edition). London: Ernst & Young and Macmillan.

Epstein, B. J. and Mirza A. A. (1997). *IAS 97*, New York: John Wiley & Sons Inc.

Financial Accounting Standards Board (1996). *The IASC-US Comparison Project: a report on the similarities and differences between IASC standards and US GAAP.* Connecticut, USA: FASB.

Financial Reporting Council (1996). *Progress Report.* London: FRC.

Grant Thornton (1990). *Audit Manual.* London: Longman.

Gray, S. J. (1980). 'The impact of international accounting differences from a security-analysis perspective: some European evidence' *Journal of Accounting Research*, Spring.

Hellman, N. (1993) 'A comparative analysis of the impact of accounting differences and return on equity'. *European Accounting Review*, 3: 495–530.

International Accounting Standards Committee (1989). *Exposure draft E 32 Comparability of Financial Statements: Proposed Amendments to International Accounting Standards 2, 5, 8, 9, 11, 16, 17, 18, 19, 21, 22, 23 and 25.* London: IASC.

International Accounting Standards Committee (1993a). *IASC Insight*, December, IASC.

International Accounting Standards Committee (1993b). *Statement of Intent: Comparability of Financial Statements.* London: IASC.

International Accounting Standards Committee (1994). *IASC Insight*, December, London: IASC.

International Accounting Standards Committee (1996a). *IASC Insight*, July, London: IASC.

International Accounting Standards Committee (1996b). *Annual Review 1996*, section on Developments in the US. London: IASC.

Joint Study (1995). *Financial Reporting in North America.* A joint study undertaken by the Canadian Institute of Chartered Accountants, the Instituto Mexicano de Contadores Públicos, A. C. and the Financial Accounting Standards Board, assisted by KPMG Peat Marwick LLP and available from any one of the three participating professional bodies.

Keegan, M. and King, H. (1996). 'Together but different'. *Accountancy* (October): 130–131.

Norton, J. (1995). 'The impact of accounting practices on the measurement of profit and equity: Australia versus the United States'. Abacus, 3(3): 178–200.

Price Waterhouse (1994): *An Introduction to US GAAP*, London: Price Waterhouse.

van der Tas, L. G. (1988): 'Measuring harmonisation of financial reporting practice'. *Accounting and Business Research*, 18(70): 157–169.

Wallace, R. S. O. (1990). 'Survival strategies of a global organization: the case of the International Accounting Standards Committee'. *Accounting Horizon:* 1–22.

Weetman, P. and Gray, S. J. (1990). 'International financial analysis and comparative accounting performance: the impact of UK versus US accounting principles on earnings'. *Journal of International Financial Management and Accounting*, 2(2/3): 111–130.

Weetman, P. and Gray, S. J. (1991). 'A comparative international analysis of the impact of accounting principles on profits: the USA versus the UK, Sweden and The Netherlands'. *Accounting and Business Research*, 21(84): 363–379.

Weetman, P., Adams, C. A. and Gray, S. J. (1993). *Issues in International Accounting Harmonisation*, Research Report No 33. Chartered Association of Certified Accountants, 39 pp.

Appendix A
Key differences between US and UK accounting policies, period 1988 to 1994, and comparison with relevant aspects of IASs. UK is compatible with IASs except where bold highlighting indicates differences.

Item	*US GAAP*	*UK accounting principles*	*IASs*
Goodwill	APB 17: Capitalise and amortise over a maximum period of 40 years.	SSAP 20: Immediate write-off against reserves. Amortisation over useful economic life is permitted but rarely applied. **SSAP 22 not compatible with IAS, FRS 10 (1997) moves closer to IAS 22 in principle but differences remain in significant details which could affect measurement aspects.**	IAS 22 Amortisation over a period up to 20 years is the required treatment. The practice of permitting goodwill on acquisition to be set against shareholders' interests was discontinued following the comparability project (Issued 1993, superseding 1983 version).
Deferred taxation	1988: For foreign registrants the situation was in transition from APB 11 (which required the deferral method and full provision) to SFAS 96, issued in 1987 but with implementation postponed, requiring the liability method with full provision. 1994: SFAS 109 (effective from 1992) requiring liability method with full provision.	SSAP 15 and Companies Act 1985 requiring the liability method with partial provision. **SSAP 15 (revised) (1978, 1985 1992) not compatible with the revised IAS 12.**	IAS 12 (issued 1979, reformatted 1995, revised Dec 1996) The 1996 revision satisfies the requirement of the core standards programme. It requires a liability method based on temporary differences and does not permit partial provision. The 1995 version required that the tax expense for the period should be calculated on the basis of 'tax effect accounting' using either the deferral or the liability method.
Pension costs	Throughout period: SFAS 87 and SFAS 88. Fundamental principle is to recognise the cost of an employee's pension over that employee's service period. The measurement rules are tightly defined and may be regarded as measuring 'current cost' of providing benefits. It is unlikely that SFAS 87 figures would precisely fulfil the requirements of SSAP 24.	SSAP 24, CA 85 and UITF 4. General principle is to recognise cost of providing pensions on a systematic and rational basis over the period during which the company benefits from the employee's services. The measurement rules allow flexibility within a principle of recognition of cost. It is unlikely that SSAP 24 figures would fulfil the requirements of SFAS 87. However, SSAP 24 (1988 amended 1992) is stated to comply with IAS 19.	IAS 19 (Issued 1983, revised 1993). Projected benefit valuation method is also allowed.
Post-retirement benefits other than pensions	1994: SFAS 106 required businesses to estimate the total future cost of providing such benefits and recognise that cost as an expense as employees render service, rather than when benefits are paid. Requirements are similar to those of SFAS 87.	UITF 6 and SSAP 24. The principles to be applied are similar to those for pension costs and accordingly SSAP 24 is applicable. Companies which use the measurement rules of SFAS 106 will be deemed to satisfy SSAP 24 principles. It is possible that measurement using the greater flexibility of SSAP 24 would not meet SFAS 106 conditions.	IAS 19 (Issued 1983, revised 1993). Benchmark treatment for all retirements is to use an accrued benefit valuation method. Projected benefit valuation method is also allowed.

Appendix A *continued*

Item	*US GAAP*	*UK accounting principles*	*IASs*
Extraordinary items	APB 30 and APB 16 Definitions unchanged throughout period.	1988: Definition in SSAP 6 superficially similar to that of US standards but more liberally applied in the UK. Consequently many items allowed as extraordinary in the UK were exceptional in the US. 1994: FRS 3 (issued 1992) emphasised the rarity of extraordinary items and effectively brought UK close to US.	IAS 8 Definitions of extraordinary items less rigorous than FRS 3. Disclosure required in income statement.
Valuation of property, plant and equipment	ARB 43 and APB 6 Require historical cost only.	CA 1985 permits valuation as an allowed alternative to historical cost. Depreciation must be based on revalued amount (SSAP 12).	IAS 16 Allows measurement subsequent to initial recognition (Issued 1993 superseding 1982) Benchmark treatment is historical cost, valuation is an allowed alternative.
Borrowing costs	SFAS 34 as amended by SFAS 42, SFAS 58 and SFAS 62 makes capitalisation compulsory for certain assets.	CA 1985 defines a fixed asset very generally, but no preferred treatment specified for borrowing costs. CA 1985 permits either capitalisation or write-off.	IAS 23 Benchmark treatment is that borrowing costs should be recognised as an expense in the period in which they occur. Allowed alternative permits capitalisation under specific conditions (Issued 1993 superseding 1984 version).
Foreign currency translation	FAS 52 requires that profit and loss account be translated at rate prevailing at time of recognition or at weighted average rate. For subsidiaries operating in hyper inflationary economics, temporal method is required.	SSAP 20 permits profit and loss account to be translated at average rate or at closing rate **SSAP 20 (1983) permits translation of income and expenses at either average rate or closing rate.** For subsidiaries operating in hyper inflationary countries, restate financial statements before translation.	IAS 21 Translate all assets and liabilities at the closing rate and income and expenses at exchange rate of date of transaction - average for the period is an acceptable approximation (Issued 1993 superseding 1983 version).
Capitalisation of development costs	SFAS 2, SFAS 68 and SFAS 86 require immediate write-off.	SSAP 13 and CA 1985 permit recognition of an asset where specific criteria are met, but choice of write-off is allowed. **SSAP 13 permits capitalisation under specific conditions but allows write-off.**	IAS 9 Requires capitalisation of development cost where specific conditions are met (Issued 1993 superseding 1978 version).
Dividends payable	Reg S-X: No provision for dividends undeclared at the year end.	CA 1985 Provision must be made for dividends relating to the financial year although not declared until after it ends.	IASs apply normal accruals requirements - UK practice is within the general principle of accruals.
Correction of fundamental errors resulting from accounting policy change	APB 20, SFAS 32 Cumulative effect of change to be shown as a separate item in profit and loss account. In certain circumstances restatement of prior year figures is allowed.	1988 SSAP 6 required adjustment to opening retained earnings and amendment of comparative information. 1994: FRS 3 continues this approach.	IAS 8 Benchmark treatment is to adjust the opening balance of retained earnings to take account of the cumulative effect on profit. Allowed alternative is to correct in the current period, giving sufficient additional information about the change (Issued 1993 superseding 1978 version).

Appendix A *continued*

Item	*US GAAP*	*UK accounting principles*	*IASs*
Business combinations	APB 16 requires purchase method for acquisitions and pooling of interests method for uniting of interests. The two are not interchangeable and specific criteria apply to each.	1988: SSAP 14 and SSAP 23 taken together meant that acquisition (purchase) accounting and merger (pooling of interests) were not necessarily mutually exclusive. 1994: FRS 2 with SSAP 23 still in place but FRS 6 was issued in Sept 1994 (effective for accounting periods commencing on or after 23 December 1994) tightening the rules on merger accounting to be stricter than US rules for pooling of interests. FRS 6 generally consistent with IAS 22	IAS 22 Defines acquisition and uniting of interest. The comparability project tightened up the definition of uniting of interest (issued 1993, superseding 1983 version).
Financial instruments	Considerable guidance in SFAS 52, SFAS 80, (relevant to 1988 and 1994 accounts) and SFAS 105, SFAS 107 and SFAS 114 (relevant to 1994 accounts).	Little authoritative guidance until FRS 4 was issued in December 1993 (effective for accounting periods ending on or after 22 June 1994). ASB issued exposure draft (1997) on disclosure aspects of financial instruments. **FRS4 (1993) prohibits 'split' accounting for capital instruments which have mixed debt and equity components.**	IAS 32 Primarily a disclosure standard. (Issued 1995) Measurement was taken as a separate project but 'split accounting' for capital instruments is required.
Restructuring costs	FAS 5 and Interpretation No 1 to APB 30 have generally resulted in restructuring costs being accrued. EITF guidance issued in 1994 was more restrictive than UK practice. Several specific standards exist in the US	Limited guidance in UK - some guidance in FRS 3 on provisions where there is a decision to terminate, but no specific standard.	No specific standard.
Revenue recognition		No specific guidance beyond the CA 85 - only subject to general requirement for prudence.	IS 18 Standard presents general principles. Revenue is recognised when it is probable that future economic benefits will flow to the enterprise and that these benefits can be measured reliably. (Issued 1993 superseding 1982 version).
Investments in marketable equity securities and debt securities	ARB 43 (applies to 1988 and 1994) plus SFAS 115 (applies to 1994 only). SFAS 115 requires an investment in debt or marketable equity securities to be classified as 'held-to-maturity', 'available-for-sale' or 'trading'. Accounting treatment depends on these categories rather than current/non-current classification.	CA 85 prescribes treatment based on classification as current or fixed. Current asset investments are normally stated at lower of cost and net market value. Under alternative accounting rules, current cost may be used. There are rules in UITF 5 for transfers from current assets to fixed assets. SSAP 19 (1981, 1992, 1994) requires revaluation of investment properties held as fixed assets. Current asset investments still under consideration; impairment under consideration.	IAS 25 current asset investments to be carried at market value or at the lower of cost and market value. Long-term assets to be carried at cost or revalued amount (Issued 1986, reformatted 1995) Project on impairment test was announced in June 1996 for general application to all intangible assets.

Appendix A *continued*

Item	*US GAAP*	*UK accounting principles*	*IASs*
Consolidation policy	Definition of control is similar to, but not an exact match to UK definition	All subsidiary undertakings must be consolidated. FRS 2 (1992) leaves almost no scope for exclusion of a subsidiary. Definition of control differs and, particularly following FRS 5 may cause consolidation of subsidiaries and quasi-subsidiaries not permitted in US. Unlikely to affect the 1988 and 1994 accounts analysed here.	IAS 27 Defines control. Allows exclusion of subsidiary if specific conditions are met. (Issued 1989, reformatted 1995).
Discontinued operations	APB 30, AIN-APB 30, EITF 85-36 and EITF 90-16. Definition differs from UK definition.	FRS 3, SSAP 22 and UITF 3. Definition differs from US definition - but reconciliations of profit measurement are rarely affected because this is a matter for separate disclosure within the overall reported profit.	IAS 8 Definition linked to US definition but less rigorous. disclosures required but, in contrast to US approach, under IAS 8 discontinued operations are to be included in the profit or loss from ordinary activities (Issued 1993, superseding 1978 version).
Stocks inventory	US permits LIFO as well as FIFO.	SSAP 9 (1975, 1980, 1988) UK encourages FIFO (LIFO allowed by SSAP 9 but not allowed for tax purposes). Does not affect reconciliations since US accepts FIFO.	IAS 2 Requires lower of cost and net realisable value. FIFO is benchmark treatment, LIFO is allowed alternative (Issued 1993 superseding 1975 version).

Sources: various SSAPs, FRSs and SFASs plus Price Waterhouse (1994), *An Introduction to US GAAP* for position at 1994 and Joint Study (1995), *Financial Reporting in North America*, various IASs and Epstein and Mirza (1997)

Abbreviations

AICPA	American Institute of Certified Public Accountants
AIN	AICPA Accounting Interpretations
APB	Accounting Principles Board
ARB	Accounting Research Bulletin
CA 85	Companies Act 1985
ED	Exposure draft
EITF	Emerging Issues Task Force
FRS	Financial Reporting Standard
Reg S-X	Regulation S-X issued by the Securities and Exchange Commission
SFAS	Statement of Financial Accounting Standards
UITF	Urgent Issues Task Force
US GAAP	Generally Accepted Accounting Principles in the US

Appendix B
List of UK companies analysed in this paper for comparison with Weetman and Gray (1991)

	Firm	*Year end for 1988 data*	*Year end for 1994 data*
1	Attwoods plc	31.7.88	31.7.94
2	Barclays Bank plc	31.12.88	31.12.94
3	BET plc	1.4.89	1.4.95
4	BOC Group plc	30.9.88	30.9.94
5	British Airways plc	31.3.89	31.3.95
6	British Gas plc	31.3.89	31.12.94
7	British Petroleum plc	31.12.88	31.12.94
8	British Steel plc	1.4.89	1.4.95
9	British Telecommunications plc	31.3.89	31.3.95
10	Cadbury Schweppes plc	31.12.88	31.12.94
11	Carlton Communications plc	30.9.88	30.9.94
12	English China Clays plc	30.9.88	31.12.94
13	Glaxo Holdings plc	30.6.89	31.12.95*
14	Hanson plc	30.9.88	30.9.94
15	ICI Group plc	31.12.88	31.12.94
16	Midland Bank plc	31.12.88	31.12.94
17	National Westminster Bank plc	31.12.88	31.12.94
18	NFC plc	1.10.88	1.10.94
19	Reuters Holdings plc	31.12.88	31.12.94
20	Signet Group plc	28.1.89	28.1.95
21	The Royal Bank of Scotland plc	30.9.88	30.9.94
22	Tomkins plc	29.4.89	29.4.95
23	United News and Media plc	31.12.88	31.12.94
24	Waterford Wedgwood plc	31.12.88	31.12.94
25	WPP Group plc	31.12.88	31.12.94

*Glaxo Holdings plc changed its accounting date so that there was an 18-month accounting period to 31 December 1995.

List of UK companies reported in Weetman and Gray (1991) not available for this work

Beazer plc	Takeover
Blue Arrow plc	Takeover
Cambridge Instrument Co plc	Not obtained
Dixons Group plc	No US listing in 1994
Huntingdon International Holdings plc	No US listing in 1994
Jaguar plc	Takeover
LEP Group plc	No US listing in 1994
Lex Service plc	No US listing in 1994
Plessey plc	Takeover
Rodime plc	Major reorientation of activity occurring
Saatchi and Saatchi Co plc	No UK listing in 1994
Shell Transport and Trading Co plc	US standards applied
Unilever plc	1994 reconciliation includes Unilever N.V.
Ward White plc	Takeover
WCRS plc (Aegis plc in 1994)	No US listing in 1994
Wellcome plc	Merger with Glaxo

Part II
Analysis of and Commentary on International Harmonization

[12]

Accounting and Business Research, Vol. 32. No. 2. pp. 105-117. 2002

Harmonisation of financial reporting before the European Company Law Directives: the case of the Nordic Companies Act

Sally Aisbitt*

Abstract—*De jure* harmonisation of financial reporting began early in the Nordic countries with initial discussions reported as early as the 1930s. Legislation implemented in the 1970s was based on a proposal for a common Nordic Companies Act. This article follows the history of this legislation and analyses it with a view to providing insights into voluntary harmonisation across multiple countries. The main lessons appear to be that (1) Germany had a measurable influence; (2) taxes played an important role which has persisted in some countries, with others resisting change until the 1980s and 1990s; (3) the Nordic countries were among the first to introduce a legal requirement for publication of a funds flow statement; (4) meeting the needs of diverse and dynamic stakeholders was addressed differentially by the Nordic countries; and (5) regional co-operation seems to have been overtaken by events on the broader international stage and the costs of compromise.

1. Introduction

The development of financial reporting in the Nordic countries (Denmark, Finland, Norway and Sweden) followed a similar pattern to other western countries: the extent and regulation of financial reporting increased with the industrial revolution and wider share ownership. In the 20th century the process continued, but was further influenced by activities in other countries as well as national needs. In requiring specific aspects of corporate organisation and reporting by law, the Nordic countries seem to have introduced legislation in similar ways to other European countries, although in general they seem to have been early to legislate. This is summarised in Table 1.

From the Table, certain trends can be identified. For example, where requirements to publish balance sheets and profit and loss accounts were introduced separately, the balance sheet was compulsory first. The significance of this has been discussed elsewhere (e.g., Edwards, 1992; Christiansen, 1995a; Nilsson, 1995), but, in general terms, the drivers for increased information about financial performance seem to be wider share ownership and scandals that highlighted the limitations of information published hitherto. It is also noticeable that the Nordic countries were early to introduce regulations for the reporting of funds and cash flow information. The final line of the Table also demonstrates the role of non-legislative bodies in producing additional regulations for financial reporting.

In the 20th century there were also some conscious efforts to amend regulations governing financial reporting to promote comparability of financial statements prepared in different Nordic countries, with a view to encouraging trade. The first such attempt was through the proposed Nordic Companies Act. This early example of voluntary harmonisation has continued relevance, given that the transition to International Accounting Standards is yet to be compulsory in most countries for most companies. The analysis of the Nordic experience in the 20th century provides useful insights for contemporary policy makers.

This article traces the development of the Act from the 1930s through to its implementation in the 1970s by a review of literature and analysis of draft and final legislation. It challenges the assumption that all language versions and all implementations of the Nordic Act were alike, leading to a common Nordic approach to accounting legislation (e.g., Flower, 1994: 239; Heurlin and Peterssohn, 1998: 1080). The implementing legislation is analysed in the context of its apparent major source, the German *Aktiengesetz* 1965. This provides an assessment of the similarities of the legislation in the Nordic countries and highlights the areas not specifically mentioned in the legislation, hence leading to possible variations in practice. This demonstrates that while the legislation in the four Nordic countries had much in common after the Nordic Act, it was not identical. Furthermore, the legislation indicates that Nordic

* The author is lecturer in accountancy at the Accounting and Finance Research Unit, The Open University Business School, Walton Hall, Milton Keynes, MK7 6AA. E-mail: S.A.Aisbitt@open.ac.uk. Dr Aisbitt is grateful for advice and suggestions from Professor Christopher Nobes (University of Reading) and an anonymous reviewer on earlier drafts of this article, and financial support from the Institute of Chartered Accountants in England and Wales.

Table 1
Earliest regulations associated with financial reporting

First	*UK*	*Germany*	*Denmark*	*Finland*	*Norway*	*Sweden*
Companies Act	1844	1794*	1917	1864	1910	1848
Balance sheet required to be published by law	1844 – 1862 and 1900	1856	1917	1895	1910	1855
Audit report required by law for generality of companies	1844 – 1862 and 1900	1931	1917	1895	1910	1895
P&l required to be published by law	1929	1884	1917	1925	1910	1910
Standardised formats for p&l and balance sheet	1981	1931	1981	1945	1957	1944
Consolidated balance sheet required to be published by law	1947	1965	1973	1978	1957	1944
Consolidated p&l required to be published by law	1947	1965	1990	1978	1976	1975
Funds flow statement required to be published by law	Not required	1998	Not required	1978	1976	1975
Funds flow statement required to be published by standard	1975	–	1979	1983	1976	1984

* The Preussisches Allgemeines Landrecht of 1794 contained the first German provisions on company law and the first uniform stock corporation law for the whole of Germany was passed in 1970 (Schröer, 1993: 336–8).

financial reporting was developing in parallel with, and perhaps influenced by, accounting elsewhere.

Finally, the discussion points out some of the pitfalls that need to be avoided, if harmonisation is to succeed. Harmonisation needs to be a continuous process, if practice is not to diverge as circumstances of countries and companies evolve, and varying stakeholders make their claims. Furthermore, the intentions of some (particularly smaller) countries can be thwarted (as well as supported) by conditions in other countries or international organisations. This is critical in the current climate, where the globalisation of capital markets is driving the accounting regulatory agenda. It is important that the contribution of smaller countries is not lost, as they concede sovereignty in the standard-setting process.

2. The proposed Nordic Companies Act

The proximity of the dates of some of the early legislation shown in Table 1 suggests that legislators were conscious of developments in other countries. This is perhaps unsurprising, given the movement of academics among the countries. For example, Heurlin and Peterssohn (1998: 1083) describe how the first professors of accounting at both Stockholm and Gothenberg Schools of Economics were German, and their successors had studied in Germany. Nilsson (1995: 228) points out that preparation of the Swedish Companies Act 1944 involved consultation with Denmark, Finland and Norway. In addition to the informal co-operation suggested by these events, there were more formal efforts to harmonise accounting legislation among the Nordic countries. Elling (1993: 582) mentions the initiation of a harmonisation project in 1934 and Alexander and Christiansen (1996) talk about the publication of a proposal in 1942, but this was halted by World War II. A Nordic Council was established in 1952 to formalise the existing links between the Nordic countries. In 1962, a Nordic common market was proposed, and this led to a common proposal for a new Companies Act in 1969 (Flower, 1994: 239). Monsen and Wallace (1995) refer to four Companies Act Proposals (Denmark in 1969, Finland in 1969, Norway in 1970, Sweden in 1971). Each country produced its own version of the proposed Act. The texts of all four versions (in one of the local languages) were published side by side.

A comparison was made of Chapter 12 of the

Table 2
Implementation of the proposed Nordic Act

Country	*Companies Act*	*Accounting Act*
Denmark	*Lov om aktieselskaber* Public Limited Companies Act 1973 *Lov om anpartsselskaber* Private Limited Companies Act 1973	
Finland	*Osakehytölaki* Companies Act 1978	*Kirjanpitolaki ja -asetus* Book-keeping Law and Statute 1973
Norway	*Lov om aksjeselskaper* Companies Act 1976	*Lov om regnskapsplikt m.v. (regnskapsloven)* Accounting Act 1977
Sweden	*Aktiebolagslag* Companies Act 1975	*Bokföringslag* Accounting Act 1976

proposed Act relating to annual accounts and group accounts as published in the proposal for the Swedish implementation of the Act (see SOU, 1971: 15: 554–83).[1] While there were differences in wording between the different language editions that could be attributed to linguistic idiosyncrasies, there were some clauses that appeared in one (or more) edition(s) and not in the others. These differences are summarised in Appendix 1. While none suggests a major difference in approach to accounting, the existence of distinctions suggests that there had been negotiation and careful consideration of the Act, such that the differences may have seemed more significant to those involved in the process than they appear now. Some of the differences clearly reflect the variations in the constitutions of the different countries, e.g., there are instances when the King can provide exemptions for companies in Sweden and Norway and no corresponding provisions in Finland or Denmark. In other cases the reasons for the variations are less obvious, e.g., Denmark requires a number of items to be disclosed which are not mentioned in the proposals for the other countries.

The proposed Nordic common market may have been inspired by the European Economic Community, and its concept of harmonisation of company law to promote free movement and trade. It is perhaps no coincidence that the Nordic proposals were published just a year after the Elmendorff Committee completed the *avant projet* for the Fourth Directive begun in 1965 and the same year that the *avant projet* for the Seventh Directive was presented to the EC Commission (Nobes, 1993). Alexander and Christiansen (1996) suggest that Denmark's 1969 proposal was influenced by anticipated future membership of the EEC. This was a general point, because at that stage all the countries were considering membership. Christiansen (1995a: 65) explains that 'an important aim of Nordic accounting harmonisation was agreement of a common definition of profit. The definition chosen followed the Swedish concept of profit, which was closely related to distribution considerations, as in Germany.'

The push for harmonisation also seems to be analogous with that within the Commonwealth of Australia at about the same time. Although uniform legislation was agreed to for all Australian states in 1961, the timing and nature of subsequent amendments varied among states and there was no strong central administration. This led to abuses in terms of interstate fraud and market manipulation. The inadequacies of the system were brought to public attention with the Rae Report in 1974. The six states and the federal government formally agreed to uniform companies and securities law in 1978 (Miller, 1994: 343).

However, the Nordic harmonisation programme did not live up to its promising start. Finland withdrew from the Nordic common market (allegedly under pressure from Russia) and as a consequence of this and/or its unique approach to accounting theory (see Section 4), abandoned its involvement in the Nordic Companies Act (Majala, 1994: 75; Flower, 1994: 240). Nevertheless the publication of a Companies Act proposal in 1969 suggests that Finland's involvement in the Nordic project had not been entirely unproductive, as will be explained in the later discussion of the details of the Acts of the 1970s. The remaining Nordic countries began to fragment with differing decisions on membership of the EEC and changes in the do-

[1] The 'Finnish text' is presented in Swedish in the document referred to. The style of Swedish used is similar to that of the Swedish text. Official Swedish translations published in Finland normally have a particular style, which is different from the Swedish used in Sweden. It is not clear whether the Swedish language 'Finnish text' used here is a somewhat unusual official Finnish version or a convenience translation produced by the Swedes for their own purposes. If this is a Swedish convenience translation, it may be that some of the nuances of the Finnish version have been lost.

mestic political situation (e.g., shortages/discovery of oil, shortages of capital, changes in governments). The commentary on the Norwegian implementation of the proposals demonstrated clear reservations (Ot. prp. nr. 19, 1974–5: 10), e.g., the relevance of a common Nordic approach is questioned if that would be different from other European countries.

Although the proposed Nordic Companies Act was not implemented as such, it strongly influenced the accounting legislation passed in the 1970s in all the Nordic countries. Committees working in these countries indicated that, where possible, it would be natural to have a standard approach between countries (Nilsson, 1995: 231). Denmark introduced the new Companies Acts (in 1973) in this way even though by that stage it had already joined the EEC. Monsen and Wallace (1995: 981) suggest that the Danish Acts were the closest to the proposed Nordic Act of any of the subsequent legislation. All the countries introduced one or more Companies Acts, which set out the accounting requirements for companies' financial statements, and all except Denmark[2] introduced an Accounting Act which applied to all businesses. There was some overlap between the Acts in each country, with Companies Acts tending to include some of the regulations from the Accounting Acts. At this stage, Denmark was the only country differentiating between public and private limited companies, presumably as a reflection of European Directives, which do this. The 1970s Acts are summarised in Table 2.

3. Nordic accounting legislation of the 1970s

In discussing the preparation of the Swedish Companies Act 1975, Nilsson (1995: 229–30) suggests that the guidelines showed awareness of EEC legislation and in particular the 'new German and French company legislation'. It is not clear what Nilsson means by this, since the only European Directives available at this stage would have been in draft form and the newest German and French 'legislation' would have been the *Aktiengesetz* 1965 and the *Plan Comptable Général* 1957 respectively. The Swedish legislation would be expected to reflect this broader European view, but could not be expected to exhibit characteristics of EC Directives, except insofar as those Directives were products of previous national legislations.

Nilsson goes on to point out that the 'principle behind the annual public reporting of companies should be the greatest possible openness; consequently, accounting would have to be made more rigorous' (Nilsson, 1995: 230). In addition to protecting creditors, financial statements should therefore provide information for management, tax authorities and employees. This suggests a radical approach, although Christiansen (1995a: 64) argues that the new Acts (Public Limited Companies Act 1973 and Private Limited Companies Act 1973) did not meet the auditing profession's expectations in Denmark: '[the Public Limited Companies Act was] primarily a codification of existing accounting practice and concentrated on broad-brush principles and requirements which did little to affect actual practice'. Norway also criticised the proposals: the need for compromises meant that it was impossible for them to be forward looking (Ot. prp. nr, 19, 1974–5: 10). The main features of the new Acts are set out below along with a comparison with the German *Aktiengesetz* 1965.[3]

3.1. Fundamental principles

The new Accounting Acts and Companies Acts all drew on a general clause that financial statements were to be prepared in accordance with 'good accounting practice' (GAP) in place of the previous general clause. The general clauses are summarised in Table 3.

GAP appears to be equivalent to the German *Grundsätze ordnungsmäßiger Buchführung* (GoB)[4] as set out in the *Aktiengesetz* 1965. German enterprises must prepare their annual accounts in accordance with GoB (§149(1) *Aktiengesetz* 1965; now in §264 (2) *Handelgesetzbuch* (Commercial Code; HGB)). The Danish commentary on the Bill implementing the Fourth Directive explains the Danish and Swedish backgrounds to the change in the general clause in the 1970s (see Table 2). The GAP clause was intended to be a new common Nordic expression, but in reality, it was simply a paraphrase of the previous general clause, in spite of the apparent harmonisation of the language used. This view was echoed by the Norwegians (Ot. prp. nr. 19, 1974–5: 154). Nevertheless, the Swedes had maintained that a general clause was necessary to provide guidance in areas where statute could not regulate in detail and to allow accounting practice to develop (*Folketingstidende*, 1980: 2974–5). This has been accepted by the other countries (e.g., Vårdal and Johnsen, 1989: 53–7).

The phrase, GAP, has been compared with the 'true and fair view' (TFV) of the subsequent European Directives by a number of authors (e.g., Elling, 1994; NOU 1995: 30: 2.3.4; Alexander and Christiansen, 1996; Aisbitt and Nobes, 2001) who

[2] The Danish Bookkeeping Act 1959 was amended in 1966, 1970 and 1986.

[3] Comparison with the *Aktiengesetz* 1965 is based on Mueller and Galbraith (1976).

[4] This phrase is often rendered as 'generally accepted accounting principles' in English. For further discuusion of the appropriateness of this translation, see Evans (2000).

Table 3
General clauses in Nordic legislation

Country	*Pre-1970s legislation*	*Post 1970s legislation*
Denmark	Ordentlig og forsigtig forretningsbrug Orderly and prudent business practice	God regnskabsskik Good accounting practice
Finland	Hyvä kauppiastapa Good businessman manner God köpmannassed* Good businessman manner	Hyvä kirjanpitotapa Good accounting practice God bokföringssed Good accounting practice
Norway	Ordentlig og forsiktig forretningsførsel Orderly and prudent management**	God regnskapsskikk Good accounting practice
Sweden	God köpmannassed Good businessman practice	God redovisningssed Good accounting practice

* The official Swedish version published in Finland is shown for the sake of completeness and for easier comparison with the other countries' expressions.
** Kinserdal (1995: 194) translates *'de grundsætninger, som gjelder for en ordentlig og forsiktig forretningsførsel'* as 'those fundamentals that exist for sufficient and conservative accounting'. Elsewhere (e.g., Johnsen, 1993) this has been translated as 'orderly and prudent business practice'. The translation in the article (by the current author) is more literal to avoid introducing interpretation of the phrase that goes beyond the words used.

have concluded that the two expressions are different although they may produce the same results. GAP is primarily producer oriented, while TFV is primarily user oriented. In this respect, GAP is closer to GoB than to TFV. Like TFV, GAP has never been defined in the legislation; however, discussions on the Swedish law are helpful:

> 'The minister went on to state that recommendations on accounting issues by those well versed in the theory as well as skilled in the practice of accountancy were of great significance for the definition. He mentioned the Industry and Commerce Stock Exchange Committee (*NBK, Näringslivets Börskommité*) and the Swedish Institute of Authorized Public Accountants (*FAR, Föreningen Auktoriserade Revisorer*).' (Nilsson, 1995: 231)

The proposal for the Swedish Companies Act (Prop. 1975: 104: 148) explains that accounting practice becomes *good* accounting practice when it is followed by 'a qualitatively representative sample of companies'. This therefore seems to reinforce the judgmental nature of the concept and the importance of professional accountants and auditors in its definition (Flower, 1994: 241–2). However, this proved problematic for Cooke (1988:100) because of the uncertainty it causes: 'one view is that if an accounting practice is adopted by a major Swedish company that procedure becomes part of general principles'. This leads to other companies changing policies, which makes cross-sectional and time-series comparisons difficult. Alexander and Christiansen (1996: 16–8) cite the use of the equity method in the 1970s to value the shares of a subsidiary in the parent company's accounts in Denmark as an example of GAP changing accepted practice without any change in law. The use of the equity method in this way is permitted by the Fourth Directive. Although there were examples of this as early as 1973 in Denmark, Alexander and Christiansen's (1996) explanation of the justification of the equity method does not make any reference to the Directive.

Again in common with the debate on TFV, there has been discussion as to whether GAP was an overriding concept. Schwencke and Alexander (1996: 14) point out that, while the Norwegian Companies Act required accounts to be prepared in accordance with GAP, the Accounting Act also required accounts to be in accordance with the provisions of the relevant statutes.[5] This is used to justify the interpretation that GAP was not overriding in Norway. The approach taken to standard setting from the mid-1970s would seem to reinforce this position. Alexander and Christiansen (1996) suggest that GAP was not overriding in Sweden. This seems more difficult to justify from a legal point of view, as there was no clause in Swedish statute comparable with that in the Norwegian Accounting Act mentioned above. Nevertheless, the importance of accounting practice already mentioned before would seem to sug-

[5] *'Den regnskapspliktige skal føre regnskap og sette opp årsregnskap i samsvar med god regnskapsskikk og bestemmelser i eller gitt i medhold av denne lov eller andre lover.'* (*Regnskapsloven*, 1977, § 4)

gest that GAP was overriding in practice, even if that was not the strict legal position. Accounting recommendations also deviated from the strict interpretation of the law (e.g., Artsberg, 1992: 123). The Finnish position seems to have been similar to the Swedish. Alexander and Christiansen (1996) are satisfied that GAP was overriding in Denmark.

Certain comparisons may be drawn here with the hierarchy of Generally Accepted Accounting Principles (GAAP) in the US. Recent enforcement procedures by the Securities and Exchange Commission (SEC) have sought to ensure the acceptability of industry practice. It has been pointed out (LaFalce, 2001) that while some of the so-called 'earnings management' techniques 'may be technically legal, they are economically indefensible'. By extension, it could be argued that such techniques do not fall within GAAP.

Christiansen (1995a: 65) considers it noteworthy that prudence was not mentioned explicitly in the 1973 general clause. However, it continued to be important in practice because of the then close relationship between financial and tax accounting in Denmark (see below). The importance of prudence as a fundamental concept continues to be debated in the context of the Fourth Directive (e.g., Schwencke, 1996; Evans and Nobes, 1996; Van Hulle, 1996). The application of prudence in the Nordic countries seems to lack the consistency it has in Germany. The general valuation principle to be applied in respect to current assets was the lower of cost and market, as in Germany.

However, an important difference from Germany arises in the attitude towards the revaluation of fixed assets. In principle, this was permitted in the Nordic countries, although there may be practical limitations, e.g., the Accounting Act in Sweden points out that revaluations cannot exceed tax values, which may have limited its application in practice. As in Germany, purchased non-consolidation goodwill could be capitalised and amortised. The maximum period of amortisation varied amongst the countries according to Companies Acts, with the Nordic countries allowing less conservative approaches:

Germany	5 years
Denmark	10 years
Finland	5–20 years
Norway	10 years
Sweden	10 years

As this related to non-consolidation goodwill, there were potential tax advantages to early write-offs, so the issue of not writing off goodwill was not relevant. This is in contrast with the debate currently taking place in the US.

Another area where prudence seems to be modified is in the treatment of long-term contracts: both Denmark and Norway specifically permitted (and still permit) accounting for profit before the contract is complete. Security for liabilities had to be disclosed and Denmark, Finland and Norway required the disclosure of unfunded pension obligations.

3.2. Untaxed reserves model

Kinserdal (1995: 195) sees the biggest difference between the Norwegian Acts of 1957 and 1976 as being the introduction of the untaxed reserves model (sometimes confusingly referred to as the tax link model). This persists in Finnish and Swedish accounting today. The untaxed reserves model was designed to address a difficulty that had arisen because companies had to record expenses in the financial statements if they were to qualify for tax deductibility. Tax regulations therefore dominated the accounting treatment of assets and expenses throughout the 20th century. The importance of tax regulations also goes some way to explaining the lack of detailed regulations (e.g., on depreciation and stock valuation) in the Accounting and Companies Acts. However the expenses which were allowable for tax purposes did not necessarily represent the economic reality of the situation, e.g., depreciation, which was allowed for tax purposes, was often more generous than that which would usually be calculated to reflect the use of an asset. Again, a similarity can be seen with Germany: Haller (1992) describes the close relationship between financial and tax accounting in Germany.

The untaxed reserves model aimed to provide users with information about the economic reality of transactions without penalising the company with unnecessary tax. The Swedish Accounting Act 1976 presented a model profit and loss account where the income and expenses were disclosed in accordance with the company's accounting policies to arrive at the *resultat före bokslutsdispositioner och skatt* (profit before appropriations and tax). The adjustments required for tax purposes were then recorded. These would usually involve movements in the inventory reserve, investment reserve and fixed asset write-downs. The integrity of the balance sheet values was retained by writing the appropriations to an untaxed reserve rather than to the specific balance sheet accounts. The untaxed reserves therefore represented a mixture of deferred tax and equity. A similar format has been used in the other three countries. While this sounds to be a neat solution, and analysts have become accustomed to regarding 'reserves' as a mixture of equity and deferred tax, it is still a different approach to that used elsewhere. Moreover, Artsberg (1996) points out the way in which untaxed reserves could be used to generate hidden reserves.

The Danish 1973 Companies Acts did not speci-

Vol. 32. No. 2. 2002 111

fy detailed profit and loss and balance sheet formats, so there was no legislation to propose or enforce the untaxed reserves model. The estimated tax liability based on the profit for the year had to be disclosed as short-term debt, but tax liabilities contingent on the realisation of assets could be shown in long-term debt or the notes. Some Danish companies followed the Swedish model, but others chose to disclose deferred tax in the US manner (Christiansen and Elling, 1993: 66). The matter was resolved shortly afterwards by the separation of tax and financial accounting with the implementation of the Fourth Directive in 1981.

3.3. Notes

The new Acts of the 1970s increased the level of disclosure in financial statements. Corresponding figures for the previous financial period were required and, where necessary, explanations were to be given to allow full comparison. As examples, disclosure was required of shares in other companies, pension liabilities, changes in equity, numbers of employees, directors' remuneration and movements in fixed assets. Again the influence of the *Aktiengesetz* 1965 seems to be apparent as it also required similar disclosure by way of notes. However, there are items which have not come from Germany, e.g., the Norwegian Companies Act 1976 mentions disclosures for leasing and inflation and the Finnish Bookkeeping Law 1973 describes the treatment of foreign currency exchange. These items indicate that the legislation went beyond emulating Germany's legislation and was designed to deal with issues which Nordic companies were currently facing. The Nordic legislators may have drawn on the debates associated with standard setting in other countries, e.g., the American Institute of Certified Public Accountants published *ARS No. 6, Reporting the Effects of Price-Level Changes* in 1963, *APB Statement No. 3, Financial Statements Restated for General Price-Level Changes* in 1969 and *ARB No. 4, Foreign Operations and Foreign Exchange* in 1939 (Choi and Mueller, 1992: 165 and 213).

3.4. Legal reserves

Another feature of German accounting which was mirrored in the 1970s Nordic legislation, except that of Finland, is the legal reserve. The principle was the same in each country, although the size of the reserve and method of creation varied.

Germany	transfer 5% of profit until reserve is at least 10% of share capital
Denmark	transfer 10% of profit until reserve is 10% of share capital, then 5% of profit until reserve is 25% of share capital
Finland	not required by law
Norway	10% of profit until reserve is 20% of share capital
Sweden	10% of profit until reserve is 20% of share capital

In this respect, the Nordic countries appear to have been more conservative than the Germans. As these reserves were compulsory for all companies, and were designed to provide a buffer for creditors, they should be distinguished from reserves accumulated in other countries with a view to smoothing income in poorer years. However, the position has since changed: legal reserves are no longer required in Denmark and Norway. The 1990s saw an increase in the proportion of finance being provided by shareholders, which may have led to a perception that protection of creditors, and hence the reserves, were no longer required.[6]

3.5. Consolidation

The proposed Nordic Act required 'group accounts' comprising a consolidated balance sheet. 1973 saw the first definition of a group in Danish legislation (Christiansen, 1995a: 64). Danish groups were required to publish a consolidated balance sheet, or a 'group statement' showing inter-company debt and the separate disclosure of the profits of the parent company and the subsidiaries. This codified what a number of companies were already practising on a voluntary basis (Christiansen, 1995a: 65). However the legislation provided little guidance on specific measurement issues. In contrast with the requirements in other countries, only the parent company proportion (rather than the full amount) of unrealised inter-company gains and losses had to be eliminated, except that there was full elimination of unrealised gains and losses on the transfer of fixed assets.

Full consolidated accounts, including an income statement, were required in Norway in the Companies Act 1976 as an extension of the 1957 law, which only required a balance sheet (Kinserdal, 1995: 196). The accounting principles used in the consolidated financial statements were to be the same as those used in the entity accounts, which meant that the tax effects percolated through into the group accounts. There was a similar requirement for consolidation in Sweden with the Accounting Act 1975. Finland also required consolidated accounts in the Companies Act 1978.

[6] A crude measure of the importance of equity is the ratio of domestic equity market capitalisation to GDP. In Denmark this rose from 22 in 1992 to 57 in 1998. The corresponding figures for Norway were 14 and 38. The move to equity was more pronounced in Sweden (31 to 117) but the conservative reserves policy was retained. (*Sources:* market capitalisation: International Finance Corporation, 1999; GDP: International Monetary Fund, 1999.)

3.6. Statement of fund flows

Although the proposed Nordic Act did not mention statements of fund flows, larger and listed companies in Sweden, Norway and Finland were required to provide a statement of fund flows following the Companies Acts of 1975, 1976 and 1978 respectively, although the legislation gave no details of form or content. This is interesting as this legislation predates any legislation requiring funds flow statements elsewhere in the world. There are records of funds flow statements in the UK as early as 1862 (Rosen and De Coster, 1969: 125), and the US seems to have followed. However, the Nordic countries may have looked to the Accounting Principles Board Opinion 3, *The Statement of Source and Application of Funds* published in 1963 in the US. This suggests that the Nordic legislators were looking beyond the existing German legislation. However, the fact that Denmark does not include this requirement may indicate that it was an area of contention in the drafting of the proposed Nordic Act and/or not fully supported by Denmark, due to a closer relationship with German/EC regulations which had no such requirement. However, by 1984, Elling and Hansen (1984: 39) were able to say that although there was no legal requirement for a funds flow statement, it was considered GAP in Denmark. This practice demonstrates the way in which GAP went beyond legal requirements. Subsequent developments in the Nordic countries have been in line with the international trend towards cash- rather than funds-based statements.

3.7. Directors' report

Christiansen (1995a: 64) sees the introduction of the directors' report in 1973 as a mandatory part of financial reporting as one of the most important changes. In principle, the directors' report was to provide the reader with information essential to the understanding of the financial position and profit of the company, which could not be derived from the accounts themselves. This requirement was also found in Finland, Sweden and Norway and seems to correspond broadly with that in Germany and the 1971 draft Directive.

3.8. Filing

Another provision of the proposed Nordic Act, which was implemented by all countries, related to the filing of annual reports. Both public and private companies (now including family companies) were required to file audited financial statements with the public Danish Commerce and Companies Agency (Christiansen 1995a: 65) following the Companies Acts 1973. At this time, a similar filing requirement was introduced for larger and listed Norwegian companies (Kinserdal, 1995: 196). This was also the case in Sweden and Finland following their new accounting legislation in the 1970s. This provision seems to be some way behind the UK which required filing of accounts as early as 1844, although the filing of audited accounts (defined as a balance sheet) did not become effective until 1907 (Edwards, 1992). However, it is perhaps understandable, given the predominance in the Nordic countries of companies with narrow share ownership financed largely by debt.

4. Distinctive features of the Finnish Accounting Act 1973

Finnish writers (e.g., Troberg, 1992; Majala, 1994; Näsi, 1995) are keen to point out the influence of accounting theory to find solutions to practical problems in Finland: this then forms the basis of legislation or provides the justification for departures from existing regulation. They argue that this approach differentiates the Finnish accounting legislation of the 1970s from that of the other Nordic countries implemented at the same time. The Accounting Act 1973 (and the Company Tax Act 1968) reflected a change in practice, which had emerged in the 1950s and 1960s based on Martti Saario's Expenditure Revenue Theory (Majala, 1994: 75–6) in addition to the proposed Nordic Companies Act as described above.

Saario put forward the Expenditure Revenue Theory of bookkeeping in his doctoral thesis in 1945, *'Realiointiperiaate ja käyttöomaisuuden poistot tuloslaskennassa'* ('The realisation principle and the depreciation of fixed assets in profit calculation'). This theory criticises the balance sheet equation or static balance method of calculating profit. In particular, the allocation of depreciation according to a pre-determined plan with no consideration of revenues was decried. It aims to present transactions from the entrepreneur's point of view. At the end of an accounting period, the profit is calculated as a result of the following calculations:

(a) the division of revenues into expenses and profit;

(b) the division of expenditures into expenses and assets.

It is assumed that the sum of profits in each period of the company's life equals the total profit of the company. If a firm is to be established or to continue, then the total profits must be positive (otherwise the company would not be started or would be liquidated). Therefore, if the total profits will not be negative, the profits of no individual period should be negative. Depreciation may therefore be ignored in a given year to avoid the calculation of a negative profit. Nonetheless, negative depreciation is not permitted. Strict matching is applied, so depreciation is calculated based on the original purchase price and the corresponding annual income, rather than the physical aspect of the assets (Majala, 1994: 71–3).

It is argued that the dominance of the Expenditure Revenue Theory and the education of accountants reduce the need for detailed regulations in the legislation (Aisbitt, 2000). However, that leads to tremendous variation in practice, as demonstrated by Jägerhorn and Troberg (1980 and 1981). Nevertheless, variation alone does not put Finland in a unique position: similar difficulties were experienced with Sweden (e.g., Cooke, 1988).

While the theoretical argument may dominate the accounting legislation, accounting practice is influenced by the constraints of the tax legislation. For example, in practice, depreciation tends to be charged to the maximum that tax rules will allow without creating a loss (which may have tax disadvantages). This is in conflict with the Theory but is understandable from management's point of view (Majala, 1994: 73). The close relationship between financial reporting and tax could be problematic. Troberg (1992: 31) points out that financial statements in Finland were criticised as being 'tax minimisation' rather than 'economic reality' statements. The variation in depreciation charge from year to year violates the consistency principle, which is fundamental in other countries. International companies gradually began showing depreciation according to plan and a separate adjustment to the actual depreciation charge. A similar approach was adopted for inventory, operating and investment reserves (Troberg, 1992: 32–3). The funds flow statement, which was compulsory for larger companies under the Companies Act 1978, would be expected to be a particularly helpful source of additional information for international users.

In spite of the claims of Finnish writers to the contrary, the Finnish Accounting Act 1973 and Companies Act 1978 still had a great deal in common with the contemporaneous legislation in the other Nordic countries in the written legislation (as shown above). The natural temptation to minimise tax liabilities is likely to have increased that likeness in practice. Some Finnish users, preparers and auditors were of the opinion that the theory would not be important for comparing Finnish financial statements internationally: what were vital were the statutory requirements (Aisbitt, 2000).

5. Conclusion

The Nordic countries essentially have a Roman law tradition, so it is understandable that financial reporting requirements would be codified in law rather than be allowed to develop through practice. However, it is interesting that another Roman law country, Germany, did not bring the requirement for a funds flow or cash flow statement into statute until 1998, although Finland, Norway and Sweden did this in the 1970s.

The German influence on accounting in the Nordic countries is apparent throughout the 20th century. German academics were the first professors in Swedish universities and their work was studied throughout the Nordic countries. The legislation at the turn of the century and in the 1970s has strong links with the preceding German legislation. However, the Nordic countries did not adopt the more rigid accounting plans followed by some other countries after German influence during the second world war (although there were accounting plans for internal accounts in some industries [e.g., ter Vehn, 1945]). As early as the 1970s, other influences could also be seen. The Nordic countries were considering membership of the EEC and the effect of other European countries and the US were apparent. The concept of GAP and its application, particularly in Sweden, seems to appeal to the common law tradition and perhaps even the British TFV.

In common with other countries, e.g., Germany, France, Italy and Belgium, the Nordic countries' financial accounts were (and still are in the case of Sweden and Finland) strongly affected by tax rules, such that the financial (or commercial) accounts were the same as the tax accounts. The necessity for financial and tax accounting to be identical was dispensed with in Denmark in 1981 and Norway in 1992. In both cases, these dates mark the end of a gradual process and reflect a combination of factors. Tax regulations had evolved so that fiscal objectives were no longer compatible with income measurement (e.g., Hansen, 1998), making the financial statements less accessible to international users. There are indications that protracted negotiations preceded the change in Norway (e.g., Fagerstrøm and Schwencke). Some changes were made to reserves for tax purposes in Sweden in the 1990s, but the link between commercial and tax accounts remains strong. Sweden recognised the value of separating tax and financial accounting when implementing the European Directives, but decided to address this as a separate issue to avoid delaying the implementation of the Directives (SOU, 1994). Breaking the tax link seems to be another example of internationalisation, and perhaps prioritising the needs of international over domestic users. It is perhaps no coincidence that these developments follow increases in foreign ownership of shares (see Oslo Stock Exchange, 1995). These in turn followed relaxation of restrictions on foreign ownership.[7]

The tax regulations were therefore influential in

[7] For details of restrictions see Oxelheim, Storehill, Randøy, V kkula, Dullum and Modén, 1998: 48.

the choice of accounting policies and the presentation of information. However, the Nordic countries recognised as early as the 1970s that the tax-based information presented in financial statements did not necessarily meet the needs of users of accounts such as investors. The introduction of the untaxed reserves model (described in Section 3.2) was designed to increase the information value of financial statements for domestic and international users.

Given the relatively small size of the Nordic countries, it is perhaps unsurprising that a small number of individuals have been able to exert significant influence. Saario's work has been discussed in Section 4, and Finnish writers claim his theory distinguishes Finland's financial reporting from that of other nations. An accounting elite has also been described by Jönsson (1984) as determining accounting policy-making in Sweden. However, the process of regulation is not entirely idiosyncratic: the framework of laws supported by professional recommendations and, later, standards is similar to that in other countries. The use of IASC standards in place of national standards in Denmark and as a source of reference in other countries for the secondary regulation to support legislation provides further evidence that the Nordic countries are not purely inward-looking.

In the period prior to the implementation of the European Company Law Directives, there appear to be two points at which financial reporting regulation clearly converges in the Nordic countries. The first, and perhaps more tenuous point, was at the start of the 20th century. The countries may have looked to one another's legislation or may all have looked to German legislation for inspiration at this early stage of development. However, given the lack of detail in the legislation in any of the Nordic countries or Germany at that time, the similarity of the Acts cannot be assumed to have led to convergence of practice.

The next period of converging legislation seems to have come in the 1970s. Denmark, Finland, Norway and Sweden seemed to introduce legislation that was broadly similar as a result of their common involvement in the project for the Nordic Companies Act. There was a conscious effort to work together and have a common framework. Parallels can be drawn with the European programme of harmonisation of company law. However, just as the harmonisation of law among members of the European Community has not necessarily resulted in standardisation of practice, the common laws in the Nordic countries will not necessarily have produced uniform financial statements. Evidence of this is recorded elsewhere (e.g., Hjorth and Petersen, 1983; Eilifsen, 1984; Cooke, 1989; Jägerhorn and Troberg, 1980 and 1981; Christiansen, 1995b; Aisbitt, 2001). In spite of its apparent similarities with the other countries' legislation, Finland's was founded in an alternative paradigm. As the legislation merely provided a framework, there was scope for variation of practice by companies within and among countries. Efforts were made to improve the quality of the information produced and perhaps to reduce the variation within a country through the publication of accounting recommendations. The bodies responsible for these recommendations operated independently in each country, although they may have referred to the work of other countries or international bodies, such as the IASC. Shortly after the final Nordic country implemented the proposed Nordic Companies Act, Denmark moved away from the Nordic model with the implementation of the Fourth Directive in 1981, as a condition of its membership of the European Community. This is therefore another factor contributing to the potential for divergence among the countries at this stage in their history.

The history seems to provoke a number of questions. From the Second World War, the Nordic countries felt that they had sufficient in common and that harmonisation was sufficiently desirable to spend 17 years working on a common Companies Act proposal. Yet even before the proposal was implemented, countries began to go their separate ways. Was it that once the proposal was complete it was felt no further co-operation was necessary? The process of formulating and implementing accounting legislation and standards and guidelines in the Nordic countries does not appear to have been explored in the literature: it concentrates on the results rather than the process. However, some clues may be found in the commentaries implementing the 1970s Acts. Co-operation seems to have proved more time-consuming and involved more compromises than the parties had anticipated. As a result, the countries may have felt that they could be more productive on their own.

By the end of the exercise, doubts even seemed to have been emerging on the validity of harmonisation at a Nordic level, when companies were trading on a European or global level. A further explanation could be found in external factors: the 1970s and 1980s were a period of political and economic change in each of the countries, and the four countries each developed in different directions, e.g., Norway discovered oil, Denmark joined the EC and Sweden suffered from an oil crisis and inflation. Interviews with practitioners and academics who had known those involved in the proposed Nordic Act did not provide alternative theories or obvious conclusions for the reason for the cessation of formal co-operation on legislation (Aisbitt, 2000). Nevertheless, there continues to be good communication between standard setters and practitioners, both on a personal level and through organisations such as *Nordiske Revisorforening* (Nordic Auditors' Association) and via the joint Nordic representation on the Board of the IASC. Thus it appears that, while the experience of the proposed Nordic Companies Act seems to have discouraged formal co-operation among legislators, it did not deter informal co-operation among individuals involved in the process. This ensures that small countries take a wider approach and draw on international best practice.

Appendix 1
Summary of differences between language editions of Chapter 12 of the proposed Nordic Companies Act

Section	*Details*	*Denmark*	*Finland*	*Norway*	*Sweden*
96§	Accounts must be passed to the auditors at least 1 month before the general meeting	✗	✓	✓	✓
	The terms of this Act apply only insofar as they do not contravene the Banking Act	✓	✗	✗	✗
98§	More detailed explanation of implications of Good Accounting Practice	✓	✗	✗	✗
	Definition of acquisition cost	✗	✓	✓	✓
99§	Definition of 'real value'	✗	✓	✓	✓
100§	Depreciation is to be charged even if the result is or thereby becomes a loss	✓	✗	✗	✗
101§	Costs of increasing share capital may not be capitalised	✓	✗	✓	✓
	Listed investments must not be shown at a value higher than the accounting year's latest listed purchase price	✓	✗	✗	✗
	Valuation of foreign work in progress can include a prudent proportion of profit	✓	✗	✗	✗
102§	Mortgages and guarantees shall be shown above the line	✗	✓	✓	✓
	Layout of the balance sheet – items were not always in precisely the same order and the following items were not specifically mentioned in all versions:				
	Tax assets	✗	✓	✗	✓
	Work in progress for foreign accounts	✓	✗	✗	✗
	Buildings	✗	✓	✓	✓
	Bank loans and similar debt	✓	✗	✗	✗
	Long term debt – pension provision	✗	✗	✗	✓
	Long term debt – other long term debt	✗	✗	✗	✓
	Dividends payable	✓	✗	✗	✗
	Unpaid dividends from previous year(s)	✓	✗	✗	✗
	Dividend for the year	✓	✗	✗	✗
	Long term debt – priority debt	✓	✗	✗	✗
	Long term debt – other secured debt	✓	✗	✗	✗
	Long term debt – convertible debt	✓	✗	✗	✗
	Long term debt – dividend bearing debt letters	✓	✗	✗	✗
	Long term debt – other debt	✓	✗	✗	✗
103§	Loans to related parties in excess of 50,000 kronor or 5% of capital (if lower) to be disclosed separately	✗	✓	✗	✓
	Loans to related parties to be disclosed separately (no *de minimis*)	✓	✗	✓	✗
	Any 3rd party guarantees not covered above must be disclosed separately	✓	✗	✓	✗
104§	Layout of p&l				
	Transfers to investment funds specifically mentioned	✓	✗	✗	✗

Appendix 1
Summary of differences between language editions of Chapter 12 of the proposed Nordic Companies Act
(continued)

Section	*Details*	*Denmark*	*Finland*	*Norway*	*Sweden*
105§ 1	The King can provide exemptions from disclosures about subsidiaries	✗	✗	✓	✓
	Information about subsidiaries can be omitted if it would be harmful to the company	✗	✓	✗	✗
105§ 3	Pension liabilities not provided in the balance sheet to be disclosed	✓	✗	✓	✓
105§ 7	Taxation value of fixed assets must be given	✗	✗	✗	✓
	For real estate the latest official valuation must be given	✓	✗	✗	✗
105§ 12	Additional disclosures regarding the calculation of profit on foreign work in progress	✓	✗	✗	✗
105§ 13	Additional disclosures regarding the tax implications of the valuation of the company's assets	✓	✗	✗	✗
105§ 14	Additional disclosures regarding tax paid in the accounting period	✓	✗	✗	✗
106§	Annual report should give details of interests in unlimited companies and their latest accounts	✓	✗	✗	✗
108§	Accounts must be filed within one month of approval	✗	✓	✓	✓
	Accounts must be filed within one month of approval and within seven months of the year end	✓	✗	✗	✗
	The King can provide exemption from filing of accounts	✗	✗	✓	✗
111§	Profit should be set aside to reserves in accordance with §40	✗	✓	✗	✓
	10% of profit should be set aside until legal reserve is 10% of share capital in accordance with §40	✓	✗	✗	✗
	10% of profit should be set aside until legal reserve is 20% of share capital	✗	✗	✓	✗
	The King can provide exemptions from establishment of legal reserves and prescriptions relating to use of legal reserves	✗	✗	✓	✗
112§	Owners of more than 10% of the share capital can demand distribution of half of the profit for the year (after statutory dispositions)	✗	✓	✓	✓

Key
✓ Item present
✗ Item not present

References

Aisbitt, S. (2000). *The Harmonisation of Financial Reporting in the Nordic Countries*. PhD thesis, University of Reading.

Aisbitt, S. (2001). 'Measurement of harmony of financial reporting within and between countries: the case of the Nordic countries'. *European Accounting Review*, 10 (1): 51–72.

Aisbitt, S. and Nobes. C. (2001). 'The true and fair view requirement in recent national implementations'. *Accounting and Business Research*, 31 (2): 83–90.

Alexander, D. and Archer, S. (1998). *The European Accounting Guide*. 3rd edition. Harcourt Brace..

Alexander, D. and Christiansen, M. (1996). 'The general clause in Danish accounting regulation'. EAA, Bergen.

Artsberg, K. (1992). *Normbildning och Redovisningsförandring*. Doctoral thesis, Lund University Press.

Artsberg, K. (1996). 'The link between commercial accounting and tax accounting in Sweden'. *European Accounting Review*, 5 (Supplement): 795–814.

Choi, F.D.S. and Mueller, G.G. (1992). *International Accounting*. 2nd edition. Prentice Hall International .

Christiansen, M. (1995a). 'The history of financial reporting in Denmark' in Walton (1995): 55–73.
Christiansen, M. (1995b). 'The measurement of international accounting comparability – some considerations'. EAA, Birmingham.
Christiansen, M. and Elling, J.O. (1993). *European Financial Reporting: Denmark*. Routledge.
Cooke, T.E. (1988). *Financial Reporting in Sweden*. ICAEW.
Cooke, T.E. (1989). 'Disclosure in the corporate annual reports of Swedish companies'. *Accounting and Business Research*, 19 (74): 113–24.
Edwards, J.R. (1992). 'Companies, corporations and accounting change, 1835–1933: a comparative study'. *Accounting and Business Research*, 23 (89): 59–73.
Eilifsen, Aa. (1984). 'En analyse av regnskapsrapporteringen til en del norske aksjeselskap for regnskapsåret 1982'. *Revisjon og Regnskap*, 3: 98–102.
Elling, J.O. (1993). 'Financial reporting in the Nordic countries. An introduction'. *European Accounting Review*, 2 (3): 581–4.
Elling, J.O. (1994). 'Denmark', in Flower (1994): 33–64.
Elling, J.O. and Hansen, C.K. (1984). 'The Fourth Directive in Denmark' in Gray, S.J. and Coenenberg, A.G. (eds) *EEC Accounting Harmonisation: Implementation and Impact of the Fourth Directive*. North Holland.
Evans, L. (2000). *'Grundsätze ordnungsmäßiger Buchführung* – a comparison with some British and American concepts'. EAA, Munich.
Evans, L. and Nobes, C.W. (1996). 'Some mysteries relating to the prudence principle in the Fourth Directive and in German and British Law'. *European Accounting Review*, 5 (2): 361–73.
Fagerstrøm, A. and Schwencke, H.R. (1994). 'Why is deferred tax treated differently in Norwegian and Swedish consolidated accounts?' Sandvika: Norwegian School of Management working paper 1994/12.
Flower, J. (ed) (1994). *The Regulation of Financial Reporting in the Nordic Countries*. Publica.
Folketingstidende (1980–81). *Fremsatte lovforslag m.v. (undtagen finans- og tillægsbevillingslovforslag)*. J.H. Schultz A/S.
Haller, A. (1992). 'The relationship of financial and tax accounting in Germany: a major reason for accounting disharmony in Europe'. *International Journal of Accounting*, 27: 310–23.
Hansen, C.K. (1998). 'Denmark', in Alexander, D. and Archer, S. (1998).
Heurlin, S. and Peterssohn, E. (1998). 'Sweden' in Alexander, D. and Archer, S. (1998).
Hjorth, J, and Petersen, C. (1983). 'En analyse af dansk koncernregnskabspraksis'. *Revisjon og Regnskap*, 3: 105–12.
International Finance Corporation (1999). *Emerging Stock Markets Factbook 1999*. 13th edition. IFC,.
International Monetary Fund (1999). *International Financial Statistics Yearbook*. International Monetary Fund.
Jägerhorn, R. and Troberg, P. (1980). 'Financial Reporting Practices in Finland 1979'. Swedish School of Economics and Business Administration working paper 56.
Jägerhorn, R. and Troberg, P. (1981). 'Financial Reporting Practices in Finland 1980'. Swedish School of Economics and Business Administration working paper 72.
Johnsen, A. (1993). 'Accounting regulation in Norway'. *European Accounting Review*, 2 (3): 617–26
Jönsson, S. (1984). 'Accounting élite and accounting policy making – the Swedish case'. *Scandinavian Journal of Management Studies*. August: 3–33.
LaFalce, J.J. (2001). Opening statement to the US House of Representatives Committee on Financial Services, Subcommittee on Capital Markets, Insurance and Government Sponsored Enterprises, 7 June 2001.
Kinserdal, A. (1995). 'The history of financial reporting in Norway' in Walton (1995): 189–202.
Majala, R. (1994). 'Finland' in Flower (1994): 65–106.
Miller, M.C. (1994). 'Australia' in Cooke, T.E. and Parker, R.H. (1994). *Financial Reporting in the West Pacific Rim*. Routledge: 333–82.
Monsen, N. and Wallace, W.A. (1995). 'Evolving financial reporting practices: a comparative study of the Nordic countries' harmonization efforts'. *Contemporary Accounting Research*, 11 (2): 973–97.
Mueller, R. and Galbraith, E.G. (1976). *The German Stock Corporation Law and The German Law on the Accounting by Major Enterprises Other than Stock Corporations*. Bilingual edition with Introduction. Fritz Knapp Verlag: Frankfurt.
Nilsson, S.-A. (1995). 'The history of financial reporting in Sweden' in Walton (1995): 221–39.
Nobes, C.W. (1993). 'The true and fair view: impact on and of the Fourth Directive'. *Accounting and Business Research*. Winter: 35–48.
NOU 1995: 30. *Ny Regnskapslov*. October.
Näsi, S. (1995). 'The history of financial reporting and auditing in Finland' in Walton (1995): 75–89.
Oslo Stock Exchange (1995). *Share Ownership Structure in Europe*. Oslo Stock Exchange.
Ot. prp. nr. 19 (1974–5). *Om lov om aksjeselskaper*.
Oxelheim, L., Stonehill, A., Randøy, T., Vikkula, K., Dullum, K.B. and Modén, K.M. (1998). *Corporate Strategies to Internationalise the Cost of Capital*. Handelshøjskolens Forlag.
Proposition (1975). 104 *om bokföringslag mm*.
Rosen, L.S. and De Coster, D.T. (1969). 'Funds flow statements: a historical perspective'. *Accounting Review*, January: 124–36.
Schröer, T. (1993). 'Company law and accounting in nineteenth-century Europe – Germany'. *European Accounting Review*, 2 (2): 335–45.
Schwencke, H.R. (1996). 'La oss beholde forsiktighetsprinsippet!'. *Revisjon og Regnskap*, 1: 12–5.
Schwencke, H.R. and Alexander, D. (1996). 'Accounting changes in Norway'. EAA, Bergen.
SOU 1971: 15 *Förslag till aktiebolagslag mm*.
SOU 1994: 17 *Års- och koncernredovisning enligt EG-direktivet*. February.
Troberg, P.H. (1992). 'Recent developments in financial reporting in Finland'. *Advances in International Accounting*, 5: 24–45.
Van Hulle, K. (1996). 'Prudence: a principle or an attitude?'. *European Accounting Review*, 5 (2): 375–82.
ter Vehn, A. (1945). *Mekanförbundets Normal-kontoplan med Kommentar*. Sveriges Mekaniska Verkstäders Förbund.
Vårdal, P. and Johnsen, A. (1989). *Norsk Regnskapslovgivning*. Bedrftsøkonomens forlag, 4e utgave.
Walton, P. (ed) (1995). *European Financial Reporting: A History*. Academic Press.

[13]

The European Accounting Review 1996, **5:2**, 317–337

Harmonizing the notes in the UK and France: a case study in *de jure* harmonization

R. H. Parker
University of Exeter, UK

ABSTRACT

This paper provides a case study of the process of *de jure* harmonization of financial reporting by examining the extent to which in the UK and France the regulations relating to the notes on the accounts (*annexe*) have been harmonized by the Fourth and Seventh Company Law Directives of the European Union and 'deharmonized' by other regulations. It looks at the requirements of the directives in relation to the notes and the reactions in the two countries to those requirements. It examines a number of areas in which implementation of the directives has been different, viz. consolidated financial statements; exemptions and extensions; financial statement formats; accounting policies; true and fair view; and tax. Finally, it explores the problem of readability and understandability and the choice between disclosure in the notes and disclosure elsewhere.

INTRODUCTION

From harmony to harmony
Through all the compass of the notes it ran

Dryden, '*A song for St Cecilia's Day*, 1687'

'Harmonization' has been defined as a 'process of increasing the compatibility of accounting practices by setting bounds to their degree of variation' (Nobes and Parker, 1995: 117). It thus represents a movement away from total diversity of accounting practices, so that a state of 'harmony' is indicated by a clustering of companies around one or a few of the available methods. Tay and Parker (1990: 73), following the lead of van der Tas (1988), distinguish between, on the one hand, *de jure* harmonization and harmony, which refer to accounting regulations and on the other hand *de facto* harmonization and harmony, which refer to the actual practices of companies. Accounting regulations are found in what is known

Address for correspondence
Department of Economics, University of Exeter, Amory Building, Rennes Drive, Exeter EX4 4RJ, UK.

 0963–8180

in French as the *droit comptable*. In the UK this covers the Companies Act 1985, applicable accounting standards (Financial Reporting Standards, FRSs; Statements of Standard Accounting Practice, SSAPs) and, for listed companies, the requirements of the London Stock Exchange. In France relevant rules are contained in, *inter alia*, the Commercial Code, the *plan comptable* and tax legislation. Both types of harmony and harmonization are worth study. What companies do is constrained, more or less heavily, by what the regulations say they ought to do, but companies may fail to comply with regulations or go beyond them. Without some knowledge of the regulations and their social and institutional context the study of practice can be rather sterile. Likewise, an analysis of regulations can be rather sterile without some understanding of practice. *De jure* and *de facto* studies may thus legitimately overlap although the conceptual distinction between them is important.

Study of the state of *de jure* international harmony involves a comparison of the regulations and the context of regulations in two or more countries at a point in time. Where the countries concerned (e.g. Australia and New Zealand) have largely similar accounting rule-making contexts it is relatively simple for the study to take the form of a line by line comparison of regulations relating to disclosure, presentation and measurement rules. Such a comparison is more difficult and arguably less useful where the countries concerned (e.g. member states of the European Union such as the UK and France) do not have similar rule-making contexts.

The study of *de jure* international harmonization can take two forms. It can involve, first, the comparison of states of relative international harmony in two or more countries at different points in time. Second, it can take the form of a study of the processes by which two or more countries move towards harmony (or disharmony) over a period of time. The former approach may be the more fruitful for Australia and New Zealand, but the latter is more interesting for the UK and France because it sheds light on the way in which regulations change and does not assume that the changes take place in two countries which differ only in that their detailed accounting regulations are not identical. It is therefore the latter approach to the study of *de jure* harmonization which is followed in the present paper.

The remainder of the paper is divided into three parts. The first part looks specifically at the process of *de jure* harmonization between the UK and France as it relates to the notes to the accounts. Within this part, the first section discusses briefly the purposes of *de jure* harmonization within the European Union and what aspects of accounting the EU has attempted to harmonize, and explains why the present study looks at the UK and France and at the notes to the accounts. The second section discusses those requirements of the Fourth and Seventh Directives which relate to the notes. The third section examines the attitudes of the UK and French legislators and standard setters to the notes, and hence their reactions to the requirements of the directives and explains in general terms how and why they were implemented differently in the two countries. The sections which follow take a more detailed look at the contrasting ways in which specific requirements of the directives, i.e. those relating to consolidated financial statements, exemptions and extensions, financial statement formats, accounting policies, a true and fair view, and tax, have been interpreted on their incorporation into UK and French national legislation. The second part of the paper looks at two areas affected by the harmonization process although not directly addressed by it: the impact of the regulation on readability and understandability; and the extent to which the directives and national regulations require certain information to be given in a specific section of the annual report and whether or not this is a matter of any importance.

The final part of the paper discusses the extent to which a *de jure* harmonization of the UK and French rules relating to the notes has been achieved.

DE JURE HARMONIZATION OF THE NOTES TO THE ACCOUNTS (*ANNEXE*)

Harmonization within the European Union

What have been the purposes of accounting harmonization within the European Union and what has the EU attempted to harmonize? It is generally agreed that a major purpose has been to increase comparability. Within the EU, at least in the Seventh Directive, there have also been two other aims: to 'improve' practice, and to assist in the control of multinational companies by host countries, although the second of these was more apparent in drafts of the directive than in the final text (Nobes and Parker, 1995: 333). The harmonization in the directives extends to concepts (e.g. the true and fair view), presentation (e.g. financial statement formats), disclosure (e.g. of accounting policies), and measurement (e.g. the valuation of inventories). However, the directives did not and were not intended to cover every aspect of financial reporting and, not surprisingly, in the words of a former chairman of the International Accounting Standards Committee:

> some of the member states did not use the Fourth Directive as a point of departure for a truly new law, but instead took existing national law, adapting that law where necessary to the requirements of the Directive [Burggraaf, 1983: 3].

This comment also applies to the Seventh Directive. Moreover, the directives do not cover the whole of company financial reporting and member states are free to continue to regulate areas of accounting not so covered.

The present paper selects two countries (the UK and France) and looks at one area, the notes or *annexe*. The UK and France have been chosen because they each represent two important, but different, accounting traditions within the EU. Previous research (e.g. Emenyonu and Gray, 1992; Walton, 1992) suggests that there is little harmonization between UK and French accounting. In France the emphasis has been, via a Commercial Code, on creditor protection and commercial transactions as well as commercial entities. Major influences on accounting are a national accounting plan (*plan comptable général*, PCG), tax legislation and (for listed companies) a securities commission (Commission des Opérations de Bourse). Traditional French accounting has been aptly described as the 'algebra of the law' (Garnier, 1947). This can be compared with the UK, where a rather strict regulatory line is drawn between incorporated and unincorporated businesses; accounting standards (FRSs and SSAPs) are of great importance; there is no national accounting plan; tax rules are a minor influence on financial reporting; and there is no securities commission with an interest in published financial statements. Furthermore, the UK professional accountancy bodies have exercised, at least until recently, more influence on accounting rules than the French Ordre des experts comptables et des comptables agréés (OECCA) (since August 1994, the Ordre des experts comptables) has had.

The notes have been chosen because although, compared with the balance sheet and profit and loss account, they are a relatively new document, in both the UK and France they now form a substantial proportion of the annual report and are the repository of much detailed information and explanation.

To what extent has *de jure* harmony been achieved? Table 1, which provides a post-directives comparison of the UK notes with the French *annexe* and is based on the evidence set out later in the paper, suggests that there exists today only a partial *de jure* harmony of concepts, presentation and disclosure.

The notes in the directives

Those responsible for drawing up the directives appear to have used the notes not only as a vehicle for *de jure* harmonization but also as a place for disclosing lack of harmonization, when they were unable to agree. There are four kinds of references to the notes in the Fourth Directive:

1 General: Article 2(1) provides that the annual accounts shall comprise the balance sheet, the profit and loss account and the notes on the accounts, and that these documents 'shall constitute a composite whole (*forment un tout*)'. This phrase is capable of different interpretations, but one certain implication must be that if the balance sheet and profit and loss account are required to be audited so also must be the notes.

Table 1 Comparison of UK notes and French *annexe*

	UK	*France*
Legislative and other requirements	Companies Act 1985 as amended 1989 FRSs, SSAPs Stock Exchange Listing Requirements	Commercial Code, as revised by Laws of 30 April 1983 and 3 January 1985 and as implemented in Decrees of 29 November 1983 and 17 February 1986 *Plan comptable général*
Relationship to balance sheet and profit and loss account	Not a separate document; but provides detail and commentary on balance sheet and profit and loss account	A separate document of equal importance. May include items which go beyond balance sheet and profit and loss account
Required only of companies	Yes	No
Exemptions	Small companies exempted from many notes; medium sized companies from some notes	Simplified *annexe* permitted for SAs and SARLs below certain size criteria and for all other business enterprises
Separation of notes to consolidated and parent company statements?	No	Yes
Standardization of format?	Not standardized	Relatively unstandardized
Prescribed tables?	No	Yes (for parent company)
Disclosure of accounting policies?	Yes, but may be separate from notes 'proper'	Yes, usually as first item of *annexe*
Relationship to true and fair view (TFV)	Additional information to give a TFV (where necessary) disclosed in notes. Departures from rules required in balance sheet and profit and loss account with explanations in the notes. In practice notes may provide data for an alternative TFV	Additional information and departures from rules must be given in the *annexe* not in the balance sheet and profit and loss account.
Relationship to tax legislation	Balance sheet and profit and loss account not directly affected by tax rules. Tax charge, including deferred taxation, must be disclosed in the notes	Effect of application of tax rules to balance sheet and profit and loss account must be disclosed in *annexe* of individual companies.
Detailed employee information	Disclosed not in notes but in Directors' Report	Disclosed not in *annexe* or *rapport de gestion* but in a separate *bilan social* (if 300+ employees)

2 Compulsory disclosures in the notes: Article 43 requires that information relating to thirteen particular items must be disclosed in the notes. Articles 15(3b), 18, 21, 29, 30, 31, 34, 35, 37, 38, 39, 40 and 42 add other specific items to this list.
3 Compulsory disclosures in the notes or elsewhere: Some Articles require disclosure of items either in the notes or elsewhere, e.g. at the foot of the balance sheet (*à la suite du bilan*) (Article 14), in the balance sheet (Articles 15 (3a), 33(2a), 33(4), 41(1)) or in the profit and loss account (Articles 35(1c)(cc), 39(1c)).
4 Exemptions: Articles 44 and 45 permit Member States to grant exemptions to certain companies and in relation to certain information.

The Seventh Directive also contains four kinds of references to the notes but places more emphasis on the disclosure of omissions, departures and derogations:

1 General: Article 16(1) provides, similarly to Article 2(1) of the Fourth Directive, that the consolidated accounts shall comprise the consolidated balance sheet, the consolidated profit and loss account, and the notes on the accounts, and that these documents shall constitute a composite whole.
2 Compulsory disclosures in the notes: Article 34 requires that information relating to thirteen particular items must be disclosed in the notes. Articles 7(2c), 19(1c), 20(3), 33(2b,c), 36(2d), 42 and 45 add other specific items to this list.
3 Omissions, departures and derogations: some Articles allow omissions or derogations which must be disclosed in the notes, e.g. Articles 5(2b), 15(3), 25(2), 26(2), 27(2), 29(2b), 29(3), 29(5), 33(3), 35(1)(b), 40(1).
4 Exemptions: Articles 5 and 6 allow member states to exclude certain undertakings to be excluded from the obligation to prepare consolidated accounts (including the notes).

Both directives also allow member states to require or permit the disclosure of information concerning acquisitions of own shares in the notes instead of in the directors' report or its French equivalent the *rapport de gestion*.

Reactions to and implementation of the directives

Reactions in the two countries to the requirements in the directives relating to the notes differed at the conceptual level and to some extent at the practical level of implementation. To understand these reactions it is necessary to look at the status of notes in each country before the Fourth

Directive. In the UK, the inclusion of notes in the annual report had been greatly encouraged by legislation. Notes were not a legal requirement and did not become a common feature until the coming into force of the Companies Act 1948. The Distillers Company, for example, first provided them in 1949 (Lee, 1979: 33). The amount of information to be provided in the notes was greatly expanded by the Companies Act 1967, which was the last Act before the implementation of the Fourth Directive to have a major effect on the rules relating to published financial statements.

In France before the implementation of the Directive in 1983 there was no requirement for notes as such, although a few large companies did provide some. There were, however, requirements to provide certain statements in addition to the balance sheet and profit and loss account, e.g. tables relating to fixed assets, investments, subsidiaries and participating interests and provisions.

Since notes were already well established, the British reaction was that the directives merely required detailed amendments to already existing requirements to provide information in notes. No conceptual issues were seen to be involved and no link was perceived with the requirement to show a true and fair view (a concept well-established in the UK, although not necessarily well understood). No books were published in the UK, as they were in France (Prost and Mai Van Thanh, 1984; Raffegeau *et al.*, 1985) devoted entirely to the notes. Authoritative British reference books (e.g. Davies *et al.*, 1994) do not devote a separate chapter to the notes.

The requirements relating to the notes in the Fourth and Seventh Directives were implemented in the Companies Acts 1981 and 1989 respectively. Most of the requirements are now to be found in Schedules 4 and 4A to the Companies Act 1985, as amended. The content of the notes has also, however, been extended by the provisions of the Statements of Standard Accounting Practice (SSAPs) of the former Accounting Standards Committee (ASC) and the Financial Reporting Standards (FRSs) of the Accounting Standards Board (ASB). For listed companies there are also Stock Exchange requirements which affect the notes. A summary of what must be disclosed is given in Hussey and Bishop (1993, Chapter 7).

In France, the requirements of the directives have been implemented in the Commercial Code, as revised by the Law of 30 April 1983 and the Accounting Decree of 29 November 1983 (especially Article 24) and in the PCG. A summary of what must be disclosed is given in Cohen (1990: 57–67).

There has been a more explicit discussion of the role of the notes in the French regulations and authoritative literature than in the British. One reason may be that the French word *annexe* does not have the same connotation as the English word notes. This is partly because notes is a plural noun and *annexe* a singular noun. As Roberts (1993: 15) puts it:

> the French word *annexe* implies a single document appended to the balance sheet and profit and loss account rather than, as is the case in the UK, a set of individual items which detail, expand and comment upon the two financial statements.

Despite the dictionary definition of an *annexe* as something attached to a principal thing, French writers (e.g. Pasqualini, 1992: 102; Colasse, 1991: 251) are clear that the *annexe* is just as important as the balance sheet and the profit and loss account. This may seem a trivial point but if the *annexe* is not just an appendage of the financial statements it is possible to argue for inclusion within it of information not related to those statements. The PCG repeats the directive in stating that the three documents form *un tout* and Article 8 of the Commercial Code as modified by the Law of 30 April 1983 goes further and uses the phrase *un tout indissociable*. Nevertheless, in the view of one French accountant (but not all) the *annexe* is the 'poor relation' of the balance sheet and the profit and loss account (Danziger, in CREFIGE, 1994: 31).

The Commercial Code goes on in Articles 9 and 11 to describe the role of the *annexe* as:

1 completing and commenting on the information given by the balance sheet and the profit and loss account;
2 supplying, when following the rules is not sufficient to give a true and fair view, additional information;
3 mentioning, in exceptional cases, derogations (departures) from an accounting requirement necessary in order to give a true and fair view;
4 describing and justifying changes in accounting policies or in presentation of the annual accounts.

There is no statement of the role of the notes in British company law or accounting standards. There is, however, some conceptual discussion in the Accounting Standards Board's draft Statement of Principles, Chapter 6 of which recognizes four primary statements (the profit and loss account, the statement of total recognized gains and losses, the balance sheet, and the cash flow statement) which 'must be read in conjunction with their related notes' (para. 3) but also states that the 'notes and primary statements form an integrated whole' (para. 11). The statement goes on to distinguish between notes to financial statements and supplementary information. The function of the notes is to (para. 11):

> amplify or explain the items in the primary statements and in certain instances [to] provide either an alternative view of a particular transaction or event to that included in those primary statements, or information on items not included.

An 'alternative view' is possible because the Companies Act requires *a* true and fair view not *the* true and fair. It is not clear, however, whether the role of the notes is explicitly to give such an alternative view or merely to provide information which enables the reader to construct his or her own view. This problem is discussed further below in the section on a true and fair view and creative accounting. Information on items not included appears in practice in the UK to be limited to the non-financial data on employees required by company law to be included in the notes rather than in the directors' report.

Supplementary information is defined by the ASB as information that is positioned outside the primary statements and notes. It may include:

> information that has a different perspective from that adopted in the financial statements, including information that is highly relevant but low in reliability, or information that is helpful to some users but not essential for all ... [It] may also include management's explanation of the information given in financial reporting and their discussion of the significance of that information [para. 12].

The ASB Statement notes that supplementary information is not required to be audited. In this it differs, for companies where an audit is required, importantly from information contained in the notes. The question of what should and should not be disclosed in the notes is discussed further below.

Consolidated financial statements

In recognition of the differences between the UK and French accounting traditions, perhaps the most striking difference between the two countries is that whereas UK companies are required to provide one set of notes to accompany both the financial statements of the parent company and those of the group, French companies with subsidiaries must provide two annexes: one for the parent company accounts and one for the consolidated accounts. These must be treated as quite separate documents (Raffegeau et al., 1993: 933). The former is sometimes omitted from published annual reports and in particular from English translations thereof. The rules relating to the *annexe* to the consolidated accounts are summarized in Corre (1989: 97–101).

In France, as in many continental European countries, the accounts of individual companies are seen by regulators to play a crucial role in creditor protection and taxation. This makes them difficult to harmonize with UK financial statements. Consolidated accounts, on the contrary, do not have this role and are more easily harmonized with UK statements. Thus, a number of measurement practices not permitted in individual company financial statements are permitted in the consolidated statements, e.g. the capitalization of finance leases (Standish, 1995: 254). Such practices must be disclosed in the notes. The two *annexes* thus help to make possible the simultaneous relatively weak harmonization of French and UK individual company financial reporting and the relatively stronger harmonization of French and UK group financial reporting.

Exemptions and extensions

In both the UK and France certain companies are granted full or partial exemption from preparing and/or publishing notes, but the rules, although in accordance with the directives, are quite different. In line with the contrasting accounting traditions of the two countries, in France but not in the UK, the requirements of the directives, including those relating to the notes, have been extended to business organizations (including sole traders, partnerships and limited partnerships) not covered by the directives. The different ways in which the exemptions and extensions have been handled provide evidence of those areas which harmonization is not intended to reach. As Nobes and Parker (1995: 130–2) argue, it may be sensible, not just easier, to direct harmonization attempts at listed companies. There are no very compelling reasons why a small family company in Nantes should present its accounts in the same way as a small family company in Exeter. There is no need to attempt to overturn long established, but differing, accounting regulations if they have proved useful in the countries concerned and are not a barrier to a free flow of financial information within the EU.

In the UK there are no accounting requirements for sole traders and partnerships. Exemptions from preparing and publishing many of the notes are granted to small companies and from some notes to medium-sized companies. These exemptions are defined in terms of turnover, balance sheet total and number of employees (the relevant figures change from time to time).

In France, in contrast, there is no formal classification into different sizes of companies. Instead, abbreviated balance sheets are permitted for business enterprises below certain levels of turnover, balance sheet total and number of employees, whereas a simplified *annexe* is permitted for SAs, SARLs and partnerships below certain levels (not the same as for the balance sheet and profit and loss account) of the three criteria. Sole traders (*personnes physiques*) with a turnover below a certain level are not required to draw up an *annexe*.

Financial statement formats

French accounting regulations have traditionally required (to British eyes) rather inflexible balance sheet and profit and loss account formats. In implementation of the Fourth Directive formats were introduced into general British companies legislation by the Companies Act 1981. In both countries relief from this inflexibility is provided in a number of ways. One way is through the notes, the content and presentation of which are much less standardized than those of the balance sheet and profit and loss account. Moreover in Britain those items in the financial statement formats in the Schedules to the Companies Act which are not preceded by a letter or a Roman numeral can be shown in the notes. This is the common practice of at least large British companies and means that, despite the directives, not only do British and French financial statements not look as similar as might be expected from a first glance at the Fourth Directive (even if the same formats are chosen), but also that the British notes contain much information that in France is shown in the financial statements themselves. It is in French not British annual reports, however, that information on the division of liabilities into current and non-current must usually be sought in the notes. Consolidated financial statement formats in France are permitted greater flexibility (see above). Those of some large French multinationals show the influence of American presentation (and, in translation, of American terminology).

This flexibility at the national level reduces international harmonization. This is accentuated by the fact that in France the notes are much less standardized than are the balance sheet and profit and loss account. While the notes as a whole are relatively unstandardized, some individual notes have become standardized. The importance of this is discussed in the section on readability below.

Accounting policies

In the UK and France before the 1970s it was often difficult to discover what a company's accounting policies were. As a result of both national and international harmonization this task has become much easier. The Fourth Directive (Article 43 (1)(1)) requires disclosure in the notes of 'the valuation methods applied to the various items in the annual accounts, and the methods employed in calculating the value adjustments'.

In the UK the disclosure of accounting policies in one place became standard practice after the publication of SSAP 2 in 1971, i.e. it preceded the implementation of the Fourth Directive. The statement of accounting policies is a required disclosure in the notes and in the *annexe* but in the UK is not always in practice clearly labelled as such. The disclosure of accounting policies in one place greatly facilitates the testing by quantitative means of harmonization of measurement practices (see e.g. van der Tas, 1988; Emenyonu and Gray, 1992; Archer *et al.*, 1995).

A true and fair view and creative accounting

Two fundamental ways in which British and French accounting differed from each other before the EU directives were the British requirement to give a true and fair view and the dominance in France of tax rules. British accountants were unwilling to let true and fair be harmonized away and there was little hope of completely removing the grip of the French fiscal authorities or of persuading French companies to give up tax benefits in the interests of improved measurement practices. True and fair, however, is a very general requirement and tax rules are very specific so, as we shall see, the 'solutions' chosen by the harmonizers had to be very different. Both, however, made use of the notes.

The EU directives require annual accounts to give a true and fair view (*une image fidèle*) but do not lay down how this is to be done. The end (truth and fairness) is to be harmonized but not the means by which it is to be achieved. This poses a problem for those who attempt to measure harmonization. Are two sets of British and French financial statements and notes more harmonized if they both give a true and fair view or if they both comply with the same set of rules, even if one or both does not give a true and fair view? In practice, researchers have implicitly assumed the latter.

The UK literature on true and fair (discussed in Parker and Nobes, 1994) places no particular emphasis on the role of the notes. The French position is quite different – possibly because both the *annexe* and *l'image fidèle* were introduced into French accounting law by the Fourth Directive. For example a COB Bulletin (quoted Prost and Mai Van Thanh, 1985: iii) as early as March 1974 refers to the need for the balance sheet and the profit and loss account to be accompanied by notes in order for a true and fair view to be communicated. The sections of the Commercial Code summarized in a previous section of this paper show that it is in the *annexe* that additional information or departures relating to a true and fair view must be given. They cannot be given in the balance sheet or the profit and loss account or as supplementary information.

In the UK but not in France, departures from detailed legal requirements or standards in order to show a true and fair view are permitted in the financial statements themselves, but readers of British as well as of French financial statements often need to read the notes, and not just the balance sheet and profit and loss account, with some care in order to obtain what is in their opinion a true and fair view. Directors, and to a lesser extent auditors (Parker and Nobes, 1994) may assume that a true and fair view is given so long as company legislation and accounting standards are not infringed. For example, the 1989 accounts of Polly Peck complied with the Companies Act and SSAP 20 on foreign exchange and disclosed in the notes that adverse exchange differences were debited to reserve, whereas substantial interest income on investments in weak currencies was credited to profit and loss account. Nevertheless, at least with hindsight, it can be queried whether or not the balance sheet and profit and loss account, together with the notes thereon, gave a true and fair view (Gwilliam and Russell, 1991).

In neither the UK nor France has accounting regulation stood still since the implementation of the EU directives. These new regulations can lead to deharmonization as well as to harmonization. An example connected with the notes is creative accounting.

Creative accounting is familiar to accountants, lawyers, bankers and financial analysts in both France and the UK. French discussions of it tend to make liberal use of borrowings of and translations of English language expressions (e.g. CREFIGE, 1994). A distinction can be made between creative accounting which is disclosed in the notes in such a way that it can be understood by an expert and creative accounting which is not so disclosed. Inclusion of the former ignores the semi-strong version of the efficient markets hypothesis.

The issue of preference shares by subsidiaries provides examples of disclosed creative accounting. Some British companies which have only small minority ordinary shareholdings in subsidiaries nevertheless have large minority interest figures (and relatively low gearing ratios) in their consolidated balance sheets. Reference to the relevant notes reveals that the minority interest consists mainly of auction preferred stock issued by a subsidiary and with a dividend rate which varies with the current rate of interest. Both the directors and auditors consider that the balance sheets give a true and fair view and make no comments on truth and fairness in the notes. Notes of this nature, once found, enable users to prepare what they may consider to be a truer and fairer view (or at least an alternative true and fair view) than that given by the financial statements alone. Companies usually state, of course, that the financial statements must be read in conjunction with the notes. It may be queried, however, whether this means that once the notes have been read the user should be placed in a position of having a *radically* alternative view of, say, a company's gearing. There is no regulatory requirement which explicitly forbids such a possibility. Perhaps some clarification is required of what is meant by the financial statements and the notes forming 'a composite whole'.

In the French context there are other reasons for the issue of preference shares by a subsidiary. Such shares, if issued by a French company, must be denominated in French francs. The company may, however, wish to make an issue in US dollars. This can be achieved by, for example, setting up a subsidiary in Luxembourg and making the issue there. In the consolidated balance sheet the issue will appear as part of the minority interest with full disclosure in the *annexe* (Bernheim in CREFIGE, 1994: 21–2).

In both these examples, disclosure in the notes makes it possible for analysts to redraw the balance sheet if they wish to do so. This disclosure approach to combating creative accounting is followed in the UK in FRS 5, paras. 30–1 of which require that the disclosure of a transaction, whether or not any assets or liabilities have been recognized, should be sufficiently detailed to enable the user to understand its commercial effect; and that where a transaction has resulted in the recognition of assets or liabilities whose nature differs from that expected of an item included under the relevant balance sheet heading, the differences should be explained. There is no equivalent regulation in France and it is uncertain whether the French *annexe* will be able to serve the same function. Danziger would like to see creative transactions disclosed in the *annexe*, but both he and Nussenbaum (CREFIGE, 1994: 30, 31, 34) agree that in practice this rarely happens. Barthès de Ruyter and Gélard (1992) in a discussion of how to combat creative accounting do not see a role in the French context for either the truth and fairness requirement or the doctrine of substance over form and make no reference to possible disclosures in the *annexe*.

Tax legislation

The drafters of the Fourth Directive used the notes not to harmonize the British and French rules relating to the influence of tax on financial statements but to draw attention to the differences. The directive provides that if fixed and current assets are the subject of exceptional value adjustments for taxation purposes alone, the amount of the adjustments and the reasons for making them shall be indicated in the notes (Articles 35 (1d), 39 (1e)).

The directive also requires (Article 43 (10) (11)), where the influence is material, disclosure in the notes of:

1 the extent to which the calculation of the profit or loss for the financial year has been affected by a valuation of the items which was made in the financial year in question or in an earlier year with a view to obtaining tax relief;
2 the difference between the tax charged for the financial year and for earlier financial years and the amount of tax payable in respect of those years.

Tax effects on accounts are easy to recognize conceptually but not so easy to quantify. It is not always obvious what depreciation method and rates a company would have used in the (hypothetical) absence of tax regulations.

The directive's requirements did not need to be implemented in the UK. They were implemented in France by Article 24 (2) (23) (24) of the 1983 Accounting Decree which calls for disclosure in the notes of: the methods which have been used to calculate depreciation and provisions, identifying separately those which have been used as a result of tax regulations; a summary of the extent to which the profit or loss of the period has been affected by the application of these tax regulations and the effects of this on the items in shareholders' funds; and an indication of any increases or decreases in future tax liabilities arising from timing differences between the tax treatment and the accounting treatment of revenues and expenses and, where the amounts are exceptional, the extent that they are expected to crystallize. In practice, depreciation is the most important item affected by tax: extra tax-driven depreciation (*amortissements dérogatoires*) is debited as an extraordinary item; the credit is to the regulated provisions (*provisions reglementées*) account. The explanations relating to these items in published accounts are, however, sometimes obscure or even absent (cf. Scheid and Walton, 1992b: 170).

The Seventh Directive contains a similar requirement to the Fourth Directive. The requirement of the directive (Article 29(5)) that adjustments made solely for tax purposes shall be eliminated in the individual accounts before consolidation has been implemented in France. The directive also requires (Article 34(11)) that the amount of deferred taxation be disclosed in the notes. Although there is no requirement in the directive that tax must be deferred this is required in the UK by SSAP 15 and in France by the 1986 Decree, giving rise to a limited amount of harmonization and in both countries a requirement to make disclosures in the notes. Methods of deferred taxation remain controversial, with the possibilities of full provision or partial provision, and the liability method or the deferral method. SSAP 15 requires a partial provision and use of the liability method. Use is made of the notes by the standard in a requirement to disclose and quantify the difference between partial provision and full provision. The position in France is much less standardized, although most large companies practice full provision combined with the liability method. This is the preference of both OECCA and the *Conseil national de la comptabilité* but other methods are also permitted and used. If partial provision is adopted this must be justified in the *annexe* and the difference between full and partial provision quantified. This is similar to the UK requirement except, of course, that in practice most French companies will not need to make this disclosure, whereas most British companies will.

READABILITY, UNDERSTANDABILITY AND FORM OF DISCLOSURE

Readability and understandability

The regulators who drew up the requirements of the Fourth and Seventh Directives did not directly address the problem of readability and understandability, but it could be argued that harmonization of the rules relating to the presentation and content of the notes in member states will achieve little if those notes are not read or not understood by users of annual reports. This is an area where harmonization must be considered to be concerned with improvement as well as comparability. In the UK, for example, a study of shareholders of the Trustee Savings Bank (Gorb *et al.*, 1989, cited Hussey and Everitt, 1991: 50–1) demonstrated that its shareholders (many of whom are likely to have no accounting skills) found the notes by far the least informative part of the bank's annual report (3 per cent found them informative when unprompted, rising to 4 per cent when prompted). There are a number of possible ways in which regulation might add to readability and/or understandability. These include exemption from disclosure of non-material items; encouragement of the use of non-technical phraseology; and the use of standardized presentation, perhaps in tabular form.

In accordance with the Directives the exclusion of non-material items from the notes is specifically permitted in both the UK and France. This regulation is in accordance with long-standing UK practice but, in the absence of a detailed definition of materiality has been interpreted much more cautiously by French companies. As a result there have been complaints in France of a lack of readability arising from the inclusion of non-material items and a lack of compliance with the 'spirit' of the Fourth Directive (de Kerviler, 1985; Pasqualini, 1992: 57–9; Scheid and Walton, 1992a: 153).

Accounting regulations often include, and require the use of, technical terms which are understood by accountants and other experts but may score low on readability tests. A distinction can thus be drawn between readability and understandability (Smith and Taffler, 1992). Thus, notes which an unsophisticated reader may find unreadable may present the sophisticated user with an opportunity rather than a problem. As Matt and Mikol (1986: 47) point out, there is a risk of conflict between the needs of those users who can profit from the *annexe* as a prime source of extra information and those users for whom such information is only an extra cause of confusion. Unsophisticated readers may continue to have a severe problem, but any attempt to make notes on some topics understandable to a reader with no knowledge of accounting runs into the difficulty of technical language. A possible solution is the provision of a glossary of terms. One British example is the 1992 annual report (reprinted in Hussey and Bishop, 1993) of Wellcome PLC, a manufacturer of health care products. However, Wellcome evidently believe medical language to be more opaque than accounting language, providing definitions of twenty-three medical terms but only five accounting terms. Matt and Mikol (1986: 48–9) do not see why auditors any more than doctors should be expected to share with the readers of their prescriptions or reports their hesitations when making technical choices. Those who want to understand technical language must, they argue, make an effort to understand the rules of the game. Indeed, sophisticated readers can benefit from complex notes to an extent not necessarily intended by company management. Weber and Wheeler (1992) show in a US context how such readers of notes, especially those relating to taxation, can extract information not otherwise available.

Adelberg (1979) distinguishes between standardized notes and non-standardized notes. He found that the latter were more easily understood by sophisticated (but non-accountant) readers than the former. He suggested (pp. 184–5) that:

> The results imply that the object language in which management and accountants encode their non-standardized messages is in the *vernacular* of sophisticated users; and that would explain why they were easier for sophisticated users to understand than … standard format footnotes … where a much greater knowledge of the accounting model is called for.

The more complex the topic, the less likely that a note can be standardized. Adelberg points out that non-standardized notes are more easily 'manipulated' by management.

Much of the information required to be disclosed in the notes could be presented in tabular form. British law and standards do not insist on tables (although they are often used) but the French PCG of 1982 requires, subject to the test of materiality, seven obligatory tables in the *annexe* of an individual company. The tables relate to fixed assets; depreciation; provisions; classification of liabilities; results and other data for the last five accounting periods; profit appropriation; subsidiaries and participating interests.

Notes or elsewhere?

It is clear from the previous discussion that the harmonization of disclosure by companies within the EU has concerned itself not just with content but also with form. It is sometimes argued that the form of a disclosure does not matter. The amount of a contingent liability, for example, is required by UK company legislation to be disclosed in the notes, but might also, in certain circumstances (e.g. if it related to a massive oil spill) reasonably also be disclosed in one or more of the balance sheet, the directors' report, the operating and financial review and the chairman's review. Which is chosen could be seen as a matter of convenience, not as a matter for national or international harmonization. The EU directives do not follow this line of reasoning. As already noted, many items must be disclosed in the notes, but for some items there is the option of disclosing information in the notes or in some other document.

The view that it is of no importance whether or not or in what manner companies disclose information in the notes or elsewhere is based on the arguments that there is no difference in cost to a company whichever reporting method is employed and that there is no difference in cost to users in looking in one place rather than another (cf. Beaver, 1973). These arguments may be valid to the extent that it does not matter where an item is required to be disclosed so long as it is required to be disclosed in that place consistently. On the other hand, it could be argued that, even for required items, at least for non- sophisticated users, putting information in the notes rather than elsewhere may lead to it being ignored on the grounds of perceived less importance or less comprehensibility. More generally, it is less costly, even for sophisticated users, to know where an item can be found, to be certain that it can be found and to know its degree of reliability. If legislation or standards do not so require it cannot be assumed that an item not disclosed in the notes will be disclosed elsewhere. A disclosure in the financial statements or in the notes in the UK may be perceived to have greater reliability than one in the directors' report, operating and financial review or chairman's review because it will be covered by the audit report. Directors of companies may have incentives to disclose items in more or less accessible places and to have them audited or not audited.

If it is accepted that whether or not an item is disclosed in the notes or elsewhere is not a trivial issue, the question needs to be asked as to which items regulators should require *not* be disclosed in the notes. The ASB Statement referred to in a previous section suggested that the notes should not contain material which although highly relevant is low in reliability, information that is helpful to some users but not essential for all, and managerial explanations. This suggests the use of two criteria both also based on the concept that the financial statements and the notes constitute a composite whole. The first is that any information given in the notes should be capable of being subjected to a financial audit (as distinct, say, from an environmental audit). The second and related criterion is that the information should be of a financial nature.

These criteria can be illustrated by looking at the rules relating to employee information. The second criterion is not followed by the Fourth Directive which requires, for example, the disclosure in the notes not only of staff costs but also of the average number of employees (Article 43, 1(9)). Both disclosures are, of course, required by UK and French law. British and French requirements depart, however, in relation to other disclosures about employees in a way that reflects the different social and financial systems of the two countries (cf. McLeay in Nobes and Parker, 1995: 377–8) and are an example of how disharmony can arise in areas not covered by the Fourth and Seventh Directives. SSAP 24's disclosure requirements (usually requiring a lengthy note) are based on the British practice of covering pension liabilities by placing funds with financial institutions. In France the question of pension provisions was debated at length in 1985–86 (Scheid and Walton, 1992a: 223–5, 319). During the debate the tax authorities not only refused to recognize such provisions but tried unsuccessfully to forbid their creation. The Commercial Code (Article 9(2)) leaves the creation of a provision, either partial or full (the preferred option of both the COB and the OECCA) to the option of the company. If there is a provision it must be mentioned in the notes.

UK law regards the directors' report, not the notes, as the suitable receptacle for information on such matters as the employment of disabled persons, health and safety at work, and employee involvement.

Much more detailed information is required by French undertakings with 300 or more employees in a *bilan social*, which is perhaps best translated as an employment report. The information covers the areas of employment; wages and related costs; health and safety conditions; other working conditions; training; industrial relations; and other relevant conditions of life within the undertaking. The requirements are set out in the Law of 12 July 1977 and the related decree of 8 December 1977. They are a result of recommendations in a 1975 Report on Company Law Reform but are not usually regarded as in any way related to the financial statements. Nevertheless, Pasqualini (1992: 211) argues that sooner or later the information contained within the *bilan social* will come within the domain of the *annexe*. Meanwhile, a few French companies (e.g. L'Air Liquide) provide an employment report as part of the annual report package.

If companies were to be required to disclose audited environmental information should it form part of the notes? It would not qualify under the second criterion suggested above as an environmental audit is not a financial audit but it is easier to support inclusion if the notes are considered as an *annexe* of equal importance to the balance sheet and profit and loss account rather than as backing up individual items in the financial statements.

NOTING THE HARMONIES

The preceding sections have set out the evidence to support and explain the statements in Table 1. It may be concluded that although the French *annexe* is a result of the harmonization process the concept behind it differs from that of the British notes. The *annexe* is a separate document; the notes are not. The notes unlike the *annexe* are required to be published by companies only. For groups there are two *annexes* but only one set of notes. The rules about exemptions, formats and tables are not the same. The *annexe*, but not the notes, is given a role in relationship to truth and fairness and the effects of tax legislation. The evidence also suggests that, to the extent that there has been harmonization, French accounting has been harmonized more with British accounting than British accounting has been harmonized with French accounting. As a result of the EU directives, the presentation of British financial statements has been influenced by the French use of formats, but British accountants do not appear to have adopted any French concepts, presentations or disclosures relating to the notes. On the other hand, although the content and the extent of the disclosures in the French *annexe* have been affected by harmonization, concepts and presentation, even when different from French accounting before the directives, have been developed very much within an existing national environment. French accounting in this area has not, as a result of the process of *de jure* harmonization, been annexed by Britain.

NOTES

A previous version of this paper was presented at the annual conference of the British Accounting Association, Winchester, March, 1994. I am grateful for the financial support of the Institute of Chartered Accountants of Scotland and the comments of C. W. Nobes, Y. Lemarchand and two anonymous referees.

REFERENCES

Adelberg, A. H. (1979) 'Narrative disclosures contained in financial reports: means of communication or manipulation?', *Accounting and Business Research*, Summer.

Alexander, D. and Archer, S. (1992) *The European Accounting Guide*, London: Academic Press.

Archer, S., Delvaille, P. and McLeay, S. (1995) 'The measurement of harmonization and the comparability of financial statement items: within-country and between-country effects', *Accounting and Business Research*, Spring.

Barthès de Ruyter, G. and Gélard, G. (1992) 'L'abus de droit. Une arme contre la comptabilité imaginative?', *Revue française de comptabilité*, October.

Beaver, W. H. (1973) 'What should be the FASB's objectives?', *Journal of Accountancy*, August.

Burggraaf, J. A. (1983) 'The political dimensions of accounting in Europe', in Bromwich, M. and Hopwood, A. G. (eds) *Accounting Standards: An International Perspective*, London: Pitman.

Cohen, E. (1990) *Analyse financière*, 2nd edn, Paris: Economica.

Colasse, B. (1991) *Comptabilité générale*, 3rd edn, Paris: Economica.

Corre, J. (1989) *Les règles de la consolidation des bilans*, 3rd edn, Paris: Dunod.

CREFIGE (Centre de Recherche Européen en Finance et Gestion) (1994) *Compte-rendu de la Table Ronde. La comptabilité créative*, Cahier de Recherche No. 9401.

Davies, M., Paterson, R. and Wilson, A. (1994) *UK GAAP*, 4th edn, London: Macmillan for Ernst and Young.

Emenyonu, E. N. and Gray, S. J. (1992) 'EC accounting harmonization: an empirical study of measurement practices in France, Germany and the UK', *Accounting and Business Research*, Winter.

Garnier, P. (1947) *La comptabilité, algèbre du droit et méthode d'observation des sciences économiques*, Paris: Dunod.

Gorb, P., Burns, R., Clarke, F., Lundholm, D. and Ross, D. (1989) *What Do Investors Really Want to Know?* London: Wolff Olins/Hall.

Gwilliam, D. and Russell, T. (1991) 'Compliance with the letter but not the spirit', *Accountancy*, April.

Hussey, R. and Everitt, H. (1991) *Summary and Simplified Financial Reporting* London: Butterworths.

Hussey, R. and Bishop, M. (1993) *Corporate Reports*, London: Woodhead-Faulkner.

Kerviler, I. de (1985) 'L'annexe en France: mais où est donc passé l'esprit de la IVe directive?', *Profession comptable*, (22).

Lee, T. A. (1984) 'Company financial statements: An essay in business history 1830–1950', in Lee, T. A. and Parker, R. H., *The Evolution of Corporate Financial Reporting*, Sunbury-on-Thames, reprinted New York: Garland Publishing.

Matt, J.-M. and Mikol, A. (1986) 'L'image fidèle, la doctrine et la loi', *Revue française de comptabilité*, December.

Nobes, C. W. and Parker, R. H. (1995) *Comparative International Accounting*, 4th edn, Hemel Hempstead: Prentice Hall.

Parker, R. H. and Nobes, C. W. (1994) *An International View of True and Fair Accounting*, London: Routledge.

Pasqualini, F. (1992) *Le principe de l'image fidèle en droit comptable*. Paris: Litec.

Prost, A. and Mai Van Thanh (1984) *Plan comptable général. L'annexe: son rôle, sa mise en place dans l'entreprise*, Paris: Sirey.

Raffegeau, J., Dufils, P. and Lopater, C. (1985) *L'annexe des comptes annuels. Guide pratique*, Paris: Editions Francis Lefebvre.

Raffegeau, J., Dufils, P., Corre, J. and Lopater, C. (1993) *Mémento pratique Francis Lefebvre comptable 1994*, Paris: Editions Francis Lefebvre.

Roberts, A. (1993) 'Reflections of a True and Fair View in France', University of Reading Discussion Paper No. 36 in Accounting, Finance and Banking.

Scheid, J.-C. and Walton, P. (1992a) *European Financial Reporting: France*, London: Routledge.

Scheid, J.-C. and Walton, P. (1992b) 'France', in Alexander and Archer.

Smith, M. and Taffler, R. (1992) 'Readability and understandability: different measures of the textual complexity of accounting narrative', *Accounting Auditing & Accountability Journal*, 5(4).

Standish, P. (1995) 'Financial reporting in France', in Nobes and Parker.

Tas, L. van der (1988) 'Measuring harmonization of financial reporting practice', *Accounting and Business Research*, Spring.

Tay, J. S. W. and Parker, R. H. (1990) 'Measuring international standardization and harmonization', *Abacus*, March.

Walton, P. (1992) 'Harmonization of accounting in France and Britain: some evidence', *Abacus*, September.

Weber, R. P. and Wheeler, J. E. (1992) 'Using income tax disclosures to explore significant economic transactions', *Accounting Horizons*, September.

The European Accounting Review 1996, **5:2**, 361–373

Some mysteries relating to the prudence principle in the Fourth Directive and in German and British law

Lisa Evans and Christopher Nobes
Napier University, and University of Reading, UK

ABSTRACT

Article 31 of the Fourth Directive, which specifies the general valuation principles to be applied in the preparation of financial statements, shows a difference in emphasis between the different language versions. Except for the English version of the Directive, all others emphasize prudence, as opposed to the other valuation principles required by the article. The earlier drafts of the Directive are examined in an attempt to trace the development of this difference between the English and the other language versions. It seems that the particular wording of Article 31 with its relatively greater weight on prudence probably results from UK influence, more specifically from SSAP 2. A possible solution is then suggested as to why this particular emphasis on prudence was not retained in the English version of the Directive. Further, it is noted that German law did not explicitly make prudence an overriding concept before the Fourth Directive and nor does the German implementation of Article 31.

INTRODUCTION

One of the key differences in accounting practices in Europe relates to differential degrees of conservatism.[1] German accounting, and to a certain extent that of most other continental member states of the European Union, tends to emphasize the principle of prudence relatively more than the other valuation principles listed in the Fourth Directive on Company Law.[2] The UK might be taken as an exemplar of the opposite view. For example, Gray (1980) proposed a conservatism index, and saw Germany as noticeably more conservative than the UK. Instances of greater German conservatism may be found in the opposition in that country to (1) the percentage-of-

Address for correspondence
Lisa Evans, Department of Accounting and Finance, Napier University, Sighthill Court, Edinburgh EH11 4BN, UK.

 0963–8180

completion method for long-term contracts (e.g. Ordelheide, 1993), and (2) the taking of gains on unsettled foreign currency monetary items.

The reasons for these differing approaches have been discussed in detail elsewhere,[3] and include the closeness of German accounting to German tax rules and the importance of creditor protection. The EC Forum spent considerable effort in 1994 and 1995 looking at 'prudence v. matching' (e.g. FEE, 1994). However, none of the publications on this subject have pointed out the following mysteries or tried to solve them:

1 Prudence was not explicitly mentioned in the first draft of the Fourth Directive or in the preceding German law.
2 The idea of explicit reference in the Fourth Directive to prudence (and an emphasis on it) seem to come from a British accounting standard.
3 Despite this, the English version of the Directive is the only one not to emphasize prudence.
4 The implementation of the Directive in German law does not carry forward the emphasis on prudence in the German version of the Directive.

THE FOURTH DIRECTIVE

The importance of prudence in German accounting is supported by the German wording of Article 31 of the Directive (see Appendix A) which, while introducing the other valuation principles with phrases which would translate, for example, as 'going concern is to be presumed'; '... consistency shall apply', etc., appears to place special emphasis[4] on prudence by stating that 'Der Grundsatz der Vorsicht muss *in jedem Fall* beachtet werden'. (Article 31 (1)(c) – emphasis added) – ('The principle of prudence must be observed *in any event*'. A more literal translation may stress this emphasis even more: 'The principle of prudence must be observed *in every case*'.)

Strangely, the English version of the Directive does not emphasize prudence. Article 31 (1)(c) reads: 'valuation must be made on a prudent basis' (see Appendix A). This may have been what led Rutteman (1984: 11) to state: 'The prudence concept they [the EEC Commission] deem to take precedence over the accruals concept, although the Directive nowhere says so.' As noted, the German version of the Directive does in fact say so. Furthermore, an examination of the other language versions shows that it is the English version of the Directive, rather than the German one, which is the exception. For example, the French version states: 'le principe de prudence doit *en tout cas* être observé ...' (emphasis added). The same stress is found in the Italian, Spanish, Portuguese and Danish versions. The Dutch version reads: 'het voorzichtigheidsbeginsel moet *steeds* in acht worden genomen ...' (emphasis added), i.e. 'the principle of prudence must always be observed ...'.

ORIGIN OF THE EMPHASIS

This raises the question of where this emphasis on prudence in the directive originates. If it had been a German influence, one might have expected to find the emphasis in the *Aktiengesetz* (*AktG*) of 1965 which formed the basis for the Fourth Directive (Nobes, 1983). However, there is no explicit mention of prudence in the *AktG*, which refers to the more detailed requirements of the Handelsgesetzbuch (*HGB*). However, although prudence is consequently referred to in the legal commentaries on the Act,[5] there is no specific emphasis on it. Furthermore, as noted in the introduction, the first draft of the Fourth Directive (1971, Article 28), which was published by the Commission before the UK, Ireland and Denmark joined the EU in 1973, does not mention prudence at all. Nevertheless, prudence is implied in the other general (valuation) principles, which deal with realization and accounting for contingencies (Article 28 (1)(b)), deficiencies becoming apparent after the balance sheet date (Article 28 (1)(c)) and a requirement to account for depreciation whether the accounts show a profit or a loss (Article 28 (1)(d)). The other valuation principles of Article 28 are consistency, separate valuation of asset and liability items, and the requirement for one year's closing balance sheet to correspond to the following year's opening balance sheet.

The situation changed by the time of the second draft (1974). The going concern and the accruals principles were introduced, and the idea of prudence was made explicit. The former subparagraphs (b) to (d) of Article 28 (as listed above) now became integrated within the new paragraph dealing with prudence (28 (c)), effectively making the realization principle a 'sub-principle of the prudence principle' (Ordelheide, 1993: 83). Also, the German version of the 1974 draft contains the explicit emphasis on prudence mentioned above, as do all the other language versions, *except for the English version.*

Incidentally, the term used in the English version of the 1974 draft was 'conservatism' (as in US documents, see *Accountancy*, 1971), rather than 'prudence', the latter only appearing in the final form of the Directive. Table 1 (see words in italics) shows how the two terms were used in various documents in English in the 1970s. There seems to be little systematic difference between the two terms, except that 'prudence' might be used to avoid the connotations of secret reserves and other practices once associated with the older word 'conservatism'. A shift such as that from 'conservatism' to 'prudence' in the wording of the drafts of the English version of the directive (between 1974 and 1978) could be achieved[6] by negotiation with the secretariat of the Council of Ministers.

Table 1 Chronology of events and publications

1961	AICPA Accounting Research Study 1: rejects *conservatism*
1965	AICPA Accounting Research Study 7: includes *conservatism*
December 1969	Accounting Standards Steering Committee formed
October 1970	APB Statement 4: *conservatism* as a 'modifying convention', not as a 'pervasive principle'
Februrary 1971	ED 2: *prudence* as overriding
November 1971	Fourth Directive first draft: no explicit reference to the concept
November 1971	SSAP 2: *prudence* as overriding
January 1973	UK joins EC (but previously observer status on Groupe d'Etudes)
July 1973	IASC formed
October 1973	Trueblood Committee reports
Februrary 1974	Fourth Directive second draft: *conservatism* emphasized
1974	UEC Recommendation No. 1 (lists four concepts, but no emphasis)
April 1974	IASC Exposure Draft E1: *prudence* as a selection criterion
January 1975	IAS 1: *prudence* as a selection criterion
July 1978	Fourth Directive: *prudence* emphasized

A further English language nuance (Rutteman, 1984: 6) is that Article 28 (in 1971 and 1974) requires that 'Only the profits *earned* at the date of the balance sheet may be included' (emphasis added), whereas Article 31 of the directive refers to 'profits made', and the British law[7] has 'profits realised' (see Appendices A and B). This change seems to be an attempt to broaden the scope of the phrase to make it less conservative. In the case of 'realised', this word was chosen[8] to be consistent with the UK's implementation in 1980 of the Second Directive's definition of distributable profits, which rests on the word 'realised'.

There were no other significant changes concerning prudence between the 1974 draft and the final Directive in any of the other language versions.[9] Article 28 of the drafts becomes Article 31 in the Directive.

If we cannot look to German precedent for the explicit inclusion of and emphasis on prudence in the 1974 draft and the final Directive, reference must be made to the main event that led to other changes from the 1971 to the 1974 version of the directive: the accession of the UK, Ireland and Denmark. It is clear that the arrival of these three countries was the cause of the insertion of the 'true and fair view' requirement in the 1974 draft (Nobes, 1993), so the above changes in the lower level accounting principles may also have resulted from this.

By 1974, the UK and Ireland had recently[10] seen the publication of the first accounting standards and, with particular relevance to the above, of SSAP 2, which lists four 'fundamental accounting concepts': going concern, accruals, consistency and prudence – with particular emphasis on prudence:

'...; provided that where the accruals concept is inconsistent with the "prudence" concept the latter prevails' (para. 14 (b)).

The influence of SSAP 2 seems to have operated through the Groupe d'Etudes, which advised the Commission on accounting matters:

> The Groupe D'Etudes has discussed this directive at considerable length and has issued two reports, the first in June last year and the second in April of this year. From the British viewpoint, we can, I feel, be satisfied with the Groupe's work, since its main recommendations include the following points:
> 1. The fundamental purposes of annual accounts should be to show a true and fair view. ...
> ...
> 3. The section on valuation rules should commence in its first article by stating that there are four basic accounting concepts – those of going concern, consistency, matching or accruals and prudence. Again *the English terms were included in the official French text of the Groupe's second report.* (Bartholomew, 1973: 424–9, emphasis added)

In the light of the above there seems little doubt that the changes proposed were UK influenced (for further evidence see, for example, the interview by Lafferty (1974) with John Grenside, one of the UK representatives in the negotiations surrounding the Fourth Directive). This may lead to the suggestion that the emphasis on prudence in relation to the other principles also originated in the UK. Another reference to the report by the Groupe d'Etudes seems relevant in this context:

> In dealing with Article 28, concerning certain general principles of valuation, the Study Group observes that the general principles include four basic concepts:
>
> 1 The going concern concept
> 2 The concept of consistency
> 3 The matching or accruals concept
> 4 The concept of prudence
>
> The application of the third concept is not prescribed as such in the provisions. ... The Study Group proposes that this concept should be incorporated in Article 28. *It states, however, that it is necessary to place these concepts in order of importance. As the concept of prudence is of primordial [sic] importance, its relationship to the concept of accruals and matching must be stated.* (*Accountancy*, 1973a: 4 – emphasis added)

A FURTHER MYSTERY

Given the apparent UK influence which seems to have led to the provisions of SSAP 2 being incorporated into the Fourth Directive, it is particularly strange that the English versions of the 1974 draft and of the final Directive are the only ones which do not retain the supremacy of prudence.

The potential explanations for the special wording in the English version seem to be:

1 a wording which was openly agreed in Council negotiations;
2 a wording lobbied for by the UK and agreed privately by the Council secretariat;
3 a wording arranged by the Council secretariat in order to make the drafting more acceptable to the UK, but not discussed with any delegation; or
4 a linguistic accident.

It is clear that (1) and (2) were not the case. None of the articles of the time, and none of the papers or the recollections[11] of the negotiators fit this explanation. If either (3) or (4) was the case, presumably the UK delegation would have objected to the wording if it had not suited them. Here, it seems useful to note that there was a change in the prevailing ethos in the UK from an emphasis on prudence to an emphasis on accruals within a relatively short time: between 1971 (the publication of SSAP 2) and 1974 (the second draft of the Fourth Directive).

A chronology of potentially relevant events is shown as Table 1. In the USA, Accounting Research Study (ARS) No. 7 of the AICPA[12] listed ten 'basic concepts', among them those which became the four of SSAP 2. By 1970, the Accounting Principles Board had downgraded conservatism to a 'modifying convention' (APB, 1970). Conservatism had also been criticized in ARS No. 1 (Moonitz, 1961) and by Sterling (1967: 131) who rejects it as 'deliberate understatement' and as a concept which 'has lost favour in accounting circles, that is not applied in practice as much as it once was' (110). This was part of a move from stewardship accounting and the protection of creditors towards the provision of information intended for financial decisions by investors. A landmark along this way was the 1973 US report of the Trueblood Committee on the objectives of financial statements.

It is clear that this trend, and increasing inflation, were already affecting the UK (Hinton, 1972: 58):

> The concept of conservatism, suitable perhaps in an era when only creditors and private owners had an interest in financial statements, is inconsistent with another basic concept, vigorously proclaimed by accountants, that accounting must be fair and free from bias. Conservatism and fairness are inconsistent concepts, since conservatism serves some users of financial statements to the detriment of others. Conservatism is basically biased; it seeks to protect the purchaser and the lender, but disregards the interests of the seller and the borrower.

Similarly, Buckley (1973) points out that the objectives of financial statements depend on the user group and change with time; in this context, he also criticizes the use of historical cost (1973: 64):

> Developed in an age when there was little or no divorce of ownership and control, stewardship accounts served the then prevailing business environment perfectly well. But now financial reporting objectives have changed; the users of financial statements want more than reports on stewardship. In addition the balance sheet of

an enterprise reflects, under generally accepted accounting principles, historic cost rather than the true value of economic resources locked up in the entity.

In 1973 the IASC was formed. In 1974 it issued its first Exposure Draft, which appears to cover much the same ground as SSAP 2. This is hardly surprising if one considers the way the IASC worked:

> It is the committee's intention to make a collection of the standards of the written work in the nine [founder] nations, and sift it to the basics. The resulting material, free from any unnecessary sophistication, will then be made into an exposure draft, and on further refinement will be published as a definite document. (*Accountancy*, 1973b: 4)

However, the resulting IAS 1 shows a move away from SSAP 2's emphasis on prudence, by not recognizing it as a fundamental assumption but only as one of three[13] considerations which 'should govern the selection and application by management of the appropriate accounting policies ...' (para. 9). This reflects the US view discussed above, which seems already to have been affecting the UK. No doubt, the involvement of US and UK representatives in the IAS 1 discussions speeded up this effect, which then fed into negotiations in Brussels from 1973. This possibility is confirmed by one of the UK negotiators of the time.[14]

Incidentally, by the stage of the negotiations in the Council of Ministers leading up to the final Directive in 1978, relatively subtle points and language differences would not have been dwelt on. National negotiators were mainly interested in achieving drafts in their own languages which could be 'lived with'.[15]

IMPLEMENTATION OF THE DIRECTIVE

The next part of the mystery is that the Directive's emphasis on prudence did not appear (at least, not directly in the words used) in the resulting laws of Germany or the UK (see Appendix B). Of course, in the case of the UK this may not be surprising because the emphasis is missing from the English version of the Directive, but how does one explain the continuing absence of the emphasis in German law, as amended by the 1985 *Bilanzrichtliniengesetz*?

Ordelheide and Pfaff (1994: 133) refer to the amended German Commercial Code, (*HGB*), §252 (1) in claiming that:

> The essential principle is the prudence principle (HGB §252 (1), No. 4). It is made concrete through the acquisition cost principle, the principle of lower of cost and market value and the realization principle, among others. In addition the following *complementary and supporting* principles should be noted:
>
> 1 The principle of balance sheet continuity (HGB §252 (1), No.1).
> 2 The 'going concern' principle (HGB §252 (1), No.2).
> 3 The principle of item-by-item valuation (HGB §252 (1), No.3).

4 The accruals principle (HGB §252 (1), No.5).
5 The consistency principle (HGB §252 (1), No.6). (emphasis added)

However, the emphasis on prudence is not obvious from a scrutiny of the German law itself (see Appendix B). *HGB* §252 does not stress the prudence principle in comparison with the other principles. It does not state that the prudence principle is the 'essential principle', nor does it define the other principles as 'complementary and supporting'. It merely requires prudence in a list of six principles all of which have to be complied with.

One can only assume that the Directive's emphasis on prudence was not explicitly included in *HGB* §252 because it was taken for granted, or could be presumed because of the more detailed valuation rules of the *HGB*, which implement the more 'prudent' options of the Fourth Directive, and because of the provisions of *Grundsätze ordnungsmässiger Buchführung* (*GoB*), which also favour a prudent approach to accounting. The context is that interpretation of a law in the Roman legal system takes more account of implicit principles than would apply in the English legal system.

The following reference to a legal commentary on the *HGB* (Baumbach *et al.*, 1989) may serve as an illustration of the preference for prudence. The *HGB* §252 (2)[16] allows departure from the detailed principles of §252 (1) in justified exceptional cases, but the legal commentary suggests that exceptions are possible from all principles except prudence:

> **Ausnahmen:** II ist hier ohne praktische Bedeutung; Ausnahmen sind idR nicht 'begründet' oder entsprechen nicht den GoB.
> (**Exceptions:** II is here without practical significance; exceptions are, as a rule, not 'justified' or do not correspond to GoB.)

SUMMARY

The supremacy of prudence over the other principles is codified in all language versions of the Fourth Directive except for the English version. This is surprising, since an examination of the development of the Directive suggests that it was particularly the British SSAP 2 which influenced Article 31 of the Fourth Directive with respect to the following:

1 the introduction of prudence as an explicit principle,
2 the supremacy of the prudence principle.

A possible reason for the omission of the emphasis on prudence in the English version of the Directive (and therefore in the Companies Act 1981) has been suggested.

A further curiosity is that German law, which otherwise places greater emphasis on prudence than does UK law, has not implemented the emphasis on it in the relevant passage of the *HGB*. This appears to be due to German *GoB* and to the detailed valuation rules of the *HGB*, in which greater emphasis on prudence as compared to the accruals principle is implicit and which implements the more prudent options of the directive.

NOTES

The authors are grateful for comments on an earlier draft to John Dyson and David Young (Napier University), Dieter Ordelheide (Goethe Universität, Frankfurt am Main), Bob Parker (University of Exeter) and Alan Roberts (University of Reading), and for advice from Sir John Grenside CBE, Frank Jenkins (of the Department of Trade and Industry), Michael Renshall CBE and Tom Watts CBE who were involved on behalf of the UK in governmental and Groupe d'Etudes negotiations of the Fourth Directive in the 1970s.

1 The words 'conservatism' and 'prudence' are used in this paper. Both can be found in official documents. There seems to be little difference in the meanings of the words.
2 See for example Ordelheide (1993: 83); Ordelheide and Pfaff (1994: 133–6); Nobes and Parker (1995: 45–7).
3 See for example Busse von Colbe (1984: 125–6); Choi and Mueller (1992: 40–3); Haller (1992); Macharzina and Langer (1995: 269); Nobes (1992: 7–23); Perera (1989).
4. Of course, it would have been possible to emphasize prudence even more by placing it as the first of the principles, or by specifically making accruals subordinate to prudence. We are grateful to Frank Jenkins for pointing this out.
5 A legal commentary on para. 39 of the *HGB* from before the implementation of the Fourth Directive (Baumbach *et al.*, 1985: 144) discusses the section of German law which influenced the content of Article 28. Paragraph 39 refers to the duty to draw up a balance sheet (*Bilanz*). The legal commentary lists, with reference to other laws and *GoB*, the following principles to be applied in doing so: clarity, truth, completeness, continuity, prudence.
6 Frank Jenkins, who was one of the representatives of the UK in these negotiations, confirms this (letter of 23 February 1995).
7 Now in Schedule 4, para. 12a to the Companies Act 1985. The word 'realised' is further defined in para. 91, in a way which refers to 'principles generally accepted'.
8 As footnote 6.
9 The German word for prudence (*Vorsicht*) did not change.
10 ED 2 (the exposure draft for SSAP 2) was published in February 1971 and the SSAP itself in November of the same year. The stress on prudence was moved from the Explanatory Note part of the ED, to the Definition of Terms part of the SSAP.
11 Sir John Grenside, Frank Jenkins, Michael Renshall and Tom Watts (see references in other footnotes) have no papers or recollections which suggest that the UK delegation was aware of or pushed for the difference in the emphasis of prudence in the English version. However, they suggest that they would have approved of the absence of emphasis.
12 American Institute of Certified Public Accountants; see Grady (1965).
13 The other two being substance over form and materiality.
14 For example, by Michael Renshall (who was involved in the negotiations at the Groupe d'Etudes and at governmental level) in a letter of 22 February 1995. However, Sir John Grenside (also closely involved) suggests that there was no

direct influence of IASC discussions (minuted telephone conversation of 28 February 1995).

15 This is recorded, in a letter of 22 February 1995 by Tom Watts, who was an honorary UK civil servant for the purposes of the Council of Ministers negotiations.

16 This implements Article 31 (2) of the Directive.

17 Amended by the 1989 Companies Act to read as follows: 11. Accounting policies shall be applied consistently within the same accounts as from one financial year to the next.

REFERENCES

Accountancy (1971) 'Accounting standards go forward', February, 54–5.

Accountancy (1973a) 'Study Group steps forward on harmonisation', May.

Accountancy (1973b) 'International accountancy: a beginning', August.

Accounting Principles Board (1970) *Statement of the Accounting Principles Board 4. Basic Concepts and Accounting Principles Underlying Financial Statements of Business Enterprises. New York: American Institute of Certified Public Accountants.*

Bartholomew, E. G. (1973) 'The EEC, company law and accountants', *The Accountant's Magazine*, August, 424–9

Baumbach, A., Duden, K. and Hopt, K. (1985) *Handelsgesetzbuch*, 26 Auflage, Munich: C. H. Beck

Baumbach, A., Duden, K. and Hopt, K. (1989) *Handelsgesetzbuch*, 28 Auflage, Munich: C. H. Beck

Buckley, A. (1973) 'The financial statement ... ', *Accountancy*, August.

Busse von Colbe, W. (1984) 'A true and fair view: a German perspective', in Gray, S. J. and Coenenberg A. G. (eds) *EEC Accounting Harmonisation: Implementation and Impact of the Fourth Directive*, North Holland: Elsevier, pp. 121–128.

Choi, F. D. S. and Mueller, G. G. (1992) *International Accounting*, New Jersey: Prentice-Hall.

FEE (1994) *Discussion Paper on the Application of Prudence and Matching in Selected European Countries.*

Grady, P. (1965) *Research Study No. 7. Inventory of Generally Accepted Accounting Principles for Business Enterprises.* New York: American Institute of Certified Public Accountants.

Gray, S. J. (1980) 'The impact of international differences from a security-analysis perspective: some European evidence', *Journal of Accounting Research*, Spring.

Haller, A. (1992) 'The relationship of financial and tax accounting in Germany: a major reason for accounting disharmony in Europe', *International Journal of Accounting*, 27: 310–23.

Hinton, P. R. (1972) 'Objectives of financial statements', *Accountancy*, November.

Lafferty, M. (1974) 'Fourth Directive .... what's in it for us?' *Accountancy*, July: 30–2.

Marcharzina, K. and Langer, K. (1995), 'Financial reporting in Germany' in Nobes and Parker (1995).

Moonitz, M. (1961) *Research Study No.1. The Basic Postulates of Accounting*. New York: American Institute of Certified Public Accountants.

Nobes, C. W. (1983), 'The evolution of the harmonising provisions of the 1980 and 1981 Companies Acts', *Accounting and Business Research*, Winter: 43–53.

Nobes, C. W. (1992) *Accounting Harmonisation in Europe: Process, Progress and Prospects*, London: Financial Times Business Information.

Nobes, C. W. (1993) 'The true and fair view requirement: impact on and of the Fourth Directive', *Accounting and Business Research*, Winter.
Nobes C. W. and Parker, R. H. (1995) *Comparative International Accounting*. Hemel Hempstead: Prentice Hall.
Ordelheide, D. (1993), 'True and fair view: a European and a German perspective', *European Accounting Review*, 1, 81–90.
Ordelheide, D. and Pfaff, D. (1994) *European Financial Reporting. Germany*, London: Routledge.
Perera, M. H. B. (1989) 'Towards a framework to analyse the impact of culture on accounting', *International Journal of Accounting*, 24, 42–56.
Rutteman, P. (1984) *The EEC Accounting Directives and their Effects*, University College Cardiff Press.
Sterling, R. R. (1967) 'Conservatism: the fundamental principle of valuation in traditional accounting', *Abacus*, 3 (2): 109–32.

APPENDIX A: ARTICLE 31, FOURTH DIRECTIVE (1978)

German Version

Artikel 31

(1) Die Mitgliedstaaten stellen sicher, daß für die Bewertung der Posten im Jahresabschluß folgende allgemeine Grundsätze gelten:

a) Eine Fortsetzung der Unternehmenstätigkeit wird unterstellt.
b) In der Anwendung der Bewertungsmethoden soll Stetigkeit bestehen.
c) Der Grundsatz der Vorsicht muß *in jedem Fall* beachtet werden. Das bedeutet insbesondere:

    aa) Nur die am Bilanzstichtag realisierten Gewinne werden ausgewiesen.
    bb) Es müssen alle voraussehbaren Risiken und zu vermutenden Verluste berücksichtigt werden, die in dem Geschäftsjahr oder einem früheren Geschäftsjahr entstanden sind, selbst wenn diese Risiken oder Verluste erst zwischen dem Bilanzstichtag und dem Tag der Aufstellung der Bilanz bekanntgeworden sind.
    cc) Wertminderungen sind unabhängig davon zu berücksichtigen, ob das Geschäftsjahr mit einem Gewinn oder einem Verlust abschließt.

d) Aufwendungen und Erträge für das Geschäftsjahr, auf das sich der Jahresabschluß bezieht, müssen berücksichtigt werden, ohne Rücksicht auf den Zeitpunkt der Ausgabe oder Einnahme dieser Aufwendung oder Erträge.

e) Die in den Aktiv und Passivposten enthaltenen Vermögensgegenstände sind einzeln zu bewerten.

f) Die Eröffnungsbilanz eines Geschäftsjahres muß mit der Schlußbilanz des vorhergehenden Geschäftsjahres übereinstimmen.

(emphasis added)

English Version

Article 31

1. The Member States shall ensure that the items shown in the annual accounts are valued in accordance with the following general principles:

(a) the company must be presumed to be carrying on its business as a going concern;
(b) the methods of valuation must be applied consistently from one financial year to another;
(c) valuation must be made on a prudent basis, and in particular:

(aa) only profits made at the balance sheet date may be included,
(bb) account must be taken of all foreseeable liabilities and potential losses arising in the course of the financial year concerned or of a previous one, even if such liabilities or losses become apparent only between the date of the balance sheet and the date on which it is drawn up,
(cc) account must be taken of all depreciation, whether the result of the financial year is a loss or a profit;

(d) account must be taken of income and charges relating to the financial year, irrespective of the date of receipt or payment of such income or charges;
(e) the components of asset and liability items must be valued separately;
(f) the opening balance sheet for each financial year must correspond to the closing balance sheet for the preceding financial year.

APPENDIX B: IMPLEMENTATION OF ARTICLE 31 INTO NATIONAL LAW

Handelsgesetzbuch Paragraph 252

Allgemeine Bewertungsgrundsätze

(1) Bei der Bewertung der im Jahresabschluß ausgewiesenen Vermögensgegenstände und Schulden gilt insbesondere folgendes:

1. Die Wertansätze in der Eröffnungsbilanz des Geschäftsjahrs müssen mit denen der Schlußbilanz des vorhergehenden Geschäftsjahrs übereinstimmen.
2. Bei der Bewertung ist von der Fortführung der Unternehmenstätigkeit auszugehen, sofern dem nicht tatsächliche oder rechtliche Gegebenheiten entgegenstehen.
3. Die Vermögensgegenstände und Schulden sind zum Abschlußstichtag einzeln zu bewerten.
4. Es ist vorsichtig zu bewerten, namentlich sind alle vorhersehbaren Risiken und Verluste, die bis zum Abschlußstichtag entstanden sind, zu berücksichtigen, selbst wenn diese erst zwischen dem Abschlußstichtag und dem Tag der Aufstellung des Jahresabschlusses bekanntgeworden sind; Gewinne sind nur zu berücksichtigen, wenn sie am Abschlußstichtag realisiert sind.

5. Aufwendungen und Erträge des Geschäftsjahrs sind unabhängig von den Zeitpunkten der entsprechenden Zahlungen im Jahresabschluß zu berücksichtigen.
6. Die auf den vorhergehenden Jahresabschlußstichtag angewandten Bewertungsmethoden sollen beibehalten werden.

Companies Act 1985, Schedule 4, Section A Accounting principles

10. The company shall be presumed to be carrying on business as a going concern.
11. Accounting policies shall be applied consistently as from one financial year to the next[17]
12. The amount of any item shall be determined on a prudent basis, and in particular—

    (a) only profits realised at the balance sheet date shall be included in the profit and loss account; and

    (b) all liabilities and losses which have arisen or are likely to arise in respect of the financial year to which the accounts relate or a previous financial year shall be taken into account, including those which only become apparent between the balance sheet date and the date on which it is signed on behalf of the board of directors in pursuance of [section 233] of this Act.

13. All income and charges relating to the financial year to which the accounts relate shall be taken into account, without regard to the date of receipt or payment.
14. In determining the aggregate amount of any item the amount of each individual asset or liability that falls to be taken into account shall be determined separately.

[15]

The European Accounting Review 1997, **6:4**, 711–720

The true and fair view override in the European Accounting Directives

Karel Van Hulle
European Commission and Katholieke Universiteit Leuven

ABSTRACT

This paper looks into the origin of the true and fair view override in the European Accounting Directives. It explains the meaning of the true and fair view override within the context of the Directives and how this principle has been implemented by the Member States of the European Union. The paper also compares the true and fair concept adopted in IAS 1 with the similar concept contained in the Accounting Directives. The paper concludes by emphasizing the usefulness of the true and fair view override within the context of an accounting regime based on a conceptual framework.

INTRODUCTION

In accordance with the European Accounting Directives, the annual and consolidated accounts must show a true and fair view. If the application of a provision in the Directives does not lead to the accounts showing a true and fair view, companies are required to depart from this provision so as to show a true and fair view. The requirement to depart from applicable rules and standards in those cases where the application of those rules and standards does not lead to the accounts showing a true and fair view is often referred to as the true and fair view override.

The true and fair view override was introduced in the Accounting Directives at the request particularly of the Danish, Dutch and UK delegations. It is an important feature of European accounting law. It requires those who prepare the accounts to apply professional judgement.

We will try to explain in this contribution how the override came into the Directives, what meaning can be attributed to it, how some Member States have implemented the concept and what significance it has, particularly in the context of international harmonization.

 0963–8180

ORIGIN OF THE TRUE AND FAIR VIEW CONCEPT IN THE DIRECTIVES

In the original proposal for a Fourth Directive, it was stated that the annual accounts should 'conform to the principles of regular and proper accounting' (draft Article 2,(2)) and that 'the annual accounts should – in the context of the provisions regarding the valuation of assets and liabilities and the lay-out of accounts – reflect as accurately as possible the company's assets, liabilities, financial position and results' (draft Article 2(3)).

In the Explanatory Memorandum to this proposal it was stated that, 'where the rules on valuation and on the structure of the accounts would not be sufficient to ensure that the accounts give a "true picture" of the company, additional information should be given in order to achieve that objective'. This wording was borrowed from the German *Aktiengesetz*. It was clear from the text that no departure from the rules was allowed in order to achieve the stated objective. The provision of additional information should be enough.

Problems arose with this text during the discussions in the Economic and Social Committee and in the European Parliament. While the European Parliament proposed the term 'true and fair view', the Economic and Social Committee suggested the wording 'as true a view as possible'.

The European Commission took up this suggestion in the amended proposal for a Fourth Directive:

> The annual accounts shall give a true and fair view of the company's assets, liabilities, financial position and results.

In the Explanatory Memorandum to this amended proposal it was stated that the principle 'implies that should the specific provisions of the Directive be of themselves insufficient to ensure that this objective is attained, the company will be legally obliged to provide further information'. The reference to the principles of regular and proper accounting was deleted 'since the requirement of a true and fair view necessarily implies that such principles must be observed'. In addition, a sentence was added in Article 2(3) stating that the annual accounts 'shall be drawn up clearly and in conformity with the provisions of the Directive'.

During the negotiations in the Council Working Party in 1974, a number of delegations questioned the usefulness of the true and fair view concept. In their view, a general concept should not prevail over specific rules. Other delegations supported the concept and insisted that there should be a requirement to depart from the provisions of the Directive if necessary in order to satisfy the true and fair view objective.

After the second reading, the idea of a departure was introduced in the text but it was still uncertain whether such a departure should be mandatory or whether it should only happen in exceptional cases. It was only after the third reading that a distinction was made in the text between the provision of additional information and a departure from the rules in exceptional cases.

MEANING OF THE TRUE AND FAIR VIEW OVERRIDE

In its present wording in Article 2 of the Fourth Directive, there can be no doubt that the true and fair view principle is an overriding principle.

In accordance with Article 2(3) of the Fourth Directive, 'the annual accounts shall give a true and fair view of the company's assets, liabilities, financial position and profit or loss'. Where application of a specific provision of the Directive would not be sufficient to give a true and fair view, additional information must be given (Article 2(4)). Where, in exceptional cases, additional information would not be enough in order to give a true and fair view, the specific provision in the Directive must be departed from (Article 2(5)). Under such circumstances, the departure must be disclosed in the notes, together with an explanation of the reasons for it and an assessment of its effect on the company's assets, liabilities, financial position and profit or loss.

A similar provision can be found in the Seventh Directive (Article 16(3)) for the consolidated accounts. However, under the Seventh Directive, the overriding character of the true and fair view requirement only has a limited application as far as the scope of the consolidation is concerned (Van Hulle, 1993: 100). The principle can only be invoked for the exclusion of a subsidiary with dissimilar activities (Article 14(1) of the Seventh Directive) and for the exclusion of subsidiaries which are immaterial (Article 13(1) of the Seventh Directive). The true and fair view override cannot be invoked to include in the scope of the consolidation undertakings which should normally not be consolidated on the basis of Article 1 of the Directive. This is the reason why Article 16(5) of the Seventh Directive refers for the override only to Articles 17 to 35 and 39 of the Directive, which deal with the preparation of consolidated accounts and not with the scope of the consolidation.

The true and fair view requirement also applies to banks and other financial institutions (Directive of 1986) and to insurance companies (Directive of 1991).

The Contact Committee on the Accounting Directives, set up by the Fourth Directive (Article 52), which is presided over by the Commission and is composed of representatives from the Member States, has also discussed the meaning of the true and fair view concept. It concluded (Commission of the EC, 1990: 2) that the application of a specific provision of the Directive can be waived only if the additional information is in itself not sufficient to give a true and fair view. It also felt that the principle must be applied in relation to a given company and not in relation to all companies or a category of companies (see also, the Interpretative Communication of 1997).

In order to prevent companies from abusing the true and fair view override as a justification for bad forms of creative accounting (Niessen, 1990: 169), some restrictions were included in the Directive. Derogations can be made only from *specific* provisions and *only in exceptional cases*. Furthermore, disclosure in the notes is required of the derogation, its justification and its effects. In order to strengthen the exceptional nature of the derogation, it was understood that the mere application of the provisions of the Directive would normally bring about a true and fair view. This understanding was incorporated in a declaration made by the Commission and the Council and included in the minutes of the Council meeting during which the Directive was adopted.

A further restriction is included in Article 2(5) of the Directive. In order to further limit the cases in which the true and fair view override can be used, Member States are allowed to define the exceptional cases and to lay down the relevant special rules. This sentence cannot be construed as an invitation to Member States or accounting standard setting bodies to develop rules or standards which depart from the provisions of the Directive by way of general measures applying to all companies (Van Hulle and Van der Tas, 1995: 951). If one goes back to the origins of this sentence, it becomes apparent that it was the Italian delegation which, during the negotiations in the Council of Ministers, wanted to further restrict the possibility for companies to use the override. As a compromise, this sentence was introduced.

Because the last sentence of Article 2(5) of the Fourth Directive is unclear, the Commission has clarified its meaning in an Interpretative Communication (1997) in which it is stated that 'In the interest of harmonisation, Member States may not use the last sentence of Article 2(5) in order to introduce an accounting rule of a general nature which is contrary to provisions of the Directive, nor can they use this sentence to create additional options allowing for accounting treatments which are not in conformity with the Directive'.

It follows from this, for instance, that Member States cannot introduce a rule or standard which would allow or require all companies to mark certain items in the balance sheet. This would indeed be contrary to the historical cost approach upon which the Directive is based. If one were to allow such departure from basic rules in the Directive, by way of an alternative rule of general application, the harmonization objective would be seriously impaired.

Another question is whether Member States can, for a specific category of companies, introduce rules which depart from provisions of the Accounting Directives on the basis of the true and fair view override. This question is more delicate. For instance, because of its general application to all limited liability companies (with the possible exclusion of banks and insurance companies) it is not excluded that certain provisions of the Directive do not sufficiently reflect the particular nature of a certain category of companies. Although the last sentence of Article 2(5) was not intended to cover such cases, its present wording seems to allow such an interpretation.

Questions have been raised concerning the wording of the true and fair view concept and notably the reference to 'financial position'. While the words 'assets and liabilities' seem to refer to the balance sheet and 'profit and loss' to the profit and loss account, the meaning of the words 'financial position' is less evident. It is understood that the reference does not introduce a further requirement in addition to those which are contained in the Directive. It cannot be implied from these words that companies would also be obliged to prepare a cash flow statement. It would appear that the words 'financial position' which are used in a number of other provisions in the Directive, refer more specifically to the solvency and liquidity of the company.

Another question which is often raised in this context is, from whose perspective should the true and fair view principle be satisfied. As the Fourth Directive introduces financial reporting requirements for a broad category of users, it follows that the needs of these users will have to be satisfied by providing financial information which is true and fair from their perspective.

The Fourth Directive contains a large number of options, which are considered equivalent, and the true and fair view is not affected by the use of these options. It could not therefore be argued that accounts which are influenced by tax rules cannot show a true and fair view, as long as the appropriate disclosures have been made in the notes on the accounts in accordance with the requirements of the Directive.

The Fourth Directive does not define the meaning of true and fair. The origin of the concept goes back to the 1948 Companies Act in the UK, a country with a common law tradition. This creates some discomfort in those Member States which have a civil law tradition and find it difficult to reconcile the overriding principle of a true and fair view with a set of specific rules, detailed layouts and a uniform chart of accounts. On the other hand, civil law countries have always invoked general concepts in their law, such as the concepts of good faith or the good housefather (*bonus pater familias*). These general concepts also require a person to depart from a strict interpretation of the law in order to achieve the higher objective.

Without the override, one could argue that the true and fair view concept is really superfluous (Zeff, 1993: 404). To the extent that the application of rules and standards is presumed to lead to accounts showing a true and fair view, the introduction of a requirement for companies to ensure that their accounts show a true and fair view does not add anything. I must therefore disagree with those who argue that the meaning of the true and fair view concept in the Directives can be reduced to a requirement for a functional (teleological) rather than a literal interpretation of the provisions in the Directives (Ordelheide, 1993: 87). It is true that a functional interpretation must be applied to European law and that a literal interpretation of the provisions in the Directives would be inappropriate but the true and fair view concept has a broader meaning as indicated before.

Although the concept of a true and fair view may have been borrowed from the UK, it has now acquired another status because of its inclusion in a Directive of the European Union. As a concept of European law, its final interpretation remains with the European Court of Justice (Ordelheide, 1993: 82; Van Hulle, 1993: 99).

The European Court of Justice has not yet had the opportunity to rule on the meaning of true and fair. However, in a surprising judgement of the Court (Case C-234/94 Waltraud Tomberger v. Gebrüder von der Wettern GmbH) of 27 June 1996 the Court ruled that a national court could rightfully decide that a parent company could include in its accounts the profits made by its subsidiary over the same financial year when the national court satisfied itself 'that the subsidiary's annual accounts for the financial year in question give a true and fair view of its assets and liabilities, financial position and profit or loss'. It is unclear how a national court would go about such an exercise. Presumably, the Court wanted to say that when the company concerned correctly applied the national accounting rules, there was no reason for criticism.

IMPLEMENTATION BY MEMBER STATES

There is no doubt that the true and fair view concept is new for most Member States. Some Member States (Germany, Austria, Finland and Sweden) were so unhappy about it that they refused to fully implement it. Where the principle has been implemented, most Member States have used the exact wording of the Directive. Some authors have tried to find differences in approach on the basis of differences in the language versions. Those who are familiar with negotiations in the European Union know that the negotiations are always conducted on the basis of one or two working languages. For the Fourth Directive, the main working language was French. While the concept of true and fair was translated from English into French using only one word (*fidèle*) instead of two words, all but one Community language uses one word in order to translate the concept of true and fair (Van Hulle, 1993: 100).

I believe that it is impossible to translate the words true and fair literally into any other Community language in a meaningful way. This cannot come as a surprise because history appears to indicate (Flint, 1982: 6) that the exact combination of the two qualifications may well be more accidental than intended.

In its analysis of the accounts published on the basis of the Fourth Directive by some 400 companies from fifteen European countries over the financial year 1989, FEE (Survey 1992: 54) discovered that only in ten cases did companies depart from national law in order to give a true and fair view. These cases related to six of the nine countries which had already implemented the Fourth Directive. Of the ten cases, five concerned listed companies (two in Denmark and one each in France, Ireland and Luxembourg) and five unlisted companies (one each in Belgium, Denmark, France, Luxembourg and the UK). Only seven companies provided a reason for the departure. Most of the cases would, in my view, not even qualify as a true and fair view override, because the practice is explicitly allowed under the law or the Directives.

The results of the FEE survey are surprising. First of all, the survey shows that the concept is now being applied in Member States other than the UK. Secondly, only one case occurred in the UK and none in the Netherlands, the countries which are usually qualified as the most ardent defenders of the true and fair view override. And, last but not least, there were only ten cases. We should therefore not overemphasize the importance of the concept. It is not *the* striking difference between financial reporting practices in Member States.

The results of the FEE survey also underline the need for proper disclosure. There can be no doubt that the Directives require the disclosure of any departure from the rules together with an explanation of the reasons for it and a statement of its effect on the assets, liabilities, financial position and profit or loss. This disclosure requirement is the necessary counterpart to the override. Where disclosure is lacking readers of the accounts may be misled because they will presume that the accounts have been prepared in accordance with the law and the applicable standards. Of course, the auditors will also have to object where a company has been applying the override without proper disclosures. The results of the FEE survey show that such is not always the case.

In continental Europe, there may be a tendency to follow the law more closely and to apply the accounting law without worrying too much about a true and fair view override. The linkage between accounting and taxation will often make it difficult for a company to apply the true and fair view override, at least in the individual accounts. It is therefore unlikely that in most continental European countries, the true and fair override will be applied in many cases, at least for the moment. On the other hand, in those Member States where the attitude towards accounting is more liberal (for instance, the Netherlands and the UK), fear of professional liability may well prevent companies and their auditors from making too much use of the override.

In a famous case, concerning the company 'Ciments Français', the Paris Court of Appeals (6 April 1994) ruled that – although the law did not specifically require the disclosure in the notes of commitments to buy shares – it followed from the general requirement that the financial statements should show a true and fair view (and of the requirement to provide additional information in the notes) that these commitments were shown in the notes to the accounts. The sanctions of the *Commission des Opérations de Bourse* against the managing director of the company were therefore upheld by the Court. Although there was no application of the override in this case, the Court attached particular importance to one of the characteristics of the true and fair view concept, i.e. additional disclosure where the application of the rules does not lead to the accounts showing a true and fair view.

INTERNATIONAL HARMONIZATION

The issue of the true and fair view concept and particularly of its overriding character came up recently during discussions concerning the adoption of an International Accounting Standard (IAS) on Presentation of Financial Statements (IAS 1). In the Exposure Draft (par. 15) it was stated:

> Financial statements should present fairly the financial position, performance and cash flows of an enterprise. In respect of transactions and events that are dealt with in International Accounting Standards, the appropriate application of International Accounting Standards, with additional disclosure when necessary, results in financial statements that present fairly such information. Additional disclosures, beyond those required by International Accounting Standards, should be made when this is necessary to achieve a fair presentation.

The lack of recognition in the Exposure Draft of the overriding character of the true and fair view concept gave rise to a heated debate.

Australia, Canada and the United States came out strongly against the override. Australia argued that bad experience with abuses of the override had led the legislator to abolish the override. Canada and the United States were not in favour of the override because they feared abuses and the maximum they were prepared to accept was to ask the International Federation of Accountants to include some kind of override test in the International Standards on Auditing. The representative of the SEC argued that – although there is an override test in the auditing standards in the US – no registrant with the SEC had ever applied the override in its financial statements.

In its comment letter to the IASC, the European Commission made strong representations in favour of the override. The lack of recognition of the override in IAS 1 would create a conflict with the Accounting Directives which would be difficult to overcome. In fact, rather than a conflict of texts, it would be a conflict between different approaches towards financial reporting. The Commission argued:

> If an override does not exist, this means that the possibility of judgement is severely restricted by the obligation of applying the codified rules. This seems to be in contradiction with the nature itself of judgement. Why is judgement necessary if in the end its result (although more correct) would not be applicable because it is not in accordance with the rules codified by the Standard?

After a heated debate at the Board meeting in Beijing, July 1997, IAS 1 was adopted with the override. The agreement was made possible by distinguishing clearly between a full application of IAS and the application of the override, by narrowing the cases in which one could invoke the override and by the inclusion of appropriate disclosures. The solution which was finally retained is very much in line with the concept of true and fair view included in the Fourth Directive.

In paragraph 10 it is stated that 'the appropriate application of IAS, with additional disclosure when necessary, results, in virtually all circumstances, in financial statements that achieve a fair presentation'. This wording is almost identical to the Council Declaration mentioned above which Member States wanted to make in order to reassure themselves as well as preparers of accounts that the application of the rules will normally lead to accounts showing a true and fair view.

In paragraph 13 the override is included with the following wording:

> In the extremely rare circumstances when management concludes that compliance with a requirement in a Standard would be misleading, and therefore that departure from a requirement is necessary to achieve a fair presentation, an enterprise should disclose:
>
> (a) that management has concluded that the financial statements fairly present the enterprise's financial position, financial performance and cash flows:
>
> (b) that it has complied in all material respects with applicable IAS except that it has departed from a Standard in order to achieve a fair presentation;
>
> (c) the Standard from which the enterprise has departed, the nature of the departure, including the treatment that the Standard would require, the reason why that treatment would be misleading in the circumstances and the treatment adopted; and
>
> (d) the financial impact of the departure on the enterprise's net profit or loss, assets, liabilities, equity and cash flows for each period presented.

The formulation of the override and the disclosures following from it are again very much in line with Article 2 of the Fourth Directive.

CONCLUDING REMARKS

The discussions within IASC have shown again that there is much confusion about the true and fair view concept. In a world of litigation it is difficult for the profession to apply professional judgement. There is a tendency to stick to the rules, whether the application of these rules in a particular case makes sense or not. Regulators are equally unhappy about overrides because they believe that the rules which they have designed are by definition perfect. This is even more so for regulators who swear by a conceptual framework which tends to be regarded as the magic formula stronger than a mathematical paradigm.

In fact, the introduction of a true and fair view override in regulation means an admission of modesty on behalf of the regulator. No regulator is perfect and the accounting rules and standards which have been designed for the majority of cases can never take account of all cases which may arise in practice.

Opponents of the true and fair view override always refer to the risk of abuse. It is clear that abuses cannot be ruled out. However, the application of the override must follow the rules which have been provided, i.e. disclosure, justification and indication of the effects. The respect of these rules must be controlled by the auditors.

I can only agree with Zeff (1993: 405) who states:

> One would hope that a conceptual framework could point towards fundamental reforms of financial reporting that might not be capable of implementation for years or decades. If financial statements would need to be prepared in conformity with Statements of Accounting Concepts, what role could such statements possibly play in promoting longer-term accounting improvement?

REFERENCES

Commission of the European Communities (1990) *The Accounting Harmonisation in the E.C.: Problems of Applying the 4th Directive on the Annual Accounts of Limited Companies*, Luxembourg: Office for Official Publications of the E.C.

Fédération des Experts-comptables de la CEE (1992) *Analysis of European Accounting and Disclosure Practices*. London: Routledge.

Flint, D. (1982) *A True and Fair View in Company Accounts*. London: Gee/Institute of Chartered Accountants of Scotland.

Niessen, H. (1990) 'Image fidèle: Réflexions sur une notion de droit communautaire en matière comptable', in Trésarrieu, J. Ph. (ed.) *Réflections sur la comptabilité: Hommage à Bertrand d'Illiers*. Paris: Economica.

Ordelheide, D. (1993) 'True and fair view: a European and a German perspective', *The European Accounting Review*, 2: 81–90.

Van Hulle, K. (1993) 'Truth and untruth about true and fair', *The European Accounting Review*, 2: 99–104.

Van Hulle, K. and Van der Tas, L. (1995) 'European Union: individual accounts', in Ordelheide, D. and KPMG (eds) *Transnational Accounting*. London: Macmillan.

Zeff, S. (1993) 'International accounting principles and auditing standards', *The European Accounting Review*, 2: 403–10.

[16]

The European Accounting Review 1999, **8:3**, 523–548

'True and fair' in the Netherlands: *inzicht* or *getrouw beeld*?

Stephen A. Zeff
Rice University, Houston

Willem Buijink
Universiteit Maastricht

Kees Camfferman
Vrije Universiteit, Amsterdam

ABSTRACT

In the Netherlands, the standard form of the opinion paragraph of the auditor's report refers to the financial statements giving a *getrouw beeld*, a phrase which in its literal meaning and material content closely resembles the British 'true and fair view'. However, in Dutch reporting law, the central overriding criterion is worded differently. According to the law, the financial statements are to give an 'insight' into financial position and results. The co-existence of these two phrases, which pre-dates the Fourth Directive, is an interesting departure from practice in other European countries. In this paper, we present an historical analysis of this phenomenon. We argue that it is related to a number of central concerns of the Dutch audit profession, in particular its desire to stay abreast of international developments and its attempts to define a proper balance between auditor responsibility and legal requirements.

'When I use a word,' Humpty Dumpty said, in a rather scornful tone, 'it means just what I choose it to mean – neither more nor less.'

Lewis Carroll, *Through the Looking-Glass*

1. INTRODUCTION

In the European Economic Community's Fourth Directive, which was approved in 1978, the overriding attribute of financial statements is, in English, that they give a 'true and fair view'. For many member states, the notion of a true and fair view, including its function as an 'override', was new, and 'serious attempts were made to translate this difficult combination

Address for correspondence
Kees Camfferman, Vrije Universiteit, Faculty of Economic Sciences and Econometrics, De Boelelaan 1105, 1081 HV Amsterdam, Netherlands. E-mail: ccamfferman@econ.vu.nl

 0963–8180

of words into the other Community languages' (Van Hulle, 1993: 100). In the Netherlands, however, there existed prior to the Fourth Directive not just one, but two concepts broadly equivalent to the British true and fair view.

First, since 1970, Dutch company law contained an overriding requirement that financial statements provide 'an insight such that a well-founded opinion can be formed concerning the financial position and income' of the company. As far as we know, this requirement in which *inzicht* (insight) is the key word, has no clear counterpart in the company legislation of any other country.

Second, the recommended standard form of the Dutch auditor's report has, since 1972, referred to *(een) getrouw beeld*. This phrase, which literally means '[a] faithful image', more closely resembles true and fair view and is ordinarily so translated into English. *Inzicht* is not mentioned in the standard form of the Dutch auditor's report.

We consider the fact that the standard form of the auditor's report does not refer to the primary attribute specified in the law as an interesting departure from practice in other countries. This difference is sometimes obscured in English translations of the Dutch law and Dutch audit reports, which may use 'true and fair view' to translate both concepts.[1] Within the Netherlands, although there is no suggestion that any difference between the two concepts has immediate significance for reporting or auditing practice, there does not appear to be a generally accepted understanding of how this dual wording has come about, or why it is necessary to retain two concepts. Therefore, this paper aims to contribute to our understanding of this issue by means of an historical analysis of the development of the central qualitative reporting attributes in the Netherlands. We argue that the phenomenon of a double criterion is the result of a quite complex historical development, and that it is related to a number of central concerns of the Dutch audit profession that predate the Fourth Directive. These concerns include in particular the desire of the Dutch audit profession to align its practices with the English-speaking world, and its attempts to maintain a balance between the professional and the legal responsibility of the auditor.

Although the focus of the paper is primarily historical, we find that the conditions that gave rise to the simultaneous use of two attributes in the Netherlands at present no longer apply; hence, a logical consequence is that one be dropped to achieve a uniform terminology. We end the paper with the observation that, while we would prefer to retain *inzicht*, we acknowledge that the retention of *getrouw beeld* would secure a greater degree of support.

Apart from its contribution to our understanding of the Dutch situation, the paper can be linked to the European accounting literature in the following ways.

First, it is generally recognized that the Netherlands is a country outside the British sphere of influence where the true and fair view concept found acceptance prior to the Fourth Directive (see, for instance, Parker and Nobes, 1994: 68–9; Walton, 1997; and Van Hulle, 1997). However, the historical background of this phenomenon is not well documented and our paper can be seen as an addition to the literature on the pre-Directive history of the true and fair concept.

Second, the paper can be related to earlier work on the question of whether a national or a 'European' conception of true and fair view prevails in the implementation of the concept in the various member states (Alexander, 1993, 1996; Ordelheide, 1993, 1996; Took, 1997; Van Hulle, 1993). Although this question is not the central focus of this paper, it does raise a new issue by drawing attention to the auditor's report as a separate context in which the meaning of true and fair is discussed. To our knowledge, the relationship between the true and fair concept in the Fourth Directive and the wording of the auditor's report has received little attention in the international literature.[2]

The paper is divided into four sections. In the first section, we review the historical evolution of the terms *getrouw*[3] and *inzicht* in the Dutch literature, in auditors' reports and in the law. This section ends with the Act on Annual Accounts of Enterprises of 1970, which was the first modern Dutch law on financial reporting and which gave the *inzicht* attribute its legal standing.

The second section discusses the factors attending the decision of the management board of the *Nederlands Instituut van Registeraccountants* (NIvRA, Dutch Institute of Registered Auditors) in 1972 to recommend a standard form for the auditor's report, which was the first time that a Dutch association of auditors had spoken on the subject. The 1972 recommendation, which was universally followed by Dutch auditors, remained unchanged until the early 1990s, and, despite several recent changes, still underpins the use of *getrouw beeld* in the opinion paragraph.

In the third and fourth sections, we describe how the situation created in the early 1970s, with the two criteria existing side by side, has continued to evolve up to the present. Two important developments discussed in these sections are the adaptation of Dutch law to the Fourth Directive (with its true and fair override) and the modifications made to the recommended auditor's report in the 1990s.

In the final section, we summarize the factors that have given rise to the two attributes and to their somewhat strained co-existence, and we present our conclusions.

2. REVIEW OF *GETROUW BEELD* AND *INZICHT* UNTIL 1972

Getrouw beeld to 1955

The first appearance of *getrouw beeld* in the auditor's report of a Dutch company was in the Unilever annual report for 1932, where it was used as the

Dutch equivalent of 'true and correct view', the wording required by the British Companies Act then in force (Zeff *et al.*, 1992: 99). *Getrouw beeld* continued to appear in the report given by the joint auditors on the Unilever financial statements even though, in 1948, the required wording according to British law became 'true and fair view'. From 1934 to the early 1970s, moreover, *getrouw en juist beeld* (faithful and correct image) appeared in the auditor's report given on the financial statements of the shipping and transport firm Wm H. Müller & Co.

These early instances of *getrouw* in auditors' reports were isolated examples, not supported by the literature. It is true that, as early as 1903, Limperg translated the attribute of true and correct view required by the British Companies Act of 1900 as *juist en getrouw beeld* (Limperg, 1903: 75), but this was not related to domestic thought on the subject. In fact, one of the essential features of the history of the auditor's report in the Netherlands is that, for a long time, many auditors preferred a report with no wording at all. In 1904, Limperg wrote that no auditor's report could be more 'eloquent' than a simple signature beneath the words, 'the Auditor' (Limperg, 1904). Subsequently, Limperg showed how this position could be derived from his theory of auditing which has exerted a great influence on the Dutch audit profession (see Camfferman and Zeff, 1994). In brief, Limperg rejected extensive auditors' reports because they suggested that the auditor could meaningfully communicate to non-auditors the variations in the scope and limitations of audits. To Limperg, this assumption was not compatible with the status of the auditor as a specialist professional.

Many auditors followed Limperg's dictum, even though they added a short caption above their signature, such as *accoord bevonden*, *juist bevonden* or *in orde bevonden* (found to be correct, in order). As will be discussed below, it was not until 1972 that the NIvRA recommended the first standard form of the auditor's report in the Netherlands.

This de-emphasis on the wording of the auditor's report ensured that there was quite a variety of wording in use when the significance of the auditor's report was discussed in the literature. During the first half of the twentieth century, one finds such discussions in terms of *waarheid* (truth) and *duidelijkheid* (clarity) (Knol, 1936; van Slooten, 1900), *juist* (correct) and *duidelijk* (clear) (Koster, 1931), and *balanswaarheid* (balance-sheet truth) (Nijst, 1928).

The most widespread wording, at least in the literature, was probably in terms of *juist* (correct), *juistheid* (correctness), or *een juist beeld* (a correct image). In its 1909 Rules of Professional Conduct, the *Nederlandsche Accountantsvereeniging* (Dutch Auditors Society) mentioned *juist beeld* in its Article 8 on auditors' reports. This wording was adopted by the *Nederlandsch Instituut van Accountants* (NIvA, Dutch Institute of Auditors, predecessor of the NIvRA) in Article 17 of its 1919 Rules of Professional Conduct, where it remained until 1946. In keeping with Limperg's views, neither organization suggested that this wording should actually appear in the auditor's report itself.

In 1946, in its Rules of Professional Conduct, the NIvA discarded *juist beeld* in favour of *goed koopmansgebruik* (sound business practice), a term that was associated with the Income Tax Law. Notwithstanding some attempts to give meaning to the latter phrase, it did not develop into a viable general qualitative criterion (see Camfferman, 1994). From the late 1940s to the 1960s, *juist* and its derivatives continued to be the coinage most commonly used when discussing the meaning of the auditor's report (Burgert, 1952; Hellema, 1960; Kleerekoper, 1967; Treffers, 1959; Vecht, 1962). Even the notion of *goed koopmansgebruik* came to be explained in terms of *juistheid* (Notes to Article 13 RBR, reproduced in NIvRA, 1975: 95).

As in the literature, there was no support during the first half of the century for the use of *getrouw*, or indeed any other wording, in guidance statements issued by any entities in the private sector or by government. The Commercial Code, whose skeletal financial reporting provisions dated from 1928/29, did not refer to any explicit qualitative criterion that the financial statements had to meet. Nor was there any legislation (until 1962) to regulate the audit profession which might have provided the basis for a particular wording. The 1928/29 financial reporting provisions in the Commercial Code did not even make mention of the 'auditor': it referred only to an unspecified 'expert' to oversee the company's accounting process and, unless the company's articles of association or the shareholders were to decide otherwise, report his findings to the supervisory board.

The earliest official support for any wording of the auditor's report was probably a 1950 decree, which required that an auditor charged with the audit of the accounts of insurance companies should report on whether the balance sheet and profit and loss account gave a *juist beeld* of the financial position and income.[4]

In 1954, though, *getrouw* gained a significant foothold in the vocabulary of Dutch auditors when it was used in the auditor's report of Klynveld, Kraayenhof & Co. that was given on the financial statements in the 1953 annual report of Royal Dutch Petroleum. It was then that the Royal Dutch/Shell Group (in which Royal Dutch Petroleum held a 60% ownership interest) was preparing to become listed on the New York Stock Exchange, and it was believed to be important that the auditor's report use language that was familiar to the US audience. Since the remaining 40% of the ownership of the Royal Dutch/Shell Group was held in Great Britain, the terminology, it was thought, should also be understandable there. *Getrouw beeld* was chosen by the audit firm as the Dutch equivalent both of the American fair presentation and the British true and fair view.[5] The Klynveld firm was the largest in the Netherlands and was the auditor of AKU (later to become part of Akzo Nobel) and Philips, which also entered the New York capital market in 1953–54. *Getrouw beeld* began to appear in the Klynveld report on the two companies' financial statements in 1954 and 1955, respectively (Zeff *et al.*, 1992: 100–1).

These instances of the use of *getrouw beeld* were connected through the Klynveld firm, and in particular its senior partner J. Kraayenhof. He was the foremost auditor in the country during the 1950s and 1960s, and played a central role in the development of financial reporting during that period. Kraayenhof was involved when, in 1955, the four employers' associations published *Het Jaarverslag* (*The Annual Report*),[6] an eighteen-page report that contained the first authoritative set of recommendations on company financial reporting. A progressive report, it was given extensive coverage in the press and was widely discussed in the professional literature. Probably owing to Kraayenhof's membership on the drafting committee, the report referred prominently to getrouw beeld as the standard of sound financial reporting (Zeff *et al.*, 1992: 94–111). The appearance of *getrouw beeld* in the committee's report as well as its use in the auditors' reports in the annual reports of several Dutch multinational enterprises did much to draw it to the attention of auditors.

Inzicht to 1955

The word *inzicht* was used occasionally in the literature before the Second World War in connection with financial statements, as in Knol (1936), where it was used to explain *duidelijk*, or in Koster (1931), where it was used to explain *juist*. However, such incidental usages did not constitute any sort of standard practice, such as clearly had become the case with *juist (-beeld)*.

After the war, *inzicht* began to figure more prominently. This occurred primarily in the context of increasing criticism of financial reporting in the financial press. Before the war, it was widely accepted that published financial statements had the limited purpose of assuring creditors of a minimum amount of capital, and of informing shareholders of the profits available for distribution, and little more. Following the war, increased demands for a greater accountability of enterprise management led to a consequent demand for more expansive financial reporting. Such demands were increasingly couched in terms of providing *inzicht*. An example was J. E. Spinosa Cattela's advocacy of financial reporting as it was then practised in the United States, which, in his view, 'gives significantly better insight for the outsider who is not an expert' than in the Netherlands (Spinosa Cattela, 1948: 17).

Inzicht received its first authoritative backing in 1954, in the address of the president of Philips, P. F. S. Otten, to the annual general meeting of shareholders. In his address, Otten declared his views on the role of enterprise leadership in providing information to shareholders. The previous year, Philips' shares had begun to be traded on the New York over-the-counter market, and the company's financial reporting had to be tailored to the requirements of the US Securities and Exchange Commission (SEC) and the demands of US investors. In his speech, which was distributed in booklet form and was extensively commented upon by the press, Otten enumerated four 'demands' that had to be satisfied if the financial statements were to give an *aanvaardbaar beeld* (acceptable image), of which two cited *inzicht* as the criterion of quality:

> 1. An explanation must be given of the overall income so that one may acquire an insight into the enterprise's activities and the way in which the income was obtained.
>
> 2. A specification must be given of the liabilities and capital and the asset components so that an insight may be acquired into solvency and liquidity.
>
> (Otten, 1954: 6)

That a company with a reputation for progressive financial reporting would adopt *inzicht* as the touchstone of its financial reporting could hardly have gone unnoticed. Otten's speech was almost certainly written by A. Goudeket, the chief internal auditor of Philips, who was the company's unquestioned authority on accounting and auditing, as well as a widely published author in the professional literature. Goudeket had, of course, played a pivotal role in Philips' entry into the New York capital market and was well informed about the norms of US financial reporting.[7] Like Kraayenhof, Goudeket was appointed to the joint committee of the employers' associations that produced the set of financial reporting recommendations *Het Jaarverslag* (*The Annual Report*) in 1955.

Like Kraayenhof, Goudeket was a strong personality, and he also succeeded in making his mark on the committee's report by inserting four 'general demands' that were closely patterned on those in the Otten address. The result was that the report stated that giving a *getrouw beeld* was the primary aim of financial statements, which was operationalized by the set of 'general demands' formulated in terms of *inzicht*.

Thanks to Kraayenhof and Goudeket, the only two auditors on a committee composed mostly of company executives, *getrouw beeld* and *inzicht* were given vital institutional backing in the report of the employers' associations. Such support was believed to carry much more weight in a report sponsored by the employers' associations than if the sponsor had been a professional accountancy body such as the NIvA. It is important to recognize that, in the 1950s, the audit profession was still unregulated by law and there was as yet no legal requirement that companies have external audits (although, by then, most listed companies had elected to have external audits).

Inzicht and *getrouw beeld* from 1955 to 1970

In the 1955 employers' report, *inzicht* was arguably subordinated to *getrouw beeld* in the sense that the former was presented as a means to achieve the latter. However, as will be seen in this section, over the next fifteen years *inzicht* became more prominent. An important reason is probably that *getrouw beeld* would appeal mainly to auditors, who could appreciate its reference to the English-language audit report. However, as seen above, the organized audit profession at the time was not prepared to give any wording of the auditor's report its official support. On the other hand, the idea that financial statements ought to give *inzicht* could easily be understood by non-auditors.

Inzicht received a boost in 1956, when a booklet containing the norms for the Sijthoff Prize for the Best Annual Report was published. Taking a cue from the Otten address of 1954 and the report of the employers' associations of 1955, the eleven-page booklet cited *inzicht* seventeen times in announcing the Sijthoff norms for praiseworthy financial reporting (Zeff *et al.*, 1992: 112–14). It did not use the word *getrouw*.

If *inzicht* did appeal to non-auditors, this became a factor of importance when, by the end of the 1950s, the improvement of company financial reporting had become part of the national political debate over the democratization of enterprise, including employee access to financial information in order to facilitate co-determination of enterprise policies. It was believed that companies should become more accountable not only to employees but also to their shareholders and the public. In the course of this lengthy and impassioned debate, there was little specific criticism of company financial reporting although there was a persistent belief that not enough information was being given.

In 1959, the 'think tank' of the Labour Party published a 175-page report entitled 'The Reform of Enterprise'.[8] The report devoted 10% of its space to an argument that financial reporting should be regulated by a Companies Commission, an SEC-like government agency. In the report, *inzicht* was given pride of place as the criterion of sound financial reporting. In 1960, the government acceded to the mounting political pressures and appointed a State Commission, known as the Verdam Commission after its chairman, to propose articles of amendment to company law. Everyone was therefore on notice that legislative reform was imminent, and reports followed in short order from the Liberal Party's 'think tank' and the employers' associations.

Both reports appeared in 1962: the Liberal Party's lengthy report[9] rejected the Labour Party's proposal for a Companies Commission and instead concentrated on the kinds of financial information that companies should report. It repeated the four 'general demands' from the 1955 report of the joint committee of the employers' associations. While *inzicht* was carried forward, *getrouw beeld* was absent. In the report produced by the council of the employers' associations,[10] in the drafting of which Goudeket and Kraayenhof again played a role, *aanvaardbaar beeld* (acceptable image), which had been favoured in Otten's 1954 address, eclipsed *getrouw beeld* in importance. *Inzicht* was invoked in connection with the committee's advocacy of replacement value accounting, which almost certainly was the handiwork of Goudeket.[11]

For its part, the Verdam Commission, acting unanimously on the report of its financial reporting subcommittee (of which Kraayenhof was a consulting member), proposed, among other things, a new law on company financial reporting. Its Articles 2 and 3, setting forth the standards of quality expected of companies' annual accounts, were included in the Act on Annual Accounts of Enterprises, passed in 1970, as follows (Article 1, containing definitions, has no bearing on the topic of this paper):

> 2. The annual accounts shall give an insight [*inzicht*] such that a well-founded opinion can be formed concerning the liabilities and capital and results of the enterprise, as well as, so far as the nature of the accounts allows, concerning the solvency and liquidity.
>
> 3. (1) The balance sheet, with the notes, shall present faithfully [*getrouw*] and consistently the amount and composition of the liabilities and capital of the enterprise at the end of the financial year.
> (2) The profit and loss account, with the notes, shall present faithfully [*getrouw*] and consistently the amount and composition of the results of the enterprise during the financial year.

In the text of the law, the order of *inzicht* and *getrouw* observed in the 1955 report of the employers' associations was reversed. When interpreting this phenomenon, one should not overemphasize the extent to which contemporaries differentiated between Articles 2 and 3. As intended by the Commission responsible for preparing the first draft, Articles 2 and 3 were frequently jointly referred to as the core of the law,[12] and the main interest of commentators was to discuss the 'override' relationship between Articles 2 and 3 on the one hand and the other more detailed requirements of the law on the other. One can therefore find instances in which the two articles together are summarized by knowledgeable authors as either 'the *inzicht* requirement' or 'the requirement to give a *getrouw beeld*' (both in IJsselmuiden, 1972: 113, 167).

Nevertheless, there were indications in the legal literature surrounding the new law that the two articles were not to be seen as interchangeable, and that the order of the two articles did imply a primary emphasis on *inzicht*. The government's explanatory memorandum to the draft law described Article 2 as stating the 'objective' or 'purpose' of financial statements and Article 3 as defining the 'nature' of financial statements which enables them to serve that purpose.[13] There are a number of indications that this definition of the relationship between the two articles did not mean that Article 2 was intended merely to play an ornamental role, or that meeting the requirements of Article 3 implied that the objective stated in Article 2 was automatically met as well.

First, the explanatory memorandum gave an indication of the difference between *inzicht* and *getrouw* by describing the applicability of the former to a wide range of disclosure, valuation and income determination issues, while the discussion of the meaning of *getrouw* was mainly limited to asset valuation and the limitations it imposed on the formation of secret reserves.

Second, the importance attached to Article 2 was underscored by a concern during the drafting stage that the *inzicht* requirement might be interpreted by the courts in terms that went well beyond current reporting practice and could lead to expectations that might be difficult to meet in practice. For that reason the clause 'so far as the nature of the accounts allows' was added during the draft stage.[14] Although some authors argued that this change made Article 3 (or 2) superfluous, the government's main advisory council argued against this and indicated that both articles might provide separate grounds for judicial proceedings.[15]

As a result, commentaries on the new Act, although they frequently referred to Articles 2 and 3 together, did make it clear that in the final analysis it was Article 2 rather than 3 which contained the more fundamental requirement (e.g. Huizenga, 1969; Sanders *et al.*, 1975) or which served as the substantial equivalent to the British true and fair view (IJsselmuiden, 1972: 36).

3. THE NIvRA RECOMMENDS A STANDARD FORM OF THE AUDITOR'S REPORT

In 1972, the NIvRA management board published a recommended standard form for the unqualified auditor's report. The recommendation included as the key phrase:

> We are of the opinion that these financial statements give a faithful image [*getrouw beeld*] of the amount and composition of the liabilities and capital of the company . . . and of the results. . . .[16]

By international standards, it is curious that the first such recommendation to emanate from an association of auditors in the Netherlands occurred only as recently as 1972. However, as seen above, the absence of such a recommendation had reflected widely held beliefs about the function of the auditor. The NIvRA's decision to make a recommendation was therefore not prompted by legal changes, such as the passage of the Act regulating the audit profession in 1962 or the Act on Annual Accounts of 1970. Apparently, the question became acute because the 'single signature' had lost its appeal. Kleerekoper (1967: 158–60) and Groeneveld (1976: 88–9), both Limperg disciples, explained the disappearance of the lone signature, and hence the need to come up with a more elaborate text, primarily in terms of foreign influence: the increasing need to translate auditors' reports into and from English, and the need to take account of the American practice of placing the auditor's report on a separate page, thus necessitating a free-standing expression of the auditor's opinion. They also pointed to a growing belief among Dutch auditors that a signature alone suggests too absolute a degree of correctness and sufficiency of the financial statements.

Evidently, the abandonment of the lone signature ushered in a period of experimentation with alternative phrasings. Bosman (1984: 9) referred to this period as one of 'proliferation in the wording of auditors' reports'. This apparently prompted the NIvRA to encourage discussion of this issue.

In a study on the auditor's report published by the NIvRA (de Jong, 1970), the author recommended that the auditor affirm that the financial statements 'give a faithful image [*getrouw beeld*] of the financial position and the results', although his reasons were less than compelling. He preferred a formulation that explicitly mentioned the requirements imposed by the new law, but he did not make clear why *inzicht* was not also a candidate for inclusion in the auditor's report.

At the suggestion of the NIvRA's management board, G. L. Groeneveld, the partner of Klynveld, Kraayenhof & Co. in charge of the Philips audit, gave an address at the NIvRA's Fall Conference in December 1970 on the auditor's report in relation to the new Act on Annual Accounts. In his address, Groeneveld stated that the old Limpergian ideal of the lone signature and the terse *accoord bevonden* (found correct) were no longer appropriate, and that it would be useful to develop a meaningful, uniform auditor's report. After considering several alternative formulations, Groeneveld expressed a preference for *getrouw weergeven* (represents faithfully) over *getrouw beeld* (faithful image) because *beeld* was superfluous and would only require further explanation (Groeneveld, 1971: 247, 260).

These proposals were discussed by J. W. Schoonderbeek and A. B. Frielink, two leading auditors. They opposed using the word *getrouw* by pointing out that it was reminiscent of the text of the new Act on Annual Accounts. They argued that the auditor's report should not follow the law too closely, in order to avoid giving the impression that the audit is limited to checking compliance with the law. Like the earlier rejection of lengthy auditors' reports, this argument drew on Limperg's theory on the role of the auditor. Under the influence of Limperg, it had been an article of faith among Dutch auditors at least since the 1930s that an audit ought never to be restricted to compliance with formal requirements (see Camfferman, 1998). It was believed that, by referring or even alluding to the law, the auditor would give precisely this undesirable impression. For this reason, and also for the reason that *getrouw* was not part of ordinary usage and made a distinctly old-fashioned impression, Schoonderbeek suggested a search for alternatives, such as *aanvaardbaar* (acceptable) and *betrouwbaar* (reliable) (Groeneveld, 1971: 253, 259, 261).

Parallel to these public discussions, the NIvRA's Committee on the Application of Professional Regulations[17] added an item to its agenda on the relation between the auditor's report and the Act on Annual Accounts that was then, in early 1969, at an advanced stage of parliamentary consideration.

The committee's initial deliberations were somewhat undirected, but early in 1971, the NIvRA's management board made a formal and rather urgent request of the committee to submit a draft standard auditor's report by 1 May, the effective date of the new law. The committee's initial reply, which was written by Groeneveld, embodied the preferred wording given in his address at the Fall Conference. The balance of the year was consumed by exchanges of views between the board and the committee and the large audit firms, which did not lead to consensus.

In January 1972 the incoming NIvRA president, C. Snoep, characterized the difference of views as a 'knotty problem' in his informal agenda for the year.[18] In 1971, the NIvRA had held a series of study conferences on the new law, and included as one of the topics for discussion the format and phrasing in the auditor's report. Although it appeared that virtually everyone acknowledged the desirability of a standard form for the report, there was no agreement on the actual wording. Among the arguments advanced against a formulation using *getrouw*, based on Article 3, was that the main criterion for a clean opinion (*inzicht*) was in fact located in Article 2.[19]

Finally, almost a year after the committee had submitted its initial response to the board's urgent request for guidance, the board published a three-page discussion paper on the standard form of the auditor's report.[20]

Reflecting differences of opinion within and between the board and its supporting committee, the paper was less a proposed recommendation than an implied request for comments on two unresolved issues.[21] First, whether the auditor's report should use the wording in the law, which might signify mere compliance with the law. And second, whether the auditor's report should use the word *getrouw*. The discussion paper presented *getrouw* as an option that could not be ignored, if only because of a lack of clearly superior alternatives, despite recognized drawbacks such as its infrequent use in the ordinary spoken language and its somewhat unspecified meaning.

Nine written reactions were received and published.[22] While all of the writers agreed that it was desirable to have a standard form of the report, their letters did not suggest even the beginning of a consensus about the standard wording. The reactions ranged from full endorsement to complete rejection of Groeneveld's earlier suggestion.

Of the nine written submissions, the joint comment by F. Graafstal and G. Timmer, both partners in Klynveld, Kraayenhof & Co., and the comment by A. B. Frielink, a partner in a smaller audit firm, are the most interesting. Frielink reacted as an outsider, but Timmer was on the NIvRA's management board in 1971, and in that capacity he had been involved at an early stage. Both reactions stated that it would be odd if the auditor's report were to appear to refer to Article 3 of the Act on Annual Accounts (i.e., with wording based on *getrouw*), rather than to what they perceived as the more general Article 2. However, rather than moving closer to the law, the commentators argued that the auditor's report should follow the law only at a distance (Graafstal and Timmer) or not at all (Frielink).

Frielink preferred the following wording:

> we are of the opinion that the financial statements satisfy the requirements of correctness [*juistheid*] and sufficiency [*toereikendheid*].

Graafstal and Timmer proposed that the standard form should read as follows:

> these financial statements give a *getrouw beeld* of the financial position . . . and of results.

They attached great importance to international aspects, and they favoured an auditor's report that, once translated, would be comfortable to an English-language audience – a view that, to them, was by far the most important consideration.[23] They also sought to adhere as much as possible to current practice in the Netherlands and asserted that:

> For us there can be no doubt that in our country the wording in which the phrase *getrouw beeld* (usually followed by 'of the financial position and the results') is used has found fairly general acceptance [p. 133].

They defended their proposal with the argument that they wanted to adhere as much as possible to 'practice in the Netherlands, in particular with respect to the large and middle-sized enterprises, as it has developed over the last decade' (p. 135).

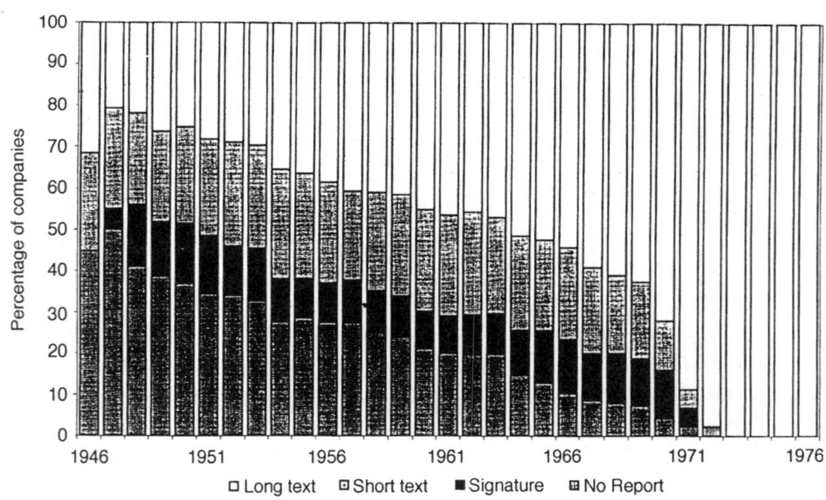

Figure 1 Types of auditor's report: Dutch listed companies, 1946–76
Note: Based on sample of 107 companies. Owing to (de)listing and data availability sample size is not equal across years.

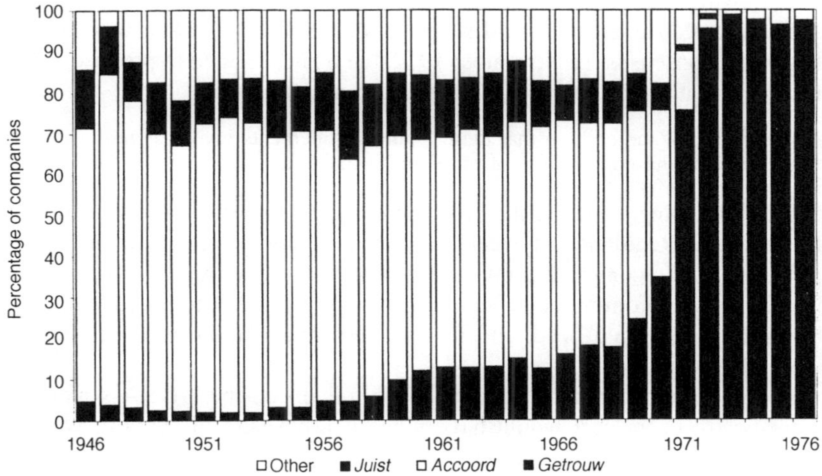

Figure 2 Key wording in auditor's report: Dutch listed companies, 1946–76
Note: Percentage of companies shown as 'short text' or 'long text' in Figure 1.

Graafstal and Timmer's assertion is not, however, borne out by a survey of auditors' reports for the period. We have studied the auditors' reports on the annual accounts of 107 listed companies over the period 1946–76.[24] Figure 1 displays the breakdown of companies according to:

1 Those that did not publish an auditor's report (gradually declining from over 40% in the 1940s to zero in 1972).[25]
2 Those publishing an auditor's report consisting of a signature only (between 10 and 15% each year until reaching 5% in 1971 and zero in 1972).
3 Those publishing an auditor's report with text, either as a caption over the signature ('short text') or as a free-standing expression of opinion ('long text').

With respect to auditors' reports containing text, Figure 2 shows the distribution of wording used in the reports. Of interest is the fact that *getrouw* was used in fewer than 20% of the reports in each year prior to 1969. The remarkable growth in the use of *getrouw* between 1970 and 1972 was associated with the efforts of the NIvRA to introduce a uniform wording, and the use of this preferred wording became virtually universal by 1973. It is difficult, therefore, to argue that *getrouw* had 'found fairly general acceptance' as a matter of free development of practice during the decade prior to 1972. Indeed, even within audit firms, there was a diversity of format and wording as among different client companies.

Following the publication of the comment letters, the NIvRA board seemed to realize that it should act with some authority, rather than attempt to forge a consensus. In November 1972, the board decided to propose a final recommendation to the NIvRA's members, as follows:

> ... we are of the opinion that these financial statements give a *getrouw beeld* of the amount and composition of the liabilities and capital ... and of the results.

Somewhat disingenuously, the board gave the Committee on Application of Professional Regulation a week in which to convey its reaction to the proposed final recommendation. As the board must have known, that was too little time for a committee of ten members to respond. The board wanted to bring the matter to a head, and its final recommendation was published in December 1972.[26]

A parallel development that may have influenced the NIvRA's management board, or at least would have given it a measure of support, was the 1972 revision of the Registered Auditors Act, in which registered auditors alone were authorized to give an opinion on the annual accounts. Their opinion, said the Act, was to be on the *getrouwheid* (fairness) of the annual accounts.

The 1972 recommendation therefore established the preference of the organized audit profession for a report couched in terms of *getrouw beeld*, even though it had not, up to that time, found widespread acceptance in practice and even though the 1970 Act had made *inzicht* at least an equally likely candidate. As if aware of a possible divergence of meaning between the two concepts, the NIvRA formally reconciled the two shortly afterwards in its new 1973 Rules of Conduct and Professional Practice.[27] In the Rules, the function of the auditor was defined as issuing opinions on *getrouwheid*, yet the criterion for issuing a clean opinion by the auditor was that the accounts in question 'give the required insight' (*het vereiste inzicht geeft*). Hence, while the auditor was to draw on the primary criterion invoked in the Act on Annual Accounts (*inzicht*) when determining whether to give a clean opinion, he or she was instructed to cite one of two secondary criteria in the Act (*getrouw*), a quality better understood internationally, in the auditor's report itself.

4. THE DUTCH ADAPTATION OF THE FOURTH DIRECTIVE: RETENTION OF *INZICHT*

When the EEC's Fourth Directive on annual accounts was approved in 1978, its key provisions on the central requirement of financial reporting and its function as an override were based on the British experience with true and fair view. In the official Dutch translation of Article 2, paragraphs 1–5, of the Directive, the central requirement was rendered as *getrouw beeld* (emphasis added in the Dutch text):

1. De jaarrekening bestaat uit de balans, de winst- en verliesrekening en de toelichting. Deze stukken vormen een geheel.	1. The annual accounts shall comprise the balance sheet, the profit and loss account and the notes to the accounts. These documents shall constitute a composite whole.
2. De jaarrekening wordt duidelijk en overeenkomstig de bepalingen van deze richtlijn opgesteld.	2. They shall be drawn up clearly and in accordance with the provisions of this Directive.
3. De jaarrekening moet een *getrouw beeld* geven van het vermogen, de financiële positie en het resultaat van de vennootschap.	3. The annual accounts shall give a true and fair view of the company's assets, liabilities, financial position and profit or loss.
4. Wanneer de toepassing van de bepalingen van deze richtlijn niet voldoende is om het in lid 3 bedoelde *getrouwe beeld* te geven, moeten aanvullende inlichtingen worden verstrekt.	4. Where the application of the provisions of this Directive would not be sufficient to give a true and fair view within the meaning of paragraph 3, additional information must be given.
5. Indien in uitzonderingsgevallen blijkt dat toepassing van een bepaling van deze richtlijn in strijd is met de in lid 3 bedoelde verplichting, dient van deze bepaling te worden afgeweken opdat een *getrouw beeld* in de zin van lid 3 wordt gegeven. Zulk een afwijking moet in de toelichting worden medegedeeld en naar behoren gemotiveerd onder vermelding van de invloed ervan op het vermogen, de financiële positie en het resultaat. De Lid-Staten kunnen de uitzonderingsgevallen nader omschrijven en de daarmee overeenstemmende afwijkende regeling vaststellen.	5. Where in exceptional cases the application of a provision of this Directive is incompatible with the obligation laid down in paragraph 3, that provision must be departed from in order to give a true and fair view within the meaning of paragraph 3. Any such departure must be disclosed in the notes on the accounts together with an explanation of the reasons for it and a statement of its effects on the assets, liabilities, financial position and profit or loss. The Member States may define the exceptional cases in question and lay down the relevant special rules.

Dutch legislation was adapted to the Fourth Directive by a new law to replace the 1970 Act on Annual Accounts of Enterprises. The main clauses of Article 2 of the Directive were incorporated in Article 362, paragraphs 1–4, Book 2, Civil Code, as follows (English translation by the authors, emphasis added to the Dutch text):

1. De jaarrekening geeft volgens normen die in het maatschappelijk verkeer als aanvaardbaar worden beschouwd een zodanig *inzicht* dat een verantwoord oordeel kan worden gevormd omtrent het vermogen en het resultaat, alsmede voorzover de aard van een jaarrekening dat toelaat, omtrent de solvabiliteit en de liquiditeit van de rechtspersoon.	1. The annual accounts shall give, in accordance with norms that are acceptable in the economic and social climate, an insight such that a well-founded opinion can be formed concerning the financial position and income, and, in so far as the nature of financial statements allows, concerning the solvency and the liquidity of the legal entity.

2. De balans met de toelichting geeft *getrouw*, duidelijk en stelselmatig de grootte van het vermogen en zijn samenstelling in actief- en passiefposten op het einde van het boekjaar weer. . . .	2. The balance sheet, together with the notes, shall represent faithfully, clearly and consistently the financial position and its composition of assets and liabilities at the end of the financial year. . . .
3. De winst- en verliesrekening met de toelichting geeft *getrouw*, duidelijk en stelselmatig de grootte van het resultaat van het boekjaar en zijn afleiding uit de posten van baten en lasten weer.	3. The profit and loss account, together with the notes, shall represent faithfully, clearly and consistently the amount of income for the financial year and its derivation from items of revenues and expenses.
4. Indien het verschaffen van het in lid 1 bedoelde *inzicht* dit vereist, verstrekt de rechtspersoon in de jaarrekening gegevens ter aanvulling van hetgeen in de bijzondere voorschriften van en krachtens deze titel wordt verlangd. Indien dit noodzakelijk is voor het verschaffen van dat *inzicht*, wijkt de rechtspersoon van die voorschriften af; de reden van deze afwijking wordt in de toelichting uiteengezet, voor zover nodig onder opgaaf van de invloed ervan op vermogen en resultaat.	4. If required for the provision of the insight referred to in paragraph 1, the legal entity shall provide information in the annual accounts in addition to what is required by the special regulations laid down in or pursuant to this section. If necessary to provide that insight, the legal entity shall deviate from those regulations; the reasons for such a deviation must be stated in the notes, where necessary with an indication of its effect on the financial position and the results.

As can be seen from these texts, the original *inzicht* criterion from the 1970 Act was retained to perform the functions of *getrouw beeld* as used in the Directive.

During the deliberations leading up to the adaptation of the Dutch law to the Fourth Directive, the Justice Ministry asked the NIvRA whether the *inzicht* criterion should be replaced by a wording based on *getrouw beeld*. The NIvRA replied that it had no objection to retaining the traditional wording.[28] Hence, notwithstanding the clear specification of *getrouw beeld* as the override in the official Dutch translation of the Fourth Directive, the Dutch legislation approved in 1983 retained *inzicht* as the primary principle in Article 362, paragraph 1, and also used *inzicht* in its rendering of the explicit override clause in the Directive (Art. 362, para. 4). *Getrouw* continued to be assigned to paragraphs 2 and 3, and so the basic structure of the 1970 Act was maintained.

The wording chosen in the Netherlands can be contrasted with that in Flemish-speaking Belgium. The Flemish version of the law incorporating the Fourth Directive used *getrouw beeld* as suggested by the Dutch version of the Directive (Lefebvre and Flower, 1994: 95). Note that in Italy, as in the Netherlands, the Fourth Directive implementation used different wording than in the Italian translation of the Directive (Took, 1997).

As part of the adaptation law, a provision was inserted (Art. 393) which expressly charged the auditor to investigate 'whether the accounts give the *inzicht* required by Article 362, para. 1'. Two years later, Article 393 was expanded to charge the auditor to 'present the outcome of his investigation in an opinion concerning the fairness [*getrouwheid*] of the annual accounts' some years after a similar provision had been inserted into the Registered Auditors Act. Hence, the auditor was expected to submit a report on 'fairness' after having completed an investigation into whether the annual accounts give an 'insight'. To the government, *inzicht* and *getrouw beeld* were clearly equivalents, as is evident from the fact that the two were used interchangeably in the Justice Ministry's explanatory memorandum attached to the draft adaptation law.[29]

That the *inzicht* requirement did not have a purely ornamental function in the late 1970s and early 1980s is shown by the important role it played in the deliberations of the Enterprise Chamber (the civil law court that considers complaints about company financial reporting). In not a few cases brought against companies that were alleged to have violated the financial reporting provisions of the law, the Chamber took the *inzicht* requirement seriously and invoked it rather more frequently than it did *getrouw weergeven*. It often used *inzicht* as a ground for judging the propriety of companies' measurement and disclosure practices.[30]

5. DEVELOPMENTS SINCE 1983

Following the adaptation of the law to the Fourth Directive, the audit profession again entered into a debate on the aptness of the standard form of the opinion in the auditor's report. While the possibility of an explicit reference to *inzicht* in the auditor's opinion was considered, the general view was that, especially given the wording of the Registered Auditors Act, it was sufficient for the auditor to give an opinion on whether the annual accounts give *een getrouw beeld*. The NIvRA's management board thereupon issued a report treating the implications of the changed financial reporting law for the auditor's report (NIvRA, 1984). The report explicitly addressed the question of whether the new law required the auditor's report to be expressed in terms of *inzicht*. While the board conceded that the law as amended in 1983 made it clear that 'the auditor's report must above all answer the question of whether the annual accounts meet the primary requirement of Article 362, paragraph 1', it nonetheless concluded that

> *inzicht* is something that the user of a set of financial statements must acquire, whereas *getrouwheid* is a demand placed on the preparer of a set of financial statements. It is true, of course, that the auditor must form an opinion on whether the accounts can reasonably be expected to allow the acquisition of insight, but this does not mean that the auditor should presume, by means of the wording of his opinion, to give a judgement that belongs to the user of that opinion.

This argument, that *inzicht*, as opposed to *getrouw beeld*, cannot be assessed completely by the auditor, can still be encountered in the literature (e.g.

Braam and Damen, 1996). However, it sits uneasily with the formal equation of the two in the NIvRA's Rules of Conduct and Professional Practice and the explicit charge to the auditor in the law to investigate whether the financial statements give the required insight (see above). Similarly, while *getrouw beeld* continues to be the attribute cited in the auditor's report, the Guidelines issued by the Council on Annual Reporting (the private-sector standard setter) appeal to *inzicht* in counselling auditors when it might be necessary to invoke the true and fair override: 'The Council considers that there are valid reasons [for departures from the Guidelines] when, with these departures, an improvement upon the insight given in annual accounts is intended and achieved'. Hence, one has the impression that *getrouw beeld* is given only when, in the auditor's opinion, an *inzicht* is conveyed, and that, notwithstanding the view of the NIvRA's management board in 1984 that 'the auditor should [not] presume . . . to give a judgement that belongs to the user', the auditor so presumes.

It is therefore likely that a more significant reason for rejecting the use of *inzicht* in the auditor's report was expressed by the following remark added by the NIvRA board in its 1984 report: 'Internationally, such wording is unusual as well'. One of the two historical reasons for preferring *getrouw* was clearly still relevant.

But the other reason, the wish to prevent a purely legal interpretation of the function of the auditor, was losing its force during the 1980s. In the 1970s, Kraayenhof still fiercely criticized a proposal to include a reference to compliance with the law in the auditor's report, adding that such a suggestion 'would have turned Limperg pale with anger' (Kraayenhof, 1976: 431). Yet, in a series of articles published in *De Accountant*, the NIvRA's journal, in the mid-1980s, proponents of a reference to the law gained the upper hand. Among them was G. G. M. Bak, an auditor and the accounting adviser to the Justice Ministry, who said,

> The audit profession must overcome its timidity and insert a reference [in the auditor's report] to the legal framework in which [the profession] has been operating now for some time. . . . Omitting such a reference can easily give the impression that the audit profession does not quite know what to do with the task [given it by the law] and maintains, from early times, its own particular system of norms, while leaving the 'legal' verification (whatever that may be) to the lawyers.
>
> (Bak, 1984: 6)

In 1991, the NIvRA's management board finally relented and changed the recommended form of the auditor's report to include an explicit reference to compliance with legal requirements. An even further step was taken when, in 1996, the NIvRA adopted a new opinion paragraph of the standard form of the auditor's report based on the format recommended by the International Federation of Accountants (IFAC), which in turn was heavily influenced by the phraseology in the US auditor's report. The new wording, which formally introduced a Dutch-language equivalent of 'generally accepted accounting principles' (*algemeen aanvaarde grondslagen van financiële verslaggeving*) into the official accounting literature, was as follows (in the NIvRA's translation):

> In our opinion, the financial statements give a true and fair view [*getrouw beeld*] of the financial position of the entity as of 31 December 19xx and of the result for the year then ended in accordance with accounting principles generally accepted in the Netherlands and comply with the financial reporting requirements included in Part 9, Book 2, of the Netherlands Civil Code.

In this version of the auditor's report, *getrouw beeld* is qualified by the reference to generally accepted accounting principles. Though the latter concept has, as yet, no well-defined meaning in the Netherlands, the proximity in wording to the auditor's report as used in the US is at least suggestive of a move in the direction of more formal, codified financial reporting rules. In this way, the motive of seeking an internationally current form for the auditor's report, which was at the origin of the introduction of *getrouw beeld* in the Netherlands, now served to overturn the traditional reticence to restrict the function of the auditor by means of formal regulations.

6. CONCLUDING REMARKS

When complex notions like the essential characteristics of financial statements have to be described by a simple phrase like true and fair, *inzicht* or *getrouw*, the dictionary meaning of words is obviously of limited help. Legislators, standard-setters and the audit profession are placed in the position of Humpty Dumpty and have to choose the meaning of words. Unlike Humpty Dumpty, though, they may be interested in genuine communication and therefore their choices can to some extent be the subject of discussion.

In the Dutch situation, while one can accept that there is no obvious basis to decide between *inzicht* and *getrouw beeld* as the overriding criterion, one can question the necessity of the two concepts existing side by side. As our historical survey has shown, the concepts have been closely related, were often used interchangeably and are currently, strictly speaking, formally defined in terms of each other in the Rules of Conduct and Professional Practice of the audit profession.

Since the law calls for *inzicht* as the primary criterion of quality in the annual accounts, with *getrouw* as one of three secondary criteria (the other two being 'clearly' and 'consistently'), it would seem logical for the criterion of quality stated in the law also to appear in the auditor's report. In other countries of the European Union, this appears to be the case (see Buijink *et al.*, 1996). In the UK, where the override originated, true and fair view is cited in the auditor's report because it is the override cited in the law.

Although our paper shows that at least three factors can be cited to explain the emergence of a double criterion, the present situation does not provide compelling arguments for the continued co-existence of the two concepts.

One factor is that the two concepts have not always been viewed as equivalents. During the 1950s and 1960s, *inzicht* connoted to some a higher aspiration for financial reporting than the status quo reflected by the *getrouw beeld* in auditors' reports. For instance, not infrequently, *inzicht* implied the use of replacement value accounting instead of historical cost. Viewed in this light, it is plausible to see the *inzicht* criterion as a kind of legacy by Goudeket, who, through the financial reporting policy of Philips and his membership on two important committees of the employers' associations, gave currency to *inzicht* as the hallmark of sound financial reporting and who also was a staunch advocate of replacement value accounting. Another difference between the two concepts is the lingering perception that *getrouw beeld* is a prerequisite for *inzicht* and that the auditor can assess the former but not the latter.

A second factor has been the long-standing desire on the part of the Dutch audit profession to keep a certain distance from the law in order to avoid giving the impression that the task of the auditor is completely defined by law or regulation. It was therefore convenient for the auditor to refer in his opinion to an attribute of the profession's choice, *getrouw beeld*, rather than to the primary attribute, *inzicht*, specified in the law.

A third – and, we believe, the most important – factor is the desire of the audit profession to be seen as following international practices, especially those in the UK and the US. This factor was responsible for the introduction of *getrouw beeld* in the recommended auditor's report in 1972 even though, until the end of the 1960s, its use was distinctly a minority practice and it was opposed by some leading auditors as archaic-looking and a break from established practice. The importance of adhering to internationally accepted practices has been a recurring argument, both at and below the surface in the Dutch literature on the auditor's report. The pressure to 'go international' continued to be strong in the 1990s, when the NIvRA formally introduced the US wording, 'generally accepted accounting principles', into the Dutch-language accounting literature by inserting it in the auditor's report.

If our analysis is correct, it shows that the Fourth Directive has played only a minor role in determining the function of the Dutch equivalent to the concept of true and fair view. By far the more important influence, both on the law and on the wording of the auditor's report, has been directly exerted by the practice of the Anglo-American audit profession. This raises an important issue related to the question of whether or not there is a 'European' conception of true and fair. The Dutch case shows the importance of the auditor's report as a context in which the meaning of true and fair is determined. As the auditor's report is currently subject to harmonization in a broader international setting than the European Union this may give rise to conflicting claims of competence to interpret the meaning of true and fair.

Leaving the broader implications to return to the Dutch situation, we conclude with the following recommendation. If one accepts that conformity with international practice should be paramount, it would seem that the next logical step would be to bring all Dutch usage in line with international practice and thus remove references altogether to *inzicht*, both in the law and therefore in the Guidelines. Therefore, the NIvRA might wish to reconsider its advice of 1981 to the Justice Ministry and now propose that all references to *inzicht* be removed from the law. As seen above, there are no formal impediments to such a change, and the inhibition against direct references to the law in the auditor's report has been largely overcome (see also Zeff *et al.*, 1999).

Yet we are of the view that Dutch law is in advance of comparable legislation in other countries in raising the aspiration for financial reporting to a level described by *inzicht* – providing a statement of purpose and a healthy challenge both to the preparers and auditors of annual accounts. In today's environment, financial reporting in many countries is inexorably becoming an exercise in compliance with detailed rules. The Dutch law contains a well-intentioned reminder that financial reporting is more than conformity with rules. It would be a pity for this reminder to disappear.

ACKNOWLEDGEMENTS

The authors wish to thank G. G. M. Bak, H. Beckman, A. J. Bosman, F. Graafstal, H. W. Hageman, H. F. J. Joosten, G. Timmer, P. A. Wessel and in particular J. W. Schoonderbeek for providing information and valuable comments on many aspects of this paper. A similar acknowledgement is due in memory of Prof. Dr A. B. Frielink RA. Two anonymous referees provided valuable comments and suggestions.

NOTES

1 See, for instance, Moret Ernst & Young (1994).
2 See Buijink *et al.* (1996) for an analysis of the wording (in English translation, which may introduce noise) of the overriding attribute in the standard auditor's report in EU member states.
3 The term *getrouw* should be separated from *beeld* (image) when examining the evolution of this terminology. Some authors accept the former, while rejecting the latter and prefer a term such as *getrouw weergeeft* (renders faithfully).
4 See KB, 8 December 1950, Stb. 545, cited in Groeneveld (1976).
5 Zeff (1990) has argued, however, that 'present fairly' is not a proper English-language translation of *geeft een* [gives a] *getrouw beeld.*
6 *Het Jaarverslag* ('s-Gravenhage: Commissie Jaarverslaggeving van het Verbond van Nederlandsche Werkgevers, het Centraal-Sociaal Werkgevers-Verbond, het Katholiek Verbond van Werkgeversvakverenigingen en het Verbond van Protestants-Christelijke Werkgevers in Nederland, 1955).

7 As it happens, J. E. Spinosa Cattela, who had appealed to 'insight' several years earlier, was formerly a member of Philips' internal audit staff and later joined an overseas firm that audited some of Philips' subsidiaries.

8 *De hervorming van de onderneming* (Amsterdam: De Arbeiderspers, 1959).

9 *Open Ondernemerschap: De groei van de onderneming en het vennootschapsrecht* ('s-Gravenhage: Martinus Nijhoff, 1962).

10 *Verslaggeving verantwoording en voorlichting door de besturen van naamloze vennootschappen* ('s-Gravenhage: Raad van Nederlandse Werkgeversverbonden, 1962).

11 Goudeket was an ardent advocate of replacement value accounting which had been practised by Philips in both its balance sheet and income statement since 1951 (see Goudeket, 1960). Almost certainly owing to Goudeket's urging, replacement value accounting was recommended in the 1955 report of the joint employers' associations. Kraayenhof, however, was not known as an advocate of replacement value accounting.

12 *Herziening van het ondernemingsrecht, Rapport van de Commissie ingesteld bij beschikking van de Minister van Justitie van 8 april 1960* ('s-Gravenhage: Staatsuitgeverij, 1968), p. 52.

13 *Bijlagen Handelingen Tweede Kamer*, 1967–1968, 9595, no. 3, p. 12.

14 See, for instance, the commentary of the NIvA management board on the draft law (NIvA, 1966).

15 *Advies inzake de wetgeving over de jaarrekening van ondernemingen*, uitgebracht aan de Minister van Justitie, 1966, No. 4 (Sociaal-Economische Raad, 1966), pp. 12–13.

16 *NIvRA Berichten*, December 1972.

17 Commissie van bijstand inzake Toepassing Beroepsregelen, CTB.

18 NIvRA Archives, DB 1972: 8.

19 See 'Wet op de jaarrekening van ondernemingen', *De Accountant*, Vol. 78, No. 9, June 1972, pp. 456–82.

20 *NIvRA Berichten*, March 1972.

21 A third issue, relating to whether the word 'consistently' (*stelselmatig*) as used in the law should also be used in the auditor's report was a major complication in the discussions covered in this section. As it is not related to the topic of this paper, it is not discussed further here.

22 *NIvRA Berichten*, June 1972.

23 Graafstal and Timmer confirmed the importance of the international aspect in an interview on 27 May 1994.

24 The 107 listed companies were selected from the holdings of annual reports in the library of the *Vrije Universiteit*, Amsterdam. Selection was at random except for the inclusion of the most prominent multinational companies.

25 Since the first law requiring companies to have an external audit did not take effect until 1971, companies had previously been required only to publish a balance sheet and profit and loss account (with few restrictions as to content), and if an external audit had been conducted there was no obligation to publish the auditor's report. Evidently, a significant number of companies elected not to publish the report of the auditor. For further discussion, see Zeff *et al.* (1992: 65–6).

26 *NIvRA berichten*, December 1972.

27 *Gedrags- en Beroepsregels Registeraccountants, GBR.*

28 Interview with H. Beckman, 18 May 1995.

29 *Bijlagen Handelingen Tweede Kamer*, 1979–80, 16326, No. 3.

30 For a discussion of the jurisprudence resulting from cases heard by the Enterprise Chamber, see Bak and Boukema (1983).

REFERENCES

Alexander, D. (1993) 'A European true and fair view?', *European Accounting Review*, 2(1): 59–80.

Alexander, D. (1996) 'Truer and fairer. Uninvited comments on invited comments', *European Accounting Review*, 5(3): 483–93.

Bak, G. G. M. (1984) 'De tekst van de goedkeurende verklaring bij de jaarrekening', *VERA-Regiosessie*. Amsterdam: NIvRA.

Bak, G. G. M. and Boukema, C. A. (1983) *Jurisprudentie inzake de jaarrekening 1977–1983*. Deventer: Fed.

Bosman, A. J. (1984) 'Hulde en respect', in Bindenga, A. J. and Nordemann, H. H. J. (eds) *Hoor en Wederhoor: Artikelen aangeboden aan Prof. Dr. A. B. Frielink*. Amsterdam: Vakgroep Bedrijfsinformatica en Accountancy, Economische Faculteit, Universiteit van Amsterdam, pp. 7–10.

Braam, G. J. M. and Damen, A. W. G. (1996) 'Inzicht of getrouw beeld? Het dualistisch karakter van de goedkeurende accountantsverklaring', in Boneco, C. M. T., de Bos, A. and Knoops, C. D. (eds) *FMA-Kroniek 1996*. Alphen aan den Rijn: Samsom, pp. 123–38.

Buijink, W., Maijoor, S., Meuwissen, R. and van Witteloostuijn, A. (1996) *The Role, Position and Liability of the Statutory Auditor within the European Union*. Luxembourg: Office for Official Publications of the European Communities.

Burgert, R. (1952) 'Publicaties van naamloze vennootschappen', in Belle, L. H., Brands, J., Brummelman, D. H., Jonkers, A. C. J. and Lindner, J. A. M. F. (eds) *Opstellen ter gelegenheid van een kwart eeuw V.A.G.A.* pp. 47–56.

Camfferman, K. (1994) 'Goed koopmansgebruik en maatschappelijk aanvaardbare normen', in Boneco, C. M. T., ter Hoeven, R. L., Speklé, R. F. and van der Wal, R. (eds) *FMA-Kroniek 1994*. Rotterdam: Vakgroep Kosten en Winstbepalingsvraagstukken, pp. 183–98.

Camfferman, K. (1998) 'Perceptions of the Royal Mail case in the Netherlands', *Accounting and Business Research*, 29(1): 43–55.

Camfferman, K. and Zeff, S. A. (1994) 'The contributions of Theodore Limperg Jr (1879-1961) to Dutch accounting and auditing', in Edwards, J. R. (ed.) *Twentieth-Century Accounting Thinkers*. London and New York: Routledge, pp. 112–41.

De Jong, J. (1970) *De accountantsverklaring aangaande een jaarrekening. NIvRA Geschriften*, Vol. 4. Amsterdam: Nederlands Instituut van Registeraccountants.

Goudeket, A. (1960) 'An application of replacement value theory', *Journal of Accountancy*, 110: 37–47.

Groeneveld, G. L. (1971) 'De accountantsverklaring en de Wet op de Jaarrekening van Ondernemingen', *De Accountant*, 77(6): 243–68.

Groeneveld, G. L. (1976) *Limperg/Groeneveld: Leer van de accountantscontrole*. Deventer: Kluwer.

Hellema, H. J. (1960) 'Artikel 16 van het Reglement van Arbeid van het NIVA', *Maandblad voor Accountancy en Bedrijfshuishoudkunde*, 34(1): 3–13.

Huizenga, P. W. (1969) *De jaarrekening van ondernemingen, Beschouwingen over de voorstellen tot wettelijke regeling*. Deventer: Kluwer.

IJsselmuiden, T. S. (1972) *Wet op de jaarrekening*. Deventer: Kluwer.

Kleerekoper, I. (1967) 'De accountantsverklaring', in Groeneveld, G. L., Kleerekoper, I., Starreveld, R. W. and Verdenius, T. J. (eds) *Stramien: Een bundel*

opstellen rond de beroepsregelen voor accountants. Deventer/Alphen aan den Rijn: Kluwer/Samsom, pp. 147–76.
Knol, H. D. M. (1936) *Civielrechtelijke aansprakelijkheid van directie en commissarissen van naamlooze vennootschappen naar Nederlandsch recht*. Zwolle: Tjeenk Willink.
Koster, J. (1931) *De onderteekening der jaarrekening*. Purmerend: J. Muusses.
Kraayenhof, J. (1976) 'Spieghel historiael', *De Accountant*, 82(8): 430–4.
Lefebvre, C. and Flower, J. (1994) *European Financial Reporting: Belgium*. London: Routledge.
Limperg, T. (1903) 'De onderteekening der balans', *Accountancy*, 1(7): 74–6.
Limperg, T. (1904) 'Enige beschouwingen over het accountants-rapport', *Accountancy*, 2(19, 23): 73–5, 124–5.
Moret Ernst & Young (1994) *Current Netherlands Accounting and Reporting Rules: Title 9, Book 2 of the Netherlands Civil Code*. Rotterdam: Moret Ernst & Young.
Nijst, J. J. M. H. (1928) 'Balanswaarheid en balansklaarheid', *Maandblad voor het Boekhouden*, 34(402): 168–71.
NIvA (1966) 'Nota van de besturen van het Nederlands Instituut van Accountants en van de Vereniging van Academisch Geschoolde Accountants inzake het voorontwerp van de commissie Verdam van Wet op de Jaarrekening van ondernemingen', *De Accountant*, 72(11): 583–95.
NIvRA (1975) *Van RBR tot GBR: De behandeling van de voorstellen tot het vaststellen van de Verordening Gedrags- en Beroepsregels Registeraccountants door de ledenvergadering van het NIVRA*. Amsterdam: NIvRA (Nederlands Instituut van Registeraccountants).
NIvRA (1984) 'De tekst van de goedkeurende verklaring bij de jaarrekening', *RADAR* 5.20. Amsterdam: NIvRA (Nederlands Instituut van Registeraccountants).
Ordelheide, D. (1993) 'True and fair view: a European and a German perspective', *European Accounting Review*, 2(1): 81–90.
Ordelheide, D. (1996) 'True and fair view: a European and a German perspective II', *European Accounting Review*, 5(3): 495–506.
Otten, P. F. S. (1954) 'Het beleid van Philips ten aanzien van de voorlichting aan aandeelhouders', Speech by Ir. P. F. S. Otten, chairman of the management board of NV Philips' Gloeilampenfabrieken, to the general meeting of shareholders.
Parker, R. H. and Nobes, C. W. (1994) *An International View of True and Fair Accounting*. London: Routledge.
Sanders, P., Groeneveld, G. L. and Burgert, R. (1975) *De Jaarrekening Nieuwe Stijl, Commentaar op de wet op de jaarrekening*. Alphen aan den Rijn: Samsom.
Spinosa Cattela, J. E. (1948) *Inleiding tot de leer van de accountantscontrôle*. Leiden: Stenfert Kroese.
Took, L. (1997) 'Whatever happened to the Quadro Fedele?', *European Accounting Review*, 6(3): 527–39.
Treffers, H. C. (1959) 'Welke is de betekenis van de arbeid van de accountant voor de commissarissen van de onderneming?', *Maatschappij-Belangen*, 123(7): 357–8.
Van Hulle, K. (1993) 'Truth and untruth about true and fair: a commentary on "A European true and fair view" ', *European Accounting Review*, 2(1): 99–104.
Van Hulle, K. (1997) 'The true and fair view override in the European Accounting Directives', *European Accounting Review*, 6(4): 711–20.
Van Slooten, G. (1900) *Verplichte openbaarmaking van balans en winst- en verliesrekening van naamlooze vennootschappen*. Den Haag: Hoekstra & Co.

Vecht, J. M. (1962) 'De niet-goedkeurende accountantsverklaring', *Maandblad voor Accountancy en Bedrijfshuishoudkunde*, 36(3): 103–14.

Walton, P. (1997) 'The true and fair view and the drafting of the Fourth Directive', *European Accounting Review*, 6(4): 721–30.

Zeff, S. A. (1990) 'The English-language equivalent of "geeft een getrouw beeld" ', *De Accountant*, 90(2): 82–3.

Zeff, S. A., Camfferman, K. and Buijink, W. (1999) 'The Royal NIVRA's adoption of IFAC's recommended auditor's report: an alternative view', *De Accountant*, 105(5): 322–4.

Zeff, S. A., van der Wel, F. and Camfferman, K. (1992) *Company Financial Reporting: A Historical and Comparative Study of the Dutch Regulatory Process*. Amsterdam: North-Holland.

[17]

Accounting and Business Research, Vol 31. No. 2. pp. 83-90. 2001

The true and fair view requirement in recent national implementations

Sally Aisbitt and Christopher Nobes*

Abstract—This note examines the implementation of the true and fair view requirement into the laws of Austria, Finland, Norway and Sweden. It builds on an earlier analysis of the 12 EU member states that had previously implemented the requirement. It is found that three of the four countries depart from the wording of the appropriate language versions of the Fourth Directive. Also, two of the countries do not implement the 'override', and the other two implement it in a way not done before, by reserving to the member state the specification of the allowed departures.

1. Introduction

The implementation and impact of the EU Fourth and Seventh Directives' true and fair view (TFV) requirement (as reproduced in Appendix 1) was examined by Nobes (1993) for 12 countries. Since that time, three new member states (Austria, Finland and Sweden) have joined the EU, and the requirement to implement the Directives has been complied with in non-EU members of the European Economic Area[1] (the largest such country being Norway). This note marshalls the facts for these four countries and puts them in the context of the earlier 12 countries. The paper looks first at the signifiers used in the Directives; then at the signifiers in national laws; then at the implementation of the 'override'.

Other researchers may wish to use these facts in order to explain the choices made or to try to assess the extent to which the implementation of the Directives is likely to contribute to the harmonisation of European financial reporting. The variations in interpretation and understanding of TFV within and between countries and over time (e.g. Nobes and Parker, 1991; Nobes, 1993) have demonstrated that this is an area where the process of harmonisation is far from complete.

* The authors are at the Open University and the University of Reading, respectively. They are grateful for advice from Kristina Artsberg (Lund University, Sweden), Harald Brandsås (Den norske Revisorforening), Sigvard Heurlin (Öhrlings PricewaterhouseCoopers, Stockholm), Pekka Pirinen (University of Jyväskylä, Finland), Gerhard Prachner (Coopers & Lybrand Inter-truehand, Vienna), and Alan Roberts (University of Reading). The authors are most grateful for the helpful suggestions on an earlier draft from the referees and the editor. Correspondence should be addressed to Professor Nobes at the Department of Economics, the University of Reading, P.O. Box 218, Whiteknights, Reading RG6 2AA. E-mail: c.wright@reading.ac.uk

The final version of this paper was accepted in November 2000.

2. Signifiers in the Directive

Nobes (1993) follows others in distinguishing between the signifier and the signified relating to the TFV, but also notes that the signifiers implemented in member state laws are not the same in all cases as those in the official versions of the Directives. For the four countries studied here, there are three new language versions of the Fourth and Seventh Directives, given that Austria is covered by the earlier German version. Table 1 shows the signifiers equivalent to 'a true and fair view' of Article 2 of the Fourth Directive for these languages. A full table for comparison of all the languages is shown as Appendix 2.

Figure 1 adds the three new language versions to the 10 others in terms of their approximate literal meanings in English. Two interesting points emerge. First, like all the earlier versions except the original[2] English, the Norwegian and Swedish versions use a unitary signifier. In the case of the Swedish version of the Directives,[3] Wennberg (1991) explained that the first drafts were produced by accountants in Sweden, under the guidance of the Justice Department for approval in Brussels. The English version of the Directive was the primary source, but the Danish version (and occasionally the German and French) was used where there were difficulties in interpretation. TFV, perhaps the most difficult requirement to interpret, seems to have been an area where recourse was made to the Danish Directive. On the other hand, the Finnish Directive, with no linguistic relative in previous versions of the Directive seems to have looked to the English and produced a dual signifier.

[1] Iceland, Liechtenstein and Norway.

[2] The evidence for this is strong and is reviewed in Nobes (1993).

[3] Wennberg gives particular emphasis to the Eighth Directive.

Figure 1
'True and fair' signifiers in the Fourth Directive

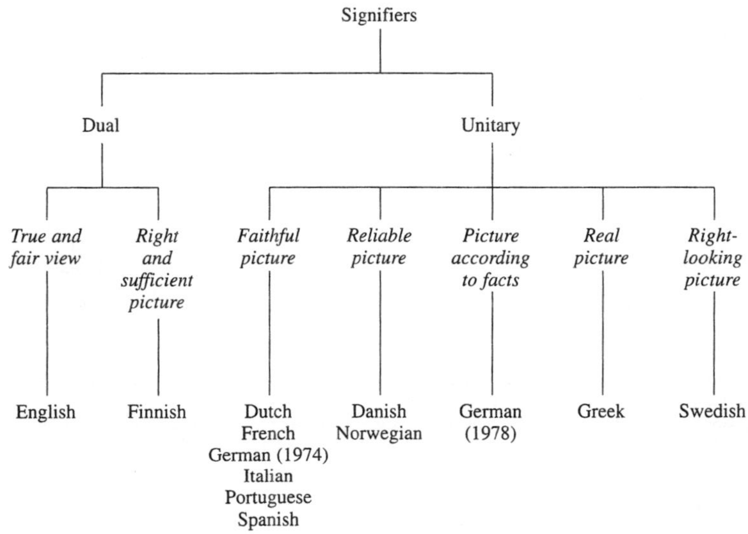

Figure 2
'True and fair' signifiers in national laws

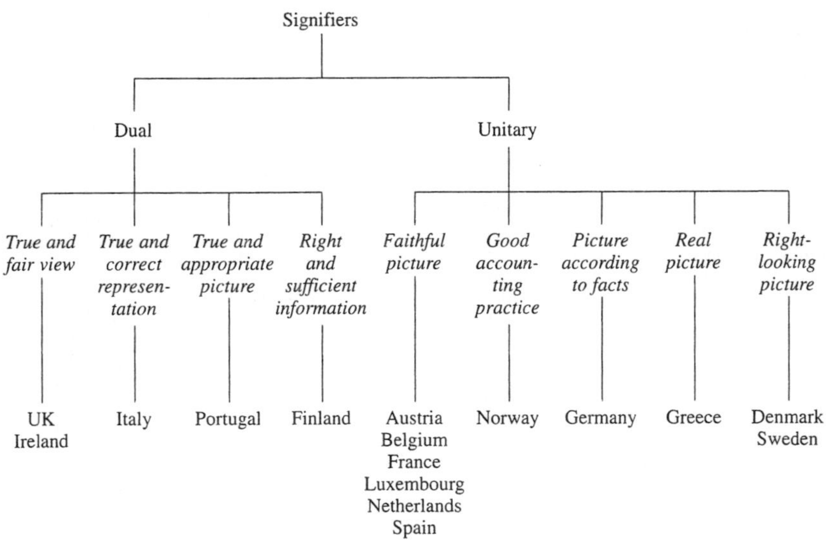

Table 1
Signifiers for a true and fair view (for translations, see Appendix 3)

Country	*Words in Directive*	*Implementation of Directive*	*Words in law if different from Directive*
Austria	ein den tatsächlichen Verhältnissen entsprechendes Bild	1990[1]	ein möglichst getreues Bild
Finland	oikea ja riittävä kuva	1992[2]	oikeat ja riittävät tiedot ... (oikea ja riittävä kuva)
	en rättvisande bild[3]		en riktig och tillräcklig bild .... (rättvisande bild)[4]
Norway	et pålitelig bilde	1998	god regnskapsskikk
Sweden	en rättvisande bild	1995	–

[1]Approximate implementation; full implementation was achieved by the *EU-Ges RÄG* of 28 June 1996, but the relevant section numbers of the ÖHGB did not change.
[2]The expression was incorporated in the Accounting Act 1992, although implementation of the Fourth Directive was not complete until the Accounting Act 1997 became effective. References in this paper are therefore to the 1997 Act.
[3]Swedish is also an official language in Finland, so Finland has two signifiers for the TFV.
[4]The paragraph heading is "Riktiga och tillräckliga uppgifter". In the Finnish version, the heading and the text use identical wording.

The second point is that the Swedish version of the Directive does not use 'faithful' as many versions of the Directive do or the similar 'reliable' as for the Danish[4] and Norwegian Directives, but uses 'right-looking', which is the same as in the Danish implementation as law (see Figure 2 and Appendix 3). Although this may not represent a significant difference, it seems to be further evidence of bureaucratic negotiation over translation as proposed in Nobes (1993), for example in the change of the German version from 1974 to 1978.

3. Signifiers in member state laws

This section deals with the words that have been used to implement the Directives' TFV requirement in national legislation. Nobes (1993) notes that several member states departed substantially or marginally from the words laid out in the Directive. This precedent is continued in three of the new implementations (i.e., except for the Swedish), as summarised on the right of Table 1. Austria departs from the Directive's *'ein den tatsächlichen Verhältnissen entsprechendes Bild'* and substitutes *'ein möglichst getreues Bild'* (ÖHGB § 195 and § 222 (2)), which is much closer to the *'einen getreuen Einblick'* of the German version of the 1974 draft of the Fourth Directive (and the 1976 draft of the Seventh Directive).

Unlike the German law (DHGB § 264 (2)), the Austrian law does not modify the requirement by adding the words 'in compliance with accepted accounting principles' (*'unter Beachtung der Grundsätze ordnungsmässiger Buchführung'* (GoB)). There is, of course, a requirement to comply with GoB, but as an additional requirement to the TFV, not as a modification of it. However, the above modification *is* to be found in the Austrian instruction on the duties of the auditors (ÖHGB § 274), as it is in the analogous German instructions (DHGB § 322). Its absence from the instructions for Austrian *preparers* may, in practice, not represent a significant difference from German law.

The Nordic countries have a long tradition of the concept of 'good accounting practice' (GAP) (Flower, 1994, p.241–2) which has some similarities to the German GoB. In the same way that the German implementation of the Fourth Directive retained this principle, the Swedish version states, in addition to the TFV requirement:

> Årsredovisningen skall upprättas på ett överskådligt sätt och i enlighet med god redovisningssed. [Annual accounts should be prepared clearly and in accordance with good accounting practice.] (*Årsredovisningslag*, SFS 1995: 1554, ch. 2, para. 2)

Other countries had also continued their former words (e.g. *'régularité et sincérité'* in France, and

[4] The Danish and Norwegian words can be literally translated as 'reliable', but this may convey the same meaning as the 'faithful' used by Nobes (1993) for Denmark.

'*inzicht*' in the Netherlands) in combination with TFV.

The Norwegian law goes further and implements the TFV concept by using the expression GAP. In complete contrast, Finland has broken away from its previous legislation by omitting references to GAP in the chapter on annual financial statements. Nevertheless, GAP is a requirement in Chapter 1 of the Act, which deals with the obligation to keep accounting records. This is not dissimilar to the Danish approach: GAP was not included in *Årsregnskabsloven* 1981 but persists in *Bogføringsloven* (see Erhvervs- og Selskabsstyrelsen, 1990) and the Stock Exchange's information requirements. The Finnish law paraphrases the wording of the Directive, but the exact phrase from the Directive is included in the law in parentheses:

> Tilinpäätöksen tulee antaa oikeat ja riittävät tiedot kirjanpitovelvollisen toiminnan tuloksesta ja taloudellisesta asemasta (*oikea ja riittävä kuva*). [The accounts shall give right and sufficient information on the reporting entity's result and on its financial position (*right and sufficient picture*).] (*Kirjanpitolaki*, 1336/1997, ch. 3, para. 2, emphasis original)

The explanation accompanying the proposal to the government for the law (RP, 1997, p.15) states that the use of the two expressions is a technical legal device to bring a number of pieces of legislation in line and to demonstrate that the two expressions are synonymous. The expression *oikeat ja riitävät tiedot* was considered to be a translation of the English term, true and fair view, from Article 2(3) of the Fourth Directive. However, the alternative phrase, *oikea ja riittävä kuva*, had already been used in previous legislation (769/1990 and 39/1889).

There may be a danger of making too much of the differences in literal wordings of signifiers. In this context, one notes that, since there are two official languages in Finland, there is an official Swedish language version of the Finnish law. In it, the above sentence uses wording that is closer to the Swedish language version of the Directive:

> Bokslutet skall ge en riktig och tillräcklig bild av resultatet av den bokföringsskyldiges verksamhet och om dennes ekonomiska ställning (*rättvisande bild*). [The accounts shall give a right and sufficient picture of the reporting entity's result and of its economic position (*right-looking picture*)]

Another detail of the wording is that the language versions examined here, except the Finnish, refer to "a" rather than "the" TFV. As noted in Nobes (1993), there are also some exceptions in other languages. However, in the Finnish language, there are no definite or indefinite articles, such concepts being conveyed by word order. This is of little consequence for the Finnish language version of the law because of the reference to "information" rather than "picture". The bracketed reference to "right-looking picture" (see in italics above) uses no article even in the Swedish language version of the Finnish law. The decisive clue is that the Swedish language version refers to "*a* right and sufficient picture" in the unbracketed text.

4. The override

As is well known (e.g. Ordelheide, 1990; Otte, 1990), the German implementation of the Fourth Directive does not comply with Article 2(5) which requires departure from the provisions of the Directive 'in exceptional cases' (see text in Appendix 1). The Austrian and Swedish implementations follow this precedent, with no mention of departure or exceptional cases, although departure in exceptional cases had been included in the first draft of the Swedish law (SOU, 1994, ch. 2. para. 2). One could argue that these implementations are examples of member states taking the option of the last sentence of Article 2 (5) (whereby the legislators may prescribe the cases of departure) but specifying no departures. This could be seen as implicit implementation of Article 2 (5).

By the time of the Swedish implementation, no national law had specified any cases of departure and few individual companies had departed from the law (e.g. Van Hulle, 1997; Jönsson Lundmark, 1996). Thorell (1995) argues, in a Swedish context, that a strong interpretation of the override would allow member states to specify departures from a provision of the Directive, which would clearly be unreasonable and would be in contravention of pronouncements from the EC Contact Committee. That Committee (EC, 1990) and Van Hulle (1993) had already supported this interpretation of the Directive. However, Alexander (1993) and Nobes (1993) argue in favour of an interpretation found in the UK whereby the standard-setters have used the override, for example in the context of investment properties and goodwill.[5] The EC Commission (EC, 1997, p.3) has subsequently confirmed that it believes that member states (and presumably standard-setters) are not allowed to promulgate general rules in contradiction of the Directive, but the authority of this statement is ambiguous, and clearly less than that of a Directive.

Contrary to this, the Finnish and Norwegian Acts implement the override using the disputed last sentence of Article 2(5). The Finnish Act specifies that the Ministry of Trade and Industry will decide when and how an entity must depart from the Act in order to give a TFV (*Kirjanpitolaki*,

[5] SSAP 19 does this by requiring investment properties (which are fixed assets with limited useful lives) not to be depreciated, in contradiction to Article 35(1)(b). Similarly, FRS 10 allows the lack of depreciation of capitalised goodwill.

1336/1997, ch. 3, para. 2). This may amount to a subtle way of arriving at a German, Austrian or Swedish result (i.e., no override) without breaking the letter of the Directive. The Finnish proposal (RP, 1997, p.15) explains that limiting the occasions when the override is permitted is essential to the system of enforcing the law. However, the Finns do not seem to have entirely ruled out the possibility of using the override. There are no examples within the Act, although the proposal (RP, 1997, pp.15–6) included an example about limiting the use of LIFO to certain companies. The override has already been the basis for a ministerial decision (Handels- och industriministeriet, 1998) allowing the use of International Accounting Standards by certain companies in their consolidated financial statements. The preamble to the decision is that:

> Handels- och industriministeriet har *med stöd av 3 kap. 2§2 mom. bokföringslagen den 30 december 1997* (1336/1997) beslutat: ...
>
> [The Ministry of Trade and Industry has decided *with the support of Chapter 3, paragraph 2§2 of the Accounting Act of 30 December 1997* (1336/1997): ...] (emphasis added)

The Norwegian law is the most interesting. The legislators have interpreted the last sentence of Article 2(5) as meaning that the law itself can specify when companies must depart from the Directives. The closest precedent for this is the UK use of standards to specify departures (see above). Early drafts of the Norwegian law included a number of 'exceptions' from the valuation rules, but the final law includes only one clear departure from the Directives:[6] the requirement that marketable investments held as part of a liquid trading portfolio should be marked to market (i.e., held at market value, with gains and losses recognised in the profit and loss account). This requirement is included in the law under the heading of '*spesielle vurderingsregler*' (special[7] valuation rules). The European Commission was already proposing to amend the Directive to allow it (EC, 1998), partly in order to be consistent with requirements of International Accounting Standards (see E 62 of 1998 leading to IAS 39). Norway was merely ahead of developments here and could take comfort from implicit approval of the change by the Commission.

The other issues included under 'special valuation rules' are of a different type in that the Norwegian law interprets or extends the Directives in particular directions, without directly overriding it. These issues are research and development, goodwill,[8] pension costs, leasing, long-term work-in-progress and currency translation. They were also unlikely to be controversial with the Commission, which had issued (EC, 1997) several imaginative[9] interpretations of the Directives which might be interpreted as suggesting that the Norwegian legislators need not have expressed their rules as departures from the Directive's provisions. For example, the Norwegian law requires the use of the closing rate of exchange for translation of foreign currency monetary balances, which is an issue not explicitly dealt with in the Directive. Most member states[10] accept or require translation at the closing rate, and the Commission (EC, 1997, p.9) regards it as acceptable under the Directives.

The objective of the Norwegian legislation (Ot. Prp., 1988–89) was said to be to move away from the legal formulations of the 1970s and towards internationally accepted practices of the 1990s. Interestingly, the EC Commission now has sympathy for this general approach, as part of supporting the work of the International Accounting Standards Committee (EC, 1995).

A related point is that the Swedish Act allows for work-in-progress to be shown at higher than cost. One could argue that this, too, is supported by the Commission's interpretation, because of its acceptance of the percentage of completion method (EC, 1997, p.8).

5. Summary

The application of the Fourth and Seventh Directives to Austria, Finland, Norway and Sweden involved three new language versions of

[6] In addition there are instances where the Norwegian Act is more prescriptive than the Directive. For example, Article 35 (3) and (4) of the Directive indicates that indirect costs and interest may be added to production cost, whereas Chapter 5, paragraph 4, amplified by Ot. Prp. (1997–8) implies that these costs must be included for enterprises other than small enterprises. The committee drafting the proposals saw any such narrowing of choice or implementation of Member State options, as well as true derogations, as departures from the Directive, i.e. as a regulated override (NOU, 1995, 2.3.4 Regulert overstyring).

[7] In the proposal from the Accounting Act Committee and the Ministry of Finance, "special valuation rules" were distinguished from "exceptions from valuation rules". The latter comprised the use of market value for financial instruments and the closing rate of exchange. It is unclear why the Parliament merged the two types.

[8] Goodwill on consolidation is not distinguished from other types of goodwill.

[9] For example, the Commission (EC, 1997, p.9) believes that gains on unsettled long-term foreign currency monetary items could be treated as 'made' (Fourth Directive, Article 31(1)(c)). The British law implemented this word as 'realised' (Companies Act 1985, Schedule 4, para. 12 (a)), and SSAP 20 (para. 65) believes that an 'override' is necessary to take such profit into the profit and loss account. Some other member states have an even more restrictive understanding of this provision.

[10] This is required in the UK and Ireland (see footnote 10). It is also the practice in Denmark, France, Greece, the Netherlands, Portugal, Spain and Sweden. (Alexander and Archer, 1995, pp. 133–4, 189, 332–3, 588–9, 685, 853–4 and 1199–2000).

the Directives. The Norwegian and Swedish versions have a unitary signifier; the Finnish a dual signifier. The Norwegian version follows the Danish Directive; the Swedish version follows the Danish law.

Three of the implementations in law depart from the appropriate language versions of the Directive. The Norwegian law retains 'good accounting practice' instead of TFV. The Finnish language version of the Finnish law has 'right and sufficient information', but the Swedish version of the Finnish law is closer to the Directive. The Austrian law departs from the German language Directive but not in order to follow the German law. All the laws refer to "a" rather than "the" TFV.

None of the laws allows directors to use judgment to depart from legal provisions in order to give a TFV. However, the Finnish law allows the government to specify departures, which it has not yet done; and the Norwegian law contains specified departures from the Fourth Directive.

References

Alexander, D. (1993). 'A European true and fair view?'. *European Accounting Review*, 2 (1).

Alexander, D. and Archer, S. (1995). *European Accounting Guide*. Harcourt Brace, 2nd edition.

EC (1990). *Accounting Harmonisation in the EC. Problems of Applying the Fourth Directive*. EC Commission.

EC (1995). *Accounting Harmonisation: A New Strategy vis-à-vis International Harmonisation*. EC Commission, COM 95 (908).

EC (1997). *Interpretative Communication Concerning Certain Articles of the Fourth and Seventh Council Directives on Accounting*. EC Commission, XV/7009/97 EN.

EC (1998). *Fair Value Accounting for Financial Instruments: A Proposal for the Amendment of the 4th Directive*. EC Commission, XV/7002/98 EN.

Erhvervs- og Selskabsstyrelsen (1990). *Bekendtgørelse om erhvervsdrivende virksomheders bogføring, årsregnskaber og opbevaring af regnskabsmateriale*, Erhvervs- og Selskabsstyrelsens bekendtgørelse nr. 598 af 21. august 1990.

Flower, J. (1994). *The Regulation of Financial Reporting in the Nordic Countries*. Publica.

Handels- och industriministeriet (1998). *Handels- och industriministeriets beslut om upprättandet av koncernbokslut i enlighet med det regelverk som används allmänt på den internationella kapitalmarknaden*, 766.

Jönsson Lundmark, B. (1996). 'Nya årsredovisningslagen inte så dålig som det påstås'. *Balans*, 4: 16–24.

Nobes, C.W. (1993). 'The true and fair view requirement: impact on and of the fourth directive'. *Accounting and Business Research*, Winter: 35–48.

Nobes, C.W. and Parker, R.H. (1991). 'True and fair: a survey of UK financial directors'. *Journal of Business Finance and Accounting*, 18 (3).

NOU (1995). *Ny Regnskapslov*. Norges Offentlige Utredninger: 30.

Ordelheide, D. (1990). 'Soft transformations of accounting rules in the 4th Directive in Germany'. *Les Cahiers Internationaux de la Comptabilité*, Editions Comptables Malesherbes, 3: 1–15.

Ot. Prp. (1988–89). Nr. 35.

Ot. Prp. (1997–98). *Om lov om årsregnskap m.v.* (regnskapsloven). Odeltings proposisjon, Nr. 42.

Otte, H-H. (1990). 'Harmonisierte Europäische Rechnungslegung'. *Zeitschrift für Betriebswirtschaft*, 42.

RP (1997). *Regeringens proposition till Riksdagen med förslag till bokföringslag samt till lagar om ändring av 11 och 12 kap. lagen om aktiebolag och 79 c § lagen om andelslag*, 173 rd.

SOU (1994). *Års- och Koncernredovisning enligt EG-direktivet*. Statens Offentilga Utredningar: 17.

Thorell, P. (1995). 'Perspektiv på den nya årsredovisningslagen'. *Balans*, 11: 31–9.

Van Hulle, K. (1993). 'Truth and untruth about true and fair'. *European Accounting Review*, May.

Van Hulle, K. (1997). 'The true and fair override in the European Accounting Directives'. *European Accounting Review*, 6 (4): 711–20.

Wennberg, I. (1991). 'Jättejobb översätta EG-regler till svenska'. *Balans*, 5:14–16.

Appendix 1

English language version of Article 2 of the Fourth Directive

1. The annual accounts shall comprise the balance sheet, the profit and loss account and the notes on the accounts. These documents shall constitute a composite whole.
2. They shall be drawn up clearly and in conformity with the provisions of this Directive.
3. The annual accounts shall give a true and fair view of the company's assets, liabilities, financial position and profit or loss.
4. Where the application of the provisions of this Directive would not be sufficient to give a true and fair view within the meaning of para. 3, additional information must be given.
5. Where in exceptional cases the application of a provision of this Directive is incompatible with the obligation laid down in para. 3, that provision must be departed from in order to give a true and fair view within the meaning of para. 3. Any such departure must be disclosed in the notes on the accounts together with an explanation of the reasons for it and a statement of its effect on the assets, liabilities, financial position and profit or loss. The Member States may define the exceptional cases in question and lay down the relevant special rules.

Appendix 2
Signifiers for a true and fair view

Country	*Words in law before Fourth Directive (first appearance)*	*Words in Directive*	*Implementation of Directive*	*Words in law if different from Directive*
UK	a true and fair view (1947)	a true and fair view	1981	–
Ireland	a true and fair view (1963)	a true and fair view	1986	–
Netherlands	1. geeft een zodanig inzicht dat een verantwoord oordeel kan worden gevormd ... 2. geeft getrouw en stelselmatig (1970)	een getrouw beeld	1983	1. (as in 1970) 2. geeft getrouw, duidelijk en stelselmatig
Denmark	–	et pålideligt billede	1981	et retvisende billede
France }	–	{une image fidèle,	1983	–
Luxembourg }		{een getrouw beeld	1984	–
Belgium }		{(in Flemish)	1985	–
Germany	–	ein den tatsächlichen Verhältnissen entsprechendes Bild	1985	Unter Beachtung der Grundsätze ordnungsmässiger Buchführung (then, as Directive)
Greece	–	tin pragmatiki ikona	1986	
Spain	–	una imagen fiel	1989	la imagen fiel ... de conformidad con las disposiciones legales[1]
Portugal	–	uma imagem fiel	1989	uma imagem verdadeira e apropriada (1989 plan)
Italy	–	un quadro fedele	1991	rappresentare in modo veritiero e corretto
Austria	–	ein den tatsächlichen Verhältnissen entsprechendes Bild	1990[2]	ein möglichst getreues Bild
Finland	–	oikea ja riittävä kuva	1992[3]	oikeat ja riittävät tiedot
Norway	–	et pålitelig bilde	1998	god regnskapsskikk
Sweden	–	en rättvisande bild	1995	en rättvisande bild

[1] The words as found in the *Código de Commercio* (Art. 34).
[2] Approximate implementation.
[3] The expression was incorporated in the Accounting Act 1992, although implementation of the Fourth Directive was not complete until the Accounting Act 1997 became effective. References in this paper are therefore to the 1997 Act.

Appendix 3

Literal translations of words in Table 1 and elsewhere

Netherlands	– geeft een zodanig inzicht dat een verantwoord oordeel kan worden gevormd	presents an insight such that a well-founded opinion can be formed
	– geeft getrouw, duidelijk en stelselmatig	presents faithfully, clearly and consistently (over time)
Denmark	– et pålideligt billede	a reliable picture
	– et retvisende billede	a right-looking (or fair-looking) picture
Germany, Austria	– (unter Beachtung der Grundsätze ordnungsmässiger Buchführung) ein den tatsächlichen Verhältnissen entsprechendes Bild	(in compliance with accepted accounting principles) a picture in accordance with the facts
	– ein möglichst getreues Bild	a picture as faithful as possible
France	– une image fidèle	a faithful picture
Greece	– tin pragmatiki ikona	the real picture
Spain	– una (la) imagen fiel ... (de conformidad con las disposiciones legales)	a (the) faithful picture ... (in conformity with the legal provisions)
Portugal	– uma imagem fiel	a loyal view
	– uma imagem verdadeira e apropriada	a true and appropriate view
Italy	– un quadro fedele	a faithful picture
	– rappresentare in modo veritiero e corretto	represent in a true and correct way
Finland	– oikea ja riittävä kuva	[a?] right (or true) and sufficient picture
	– oikeat ja riittävät tiedot	right (or true) and sufficient information
	– en riktig och tillräcklig bild	a right (or true) and sufficient picture
	– riktiga och tillräckliga uppgifter	right (or true) and sufficient information
Norway	– et pålitelig bilde	a reliable picture
	– god regnskapsskikk	good accounting practice
Sweden	– en rättvisande bild	a right-looking (or fair-looking) picture

[18]

The International Journal of Accounting

The Reintroduction of the True and Fair Override and Harmonization with IASC Standards in Australia: Lessons from the EU and Implications for Financial Reporting and International Trade

Alan S. Dunk and Alan Kilgore
University of Western Sydney, Nepean, Australia

Key Words: True and fair view; Override; Harmonization; Accounting directives; Internationalization

Abstract: *Two issues currently facing Australia having implications for financial reporting and trade are first, calls for the reintroduction of the true and fair view (TFV) override and second, the move to harmonize Australian accounting standards with those of the International Accounting Standards Committee (IASC). The purpose of the article is to examine the likely effects of such moves given the increasing globalization of both financial and product markets. The conclusions of the article suggest first, a reintroduction of the TFV override would be consistent with its role in the Fourth Directive as the fundamental principle of financial reporting. Second, harmonization with IASs by default will allow an override, as IAS 1 now provides for one. Third, Australia's harmonization of financial reporting requirements with the wider global community may be impeded because of inconsistencies between IASs, US GAAP, and EU Directives. Hence, the proposed reintroduction of the TFV override together with IASC reporting is unlikely to enhance Australia's link to the wider global community, leading to potential negative consequences in both financial and product markets.*

Two issues currently facing Australia having implications for financial reporting and trade are first, calls for the reintroduction of the true and fair view (TFV) override and second, the move to harmonize Australian accounting standards with those of the International Accounting Standards Committee (IASC). Prior to 1991, Australia had allowed the application of a TFV override when necessary. Under the 1983 amendments to the Corporations Act, if it were considered that the preparation of financial statements in accordance with a particular standard would fail to give a TFV, then directors were permitted to depart from the standard, thereby providing them with an

Direct all correspondence to: Alan S. Dunk, School of Accounting, University of Western Sydney, Nepean, P.O. Box 10, Kingswood, NSW 2747, Australia; E-mail: a.dunk@nepean.uws.edu.au

The International Journal of Accounting, Vol. 35, No. 2, pp. 213–226 ISSN: 0020-7063.

override (Deegan et al., 1994). A number of companies subsequently took the position that compliance with one or more approved accounting standards would not give a TFV (McGregor, 1992).

McGregor (1992) reported that for the period June 1990 to June 1991, there were 114 separate cases of non-compliance with 16 approved accounting standards by Australian companies. This suggests, as proposed by Deegan et al. (1994), that the TFV override might have been used by company directors as justification for not complying with particular accounting standards. As the meaning of TFV was unclear in both the Corporations Law and the standards, they argued that some directors may have opportunistically invoked the override on the basis that it would have been difficult for regulators to prove that their disclosure practices were not motivated by TFV considerations.

In 1991, however, the true and fair override was removed (Nobes, 1993). The Australian Corporations Act now provides that if financial statements prepared in accordance with applicable approved accounting standards and the prescribed requirements of the law do not otherwise give a TFV, then directors need to make available such information and explanation as will give a TFV (Nobes, 1993; Deegan et al., 1994). Consequently, directors are required to comply with existing accounting standards, even if they believe that they may not be appropriate (Deegan et al., 1994). In eliminating the TFV override, the amendment mandates adherence to accounting standards approved by the Accounting Standards Review Board (ASRB) (Deegan et al., 1994).

Against this backdrop, calls have been made for the reintroduction of the TFV override. Gearin and Khandelwal (1995) reported that the debate about whether a TFV override should be allowed once more over Australian accounting standards has been gathering strength. There is little agreement, however, as to whether this proposition should proceed. Moreover, they argued that since globalization, consistency, and comparability of financial information is crucial to international users, a TFV override could seriously affect the international perception of the quality of Australian financial statements in an environment in which international requirements are allegedly becoming increasingly standards-based. This may have considerable ramifications for the Australian Accounting Standards Board (AASB), as it intends to ensure that Australian standards are consistent with those of the IASC in the near term. An override may provide additional reporting flexibility not envisioned by the IASC in 1996 (IASC, 1996), but now forming part of IAS 1 (IASC, 1997). How the AASB will resolve this dilemma is unclear.

The purpose of the article is to explore the issues surrounding the use of the TFV and to consider implications likely to follow in Australia from the proposed reintroduction of the override together with the employment of IASC consistent standards. First, the article examines the TFV override within the framework primarily of the Fourth Directive in harmonizing financial reporting between EU member states, together with its role in facilitating international harmonization. Second, it explores the proposed linking of Australian accounting standards with those of the IASC from an international perspective.

The structure of the article is as follows. In the next section, the proposal to reintroduce the TFV override into Australia and the EU's experience with the application of the TFV provision are reviewed. The subsequent section draws together issues relating to the proposed linking of Australian standards to those of the IASC. In the final section, a number of conclusions are drawn with respect to the reintroduction of the TFV override and the use of IASC consistent accounting standards in Australia.

THE TFV REINTRODUCTION PROPOSAL AND THE EU EXPERIENCE

The removal of the TFV override by the Australian Corporations Act in 1991 has resulted in additional disclosures in corporate financial reports. For example, two sets of financial statements have been presented by both QBE Insurance and NRMA since 1992, the first set following the requirements of AASB 1023 and the second set "using their own preferred approach," which the respective directors believed better reflected a TFV (Deegan et al., 1994). Similarly, Washington H. Soul Pattinson has issued two sets of financial statements since 1992, one set referred to as "ASC Standard Consolidated" and the second set referred to as "True and Fair Consolidated." In the opinion of the directors, the "application of AASB 1024 has not resulted in the financial statements giving a true and fair view" (Annual Report, 1996). Hence, the issue of what constitutes a TFV may have been legislatively resolved, but not from the perspective of the directors of some major corporations.

Support for the reemergence of a TFV override has been building in Australia. Bice (1997) reported that the Australian Institute of Company Directors has called on the Australian Government to reintroduce the directors' option to override accounting standards, arguing that on occasions, they may not reflect an entity's economic reality. Although previously adopted by a number of countries including Australia, the TFV, together with an override facility, more recently has been implemented by member states of the EU via the Fourth Directive to contribute to the harmonization of accounting practice between them (Nobes and Parker, 1991; Van Hulle, 1993a; Alexander, 1996). The TFV concept, together with the accounting rules embodied in the Directives, have been incorporated into the law of each EU member state (Higson and Blake, 1993; Van Hulle, 1993b). Implications arise from the EU's experience with the TFV as to the possible financial reporting outcomes if the TFV is reintroduced into Australia.

The EU Experience

One major feature of the requirements of the Fourth Directive is that the TFV prevails over specific accounting provisions where circumstances justify it (Burlaud, 1993; Thorell and Whittington, 1994; Van Hulle, 1997). If a particular requirement of the Directive is not sufficient to give a TFV, additional information must be given and in exceptional cases where that information would not be enough to give a TFV, the specific provision in the Directive must be departed from (Burlaud, 1993; Van Hulle, 1993a). Under such circumstances, the departure must be disclosed in the notes, together with an explanation of the reasons for it and an assessment of its effect on the company's assets, liabilities, financial position and profit, or loss (Van Hulle, 1993a; Alexander, 1996).

Using the TFV as an override means that it is intended to be the governing criterion by which financial statements are to be judged (Zeff, 1993). In being the statutory objective of financial reporting, the TFV principle has achieved significant symbolic status within the EU (Houghton, 1987; Walton, 1993). Forker and Greenwood (1995) argued that the TFV provides scope to depart from the mechanical application of accounting rules. In the context of EU harmonization particularly, and with the increased formal regulation of accounting, the TFV has an essential role to play as a defense against the unsuitability of general rules in specific circumstances (Forker and Greenwood, 1995). In such instances, comparability is attained by disclosing the quantified effect of the departure from the rule (Forker and Greenwood, 1995). Consequently, the TFV override is frequently argued to provide scope for the exercise of professional judgment in specific cases, particularly with the need to depart from accounting rules (Hopwood, 1994; Forker and Greenwood, 1995). Given the diversity of legal and institutional frameworks that exist across countries within the EU, reflecting a TFV while preserving comparability is seen as crucial to the success of the EU harmonization program (Van Hulle, 1993a; Thorell and Whittington, 1994; Forker and Greenwood, 1995). Moreover, Van Hulle (1993a) argued that the TFV adds flexibility to financial reporting because of the socio-economic and cultural differences between EU member states.

Forker and Greenwood (1995) warned, however, that broad-based flexibility facilitates discretionary compliance, thereby undermining the comparability of accounts and restricting the scope of accounting regulators to outlaw unsatisfactory practice. The EU has taken the position that it is not necessary to develop uniform rules, and as such, options are acceptable as long as they can be considered equivalent and are supplemented by appropriate disclosures in the notes (Van Hulle, 1993b). Moreover, Adams et al. (1993) reported that the EU does not regard the availability of options as undermining the objective of international comparability. In what may be interpreted as an implied form of justification for this perspective, Thorell and Whittington (1994) argued that even though standardization may eliminate some ambiguity, it is unlikely to lead to uniform accounting practice as the variety of business circumstances and the methods of describing them will invariably necessitate a degree of choice being allowed by those standards.

Nevertheless, concerns have been expressed on whether the TFV provisions of the Fourth Directive have promoted harmonized financial reporting in the EU. For example, Van Hulle (1993a) noted that it is possible for annual accounts to be true and fair in one member state and not in another. Despite being true and fair in their country of origin, he indicated that for them to be true and fair in another member state requires different explanation and elaboration, given the provisions of the Fourth Directive. Although the Directive has achieved a uniform minimum degree of regulation of accounting, Thorell and Whittington (1994) argued that it has been more effective in the areas of format and disclosure than measurement.

Despite its importance, the meaning of the TFV concept remains unclear even though the literature contains numerous attempts to define it (e.g. Rutherford, 1985; Houghton, 1987; Stewart, 1988; Alexander, 1993, 1996; Nobes, 1993; Ordelheide, 1993, 1996; Walton, 1993). Walton (1993) reported that a contemporary view considers the TFV as no more than a code for generally accepted accounting practice, which in turn reflects pragmatic responses to measurement problems. Numerous studies have empirically explored the perceived meaning of the TFV phrase, together with its implications for practice, if the override were to be reintroduced into Australian Corporations Law.

For example, Nobes and Parker (1991) concluded from their study of 463 UK companies that they take no specific action to ensure that accounts give a TFV. Moreover, and of some concern, they reported that true and fair was not seen as inconsistent with creative accounting and income smoothing. In a later study, Higson and Blake (1993) interviewed 22 technical audit partners from the top 30 UK firms and found that a significant number of them considered the concept as being vague, ambiguous, and misleading. Sucher et al. (1996) reported that the TFV principle in the Czech Republic differs in what it signifies to initiators, users, and preparers of financial statements. Such variance in perspectives is unlikely to be conducive to financial reporting harmony and transparency if the override were to be reintroduced into Australia.

Higson and Blake (1993) expressed concern that in Australia and the UK, the TFV has been shown to be too vague to form the basis for legal action. They reported that in the UK, there has only been one minor prosecution of failure to provide a TFV. There have been no TFV prosecutions in Australia (Deegan et al., 1994). In a study conducted by the Fédération des Experts-comptables de la CEE (1992), 475 European companies' financial statements were examined and it was found that only 10 used the TFV override to depart from national law, out of six of the nine countries that had implemented the Fourth Directive (Van Hulle, 1993a). Given there were only 10, it has been suggested that the importance of the TFV concept should not be overemphasized (e.g. Higson and Blake, 1993; Van Hulle, 1993a).

Clearly, the weight of evidence suggests, however, that the implementation of the TFV principle in the context of the EU has contributed to the harmonization of accounting regulation within the framework facilitated by the accounting Directives[1] (e.g. Alexander, 1993; Van Hulle, 1993a). Even though its meaning has not been well-articulated, it has enabled diverse national groupings to consolidate the main thrust of their financial reporting. This has come at what might be considered a cost, that is, the considerable flexibility it provides both within and between member states in their corporate reporting requirements. The variance that the TFV override would provide may reflect negatively on the comparability and quality of financial reports prepared in Australia. Whether this matters might be considered in terms of potential effects on international harmonization.

The TFV and International Harmonization

Thorell and Whittington (1994) argued that the development of global capital markets has provided an impetus for the international harmonization of accounting particularly for those companies whose shares are traded on these markets and which have to satisfy the information needs of investors of different countries. Companies are no longer limited in their fund raising and investment activities to their home countries, and as such, this brings into focus the issue of the accounting practices that underlie the numbers on which cross-border financing and investment decisions are predicated (Emenyou and Gray, 1996). Thorell and Whittington (1994) argued that harmonizing the accounting standards of different countries should, in principle, first, assist in comparing the financial information of companies based in different countries, and second, make it easier for firms to engage in cross-border activities, such as raising finance.

These considerations raise the question of whether the application of the TFV override is conducive to international trade and finance, although it may have utility in managing differences in accounting regulation within a specific group of countries. The EU experience may provide guidance to Australia not only in terms of whether to support the reintroduction of the TFV override, but also whether the adoption of specific accounting standards might either hinder or facilitate international corporate operations. Although the provision of a TFV override helped to facilitate harmonization across member states of the EU, such a facility is not an issue in the Australian context as applicable laws and standards are implemented at the national level.

LINKING AUSTRALIAN STANDARDS TO THOSE OF THE IASC

The AASB plans to ensure that Australian accounting standards comply with IASs (Peirson and McBride, 1997). The AASB's program of harmonization involves both the modification of existing standards and the development of new ones (Peirson and McBride, 1997). In order to address effectively problems in various exposure drafts and standards, the planned December 1998 AASB deadline for completion of the harmonization program has been extended (Institute of Chartered Accountants in Australia (ICAA), 1998; Ravlic, 1998). The objective of the AASB is consistent with the goal of the IASC and the International Organization of Securities Commissions (IOSCO) for the completion of a core set of IASs to be used in the preparation of financial reports for cross-border fund raising and stock exchange listing (Peirson and McBride, 1997). Spencer (1998) reported that the AASB believes the IASC standards represent the best prospect for achieving a globally accepted set of standards within a reasonable period of time.

Although the IASC is an accounting standard setting body, its standards are not enforceable by law; hence, compliance is purely voluntary, relying for their implementation on their constituencies to encourage harmonization of national bodies with its standards (Adams et al., 1993; Van Hulle, 1993b; Thorell and Whittington, 1994). Endorsement by both IOSCO and member Securities Commissions is an essential prerequisite for the enforcement of IASs and ultimately for the global harmonization of accounting standards (Peirson and McBride, 1997; Weetman et al., 1998). Sharpe (1998) argued that international users of financial information have neither the time nor the desire to understand Australian accounting standards, and as such, IASs provide the way forward.

In their 1996 E53 exposure draft, the IASC proposed that financial statements should present fairly an enterprise's financial performance and position. For financial statements prepared using IASs, a fair presentation was suggested to require compliance in all material respects with all applicable standards (IASC, 1996). This proposal, together with a requirement to report that financial statements comply with IASs, with details of any departures, was designed to enhance the reliability and comparability of financial statements (IASC, 1996).

The position taken by the IASC in 1996 on international comparability has received support. Emenyou and Gray (1996) argued that "the increasing trend of multinationality of companies raises serious questions as to the adequacy and suitability of ethnocentric accounting guidelines, as conflicting standards of national reporting pose additional problems and costs both for multinational corporations and information users." Carsberg (1998) stressed that the IASC is trying to achieve international accounting harmonization to address such concerns.

Underlying the position taken by the AASB in adopting IASC standards is the presumption that they represent the position taken internationally. There is little evidence, however, that IASC standards are now, or are becoming, globally accepted. They have been difficult to gain acceptance in countries such as Japan, where professional accounting

Table 1. Countries' Share of World Market Capitalization

Country	%
Australia	1.25
France	3.21
Germany	3.86
Hong Kong, China	1.21
Japan	11.63
Malaysia	0.23
Singapore	0.18
Switzerland	3.04
UK	10.90
US	51.67

Adapted from the *Australian Financial Review*, January 20, 1998, as reported in Spencer (1998).

organizations do not have a significant role in the standard setting process (Emenyou and Gray, 1996). Although Gould (1995) argued that the IASC has served the accounting profession well in establishing a framework within which international accounting reporting standards can be debated, and however great the perceived need for common standards, there is little evidence of increasing support for IASs. He concluded that the concept of common standards has appeal, but it is unlikely to be accepted in practice, and furthermore, even though the IASC effort is notable, it does not appear to be sufficient for internationally accepted accounting standards. This suggests that the objective of the AASB to link Australian standards with those of the IASC will not materially add value to international harmonization on the grounds that first, there is very little evidence that such harmonization exists and second, it is far from clear that IASs are the appropriate vehicle for an attempt at building harmonization. Furthermore, Spencer (1998) argued that IASC standards are not as rigorous as Australian standards, due in part to the alternative accounting policies they currently allow.

In terms of international acceptance, Spencer (1998) reported that only a few countries so far have adopted the substance of IASC standards and emphasized that none of them, as Table 1 indicates, is significant in terms of world market capitalization. He argued that IASC standards would need to be accepted for domestic reporting purposes in countries like the US, the UK, and Japan if they are to be considered internationally accepted.

For example, difficulties have been encountered by a number of large European companies listed on stock exchanges outside Europe, most commonly the NYSE, in meeting reporting requirements (Cairns, 1997; Flower, 1997). Flower (1997) reported that the financial statements prepared by these companies in accordance with national legislation, and based on the accounting Directives, are not sufficient for international capital market purposes. Batt (1998) indicated that under new French law, listed companies will continue to be permitted to prepare consolidated accounts in accordance with IASs. However, if the accounts of those French companies conflict with EU Directives, Barthes, the president of the Conseil National de la Comptabilité and a former IASC chairman was reported to have specified that "they will have to publish two sets of accounts—one according to French rules and one according to IASs" (Cairns, 1998). Thorell and Whittington (1994) warned that a process of internal harmonization, which increases differences between EU members and the rest of the world, might be damaging to the EU's economic competitiveness in the global economy. Until the harmonization matter is clarified, both Flower (1997) and Batt (1998) warned that there is a risk that large companies will be increasingly drawn towards US GAAP. In the US, the governing criterion is conformity with GAAP, as financial statements are required to be presented fairly in conformity with generally accepted accounting principles (Nobes, 1993; Zeff, 1993).

Diversity Reduction

Evidence of one resultant outcome of the adoption of IASC standards would be a reduction in the diversity of accounting practice internationally. Emenyou and Gray (1996) examined the extent to which accounting measurement and associated disclosure practices of major companies in France, Germany, Japan, the UK, and the USA have become less diverse in the context of efforts made since the 1970s; that is, the period essentially since the formation of the IASC to reduce or eliminate differences in accounting policies and practices internationally. They found from their analysis of the financial reports of 293 companies that the impact of efforts to reduce international accounting diversity over the 20-year period from 1971–1972 to 1991–1992 has been quite modest. They reported that the average reduction in diversity was only 10.8 percent, and that of the 26 major accounting measurement issues they identified, the results showed that 14 reduced diversity and 12 increased diversity. Emenyou and Gray (1996) concluded that international harmonization remains a desirable but elusive objective.

In a study by Adams et al. (1993) of 17 Finnish companies listed on the London Stock Exchange for the period 1989–1991, an analysis of their corporate reports indicated major differences between Finnish accounting standards and IASs to the extent that there were significant quantitative differences relating to profit or loss and balance sheet equity. They also found that there was a lack of consistency in the presentation of statements reconciling Finnish accounting standards with IASs. Although Finnish companies produced supplementary financial statements in conformity with IASs, the study indicated that users would not be aware of many of the problems inherent in the adjustment process or the need to provide more specific descriptions of accounting policies used by them. Moreover, Gould (1995) reported that there are material differences between IASs and German regulatory requirements, and as such, it is unlikely that IASs would replace current German provisions. Although this may be the case, German legislation of 1998 provides for German listed enterprises to produce consolidated financial statements in compliance with either the German Commercial Code, US GAAP, or IASs (IASC, 1999).

The User's Perspective

In attempting to shed light on the user's perspective, Kenny and Larson (1993) investigated the role of lobbying in accounting standard setting and found that few firms lobbied the IASC. Of the 50 respondents to ED35, 15 were from industry or financial institutions, while the remaining 35 were from professional organizations and standard setting bodies. They speculated that the dearth of corporate respondents to

ED35 implied that multinational corporations did not see the IASC as a serious regulatory organization.

Nevertheless, Hopwood (1994) argued that although much is made of the functional nature of accounting reports and the needs of capital market users in setting accounting policy, he remarked that such users are rarely present. Hopwood (1994) reported that they are often referred to indirectly by representatives of the audit industry or capital market regulators who claim to articulate the needs, interests, and perspectives of the user community. Moreover, Hopwood (1994) disagreed that the process of international accounting harmonization is necessarily demand-driven by the needs of international business as there is little evidence supporting such a claim. No appeal, he emphasized, is made either to supportive empirical studies or to the views of the user community. The user perspective, Hopwood (1994) concluded, is taken to be one of such obviousness that it requires neither a physical manifestation nor an appeal to conventionally accepted evidential bases. If so, this suggests that the demand for IASC standards is not overwhelming. How this might impact the Australian proposal is of some concern.

The IASC and the Provision of an Override

The IASC's position, with respect to the use of an override, has changed. The IASC Board rejected in 1996 the use of an override stating (p. 4) that an "override would impair the ability of international investors to rely on the comparability of financial statements prepared in accordance with International Accounting Standards." The revised version of IAS 1 (IASC, 1997), however, now allows at paragraph 13 an override, "in the extremely rare circumstances when management concludes that compliance with a requirement in a standard would be misleading, and therefore that departure from a requirement is necessary to achieve a fair presentation . . . ." This provision stands in stark contrast with the current requirement under Australian Corporations Law that financial statements are to adhere to accounting standards approved by the AASB, without recourse to an override.

The prospect of the reintroduction of an override in Australia adds a degree of complexity to the IASC move. The Securities Institute of Australia argued in its submission to the Australian Government's Corporate Law Economic Reform Program that Australia should move towards US accounting standards, which it says are recognized as world's best practice (Bice, 1997). If US standards are the way forward as a means of enhancing international harmonization, then the adoption of standards consistent with those of the IASC may not be constructive. Furthermore, as the US SEC currently views IASs as being not sufficiently comprehensive in terms of coverage and quality (e.g., Hegarty, 1997; Sharpe, 1998), then linking Australian standards to those of the IASC may be fraught with difficulty.

Although Crofts (1998) argued that there are important differences between IASs and US GAAP, Gould (1995) reported that increased competition in the international securities markets may pressure the SEC into considering IASs as appropriate for US securities filings. The Chairman of the FASB objected to this, on the grounds that the US accounting and reporting system is the most sophisticated in the world (Gould, 1995). Importantly, the SEC has set three conditions, which will have to be met before considering to endorse IASs. These requirements are that a core set of standards have to be completed, those

Table 2. Financial Reporting in Transition

	EU	*USA*	*Australia*
Financial reporting focus	TFV; override; interpreted by individual member states	present fairly in accordance with GAAP	TFV; no override, though being lobbied
IASC standards	no link	no link	planned by middle of 1999; present fairly, override
Link to EU directives		no link	no link
Link to SEC requirements	no link		no link

standards have to be of high quality, and they will have to be rigorously interpreted and applied (Hegarty, 1997; Sutton, 1997; Sharpe, 1998). According to Gould (1995), the FASB chairman suggested that it would be inappropriate to require US registrants to comply with a strict system while allowing foreign registrants to follow one that is less strict. Sutton (1997) reported that the SEC provides a regulatory system based on the principle of full disclosure, supported by market oversight and enforcement. As such, he argued that investors have confidence in the integrity of US capital markets. Sending an implicit message, Sutton (1997) concluded from his perspective as Chief Accountant of the SEC that the tenets, which have proven successful in the US, will be equally so in the international capital market environment.

Table 2 provides a summary of the financial reporting focus, the use of IASC standards, the application EU Directives as well as SEC requirements in the context of the EU, the USA, and Australia. The table illustrates that there is little evidence of international harmonization in terms of either the TFV or presenting fairly, apart from the nature of the underlying standards used.

CONCLUSIONS

The analysis of the theoretical and empirical literature suggests the following. First, a reintroduction of the TFV override in Australia would be consistent with its role in the Fourth Directive as a fundamental principle of financial reporting. Second, harmonization with IASs by default will allow an override, as IAS 1 now provides for one. Third, Australia's harmonization of financial reporting requirements with the wider global community would confront a number of impediments because of inconsistencies between IASs, US GAAP, and EU Directives. Hence, the proposed reintroduction of the TFV override, together with IASC consistent reporting, is unlikely to enhance Australia's link to the wider world community, particularly if the move to US GAAP gains further momentum. As such, this could lead to potential negative consequences in both financial and product markets. Nevertheless, Hegarty (1997) argued that purely national regimes are not conducive to the internationalization of markets, since differences in approach give rise to barriers to trade and investment.

Based on Emenyou and Gray's (1996) results, moves to link Australian accounting standards to those of the IASC may be premature, since there is little evidence to suggest that this necessarily will improve international product and financial relations for companies reporting under Australian requirements. This does not mean that the Australian and IASC standards will be the same, as some IASs contain alternatives not considered appropriate to the Australian context (ICAA, 1998). Furthermore, it is difficult to envisage how such standards will interface effectively with the current TFV provision and the prospective one of presenting fairly, as required by IAS 1. The EU experience has shown that as the meaning of TFV differs between member states (Alexander, 1993; Burlaud, 1993), then its contribution to the consistency of financial reporting is far from clear. As Forker and Greenwood (1995) noted, reporting flexibility undermines the comparability of accounts. Moreover, if as Van Hulle (1993a) indicated that it is possible for annual accounts to be true and fair in one member state but not in another, then Australia's re-adoption of a TFV override or its introduction through IAS 1 can hardly facilitate Australia's contribution to effective global reporting consistency.

The evidence is quite clear that the flexibility allowed by a TFV override does not contribute to financial statement comparability. In terms of corporate oversight, the TFV requirement has been argued to be too vague to form the basis of legal action in the UK or Australia and as such, it is hard to consider how it would further Australia's interest through its reintroduction. As the literature has warned, inconsistencies facilitated through flexibility associated with the TFV in terms of the EU's accounting Directives or through IAS 1 may precipitate a greater move towards the adoption by capital market participants of US reporting standards. This is not a position that we necessarily advocate, but one that is receiving increasing support in the literature (e.g. Irvine, 1999; McGregor, 1999).

A grave concern arising from the reintroduction of an override either by way of a TFV override or one provided by way of IASs may potentially allow company directors to act opportunistically. Moreover, the introduction of IASC consistent standards will substitute the current position of uniformity of practice for flexibility of practice, reflecting compromises inherent in IASs. Those companies seeking to raise capital on international markets may be further motivated to adopt US GAAP.

The essential implications of Australia harmonizing its standards with those of the IASC are as follows. For internal purposes, Australian reporting companies will incur transaction costs in adapting to IASC harmonized standards, together with the need to explain to domestic and international investors the nature and the effect of those changes. The major impact will be felt by companies continuing or contemplating external listings. IASs are not generally accepted in the EU nor are they accepted in the US. Hence, there is little incentive, other than regulatory, to adopt IASs. Anecdotal evidence suggests that recent capital raisings by Australian companies have not been impeded by non-harmonized standards. This implies that overseas investors are comfortable with the current Australian regulatory reporting system. If so, then the undue haste to harmonize with IASC standards is of some concern. The incremental benefits of this approach have not been demonstrated.

Acknowledgments: Thanks are due to David Alexander, Harry Fechner, Jane Godfrey, Sharron Leahy, Janice Loftus, Chris Nobes, and other participants at presentations at the University of Western Sydney, Nepean, the 1998 Annual Congress of the European Accounting Association, and the 1998 International Accounting Education and Research/Center for International Education and Research in Accounting Conference. The helpful comments of the two anonymous reviewers are also acknowledged.

NOTE

1. However, as emphasized by one reviewer, harmonization of regulation does not necessarily imply harmonization of practices.

REFERENCES

Adams, C.A., P. Weetman, and S.J. Gray. 1993. "Reconciling National with International Accounting Standards." *European Accounting Review, 2*(3): 471–494.

Alexander, D. 1993. "A European True and Fair View?" *European Accounting Review, 2*(1): 59–80.

Alexander, D. 1996. "Truer and Fairer. Uninvited Comments on Invited Comments." *European Accounting Review, 5*(3): 483–493.

Annual Report. 1996. Washington H. Soul Pattinson.

Batt, M.C. 1998. "European Accounting Harmonization." *Accountancy, 121*(125b): 70–71.

Bice, K. 1997. "Review Rekindles Debate Over Accounting Standards." *Australian Financial Review,* (May 22): 11.

Burlaud, A. 1993. "Commentary on the Article by David Alexander "A European True and Fair View?"" *European Accounting Review, 2*(1): 95–98.

Cairns, D. 1997. "The Future Shape of Harmonization: A Reply." *European Accounting Review, 6*(2): 305–348.

Cairns, D. 1998. "Europe and IOSCO at the Forefront." *FT World Accounting Report,* (April): 6–7.

Carsberg, B. 1998. "Future Directions of Financial Reporting." In *Performance Measurement in the Digital Age*, pp. 31–40.

Crofts, L. 1998. "Bridging the GAAP: 1." *Accountancy, 121*(125b): 128–129.

Deegan, C., P. Kent, and C.J. Lin. 1994. "The True and Fair View: A Study of Australian Auditors' Application of the Concept." *Australian Accounting Review, 4*(1): 2–12.

Emenyou, E.N. and S.J. Gray. 1996. "International Accounting Harmonization and the Major Developed Stock Market Countries: An Empirical Study." *International Journal of Accounting, 31*(3): 269–279.

Fédération des Experts-comptables de la CEE. 1992. *Analysis of European Accounting and Disclosure Practices*. 1997. London: Routledge.

Flower, J. 1997. "The Future Shape of Harmonization: The EU versus the IASC versus the SEC." *European Accounting Review, 6*(2): 281–303.

Forker, J. and M. Greenwood. 1995. "European Harmonization and the True and Fair View: The Case of Long-Term Contracts in the UK." *European Accounting Review, 4*(1): 1–31.

Gearin, M. and S. Khandelwal. 1995. "A True and Fair View or Mandatory Standard?" *Australian Accountant, 65*(5): 12–16.

Gould, J.D. 1995. "A Second Opinion on International Accounting Standards." *CPA Journal, 65*(1): 50–52.

Hegarty, J. 1997. "Accounting for the Global Economy: Is National Regulation Deemed to Disappear?" *Accounting Horizons, 11*(4): 75–90.

Higson, A. and J. Blake. 1993. "The True and Fair View Concept—A Formula for International Disharmony: Some Empirical Evidence." *International Journal of Accounting, 28*: 104–115.

Hopwood, A.G. 1994. "Some Reflections on "The Harmonization of Accounting within the EU." " *European Accounting Review, 3*(2): 241–253.

Houghton, K.A. 1987. "True and Fair View: An Empirical Study of Connotative Meaning." *Accounting, Organizations and Society, 12*(2): 143–152.

Institute of Chartered Accountants in Australia (ICAA). 1998. *Major Changes and New Directives in Accounting and Auditing*. Institute of Chartered Accountants in Australia: Sydney.

International Accounting Standards Committee (IASC). 1996. *Presentation of Financial Statements: Exposure Draft E53*. IASC: London.

International Accounting Standards Committee (IASC). 1997. *International Accounting Standard IAS 1* (July).

International Accounting Standards Committee (IASC). 1999. "Farewell Commercial Code Accounting." *IASC Insight,* (March).

Irvine, J. 1999. "IAS in Europe: Too Much or Too Little?" *Accountancy International, 123*(1267): 21.

Kenny, S.V. and R.K. Larson. 1993. "Lobbying Behaviour and the Development of International Accounting Standards." *European Accounting Review, 2*(3): 531–554.

McGregor, W. 1992. "True and Fair—An Accounting Anachronism." *Australian Accountant, 62*(1): 68–71.

McGregor, W. 1999. "An Insider's View of the Current State and Future Direction of International Accounting Standard Setting." *Accounting Horizons, 13*(2): 159–168.

Nobes, C. 1993. "The True and Fair View Requirement: Impact on and of the Fourth Directive." *Accounting and Business Research, 24*(93): 35–48.

Nobes, C.W. and R.H. Parker. 1991. "True and Fair: A Survey of UK Financial Directors." *Journal of Business Finance and Accounting, 18*(3): 359–375.

Ordelheide, D. 1993. "True and Fair View: A European and a German Perspective." *European Accounting Review, 2*(1): 81–90.

Ordelheide, D. 1996. "True and Fair View: A European and a German Perspective II." *European Accounting Review, 5*(3): 495–506.

Peirson, G. and P. McBride. 1997. "More on International Harmonization in Australia." *CPA Communique, 75*: 1–4.

Ravlic, T. 1998. "Harmonization: Worth the Pain?" *Australian CPA, 68*(8): 47–48.

Rutherford, B.A. 1985. "The True and Fair View Doctrine: A Search for Explication." *Journal of Business Finance and Accounting, 12*(4): 483–494.

Sharpe, M. 1998. "Looking for Harmony: Building a Global Framework." *Australian Accountant, 68*(2): 16–18.

Spencer, K. 1998. "The View from the AASB: Take it Easy, Get it Right." *Australian Accountant, 68*(2): 20–21.

Stewart, I.C. 1988. "The Explication of the True and Fair View Doctrine: A Comment." *Journal of Business Finance and Accounting, 15*(1): 115–123.

Sucher, P., W. Seal, and I. Zelenka. 1996. "True and Fair in the Czech Republic: A Note on Local Perceptions." *European Accounting Review, 5*(3): 545–557.

Sutton, M.H. 1997. "Financial Reporting in U.S. Capital Markets: International Dimensions." *Accounting Horizons, 11*(2): 96–102.

Thorell, P. and G. Whittington. 1994. "The Harmonization of Accounting within the EU: Problems, Perspectives and Strategies." *European Accounting Review, 3*(2): 215–239.

Van Hulle, K. 1993a. "Truth and Untruth about True and Fair: A Commentary on "A European True and Fair View" Comment." *European Accounting Review, 2*(1): 99–104.

Van Hulle, K. 1993b. "Harmonization of Accounting Standards in the EC: Is it the Beginning or is it the End?" *European Accounting Review, 2*(2): 387–396.

Van Hulle, K. 1997. "The True and Fair View Override in the European Accounting Directives." *European Accounting Review, 6*(4): 711–720.

Walton, P. 1993. "Introduction: The True and Fair View in British Accounting." *European Accounting Review, 2*(1): 49–58.

Weetman, P., A.E. Jones, C.A. Adams, and S.J. Gray. 1998. "Profit Measurement and UK Accounting Standards: A Case of Increasing Disharmony in Relation to US GAAP and IASs." *Accounting and Business Research, 28*(1): 189–208.

Zeff, S.A. 1993. "International Accounting Principles and Auditing Standards." *European Accounting Review, 2*(2): 403–410.

[19]

© 2001 American Accounting Association
Accounting Horizons
Vol. 15 No. 2
June 2001
pp. 171–182

COMMENTARY

International Harmonization: Cautions from the Australian Experience

Peter H. Collett, Jayne M. Godfrey, and Sue L. Hrasky

Peter H. Collett is a Lecturer, Jayne M. Godfrey is a Professor, and Sue L. Hrasky is a Lecturer, all at the University of Tasmania.

SYNOPSIS: Global harmonization of accounting is a challenging and controversial issue currently confronting accounting standard setters and market regulators internationally. To date, Australia is further along in its international harmonization program than any other country with an established standard-setting regime. While no country's national standard-setting arrangements are likely to be subject to political pressures identical to those recently exerted in Australia, there are lessons to be learned from the Australian events. Given the political nature of standard setting, it is not surprising that the Australian experience indicates that pushes for harmonization are not necessarily what they seem. This paper describes the Australian experience and identifies some of the political drivers of recent standard-setting reform initiatives. It demonstrates how the rhetoric of harmonization can divert attention from politically motivated changes to the fundamental basis of standard setting. Using the harmonization banner to garner support in principle, parties with vested interests can push regulatory agendas that potentially subrogate user needs.

INTRODUCTION

Global harmonization of accounting is arguably the most challenging and controversial issue currently confronting accounting standard setters and market regulators. Recent discussions focus on experience from North America, the United Kingdom, and continental Europe (for example, Hegarty 1997; Sutton 1997; Zarzeski 1996; Bayless et al. 1996). However, a past chair of the International Accounting Standards Committee (IASC) and the immediate past chair of the Australian Accounting Standards Board (AASB) both argued that Australia has progressed further in its international harmonization program than any other country with an established standard-setting regime (Sharpe 1998, 18; Spencer 1998, 20). It is likely, therefore, that other national accounting regulators, particularly those in countries with rigorous accounting standards and strong regulatory enforcement, can benefit from an understanding of Australia's harmonization experience.

Editor's Note: During 1995 to 1999, Professor Jayne Godfrey was a member of the Australian Accounting Standards Board (AASB). The views expressed in this paper are the personal views of the authors and do not necessarily reflect those of the AASB.

The extent to which embracing harmonization is allowed to impact on domestic standard-setting arrangements needs to be considered carefully by countries that have been at the forefront of standard setting. Australia is one of these countries, having played an active and influential role in international accounting development since the concept of an International Accounting Standards Committee was developed in Sydney, Australia, at the 1972 World Accounting Congress. Australia is represented on the IASC with full voting rights, and two Australian representatives served as chair of the Committee. International links are also maintained through the AASB's membership of the G4+1, a body comprised of the national standard setters from the U.S., Canada, U.K., Australia, and New Zealand plus the IASC. The immediate past chair of the AASB also chaired the G4+1. While the G4+1 never enjoyed legal status, it has been influential in the development of an integrated approach to standard setting across its member countries and the IASC.[1]

As in many countries, Australian regulators debate the merits of international harmonization of accounting standards. Not surprisingly, given the political nature of standard setting, Australian experience to date indicates that pushes for harmonization are not necessarily what they seem. This paper describes the Australian experience, and reveals some of the political drivers of recent standard-setting reform initiatives. This experience demonstrates how the rhetoric of harmonization is used to divert attention from other politically motivated changes to the fundamental basis of standard setting.

AUSTRALIAN ACCOUNTING STANDARD SETTING

Introduction of Mandatory Accounting Standards

Since the early 1980s, standard setting in Australia has been controversial in terms of the institutional standard-setting arrangements in place and the regulations introduced by the standard-setting bodies. Prior to 1984, standards were developed by the Australian Accounting Research Foundation (AARF) on behalf of Australia's two professional accounting bodies, the Australian Society of Accountants (later the Australian Society of CPAs or ASCPA, and now CPA Australia) and The Institute of Chartered Accountants In Australia (ICAA). These two bodies funded the AARF and were able to influence the standards with which their members were directed to comply. The AARF standards had no legal status, though, and noncompliance was common.

During the early 1980s, pressures mounted for accounting standards with legislated penalties for noncompliance. To some extent, this pressure was exerted by the professional bodies that sought enforceability of their standards, and the credibility that ensues from legislative backing. Pressure also arose from public concerns about the quality of financial reporting during the corporate excesses and collapses of the late 1970s and early 1980s. The apparent regulation of the profession, by the profession, and for the profession, was viewed as inadequate and ineffective. As Watts and Zimmerman (1986) describe it, the business environment provided a "crisis" that politicians could claim to resolve through accounting regulation.

[1] Despite the fact that the interactions of the members of the G4+1 facilitate it, the G4+1 does not have a stated objective to develop an integrated approach to standard setting across its member countries and the IASC. For a comprehensive description and explanation of the evolution of the G4+1 and an understanding of its current activities and of its future in international accounting, see Beresford (2000).

In January 1984, the Australian government established the Accounting Standards Review Board (ASRB). The ASRB reviewed and endorsed accounting standards developed by AARF and gave them legislative status. The ASRB was funded by government, and took its directives from, and was accountable to, the federal Attorney General's Department. Comprising both members of the accounting profession and members who were not professional accountants, the ASRB was intended to be independent of the profession. But early on, the ASRB recognized that the accounting bodies retained primary responsibility for developing the accounting standards that they approved (ASRB Release 100 [ASRB 1985]), and only one approved standard ever emerged from a source other than the profession.[2]

In the meantime, the Accounting Standards Board (AcSB) of the two professional bodies issued accounting standards on behalf of the profession but without legislative backing and enforcement. The AcSB put these standards to the ASRB for approval. Although preferring self-regulation, the profession determined that this was not feasible in the environment at the time. For standards to be generally accepted and politically viable, they needed to be set by the democratic processes of a representative body (Hines 1983, 25).

Demise of the ASRB

The ASRB lasted only one full term before political pressures led to its replacement. These pressures emanated partly from the profession that became increasingly disenchanted with the structure of the ASRB, and regretted its loss of control over the standard-setting process and outcomes. Differences between decisions on key accounting issues made by the profession's own AcSB and Public Sector Accounting Standards Board (PSASB) on the one hand, and the ASRB on the other, created a rift between the profession and the ASRB. For example, in 1987 the ASRB reversed foreign currency accounting rules issued by the profession.[3] Ironically, pressures on the ASRB also arose at this time from a perceived capture of the ASRB's processes by the profession (Walker 1987).

Currently, standards in Australia are developed by the Australian Accounting Standards Board (AASB), established in 1989 under the Australian Securities Commission Act, replacing the ASRB. Decisions made by the AASB caused controversy on a number of occasions.

The ASRB: Controversy and Criticism

In March 1992, Statement of Accounting Concepts 4, *Definition and Recognition of the Elements of Financial Statements* (SAC4) (AASB 1992b), became the most controversial promulgation by a standard-setting body in Australia's history. After harsh criticism

---

[2] The requirements of ASRB 1003, *Foreign Currency Translation—Disclosure*, which came into effect in 1985, were developed by the National Companies and Securities Commission (NCSC). The NCSC was the chief corporate regulatory body at that time. This standard was subsequently replaced by ASRB 1012 (ASRB 1987), *Foreign Currency Translation*, developed by AARF.

[3] The AcSB and the PSASB preferred to defer and amortize unrealized foreign currency gains and losses; the ASRB required immediate recognition of those gains and losses. The outcome of discussions between the two standard-setting bodies in 1987 is that immediate recognition is now required. This contrasts with the requirements to defer and amortize introduced by the profession in 1985 when it controlled the standard-setting process. In 1988 the ASRB and the AcSB merged, and the ASRB issued both the legislatively backed standards and the professional standards that did not have the force of law. The two sets of standards became identical in their content.

and intensive lobbying by corporate Australia, the mandatory status of SAC4 was withdrawn. SAC4 was subsequently revised and reissued in May 1995. It remains nonmandatory. The revised SAC4 is less specific and less controversial than its predecessor. The most influential lobbyist in the process was the G100, a group of chief financial officers of approximately 100 of the largest companies in Australia.[4]

A more recent decision of the AASB resulted in an unprecedented development. In February 2000 the Australian Senate disallowed two paragraphs of a standard passed on to it by the AASB for endorsement. The disallowed paragraphs formed part of Accounting Standard AASB 1015, *Acquisition of Assets*, issued by the AASB in November 1999. The effect of the disallowance is that for reconstructions within an economic entity, exchanges cannot be valued at their carrying amounts, an option permitted under the disallowed paragraphs. Instead, the purchase method of accounting for such exchanges is now obligatory.

Outcomes of the type described above, along with the associated political debates, erode both the standing of AARF as the research support to the AASB and, to some degree, the AASB itself. Other factors combined to render Australian standard-setting institutional arrangements vulnerable to reform proposals:

- Business perceptions that the Australian accounting standard-setting approach is too academic and insufficiently business oriented. For example, in a direct jibe at the AASB and AARF, the Chair of the Australian Stock Exchange (ASX) commented that there was no future in Australia being an island of accounting purity (Wood 1996).
- A review of AARF in 1995, commissioned by the profession, found that AARF was under-resourced and was not in a position to adequately support the current standard-setting arrangements. Since that review the AARF staff profile further declined due to resignations, most significantly at senior levels, and morale is low. This culminated in the April 1999 resignation of AARF's executive director.

Corporate Law Economic Reform Program

Coinciding with this climate of disquiet about standard setting in Australia, the Australian government undertook a major campaign to reform institutional arrangements affecting business. The first set of proposals produced by the Corporate Law Economic Reform Program (CLERP) in 1997 related to accounting standard setting.[5] Far-reaching changes to the institutional arrangements for standard setting in Australia were proposed and were subsequently enacted in legislation.[6]

Under this legislation, the Financial Reporting Council (FRC) was established to provide broad oversight of the standard-setting process in Australia. It appoints the members of a reconstituted AASB (apart from the Chairman who is appointed directly by the federal Treasurer), and it is required to give direction to the AASB on matters of general policy and procedures. While the FRC was not given the power to direct the

[4] The G100 continues to play a dominant role in the direction of standard setting in Australia. For example, it commissioned a report on measurement that promotes modified historical cost accounting, the measurement method preferred by some of the most influential G100 members.

[5] Corporate Law Economic Reform Program Proposals for Reform Paper No. 1, *Accounting Standards: Building International Opportunities for Australian Business* (Commonwealth of Australia 1997).

[6] Corporate Law Economic Reform Program Act 1999 which, among other initiatives, repealed Part 12—Accounting Standards, Australian Securities and Investment Commission Act 1989.

AASB in the development of particular standards or to veto a standard recommended by the AASB, it has the potential to exert a powerful influence over standard setting in Australia. For example, its functions include monitoring the AASB's priorities, the effectiveness of the AASB's consultative mechanisms, and the general relevance and effectiveness of accounting standards.[7]

The implications of these reforms for Australia and its approach to the international harmonization of accounting standards are likely to be profound. As explained in "Recent Reforms in Australia" below, the reform program provided a platform for lobbyists to strongly push an international harmonization agenda, and the legislation emanating from CLERP does promote the development of a single set of accounting standards for worldwide use. This represents a significant change to the approach to harmonization taken for some years by the AASB. The AASB approach is explained in the following section.

AASB APPROACH TO INTERNATIONAL HARMONIZATION

The AASB originally adopted an approach to harmonization based on a "philosophy of internationalisation" (AASB 1994, 23). This involved examining the pronouncements of the IASC, New Zealand, the U.S., the U.K., Canada, and South Africa before issuing exposure drafts of proposed Australian accounting standards. The objective was to ensure that Australian standards reflected and required best international practice. There were very few instances where Australian requirements differed from the position taken by these other jurisdictions (AASB 1994, 23). Where an IAS existed, the Australian standard included a statement of "Compatibility with International Accounting Standards" that indicated whether the requirements of the Australian standard were consistent with those of the IAS. In the few cases of inconsistencies, this statement explained the inconsistency and indicated what was required under the relevant IAS.

Since 1996, the AASB adopted a stronger policy of international harmonization whereby compliance with Australian accounting standards ensures compliance with IASs promulgated by the IASC unless there are sound reasons why compliance is inappropriate within the Australian institutional setting. Hence, it is envisioned that entities reporting under Australian accounting standards will also meet the requirements of those jurisdictions where reporting under IASs is permitted. This does not mean that Australian requirements are identical to those of IASs. Compliance with IASs does not necessarily ensure compliance with Australian standards. IASs often allow more accounting method choices than do the corresponding Australian standards.

The harmonization program involves the AASB in reviewing existing and draft standards to ensure consistency with IASs, and the AASB provides input, via submissions, to the development of IASs. Australia benefited from a re-examination of several of its older and less rigorous standards during the harmonization process. For example, a review of the depreciation accounting standard ensured more consistent treatments of tangible and intangible assets. Also, the accounting for borrowing costs is now subject to regulation.

[7] Section 225, Australian Securities and Investment Commission Act.

Rationale for this Approach to Harmonization

The AASB embarked on its harmonization program because it expected a number of benefits to flow from reducing diversity in international accounting practice, most notably:

- increased comparability of financial statements internationally, encouraging the flow of international investment;
- decreased cost of capital due to removal or reductions in premiums associated with the risk of not fully understanding the financial report of an entity reporting under a different accounting regime; and
- lower reporting costs achieved by obviating the need for an entity to produce two or more sets of financial reports to satisfy differing sets of standards, listing rules or other regulations (AASB 1994, 11).

By reviewing international developments and incorporating international best practice, the AASB ensures that Australian standards are compatible with those of the IASC and informed by the global public interest. In those jurisdictions where the use of IASs is accepted, reports produced using Australian standards should be both comparable and understandable. This result is achieved without businesses incurring the cost of restating or reconciling items, or producing an additional set of reports to satisfy different accounting rules.

However, in pursuing harmonization, the AASB follows the philosophy that high-quality financial reporting is fundamental to the efficient operation of capital markets, both locally and globally. It has not sought international comparability when the quality of Australian accounting standards is compromised (AASB 1994, 1), and it rejected outright adoption of IASs as a replacement for domestic standards.

There are persuasive arguments to support the position taken by the AASB.

International Differences

Diversity in reporting regimes results from an evolutionary process that reflects each jurisdiction's cultural, political, legal, and economic differences (Hegarty 1997, 75; Zarzeski 1996, 35). The AASB recognizes that legitimate differences cause accounting standards to develop differently between countries:

- differences in concentrations of ownership create differing degrees of reliance on general-purpose financial reports. Standards tend to be more highly developed in jurisdictions where ownership is less concentrated;
- variation in the optimal debt-to-equity ratio across countries results in differing preferences for the mix of information provided; and
- alternative legal structures and legal systems impacts accounting standards (AASB 1994).

International accounting standards are not necessarily to be preferred over their national counterparts. In some cases they are unsuitable for the particular national environment. Fundamentally different institutional environments require that some differences in standards between countries remain, and any country that adopts nondomestic standards *carte blanche* must worry about whether the users of reports will be serviced less well than at present.

Universal International Adoption

A major benefit claimed for harmonization is that enhanced comparability between the reports of different jurisdictions will facilitate investment flows in international markets and enhance the operating efficiency of international markets. However, there presently are relatively few entities following these standards (Spencer 1998, 20). As of 1998, only eight countries had adopted IASs in their entirety;[8] none of those are significant in terms of world market capitalization.

The Commission of the European Communities intends to require all listed EU companies to prepare consolidated accounts using IASs, beginning no later than 2005. However, it acknowledges that IASs could be inappropriate and possibly invalid for the preparation of individual accounts, given various national regulatory and taxation requirements. Furthermore, the EU sees the need for an endorsement mechanism to exercise oversight of the IASs, so that only endorsed standards could be used (Commission of the European Communities 2000).

In May 2000, IOSCO completed its assessment of IASs and recommended that its members allow incoming multinational users to use 30 IASs for cross-border listings and offerings. It noted, however, that "supplemental treatments" may be necessary "to address outstanding issues at a national or regional level" (IOSCO 2000).

Importantly, national regulators in countries with major capital markets, including the U.S., the U.K., and Japan,[9] are not prepared to accept IASs as replacements for their own standards, nor are they prepared to base their national accounting standards on IASs (Sutton 1997). This undermines the argument that individual countries should adopt IASs because the IASC core set of standards will be acceptable to each major national constituency.

Some evidence suggests that it is unnecessary to have international conformity between standards anyway. For example, Lev and Sougianis (1996) report that U.S. investors react to reported research and development (R&D) expenditure *as if* it is capitalized as required by national jurisdictions such as Australia and allowed under IASs. Investors did not respond to reported earnings as if the R&D was expensed, despite the requirement in the U.S. to treat it that way.

Rigor of Standards

A major concern with IASs is that in the past they often emerged from a process of much greater compromise than that required for national standard setting (AASB 1994, 15). IASs are designed to provide guidance in jurisdictions with differing accounting frameworks; some jurisdictions are taxation-based and others have conceptual frameworks in place. With such diverse jurisdictions, the IASC approach traditionally was not tailored to nations with strong standard-setting arrangements already in place, such as the G4+1 countries. If IASs were adopted for domestic use in these nations, the quality of domestic financial reporting could decline. This concern was expressed by Jim Leisenring, the vice-chairman of the FASB and U.S. observer on the IASC in 1996, who commented that:

> the compromise necessary to reach an agreement on an international standard often leads to some purposeful ambiguity. That ambiguity brings about very wide latitude in the application of the standards. (Bayless et al. 1996, 15)

This view is consistent with Hegarty's (1997, 88) suggestion that international standards at best provide "a safety net of common minimum standards," and with the

---

[8] These countries are Croatia, Cyprus, Latvia, Malta, Oman, Pakistan, Trinidad, and Tobago.

[9] These three countries currently account for approximately 74 percent of world market capitalization.

following statement made by the chairman of the Australian Securities Commission, Alan Cameron:

> IASC standards are generally more permissive and less comprehensive than are domestic standards in Australia and other major economies. Work being done by the IASC towards improving the quality of its standards should be encouraged. But, ultimately IASC standards will always be the result of a complex set of compromises between numerous jurisdictions, and may never be aimed specifically at Australia's needs and circumstances. (Spencer 1998, 21)

It is possible that these concerns about the quality of IASs may need to be modified in the future. The IASC was recently restructured and has a new mandate to develop a set of high-quality, understandable, and enforceable global accounting standards. It remains to be seen whether the constraints and difficulties that impeded the development of IASs to date can be overcome.

RECENT REFORMS IN AUSTRALIA

CLERP and the Move toward IAS Adoption

If one accepts the arguments presented above, it is not appropriate for a country with its own rigorous and comprehensive standards that already reflect a global perspective to replace those standards with IASs. Although this is the exact position taken to date by the AASB, and despite the compelling reasons for maintaining this approach, recent developments in Australia suggest this position is seriously threatened.

As explained in the "Australian Accounting Standard Setting" section, the Corporate Law Economic Reform Program (CLERP) produced legislation with far-reaching implications for standard setting in Australia. Sections of this legislation affect the approach taken to international harmonization in the future. While the legislation does fall short of requiring immediate and outright adoption of IASs by Australia, it represents a significant shift from the AASB's position at the time. For example, it requires the AASB to participate in and contribute to the development of a single set of accounting standards for worldwide use.[10]

It is worth noting that the original CLERP Paper No. 1, which was the basis for this legislation, conceded that IASs in 1997 were not "of a quality and level of international acceptance whereby Australia can simply adopt them" (Commonwealth of Australia 1997, 24). Nevertheless, it anticipated that the "Australian standard setting body should adopt IASC standards from 1 January 1999..." (Commonwealth of Australia 1997, 26). The fact that this timetable was not met does not negate the intention of the original Paper or the resulting legislation: Australia is to work toward replacing its own accounting standards with a set of internationally recognized standards. The legislation also ensures that the harmonization policy that it embodies cannot be thwarted by the AASB, requiring that body to comply with any direction given to it by the Minister about the role of IASs.[11]

Opposition to the Adoption of IASs

It is illuminating to consider how the departure from the position taken to date by the AASB came into effect. The case for reform appears totally based on selected

[10] Section 227 (1) (d), Australian Securities and Investment Commission Act.

[11] Section 233, Australian Securities and Investment Commission Act.

anecdotal evidence (Collett et al. 1998). For example, the CLERP Paper explains that the push for reform emanates from "criticisms made to the Government from time to time" (Commonwealth of Australia 1997, 11). While anecdotal evidence can be a useful instigator of change, researchers are familiar with its limitations

Not only is there no compelling argument for the reform proposals, but also a variety of interested parties are united in their opposition to adopting IASs. The G100, representing corporate Australia, did initially argue strongly for international harmonization of Australian accounting standards, providing much of the impetus for the reform program. However, its position changed due to dissatisfaction with some recent IASC standards thought to impose heavier burdens on preparers of accounts than the corresponding Australian accounting standards.[12]

Opposition also came from the Big 5 accounting firms, the professional accounting bodies, and the major banks; all presented submissions cautioning against premature adoption of IASs, and supporting the current harmonization policy of the AASB. If the benefits claimed to flow to business from outright adoption of IASs were real and achievable, then adoption would have presumably attracted and retained the overwhelming support of Australian businesses.

The Australian Securities and Investment Commission (ASIC), responsible for corporate regulation in Australia, highlighted in its submission the potential loss of quality in accounting standards flowing from a hasty adoption of IASs. Taking the same view was the Accounting Association of Australia and New Zealand, the premier body of Australian and New Zealand accounting academics. In the U.S., the FASB stated that it regarded the CLERP proposals as a backward step, and the U.K. Accounting Standards Board cautioned against early adoption.

The reasons these groups give for opposing the adoption of IASs in Australia are not necessarily consistent. Although some groups anticipate a reduction in the quality of standards, another group's concerns are that at least some IASs impose a greater burden on businesses than do their Australian counterparts. Nevertheless, widespread opposition to the proposal does exist. It is worth noting that one important group failed to make any contribution to the debate—accounting-report users. The user group is relatively ineffectual in Australia. Not one user-group representative lodged a written submission on the CLERP proposals.[13]

The Reforms Proceed: The Role of the ASX

Given the concerted opposition to the reform proposals, and the absence of a systematic case for reform, one wonders why they were legislated anyway, albeit in modified form. Horngren's (1973, 61) comment that "the setting of accounting standards is as much a product of political action as of flawless logic or empirical findings" is pertinent. It is important to understand where the real impetus for the radical changes suggested in the CLERP proposals originated. If corporate Australia, users, preparers, the accounting profession, and key regulators were not driving the CLERP reforms, then who, or what, was the force behind these radical proposals?

---

[12] Most notable among the standards that Australian business argues will impose costs upon them are IAS No. 12, *Income Taxes*; IAS No. 17, *Leases*; IAS No. 38, *Intangible Assets;* and IAS No. 39, *Financial Instruments: Recognition and Measurement*.

[13] This failure to lobby should be viewed in the context of a geographically dispersed group of users with varying needs for financial statement information. Coalition costs can be prohibitive to a representative body seeking to present a single view (Watts and Zimmerman 1986).

Collett et al. (1998) identify revealing comments by the then chair of the AASB:

> (t)he Australian Stock Exchange would prefer that Australian companies could prepare financial statements in accordance with IASC standards rather than Australian standards. Unless this is permitted, the Exchange perceives that Australian companies may decide to list on other exchanges which permit IASC's standards to be the basis for financial reports rather than maintaining their Australian listing.

The ASX is actively involved in the harmonization debate. Eighty-seven percent of respondents to an ASX survey favored a form of international harmonization allowing companies complying with Australian accounting standards to also comply with IASs, a position consistent with AASB policy to date. Although the majority of respondents did not support outright adoption of IASs, the ASX used the survey support to advocate its own harmonization agenda.

In a related move, the ASX used a levy imposed on listed companies to fund the current international harmonization program. The arrangement ceased in 1999. It placed the ASX in a powerful position since the ASX paid the funding in discrete allocations to the AARF, contingent upon the AASB meeting targets in the harmonization process. The ASX was instrumental in setting these targets and deciding whether the funding was to be withheld. On one occasion, the funding was paid only after some debate about whether the six-monthly targets were achieved.

It appears that the main impetus for the changes comes from the ASX. Indeed, the ASX was the only organization other than the IASC to make a written submission supporting the immediate adoption of IASs. At the time, the ASX planned to float as a public company. Through standard-setting reforms that reduce reporting requirements, it is likely that the ASX sought to facilitate offshore listings. Increased listings and easier access to offshore capital would boost the value of the Exchange and the success of the initial public offering.

Implications of the Reform Proposals

The potential implications of the new legislation are profound in terms of investor protection and the international reputation and effectiveness of Australian standard setters. One key concern with the legislation is the apparent movement away from investor protection as a primary purpose of accounting regulation. The view that international harmonization may have this consequence was expressed in a recent AAA forum (Bayless et al. 1996). The original CLERP proposals, and to a lesser extent the later legislation, reveal a definite and deliberate movement away from an emphasis on the interests of financial information users to an emphasis on broader macro-economic objectives. In particular, there is an emphasis on ensuring that accounting standards make Australian firms more competitive, for example, by lowering their cost of capital. In Reform Proposal No. 2 the subordination of user needs in favor of benefits to corporate business was made explicit:

> (t)he *ultimate objective* for the setting of accounting standards in Australia should be the production of high quality accounting standards *that facilitate Australian business* by leading to lower costs of capital and enabling Australian companies to compete on an equal footing overseas, while also maintaining investor confidence. (Commonwealth of Australia 1997, 1) (emphasis added).

In the legislation that followed, the substance of this objective is retained, but it is not given explicit primacy over user needs. User needs are still recognized as important in the development of accounting standards, but there is no clear statement that user needs dominate business needs. The original CLERP Paper reflects an entrenched business bias. It states that preparers of reports should interpret accounting standards from a "commercial perspective." Although the phraseology has changed, the door is open for commercial objectives to dominate the development of accounting standards relative to users' interests.

Another risk that any major standard-setting country faces by prematurely and mechanically adopting international accounting standards is the risk of diminishing its reputation and effectiveness in the international accounting arena. This is also likely to be associated with an erosion of technical support for, and expertise in, the standard-setting process, which must further diminish innovation and effectiveness. In Australia, after key personnel resigned from AARF, technical support is provided largely by short-term contract staff hired for specific projects. Uncertainty surrounding developments in the standard-setting process was cited as the reason (McGregor 1999).

Australian standard setters have been leaders in the development of international accounting initiatives. For example, the concept of "control" given precedence by Australian regulators in AASB 1024, *Consolidated Accounts* (1992a) now prevails over "ownership" in what is considered best practice accounting for consolidated statements internationally, including within the U.S.[14] Moreover, despite the fact that IASC Board members are to be appointed as individuals in their own right rather than as national delegates after the IASC re-structuring, the ability of a member from Australia to influence an IAS project might be reduced once it becomes apparent that Australia intends to automatically adopt IASs regardless of their content.

CONCLUSIONS: LESSONS AND WARNINGS

Running under the harmonization banner to garner support in principle, one particular party with a vested interest managed to push the Australian regulatory agenda, and subrogate the primacy of user needs in accounting standard setting. Legislation now contains what will be the first legislated recognition of business needs as a key objective of standard setting.

No country's national standard-setting arrangements are likely to be subject to pressures identical to those recently experienced in Australia. However, the globalization of accounting and the worldwide attention currently focused upon international harmonization mean that there are pertinent generalizations to be drawn from the Australian experience. Certain questions must be asked about reform initiatives in any country. For example, are the stated objectives legitimate or is there an alternative agenda? Will the reforms, if implemented, represent a backward step in relation to the nation's current standard-setting objectives and in relation to standard setting globally? Although the reform rhetoric may be couched in terms of objectives of global harmonization and benefits to domestic entities, the reality may be that this rhetoric diverts attention from the interests being advanced by politically influential parties.

---

[14] At the time of this writing, the FASB has an exposure draft favoring effective control over legal ownership in determining when to prepare consolidated statements. However, a final statement has not yet been issued.

REFERENCES

Accounting Standards Review Board (ASRB). 1985. *Criteria for the Evaluation of Accounting Standards*. Release 100. Caulfield, Victoria: ASRB.

———. 1987. *Foreign Currency Translation*. ASRB 1012. Town, Province: Publisher/Publishing Body.

Australian Accounting Standards Board (AASB). 1992a. *Consolidated Accounts*. AASB 1024. Caulfield, Victoria: AASB.

———. 1992b. *Definition and Recognition of the Elements of Financial Statements*. Statement of Accounting Concepts 4. Caulfield, Victoria: AASB.

———. 1994. *Towards International Comparability of Financial Reporting*. Caulfield, Victoria: AASB.

Bayless, R., J. Cockrane, T. Harris, J. Leisenring, J. McLaughin, and J. P. Wirtz. 1996. International access to U.S. capital markets—An AAA forum on accounting policy. *Accounting Horizons* (10): 75–94.

Beresford, D. R. 2000. A newcomer on the international scene. *The CPA Journal*. Available at http://www.nysscpa.org/cpajournal/2000/0300/f14300a.htm.

Collett, P., J. Godfrey, and S. Hrasky. 1998. Standard-setting in Australia: Implications of recent radical reform proposals. *Australian Accounting Review* (8): 9–17.

Commission of the European Communities. 2000. *EU Financial Reporting Strategy: The Way Forward*. Communication from the Commission to the Council and the European Parliament. June. Brussels, Belgium: Commission of European Communities.

Commonwealth of Australia. 1997. *Accounting Standards: Building International Opportunities for Australian Business*. Corporate Law Economic Reform Program Paper No. 1. Canberra, Australia: AGPS.

Hegarty, J. 1997. Accounting for the global economy: Is national regulation doomed to disappear? *Accounting Horizons* (11): 75–90.

Hines, R. 1983. Economic consequences of accounting standards: Reason for ASRB. *Chartered Accountant in Australia* (54): 25.

Horngren, C. T. 1973. The marketing of accounting standards. *Journal of Accountancy* (October): 61–66.

International Accounting Standards Committee (IASC). 1997. *International Accounting Standards*. London, U.K.: IASC.

International Organisation of Securities Commissions (IOSCO). 2000. *IASC Standards*. Press release. May. Sydney, Australia: IOSCO.

Lev., B., and T. Sougiannis. 1996. The capitalization, amortization, and value-relevance of R&D. *Journal of Accounting and Economics* 21: 107–138.

McGregor, W. 1999. The standards revolution: The view from the AARF. *Australian CPA* (April): 32–33.

Sharpe, M. 1998. Looking for harmony: Building a global framework. *Australian Accountant*: 16–18.

Spencer, K. 1998. The view from the AASB: Take it easy, get it right. *Australian Accountant* March: 20–22.

Sutton, M. H. 1997. Financial reporting in U.S. capital markets: International dimensions. *Accounting Horizons* 11: 96–102.

Walker, R. 1987. Australia's ASRB—A case study of political activity and regulatory "Capture." *Accounting and Business Research* 67 (17): 269–286.

Watts, R., and J. Zimmerman. 1986. *Positive Accounting Theory*. Englewood Cliffs, NJ: Prentice Hall.

Wood, C. 1996. Standards levy gets harmonious response. *Business Review Weekly* 26 (August): 92.

Zarzeski, M. T. 1996. Spontaneous harmonization effects of culture and market forces on accounting disclosure practices. *Accounting Horizons* 10: 18–37.

[20]

The European Accounting Review 1995, **4:1**, 155–164

European Union accounting harmonization

The case of leased assets in the United Kingdom and Germany

Neil Garrod and Isabel Sieringhaus
University of Glasgow and
University of Münster

INTRODUCTION

With the magic date of 31 December 1992 having passed and the reality of the single market upon us, it is an appropriate time to assess the extent of accounting harmonization with regard to reporting practice across the EU countries. In this paper we contribute to the debate and extant evidence by comparing the reporting practice regarding leased assets in the UK and Germany.

In the UK, SSAP 21: 'Accounting for leases and hire purchase contracts', issued in 1984, regulates accounting for leasing. Like all other SSAPs it is not law but professional bodies as well as the London Stock Exchange expect compliance.

In Germany, the re-formation of the Code of Commercial Law in 1985, by which the Fourth and Seventh Directives were enacted, does not include any regulation concerning accounting for leases. Only 285 no. 3 of the Commercial Code (1985) requires, following Art. 43 I no. 7 of the Fourth Directive, disclosure of 'other financial commitments' inclusive of lease commitments. The Institute der Wirtschaftsprüfer (IdW), a professional body of chartered accountants, issued two guidelines[1] concerning accounting for lease by lessee and accounting for lease by lessor in 1973 and 1989, respectively. However, the first guideline issued in 1973 was often criticized and was consequently temporarily suspended in 1974 and finally totally abolished in 1990. Because of the missing accounting regulations, the

Address for correspondence
Department of Accounting and Finance, University of Glasgow, 65–71 Southpark Avenue, Glasgow G12 8LE, UK.

 0963–8180

appropriate tax provisions are, in practice, also applied for financial accounting although this application is disputed (Feinen, 1990).

The major issue addressed by lease accounting regulation is to whom the leased assets are assigned, i.e. who has to capitalize the leased asset: the lessee or the lessor? The criteria which lead to an assignment to the lessor vary in the UK and Germany and are set out in the next section.

CRITERIA OF ASSIGNMENT OF LEASED ASSETS TO THE LESSEE OR THE LESSOR

UK regulations

SSAP 21 classifies leases into finance leases and operating leases (SSAP 21, Art. 6). A criterion differentiating between finance leases and operating leases is not really specified. Only general definitions are given which allow subjective interpretations. 'A finance lease is a lease that transfers substantially all the risks and rewards of ownership of an asset to the lessee' (SSAP 21, Art. 15) whereas 'an operating lease is a lease other than a finance lease' (SSAP 21, Art. 17). SSAP 21 states that all the risks and rewards of ownership will be transferred 'if at the inception of a lease the present value of the minimum lease payments, including any initial payment, amounts to substantially all (normally 90 per cent or more) of the fair value of the leased assets' (SSAP 21, Art. 15) – but this concrete definition of the general criterion should be viewed as a refutable presumption. The decisive factor is the transfer of substantially all the risks and rewards of ownership. This could even happen if the present value of the minimum lease payments is less than 90 per cent of the fair value of the leased asset. Alternatively, the lease could be classified as an operating lease although the present value of the lease payments is greater than 90 per cent of the fair value.

Therefore, in addition to this 90 per cent test, another test, the so-called condition test, is carried out: the terms of the contract between the lessor and lessee are investigated in order to find factors influencing the decision as to whether substantially all the risks and rewards of ownership have been passed on. Such important factors are the lease term, the cancellation provisions and renewal options.

A contract which 'contains a provision giving the hirer an option to acquire a legal title to the asset upon the fulfilment of certain conditions stated in the contract' is defined as a hire purchase contract (SSAP 21, Art. 18). Accounting for such hire purchase contracts is also regulated through SSAP 21. Hire purchase contracts are accounted for like finance leases or operating leases depending on whether they are of a financing nature or not (SSAP 21, Art. 31).

If the conditions of the lease agreement lead to the lease being classified as a finance lease then the assets are assigned to the lessee who, in turn, has to capitalize those assets. If not then it is classified as an operating lease and the lessor must capitalize the leased assets.

German regulations

The Code of Commercial Law (1985) does not contain any regulations concerning the assignment of leased assets of one party to a lease contract, as has already been mentioned.

The IdW disclosed in its guideline of 1973 that the decisive factor influencing the assignment of leased assets should be the economic title, independent of the legal title. If the economic title is passed on to the lessee, the lease will be regarded as a finance lease and the asset will be assigned to the lessee. Criteria characterizing finance leases are enumerated in an exemplary way (IdW, 1973: 101). Moreover, even if the economic title is not passed on to the lessee or if it is not clear whether the economic title has been transferred, the IdW could put forward the motion to assign leased assets to the lessee (IdW, 1973: 102). The rationale behind this last suggestion of the IdW is that the purpose of annual accounts is to show a true and fair view of a company's demands for lease commitments (Forster, 1973: 82). However, this opinion has been criticized as being incompatible with the German GAAP, resulting in its suspension in 1974 and finally its abolition in 1990.

Because of the lack of law regulations or regulations by professional bodies – which has not changed even on transforming the Fourth Directive into law – tax law provisions concerning accounting for leases are in practice applied to financial accounting as well (Feinen, 1990: 117). The Federal Court in charge of tax matters enacted a verdict about accounting for leases in 1970. The economist's viewpoint is supposed to determine tax accounting for leases which must be examined for every single case (Federal Court verdict of 26 January 1970, Art. A, I, II). The Federal Court itemized the following rules fixing finance leased assets to be assigned to the lessee (Federal Court verdict of 26 January 1970, Art. A, III–V):

- The useful life of the leased asset is much longer than the lease term and the contract contains an option giving the lessee the right to acquire the asset or to renew the contract. The agreed option price or the follow-up lease payments are therefore less than the usual disposal price or the usual lease payments.
- The lease term is appropriate to the useful life of the asset regardless of any contractual options.
- The leased asset is specially produced for the lessee and cannot be used by anybody else.

The reason given for the verdict is that the lessee has to account for assets for which he receives the economic title giving him all the risks and rewards and excluding the lessor from such risks and rewards. Therefore the legal title does not enter into the assignment of the asset (Grieger, 1970).

The general rules given in the verdict have been specified by several edicts issued by the Federal Ministry of Finance in 1971, 1972 and 1975. Each of these edicts deals with a different kind of lease contract. The first edict (1971) regulates accounting for those lease contracts where the minimum lease payments cover at least the original costs of the lessor. Accounting for leasehold real estate is standardized by the second edict (1972). The third edict sets the policy of how to account for lease contracts where the minimum lease payments do not cover the original costs of the lessor.

The edict of 1971 defines finance leasing as a binding contract ensuring that the original costs are covered by the minimum lease payments (Art. II, 1). It is argued that in such a case the lessee bears all the risk of ownership (Rau, 1971). Furthermore, the edict characterizes those finance leased assets assigned to the lessee or the lessor, respectively, depending on various terms of the lease contract. This can be best illustrated by Table 1 (Art. III).

Depending on the relation between lease term and useful life as well as on other conditions of the lease contract, it may be argued that the lessor's claim for return is so immaterial that the lessee takes all the rewards. Consequently, the lessee has to capitalize the asset (Rau, 1971).

The edict issued in 1975 deals with those lease contracts which do not ensure an amortization of the original cost solely by the minimum lease payments but by other provisions of the contract (Art. 1). This edict concerns only those lease contracts where the lease term lies between 40 and 90 per cent of the useful life of the asset. Moreover, it does not deal with

Table 1

		Lease term		
Other terms		*<40% of useful life*	*40%–90% of useful life*	*>90% of useful life*
Without option		Lessee	Lessor	Lessee
With purchase option	+	Lessee	Lessee	Lessee
	–	Lessee	Lessor	Lessee
With renewal option	+	Lessee	Lessor	Lessee
	–	Lessee	Lessor	Lessee

Notes

+, option price is less than the remaining book value or the follow-up lease payments amount to less than the remaining book value.

–, option price or follow-up lease payments are at least appropriate to the remaining book value.

all possible kinds of contracts but only with the contracts listed below (Art. 2).

1 The lease contract contains the provision giving the lessor an option to request the lessee to buy the leased asset. In such a case the leased asset has to be assigned to the lessor.
2 The lessee and lessor agree to sell the leased asset after the lease term had expired. If the selling price is higher than the amortized cost and if the lessor gets 25 per cent of this difference the lessor will have to account for the leased asset. If they reconcile that the lessor gets less than 25 per cent of the difference the lessee will have to account for the lease.
3 The lessee is allowed to cancel the contract after 40 per cent of the useful life has passed, at the earliest. The payment following the cancellation ensures the amortization of the lessor's original costs. In such a case the lessor has to capitalize the asset.

On concluding one of these kinds of contracts, all risks are transferred to the lessee since the amortization of the original cost is ensured by the conditions of the contract (Müller-Schwerin, 1990). However, the rewards are not totally transferred. Assume, for example, a contract giving the lessor the option of requesting the lessee to buy the leased asset. In such a case the lessor obtains a right but not an obligation so that he still gets the possibility to sell the asset to a third party in order to attain a higher profit (Ministry of Finance edict of 22 December 1975, Art. 2).

The edicts have been discussed extensively and criticized in that they do not comply totally with earlier legal verdicts (Stobbe, 1990).

Despite these criticisms directed at the edicts themselves, there has been debate about whether it should be allowed to apply the tax law provisions on financial accounting at all (e.g. Runge, 1971; Knapp, 1972). The most discussed question has been whether the lessee should get the right of disposal as is required to capitalize assets. In the case of contracts which do not contain any option or which contain a renewal option, the literature states that the lessee never gets the right of disposal so that he never has to account for leases (Knapp, 1972; Baetge and Ballwieser, 1978). However, if a purchase option is decided upon, the literature disagrees as to whether the lessee ever gets the right of disposal or not (e.g. Döllerer, 1971; Knapp, 1972; Leffson, 1976).

The discussion as yet has offered no solution, and thus in practice financial accounting for leases will continue to be based on tax law provisions.

A critical comparison of the regulations

When initially comparing the UK and German regulations it seems that their general intentions are very similar. Both state that the decisive factor is the transfer of the economic title independent of the legal title. If risks and rewards of ownership are passed on to the lessee, i.e. if the economic title is transferred to the lessee, he will be the one to capitalize the leased asset.

However, the criteria determining when such a transfer will happen are different in the UK and Germany. First, although both countries use the item 'finance lease' the definitions vary dramatically. Furthermore, assignment regulations following a finance lease are different.

In the UK all contracts assuring a transfer of risks and rewards are defined as finance leases and always follow capitalization by the lessee. In contrast, in Germany binding contracts which contain the provision that the original costs are amortized, ensuring only the transfer of the risks, are stated as finance lease. Moreover, accounting for such finance lease contracts is dependent on further factors.

The UK criteria following an assignment to the lessee have not really been outlined, whereas the German tax law provisions give strict rules. This makes a straight comparison very difficult.

Assuming that in the UK the decision of assignment is based largely on the relationship between the present value of the minimum lease payments and the fair value of the asset, and further, that this relationship is appropriate to the German required equivalence of the original cost and the amount of lease payments, accounting for leases could be different in both countries. In such a case a UK lessee is required to capitalize the asset anyway, whilst a capitalization by the German lessee is dependent on the conclusion of certain combinations of other contractual conditions.

Furthermore, considering that the 90 per cent mark is viewed as a refutable presumption, a lease contract may be defined as a finance lease in the UK if contract conditions other than the relationship between the present value and the fair value ensure that the risks and rewards are transferred. On the other hand, in Germany, leases which do not secure an amortization of the original costs are assigned to the lessor.

The comparisons show that the potential interpretations of the UK regulation give rise to the possibility that similar contracts are accounted for in different ways in the UK and in Germany.

Here it should be mentioned that the conditions of a lease contract can be influenced by the lessee and the lessor in order to achieve an assignment to the lessor which is preferred in both countries for tax and liquidity reasons. These manipulations seem to be easier in Germany since the lack of fulfilment of only one of the stated criteria means assignment to the lessor. However, whether and how often the lease contracts are manipulated in order to achieve capitalization of the asset by the lessor is not included in the matter of this paper and demands further empirical study.

ACCOUNTING FOR LEASED ASSETS ASSIGNED TO THE LESSEE

UK regulations

At the inception, a finance lease should be capitalized at the amount of the present value of the minimum lease payments on the asset side in the lessee's balance sheet. A corresponding sum is to be recorded as an obligation. The present value is calculated by discounting the lease payments at the implicit interest rate (SSAP 21, Art. 32). Instead of recording the present value of the minimum lease payments it will be allowed to use the fair value of the asset if both amounts are appropriate – as is often the case in practice (SSAP 21, Art. 33).

The initial equivalence of the asset side and the liability side changes over the lease term. The asset is depreciated over the lease term or if shorter over the useful life of the asset (SSAP 21, Art. 36). By contrast, the liability is reduced by the rentals payable. The rentals payable are thereby allocated between the finance charge and the reduction of the obligation. The allocation should be carried out in such a way that a constant periodic rate of charge on the outstanding liabilities will be produced (SSAP 21, Art. 35).

The UK GAAP states three methods of how to divide the rentals payable: the actuarial method is the one which guarantees a constant periodic rate of charge but this method is very complex and difficult to calculate. Therefore the sum-of-the-digits method, also called the 'rule of 78' method, which is easier to calculate but still achieves a good approximation of the constant periodic rate is often used. Moreover, SSAP 21 explicitly allows a reasonable approximation to be used. The third method, the straight-line method, is less frequently used because it is argued that this method is too inaccurate (Davies *et al.*, 1989).

Besides the records made in the balance sheet and the earning statement as mentioned above, the lessee is required to make further disclosures in his notes (SSAP 21, Art. 49–53 and 57). Gross amount, accumulated depreciation, net amount and depreciation allocated to the period for finance lease are expected to be disclosed. The lessee thus has the option of reporting these sums separately to the owned fixed assets or integrated with the owned fixed assets. The latter treatment, however, demands that the proportion of assets held under finance leases included in the overall total amount should also be disclosed in note form. Furthermore, the net obligations should be reported. The amount is to be split into obligations payable in the next year, in the second to fifth years and the aggregated amounts payable thereafter. Finally, finance charges and the valuation method should be disclosed.

German regulations

As in the case of the assignment question discussed above, recording leased assets in the balance sheet is not regulated by law. Moreover, the tax law provisions, which are used in practice for the assignment decision, on the valuation of leased assets have been heavily criticized.

The edict of 1971 demands a capitalization on the asset side at the amount of the original cost of the lessee. An obligation due to the lessor of the amount of the original cost is entered on the liability side (Art V, 1). The problem arising from using this method is that the lessee normally does not know the original costs unless he has been told by the lessor (Baetge and Ballwieser, 1978). The asset is depreciated over its useful life. The liability is amortized over the lease term by the rentals payable. The rentals payable should be allocated in such a way that the finance charges decrease over time while the reduction of the obligation increases (Art. V, 1).

Because of the practical problems associated with the method stated above, another method is discussed in the literature. The IdW suggests in its guideline of 1973 to capitalize the asset at an amount of the present value of the lease payments and to enter a corresponding sum on the liability side of the balance sheet. The present value should be derived by discounting the payments at a reasonable discount rate (IdW, 1973: Art. V). This is the precise point where the problem of this method lies. Nothing is mentioned, however, either in the guideline itself or in the explanation given, as to the meaning of a reasonable discount rate (Lefhalm, 1973). The controversial discussion concerning the valuation methods of leased assets is still going on, so that even now it is up to the auditor to decide which method is appropriate for the German GAAP (Leffson, 1976; Küting and Weber, 1991; Adler *et al.*, 1993).

Requirements concerning further disclosure in the notes are not given by law or any other regulations. The 285 I No. 3 of the Commercial Code requiring the disclosure of financial commitments is not meant for those leased assets assigned to the lessee, since the paragraph demands the disclosure only for those commitments which have not already been entered on the liability side. The only disclosure to be made in the lessee's notes in case the lease is assigned to him is about the valuation method used (284 II No. 1 of the Commercial Code, 1985).

ACCOUNTING FOR LEASED ASSETS ASSIGNED TO THE LESSOR

The UK and Germany agree that leased assets assigned to the lessor are not capitalized by the lessee. The rentals payable should be charged as an expense in both countries as is the case for hire contracts. However, in considering this agreement it is important to be aware that the criteria resulting in assignment to the lessor vary considerably between the UK and Germany as discussed above.

More important, with respect to this paper, are the different requirements concerning notes. SSAP 21 demands the total of operating lease rentals to be charged as an expense so that the commitments made during the next years can be disclosed. Moreover, the charge or the commitments should be analysed with respect to asset classes or with respect to the maturity of the commitments, respectively (SSAP 21, Art. 55–57). By contrast, 285 I No. 3 of the Commercial Code already mentioned above requires a disclosure of all other financial commitments including lease commitments whereby the lease is assigned to the lessor. However, the disclosure is to be made in one sum, so that isolation of the lease commitments is impossible.

A FINAL COMPARISON

The expositions above have made clear that lease accounting regulations are ambiguous in both countries. The main problem lies in the different regulations concerning the assignment of leased assets. Most leases which are assigned to the lessee in Germany would be assigned to a UK lessee whilst the reverse is not necessarily the case. In addition, the valuation of assets may vary between the countries. However, since the Fourth Directive requires disclosure of valuation methods, this difference can be viewed as less important. Whilst the UK lessee is expected to make a detailed disclosure, notes of German companies do not give further information with respect to lease commitments.

NOTE

1 These guidelines issued by the IdW are not law but all chartered accountants who are members of the professional body are committed to following such experts.

REFERENCES

Accounting Standards Committee (1984) *SSAP 21: Accounting for Leases and Hire Purchase Contracts*, August.

Adler, Düring and Schmalz (1993) *Rechnungslegung and Prüfung der Unternekmen*, Stuttgart.

Baetge, Jörg, and Ballwieser, Wolfgang (1978) 'Ansatz und Ausweis von Leasingobjekten in Handelseund Steuerbilanz', *Die Betriebswirtschaft*, 38: 3–19.

Companies Act (1981) London: HMSO.

Council of the European Communities (1979) *Fourth Council Directive for Coordination of National Legislation Regarding the Annual Accounts of Limited Companies*, Brussels.

Davies, Mike, Paterson, Ron, and Wilson, Allister (1989) *UK GAAP – Generally Accepted Accounting Practice in the United Kingdom*, London.

Döllerer, Georg (1971) 'Leasing – wirtschaftliches Eigentum oder Nutzungsrecht?', *Der Betriebs-Berater*, 26: 535–40.
Feinen, Klaus (1990) *Das Leasinggeschäft*, 3rd edn, Frankfurt am Main.
Forster, Karl-Heniz (1973) 'Zur Leasing-Stellungnahme des HFA', *Die Wirtschaftsprüfung*, 26: 81–3.
Grieger, Rudolf (1970) 'Die handelsrechtliche und steuerrechtliche Behandlung des Leasing', *Wertpapier-Mitteiling*, 24: 302–13.
IdW (1973) 'Stellungnahme HFA 1/73', *Die Wirtschaftsprüfund*, 26: 101–2.
Knapp, Lotte (1972) 'Leasing in der Handelsbilanz', *Der Betrieb*, 25: 541–9.
Küting, K. and Weber, C. (1991) *Handbach der Rechnungslegung*, Stuttgart.
Leffson, Ulrich (1976) 'Die Darstellung von Leasingverägen im Jahresabschlub', *Der Betrieb*, 29: 637–41, 685–90.
Lefhalm, Heinz-Wilheim (1973) 'Zur Bewertung der Leasing-Gegenstände und Leasing-Verpflichtungen in der Handels-bilanz des Leasingnehmers', *Der Betrieb*, 26: 2149–56.
Müller-Schwerin, Eberhard (1990) 'Der Teilamortisationserlab und das Leasinggeschäft, *Zeitschrift für das gesamte Kreditwesen*, 43: 548–52.
Rau, Hans-Gerd (1971) 'Steuerliche Behandlung des Leasing', *Der Betrieb*, 24: 3–14.
Runge, Berndt (1971) 'Finanzierungs-Leasing in der Behandlung der Finanzverwaltung', *Der Betrieb*, 24: 963–76.
Stobbe, Thomas (1990) 'Ist der Mabgeblich-keitsgrundsatz bei der Zurechnung des wirtschaftlichen Eigentums anwendbar?', *Der Betriebs-Berater*, 43: 518–25.

Pergamon

The International Journal of Accounting
36 (2001) 147–167

The International Journal of Accounting

Accounting for brands in France and Germany compared with IAS 38 (intangible assets): An illustration of the difficulty of international harmonization

Hervé Stolowy[a,*], Axel Haller[b], Volker Klockhaus[c]

[a]*Department of Accounting and Management Control, HEC School of Management (Groupe HEC), 1, rue de la Libération, 78351 Jouy en Josas Cedex, France*
[b]*Johannes Kepler, University of Linz, Linz, Austria*
[c]*University of Cologne, Cologne, Germany*

Abstract

This paper compares the positions taken by IAS 38 over brands and the related treatments in France and Germany. Despite many points of convergence, the paper shows that these two countries, often to be found in the same cluster of national accounting systems (the "Continental-European" model), have adopted very different solutions in relation to each other and to IAS 38. The results of the study highlight the difficulty of international harmonization. They also show that as far as the qualitative characteristics of accounting are concerned, the frequently made association between Anglo-American accounting philosophy and "relevance," and between Continental-European accounting philosophy and "reliability," may not apply when it comes to brand accounting. To resolve this international "disharmony," our paper militates in favor of disclosure of additional information. © 2001 University of Illinois. All rights reserved.

Keywords: Brands; International accounting standards; IASC; Intangible assets; International harmonization

1. Introduction

Intangibles have become an increasingly important factor in economic life and the success of corporate activities (Duizabo & Guillaume, 1996; Ochs, 1996). For the majority of

* Corresponding author. Tel.: +33-1-39-67-9442; fax: +33-1-39-67-7086.
E-mail address: stolowy@hec.fr (H. Stolowy).

PII: S0020-7063(01)00092-9

companies, intangibles are essential for progress and a considerable part of the corporate value. One type of the very broad spectrum of corporate intangibles is brands. Brands can be defined as any word, tone, symbol or design to identify and distinguish one product or group of products from other products (Plasseraud, Plasseraud, & Dehaut, 1994). However, brands are more than just the name or sign. In a broader sense, they create a unique image of the branded product or service, its quality and attributes as perceived by customers (Meffert & Burmann, 1998, p. 81; Smith, 1997, pp. 38–44; see also Kapferer, 1998). In the consumer product industry particularly, they are regarded as a key competitive factor influencing consumer preferences for a product and, therefore, the corporate sales level.[1]

Because of the importance of brands for the economic development of certain businesses, their accounting treatment has been a matter of debate and controversy in many countries, for example, in Australia and the United Kingdom, where companies such as Grand Metropolitan and Rank Hovis McDougall decided in 1988 to include the value of brand names, either purchased or internally developed, in their consolidated balance sheets (among others see Barwise, Higson, Likierman, & Marsh, 1989; Power, 1992). In France, too, the consequence of accounting for intangible assets, including brands, is important for certain companies because of their potential relative significance in the presentation of the balance sheet. For example, in 1998, brands represented 22.8% of the balance sheet total for "Rémy Cointreau" and 11.9% for "Danone" (X, 1999a). The most remarkable transaction concerning brands in Germany was the acquisition of the "Rolls-Royce" and "Bentley" brands by BMW and VW in 1998. For Beiersdorf there is an assumption that the "Nivea" brand is more valuable than the balance sheet total (Breit, 1997).

Against this background, the International Accounting Standards Committee (IASC) issued its International Accounting Standard 38 in July 1998 (IAS 38, intangible assets, see Gélard, 1998; IASC, 1998b), following the publication of two Exposure Drafts (E50, June 1995, see Gélard, 1995; IASC, 1995; X, 1995a, 1995b and E60, August 1997, see IASC, 1997). The standard sets out proposals for the recognition, measurement, amortization, and disclosure of intangible assets. Accounting treatment of brands is included in the scope of this text.

It is often stressed that the process and outcome of IASC standard setting are very much influenced by the Anglo-American accounting approach, which theoretically emphasizes "relevance." This is considered one of the major reasons why countries with other accounting approaches are clearly reluctant to adopt the international accounting standards. That is particularly true of countries belonging to the "Continental-European conception," which is supposed to stress reliability, objectivity, and prudence in income calculation. It is thus highly interesting to examine whether the treatment described in IAS 38 differs from accounting practice in Continental-European countries, and to consider if the content of the standard could easily be adopted by enterprises in those countries. This is the main objective

[1] An empirical study (sample of 400 companies) carried out in Germany indicates that more than 80% of managers are convinced that the importance of brands has increased considerably during the last few years. At the same time, taking all industries together, brand values represent on average 56% of the market values of German companies (Wermelkirchen, 1999).

of our paper, which compares the positions taken by standard IAS 38 over brands with the related treatments[2] in two countries not often studied together: France and Germany.

The remainder of our paper proceeds as follows. The next section presents the recognition of brands as an asset, covering such fundamental problems as the definition of intangible assets, the principles governing the recognition of brands (acquired or self-generated) and initial measurement of brands. Section 3 describes the subsequent measurement (amortization, revaluation, and value recovery) and Section 4 suggests some limitations of our study and directions for future research. Section 5 presents the conclusions.

2. Recognition of brands as an asset and initial measurement

Because brands are intangible items, their recognition on the balance sheet primarily depends on their compliance with the definition of intangible assets. The classification of intangibles as assets is therefore the preliminary step in our investigation.

2.1. Definition of intangible assets

IAS 38 (para. 7) defines an intangible asset as an "identifiable nonmonetary asset without physical substance held for use in the production or supply of goods or services, for rental to others, or for administrative purposes." An asset "is a resource (a) controlled by an enterprise as a result of past events; and (b) from which future economic benefits are expected to flow to the enterprise." The standard indicates (IAS 38, para. 8) that "enterprises frequently expend resources, or incur liabilities, on the acquisition, development, maintenance or enhancement of intangible resources such as . . . trademarks (including brand names and publishing titles)." Not all intangible items meet the characteristics of an intangible asset, that is, "identifiability, control over the resource and existence of future economic benefits" (IAS 38, para. 9).

IAS 38 requires an intangible asset to be "identifiable to distinguish it clearly from goodwill" (para. 10), which is the case "if the asset is separable" (para. 11). Separability exists "if the enterprise could rent, sell, exchange or distribute the specific future economic benefits attributable to the asset without also disposing of future economic benefits that flow from other assets used in the same revenue earning activity" (para. 11). But it may also be possible to prove the identifiability of an asset in some other way (see IAS 38, para. 12). IAS 38 assumes that "an enterprise controls an asset" if it "has the power to obtain the future economic benefits flowing from the underlying resource and also can restrict the access of others to those benefits" (para. 13). Future economic benefits may "include revenue from the sale of products or services, cost savings, or other benefits resulting from the use of the asset by the enterprise" (para. 17).

The definition and explanations given by IAS 38 are much more detailed than German and (particularly) French texts on the subject. In Germany, intangible assets, like tangible assets, are not legally defined. The general definition of an asset, derived in German accounting tradition

[2] The notion of "treatments" comprises accounting rules, principles, and company practices.

from the "principles of proper accounting" (*Grundsätze ordnungsmäßiger Buchführung*) and the purposes of financial accounting, in fact applies to tangibles as well as intangibles. Thus, intangible assets are all items that correspond to the general asset definition, and are fixed but not tangible (i.e., without physical substance) or financial (Haller, 1998, p. 564). The major formal difference compared to the IASC definition is that the German definition does not explicitly stress the characteristic of a "future economic benefit." It speaks about an "economic value" inherent to an item, and this generally but not necessarily implicitly incorporates the idea of a future economic benefit (Hommel, 1997, p. 352; Moxter, 1986, pp. 246–247). The two predominant components of the German asset definition are quite similar to the IASC approach, in that an asset must be identifiable and independently and reliably measurable (Baetge, 1996, pp. 148–155; Haller, 1998, p. 575; Hommel, 1997). Identifiability means that the item can be separated from the business and its economic benefits can be disposed of separately in any form. Thus, in terms of separability of the item from the enterprise, and its independent and reliable measurability, the definition of intangible assets in Germany is quite similar to that given by the IASC (Haller, 1998, p. 575; Hommel, 1997, p. 363).

In France, however, the General Accounting Plan (*Plan comptable général*) 1982 (CNC, 1986, I.33; Orsini, Gould, Mc Allister, & Parikh, 1998) defines intangible assets as being fixed assets other than tangible or financial assets, with a fixed asset being defined as an asset acquired for long-term use in the operation of the business. The general definition of an asset is "... an element of net worth which has a positive economic value for the firm." (The concepts of "identifiability" and "separability" are not dealt with). Therefore, intangible assets are recognized only by comparison with tangible assets, which correspond to real rights over tangible objects. The new version of the General Accounting Plan, dating from 29 April 1999 (X, 1999c), no longer provides a definition of intangible assets. However, the general opinion is that the definition given in 1982 is still valid.

It could therefore be claimed that the German and French definitions of intangible assets are not in contradiction with the IAS 38, but are simply less specific. Nevertheless, they are not totally comparable because of the differences in the general asset definition regarding the characteristic of "future economic benefits" (see Table 1).

2.2. Principles for recognition of brands

In IAS 38 (brands are mentioned on several occasions, most importantly in the overall definition of intangible assets), and also the accounting rules in France and Germany, brands are regarded as a type of intangible item whose recognition could become possible or even necessary.

Table 1
Definition of intangible assets

IAS 38	France	Germany
Identifiable, nonmonetary assets without physical substance	Fixed assets other than tangible or financial	No legal definition. In practice: fixed assets other than tangible or financial

IAS 38 has made a considerable effort to clarify matters by indicating (para. 18) that an intangible item should be recognized as an asset if it "meets the definition of an intangible asset" mentioned above, plus two additional "recognition criteria set out in the Standard":

(a) "it is probable that the future economic benefits that are attributable to the asset will flow to the enterprise"; and
(b) "the cost of the asset to the enterprise can be measured reliably" (para. 19).

Before looking into the possibilities for recognizing brands in France and Germany, we should remember that Articles 9 and 10 of the Fourth Directive, No. 78/660/EEC of 25 July 1978, stipulate that, in order to be included in balance sheet assets, brands should be:

- either "acquired for valuable consideration and need not be shown under goodwill";
- or "created by the undertaking itself, in so far as national law permits their being shown as assets" (EEC, 1978, Article 9 C.).

This European Directive lacks precision and therefore leaves European Union countries considerable scope for initiative. In France and Germany, this part of the Directive was turned into a simple rule concerning the format of the balance sheet. Although France goes so far as to cite brands in the balance sheet headings for intangible assets, they are not explicitly mentioned in the corresponding balance sheet position under German rules (HGB -*Handelsgesetzbuch* (Commercial Code) – para. 266 [2]), but they are covered as they belong to the term *gewerbliche Schutzrechte* (industrial property rights), which are mentioned in the national rule.

Looking at the conditions of recognition in more detail, differences between the three regarded sets of rules become obvious.

2.2.1. Probability of future economic benefits

According to IAS 38 (para. 20), "an enterprise should assess the probability of future economic benefits by using reasonable and supportable assumptions that represent management's best estimate of the set of economic conditions that will exist over the useful life of the asset." In Germany, as already mentioned, future economic benefits are not explicitly referred to in the intangible asset definition. In France, the same applies for individual financial statements. However, the new regulation on consolidated accounts (X, 1999b, para. 2111) includes the requirement of future economic benefits.

2.2.2. Reliable measurement of cost

Brand value, as a key management responsibility, should be assessed, monitored, maintained, and enhanced for the following reasons: (1) maximization of shareholder value through maximization of brand value, (2) estimation of the value of a company in the context of mergers and acquisitions, (3) determination of royalties for brands, and (4) for accounting purposes. While many companies include brands on balance sheets, many also charge subsidiaries for access to and use of brands (e.g., Nestlé), and many companies are acquired as much for their brands as for their tangible assets (e.g., Nabisco, Jaguar). Brands must also be valued because they are increasingly the subject of litigation. The more valuable they are perceived, the more companies are prepared to spend to defend their values. One role of assessing the value of brands is to convince the courts of the gravity of the offense and to help the court assess the damage in settlement.

Besides the need to identify the asset, the key issue in brand valuation is the selection of an appropriate valuation method, which is based on a subjective process emphasizing economic benefits. Various valuation methods are discussed and proposed in literature and used in practice. In general, these methods can be divided into three approaches: the cost approach (historical cost method or replacement cost method), the income approach (namely the royalty-relief method, and all types of discounted cash-flow and earnings methods), and the market approach (comparison with other transactions) (see among others Barwise et al., 1989, pp. 53–76; Haigh & Perrier, 1997; Kahn, 1997; La Villeguérin, 2000/2001; Medus, 1990; Nussenbaum, 1991; Reilly & Schweihs, 1998, pp. 426–433; Roeb, 1994, pp. 80–133; Sattler, 1995; Smith, 1997; Viale, 1991).

In practice, the accounting policy followed for brand recognition and, in particular, the choice of a valuation method, depends on the way the brands have been obtained by the enterprise: separate acquisition (including acquisition without charge or by exchange), acquisition as part of a business combination (mergers or acquisition of subsidiaries), or internal generation.

2.2.2.1. Separate acquisition. According to IAS 38 (para. 23), "if an intangible asset is acquired separately," its cost "can usually be measured reliably." This is particularly so when the purchase consideration is in the form of cash or other monetary assets." When a brand is acquired by exchange (or as part of an exchange) with another asset (tangible or intangible), it must be measured at its fair value, "which is equivalent to the fair value of the asset given up adjusted by the amount of any cash or cash equivalents transferred" (IAS 38, para. 34).

In France, brands acquired for a consideration are treated as intangible fixed assets and as such are recorded under the heading *Concessions et droits similaires, brevets, licences, marques, procédés, logiciels, droits et valeurs similaires* (Concessions and similar rights, patents, licenses, brands, processes, software, rights, and similar assets). Like all other assets, the value recorded is the acquisition cost paid (La Villeguérin, 2000/2001; Viale & Lafay, 1990). An asset acquired by way of an exchange should be recognized at its market value, which is the price that would have been paid under normal market conditions (i.e., in an arm's-length relationship). Measurement of acquired brands is therefore similar under IAS 38 and French rules. Furthermore, the National Accounting Council (*Conseil national de la comptabilité, CNC*), the standard-setting body attached to the Ministry of Economy and Finance, set up a committee to work on brands in 1990–1991. This committee issued a report (CNC, 1992) in April 1992: it refers to acquired brands without discussing their recognition and measurement.

In Germany, until the adoption of the *Markengesetz* (MarkenG, Brands Act of October 25, 1994), it was not possible to sell a brand separately, but only with the whole enterprise or with the business of an enterprise possessing the brand. Today, a brand itself can be sold separately without any connection to the sale of the whole enterprise or parts of it (MarkenG, para. 27).

Because reliable cost measurement is the predominant requirement for recognition of an intangible asset, recognition depends on the acquisition being for a consideration, which gives a reliable indication for measurement. Therefore, a brand, like all other intangible assets, must be recognized at acquisition cost if it has been acquired for a consideration (Coenenberg, 1996, pp. 83; Keitz, 1997, pp. 66–68). Brands acquired by way of exchange can be initially measured either at the fair value of the asset given up or at its carrying amount (Knop & Küting, 1995, pp. 1047–1048).

In the event of separate acquisition of a brand, IAS 38 and both French and German accounting rules require initial measurement of the brand to be based on the acquisition cost, and so only the historical cost approach is appropriate. The definition of acquisition cost is similar in the three sets of rules. It comprises purchase price, including any import duties and nonrefundable purchase taxes, and any directly attributable expenditure on preparing the asset for its intended use. There is only one difference, relating to the treatment of professional fees and legal charges, which are not included in France. With regard to brands acquired by way of exchange, the three sets of rules are similar.

2.2.2.2. Acquisition as part of a business combination (merger or consolidated financial statements). IAS 38 (para. 27–32) covers the treatment of intangibles acquired as part of a business combination as defined in IAS 22 (IASC, 1998a). In this context, the cost of an intangible asset "is based on its fair value at the date of acquisition" (IAS 38, para. 27). Judgement is needed to determine whether the fair value of the intangible asset can be ascertained with sufficient reliability. In such cases, IAS 38 (para. 28) states that "quoted market prices in an active market provide the most reliable measurement of fair value." "If no active market exists for an asset, its cost reflects the amount that the enterprise would have paid, at the date of the acquisition, for the asset in an arm's length transaction between knowledgeable, and willing parties, based on the best information available" (para. 29). IAS 38 also cites several other methods to estimate the fair value, e.g., multiplicators or discounted cash flows (IAS 38, para. 30), and concludes, "if the cost (i.e., fair value) of an intangible asset . . . cannot be measured reliably, that asset is not recognized as a separate intangible asset but is included in goodwill (IAS 38, para. 31-b)."

Because it is usually difficult to arrive at separate evaluations of brands acquired as part of a business combination, then as we understand IAS 38, the first consolidation will only seldom lead to separate recognition of a brand because of the lack of sufficient reliability in measurement (see also Harding, 1995, p. 9). IAS 38 actually leaves companies the option of whether to separate the brand or to include it in goodwill. Additionally, the Basis for Conclusions for IAS 38, para. 37-b (IASC, 1998c), a separate document prepared by the IASC Staff giving their reasons for supporting or rejecting alternatives on certain specific issues, does not explicitly require an active market for an intangible asset to be separated from goodwill in a business combination and measured at fair value. In the final analysis, as the treatment of goodwill is consistent with that of intangible assets, separate recognition of brands is only a question of disclosure and additional information and has no material impact on net income (at least as long as amortization is the same for goodwill and brands) (IASC, 1998c, para. 57–59).

The Fourth (EEC, 1978) and Seventh European Directives (EEC, 1983) do not include any explicit advice on how to treat intangible assets acquired through a merger or with a subsidiary. Implicitly, however, it can be concluded that such assets, if identifiable, should be recognized and measured separately.

The position taken by the IASC differs slightly from French rules and practice. In France, when an enterprise is first included in consolidated accounts, brands may be capitalized in recording the difference between the cost of acquiring a company and the proportion of the net assets acquired, including profits for the accounting year to date. This difference comprises two elements firstly, the positive or negative valuation differences on certain identifiable assets when restated at fair value, and secondly, a remainder, which cannot be allocated, called the "acquisition difference" (goodwill). With respect to valuation differences, the National Accounting Council specifies, in an Opinion dated January 15, 1990 (CNC, 1990), that "among these identifiable elements should be included intangible assets, which have not been included in the individual company accounts: commercial networks, market shares, databases, etc." The CNC opinion does not mention brands specifically, but commentators (and French companies) made two remarks following the publication of the Opinion:

- logically, it is possible to argue that brands are more easily identifiable than market shares, which are explicitly mentioned in the Opinion;
- the presence of the "etc." at the end of the sentence leaves the list open to additional items.

Consequently, in practice a certain number of French companies allocate a part of the difference on first consolidation to brands. In fact, according to the annual review by a group of accounting firms of published annual reports for 1998 (X, 1999a), 48 of the hundred groups reviewed allocate a part of the consolidation difference to brands, and in some cases the brands concerned amount to more than 20% of the balance sheet total.

To confirm the analysis of the 1990 Opinion by commentators, the new regulation on consolidated financial statements (X, 1999b, para. 2111) explicitly quotes brands in the list of identifiable intangible assets, thus clearly saying that brands can be recognized as assets within the context of a business combination.

As far as the valuation of brands is concerned, several methods exist side by side, as presented in literature and more particularly in the National Accounting Council report (CNC, 1992). Methods based on the capacity to generate future cash flows (or profitability methods) can be used to value a brand in the context of a merger or the first consolidation of an acquisition, in order to separate the valuation difference into identifiable components. The royalty-relief method is the most standard approach and, if applicable, the most often used for brand valuation in France (La Villeguérin, 2000/2001).

In Germany, if the acquisition cost is higher than the proportional net asset value of the acquired subsidiary, the difference on first consolidation must be allocated between the various assets, or offset against certain liabilities of the acquired company (HGB, para. 301 al. 1, s. 3). The portion of the consolidation difference that cannot be allocated to specific assets has to be treated as goodwill (*Geschäfts- und Firmenwert*) (HGB, para. 268 al. 2) and recorded under the balance sheet heading of intangible assets.

Under the generally accepted principles, there is certainly no option on separate recognition of brands, since it is either obligatory (HGB, para. 246, al. 1) or forbidden (HGB, para. 248 al. 2). If the purchased company possesses (internally generated) brands, the acquiring company must recognize the brand in its balance sheet if there is a reliable basis of measurement (Rohnke, 1992; Stein & Ortmann, 1996, p. 788). Because of the difficulties mentioned above in determining identifiable intangibles and measuring them reliably, the majority of German companies include the vague amount corresponding to intangibles acquired with a subsidiary in goodwill. Nevertheless, some authors refer to a possible price arrangement for specific items in the contract of sale or in the underlying valuations, which might be a value indication (Richter, 1990, p. 23), while some also list several of the abovementioned methods for brand valuation and give practical advice for their use (Rohnke, 1992).

While France believes that measurement of brands is sufficiently reliable, the IASC and Germany have concluded otherwise. How can this difference be excplained? One answer could be France's long tradition and a great amount of literature dealing with the valuation of brands. Therefore, the reliability argument is not considered an obstacle to putting "relevance" first. Another reason relates to the fact, already referred to, that separability is not a specific characteristic in the French definition of an asset. Therefore, there is no need to comply with a "separability" or "identifiability" requirement in recognizing a brand. A more practical reason for the transfer from goodwill to brands of part of the difference on first consolidation could be the positive effect on income for French companies, as brands are regarded as nonamortizable[3] (see below, Section 3).

2.2.2.3. Internal generation. As IAS 38 (para. 39) points out, "it is sometimes difficult to assess whether an internally generated intangible asset qualifies for recognition." The standard indicates that, with regard to intangible assets "arising from development (or from the development phase of an internal project)," special conditions that give more concrete guidance for recognition must be met (para. 45, a–f). They are "the technical feasibility of completing the intangible asset so that it will be available for use or sale," the "intention to complete the intangible asset and use or sell it," "the ability to use or sell the intangible asset," the demonstration of probable future economic benefits, "the availability of adequate technical, financial and other resources to complete the development and to use or sell the intangible asset" and the "ability of the enterprise to measure the expenditure attributable to the intangible asset during its development reliably."

Most surprisingly, without taking into account whether the concrete conditions are fulfilled or not, IAS 38 (para. 51) states specifically that "internally generated brands . . . should not be recognized as intangible assets." This is because the IASC believes "that expenditure on

[3] This reasoning is in conformity with the experience of the UK before FRS 10 (ASB, 1997) was adopted. The treatment of brands was in practice affected by considerations concerning its effect not on taxable income but on critical accounting ratios (Muller III, 1999).

internally generated brands ... cannot be distinguished from the cost of developing the business as a whole" (IAS 38, para. 52). With this concrete prohibition, the IASC is taking a very prudent point of view that stresses reliability.

In principle, the French viewpoint is opposed to the IAS, but in practice, it conforms to it. The General Accounting Plan even includes a specific balance sheet heading to record "expenses incurred to obtain the benefit that comes from the protection afforded ... to the beneficiary of the operating rights ... to a brand" (CNC, 1986, I.25; X, 1999c, para. 441). Based on a broad interpretation of this heading, enterprises could include self-generated brands in their balance sheets. However, in practice, French companies do not recognize internally generated brands as assets. The major arguments against it are the high degree of uncertainty as to the nature of expenses that can be capitalized, and the impact on taxable income, given the close interdependence of financial accounting and taxation in France.

The first of these arguments against recognition is highly debatable, especially as the CNC report (CNC, 1992) states that an intangible item developed internally by an enterprise should be included in the balance sheet fixed assets if:

- it is possible to demonstrate, with reasonable probability, that the item is capable of generating future economic benefits in favor of the enterprise;
- it is intended to be used durably in the enterprise;
- and its cost can be calculated in a reliable way, with the help of a specific individual project.

The CNC report, modeled on the measures adopted in the CNC opinion on computer software (CNC, 1987), undertakes an in-depth study of the process of brand creation and proposes step-by-step solutions for recording a brand as an asset, based on the different stages of this process. All the reasoning is based on the concept of a "project," where the following seven criteria must be met to record the output (brand) as an asset:

1. Specification of the output (brand) (answer to the question: what?);
2. Identification of the process to develop this output (brand) (answer to the question: how?);
3. Allocation of human, financial, commercial ... means (resources) to the project (answer to the question: with what resources?);
4. Implementation of management tools to control the process, in order to (a) measure the cost of the brand created, (b) match the expenses to the different steps of the project, (c) evaluate, at each step, the probability of commercial success or failure (answer to the question: with what control tools?);
5. Explicit commitment to produce the output (use the brand) whose development is in process;
6. Reasonable probability of generating future advantages (commercial profitability);
7. Long-term use of the output produced (brand created).

If Criteria 1 to 5 are satisfied, we have a real "project." If Criteria 1 to 5 plus 6 and 7 are satisfied, the output (brand) can be capitalized. The report goes on to describe the different phases of development of a brand and explains when (at which phase) the brand can be recorded as an asset.

For determining the production cost of a brand produced by the enterprise for its own use, current accounting discussion in France has concluded that this method is:

- reliable, through use of the project concept applied to the brand creation process (see above);
- relevant, according to the CNC (1992), particularly for valuing a recent brand with a serious chance of commercial profitability but which has not yet attained its full maturity.

This production cost method leads to separate valuation of the brand, and the result is relatively objective in the way it is determined (project) and consistent with the standard accounting measurement approach based on costs. Unfortunately, the CNC report has never been turned into a standard, probably because of the taxation effect already mentioned.

We have not discovered any official indications in Germany of a similar reflection to that undertaken in France concerning the recognition of self-generated brands. On the contrary, in Germany, the recognition of internally generated noncurrent intangible assets is illegal because of the lack of sufficient reliability of measurement (HGB, para. 248, al. 2; Adler, Düring, & Schmaltz, 1995, No. 23 to HGB, para. 248). Without any doubt, brands are covered by this ban.

The ideas contained in the CNC report are very interesting and show that, contrary to what is affirmed in IAS 38, solutions exist to calculate the cost of internally generated brands. It may seem surprising to find a method that is considered both reliable and relevant in France, although the IASC and Germany believe that reliability is impossible in the field of internally generated brands, especially given that the criteria (Steps 1 to 7) proposed by the CNC are quite close to the requirements indicated in IAS 38 (para. 45). We do not think that the French proposal is less rigorous than systems applied elsewhere, or that French "specialists" are somehow "cleverer." We believe that the cultural weight of "reliability" is very important elsewhere and that the French proposal still includes assumptions that leave it open to criticism and discourage other countries from following its lead.

3. Measurement after initial recognition

When brands are recognized separately, their value must be examined at the balance sheet date. This may result in (1) amortization, (2) revaluation, or (3) a possible write-down or write-up.

3.1. General reflections on brand amortization

There is considerable discussion about whether a brand should be subject to amortization at all, and how to determine its useful life. The main arguments against a definite useful life, and therefore against amortization of brands, are as follows:

- In many countries the legal protection of brands is unlimited, or at least renewable indefinitely (e.g., for Community Trademarks within the European Union, in France, Germany, and the USA). Hence from a legal point of view, the use of a brand is not limited for its owner.
- Some brands are very old, sometimes reaching 150 years in certain sectors: in France, for instance, 150 years for champagnes such as "Moët," or cognacs like "Martell" and "Rémy Martin"; 100 to 150 years for mineral water ("Evian," "Vittel," "Badoit," etc.); 50 to 100 years for spaghetti ("Lustucru"), chocolate ("Lanvin"), and pastis ("Ricard") (CNC, 1992). Other examples of "old" brand names are "The Times," "Coca-Cola," and "Walt Disney." Although the useful life cannot be known with certainty, particularly in advance, age is an ex post facto proof of a long economic life.
- Some authors argue that the value of a brand is maintained or even increased by huge advertising expenses, which are recognized as expenses and do not therefore justify amortization or a limitation of the useful life. In a similar situation, the useful life of tangible assets would be estimated based on the assumption of regular maintenance. In addition to this, amortization of the brand would result in double impact on the profit margins (amortization and maintenance) (Harding, 1997, pp. 81–84; Pizzey, 1991, p. 26).
- There are no doubts about the possibility of a brand value declining, but there are doubts about the regularity of the decline. Consequently, brands should be subject to write-downs if necessary but not to regular amortization (Smith, 1997, pp. 104–123; Wild & Scicluna, 1997, pp. 94–96).

Those in favor of amortization and a limited useful life for brands put forward the following responses to these arguments:

- For the purposes of financial accounting, the economic approach is more relevant than a legal point of view (Barth & Kneisel, 1997, p. 474). Although the legal right to use a brand might last indefinitely, the ability to achieve future economic benefits from this brand is what settles the question of amortization and useful life. It is not the legal aspect of a brand that creates future economic benefits but the higher sales of products, the stabilized connections between customers and the branded products, and the savings on advertising expenses (Barwise et al., 1989, pp. 29–32; Gold, 1998, p. 958; Meffert & Burmann, 1998, p. 87; Stein & Ortmann, 1996, p. 790). Brands are closely connected with the product sold under the brand. But products, their technology, customer expectations, and market conditions change constantly. So if the brand is not supported by management action to anticipate or oppose these changes, the value of the brand diminishes quickly (this conclusion has been reached from several different perspectives, see Barwise et al., 1989, pp. 32–38; Meffert & Burmann, 1998). The question raised by this argumentation is whether, from this point of view, the brand is still an identifiable and separable asset, or whether it is in fact too closely connected to the products or services to allow separate recognition.
- The expenses incurred to maintain a brand, e.g., advertising costs, are not an argument in favor of an indefinite life. The value of a brand is a certain customer connection that

leads to higher sales. With time this connection loses strength, then advertising creates new customer connections. So even when sales levels are constant, they are in fact different in substance from the original sales. This line of thought thus concludes that the purchased brand is eventually replaced by an internally generated brand, which should not be recognized as an asset (Barth & Kneisel, 1997, pp. 476–477; Boorberg, Strüngmann, & Wendelin, 1998, p. 1115).

- Just as there seem to be examples of brands always keeping their value, there are also brands that have vanished, like "Steinhäger" (spirit), "Simca" and "Triumph" (cars) (Harding, 1997, p. 82; Stein & Ortmann, 1996, p. 791).

In the end, the debate over brand amortization is based on how we understand the function of amortization. If amortization should reflect current value, there seem to be more objections than reasons for its application; if amortization is to distribute the recognized amount over a limited time, there are more arguments in favor of regular amortization (Barth & Kneisel, 1997, p. 474). The rules of the IASC, France, and Germany clearly reflect this discrepancy.

3.2. Amortization of brands under IAS, French, and German accounting rules

According to IAS 38 (para. 63), "after initial recognition, an intangible asset should be carried at its cost less any accumulated amortization and any accumulated impairment losses." Later, the standard states (para. 79) that "the depreciable amount of an intangible asset should be allocated on a systematic basis over the best estimate of its useful life" and that "there is a rebuttable presumption that the useful life of an intangible asset will not exceed 20 years." In the case of control "achieved through legal rights that have been granted for a finite period," the standard adds that "the useful life of the intangible asset should not exceed the period of the legal rights unless: (a) the legal rights are renewable and (b) renewal is virtually certain" (para. 85). However, because of the existence of economic factors, "the useful life is the shorter of the periods determined by" economic and legal "factors" (para. 86).

Moreover, "in rare cases, there may be persuasive evidence that the useful life of an intangible asset will be a specific period longer than 20 years. In these cases, the presumption that the useful life generally does not exceed 20 years is rebutted and the enterprise (a) amortizes the intangible asset over the best estimate of its useful life; (b) estimates the recoverable amount of the intangible asset at least annually in order to identify any impairment loss...; and (c) discloses the reasons why the presumption is rebutted and the factor(s) that played a significant role in determining the useful life of the asset" (para. 83).

The idea that the asset may never be amortized is explicitly mentioned, as the standard adds that "the useful life of an intangible asset may be very long but it is always finite" (para. 84).

Article 35 of the Fourth European Directive of 1978 (para. 1. b) stipulates that "the purchase price or production cost of fixed assets with limited useful economic lives must be reduced by value adjustments calculated to write off the value of such assets systematically over their useful economic lives." This article gives a general definition of depreciation. However, the Directive does not provide any special guidance for brands, in contrast to formation expenses (article 34) and costs of research and development (article 37, para. 2). Once again, member states enjoy the widest latitude in dealing with brand amortization.

In France, the depreciable nature of brands was the subject of considerable debate in the report on brands mentioned above (CNC, 1992), due to a lack of clarity in the General Accounting Plan. The Plan seems (implicitly) to exclude amortization of acquired brands, because they are not mentioned in the asset subheading "Amortization of concessions, patents..." whereas they are included in the asset heading "Concessions, patents... brands..." At the same time, a write-down expense is allowed, if necessary: the asset subheading "Write-down (provision) expense for intangible assets: concessions..." includes brands explicitly. Considering matters from a conceptual point of view, the CNC report added that there is no irreversible amortization of a brand, and so it concluded that a brand (acquired or internally generated) should not be amortized. Instead, a regular test of impairment should be implemented.

In Germany, recognized intangible assets, with the exception of the acquired goodwill, have to be amortized over their useful life. In this country, recent discussions dealt with the question of whether a brand has a determined useful life and, if so, what the appropriate period is for financial accounting purposes. In 1996, the federal court for tax affairs (*Bundesfinanzhof*) ruled that there is no reliable estimation for a specific limitation of the useful life and amortization of brands: therefore, brands should not be subject to amortization. In reaction, the ministry of finance took a contrary position in 1998, declaring that it generally supposes a useful life for brands to be 15 years (the same as for goodwill) if the owner cannot justify a shorter period. Since accounting for tax purposes and financial accounting are closely connected in Germany (see Haller, 1992), these statements are in fact relevant for financial accounting, too.

Since the decision of 1996, several comments have been published in literature (see among others Barth & Kneisel, 1997; Boorberg et al., 1998). Nearly all authors criticize the decision of the federal court; in doing so they put forward a range of arguments (most of them included in the list above), and recommend amortization of brands (exception: Fick, 1997). Even the presumption of 15 years is considered too long. Instead, a useful life of between 3 and 5 years is proposed. This shorter period is justified by the prudence principle, as there is no reliable measurement, or by reference to life cycles (Meffert & Burmann, 1998, pp. 96–118; Stein & Ortmann, 1996). For extremely strong brands only, a longer useful life may be applied (Boorberg et al., 1998, pp. 1114–1116). These arguments correspond to the general opinion before the 1996 court ruling (Richter, 1990). Because of the range of opinions, the question of applying amortization remains unclear for both financial and tax accounting purposes.

A brand acquired in an acquisition of a whole enterprise (in a merger or other business combination) and which is not reliably separately identifiable is, as mentioned above, included in goodwill. This goodwill (and therefore the brand, being part of it) can, in Germany, be either amortized over a maximum of 4 years or a longer useful life, or treated directly as an expense. If the company opts to amortize intangible assets over more than 4 years, a useful life of 15 years is usually applied in the financial accounts due to a corresponding fiscal regulation. Goodwill arising from a business combination can additionally be set off against reserves. The considerable number of options in the treatment of goodwill arising from a business combination shows that in Germany it is significant whether a brand is separated from the goodwill and recognized as an identifiable asset or incorporated in the goodwill. Whereas in the first case it must be amortized over its useful life, in the second it can be amortized over a period of up to 4 years, amortized over the useful life of the goodwill, directly expensed, or set off against reserves. This means it really matters how a brand acquired in a business combination is recorded.

And so a general divergence emerges between the German and French accounting conceptions regarding the amortization of brands, resulting—as already seen—from different perceptions of the function of depreciation. According to HGB, para. 253, al. 2, s. 2 the dominant objective of normal depreciation in Germany is not to take account of a fall in value but to spread the cost over the useful life (Coenenberg, 1996, p. 130; Döring, 1995, pp. 926–928; Moxter, 1996, pp. 215–217). The same reasoning is followed by the IASC (1998, para. 46). The purpose of amortization is therefore clearly defined under IAS and German rules, whereas in the French General Accounting Plan amortization "hesitates between the objective of assessing depreciation and that of spreading costs" (Klee, 1992, p. 50).

There are thus important differences between Germany and France with respect to both the concept and the period of brand amortization. Whilst in Germany brands are treated as amortizable assets with relatively short lives, in France brands are nonamortizable intangible fixed assets. IAS 38, with its rebuttable presumption of a useful life no longer than 20 years, lies somewhere in between these positions, albeit closer to the German position (see Table 2).

3.3. Revaluation

For the valuation of intangible assets at the end of the financial year, IAS 38 defines a benchmark treatment and an allowed alternative treatment (para. 63–64). The benchmark treatment is based on the initial measurement minus accumulated amortization and accumulated impairment losses, as explained above. Under the allowed alternative treatment, "an intangible asset should be carried at a revalued amount, being its fair value at the date of the revaluation less any subsequent accumulated amortization and any subsequent accumulated impairment losses. ... Fair value should be estimated by reference to an active market" (para. 64). However, as IAS 38, para. 67 specifies, "an active market cannot exist for brands," as is the case for other intangible assets, like newspapers, mastheads, publishing rights etc., because "the transactions are relatively infrequent." Therefore, the prices for recent transactions do "not provide sufficient evidence of the fair value" of other

Table 2
Amortization of brands

IAS 38	France	Germany
• Amortization required over the useful life • 20 years normally the maximum (rebuttable presumption) • Disclosure if the amortization period exceeds 20 years • Impairment test if amortization period > 20 years	No amortization Impairment possible	Amortization required Generally over 3–5 years, limited possibility over 20 years

brands. Due to this lack of a reliable measurement basis, IAS 38 appears not to allow revaluation of brands.

The situation is absolutely clear in Germany and France. There, in accordance with the Fourth European Directive (Article 33, para. 1), the revaluation of intangible assets is generally not allowed. In Germany, due to the strong principle of prudence, revaluation is not allowed for any asset. In France, the general revaluation option is limited (as it is in Article 33 para. 1 of the Fourth Directive) to tangible fixed and financial assets.

In practice, the positions taken by IAS 38 and the French and German laws lead to the same result: revaluation of brands is forbidden.

3.4. Recovery of the carrying amount

Brands may be subject to a write-down because of extraordinary conditions that lead to an unexpected decline in value. Examples of such circumstances are a loss of customer confidence because of an event such as the "Elch-Test" for Daimler-Benz or a loss of image such as "Brent Spar" was for Shell (Meffert & Burmann, 1998, pp. 118–119).

To determine whether or not an intangible asset is impaired, an enterprise applies IAS 36 ("Impairment of Assets"). In addition to the requirement included in this standard, IAS 38 adds that "an enterprise should estimate the recoverable amount of the following intangible assets at least at each financial year end, even if there is no indication that the asset is impaired: (a) an intangible asset that is not yet available for use; and (b) an intangible asset that is amortized over a period exceeding 20 years from the date when the asset is available for use" (para. 99).

This mandatory write-down, in the case of impairment, is a direct consequence of the worldwide-applied principle of "lower of cost or market." Therefore it is compatible with the French and German rules.

In France, the *Commission des Opérations de Bourse* (COB — French equivalent of the Securities and Exchange Commission) also indicates that management is responsible for determining the objective and verifiable numeric criteria upon which the value of elements of intangible assets may be based year by year (COB, 1991, p. 10; X, 1991).

German rules regarding write-downs differentiate between state-owned corporations and private companies, current and noncurrent assets, and whether the decline in value is expected to last for a longer or shorter period. In the standard case of a state-owned company whose brands are classified as noncurrent assets, the brand must be written down to its fair value if an event has decreased the value of the brand for quite a long time. If there is a recovery of value later, the company must restate the brand at the lower of cost or market (HGB, para. 280).

4. Limitations and directions for future research

The topic of brand valuation has not been developed further here because it represents a separate topic in itself. The reliability and relevance of each of the methods in either Germany or France or within the context of IASC standards is open to discussion. It would also be interesting to address the following questions:

- How do industry norms for tradable assets (e.g., landing slots, franchise rights) differ in France and Germany?
- What are the limits of market valuation?
- How do companies deal with the following problems encountered in the use of royalty-relief methods: selection and determination of royalty rates, discount rates, protection/renewal and length of brand life, and calculation of discounted value on the basis of a terminal value or to perpetuity?

Harmonization efforts are long-run and evolutionary in nature, with the market ultimately determining which of the existing alternatives will prevail. Harmonization also requires countries to change their domestic practices at some point — at least for multinational reporting. In this context, our conclusions on the difficulty of harmonization may by limited by the fact that any assessment as to whether harmonization initiatives have worked or are working is difficult on a spot basis.

5. Conclusion

The Fourth and Seventh European Directives allow wide latitude for the treatment of brands, in relation to their capitalization, their valuation and amortization, and the treatment of the difference arising on first consolidation. This partly explains the emergence of accounting solutions that may be divergent or even contradictory in different European countries, as in the examples studied, France and Germany. Table 3 presents the major differences between the three sets of rules.

Firstly, it becomes obvious that with regard to self-generated brands German standards have more in common with the IASC opinion than with leading accounting assumptions in France. In consolidated financial statements, as far as brands are concerned, France clearly has no hesitation in breaking away from the focus on the prudence principle and

Table 3
Fundamental differences

	IAS 38	France	Germany
Capitalization of internally generated brands	Impossible	Might be possible	Impossible
	Reliability	*Relevance*	*Reliability*
Allocation to brands of the difference arising on first consolidation	Possible in theory, difficult in practice	Possible and widely practiced	Possible in theory, difficult in practice
	Reliability	*Relevance*	*Reliability*
Amortization	20 years	No amortization	Short amortization
	Reliability/relevance	*Relevance*	*Reliability*

moving towards a more economic approach to accounting. Most surprisingly, the IASC stresses the reliability aspect ("separability," "identifiability," and "reliable measurement of cost") over the relevance aspect in connection with brands. Finally, regarding the concept and period of amortization of brands, the IASC's position is closer to Germany than France.

Brand accounting is the focus point of the conflicting relationship between the major characteristics of accounting data, 'relevance" and "reliability." This research shows that the frequently stated association between the Anglo-American accounting philosophy and "relevance," and between the Continental-European philosophy and "reliability," may not apply when it comes to brand accounting (see Table 3). It also questions the research concept of clustering national accounting systems, because France and Germany, two countries often found together in the "Continental-European cluster" (Choi, Frost, & Meek, 1999, p. 37), have adopted very different solutions for brand accounting in relation to each other and to the IASC.

Although we worked on a spot basis (see above), this paper seems to be a good illustration of the difficulty of international accounting harmonization. It could be worthwhile to think about other ways of making accounting comparable in the meantime, in order to avoid fundamental opposition (we find it difficult to imagine French companies starting to amortize brands, even over 20 years), for example by providing additional information in the notes. One idea could be the disclosure of an additional statement of the breakdown, changes, and values for the most important groups of intangible assets in a corporation (Haller, 1998, pp. 583–591). This should show to what extent the corporate value is made up of different sorts of intangibles. Such a statement would have to be accompanied by additional information, e.g., explaining the brand(s) and its (their) valuation. Our reflections demonstrate that brands in particular and intangibles in general are set to remain a major accounting challenge in the future.

Acknowledgments

The authors thank participants of the 1999 "Emerging Issues in International Accounting" Conference (CIERA and Niagara University) and two anonymous reviewers for helpful comments and suggestions. They also thank Ann Gallon for helping to finalize the English-language version of the paper. The present paper was made possible by financial support from the Research Center of the HEC School of Management (Paris) and the European Commission (TSER project "MERITUM" - MEasuRing Intangibles To Understand and improve innovation Management).

References

Adler, H., Düring, W., & Schmaltz, K. (1995). *Rechnungslegung und Prüfung der Unternehmen* (6th ed.). Schäffer-Poeschel Verlag, Stuttgart.

Accounting Standards Board (ASB) (1997). *Goodwill and intangible assets*. Financial Reporting Standard 10, (December).
Baetge, J. (1996). *Bilanzen* (4th ed.). IDW Verlag, Düsseldorf.
Barth, T., & Kneisel, H. (1997). Entgeltlich erworbene Warenzeichen in der Handels- und Steuerbilanz. *Die Wirtschaftsprüfung*, *50*, 473–479.
Barwise, P., Higson, C., Likierman, A., & Marsh, P. (1989). *Accounting for brands*, London Business School and ICAEW (London).
Boorberg, W., Strüngemann, T., & Wendelin, B. (1998). Zur Abnutzbarkeit entgeltlich erworbener Warenzeichen und Arzneimittelzulassungen. *Deutsches Steuerrecht*, *36*, 1113–1118.
Breit, H. V. (1997). Starke Marken sind Garanten für Wachstum in stagnierenden Märkten. *Blick durch die Wirtschaft*, *10*, 1 (October).
Choi, F. D. S., Frost, C. A., & Meek, G. K. (1999). *International accounting* (3rd ed.). Prentice Hall Upper Saddle River, NJ.
Conseil national de la comptabilité (CNC) (1986). *Plan comptable général* (4th ed.) (Paris).
Conseil national de la comptabilité (CNC) (1987). *Avis relatif au traitement comptable des logiciels*. Document No. 66 (April).
Conseil national de la comptabilité (CNC) (1990). *Avis relatif au traitement comptable de l'écart d'aquisition*. Document No. 85 (January).
Conseil national de la comptabilité (CNC) (1992). *Les marques : un actif pour l'entreprise?* Document No. 94 (April).
Commission des Opérations de Bourse (COB) (1991). Nécessité de la vérification périodique des actifs financiers et des actifs incorporels. *Bulletin*, *243*, 3–12 (January).
Coenenberg, A. (1996). *Jahresabschluß und Jahresabschlußanalyse* (16th ed.) mi-Verlag (Landsberg a. L.).
Döring, U. (1995). Commentary on HGB, para. 253. In: K. Küting, & C.-P. Weber (Eds.), *Handbuch der Rechnungslegung, Band Ia*, pp. 877–970 (4th ed.). Schäffer-Poeschel Verlag, Stuttgart.
Duizabo, S., & Guillaume, N. (1996). Approche d'une nouvelle typologie des actifs immatériels. *Echanges*, *119*, 34–39 (January).
European Economic Community (EEC) (1978). 4th Directive on the annual accounts of certain types of companies no 78/660/EEC. *Official Journal of the European Communities*, (August 14).
European Economic Community (EEC) (1983). 7th Directive on consolidated accounts of companies no. 83/349/EEC. *Official Journal of the European Communities*, (July 18).
Fick, H. P. (1997). Planmäßige Abschreibung auf Warenzeichen. *Die steuerliche Betriebsprüfung*, *37*, 107–108.
Gélard, G. (1995). Les immobilisations incorporelles — l'exposé-sondage E50 de l'IASC. *L'Actualité Fiduciaire*, *788*, 45–50 (September).
Gélard, G. (1998). Immobilisations incorporelles — la norme 38 de l'IASC. *Echanges*, *149*, 46–49 (November).
Gold, G. (1998). Steuerliche Abschreibungsmöglichkeiten für Marken? *Der Betrieb*, *51*, 956–959.
Haigh, D., & Perrier, R. (1997). Valuation of trade marks and brand names. In: R. Perrier (Ed.), *Brand valuation* (3rd ed.) pp. 35–42, Premier, London.
Haller, A. (1992). The relationship of financial and tax accounting in Germany: a major reason for accounting disharmony in Europe. *International Journal of Accounting*, *27*, 310–323.
Haller, A. (1998). Immaterielle Vermögenswerte — Wesentliche Herausforderung für die Zukunft der Unternehmensrechnung. In: H. P. von Möller, & F. Schmidt (Eds.), *Rechnungswesen als Instrument für Führungsentscheidungen, Festschrift für A. Coenenberg* (pp. 561–596). Schäffer-Poeschel Verlag, Stuttgart.
Harding, T. (1995). Intangible: a question of reliability. *IASC Insight, 8–9* (June) IASC, London.
Harding, T. (1997). Brands from the standards setters' perspective. In: R. Perrier (Ed.), *Brand valuation* (3rd ed.) pp. 73–86, Premier, London.
Hommel, M. (1997). Internationale Bilanzrechtskonzeptionen und immaterielle Vermögensgegenstände. *Zeitschrift für betriebswirtschaftliche Forschung*, *49*, 345–369.
IASC (1995). *Intangible assets*. Proposed International Accounting Standard, Exposure Draft E50, London.
IASC (1997). *Intangible assets*. Proposed International Accounting Standard, Exposure Draft E60, London.
IASC (1998a). *Business combinations*. International Accounting Standard 22, London.

IASC (1998b). *Intangible assets*. International Accounting Standard 38, London.

IASC (1998c). *Basis for conclusions: IAS 38, Intangible assets, IAS 22 (revised 1998)*. Business combinations and summary of changes to E60 and IAS 22 (October), London.

Kahn, O. (1997). Evaluation de la marque, une méthode spécifique. *Revue Française de Comptabilité, 286*, 73–78 (February).

Kapferer, J.-N. (1998). *Les marques, capital de l'entreprise. Créer et développer des marques fortes* (3rd ed.). Paris: Editions d'Organisation.

Keitz, I. (1997). *Immaterielle Güter in der internationalen Rechnungslegung*. IDW Verlag (Düsseldorf).

Klee, L. (1992). La comptabilité allemande. *Revue Fiduciaire Comptable, 175*, 33–69 (May).

Knop, W., & Küting, K. (1995). Commentary on HGB para. 255. In: K. Küting, & C.-P. Weber (Eds.), *Handbuch der Rechnungslegung, Band Ia*, pp. 1011–1149 (4th ed.). Schäffer-Poeschel Verlag, Stuttgart.

La Villeguérin (de), E., (Ed.). (2000). *Dictionnaire fiduciaire comptable* (7th ed., 2001). Paris: La Villeguerin Éditions (See namely headings: Marques, Immobilisations incorporelles, Immobilisations corporelles, Ecart de première consolidation).

Medus, J.-L. (1990). Méthodes de valorisation d'une marque. *Revue du Financier, 73*, 11–16 (January–February).

Meffert, H., & Burmann, C. (1998). Abnutzbarkeit und Nutzungsdauer von Marken — Ein Beitrag zur steuerlichen Behandlung von Warenzeichen. In H. von Meffert, & N. Krawitz (Eds.), *Unternehmensrechnung und -besteuerung. Festschrift zum 65. Geb. von D. Börner* (pp. 75–126). Gabler Verlag, Wiesbaden.

Moxter, A. (1986). Immaterielle Vermögensgegenstände des Anlagevermögens. In: U. Leffson, D. Rückle, & B. Grossfeld (Eds.), *Handwörterbuch unbestimmter Rechtsbegriffe im Bilanzrecht des HGB* (pp. 246–250). Schmidt Verlag, Köln.

Moxter, A. (1996). *Bilanzrechtsprechung* (4th ed.). Mohr Verlag, Tübingen.

Muller, K. A. III (1999). An examination of the voluntary recognition of acquired brand names in the United Kingdom. *Journal of Accounting and Economics, 26*, 179–191.

Nussenbaum, M. (1991). Les marques : un actif à évaluer. *Banque, 515*, 401–408 (April).

Ochs, P. (1996). Mieux mesurer l'investissement immatériel. *Echanges, 570*, 48–50 (May).

Orsini L. L., Gould, J. D. Mc Allister, J. E, & Parikh, R. N. (Eds.) (1998). *World accounting* (Ed. Matthew Bender). Release No. 16 (November).

Pizzey, A. (1991). Accounting for goodwill and brands. *Management Accounting London, 69* (8), 22–26.

Plasseraud, Y., Plasseraud, C., & Dehaut, M. (1994). *Marques — Création, Valorisation, Protection*. Paris: Editions Francis Lefebvre, Collection Dossiers pratiques.

Power, M. (1992). The politics of brand accounting in the United Kingdom. *European Accounting Review, 1* (1), 39–68.

Reilly, R. F., & Schweihs, R. P. (1998). *Valuing intangible assets*. Mc Graw Hill (New York).

Richter, M. (1990). Die immateriellen Anlagewerte. In: *Handbuch des Jahresabschlusses in Einzeldarstellungen* (2nd ed.) (Abt. II/2, Schmidt Verlag, Köln).

Roeb, T. (1994). *Markenwert — Begriff, Berechnung Bestimmungsfaktoren*. Verlag Mainz, Aachen.

Rohnke, C. (1992). Bewertung von Warenzeichen beim Unternehmenskauf. *Der Betrieb, 45*, 1941–1945 (September).

Sattler, H. (1995). Markenbewertung. *Zeitschrift für Betriebswirtschaft, 65*, 663–682.

Smith, G. V. (1997). *Trademark valuation*. John Wiley & Sons (New York).

Stein, C., & Ortmann, M. (1996). Bilanzierung und Bewertung von Warenzeichen. *Der Betriebs-Berater, 51* (15), 787–792.

Viale, F. (1991). Les marques : de la théorie à la pratique. *Revue Fiduciaire Comptable, 166*, 31–40 (July).

Viale, F., & Lafay, F. (1990). Les marques : un nouvel enjeu pour les entreprises. *Revue Française de Comptabilité, 216*, 92–99 (October).

Wermelkirchen, S. (1999). Kraft des Namens. *Wirtschaftswoche*, 154–160 (18th November).

Wild, K., & Scicluna, M. (1997). Accounting for brands: the practitioner's perspective. In: R. Perrier (Ed.), *Brand valuation* (3rd ed.) pp. 87–98. Premier, London.

X. (1991). Quelle est la position de la COB en matière d'évaluation des marques ? *Bulletin Comptable et Financier Francis Lefebvre, 52* (September): 72–74.

X. (1995a). Immobilisations incorporelles — projet de norme comptable internationale E50 de l'IASC. *Bulletin Comptable et Financier Francis Lefebvre, 68* (September): 25–32.

X. (1995b). Immobilisations incorporelles — Projet de norme IASC. *Revue Fiduciaire Comptable, 214* (December): 7–10.

X. (1999a). *L'information financière en 1998: 100 groupes industriels et commerciaux.* Paris: CPC.

X. (1999b). *Arrêté du 22 juin 1999 portant homologation du règlement 99-02 du 29 avril 1999 du Comité de la réglementation comptable* ("Arrêté" of June 22, 1999, approving the regulation No. 99-02 of April 29, 1999, of the Accounting Regulation Committee), Paris.

X. (1999c). *Arrêté du 22 juin 1999 portant homologation du règlement 99-03 du 29 avril 1999 du Comité de la réglementation comptable* ("Arrêté" of June 22, 1999, approving the regulation No. 99-03 of April 29, 1999, of the Accounting Regulation Committee), Paris.

The European Accounting Review 1998, **7:1**, 125–148

Accounting in Europe

Harmonization of the structure of audit firms: incorporation in the UK and Germany

Lisa Evans and Christopher Nobes
Napier University and University of Reading, UK

ABSTRACT

The Eighth EU Council Directive addresses the harmonization of the conditions for the approval of auditors This paper deals specifically with the approval of incorporated audit firms, which is regulated by Article 2 of the Directive, and with the extent to which the Eighth Directive has improved *de jure* harmonization of the rules for incorporated audit firms between UK and German law. The development of Article 2 from the proposal to the final version of the Directive is studied, as is the implementation of Article 2 into UK and German law and the reasoning behind the choices made by both Member States in this process. Although considerable changes were made to the laws of both countries, little greater *de jure* harmony was achieved.

INTRODUCTION

The Eighth EU Council Directive addresses the harmonization of the conditions for the approval of auditors. A working party had prepared an *avant projet* of a Directive to deal with the minimum qualification of auditors as early as May 1972, but the official Proposal (hereafter 1978 Draft) for the Directive was not published until 1978; the Amended Proposal (hereafter 1979 Draft) in 1979; and the final version in 1984. A chronology of the development of the Eighth Directive is given in Table 1.

This paper deals specifically with the rules relating to incorporated audit firms, which are found in Article 2 of the Directive. Van Hulle (1992) argues that this is one of the areas not satisfactorily resolved by the Eighth Directive because considerable national differences remain. He suggests that further initiatives by the Commission may be necessary. Similarly, Nordemann

Address for correspondence
Lisa Evans, Department of Accounting and Finance, Napier University, Sighthill Court, Edinburgh EH11 4BN, UK.

 0963–8180

Table 1 Chronology of the development of the Eighth Directive

(Unpublished) draft prepared by working party of Commission	30.05.72
Proposal for Eighth Directive (No. C 112/6)	13.05.78
Amendments proposed by European Parliament (No. C 140/154)	05.06.79
Opinion of the Economic and Social Committee (No. C 171/30)	09.07.79
Amended Proposal for Eighth Directive (No. C 317/6)	18.12.79
Council of Ministers/Working Party: revised (unpublished) drafts	1980–84
Eighth Council Directive (No. L 126/20)	10.04.84

(The items in bold print are publications in the *Official Journal of the European Communities*. For the Proposal and the Amended Proposal the actual issue dates were somewhat earlier, i.e. the Proposal dates from 24.4.1978 and the Amended Proposal from 5.12.1979.)

(1989) implicitly suggests that the Directive did not help harmonization of the authorization of firms.

The aim of this paper is to establish the extent to which the Eighth Directive has improved *de jure* harmony of the rules for incorporated audit firms between UK and German law. It examines the development of Article 2 from the draft to the adopted version of the Directive, examines UK and German views voiced during this process and, as far as possible, identifies probable influences of these two Member States. It further examines the implementation of Article 2 into UK and German law and the reasoning behind the choices made in this process.

UK and German law were chosen as case studies for this paper for a number of connected reasons. The two countries represent opposing accounting traditions, as has been suggested by the classifications carried out, for example, by Mueller (1967, 1968), Nair and Frank (1980), Nobes (1983, 1984/1992), or through studies based on Hofstede's (1984) identification of cultural patterns such as Gray (1988), Perera (1989) and Perera and Mathews (1990).

The two countries are often quoted as representatives of the Anglo-Saxon (or Anglo-American) and the continental European accounting traditions (see Perera, 1989 – who in turn refers to Mueller, 1967, and to Nobes, 1983, 1984/1992); or as representatives of the micro- and the macro-uniform-based systems (Nobes, 1983). Further they are often referred to as examples of different degrees of influence by the accounting professions on accounting regulation, different degrees of the professions' self-regulation versus state regulation, and of differing emphases on 'professionalism' (see, for example, Perera, 1989). This is related to a further important difference, i.e. that the UK has a common law-based legal system, while that of Germany is based on codified Roman law (David and Brierley, 1978). This legal difference has, *inter alia*, a significant influence on each country's interpretation of the 'true and fair view' principle. Further, there are differences in sources of finance for enterprises and, related to this, the importance of capital markets. While in Germany finance has traditionally been provided by banks (both as equity owners and as lenders), in the UK large companies have placed more reliance on finance through 'external' shareholders.[1] This latter difference in particular has also led to a greater emphasis on audit and publication requirements in the UK (Nobes and Parker, 1995).

However, Vieten (1995) challenges, in particular, the distinction between statutory control in Germany on the one hand, and a strong profession in the UK on the other. He points out that the traditionally claimed dichotomy between the UK and German accounting systems may no longer hold true for the professional frameworks in that, due to European company law harmonization, a near convergence has been achieved mainly because 'By increasing the scope for government intervention Britain is moving closer to the German system . . .' (Vieten, 1995: 495). However, apart from the apparent trend towards a stronger influence by the state in the UK, Vieten highlights more differences than similarities, thereby indicating that the old categorizations are still at least partly valid. Vieten himself points out that '. . . the audit objective under German law is to test for accordance with the relevant legislation' (*ibid.*: 500), rather than mainly to give an opinion on the true and fair view. This appears to be one of the essential differences between UK and German auditing, and may well lie at the heart of or be symptomatic of the old distinctions.

Categorization attempts are, almost by definition, simplifications, and Vieten does succeed in making the reader aware that the categorization may be subject to change, that the boundaries of the dichotomy may well be shifting and that the classifications are not always clear-cut. However, similar issues with respect to recent changes and their effect on the 'classification by regulation' were raised by Nobes (1984/1992).[2]

REGULATION BEFORE IMPLEMENTATION OF ARTICLE 2 OF THE DIRECTIVE

UK

According to the Companies Act (CA) 1985 s.389(6), audit firms were not allowed to incorporate in the UK. This restriction dated from the 1928 Act and had been instigated by the Institute of Chartered Accountants in England and Wales (ICAEW):

> . . . on the grounds that only individual auditors were in a position to express a personal audit opinion and take full responsibility for that opinion. This in turn reflected the generally accepted view of the time that the partnership structure was the appropriate form of business organisation for professional men.
>
> (Department of Trade and Industry – DTI, 1986: 61)

Germany

Section 5 (paragraphs 27 to 36) of the *Wirtschaftsprüferordnung* (WPO – Regulation for Auditors) deals with firms of *Wirtschaftsprüfer* (WP – auditors). Paragraph 27 specified, and still specifies, what legal forms are allowed for firms of WP: *Aktiengesellschaft* (AG – approximately equivalent to a public limited company), *Kommanditgesellschaft auf Aktien* (KGaA – a public company with at least one personally liable member), *Gesellschaft mit beschränkter Haftung* (GmbH – private limited company), *offene Handelsgesellschaft* (OHG – a form of partnership) or *Kommanditgesellschaft* (KG – limited partnership).[3,4]

Before the implementation of the Eighth Directive, paragraph 28 of the WPO specified (*inter alia*) that:

- the members of the supervisory board and of the management and the personally liable *Gesellschafter*[5] must be WP;
- under certain conditions *vereidigte Buchprüfer* (vBP – 'sworn-in' auditors[6]), *Steuerberater* (StB – qualified tax advisors) or experts from other areas who are not WP may be permitted to become members of the supervisory board, of the management, or personally liable *Gesellschafter*; although the number of these persons may not exceed the number of WP in the above positions;
- for the AG and KGaA the shares must be registered and may be transferred only with the agreement of the firm; the latter also applies to the transfer of shares in a GmbH.[7]

There was no reference to share ownership or voting rights.

Paragraph 34 dealt (and still deals) with the withdrawal of the authorization of firms of auditors, where the conditions for approval are no longer met. In some circumstances (para. 34 (1)(2)) authorization may not be withdrawn if the firm meets the required conditions within a specified time span.

ARTICLE 2 AND ITS DEVELOPMENT

Article 2 of the Directive (see Appendix) outlines the rules for approval of persons or firms. Only approved persons shall carry out statutory audits. Natural persons, as well as firms, may be authorized by the authorities of the Member States. Natural persons would have to fulfil the detailed requirements of the Directive about the qualification of auditors. Firms would have to fulfil the following conditions:

- the natural persons carrying out audits on behalf of the firms would have to meet the requirements of the Directive about the qualification of auditors;
- natural persons or firms meeting these requirements must hold the majority of the firm's voting rights; and
- natural persons or firms meeting these requirements must make up the majority of the firm's administrative or management body (unless there are only two such members, in which case it is sufficient for one of the two to meet the requirements).

The Directive offers an exemption to the second of these conditions (extract from Art. 2 (1)(b)(ii)):

> However, those Member States which do not impose such majority at the time of the adoption of this Directive need not impose it provided that all the shares in a firm of auditors are registered and can be transferred only with the agreement of the firm of auditors and/or, where the Member State so provides, with the approval of the competent authority.

The Directive also provides that the Member States may allow the authoritative bodies governing auditing to be professional associations.

The 1978 Draft had been less comprehensive than this (see Appendix). It did not require that the majority of members of management and administrative bodies be made up of persons qualifying as auditors under the conditions of the Directive. The 1979 Draft dropped a clause which had qualified the majority ownership requirement by restricting it to companies formed after implementation of the Directive. However, an idea similar to this exemption, but going even further, was reintroduced in the final Directive (see quotation above).

There are provisions concerning the non-interference by persons who are not themselves qualified as auditors. However, these became far less detailed between the Drafts (see Article 2 (2)(a)) and the final version, and they were moved to Article 27 (in the section: 'Professional integrity and independence'). A provision dealing with confidentiality was also relaxed in the 1979 Draft to the effect that audit reports and documents were no longer required to be withheld from the knowledge of non-qualified persons in the firm; this provision was dropped in the final version. In addition, the final version (Article 2 (1)(b)(iii)) introduced the requirement for the management and administrative bodies of firms to consist of a majority of qualified auditors or firms. At the same time it introduced the escape clause quoted above concerning the firm's ownership.

It appears, therefore, from Article 2 in the final version that ownership, but not administration and management, may be in the hands of a majority of persons or firms not qualifying under the provisions of the Directive. However, this concession concerning ownership only applies to Member States which had not imposed this requirement regarding majority previously; in other Member States, ownership too would have to be in the hands of a majority of persons or firms meeting the requirements of the Directive.

POSSIBLE INFLUENCES ON THE DIRECTIVE

It is clear that the idea of incorporation of audit firms has continental rather than British antecedents, but that both German and UK views were, to some extent, accommodated by the re-drafting.

British views

The 1978 Draft's Article 2 proposed to offer the Member State option to allow audit firms to incorporate. There does not appear to have been any resistance to this from the UK government, presumably because it would have been desirable from a UK point of view to have as many options as possible. However, the option represented a major change for UK legislation, and it caused a mixed reaction from the profession. Bartholomew (1978: 334) sees the following difficulties with the Draft's requirement that Member States shall approve only 'natural persons who satisfy at least the conditions specified in the following Articles' to carry out statutory audits and which denies others not so qualified access to all documents relating to the audit:

- This might require the exclusion of partners in accounting firms who would not be auditors under the Directive's rules, but whose specialism (e.g. taxation) might be required for the completion of the audit. As can be seen from Table 2, this requirement was substantially weakened in the 1979 Draft and dropped in the final version.
- It might cause problems for (a) quality control reviews of international firms, if these reviews were carried out by personnel not qualified under the provisions of the Directive, and (b) audits of multinational companies involving such personnel.

Similar points (with reference to Article 2) were made in a letter and a memorandum by the Consultative Committee of Accounting Bodies (CCAB) to the Department of Trade (*Accountancy*, 1981).

German views

German legislation before the Directive allowed audit firms to be incorporated and would have met the requirements of Article 2 (albeit by taking advantage of the exemption clause with respect to voting rights) except for two points:

- The Directive required the majority of the members of administrative or management bodies to be qualified auditors under its rules, while the German law merely required that non-WP should *not exceed* the number of WP on the supervisory board, the management, or as personally liable *Gesellschafter*.
- Following from this, German law did not have (and did not require) any exemption for cases where the relevant bodies were made up of only two persons.

Niessen (1984) claims that, due to the differences in the Member States' legislation, the provisions concerning firms of auditors were very much contested during the negotiations. This led to a weakening of the provision concerning the majority of voting rights for the benefit of those Member

States for whom this rule would have been new. Niessen claims that, without this compromise, the finalization of the Directive would not have been possible.

Bartholomew (1978: 334) suggests that this exemption was introduced for the benefit of Germany, in order to prevent legal difficulties. Due to their historical development, the large German audit firms were often owned by banks or the State. Had Article 2 been implemented without the exemption, these owners would have been barred, which would have violated the German constitution and could have given cause to legal proceedings against the State. In the most bizarre case, the State (as majority owner of Treuarbeit AG) would have to have dispossessed itself.[8]

This suggested cause of the exemption is also supported by the following quote from Strobel (1984), which further highlights the German concern:

> The principle of the liberal profession in auditing is an obstacle for firms of auditors. If those circles which wanted to limit the Directive to a strictly liberal profession basis had succeeded, this would have meant the end of our large firms of auditors and thereby also of the concentration of audit firms. *Meanwhile,* inter alia *the German side of negotiations has achieved a solution* which leaves our concentration of audit firms untouched and *thereby also secures the existence of Treuarbeit AG, which is owned by the Federation and the Länder, as well as that of similar firms.*[9]
>
> (Strobel, 1984: 954 translation – emphases added)

It appears, however, that the latter part of Strobel's argument, i.e. the continued existence of state-owned firms (or others with a majority of outsider participation) is the more valid one. For example, English[10] experience has shown that the ban on firms being legal entities is no obstacle to a concentration of the firms.

The 'price' of the Directive's exemption clause in Article 2 (1)(b)(ii) (as discussed above, i.e. that the majority of voting rights need not be held by auditors fulfilling the Directive's conditions if '. . . all the shares in a firm of auditors are registered and can be transferred only with the agreement of the firm of auditors . . .') was no problem from a German point of view since this provision already existed.

Other German concerns included the following:

- A desire for a tightening of the provisions of Article 2 is apparent in the suggestions made by a body representing German accounting academics (von Wysocki, 1979). With respect to Article 2 (2)(a) of the draft (see Appendix), they recommended further regulation to ensure independent and unbiased audit work by firms in which outsiders have an interest. To achieve this, they suggest a strengthening of the technical/professional position of the supervisory board or the management.
- Lück (1979), also commenting on the Proposal, welcomed the provision preventing non-auditors from owning a majority of the share capital of firms of WP. However, he thought that the provisions did not go far

enough, since they did not appear sufficiently able to prevent interconnections between firms of auditors and outsiders, even audit clients. He suggested that the Commission should reconsider the question of whether outsiders should be excluded from participation altogether.

- Another point of criticism is the wording of Article 2 (2)(a) (see Lück, 1979; and Wirtschaftsprüferkammer und Institut der Wirtschaftsprüfer in Deutschland e.V. (WPK and IdW – the Chamber of Auditors and the Institute of Auditors in Germany), 1979). With reference to the provisions concerning the assignment of audit staff, confidentiality and access to audit documents, Lück points out that there is a paradox in the regulations because the Directive allows management participation of non-auditors, but effectively prevents this through detailed rules which tie their hands. The WPK and IdW argue that, for specific issues, the auditor may need to rely on the expertise of non-auditors (who may belong to the audit firm's management). They therefore suggest a wording according to which the audit documents would not be withheld from non-auditors as long as these work for the firm of auditors and are subject to the same secrecy rules as the auditors.
- The body representing German accounting academics would have preferred ownership of new firms to be exclusively in the hands of auditors, although they acknowledge that the constitutional implications would have to be considered for existing firms (Sieben and von Wysocki, 1979).

Similar concerns were voiced in the UK with respect to the original restrictive wording of Article 2 (a), especially sub-paragraphs (1) and (3). The problems were addressed in the 1979 Draft and the provisions were considerably watered down in the final version (as discussed in the previous section). Although some German commentators suggested a tightening of the rules on participation of outsiders, the main German influence appears to have been the introduction of the exemption clause with respect to majority of ownership/voting rights (see above – e.g. Bartholomew, 1978; Strobel, 1984).

IMPLEMENTATION IN THE UK

Department of Trade and Industry (DTI) consultation

In 1986 the DTI published a consultative document inviting comments on both the implementation of the Eighth Directive and other issues which the necessary review of the legislation would give an opportunity to address. While it was felt that to comply with the minimum requirements of the Directive would require little change to legislation, the DTI also sought correspondents' views on such matters (partly related to the implementation of the Directive) as the incorporation of audit firms or the legislation on auditors' qualifications.

As mentioned above, according to the CA 1985, corporate entities could not be appointed as auditors. However, the DTI document suggests that, to some extent, the arguments made against incorporation had in recent years lost relevance. The DTI summarized the main arguments in favour of incorporation as follows:

- Incorporation would better enable audit firms to adopt management structures corresponding to their size and business diversity.
- Firms could more easily compete with companies in other industries in attracting specialist staff (e.g. by offering perks such as share ownership and by avoiding the conflict inherent in the requirement for all partners of accounting firms to be accountants – although the latter is, of course, an issue not necessarily linked to incorporation).
- Incorporation would have certain financial advantages, in particular with reference to raising capital.
- Incorporation would place firms on a similar footing to incorporated firms in other European countries. There might thus be advantages with respect to competition and rules on mutual recognition.
- Other financial services companies might be able to be authorized to audit if the companies met the legislation's minimum requirements. (This argument would of course not be congenial to accountants, since it would be against their interests to see the market or audit services opened to non-accountants.)
- There might be certain advantages with respect to limiting auditors' liability (in that, by forming a limited liability company, individuals would be protected against personal bankruptcy in cases of litigation).

The following arguments were made against incorporation:

- The partnership structure places responsibility on the individual partners and is therefore the most appropriate business form for accountants.
- Lack of personal liability, and the possibility of non-auditors as part-owners, would represent a risk to independence and integrity.
- Directors or employees of audit firms would have less incentive for 'adopting the highest professional standards' (DTI, 1986: 67) (presumably because they would not necessarily be the (only) owners of the business). The quality of service provided might be reduced.
- Outside ownership might negatively affect partners' commitment to the audit firm.

The document further sought views on any additional safeguards beyond the requirements of the Directive that might be adopted if incorporation was to be allowed. This could, in particular, address:

- the requirements of the Directive's Article 2 (presumably with reference to the provision that the majority of shareholders or members of the administrative or management bodies should be auditors[11]);
- any rules on integrity and independence over and above those applying to partnerships and sole practitioners (e.g. with respect to outside shareholders; for example, it was suggested that such shareholders should not be allowed to be audit clients or companies related to them);
- the requirement for indemnity insurance.

Response from firms

KPMG Peat Marwick McLintock (1987) was one of the UK audit firms expressing their views on incorporation. They did not object in principle to incorporation and did not perceive this to have a negative effect on the public interest, but objected to the idea of outside shareholders. Their objection was not based on concerns about auditor competence and the resulting quality of the audit, but rather on concerns about auditor independence and confidentiality. The most obvious problem, i.e. the audit client holding shares in the audit firm, had been addressed by the DTI. KPMG felt that the same person should not be allowed to hold a directorship with the auditor *and* his client.[12] They were further concerned about:

> situations where the outside interest in the corporate auditor also has a financial interest in a company being audited by the corporate auditor. These interests are not restricted to share interests but also include loans to that other company. We . . . suggest that an interest as a commercial competitor, or as a potential predator, should also be regarded as an interest which could affect independence [*ibid.*: 4].

It was further felt that outside interests would raise public concern about confidentiality, even if this were addressed by rules on the security of confidential information.

As a further argument against outside interests, reference was made to developments in Germany (cf. 'Implementation in Germany', below):

> Germany, by contrast, is a leading international business country which has allowed audits to be carried out by corporate auditors, and previously with no restriction on the extent of outside interests . . . in 1985 the German Government introduced a law which requires all new corporate auditors to be wholly owned by persons working in the business of the corporate auditor and with a majority of voting shares being held by qualifying interests. Further, for existing corporate auditors the law effectively requires that all further issues of shares, or sales of shares by outside interests, are to be qualifying interests or other internal interests.
>
> . . .
>
> At a time when there is no indication of any relaxation of the independence environment in the international business world, and when a leading member of the Community, Germany, is taking steps to strengthen independence, we think it

Table 2 Views of large accounting firms on five incorporation issues (Source: *Accountancy Age*, 1988: 5)

Firm	*1*	*2*	*3*	*4*	*5*
Arthur Andersen	0%	49%	total ban	yes	yes
BDO Binder Hamlyn	49.9%	49.9%	49.9%	no	no
Clark Whitehill	25%	19.9%	total ban	yes	yes
Ernst & Whinney	49.9%	25%	25%	no	no
Hodgson Impey	25%	25%	25%	no	no
Moores & Rowland	25%	49%	total ban	no	no
Neville Russell	49.9%	25%	total ban	no	yes
Peat Marwick McLintock	49.9%	25%	total ban	no	no
Robson Rhodes	49.9%	25%	allowed: no limit specified	no	no

1: Limit on voting shares for non-auditors in firm
2: Limit on percentage of shares allowed to outsiders
3: Limit on outsiders' voting rights
4: Ban on outsider-shareholder directors
5: Ban on outsider-shareholders influencing appointment of director

> would be astonishing if the UK were to introduce legislation which could lead to a weakening of the independence environment [*ibid.*: 6].

However, KPMG's views,[13] in particular with respect to outside shareholders, were not totally shared by all the other large firms. Table 2 shows a summary of the views of a number of large firms.

The Law

The UK implemented the Eighth Directive through the Companies Act 1989. This resulted in few practical changes: its main impact appears to have been that more rules were laid down in legislation, instead of being left to the accounting profession. One of the more important changes was the removal of the prohibition for auditors to incorporate (with effect from 1 October 1991). Section 25 of the 1989 Act states that:

> (1) a person is eligible for appointment as company auditor only if he –
>
> (a) is a member of a recognized supervisory body,[14] and
> (b) is eligible for the appointment under the rules of that body.
>
> (2) An individual or a firm may be appointed as company auditor.
>
> . . .

'Firm' can refer to a partnership or to a body corporate. This effectively removes the old prohibition of CA 1985 s.389(6).

Part II of the Act's Schedule 11 lays down the following minimum rule for Recognized Supervisory Bodies (RSBs):

4. – (1) The body must have rules to the effect that a person is not eligible for appointment as company auditor unless –
   (a) in the case of an individual, he holds an appropriate qualification;
   (b) in the case of a firm –
      (i) the individuals responsible for company audit work on behalf of the firm hold an appropriate qualification, and
      (ii) the firm is controlled by qualified persons (. . .).

The profession's implementation

In May 1989 the Independence and Incorporation Committee of the three Chartered Institutes published a report summarizing the responses (by auditors, users and preparers of accounts) to a Consultative Document which they had issued (ICAEW, ICAS, ICAI, 1988b).[15] They recommended that:

- At least 75% of shareholders' voting rights in an incorporated audit firm should be held by auditors.
- At least 75% of the voting rights on the board of directors of an incorporated audit firm should be held by auditors.
- Restrictions imposed on the ownership and management of incorporated firms of auditors should also apply, with appropriate adjustments, to partnerships.
- Other restrictions imposed by professional guidance in order to safeguard independence should apply equally to partners in audit firms and to shareholders and directors of incorporated firms of auditors.

(ICAEW, 1989: 1)

The Institutes' report addresses the importance of independence, in particular in the UK's environment, which involves the exercise of professional judgement and the overriding importance of the true and fair view, rather than the '. . . mechanical compliance with detailed rules . . .' (ICAEW, ICAS, ICAI, 1989: 8). In this context it was pointed out that independence and integrity are mental attitudes which should be protected and developed by the ethos of the firms, and which cannot be assured through detailed rules or procedures relating to any one particular audit.

The independence and integrity of audit firms would be endangered, according to the Institutes, if ownership or control were in the hands of outsiders – this might lead to a greater emphasis on profit-orientation as opposed to independence and integrity. On the other hand, it was suggested that, for example, a 51% majority of ownership or management rights in the hands of auditors would not necessarily guarantee control. It was suggested that 5% or 10% outside ownership would be no threat. However, 30% would give a certain amount of influence to outsiders. This led the Institutes to suggest that a minimum of a 75% majority of voting rights should be owned,[16] and, on the board of directors, 75% of the voting rights should be held by auditors. No other restrictions on the holding of the minority interests were deemed necessary. The Institutes would not require the remaining 25% of shares or voting rights to be held by non-auditor *insiders* (i.e. persons working for the firm). The requirement relating to shares should relate to voting rights as well as to all share capital in aggregate. Further, restrictions should be imposed on group structures, in order to avoid dilution of control.

It was further suggested that outsiders and non-auditor insiders should be made subject to the rules of the Institutes. The Institutes would, in this respect, monitor and impose sanctions on the firms, which should satisfy the criterion of being 'fit and proper persons'.[17] The Institutes further suggested that '. . . the transfer of shares in an audit firm should be subject to approval by the Board'. This would require consideration of the rules for 'fit and proper persons' and thus prevent shares from being freely traded (*ibid.*: 11–12).[18]

Richards (1990) points out that the DTI considered the above suggestions to be going too far and to be detrimental to competition.[19] Similar concerns were voiced by Sir Gordon Borrie, the then Director General of Fair Trading, in a report addressed to the DTI (*CA Magazine*, 1991a). However, 'The profession's initial reaction to Sir Gordon's report has been one of slight bewilderment: the prospect of auditing firms being run by unqualified operators is not likely to silence critics of the present system' (*ibid.*: 60). The Institutes subsequently defended their position (and criticized that of the Director General) in a letter to the Corporate Affairs Minister in which the need for prevalence of auditor independence over competition considerations was stressed (*CA Magazine*, 1991b). However:

> After discussions with the DTI, the Institutes made modifications to peripheral ownership rules but these still did not persuade OFT director general Sir Gordon Borrie to change his mind. Corporate Affairs Minister John Redwood then used his powers under the 1989 Companies Act to overrule his objections.
>
> (*Accountancy*, 1991: 10)

It appears that, possibly due to the profession's self-imposed restrictions, there was no immediate interest in incorporation, in particular not from the large firms (*Accountancy*, 1989). A survey commissioned by Arthur Young showed a lack of interest in accounting firms by investors. This was partly blamed on accounting firms' traditional lack of disclosure (*Accountant's Magazine*, 1988: 5).

Summary for the UK

In summary, UK legislation implements only the minimum requirement of Article 2, which is that a firm of auditors must be controlled by qualified persons (where this is defined mainly with respect to voting rights). However, the Institutes felt that it would not be sufficient to safeguard auditor independence if control meant only a mere majority of voting rights. In their capacity as Recognized Supervisory Bodies they therefore implemented a requirement that at least 75% of voting rights should be held by qualified auditors. This also applies to voting rights on the management body. The

Association of Chartered Certified Accountants (ACCA) and the Association of Authorised Public Accountants (AAPA) only require the majority of voting rights to be held by qualified auditors; qualified auditors also need to hold only a majority of the voting rights on the management body.

IMPLEMENTATION IN GERMANY

The changes to paragraphs 28 and 34[20] of the WPO which were necessary to implement Article 2 of the Directive were introduced in the *Bilanzrichtliniengesetz* (BiRiLiG – Accounting Directives Law) of 1985. Paragraph 28 was changed as follows: the word 'exceed' was substituted with 'reach' (*erreichen*), i.e. it was established that WP must form at least a majority of the supervisory or management board members or personally liable *Gesellschafter*. Further, the following phrase was introduced: 'if the firm has only two supervisory board members, managers or personally liable *Gesellschafter*, then one of them must be a *Wirtschaftsprüfer*'.

A new sub-paragraph 4 was introduced into Paragraph 28, listing (*inter alia*) the following further conditions for the authorization of firms of auditors:

- only WP, firms of WP meeting the conditions of the sub-paragraph, or, provided they are employed by the firm, vBP, StB, *Steuerbevollmächtigte* (StBv – a lower qualification of tax advisor), lawyers or other persons whose position as member of the supervisory or management bodies or as personally liable *Gesellschafter* has been specially authorized may be *Gesellschafter*;
- the shares in the firm may not be held on behalf of third parties;
- WP or firms of WP must hold the majority of the shares and the voting rights in the firm (this also applies to the capital/shareholding of the limited partners in a KG);
- the articles of association (or, respectively, the partnership contracts) must specify that only those *Gesellschafter* may exercise their specific rights (*Gesellschafterrechte*) who are WP.

For existing firms, the new rules would only apply in cases of sale or succession.

A report by three members of the *Bundestag* who were members of the drafting committee explains the reasoning behind the changes as follows:

> A *Kapitalbindung* (a form of capital/financial tie) is introduced for firms of WP and vBP. The Legal Committee is of the opinion that the participation of outsiders in the profession can only be reconciled with the practising of a liberal profession with great difficulty. Even the authorisation of corporations to carry out these activities is questionable, because a legal person is placed between the auditor and his client. Thereby the responsibilities may become obscured and numerous dependencies may be established.[21]
>
> (BD 10/4268: 93 translation)

The report further points out that, since 1931, when the profession began to be regulated, outsiders, in particular credit institutions, had been giving up their stakes in firms of WP. This was apparently due to the fact that outside ownership was not customary internationally, and also to growing doubts in Germany about auditor independence where firms were partly owned by outsiders.

On the other hand, a trend apparently began to emerge for medium-sized firms of WP to be founded by non-auditors, in particular by members of consulting professions who would like to be able to offer their clients the additional service of an audit. It appears that their motivation was two-fold: they would be able to influence the audit, and they would not lose the consultation fees to an audit firm providing both services. It was felt, therefore, that the legislator would have to take steps to prevent auditors from being gradually restricted to being employees of corporations partly owned by non-auditors, instead of continuing the independent tradition of the liberal professions.

This new legislation was felt to have far-reaching consequences. In particular, after 31 December 1987 it would be impossible for existing firms not fulfilling the new requirements to participate in the foundation of new firms (IdW, 1986).

In summary, Germany implemented changes going much further than Article 2 of the Eighth Directive and further than the UK implementation.

SUMMARY AND CONCLUSIONS

The above discussion has highlighted a number of issues symptomatic of the differing accounting and legal traditions in the UK and in Germany. In accordance with prior classifications (see 'Introduction', above), in the UK a self-regulating accounting and auditing profession and a common law legal system are apparent. These issues are linked to an emphasis on professional judgement and the principle of the true and fair view. In Germany, a more state-controlled, 'weaker' profession is apparent, as is a civil law-based legal system with greater emphasis on compliance with detailed rules, which also reflects on the audit (see above).

The review of the legislative changes brought about by the implementation of the Eighth Directive supports this distinction, in that the UK government effectively delegated the authority over the approval of auditors to the profession. Even at the level of the legislative changes, which implement only the minimum requirements of Article 2, the UK profession was heavily involved in the consultation process. Even more typical however is the fact that it *was* just the minimum requirements which were made law, while the profession laid down the more detailed and stricter rules, which went beyond the requirements of the Directive. The profession's desire to lay down stricter rules was linked to the importance placed on independence especially in an environment involving the exercise of professional judgement.

In Germany, however, in spite of some consultation of other parties, the legislative process, and thus the rule-making for auditors, was very much in the hands of the government. The stricter rules, going beyond the requirements of the Directive, were laid down in statute.

The second main issue illustrated here relates to the content of the detailed rules. The above discussion outlined the reversal of the attitudes and legal provisions concerning the incorporation of audit firms in the UK and in Germany. The attitude in the UK before the implementation of the Eighth Directive appeared to be that '. . . the partnership structure was the appropriate form of business organisation for professional men' (DTI, 1986: 61) and the idea of outside interests in an audit firm was met with concern. By contrast, in Germany, the majority of audit firms had chosen to organize themselves as corporate entities, and outside interests were allowed and fairly common. With the implementation of the Eighth Directive, the UK dropped the prohibition of incorporation and allowed outside interests – though after considerable debate and discussion of concerns voiced by the profession. German legislation, on the other hand, now prohibits shareholdings by outsiders in new firms. Although it could be argued that some degree of harmonization has been achieved in that both countries now permit incorporation, the legal situation regarding ownership of audit firms reflects a reversal of the original position.

Havermann (1993), with reference to the pre-Eighth Directive situation, comments on the astonishment of UK accountants when they were told that WP were allowed to organize themselves in corporations, in which outsiders were allowed to hold shares. He points out that, since then, the situation has started to turn into the reverse, i.e. while German law does not permit outsider-shareholdings in new firms of WP, UK law now allows both incorporation of audit firms and outsider-shareholdings. This raises the question of whether this shift implies a changing perception of auditors and audit in both countries, i.e. perhaps greater emphasis on commercialism in the UK, and greater emphasis on independence and 'professionalism' in Germany. It further raises the question of the extent to which the organizational culture of the international Big Six firms affects such changes.

Considering the reversal of the original position in the UK and Germany, Nordemann (1989) points out that it is questionable whether the Eighth Directive improved the situation in the way intended by the Commission.

This may be due to the fact that harmonization as proposed by the European Commission deals with convergence of detailed rules, but not with the underlying issues. While there are differing cultures and traditions with respect to the financing of companies, and thus also with respect to ownership structures, accountability and the role of the audit, it is not surprising that harmonization of the detailed rules will remain superficial.

In summary, if the UK and Germany had taken advantage of certain options allowed by Article 2, very little change would have been required to their rules on authorization of audit firms. However, triggered by the requirement to implement the Eighth Directive, both countries made choices in their implementations which, to an extent, reversed their original positions.

ACKNOWLEDGEMENTS

The authors are grateful for comments on earlier versions from John Dyson and Nicholas Grier (Napier University), Liesel Knorr (IASC), Brenda Porter (Cranfield University), and David Hatherly (University of Edinburgh). We are also grateful for helpful comments from two anonymous referees.

NOTES

1 Other symptoms of this difference are that there is a lower number of listed companies in Germany, that share capital is less distributed in Germany and that small investors are 'less important'. Because of these differences the German system tends to emphasize creditor protection while the UK system emphasizes shareholder protection. These differences in turn explain the relative importance given to the prudence principle on the one hand, and the true and fair view principle on the other hand.

2 Nobes (1992) also makes the point that apparent similarities may be either homologues (i.e. things derived from the same origin, but possibly different in appearance) or analogues (i.e. things often similar in appearance and serving similar purposes, but of different origins). He refers to David and Brierley (1978), who point out that for the classification of legal systems it is important not to be misled by superficial similarities. Nobes therefore suggests that one needs to look for homologues when classifying accounting systems.

3 Since 1995 it is also possible for WP to organize themselves in a different form of partnership, the *Partnerschaftsgesellschaft*.

4 Another research project currently undertaken by the authors suggests that determinants for the choice of legal form of audit firms in Germany are mainly organizational and legal considerations, taxation, liability considerations and publication requirements, but also historical factors (see also, for example, Havermann, 1993; Schruff, 1992; Markus, 1996).

5 The term '*Gesellschafter*' has not been translated because of its ambiguity: it can mean 'partner', e.g. a partner in a KG, or 'shareholder', as e.g. in a GmbH or AG. Here it refers to a partner in a KG. The equivalent English term would be 'member', but this would be confusing in this context.

6 A lower qualification than that of WP with lower entry requirements; entry to this branch of the profession had been closed since 1961 but it was revived with the implementation of the *Bilanzrichtliniengesetz* (BiRiLiG – Accounting Directives Law).

7 Teckemeyer (1986) suggests that, due to these provisions, further regulation about share-ownership in firms of WP had been considered unnecessary until the passing of the BiRiLiG

8 We are grateful to Professor Dr Lothar Schruff (University of Göttingen) for pointing this out.

9 'Das prüferische Freiberuflerprinzip steht Prüfungsgesellschaften im Wege. Hätten jene Kreise obsiegt, die die Prüferrichtlinie auf eine strenge Freiberuflerschaft festlegen wollten, so hätte dies das Ende unserer großen Prüfungsgesellschaften und damit auch der Prüfungskonzentration bedeutet. *Indessen hat u.a. die deutsche Verhandlungsseite eine Lösung erziehlt*, die unsere Prüfungskonzentration unangetastet läßt und *dabei auch die Existenz der im Bundes- und Länderbesitz stehenden Treuarbeit AG sowie ähnlicher Gesellschaften sichert*' (emphases added). Vieten (1995: 508) defines 'liberal professions' (*freie Berufe*) as follows: ' "Free" occupation is a technical term in the German context, denoting a specifically state-sponsored profession, whose function is not to be regarded as a commercial activity.'

10 As opposed to Scottish law, under which partnerships are legal entities.

11 For example, the DTI intended to restrict the period (Art. 2 (1)) allowed for incorporated audit firms which ceased to comply with the requirements of Article 2 to correct the situation from the Directive's two years to three months.

12 'Nevertheless, we note, and welcome, the Department's proposal to introduce legislation prohibiting a corporate auditor from auditing a company in which it holds shares or which conversely, has an interest in the shares of the corporate auditor. We note the proposal that the prohibition might be extended to cases where the corporate auditor and a potential client have a common director, and in our view this would be essential' (KPMG-Peat Marwick McLintock, 1987: 3) The Government's proposals were *inter alia* published in *The Accountant's Magazine*, Feb. 1988: 16–17. It was clearly intended that a blanket prohibition as outlined above should be included in the legislation implementing the Eighth Directive. This would presumably have taken the form of a Statutory Instrument under section 27(2) of the Companies Act 1989. However, to date, no such Statutory Instrument appears to have been passed, and the above situations remain regulated under the professional bodies' Ethical Guides, which, as rules of the RSBs, have gained quasi-legal status.

13 KPMG's reported views in Table 2 appear to have been modified slightly since its 1987 publication. For a more detailed discussion of the firms' views on these and related issues see *Accountancy Age*, 1988: 5.

14 Recognized Supervisory Body is defined in the CA 1989 as

> . . . a body established in the United Kingdom (. . .) which maintains and enforces rules as to –
>
> (a) the eligibility of persons to seek appointment as company auditors, and
> (b) the conduct of company audit work,
>
> which are binding on seeking appointment or acting as company auditors either because they are members of that body or because they are otherwise subject to its control.

The four professional bodies whose members had been authorized to audit previously under the CA 1985, namely the ICAEW, the Institute of Chartered Accountants of Scotland (ICAS), the Institute of Chartered Accountants in Ireland (ICAI) and the Association of Chartered Certified Accountants (ACCA), gained recognition as RSBs, and were later joined by a fifth body, the Association of Authorised Public Accountants (AAPA).

15 This was preceded by an earlier report of the three Institutes' Working Party on Independence and Incorporation (ICAEW, ICAS, ICAI, 1988a), which had recommended, *inter alia*, that non-auditors employed by the firm should be allowed to hold up to 49% of shares while 'outsiders' should be allowed to hold only non-voting shares, and no more than 25% of all shares, and that they should not be allowed to appoint or influence the appointment of the firm's management. The recommendations of this publication were apparently a compromise, in particular with respect to outside shareholdings, which the English Institute would have preferred to outlaw (see *Accountancy*, 1988).

16 '75% control is also relevant to UK company law requirements on special and extraordinary resolutions, which are necessary for (i) alteration of the company's objects, (ii) alteration of the company's articles, (iii) reduction of the company's capital, and (iv) certain measures relating to a members' voluntary winding up of the company' (ICAEW, ICAS, ICAI, 1989: 10).

17 This implements the requirement of the Directive's Article 3 that auditors must be persons of 'good repute'.

18 The Institutes further supported the following suggestions:

- to apply the rules relating to incorporated businesses also to partnerships (this would in effect mean that up to 25% of the partners in a partnership could be outsiders);
- to apply the rules and percentages suggested to all firms; no exemptions would be permitted on grounds of size (with no use of the exemption permitted by the Directive's Article 2(1) (iii)); and
- to require additional disclosure for the register of auditors and firms: beneficial shareholders should be disclosed; a distinction should be made on the register between non-auditors and outsiders; and the shareholding held by each representative of these groups should be disclosed.

19 See also a further consultative document published by the DTI in December 1989, which addresses specifically this issue.

20 There was only a very small change to paragraph 34, concerning the time span allowed to correct certain situations in which the conditions for approval were no longer met.

21 'Es wird eine Kapitalbindung für Wirtschaftsprüfungs- und Buchprüfungsgesellschaften eingeführt. Der Rechtsausschuß ist der Auffassung, daß die Beteiligung Berufsfremder an solchen Gesellschaften mit der Ausübung eines freien Berufs nur schwer vereinbar ist. Bereits die Zulassung von Kapitalgesellschaften für die Ausübung dieser Tätigkeiten ist bedenklich, weil eine juristische Person zwischen den Prüfer und seinen Mandanten gestellt wird. Die Verantwortlichkeiten können dadurch verwischt und zahlreiche Abhängigkeiten begründet werden.'

REFERENCES

Accountancy (1981) 'CCAB demands changes to Eighth Directive on auditors', February: 6.
Accountancy (1988) 'Compromise reached, debate goes on', March: 5.
Accountancy (1989) 'Few takers for "important freedoms"?', September: 9.
Accountancy (1991) 'RSBs at the ready', September: 10.
Accountancy Age (1988) '. . . still divided over incorporation', 20 October: 5.

The Accountant's Magazine (1988) 'Safeguarding auditors' independence', March: 5.

Bartholomew, E. G. (1978) 'The EEC and auditors' qualifications', *Accountant's Magazine*, August: 333-5.

CA Magazine (1991a) 'Auditing rules attacked by Borrie', May: 60.

CA Magazine (1991b) 'Audit regulations report challenged', July: 59–60.

Clayton, M. (1984) 'Eighth Directive: the UK's successful bargain', *Accountancy*, April: 16–17.

Council of the European Communities (1978) 'Proposal for an Eighth Directive . . .', *Official Journal of the European Communities* No. C 112, 13.5.1978: 6–10.

Council of the European Communities (1979) 'Amended Proposal for an Eighth Directive . . .', *Official Journal of the European Communities* No. C 317, 18.12.1979: 6–15.

Council of the European Communities (1984) 'Eighth Council Directive', 84/253/EEC, *Official Journal of the European Communities* No. L 126, 12.5.1984: 20–6.

David, R. and Brierley, J. E. C. (1978) *Major Legal Systems in the World Today*. London: Stevens.

Department of Trade and Industry (1986) *Regulation of Auditors. Implementation of the EC Eighth Company Law Directive. A Consultative Document.*

Department of Trade and Industry (1989) *Ownership and Control of Firms of Auditors under the Companies Act 1989. A Consultative Document by the Department of Trade and Industry.*

Deutscher Bundestag (1985a) *Bundestags-Drucksache BD 10/3440*. Bonn: Verlag Dr. Hans Heger.

Deutscher Bundestag (1985b) *Bundestags-Drucksache BD 10/4268*. Bonn: Verlag Dr. Hans Heger.

Gray, S. J. (1988) 'Towards a theory of cultural influence on the development of accounting systems internationally', *Abacus*, 24(1): 1–15.

Havermann, H. (1993) 'Die Wirtschaftsprüfungsgesellschaft – Struktur und Strategie eines modernen Dienstleistungsunternehmens', in Baetge, J. (ed.) *Rechnungslegung und Prüfung – Perspektiven für die neunziger Jahre*. Düsseldorf: IdW-Verlag, pp. 41–59.

Hofstede, G. (1984) *Culture's Consequences, International Differences in Work-related Values*, abridged edition. Beverly Hills: Sage Publications.

Institut der Wirtschaftsprüfer e.V. (1986) *Wirtschaftsprüferhandbuch*. Düsseldorf: IdW-Verlag.

Institute of Chartered Accountants in England and Wales (1989) *The Companies Bill: Part II*. News Release.

Institute of Chartered Accountants in England and Wales, Institute of Chartered Accountants of Scotland, Institute of Chartered Accountants in Ireland (1988a) *Report of the Working Party on Independence and Incorporation*. February.

Institute of Chartered Accountants in England and Wales, Institute of Chartered Accountants of Scotland, Institute of Chartered Accountants in Ireland (1988b) *Independence and Incorporation. A Consultative Document*. October.

Institute of Chartered Accountants in England and Wales, Institute of Chartered Accountants of Scotland, Institute of Chartered Accountants in Ireland (1989) *Report of the Independence and Incorporation Committee*. May.

KPMG Peat Marwick McLintock (1987) *Independence and Incorporation of Auditors. Submission by Peat Marwick McLintock*. October 1987.

Lück, W. (1979) 'Zur Harmonisierung nationaler Rechtsvorschriften bei der Zulassung als Abschlußprüfer in der EG. Analyse des Vorschlags einer 8. EG-Richtlinie', *Der Betrieb*, 7: 317–24.

Markus, H. B. (1996) *Der Wirtschaftsprüfer. Entstehung und Entwicklung des Berufes im nationalen und internationalen Bereich*. München: Verlag C. H. Beck.

Mueller, G. G. (1967) *International Accounting*. New York: Macmillan.

Mueller, G. G. (1968) 'Accounting principles generally accepted in the United States versus those generally accepted elsewhere', *International Journal of Accounting Education and Research*, 3(2): 91–103.

Nair, R. D. and Frank, W. G. (1980) 'The impact of disclosure and measurement practices on international accounting classifications', *Accounting Review*, LV(3): 426–50.

Niessen, H. (1984) 'Die Regelung der Europäischen Gemeinschaft über die Zulassung der Abschlußprüfer als Teil der Koordinierung des Gesellschaftsrechts', *Die Wirtschaftsprüfung*, 15/16: 408–12.

Nobes, C. (1983) 'A judgemental international classification of financial reporting practices', *Journal of Business Finance and Accounting*, 10(1): 1–19.

Nobes, C. (1984/1992) *International Classification of Financial Reporting*, first and second editions. London: Routledge.

Nobes, C. and Parker, R. (1995) *Comparative International Accounting*, fourth edition. Hemel Hempstead Prentice-Hall.

Nordemann, H. H. J. (1989) 'Der Europäische Wirtschaftsprüfer – Mythos oder Realität?', *Die Wirtschaftsprüfung*, 23/24: 671–9.

Perera, M. H. B. (1989) 'Towards a framework to analyse the impact of culture on accounting', *International Journal of Accounting*, 24: 42–56.

Perera, M. H. B. and Mathews, M. R. (1990) 'The cultural relativity of accounting and international patterns of social accounting', *Advances in International Accounting*, 3: 215–51.

Richards, H. (1990) 'Auditors and supervision', *Accountant's Magazine*, April: 40–1.

Schruff, L. (1992) 'Wirtschaftsprüfer, Formen der Berufsausübung', in Coenenberg, A. G. and Wysocki, K. (eds) *Handwörterbuch der Revision*. Stuttgart: C. E. Poeschel Verlag, pp. 2190–9.

Sieben, G. and von Wysocki, K. (1979) 'Empfehlungen zum Vorschlag einer 8. EG-Richtlinie der Kommission Rechnungswesen im Verband der Hochschullehrer für Betriebswirtschaft e.V.', *Betriebswirtschaftliche Forschung und Praxis*, 5: 423–33.

Strobel, W. (1984) 'Die neue EG-Prüferrichtlinie und ihre berufsständische Bedeutung', *Der Betriebs-Berater*, 15: 951–61.

Teckemeyer, H. (1986) 'Wirtschaftsprüfer-Examen, vereidigte Buchprüfer-Examen, Anerkennung von Wirtschaftsprüfungsgesellschaften – gestern und heute', *Die Wirtschaftsprüfung*, 23: 650–9.

Van Hulle, K. (1992) 'Wirtschaftsprüfung, EG', in *Handwörterbuch der Revision*, second edition. Stuttgart: C. E. Poeschel Verlag, columns 2225–34.

Vieten, H. (1995) 'Auditing in Britain and Germany compared: professions, knowledge and the state', *European Accounting Review*, 4(3): 485–511.

von Wysocki, K. (1979) 'Zur endgültigen Fassung der 7. und 8. EG-Richtlinie. Vorschläge der Kommission Rechnungswesen im Verband der Hochschullehrer für Betriebswirtschaft e.V.', *Der Betrieb*, 31: 1472–3.

Wirtschaftsprüferkammer (ed.) (1994) *Gesetz über eine Berufsordnung der Wirtschaftsprüfer (Wirtschaftsprüferordnung).* Düsseldorf: IdW-Verlag.
Wirtschaftsprüferkammer und Institut der Wirtschaftsprüfer in Deutschland e.V. (1979) 'Zum Vorschlag einer 8. EG-Richtlinie über die Zulassung der mit der Pflichtprüfung des Jahresabschlusses von Kapitalgesellschaften beauftragten Personen. Stellungnahme der Wirtschaftsprüferkammer und des Instituts der Wirtschaftsprüfer in Deutschland e.V.', *Der Betrieb*, 29: 1378–82.

APPENDIX: ARTICLE 2, EIGHTH DIRECTIVE

Art.	*1978 Draft*	*1979 Draft*	*Art.*	*Final Version*
	Member States shall approve to carry out statutory audits of the annual accounts of the companies referred to in Article 1 only:	unchanged	1	Statutory audits of the documents referred to in Article 1 (1) shall be carried out only by approved persons. The authorities of the Member States may approve only:
1	natural persons who satisfy at least the conditions specified in the following Articles;	unchanged	1(a)	natural persons who satisfy at least the conditions laid down in Articles 3 to 19;
2	legal persons or other types of professional companies or associations which satisfy the following conditions:	unchanged	1(b)	firms of auditors which satisfy at least the following conditions:
2(a)	The partners, members, persons responsible for the management, administration, direction or supervision of such professional companies or associations who do not personally fulfil the conditions laid down in this Directive shall exercise no influence over the statutory audits carried out under the auspices of such approved professional companies or associations.	unchanged	27	Member States shall ensure that at least the members and shareholders of approved firms of auditors and the members of the administrative, management and supervisory bodies of such firms who do not personally satisfy the conditions laid down in Articles 3 to 19 in a particular Member State do not intervene in the execution of audits in any way which jeopardizes the independence of the natural persons auditing the documents referred to in Article 1 (1) on behalf of such firms of auditors.

Art.	*1978 Draft*	*1979 Draft*	*Art.*	*Final Version*
	The law shall, in particular, ensure:	The law shall, in particular, ensure:		
-	that the abovementioned persons may not participate in the appointment or removal of auditors and that they may not issue to the latter any instruction regarding the carrying out of audits;	that the above-mentioned persons may not intervene in the choice of natural persons acting as auditors on behalf of the company or association and that they may not issue to the latter any instruction regarding the carrying out of audits;		
-	that such persons shall not hold a majority of the capital of such professional companies or associations constituted after the entry into force of measures implementing this Directive and that they may not thereafter increase their holding so as to obtain a majority of the capital of existing professional companies or associations;	that such persons do not hold a majority of the capital or voting rights of such professional companies or associations;	1(b) (ii)	a majority of the voting rights must be held by natural persons or firms of auditors who satisfy at least the conditions imposed in Articles 3 to 19 with the exception of Article 11 (1) (b); the Member States may provide that such natural persons or firms of auditors must also be approved. However, those Member States which do not impose such majority at the time of the adoption of this Directive need not impose it provided that all the shares in a firm of auditors are registered and can be transferred only with the agreement of the firm of auditors and/or, where the Member State so provides, with the approval of the competent authority;
	[no equivalent]	[no equivalent]	1(b) (iii)	a majority of the members of the administrative or management body of a firm of auditors must be natural persons or firms of auditors who satisfy at least the conditions imposed in Articles 3 to 19; the Member States may provide that such

continued overleaf

Art.	1978 Draft	1979 Draft	Art.	Final Version
				natural persons or firms of auditors must also be approved. Where such body has no more than two members, one of those members must satisfy at least those conditions.
-	that the confidentiality of audit reports produced by the auditors and all documents relating thereto is protected and that these are withheld from knowledge of the abovementioned persons.	that the confidentiality of audit reports and all documents relating thereto is protected.		[no equivalent]
(b)	The natural persons who are responsible for the audit and certification of annual accounts carried out under the auspices of the professional company or association in the Member State in which approval is sought, shall satisfy at least the conditions specified in the following Articles.	unchanged	1(b) (i)	the natural persons who carry out statutory audits of the documents referred to in Article 1 on behalf of firms of auditors must satisfy at least the conditions imposed in Articles 3 to 19; the Member States may provide that such natural persons must also be approved;
	[no equivalent]	[no equivalent]	1(b)	Without prejudice to Article 14 (2), the approval of a firm of auditors must be withdrawn when any of the conditions imposed in (b) is no longer fulfilled. The Member State may, however, provide for a period of grace of not more than two years for the purpose of meeting the requirements imposed in (b) (ii) and (iii).
	[no equivalent]	[no equivalent]	2	For the purposes of this Directive, the authorities of the Member States may be professional associations provided that they are authorized by national law to grant approval as defined in this Directive.

[23]

© 2001 American Accounting Association
Accounting Horizons
Vol. 15 No. 3
September 2001
pp. 257–271

Why Not Allow FASB and IASB Standards to Compete in the U.S.?

Ronald A. Dye and Shyam Sunder

Ronald A. Dye is a Professor at Northwestern University and Shyam Sunder is a Professor at Yale University.

SYNOPSIS: This paper discusses arguments for and against introducing competition into the accounting standard-setting process in the U.S. by allowing individual corporations to issue financial reports prepared in accordance with either FASB or IASB rules. The paper examines several arguments supporting the status quo, including (1) the FASB's experience and world leadership in making accounting rules; (2) the increased risk of a "race to the bottom" under regulatory competition; (3) the inability of most users of financial reports to understand the complex technical issues underlying accounting standards; (4) the possibility that IASB's standards will be diluted to gain international acceptance, allowing additional opportunities for earnings management; (5) the risks of the IASB being deadlocked or captured by interests hostile to business; (6) the costs of experimentation in standard setting; and (7) economies from network externalities. Arguments examined on the other side include how competition will (1) help meet the needs of globalized businesses; (2) increase the likelihood that the accounting standards will be efficient; (3) help protect standard setters from undue pressure from interest groups; (4) allow different standards to develop for different corporate clienteles; (5) allow corporations to send more informative signals by their choice of accounting standards; (6) protect corporations against capture of regulatory body by narrow interests; and (7) not affect network externalities at national or global scales.

Keywords: accounting standards; regulatory competition; international.

INTRODUCTION

This essay is written in the form of a debate between two individuals, M and C, over the appropriateness of introducing competition into the accounting standard-setting process. It is motivated by current discussions over whether standards promulgated by the International Accounting Standards Board (IASB) should be an acceptable substitute for those developed by the Financial Accounting Standard Board (FASB) in the U.S. At present, the Securities and Exchange Commission effectively allows the FASB to take the lead in formulating financial accounting standards for U.S. businesses.

We benefited from comments of two anonymous referees, Bryan Carsberg, Karel van Hulle, Edmund Jenkins, James Leisenring, Katherine Schipper, Stephen A. Zeff, and workshop participants at Carnegie Mellon University, Hong Kong University of Science and Technology, and Nanyang Technological University. We alone are responsible for the paper.

Submitted: March 2001
Accepted: May 2001
Corresponding author: Shyam Sunder
Email: shyam.sunder@yale.edu

Expanding the set of acceptable standard-setting bodies will significantly change the financial-reporting environment.

The desirability of introducing competition in standard setting varies with the issue being evaluated. We evaluate the pros and cons of competition by organizing this discussion between M (for monopoly) and C (for competition) around several of the major issues commonly raised. We provide section labels to demark the discussion of distinct issues.

IF IT'S NOT BROKEN, DON'T FIX IT

M1: The FASB has done a good job of dealing with many complex accounting issues over the past quarter century. It is the unquestioned leader in setting financial accounting standards in the world. Its standards serve as the model for a large number of other countries; some countries adapt its standards to suit their local conditions. The FASB standard-setting process is "open," encouraging participation by all interested constituencies. The FASB does not shy away from taking up difficult, even unpopular, stands on tough issues. Even many opponents of its proposals came to support its actions. It has acknowledged expertise; it has an established tradition; it has a worldwide reputation for visionary leadership in setting standards. Why change things now?

THE WORLD HAS CHANGED

C1: I agree with much of what you said. The FASB's pronouncements are often used as a model by many other countries, as well as by the IASB itself. No other standard-setting body in the world comes even close to matching the FASB's achievements. An argument for change now need not be read as a criticism of the FASB's past accomplishments and leadership. However, we must also look at the present and into the future.

The economic map of the world has changed over the past quarter century, and it continues to change. The U.S. economy, its capital markets, and U.S.-based multinational corporations are still the largest in the world. However, even though the U.S. economy continues to grow, faster growth in other parts of the world elevates the relative importance of other economies, their capital markets, and corporations based outside the U.S. In addition, capital flows more freely across national boundaries now than in the past. As a result, an increasing proportion of the holders of securities reside outside the legal jurisdiction in which the issuers of the securities reside. For example, a corporation chartered in the state of Delaware has shareholders, plants, employees, customers, and vendors scattered all over the globe, diluting the meaning and relevance of its national identity.

If we assume that certain standards are useful for promoting commerce, cross-boundary commerce requires cross-boundary standards. This is what the IASB is trying to do in the field of accounting, for the U.S. and for the world economy. There are parallels between the IASB's efforts and the federal laws that regulate interstate commerce and securities in the U.S. Over a century ago, the state of New York dominated the U.S. economy, and the laws and practices of that state influenced business conventions throughout the country.[1] As the economies of the

[1] See, for example, Carey's (1970) discussion of the importance of New York State's role in the development of accounting and auditing standards.

other parts of the U.S. developed, the national role of the state of New York diminished. Given the continuing development of the world economy, the FASB may not be able to continue its predominant role in determining national and international accounting standards.

I could make many arguments why it is desirable to allow the IASB to take the lead in formulating accounting standards in the U.S. Instead, I propose a more conservative course of allowing both the FASB and IASB standards to operate in the U.S. for five to ten years. With the insights generated by this experience, we could then decide whether to depend on either the FASB's or the IASB's standards, or to allow the standards developed by both to continue to operate in parallel.

COMPETITION MAY INDUCE A RACE TO THE BOTTOM

M2: Let us consider the suggestion that the U.S. allow each reporting organization to choose whether it wishes to publish its financial reports according to the FASB's or IASB's accounting standards. Presumably, firms will not be allowed to pick and choose among individual standards, and financial reports will be clearly labeled to inform the reader of the set of standards they conform to. However, I doubt if the average reader of financial reports has the accounting and financial expertise to distinguish between the information provided by financial reports prepared under the two sets of standards. How many people understand the meaning and implication of the UL (Underwriters Laboratories) stamp at the bottom of their toaster? And, using a toaster is easier than reading financial statements. I fear that allowing two sets of standards will induce a "race to the bottom," and erase the hard-won gains of financial reporting in the U.S. over the past half-century.

C2: What do you mean by a "race to the bottom"?

M3: A "race to the bottom" is a degradation of the quality and/or quantity of standards resulting from competition between standard-setting bodies.[2] It is closely linked to Gresham's Law—bad money drives out good money—and it applies to many forms of regulation. For example, in their quest to compete for depositors, countries such as Switzerland and the Cayman Islands simplified their banking regulations. Consequently, their banks became havens for illegitimately obtained money from all over the world. Similarly, some U.S. states and municipalities gave such large tax breaks to attract new businesses that their financial viability was threatened.

The same may happen to accounting standards if alternatives to FASB rules are permitted in the U.S. The financial reports of public corporations are prepared by their managers. Viewing accounting standards as a burden, managers prefer to comply with the least rigorous and demanding standards available. Requests for new accounting standards rarely originate from corporate executives who prepare financial reports. Whenever the FASB proposes a new standard, one can be reasonably sure that the Financial Executives International will resist the idea.[3] Moreover, managers seem to exploit whatever flexibility exists in accounting standards to present themselves, or their firms, in better light than indicated by their underlying performance.[4]

---

2 See Monks and Minow (1995) or Easterbrook and Fischel (1991) for further discussion of the "race to the bottom."

3 See Parfet (2000, 484).

4 As an example of analytical model of managers' demand for earnings management, see Dye (1988).

Moreover, the FASB pays for many of its operating costs through the sale of publications, and through contributions from various constituents, including firms subject to FASB's rules. Given the freedom to choose between alternative sets of standards, firms are likely to buy the publications of, and make contributions to, the body whose standards they adopt. In addition to this link between the adoption of standards and the revenues of the standard-setting bodies, there is also the question of the respect and authority that derives from having many firms comply with a given body's standards. In their attempt to attract a larger following, and knowing that the firms prefer the least-demanding standards, the standard-setting bodies will tend to issue standards that pander to the reporting firms. What is worse, you won't have to wait for arrival of actual competition among standard setters before observing a reduction in the quality of accounting standards; even the anticipation of competition will lower the quality of standards.[5]

C3: Won't standard setting actually improve with increased competition?

M4: It is difficult for me to imagine that FASB's Standard No. 106, *Other Post Retirement Employee Benefits,* for example, could have been issued in a competitive environment. It was fought tooth and nail by business firms, even though many critics of that proposal are now glad that the FASB persevered in spite of their original objections.[6]

The argument that competition is good because it pushes organizations to be more responsive to their constituents can be taken only so far. In some instances, markets break down, and the consequences of competition can be worse than monopoly. If air pollution standards were set locally by individual municipalities, each might seek to attract industry by lowering its own standards with the expectation that a significant part of the cost of pollution will be borne by the residents of neighboring towns. In order to avoid this "race to the bottom," these standards are set by the federal government at the national level.

In any case, as I mentioned earlier, the process for setting accounting standards in the U.S. already has many desirable attributes: it is transparent and subject to detailed public scrutiny. Moreover, it is highly responsive to its constituents, which include both the investing public and the business community. Making the process more responsive, by allowing competition between standard-setting bodies, is only likely to create inappropriate pressure for lowering standards.

COMPETITION NEED NOT BE EQUATED TO "RACE TO THE BOTTOM"

C4: After hearing your argument, I agree that unbridled market competition is not a perfect solution to the problem of standard setting. We should look at the restraints that exist in the system to keep the potentially undesirable consequences of free competition under control. We also need to review the benefits of a limited amount of competition in this field.

If we allow competition in the creation of accounting standards, we will not do so in a vacuum. Acceptance of IASB standards in other countries is subject to the approval of local authorities. So is the approval of any changes in GAAP in the

---

[5] This is similar to how the threat of competition from firms not presently in a market can discipline the prices set by firms already in the market. See, e.g., Baumol et al. (1982).

[6] See Parfet (2000, p. 484).

U.S. Even today in the U.S., the SEC reviews all proposals and pronouncements of the FASB before deciding to support them. We will certainly continue this process if we allow IASB standards to compete with those of the FASB. If the SEC judges that either body is trying to "race the other to the bottom," it can withdraw its support and undermine the credibility of the offending standard setter. This threat will restrain the tendency of standards to "race to the bottom."

Moreover, all markets do not necessarily "race to the bottom." Competing bodies for standardization and certification of products and membership exist in many fields, such as engineering and education, in virtually all countries. The resulting standards are not necessarily watered down.[7] Producing sloppy standards enhances neither the reputations of those who set or comply with the standards nor the demand for their services. The same is true of competition among the 50 states in the U.S. with respect to corporate charters (see Dodd and Leftwich 1980).

I am also not convinced that managers always prefer or select the most aggressive reporting behavior permitted under prevailing rules. Conservatism has a long-standing and respected tradition among accountants and managers. Some firms and their managers attach considerable value to being known for reporting "high quality" earnings and are rewarded by the capital markets with lower cost of capital. In 1993, Daimler-Benz of Germany chose to adopt the stricter and more transparent U.S. standards in the hope of gaining these benefits.[8] Firms that adopt aggressive reporting behavior often experience large drops in value when the investing public becomes aware of their aggressiveness, and the managers of such firms sometimes get fired. Managers have substantial incentives to protect their reputations by adhering to conservative reporting practices. In short, there is an implicit demand by managers of public corporations for quality accounting standards and disclosures.[9]

M5: Although some of the details of your argument make sense to me, I want to return to the analogy between competition among accounting standard setters and competition among jurisdictions in setting pollution standards mentioned previously. In both cases, the problem is the existence of "externalities," or "spillover" costs or benefits arising when one party's actions result in uncompensated gains or losses to other parties. Pollution creates an externality except in those rare instances where the polluter reimburses those harmed by the pollution.[10] When individual jurisdictions set pollution standards, they capture the benefits of relaxed pollution

[7] There is historical evidence that competition for members among accounting groups need not destabilize membership standards. In the United Kingdom, and in Canada, three institutes of accountants compete in overlapping markets. The membership requirements of these institutes do not seem to be progressively slackening over time. This should not be surprising: these institutes must worry about the reputation of their members and the demand for their services when setting the height of the bar for admission. Setting the bar low enhances neither their reputations nor the demand for their services.

[8] "[Y]ou have to have access to global capital. That means listing on the leading stock markets. And it means presenting your financial accounts to the standards of the transparency demanded by investors" (Jürgen Schrempp, Chairman of Daimler Benz to Graham Bowley ([1997]).

[9] William Parfet (2000, 481–482), the chairman and CEO of MPI Research, Inc., said about managers' behavior in preparing firms' accounting reports, "To use a sports analogy, we want to win, but we want to win playing by the rules."

[10] When no individual has property rights over the fish in a body of water, unregulated competitive fishing leads to depletion of stocks. This is a classic example of inefficient use of a resource in presence of an externality, and often goes by the name "the tragedy of the commons." See, e.g., Stiglitz (1997).

restrictions. These benefits include attracting businesses seeking to avoid the costs of complying with pollution-related regulations, without bearing any of the costs imposed by pollution outside of their jurisdictions. The net result is too much pollution. There is a similar externality produced by standard-setting bodies. In evaluating General Motors, an investor looks not only at GM's financial statements, but also compares them to the financial statements of Ford. If Ford chooses to comply with a different set of reporting standards, then evaluation of GM becomes more difficult and less precise. Externalities of this sort pose problems only when there are multiple, competing jurisdictions. Why introduce this problem into the U.S. financial-reporting environment by inviting the IASB to compete with the FASB in the U.S.?

C5: It is interesting that you present the example of why there are national, and not municipal, standards for air pollution. Just as air travels from one municipal jurisdiction to another—making air quality difficult to control satisfactorily by local standards—capital also travels across national boundaries, making it difficult to control by national standards. This argument lies at the heart of the case for giving the IASB a fair trial in the U.S.

Achieving the right balance in air pollution controls is not a trivial problem. However, neither is choosing the right level of accounting standards. The most difficult problem in developing accounting standards, it seems to me, entails determining the right balance between "excessive" and "insufficient" standardization. The value of financial reporting is diminished at either extreme. Insufficient standards make it difficult for financial statement readers to identify the principles firms applied in constructing the statements. Excessive or inordinately narrow standards may prevent firms from selecting a reporting procedure that accurately conveys the substance of their economic situation.

Competition can help the economy "zero in" on the right level of accounting standards. It is difficult to conduct a social cost-benefit analysis of proposals for new standards, or for eliminating existing ones. Estimates of the economic consequences of such proposals are notoriously inaccurate. Asking firms or others to furnish their own estimates of the economic consequences of an accounting proposal runs into two problems. First, only those people or firms whose individual gains or losses are sufficiently large respond to such solicitations, resulting in a selection bias. Second, when they do respond, firms and other interested parties have obvious incentives to exaggerate their estimates in the hope of influencing the adopted policy.

Because accurate social cost-benefit analyses are difficult to conduct, accounting rules actually implemented may be inappropriate. Moreover, the difficulties attending the assessment of standards makes standard-setters susceptible to the so-called Law of the Instrument;[11] that is, standard setters may recommend the promulgation of increasingly more standards even when better alternatives exist. The resulting standards do not achieve the best social outcomes. This may account for the explosive growth of standards during the years since the creation of the FASB.

---

[11] "I call it *the law of the instrument*, and it may be formulated as follows: Give a small boy a hammer, and he will find that everything he encounters needs pounding" (Kaplan 1964, 28) (emphasis in the original).

Competition among standard-setting organizations can eliminate some of these problems and increase the efficiency of standards. Reactions to competing standards furnish each standard-setting organization with real feedback from their constituents. Instead of posturing as they often do at present, firms will "vote with their feet" in adopting or rejecting standards.[12] Competing standard-setting organizations are likely to be more responsive to demands for better standards than is a monolithic standard setter. If one set of standards is deficient relative to another, then competition will eliminate the former. Both insufficient and excessive standard setting will be curtailed as a consequence.

SURVIVAL OF THE FITTEST AND VOTING BY FEET

M6: Your argument seems to be a variation on the Darwinian "survival of the fittest" line of reasoning. Following this logic, one can make a case for not having any standards at all. After all, standards are a form of social norm or custom, and customs tend to evolve to efficient forms over time. This is the basic premise of the law and economics movement championed by Posner (1992) and others: the common law will eventually lead to socially efficient rules of behavior over time. Since the law does not face competition from other laws in a society, but is presumed to become efficient eventually, why shouldn't we expect accounting standards to become efficient over time, also—with or without competition?

C6: I agree that, like all social norms, accounting standards may converge to efficient rules over time with or without competition. However, and also like social norms, the evolution of accounting standards toward efficiency is neither rapid nor certain. Under rapid and continual change, accounting standards can permanently lag behind current business conditions, causing resources to be misallocated. Thus, there is a demand for organizations that develop financial-reporting standards. If we must have some formal standard-setting body, it is sensible not to allow any single body to have monopoly control of this process. A single source of accounting standards doesn't allow firms to "vote with their feet," and hence increases the chance of errors being perpetuated over the long term.

PEOPLE MAY NOT KNOW WHAT IS GOOD FOR THEM

M7: This "voting by their feet" argument assumes that people who make these decisions have sufficient understanding of the alternatives on hand to know the consequences of each option and to choose correctly what is in their best interest. I know that it sounds like an elitist argument, but years of experience with standard setting lead me to a different conclusion. The issues involved in setting accounting standards are technically quite complex, and it is not realistic to expect more than a handful of people to make the effort to gain more than superficial understanding of these issues. People do not always know what is in their own best interest when it comes to accounting. I already gave the example of the FASB's standard, *Other Post-Retirement Employee Benefits,* and there are many other examples. If the FASB could ever get its original proposal for a new standard on accounting for employee stock options approved, I believe firms will then ultimately understand that it was in their own best interest to recognize these expenses. The FASB has

[12] See Tiebout (1956) for the effects of competition between jurisdictions on the efficiency of the provision of local public goods. See, also, Tjiong (2000) for some counterarguments.

little chance of reaching that stage in such a politically charged issue. In any case, that is the reason why we need panels of experts like the FASB and IASB rather than referendums to set accounting standards.

C7: Your concern about the receptivity of business to new accounting standards such as those involving accounting for stock options or post-retirement benefits actually provides another reason for allowing competition between standard-setting bodies. Let's take the debate on accounting for derivatives. Alan Greenspan, Chairman of the Federal Reserve Board, agreed with the major banks' objections to mark-to-market accounting for derivatives. It was not until Congress introduced legislation to intervene in this matter, citing his position, that Mr. Greenspan reiterated his support for the independence of the FASB's process. With multiple sets of standards, the political pressures on the FASB, or any other standard-setting body adventurous enough to propose significant new reporting requirements, would be lower. That body could say, "Look, if you don't like these standards, opt out and select another set." The net result of introducing competition in standard setting might be just the opposite of what you call a "race to the bottom." Competition could reduce the lobbying pressure on any single standard-setting body compared to the present regime in which a single authoritative accounting body is subjected to considerable political pressure whenever it proposes an accounting innovation.

THE U.S. IS DIFFERENT (BETTER?) THAN THE REST OF THE WORLD

M8: Your argument implies that the IASB could serve as a foil for the FASB. Think about the specifics of how international accounting standards are set. Instead of developing in a vacuum, they respond to specific institutional settings. German accounting rules, for example, permit a plethora of "reserve" accounts. Lack of disclosure about these accounts makes it difficult for the reader to assess the value of a firm from its financial statements. Yet, this opacity of financial reports presents no problem for German banks—historically the principal source of capital for German firms. As lenders, these banks are privy to additional information not available to the general readers of German firms' financial statements. A representative of the bank often sits on the firm's board of directors. Under this financing and corporate governance structure, German GAAP does not hinder financing of German firms. However, financing and corporate governance structures in the U.S. are different. Individuals and other "nonbank" financial institutions hold much of the equity and debt issued by U.S. firms. Allowing U.S. firms the freedom to issue opaque statements loaded with reserve accounts will not work well because the providers of capital do not have access to the information hidden behind the reserve accounts.

Moreover, international accounting standards necessarily gloss over the variations in the functioning of national capital markets. They tend to be based on one of two strategies. One strategy is to base the international standards on standards already in force someplace. If sufficient support is not forthcoming for any existing standard, then a new standard is drafted. The new standard needs to gain substantial support from countries with diverse accounting practices and institutions. Often, the outcome of this process is a "minimum common denominator standard," which is just another way of phrasing "the race to the bottom" we discussed earlier. Unless the standards chosen are modeled after the practices of a country with a strong bias in favor of equal access to information, the outcome will be a step backward for investors. Since the U.S. is the leader in standard setting, forcing U.S. standard setters to compromise their principles for the sake of international harmonization will only have the effect of watering down U.S. GAAP. This is not the best outcome for participants in the U.S. securities markets.

C8: We both agree that business environments vary across countries. Let us also agree that in an ideal world it might be best to develop a unique set of ideal accounting standards for each environment. However, even within a legal jurisdiction, organizations of different sizes operate in different industries and in regions with different business environments. In fact, one could make a good argument that there is less difference between the business environments of Exxon and British Petroleum than between Exxon and Paradise Inc., a small Florida confectioner traded on the NASDAQ. So the problem you rightly point to is not unique to international accounting standard setting.

Fortunately, the resolution on the table leads to a reasonable solution to the problem. Under a competitive standard-setting system, the harmonization of reporting standards across the globe can proceed at a voluntary pace determined by local conditions. Firms with local clientele and little or no international exposure may find comfort in conforming to locally optimized standards written by their domestic standard-setting body, such as the FASB in the U.S. Other firms with international clienteles will choose to conform to international standards if they believe they are better off by doing so. This two-tiered system allows more freedom of choice to firms in all countries. Instead of suppressing it, such an approach will actually promote the legitimization of local standard-setting bodies. Within the U.S., for example, various stock exchanges compete by setting their own standards for listing firms. This competition creates a multitiered market that is healthy for the securities industry. It led to an equilibrium in which the New York Stock Exchange coexists with the NASDAQ, several regional exchanges, and even the Vancouver Stock Exchange with its reputation for trading highly speculative securities. Introducing competition between the IASB and local standard-setting bodies will encourage similar healthy competition in setting accounting standards.

Moreover, the possibility of segmentation of accounting standards is not new to the U.S. There has been much discussion about the "Little GAAP, Big GAAP" controversy over adjusting reporting standards for clientele effects. Competition between IASB and the FASB will respond to clienteles on a global scale. In short, I agree that, while there may be a problem resulting from IASB standards not being directly competitive with U.S. GAAP, there is a simple resolution of the problem—just introduce more competition!

BROADER AGREEMENT MEANS WEAKER STANDARDS

M9: You turned my own argument against me. But it is not that simple. Because the IASB must gain approval from a much larger constituency, the number of things they can agree on must be smaller than what the FASB agrees on. A possible result is lax standards compared to those of the FASB. Lax IASB standards allow firms more opportunity to manage their earnings, making financial reports less useful to investors. One of the costs associated with reaching the political consensus necessary to get international standards adopted is that the standards must be constructed relatively broadly and less specifically. Broad standards create more ambiguities and enhance chances that opportunistic, if not illegal, accounting treatments are blessed by generally accepted accounting principles. Earnings and balance-sheet management is one consequence of this vagueness. Earnings management misleads and harms investors who read and rely on the financial statements of culpable firms. A firm may be made to look more profitable and less risky. This practice injures not only the investors in the culpable firm, but also harms investors in other firms who may make invalid comparisons among the financial statements of firms that do/do not manipulate their earnings.

UNIFORMITY OF FORM OR UNIFORMITY OF SUBSTANCE

C9: Achieving uniformity and comparability of financial reports across firms and across time is a difficult problem in financial accounting. Contrary to popular belief, more detailed and more rigid or "uniform" standards that allow fewer options to managers do not make financial reports more comparable, or more informative. Statement of Financial Accounting Standards No. 2 is a good example. It requires all research and development outlays to be expensed, allowing managers no discretion when accounting for such costs. As a consequence, two firms that spend equal amounts on research report identical financial results, even when one's research is successful and the other's research yields no usable results. The idea that detailed rules lead to uniform and comparable results can be easily rejected on the basis of the exponential growth of the Internal Revenue Code, and the public dissatisfaction with the inequities of the tax burden and the administration of the Code.[13]

When you permit firms to choose from a set of accounting alternatives, firms do not necessarily reduce the amount of information they reveal to the readers of their reports, as long as the method they choose is also disclosed in the reports. Their choice among methods reveals what they know to the discriminating reader, just as the choice of an auto insurance policy with a low deductible reveals a policyholder's private information to an insurance company (see Levine 1996). By choosing a low-deductible policy, the policyholder reveals his/her high driving risk and high aversion to financial risk. Financial analysts continually scrutinize the choice of accounting methods by firms to assess the quality of firms and the quality of their management. Nothing generates a faster sell decision by an experienced analyst than a financial report in which management enlists all possible accounting tricks to burnish the report. Managers cannot resort to such methods without also revealing to knowledgeable readers that their firm is in a desperate condition. By eliminating such options in favor of "tight" standards, we also close off yet another channel of communication from the firm to the investing public.

Besides, managers who wish to be in the good graces of shareholders and analysts, and have confidence in the prospects of their firm, always have the option of revealing more than the applicable standards require. Adding IASB to FASB standards will not change any of this.

[13] Also see Havighurst (1965); Sunder (1997, 143–145).

INTERNATIONAL STANDARDS BODY MAY BE CAPTURED BY NONBUSINESS INTERESTS

M10: I want to step back to an earlier point about how the nature and extent of lobbying might be affected by competition between standard setters. You think that introducing competition will take the heat off a single standard-setting body and so, in principle, induce that body to be more adventurous in choosing innovative, even aggressive, standards. Contrary to your conjecture, I think competition will exacerbate, not relieve, lobbying pressures. We know how children try to play one parent against the other to get what they want. Competition between standard setters to attract client firms will only make them more susceptible to such pressures. It is easier to take a hard line when you are the only game in town.

Moreover, I worry about the pressures that could be brought to bear on the IASB. In the U.S., some accountants complain about the excessive influence of the Financial Executives International and the Business Roundtable in the standard-setting process. However, lobbying pressure from nonbusiness interests could be even worse. Think of the IASB as the United Nations of accounting boards. It is a voluntary association created by accounting organizations across 114 countries. If environmental or governmental interests in enough countries dominate business interests, then the IASB might be induced to issue standards unacceptable or irrelevant to business firms. International labor unions, various governmental groups, environmental and consumer groups may all try to sway IASB standards. One possible result of all this pressure is for the business community to stay away from IASB standards entirely. The conflicts among business, accounting, and other groups I mentioned could produce a deadlocked, paralyzed IASB—a paper tiger.

C10: Early in this conversation, you argued against more than one standard-setting body because the resulting competition would pose a serious challenge to the FASB, and that is undesirable. Now, you're saying that it is undesirable to have more than one standard-setting body because it wouldn't create viable competition. You can't have it both ways.

The possibility of IASB standards being co-opted by nonbusiness interests is remote. Even if that happens, the business community will not sit and watch from the sidelines any more than they did when the FASB's standards became mandatory in the U.S. Business will have a significant voice in all standard-setting decisions. Moreover, when businesses can choose which set of standards to adopt, neither the IASB nor any other standard-setting body can afford to write standards that alienate the business community. Even if your worst fears came true, and the IASB were captured by interests hostile to business, under the proposal we are debating the business community could simply ignore those standards and carry on.

My overall argument is simple: either IASB would be a viable alternative or it wouldn't; let's experiment by giving it a chance! The costs of conducting the experiment aren't that high. How can you lose?[14]

[14] The importance of "experimenting," or taking an action that may not be the best possible given current information, in hopes of making improved future decisions based on additional information collected today, has been the subject of intense study in the statistics literature. These problems have been classically referred to as "bandit" problems. See Berry and Fristed (1985) for an overview. This literature occasionally receives attention in economics as well. See, e.g., Grossman et al. (1977) for the earliest such treatment in economics. An interesting discussion about how successful firms may be averse to innovating, and consequently lose what made them successful, may be found in Christensen (1997).

THE COST OF STANDARDS AND EXPERIMENTATION

M11: The cost of failed experimentation with accounting standard-setting mechanisms is not low. Let's go through the list. Costs of standards include: (1) the costs incurred by the standard-setting body and the constituents in the formulation of standards; (2) the direct costs of implementing the standards by firms preparing the financial statements; and (3) the indirect costs of various agents adjusting their behavior to the new standard, and the economic consequences of the altered behavior. Most of our debate so far has centered on the third category. However, the costs in the first two categories are not small. Indeed, much of the opposition from business to new proposals for accounting standards is based on business' beliefs that their benefits do not exceed their costs.

The duplication of effort in evaluating competing standards is inevitable and wasteful. On top of this, firms may incur significant implementation costs if they decide to switch between competing standards. In addition, competing standard-setting groups lack the incentives to engage in due diligence when developing standards. Since the output of a standard-setting body is what economists call a "public good," a competing standard-setting body can use the concepts and ideas underlying a standard for free without incurring the cost of developing it. A developer of standards has no enforceable property right to its ideas and concepts. In contrast, a monopoly standard-setting body has the appropriate incentives to do due diligence without wasteful duplication.

C11: Keeping your three cost categories in mind, I agree that it is easier to estimate the costs in the first and second categories than in the third.[15] But the third category of costs is an order of magnitude higher than the other two. In a competitive environment, the standard-setters have reasons to minimize the sum of all three costs—essentially minimizing the third element. This inherent tendency of a competitive system is absent in a monopoly regime.

While your schema of costs is quite comprehensive, it is difficult in practice to provide reasonably precise estimates of any but the most trivial of these costs. Consider just one of the costs that is difficult to evaluate: the cost of obtaining "representative" standards board members. No standard-setting body can perfectly represent of all its constituencies. Limitations on the feasible size of such a body, and the large number of interests in society on which its actions may impinge, ensure that the constitution of such bodies must be less than perfectly representative. Competition among standard-setting bodies reduces the import of such imperfections. It ensures that such bodies must take into account the interests of various constituents even if they are not directly represented on the body itself. Disgruntled interests can shift their allegiances to the competition. This argument is invoked against federal chartering of corporations in the U.S. All 50 states of the union compete vigorously in the market for corporate charters, and Delaware seems to have won a lion's share of the market by designing laws, or

[15] Accounting and management generally are plagued with instances in which decisions are based on the easily assembled or computed information, rather than information most relevant to the decision at hand. A classic example is the emphasis on the "total costs of quality," consisting of appraisal, prevention, internal failure, and external failure costs (see, e.g., Kaplan and Ittner 1988). While the existence of these costs cannot be denied, they probably are an order of magnitude smaller than the effects of quality on customer demand.

"standards," attractive to various corporate constituents. In the 1980s, when some states tried to pass laws in support of corporate takeover defenses, economists argued that such laws only drive business away from the states that enact them. In brief, the composition of a standard-setting body becomes less critical when standard-setting bodies have to compete.

As I mentioned earlier, the costs of setting standards are difficult to quantify. To evaluate a monopoly standard-setter, one needs to know the magnitude of various costs. With competition among standard setters, there is less of a need to make such judgments. Competition helps ensure that the right amount of time, money, and effort is devoted to each of the activities the various standard setters engage in.

M12: There are other costs of competition. Economists study network externalities—the benefits of having multiple customers adhere to the same standard.[16] The telephone and facsimile machine provide classic examples of network externalities. One telephone, or one facsimile machine, is not of much use by itself. The usefulness of a telephone, or facsimile machine increases with the number of others who use compatible machines. Accounting standards also have network externalities. Using or interpreting financial reports to infer a firm's economic condition and performance is prone to error. If multiple firms adhere to the same set of standards, readers can compare across firms and interpret the reports better. This is a big advantage of having a single set of standards, and hence a single standard setter. I can only imagine the consequences if each firm reported by its own unique set of "standards."

As another example, think about the rationale for a single set of health and sanitation standards for restaurants in a city. Diners could go into a restaurant and ask themselves, "Is the set of health standards used here appropriate for what I would like to order for lunch today?" Instead, they prefer to have experts set uniform standards to ensure that all food served in all restaurants is safe. Analogously, investors don't want to have to wade into technical arguments about variations in GAAP when interpreting a firm's financial reports. You win investors' trust, and eliminate their confusion, by having all financial reports prepared in accordance with one GAAP.

C12: I agree that network externalities apply to accounting standards. Without such externalities, each firm could follow its own rules and there will be little need for standards (see Sunder 1997 chap. 11). The critical issue is how the magnitude of network externalities of accounting standards changes with the number of conforming firms. The economics literature typically assumes that the benefit of using a common standard increases with the number of consumers, according to some functional relationship. We do not know this function. It is possible that the rate of increase in benefit drops significantly as the numbers grow, in which case the advantage of adhering to a single set of standards in a large economy is minimal.

Let's consider the following thought experiment for the network externalities associated with telephones. Suppose everyone in the U.S. has a phone, but no one in Russia does. Under this hypothetical situation, it is not clear that most U.S. residents would get much added benefit if all Russians were given phones. We

[16] See Farrell and Saloner (1985) for an early reference.

should expect the incremental network externalities associated with more users to become small at some point. While network externalities may be important, we should not overstate their magnitude.

If the potential benefits from network externalities diminish rapidly with the number of firms adhering to the standards, then competing standard setters may do as well as a monopolist standard setter. This is true even without considering the other benefits of competition I mentioned earlier.

Your analogy with uniform sanitation code is inappropriate. First, investors do not have to know the details of GAAP, only their investment advisors do. People order and eat their meals without professional advisors at their side. Second, U.S. GAAP already permits many financial-reporting alternatives, forcing investors and analysts to cope with the different choices firms make.

M13: Perhaps the largest of the costs of accounting standards we haven't discussed yet is their effect on the risks borne by investors and the risk premium investors demand when pricing securities. Reporting standards cannot reduce the risk arising from the covariance between the market and firm returns. They can affect portrayal of the risk associated with the firm's cash flows. A monopoly standard setter, concerned with the risk borne by the shareholders of firms that adhere to its standards, could attempt to minimize this latter risk premium in the aggregate. Would competition among several standard setters do as well?

C13: I believe that competitive standard setters would do better. If the only objective of standard setters is to minimize the "informational" risk premium, then there will be no difference in the disclosures proposed by a monopoly standard setter and a set of competitive standard setters.[17] However, socially concerned standard setters must also consider whether increased disclosures result in firms' disclosing proprietary information to their competitors. When such proprietary costs are taken into account, it is very difficult to determine efficient or optimal standards. As I stated above, competitive standard-setting bodies are more likely to make the right choices in such tough decision-making circumstances.

SUMMARY

M14: I think we have put as many issues on the table as is possible in one debate, so let me summarize. I do not believe we need to fix something that is not broken. You believe in laissez faire competition, even in fields where the presence of externalities mitigates against the advantages of competition. As a practical matter, the SEC will never countenance the "choice" solution you propose. As a regulatory agency, the SEC has low tolerance for ambiguity and always champions the cause of uniformity over flexibility, even when, in your opinion, such uniformity is more a matter of form than substance. It is the least likely body to accept a regime under which companies subject to its jurisdiction can choose their own accounting standards. Of course, that does not mean that we shouldn't discuss and debate it. Do you have any final thoughts?

---

[17] See Dye (1990).

C14: Informed by a wider debate of this kind, we could make a better decision about opening the U.S. to the IASB standards. I wish we could elicit the best arguments by inviting more people to participate in this debate, even offering a prize to the person who makes the most persuasive case. However, I guess to be consistent with the philosophical position you advanced throughout this debate, you prefer a debate with only one person present, whose assertions are final and binding.

REFERENCES

Baumol, W., J. Panzar, and R. Willig. 1982. *Contestable Markets and the Theory of Industry Structure*. New York, NY: Harcourt, Brace and Jovanovich.

Berry, D., and B. Fristedt. 1985. *Bandit Problems: Sequential Allocation of Experiments*. London, U.K.: Chapman and Hall.

Bowley, Graham. 1997. Corporate culture and a community contribution. *Financial Times* (October 31): 16.

Carey, J., 1970. *The Rise of the Accounting Profession: To Responsibility and Authority 1937–1969*. New York, NY: AICPA.

Christensen, C. 1997. *The Innovator's Dilemma*. Cambridge, MA: Harvard Business Press.

Dodd, P., and R. Leftwich. 1980. The market for corporate charters: "Unhealthy competition" versus federal regulation. *Journal of Business* 53: 259–283.

Dye, R. 1988. Earnings management in an overlapping generations model. *Journal of Accounting Research* 26 (Autumn): 195–235.

———. 1990. Mandatory vs. voluntary disclosures: The cases of real vs. financial externalities. *The Accounting Review* 65 (January): 1–24.

Easterbrook, F., and D. Fischel. 1991. *The Economic Structure of Corporate Law*. Cambridge, MA: Harvard University Press.

Farrell, J., and G. Saloner. 1985. Standardization, compatibility, and innovation. *Rand Journal of Economics* 16 (Spring): 70–83.

Grossman, S. J., R. E. Kihlstrom, and L. J. Mirman. 1977. A Bayesian approach to the production of information and learning by doing. *Review of Economic Studies* 44 (October): 533–547.

Havighurst, Clark C., editor. 1965. *Uniformity in Financial Accounting. Law and Contemporary Problems*. Vol. XXX. Durham, NC: Duke University.

Kaplan, A. 1964. *The Conduct of Inquiry: Methodology for Behavioral Science*. San Francisco, CA: Chandler Pub. Co.

Kaplan, R., and C. Ittner. 1988. *Texas Instruments: Cost of Quality (A)*. HBR Case Studies. Boston, MA: HBS Publishing.

Levine, C. 1996. Conservatism, contracts and information revelation. Doctoral dissertation, Carnegie Mellon University.

Monks, R., and N. Minow. 1995. *Corporate Governance*. Oxford, U.K.: Blackwell.

Parfet, W. U. 2000. Accounting subjectivity and earnings management: A preparer perspective. *Accounting Horizons* 14 (December): 481–488.

Posner, R. 1992. *The Economic Analysis of Law*. 4th edition. Boston, MA: Little Brown and Company.

Stiglitz, J. E. 1997. *Economics*. Second edition. New York, NY: W. W. Norton.

Sunder, S. 1997. *Theory of Accounting and Control*. Cincinnati, OH: Thomson Learning.

Tiebout, C. M. 1956. A pure theory of local expenditures. *Journal of Political Economy* 64 (October): 416–424.

Tjiong, H. I. T. 2000. *Breaking the Spell of Regulatory Competition: Reframing the Problem of Regulatory Exit*. Bonn, Germany: Max-Planck-Projektgruppe Recht der Gemeinschaftsguter.

[24]

Accounting Horizons
Vol. 16 No. 1
March 2002
pp. 43–54

COMMENTARY

"Political" Lobbying on Proposed Standards: A Challenge to the IASB

Stephen A. Zeff

Stephen A. Zeff is a Professor at Rice University.

INTRODUCTION

Now that the International Accounting Standards Board (IASB) has emerged from the restructuring of the International Accounting Standards Committee's (IASC) board, it seeks to establish high-quality International Financial Reporting Standards (IFRSs) and to engineer convergence at that level with eight leading national standard setters via a formal process of liaison.

One obstacle lying in the IASB's path is the set of "political" pressures that may be triggered by any board initiative to prescribe specific accounting treatments, eliminate alternative treatments, impose additional disclosure requirements, or tighten the allowed interpretations. I define "political" to mean self-interested considerations or pleadings by preparers and others that may be detrimental to the interests of investors and other users, a phenomenon that has been associated with the term "economic consequences" (see Zeff 1978). The IASB's initiatives will prescribe acceptable standards with greater specificity and provide less room for flexibility. Because the European Commission (EC) has given notice that, no later than 2005, all listed European Union (EU) companies must adopt "endorsed" IFRSs in their consolidated statements, EU companies will see the stakes as being much higher than they were with the standards issued by the old IASC board. Much depends, of course, on how effectively the several countries' regulators enforce compliance with IFRSs.

This article relates numerous attempts by industry and other affected parties, both in the U.S. and other countries, to move aggressively to prevent an accounting standard setter from imposing an objectionable requirement. They exemplify the lengths to which the powerful critics of proposed standards will go to defend their self-interests.

This paper served as the basis for a plenary address at the International Workshop on Accounting and Regulation, in Siena, Italy, on September 27, 2001. The conference was sponsored by the European Institute for Advanced Studies in Management. The author is grateful for the comments of Dennis Beresford, David Cairns, and Elizabeth Tebeaux on an earlier draft. The comments of the reviewer are much appreciated. The responsibility for what remains is entirely the author's.

RECENT DEVELOPMENTS

The "political" pressures may emerge in very different degrees and strength of feeling across the eight countries whose standard setters are to act in liaison with the IASB.[1] Such pressures could impede the effort to achieve convergence at a high level of quality. Lobbying may originate in other countries as well. Already, at the IASB's inaugural meeting with its Standards Advisory Council (SAC) in July 2001, it was reported that a major Swiss company, later revealed to be Novartis, had written to Sir David Tweedie, chairman of the IASB, that it will consider switching from IFRSs to U.S. GAAP if the IASB does not change its standard that requires the amortization of goodwill over 20 years. It was said that Novartis was concerned that it will be placed at a strategic disadvantage if the IASB does not adopt a standard on goodwill that converges with the FASB's Statement of Financial Accounting Standards (SFAS) No. 142. As a Swiss company, Novartis will not be required to continue using IFRSs in its primary financial statements under the EC's 2005 initiative unless the Swiss government passes a law to that effect.

Some European companies have other reasons for considering a switch to U.S. GAAP. One researcher has found that the chief financial officers (CFOs) of a number of major Swiss companies are attracted to U.S. GAAP because preparers in the U.S. are well organized and constitute a powerful lobby—a source of comfort to CFOs.[2] As noted below, such bodies as Financial Executives International (FEI, formerly the Financial Executives Institute) and The Business Roundtable have forcefully presented industry's views on proposed accounting standards to the FASB for many years. (The Business Roundtable is composed of the chief executive officers of some 150 of the largest U.S. corporations.)

Also at the SAC/IASB meeting in July, Phil Livingston, the full-time president and chief executive officer of FEI, told the IASB that it should leave stock option accounting off of its agenda. He described the exchange of views as "tense," and, in a subsequent report to FEI members dated July 25, he recounted what he said as follows:

> I gave a strong statement that we had been through 10 years of debate on this subject in the U.S., and were not interested in reopening the huge wounds that resulted from the battle with the FASB. I said that the issues here had been debated over and over again, and it was not possible to state a new argument for either side. Neither side has changed its view of this issue, and neither will. I suggested that they recognize the reality that stock option accounting is not going to change in the U.S. Therefore, they should get the issue off their plate and adopt a disclosure-based standard using whatever valuation method they deem theoretically correct. (Livingston 2001)

An article raising ominous consequences for the IASB, if it goes further on accounting for stock options than the FASB, was published in the *Wall Street Journal* (2001). I suspect that the idea for the article was "planted" by FEI in order to spread word of the IASB's intention. FEI again took aim at the IASB when it learned of the Board's tentative decision at its September meeting to measure employee stock options at fair value

---

1 The eight countries are Australia, Canada, France, Germany, Japan, New Zealand, the United Kingdom, and the United States.

2 This finding was communicated to the author by Giorgio Behr, the chairman of the Swiss accounting standards board, in an email message dated August 29, 2001.

and to recognize the corresponding expense in the income statement.[3] In a press release issued on September 21, FEI denounced this tentative decision. The senior finance officers of three major U.S. companies, including Pfizer, Inc., whose chairman and chief executive officer serves on IASB's board of trustees, were quoted in the release as opposing the IASB's initiative on this subject. Phil Ameen, the comptroller of General Electric Company, threatened that the board's "[tentative decision], if sustained, will portend a quick erosion of corporate participation and support" for the IASB. He added, "Competing national accounting standards will become the global standards, with little competition from the IASB." The FEI release stated, "Expense recognition can only lead to greater international divergence and a significant step back for the future of global accounting standards" (for the FEI press release, see http://www.fei.org; also see Hinchman 2001; Livingston 2001).

Congress has entered the picture. On October 12, 2001 the chairman of the U.S. House of Representatives' Committee on Financial Services was reported by the *New York Times* "to be carrying water" for FEI when he recently wrote a letter to the SEC chairman to warn of the adverse consequences of the IASB's tentative proposal on accounting for employee stock options (Morgenson 2001). The House member sent similar letters to the FASB chairman and to the chairman of IASB's board of trustees (letters dated October 12 from Rep. Michael G. Oxley to Harvey L. Pitt, Edmund Jenkins, and Paul A. Volcker).

These are in the nature of threats, and talk is cheap. But the FASB and the U.K. Accounting Standards Board know from experience that such threats can materialize into action.

Another possible source of "political" intrusion in the work of the IASB might come from the EC's screening mechanism, which was established during the first half of 2001. Its objective is to determine whether IFRSs should receive legal endorsement for use by EU companies in their consolidated financial statements under the EC's 2005 initiative, mentioned above. The EC stimulated the creation of a new private-sector body, the European Financial Reporting Advisory Group (EFRAG), which in turn formed a Technical Expert Group (TEG) to advise the EC on the appropriateness of IFRSs for use in the EU. The 11-member TEG is composed of representatives from the accounting profession, stock exchanges, accounting standard setters, financial analysts, and financial statement preparers. A final decision on whether to endorse IFRSs will be made by an Accounting Regulatory Committee (ARC), chaired by the EC and composed of government representatives from all of the EU member states, which "will operate at the political level under established EU rules for decision-making by regulatory committees" (EU 2001). The ARC will act on proposals received from the EC. At this early stage, it is not known whether the effect of these two new committees will be to introduce "political" considerations into the deliberations of the IASB. Some envision the EC's screening mechanism as the first step toward establishing a European Accounting Standards Board, an option that the EC considered adopting in 1995 (*Insight* 1996).

---

[3] See IASB's *Update* for September 2001, as supplemented by the report in Deloitte Touche Tohmatsu's IAS PLUS web site (http://www.iasplus.com). Walton (2001) reports that the German standard setter issued an exposure draft in June 2001, favoring fair value treatment and the recognition of the corresponding expense in the income statement, as of the *grant* date. A G4+1 paper (Crook 2000) is being used by the IASB as the basis for its deliberations. It calls for use of the *vesting* date, which occurs after most of the employees' services anticipated by the grant of stock options are rendered.

"Political" considerations affected the IASB's predecessor. In 1992, a proposal before the IASC board was defeated by "political" opposition, before companies faced any real regulatory pressure to adopt International Accounting Standards (IASs). Hence, the seeds of discontent can be sown even in circumstances when adherence to IASs is voluntary.

IASC'S EMBARRASSING REVERSAL ON LIFO IN 1992

At its meeting in October 1992, the IASC board was poised to eliminate LIFO as an allowed alternative treatment, as part of the board's Comparability/Improvements project, set forth in its Statement of Intent of July 1990, *Comparability of Financial Statements* (IASC 1990, 19). Since April 1992, it had been known that the International Organization of Securities Commissions (IOSCO) opposed eliminating LIFO, which had come as a shock to the board.[4] Although the U.S. and Canadian accounting bodies had made it known that they favored retaining LIFO as an allowed alternative treatment, in the end they demonstrated solidarity with the Comparability/Improvements project and voted to eliminate LIFO.[5] But, at the decisive board meeting, the delegations from Korea, Japan, Germany, and Italy, whose accountancy bodies' comment letters also favored retention, all voted against the proposal, thus defeating it in a 10-4 vote (see Cairns 1998). A three-quarters vote was required for approval, 11-3 in this case. The four delegations voting against the elimination were evidently pressured not to eliminate LIFO as an option by companies in these countries—where LIFO was allowable for income tax purposes, and financial reporting was linked to tax rules. Thus, in the IASC boardroom, where the supporters of international harmonization expected to find their most articulate and committed exponents, "political" pressure succeeded in defeating one of the objectives of the IASC board's Comparability/Improvements project. This "political" intervention occurred before the government regulators in any of the countries represented by the four dissenting delegations contemplated requiring companies to adopt IASs.

U.K. ACCOUNTANCY PROFESSION'S SUDDEN *VOLTE-FACE* ON DEFERRED TAX ACCOUNTING IN THE MID-1970s

Another example of the power of "political" pressures, again when no enforcement mechanism other than the external auditor existed, occurred in 1975–78 in the U.K. In August 1975, the governing Councils of the accountancy bodies sponsoring the U.K. Accounting Standards Committee (ASC) approved Statement of Standard Accounting Practice (SSAP) No. 11, *Accounting for Deferred Taxation*. The Standard embraced the "comprehensive tax allocation" approach, by which all timing differences were to be recognized and deferred, a method that the U.S. Accounting Principles Board had adopted in its Opinion No. 11, issued in 1967. The objective was to harmonize with the Americans.

But big industry began to voice strong "political" objections. The 1970s were an inflationary decade in the U.K., and the annualized inflation rate topped 25 percent in August 1975. Since 1972, companies had been deducting 100 percent first-year tax allowances on

[4] For a news report on this episode, see *Insight* (1992). Also see Cairns (1999, 495–496). I gathered additional information on this matter from Arthur R. Wyatt, the IASC chairman at the time.

[5] The American Institute of Certified Public Accountants and the Institute of Management Accountants, the bodies whose representatives composed the U.S. delegation on the IASC board, had no power to eliminate LIFO as an option in U.S. GAAP. Only the FASB had that authority, and the board would obey the norms of its elaborate due process, if it had attempted to make such a change.

many fixed assets, while displaying the usual depreciation allowances in their published accounts. Moreover, in 1974 the Government began granting stock appreciation relief for merchandise inventories for tax purposes, a variation on LIFO, which was not acceptable under U.K. GAAP. In view of the steep inflation, the notional income tax expense and the corresponding balance in companies' deferred tax accounts under comprehensive tax allocation would have been enormous. When Tony Benn, the secretary of state for industry in the Labour Government, openly advocated a gradual nationalization of industry, some companies nervously feared the Government might interpret the large deferred tax balances as amounts owed to the Government that might serve as the pretext for a takeover. The *Financial Times* reported, "The suggestion was that a future Government might call in all the deferred tax, or nationalise companies instead" (Lafferty 1978; see Appleyard 1978).

On June 14, 1976, the powerful Confederation of British Industry (CBI) wrote a letter to the ASC on behalf of 60 large companies (letter from Campbell Adamson to Sir Ronald Leach). The CBI articulated three complaints: (1) "the deferred taxation [balance] will inevitably continue to grow and grow in the vast majority of cases where companies continue trading in normal circumstances"; (2) the balance would be costly to calculate; and (3) SSAP No. 11 "is inequitable as regards current shareholders." The CBI predicted "that a growing number of companies will choose not to comply with the Standard" and thus will take a qualified auditor's report. The CBI therefore urged the ASC to reconsider SSAP No. 11.

Within the ASC, the need to develop a current cost accounting standard became a factor in the treatment of deferred taxation. The ASC was contemplating a standard that would show depreciation expense and cost of sales at current cost, which would be incongruous with an income tax expense based on historical cost profit. In October 1976, the ASC announced that it was reviewing SSAP No. 11 and asked the professional bodies' Councils to defer its date of implementation, which they did. In May 1977, the ASC issued ED (Exposure Draft) No. 19, which proposed partial deferred taxation to be applicable only to short-term timing differences and not to those that might persist well into the future. This outcome is exactly what industry wanted, and in October 1978 the Councils announced that they were replacing SSAP No. 11 with SSAP No. 15, which endorsed partial deferred taxation as the only appropriate accounting treatment.

Clearing banks were also upset with SSAP No. 11. They were just becoming active in long-term leasing, and the Standard would have forced them to take a large charge against their shareholders' equity at a time when U.S. banks were preparing to invade their market. The U.K. government was also unhappy with SSAP No. 11, as it would have required companies to display a much larger notional income tax expense in their published accounts than the amount actually due, as if they had not been accorded substantial tax relief for the rising cost of fixed assets and merchandise. The cumulative effect of "political" pressures from all three sides—big industry, the clearing banks, and government—played a major role in persuading the ASC and the governing Councils of the accountancy profession to reverse themselves.[6] To be fair, the need to issue a current cost accounting standard also helped turned the tide. Yet, on balance, this attempt by the ASC and the Councils to achieve a harmonization with the Americans was undermined by "political" pressure.

---

[6] See also Hope and Briggs (1982). The discussion in this section draws heavily on Zeff (1988, 21–22).

In the 1990s, the U.K.'s Accounting Standards Board also faced "political" pressures and a great deal of contentiousness on such subjects as (1) accounting for securitizations (Financial Reporting Standard No. 5),[7] (2) the Government's Private Finance Initiative (1998 amendment to FRS No. 5),[8] and (3) provisions for future operating losses in acquisition accounting (FRS No. 7).[9]

AUSTRALIAN SENATE VETOES PART OF AN ACCOUNTING STANDARD

Recently, the Australian Parliament administered a jarring rebuff to the national standard setter. In February 2000, two opposition political parties represented in the Australian Senate sponsored a "disallowance motion," which voided an optional treatment approved by the Australian Accounting Standards Board (AASB) as part of AASB No. 1015, dealing with reconstructions within an economic entity.[10] The Standard had been approved by a 5-4 vote; the dissenters all disapproved of the optional treatment. The optional treatment permitted companies to record acquisitions of assets falling within internal reconstructions at book value instead of at fair value. The Senators regarded the book value method as "inconsistent with the provisions in the legislation dealing with standards that demanded comparability and consistency between reporting periods and between entities" (Ravlic 2000, 16), and therefore not in the best interests of the investment community. While the optional treatment had its detractors, including the Australian Securities and Investments Commission, this was the first time that the Senate invoked its authority to disallow an accounting practice approved by the AASB. This experience illustrates how partisan politics can affect accounting standards. The laws that underpin the current accounting standard-setting regimes in both Australia and New Zealand authorize Parliament to overturn their Standards. It could happen again.

During the 1990s, the AASB was subjected to "political" pressure on a number of issues, notably in the wake of Statement of Accounting Concepts (SAC) No. 4, *Definition and Recognition of the Elements of Financial Statements*, issued in March 1992. This mandatory concepts statement implied in an appendix that virtually all leases should be brought into the balance sheet. The standard-setting establishment came under virtual assault from all sides until it decided, in an embarrassing reversal in 1993, that the concepts statements would no longer be mandatory.[11]

IMPORTANCE OF "POLITICAL" PRESSURE IN THE UNITED STATES

The impact of "political" pressure is even greater in settings where a strong enforcement mechanism exists, as in the United States. The Securities and Exchange Commission (SEC), a powerful federal government agency, possesses authority to prescribe the financial reporting used by the approximately 14,000 publicly traded companies in the U.S. Beginning in the late 1930s, the SEC looked to the public accounting profession and, since 1973, to the independent FASB as the authoritative source of most of what constitutes U.S. GAAP. Once the FASB issues a Standard, except in rare instances

[7] See, e.g., Barclays Bank's unusual, four-page advertising insert in the February 1, 1992 issue of *The Economist*, contesting the ASB's position on accounting for securitizations, and *Accountancy* (1992).

[8] See, e.g., *The Accountant* (1998a, 1998b, 1998c) and *Accountancy* (1998).

[9] See, e.g., *Accountancy* (1993, 1994).

[10] This section is based on Ravlic (2000). Also see Collett et al. (2001, 174). For more on the "political" dimension of standard setting in Australia, see Stoddart (2000).

[11] See, e.g., Burrows (1996, 196–199) and Miller (1995, 7, 9).

when the SEC regards the Standard as an unacceptable norm, the SEC requires all publicly traded companies to adopt it forthwith. If such companies fail to do so, or if they implement the Standard in a way that is unacceptable to the SEC's accounting staff, then the SEC requires them to revise and reissue their defective financial statements. Otherwise, these companies are rebuked by the SEC, which would immediately issue an order to stop the trading of their securities in the U.S. securities market. In the case of companies proposing to make an initial public offering, the SEC intervenes to interdict that offering unless the companies comply with the Standard in an acceptable manner. The SEC, therefore, is a potent force in securing compliance with accounting standards in the U.S. Consequently, if companies find a proposed FASB Standard to be objectionable, then they will lobby the FASB to prevent its issuance in order to avoid the inevitable intervention by the SEC.

Even though the SEC does not allow U.S. companies to use IASB Standards, when the IASB adds a topic to its agenda, this act places pressure on the eight collaborating national standard setters, of which the FASB is one, to converge toward what the IASB finally decides. Thus, the FASB may occasionally find itself operating in the wake of the IASB. For this reason, U.S. companies are expected to keep a close eye on the IASB's agenda decisions, just as FEI did with respect to accounting for employee stock options.

Because of rigorous enforcement in the U.S., it is likely that a controversial, proposed IASB standard would generate much stronger negative reaction in the U.S. than in the other seven countries collaborating with the IASB. The confrontational climate in the U.S., epitomized by the high incidence of litigation and the traditionally intense lobbying of legislators at both the federal and state levels, virtually assures this result. In particular, the FEI, The Business Roundtable, and various U.S. industry-specific trade associations have organized powerful lobbies to confront the FASB and its predecessors on proposed standards that their members found to be objectionable.[12]

In the 1990s, the FASB was successfully lobbied to reconsider, or reverse itself on, three important proposed Standards: accounting for marketable securities, stock-based compensation (i.e., stock options), and intangibles. In all three instances, the commercial bank and company sectors used their contacts and connections in the federal government, including bank regulatory agencies, Secretaries of Government Departments, and members of Congress, to provide "political" leverage in their efforts to convince the FASB to reconsider its thinking on these contentious subjects. In a fourth instance, on derivative securities, the lobbying effort did not succeed in persuading the FASB to roll back its position.[13]

Marketable Securities

In the first of the three successful lobbying sorties (1990–93), the American Bankers Association (ABA)—abetted by letters sent by the chairman of the Federal Reserve Board, the chairman of the Federal Deposit Insurance Corporation, the Secretary of the Treasury, and two United States Senators—pressured the FASB either directly or indirectly.

[12] See, e.g., Van Riper (1994), Gorton (1991), Miller et al. (1998, Chapter 5), Zeff (1972, 178–180, 200–202, 212–216, and 219–221), and Zeff (1993, 130–142). The FEI was also active in opposing a proposed concepts statement (see Miller 1990).

[13] This article does not treat the successive attempts by the FEI in 1985, The Business Roundtable in 1988, and the FEI again in 1996 to dilute the effectiveness of the FASB. See Van Riper (1994, Chapters 8 and 9) and Miller et al. (1998, 177–194).

Even though the FASB had strong SEC support, the ABA pushed the FASB to retreat from a position that it was considering, namely, that all marketable securities be shown at fair value and that the year-to-year change in fair value be taken into earnings.[14] The banking industry feared the earnings volatility that would result from taking the changes in fair value of such holdings directly to earnings. Instead, in its September 1992 Exposure Draft and in Statement of Financial Accounting Standards (SFAS) No. 115, issued in May 1993, the FASB created the portfolio of "available for sale" securities, whose year-to-year change in fair value is taken to shareholders' equity instead of to earnings. SFAS No. 115 was approved by a vote of 5-2,[15] and the two dissenters argued for including in earnings all unrealized changes in the fair value of debt and equity securities.

Stock Options

In the second successful lobbying campaign, carried out during 1992–95, industry reacted fiercely to the FASB's Exposure Draft that would have required companies conferring stock options upon employees to estimate the fair value of the options and record a corresponding expense in their income statements. Trade associations and companies in the entrepreneurial sector, in particular, pressured prominent members of the House and Senate to introduce a series of bills aimed at frustrating any attempt by the FASB to move ahead with its proposal. At one point, the Senate passed a "sense of the Senate" resolution urging the FASB not to proceed with its initiative on accounting for employee stock options, citing its "grave economic consequences particularly for business in new-growth sectors which rely heavily on employee entrepreneurship."[16] Congressional pressure became so intense and unrelenting that the SEC chairman feared that the FASB's approval of its stock option accounting proposal would "jeopardize private sector control of accounting standards-setting" (*CPA Journal* 2001, 28). In the end, under the gun from key members of Congress, the FASB could do no more than issue SFAS No. 123, by a 5-2 vote, requiring footnote disclosure of the estimated dilutive effect of stock options on reported earnings (for an account of this episode, see Zeff [1997]). Both dissenters argued that the compensation associated with employee stock options should be recognized in the body of the financial statements, not in the footnotes.

Business Combinations and Intangibles

The third of the successful lobbying actions, during 1996–2001, dealt with accounting for business combinations and intangibles, chiefly goodwill. The SEC had urged the FASB to add this issue to its agenda. In its Exposure Draft issued in September 1999, the FASB called for elimination of the pooling-of-interests method of accounting for business combinations and for the mandatory amortization of goodwill over a maximum of 20 years. This provision on goodwill would have brought the FASB's standard on the subject into line with that of the IASC.

---

[14] The board's first tentative position on "mark-to-market" accounting, as fair value accounting was then called, was that the unrealized holding gains and losses on securities not classified as current assets or trading securities should not be taken to earnings (*FASB Action Alert*, November 13, 1991, p. 3). Two meetings later, the board reversed itself, and it tentatively decided that all unrealized holding gains and losses should be taken to earnings (*FASB Action Alert*, December 4, 1991). Also see Kirk (1991), Berton (1992), Worthy (1992), and *The Economist* (1992).

[15] Since January 1991, all FASB Statements must be approved by at least a two-thirds majority, 5-2 when seven members are voting.

[16] *Congressional Record—Senate*, May 3, 1994, S 5032.

Industry, led by the FEI, objected especially to the mandatory amortization of goodwill, and it appealed to members of Congress for relief. In March and May 2000, a Senate committee and House subcommittee held one-day hearings that were "dominated by the views of those opposed to the FASB position on accounting for business combinations."[17] The chairman of the Senate committee expressed concern over the mandatory amortization of goodwill, and he proposed a periodic impairment test as a better solution. He reiterated this view at a Roundtable Discussion on Accounting for Goodwill, which his committee held in June to discuss the issue further. Then, in October, a House member introduced a bill to create a commission to study afresh the entire subject of accounting for business combinations and goodwill, an obvious delaying tactic. During 2000–01, two sets of letters signed by Senators were sent to the FASB chairman.

Eventually, in February 2001, the FASB rushed out a second Exposure Draft that called for a periodic impairment test for goodwill and disallowed amortization, a position that the board concluded it could support in principle. After making further amendments, the board unanimously approved SFAS Nos. 141 and 142, which outlawed the pooling-of-interests method and specified a periodic impairment test for goodwill. Again, the persistent lobbying of the FASB by way of Congress succeeded in persuading the board to reconsider. Ironically, SFAS No. 142 on goodwill brought the FASB's standard into conflict with the comparable IASC standard.

Industry also fought the FASB's fair value proposal on accounting for derivative securities, and blocking bills were again introduced in the House and Senate. In October 1997, a House subcommittee held a one-day hearing as a reaction to the FASB's Exposure Draft. In February 1998, the subcommittee chairman introduced a bill euphemistically called the Financial Accounting Fairness Act of 1998 (H.R. 3165). If enacted, then this bill would instruct the SEC to review each FASB Standard to ascertain whether it "will promote efficiency, competition, and capital formation" in addition to protecting investor interests, and it would require the SEC to consult with federal banking agencies on any FASB Standards affecting the banking sector. In March and October 1997, a Senate subcommittee held two days of hearings under the title "Derivatives Disclosure and Accounting." In November 1997, one of the subcommittee's members introduced a bill, dubbed the Accurate Accounting Standards Certification Act of 1997 (S. 1560), to prevent any FASB Standard from being applied to banking institutions unless the appropriate federal banking agency certified its acceptability to Congress.

Clearly, members of Congress had been approached by those opposed to the FASB's Exposure Draft. Earlier, in August 1997, the chairman of the Federal Reserve Board urged the FASB to soften its proposal considerably and not require public companies to take the changes in the fair value of their derivatives contracts to earnings (see MacDonald 1997b; MacDonald and Frank 1997). All of these interventions, deliberately aimed at crippling the board's initiative on accounting for derivatives, did not, in the end, prevent it from moving ahead with its intended norms in SFAS No. 133.

A Further FASB Initiative to which Industry Objected

SFAS No. 130, issued in June 1997, deals with the display of "comprehensive income." Industry strongly objected to this initiative, although it seems that the dialogue fell within the bounds of the give-and-take that the FASB expects to occur during the

[17] See Beresford (2001, 80). In an appendix to his article, Beresford lists the Congressional hearings held on FASB projects from 1976 to the present. Much of this section is based on the Beresford article.

comment process, and that "political" pressure was not applied. The financial analyst community had urged the FASB to develop a standard on the reporting of comprehensive income (see Knutson 1993, 63). Comprehensive income, defined as the change in net assets excluding transactions with owners, embraces net income as we currently know it plus *other comprehensive income* (OCI). Items carried directly to shareholders' equity—such as unrealized gains and losses on "available for sale" securities and certain derivative financial instruments, and foreign currency translation adjustments arising under the current rate method—are grouped in OCI. The board's July 1996 Exposure Draft required that OCI be displayed either in a new section at the bottom of the income statement or in a separate statement of financial performance. The FEI's committee on corporate reporting disagreed strongly with the board's draft.[18] The committee did not want the items included in OCI to be reflected in a comprehensive earnings per share. By a vote of 5 to 2, the board reluctantly acceded to a third and much less prominent place for displaying OCI—the statement of changes in equity. Close observers stated that SFAS No. 130 was issued "in the face of substantial opposition by the preparer community" (Miller et al. 1998, 113; see also MacDonald 1997a).

CONCLUSION

The specter of "political" challenges such as those recounted in this article should give pause to members of the IASB and the eight national standard setters with which it is collaborating when they propose to develop a Standard on a sensitive and controversial topic. Notwithstanding this specter, all who are interested in sound and useful financial reporting hope that the Board will not retreat from sensitive and controversial issues in need of high-quality reporting standards.

[18] For a summary of the committee's views, see *Financial Executive* (1996).

REFERENCES

Accountancy. 1992. ASB reaches compromise. (December): 13.
———. 1993. ASB takes on the giants. (May): 11.
———. 1994. ASB set to make powerful enemies. (June): 10.
———. 1998. ASB takes blows over PFI. (April): 12.
Accountant, The. 1998a. ASB locks horns with Treasury over PFI. (June): 10.
———. 1998b. Deferred ASB ruling triggers political row. (October): 3.
———. 1998c. New guidance jeopardises government capital scheme. (December/January): 1.
Appleyard, B. 1978. Corporation tax rules revised in new standards for accountants. *The Times* (October 16): 19.
Beresford, D. R. 2001. Congress looks at accounting for business combinations. *Accounting Horizons* (March): 73–86.
Berton, L. 1992. FASB balks at current-market rules for banks as member switches his vote. *Wall Street Journal* (January 16): A3.
Burrows, G. 1996. *The Foundation: A History of the Australian Accounting Research Foundation 1966–91*. Caulfield, Victoria, Australia: Australian Accounting Research Foundation.
Cairns, D. 1998. Twists in the tale of the SIC's deliberations. *Accountancy* (International Edition) (January): 65.
———. 1999. *Applying International Accounting Standards*. London, U.K.: Butterworths.

Collett, P. H., J. M. Godfrey, and S. L. Hrasky. 2001. International harmonization: Cautions from the Australian experience. *Accounting Horizons* (June): 171–182.

CPA Journal. 2001. Arthur Levitt remembered: Four personal commentaries on the longest-serving SEC chairman in U.S. history. (May): 25–26, 28+.

Crook, K. 2000. *Accounting for Share-Based Payment*. Norwalk, CT: Financial Accounting Standards Board.

Economist, The. 1992. Bank accounting: The truth will out. (May 9): 98, 100.

European Union (EU). 2001. Financial reporting: Commission welcomes creation of European technical expert group. Press Release (June 26).

Financial Executive. 1996. Thumbs down on comprehensive income draft. (November/December): 53–54.

Gorton, D. E. 1991. The SEC decision not to support SFAS 19: A case study of the effect of lobbying on standard setting. *Accounting Horizons* (March): 29–41.

Hinchman, G. 2001. Fasten seat belts: Bumpy ride for stock option accounting. *Financial Executive* (September): 68.

Hope, T., and J. Briggs. 1982. Accounting policy making—Some lessons from the deferred taxation debate. *Accounting and Business Research* (Spring): 83–96.

Insight. 1992. Board approves first three revised standards. (December): 1, 14–15.

———. 1996. EU puts weight behind IASC. (March): 1, 3.

International Accounting Standards Committee (IASC). 1990. *Comparability of Financial Statements*. Statement of Intent. London, U.K.: IASC.

Kirk, D. J. 1991. Competitive disadvantage and mark-to-market accounting. *Accounting Horizons* (June): 98–106.

Knutson, P. H. 1993. *Financial Reporting in the 1990s and BEYOND*. Charlottesville, VA: Association for Investment Management and Research.

Lafferty, M. 1978. New standard issued on deferred taxation. *Financial Times* (October 16).

Livingston, P. 2001. Options accounting should follow U.S. course. *Financial Executive* (November): 6.

MacDonald, E. 1997a. FASB asks for additional profit data, but backs down on a major provision. *Wall Street Journal* (July 2): B2.

———. 1997b. Greenspan urges FASB to drop plan on adjusting earnings for derivatives. *Wall Street Journal* (August 7): A8.

———, and S. E. Frank. 1997. FASB rejects Fed chairman's request to soften proposed rule on derivatives. *Wall Street Journal* (August 12): A2.

Miller, M. C. 1995. Goodwill discontent: The meshing of Australian and international accounting policy. *Australian Accounting Review* (June): 3–16.

Miller, P. B. W. 1990. The conceptual framework as reformation and counterreformation. *Accounting Horizons* (June): 23–32.

———, R. J. Redding, and P. R. Bahnson. 1998. *The FASB: The People, the Process, and the Politics*. Burr Ridge, IL: Irwin/McGraw-Hill.

Morgenson, G. 2001. Time to look at stock options' real cost. *New York Times* (October 21): Section 3, 1.

Ravlic, T. 2000. When the politicians step in. *Accounting & Business* (April): 16–17.

Stoddart, E. K. 2000. Political influences in changes to setting Australian accounting standards. *Critical Perspectives on Accounting* (December): 713–740.

Van Riper, R. 1994. *Setting Standards for Financial Reporting: FASB and the Struggle for Control of a Critical Process*. Westport, CT: Quorum Books.

Wall Street Journal. 2001. Global accounting faces stock-option tiff. (August 28): C14.

Walton, P. 2001. German stock option draft. *World Accounting Report* (September): 14.

Worthy, F. S. 1992. The battle of the bean counters. *Fortune* (June 1): 117–118, 122+.

Zeff, S. A. 1972. *Forging Accounting Principles in Five Countries: A History and an Analysis of Trends*. Champaign, IL: Stipes Publishing.

———. 1978. The rise of "economic consequences." *Journal of Accountancy* (December): 56–63.
———. 1988. Setting accounting standards: Some lessons from the U.S. experience. *The Accountant's Magazine* (January): 20–22.
———. 1993. The politics of accounting standards. *Economia Aziendale* (August): 123–142.
———. 1997. The U.S. senate votes on accounting for employee stock options. In *Readings & Notes on Financial Accounting*, edited by S. Zeff, and B. G. Dharan, 507–517. New York, NY: McGraw-Hill.

Name Index